A Performer's Guide to
Seventeenth-Century Music

Early Music America

Performer's Guides to Early Music

Jeffery T. Kite-Powell, Series Editor

PUBLISHED

A Performer's Guide to Renaissance Music
Jeffery T. Kite-Powell, Editor

A Performer's Guide to Seventeenth-Century Music
Stewart Carter, Editor

A Performer's Guide to Seventeenth-Century Music

Edited by

STEWART CARTER

SCHIRMER BOOKS
An Imprint of Simon & Schuster Macmillan
NEW YORK

Prentice Hall International
LONDON • MEXICO CITY • NEW DELHI • SINGAPORE • SYDNEY • TORONTO

Schirmer Books
An Imprint of Simon & Schuster Macmillan
1633 Broadway
New York, NY 10019

Library of Congress Catalog Card Number: 97-1310

Printed in the United States of America

Printing number
1 2 3 4 5 6 7 8 9 10

Library of Congress Cataloging-in-Publication Data

A performer's guide to seventeenth-century music / edited by Stewart Carter.
      p.   cm.—(Performer's guides to early music)
   Includes bibliographical references and index.
   ISBN 0-02-870492-4
   1. Performance practice (Music)—17th century.   I. Carter,
Stewart Arlen.   II. Series.
ML457.P49 1997
781.4'3'09032—dc21   97-1310
                                                      CIP
                                                     MN

Contents

CONTENTS

Contributors

Jack Ashworth is Professor of Music History and Director of the Early Music Ensemble at the University of Louisville, where he has taught since receiving the D.M.A. from Stanford in 1977. He is a performer on keyboards, specializing in continuo realization, and plays historical winds and strings as well. He is currently president of the Viola da Gamba Society of America.

Soprano **Julianne Baird** has appeared with major ensembles throughout the world, including the New York Philharmonic, the Cleveland Orchestra, the St. Paul Chamber Orchestra, the Orquesta Sinfonica Nacional (Mexico), Mostly Mozart, and Helicon Ensemble. Her discography comprises more than sixty-five recordings, on such labels as Decca, DGG, Dorian, Omega, Newport Classics, Nonesuch, and Vox cum Laude. Her book *Introduction to "The Art of Singing" by Johann Friedrich Agricola* was published by Cambridge University Press in 1995. She is currently on the faculty of Rutgers University.

Stewart Carter is executive editor of the *Historic Brass Society Journal*, general editor of Bucina: The Historic Brass Society Series, and former editor of *Historical Performance*. He has published articles and reviews in *Early Music, Performance Practice Review, MLA Notes, The New Grove Dictionary of Women in Music, The American Recorder, Historic Brass Society Journal*, and *Historical Performance*. An active performer on sackbut and recorder, he has taught at early music workshops throughout the United States, and serves annually on the faculty of the Amherst Early Music Festival. He received the Ph.D. in musicology from Stanford University. He is Professor of Music at Wake Forest University, and in the spring of 1997 he was Visiting Research Professor at the Shrine to Music Museum of the University of South Dakota.

Stuart Cheney is a Ph.D. candidate in musicology at the University of Maryland, where he is writing his dissertation on French variation practices of the seventeenth century. He has also written articles about and edited viol music from this period.

Barbara Coeyman holds a Ph.D. from the Graduate Center of the City University of New York, where she wrote a dissertation on Delalande's music for the French court. She has several recent publications on French Baroque composers and on theaters and other settings for Baroque opera, and has also written about Baroque dance. She has served as teacher and coach in various early music organizations, including the Viola da Gamba Society of America. Her research has been funded by the National Endowment for the Humanities, Harvard University, and the American Philosophical Society. She is founding vice-president of the Society for Seventeenth-Century Music, and she has served on the faculty of West Virginia University for the past eleven years.

John Michael Cooper is Assistant Professor of Music at Illinois Wesleyan University. He has published articles, reviews, and translations on Felix Mendelssohn Bartholdy, Robert Schumann, Johannes Brahms, and Antonin Dvořák, as well as on *tableaux vivants* and Baroque timpani. His edition of the unpublished revision of Mendelssohn's "Italian" Symphony will be published by Ludwig-Reichert-Verlag (Wiesbaden) in 1997, and he is currently completing *Felix Mendelssohn Bartholdy: A Guide to Research* (to be published by Garland Press) and a monograph on Mendelssohn's "Italian" Symphony (to be published by Oxford University Press).

Bruce Dickey is a performer and researcher who has devoted himself since 1975 to the revival of the cornett, an instrument to which he was attracted while pursuing a master's degree in musicology at Indiana University. He has taught cornett and seventeenth-century performance practice at the Schola Cantorum Basiliensis in Basel since 1976. Founder and codirector of the ensemble Concerto Palatino, he has performed extensively throughout the world and can be heard on more than sixty recordings. He is also active in research on performance practice, and has just published, together with Michael Collver, *A Catalog of Music for the Cornett* (Bloomington: Indiana University Press, 1996). In 1981 he moved to Italy, partly to be closer to the origin and source material for his instrument and its music.

David Douglass is the founder and director of The King's Noyse, a Renaissance violin band. He has been a leader in the recreation of the sound, style, and technique of the early violin. Mr. Douglass frequently performs with such ensembles as The Harp Consort, The Musicians of Swanne Alley, and The Folger Consort, playing viola da gamba and medieval stringed instruments in addition to the violin. He has lectured and published articles on early violin history, technique, and repertoire. He teaches at many summer early music courses and workshops, including those of the Vancouver and San Francisco Early Music Societies, and he has been Artist Faculty at the Aston Magna Academy. He has recorded for the Harmonia Mundi USA, Virgin, Erato, BMG, Berlin Classics, and Auvida-Astree labels.

Anne Harrington Heider is Associate Professor of Choral Music and Director of Choral Ensembles at Chicago Musical College of Roosevelt University. She is also artistic director of the professional vocal ensemble His Majesties Clerkes. Her research in early music has been supported by the Newberry Library, the National Endowment for the Humanities, and Roosevelt University. Her critical editions of music by Claude Le Jeune were published by A-R Editions in their series Recent Researches in the Music of the Renaissance.

George Houle is an oboist and gambist who enjoys performing the music of the fifteenth through the eighteenth centuries. He was Professor of Music at Stanford University, where he taught music history and performance practices of Renaissance and Baroque music.

During a career spanning over a quarter century **Mark Kroll** has performed throughout North and South America and Europe. He has recorded repertoire for solo harpischord and fortepiano, as well as major works for keyboard with other instruments. He has made numerous radio and TV appearances in the United States and abroad, and appeared as concert soloist with several major orchestras. His honors include grants from the NEA, DAAD, IREX, and the Martha Baird Rockefeller Fund. He served as Fulbright Professor and Artist-in-Residence in Yugoslavia, and Visiting Professor at the Würzburg Conservatory in Germany. He is Professor of Music at Boston University, where he directs the Early Music Series and serves as Chairman of the Department of Historical Performance.

As a lute and theorbo player, **Kevin Mason** has performed throughout the United States and in Canada, England, Germany, and Holland as guest artist with such early-music ensembles as The King's Noyse, The Newberry Consort, Pomerium Musices, Les Filles de St. Colombe, Concert Royal, Tafelmusik Baroque Orchestra of Toronto, The New World Consort of Vancouver, Ensemble Chanterelle, and The London Early Music Group. He founded, directed, and performed with Orpheus Band, a Chicago-based group that specializes in seventeenth-century music for strings and strings with voices. He has recorded for RCA, Nonesuch, Classic Digital, and Harmonia Mundi USA. He holds a Ph.D. in Historical Performance Practices from Washington University, St. Louis. His book *The Chitarrone and its Repertoire in Early Seventeenth Century Italy* was published by Boethius Press in 1989.

James Middleton, founder and artistic director of Ex Machina Antique Music Theater Company, has been called "the P. T. Barnum of the Baroque" for his re-creations of Baroque stagecraft. His productions have been seen in cities throughout the United States. He is a frequent guest artist at U.S. colleges and universities and has lectured and conducted workshops for Mexico's Instituto Nacional de Bellas Artes. A faculty member of the Amherst Early Music Institute, he was recently named a fellow of the Aston Magna Academy for his work in the area of Latin American Music.

Herbert W. Myers is Lecturer in Renaissance winds and curator of the instrument collection at Stanford University, from which he holds a D.M.A. in Performance Practices of Early Music. As a member of the New York Pro Musica from 1970–73 he toured North and South America, performing on a wide range of early winds and strings. He currently performs with The Whole Noyse and Magnificat. He has published articles in *Early Music, Historical Performance, The American Recorder, Strings*, and the *Journal of the American Musical Instrument Society*.

Paul O'Dette is a lutenist and researcher specializing in Renaissance and early Baroque music. He can be heard on more than 100 recordings as a soloist as well as continuo player. His five-CD set of the lute music of John Dowland was awarded the Diapason d'Or. Director of Early Music at the Eastman School of Music, Mr. O'Dette is also co-director of the Musicians of Swanne Alley and artistic director of the Boston Early Music Festival. In collaboration with Patrick O'Brien, he is currently writing a method book for the Renaissance lute.

Dorothy Olsson received the M.M. in musicology from the Manhattan School of Music and the Ph.D. in Performance Studies from New York University, the latter with a dissertation on early-twentieth-century dance. She is director of the New York Historical Dance Company and has given numerous workshops on historical dance. She has choreographed for and performed with Piffaro (Philadelphia Renaissance Wind Band), the Folger Consort, Parthenia—A Consort of Viols, the Philadelphia Classical Symphony, Western Wind Vocal Ensemble, OperaDelaware, and the New Dance Group. She teaches historical dance at the Amherst Early Music Festival, where she has directed several historical theatrical productions. She is currently Adjunct Assistant Professor of Dance Education at New York University.

Steven Plank is Professor of Musicology at Oberlin College. He is the author of *The Way to Heavens Doore: An Introduction to Liturgical Process and Musical Style* (Scarecrow, 1994), as well as many articles devoted to contextual studies of seventeenth-century music. He is also active as a conductor, organist, and trumpeter.

Sally Sanford, soprano, has appeared in recital, oratorio, Baroque opera, and staged medieval drama in Europe, Canada, and throughout the United States. Active also as a scholar and teacher, she is frequently invited to lecture and give master classes in historical singing styles and techniques at colleges and universities. She has performed with many distinguished early music ensembles and is a founding member of Ensemble Chanterelle, a trio that specializes in seventeenth-century music. She is associate director and a regular artist faculty member of the Aston Magna Academy and has recently been appointed to the music faculty of Wellesley College.

Gary Towne received the Ph.D. in musicology from the University of California, Santa Barbara with a dissertation on Gaspar de Albertis and sacred music in sixteenth-century Bergamo. He has published articles and reviews in *Musica disciplina, Journal of Musicology, The Historic Brass Society Journal*, and *Archivio storico bergamasco*. He currently teaches music history and directs the Collegium musicum at the University of North Dakota. He is currently working on an edition of the music of Albertis for *Corpus mensurabilis musicae* and a history of musical institutions in medieval and Renaissance Bergamo.

Preface

It is trite, but nonetheless accurate, to say that the seventeenth century was an age of transition between the High Renaissance and the High Baroque. This era was in fact long ignored by music historians. An earlier age, which liked to think of musical periods as dominated by great men, dubbed the Renaissance the Age of Palestrina and Lasso, and the Baroque the Age of Bach and Handel. Even the Early Music Movement, in its "earlier" stages, regarded the seventeenth century as an awkward stepchild; the music was either overripe Lasso or incipient Bach. Until fairly recently, the term "Baroque Performance Practice" was understood to refer primarily to the period of 1680 to 1750.

But recent research and recent performers have begun to change all that. There are now ensembles and individual performers who specialize in this repertory, and performances of the Monteverdi 1610 Vespers are ubiquitous. There is also a scholarly organization, the Society for Seventeenth-Century Music, devoted to this era. Yet just a few years ago, one could not find a period instrument recording of Corelli's trio sonatas listed in the Schwann Catalogue.

When this series of Performer's Guides was launched a few years ago, it was initially planned that there would be just one Baroque volume. Subsequent discussions made it clear that the subject matter was too vast to handle in a single volume, and so the seventeenth century was separated from the late Baroque. But apart from mere convenience, is there a compelling reason to treat the seventeenth century separately? Are there qualities that set the seventeenth century apart and make it unique? Historical watersheds rarely oblige us by falling neatly into years with round numbers, but at the beginning of the seventeenth century, this nearly happened in music. In Italy, the rise of monody and opera and the cataclysmic changes in texture did take place very close to 1600, thereby making that year a convenient dividing line on the early end of our spectrum.

The latter end of our period is well defined chronologically, but considerably less so stylistically. Some would argue that the Baroque style reached full maturity around 1680. All of the published works of Corelli—arguably one of the first masters of the mature Baroque and one who exerted immeasurable influence on musical style throughout

Europe—appeared after this date. The last works of Lully, who almost single-handedly created the French Baroque style, similarly appeared after 1680, as did the mature works of Purcell, the giant of the English Baroque.

So our century includes both the dawn of the Baroque and the beginnings of its maturity. But what holds it together stylistically? The characteristics of the Baroque that distinguish it from the Renaissance and mark it as a unique—even revolutionary—period are well known: the new texture of the "firm bass and florid treble," supplanting the old equal-voiced style; the rise of harmony and consequent downgrading—though not the disappearance—of counterpoint; the rise of instrumental music; the rise of solo music; the concertato style; the basso continuo; a new attitude toward the relationship between words and music; a new attitude toward emotional content in music; and the birth of new genres such as opera, oratorio, and sonata.

The changes that were wrought in Italy in the early seventeenth century were unusual in many respects. First, the rapidity and profundity of the change were unparalleled in the history of music up to that time. Never before had music changed so radically so quickly, and never before had theorists led the way, at least in part, toward stylistic change. Theorists of the Middle Ages and Renaissance described and explained music as they knew it; rarely did they advocate stylistic change. The members of the Florentine Camerata, most of them musical amateurs, probably just did not share the reverence for the received tradition of music that is evident in the writings of most earlier theorists.

Thoughts and ideas, then, led the way. This was a philosophical revolution as much as a musical one; or perhaps more accurately, the philosophical revolution precipitated the musical one. And it is probably safe to say that no one can fully understand the performance practices of the seventeenth century without some knowledge at least of its theoretical and philosophical underpinnings. Prominent among these is the widely cited but imperfectly understood Doctrine of Affections.

The idea that music had the power to move human affections was not new. Similar ideas had been propounded by the ancient Greeks, who served as the inspiration not only for the Baroque theories of the Affections, but for early Baroque solo song (today called monody) as well. In the opinion of some modern writers, this belief in the power of music to move human passions is the most salient element uniting the entire spectrum of Baroque music. It is impossible to understand Baroque music—particularly Italian music of the early seventeenth century—without grasping the essential elements of the Doctrine of Affections. For readers who wish to explore this matter further, the writings of Claude Palisca (see bibliography) are a good place to start.

Every performer of Baroque music must come to grips with the Doctrine of Affections on some level. But most of you who read this book will do so in search of practical information. The novice early music performer will find here a wealth of strategies for approaching a vast but little-known—and sometimes quirky—repertory. But experienced performers familiar only with the late Baroque may also find themselves enlightened. In many respects, the seventeenth century is a different period. Consider the following aphorisms that were more or less "gospel" among performers of late Baroque music thirty-odd years ago:

1. The trill begins on the upper auxiliary.
2. When realizing the basso continuo, use harpsichord in secular music, organ in sacred music.
3. Crescendo and diminuendo were not used in Baroque music; apply terrace dynamics instead.

Then there is the shopworn trick question, "How many performers are required to perform a trio sonata?," and its smug answer, "Four—two treble parts, a keyboard instrument, and a melodic bass to double the continuo line."

The above generalizations are riddled with misinformation, and the grains of truth contained therein are less true of seventeenth-century than of early-eighteenth-century music. Even among today's relatively well-informed professional performers of Baroque music there persist many disturbing misunderstandings of the essence and the details of seventeenth-century music. More disturbing still, however, is an attitude discernible among all too many musicians that "one style suits all," that is, you play Monteverdi much as you would play Bach—or worse still, Mozart. A case in point concerns the violin: an instrument set up according to mid-eighteenth-century specifications is simply not the instrument that Monteverdi or Schütz knew. But who will know? The purchaser of the latest CD of seventeenth-century music examines the jacket notes and is satisfied to see that the instrumentalists are using "Baroque" instruments—whatever that means!

This is not to say that the Collegium director at Generic State University should cancel a performance of the Monteverdi Vespers because he or she doesn't have access to early-seventeenth-century violins. Far from it. We can't recreate a truly "authentic" performance; we can only approximate it. And often we have to make compromises—lots of them. But when we do, let's be honest about it. Trumpet-maker Robert Barclay argues this point rather persuasively with regard to vent holes on valveless trumpets. Play the instrument if you want, he says, but don't call it a "Baroque trumpet" or a "natural trumpet," because it isn't either one.

It is hoped that this book will help us get closer to "the way they did it." None of us will make it all the way, but the more we learn about what seventeenth-century musicians did, the better we will understand their music.

I

VOCAL ISSUES

1

Solo Singing 1

Sally Sanford

*Divers Nations have divers fashions, and differ in habite, diet, stud-
ies, speech and song. Hence it is that the English doe carroll; the
French sing; the Spaniards weepe; the Italians . . . caper with their
voyces; the others barke; but the Germans (which I am ashamed to
utter) doe howle like wolves.*

Andreas Ornithoparcus, *Musicae active micrologus* (1515),
translated by John Dowland, 1609[1]

*As to the Italians, in their recitatives they observe many things of which
ours are deprived, because they represent as much as they can the passions and affections of the soul and the spirit, as, for example, anger,
furor, disdain, rage, the frailties of the heart, and many other passions,
with a violence so strange that one would almost say they are touched
by the same emotions they are representing in the song; whereas our
French are content to tickle the ear, and have a perpetual sweetness in
their songs, which deprives them of energy.*

Marin Mersenne, *Harmonie universelle*, 1636[2]

Although one might assume that the human voice has not changed
over the centuries, many elements of seventeenth-century vocal performance practice differed considerably from modern singing, as well
as from country to country. There was no single method of singing seventeenth-century music; indeed, there were several distinct national
schools, each of which evolved during the course of the century. The
differences between French and Italian singing were widely recognized
in this period, and the merits of each were debated well into the eighteenth century.[3] There were also distinctive features in German, English,
and Spanish singing.

Though the Italian school was the most influential outside its borders, much less source material by Italians survives than by Germans.
In reading the sources, confusion inevitably rises regarding terminology and the repertoire(s) and region(s) to which they apply. Writers use
the same term, such as *tremolo*, with different meanings, which in turn
may not correspond to modern usage. Though laryngology was not an

established science in the seventeenth century, some writers ventured into the area of vocal physiology, frequently creating more confusion than clarification.

Examining the linkages among treatises reveals both continuity and evolution within a national style over time and crosscurrents among regions. Figure 1.1 shows this linkage for Italian and German sources. While there was considerable musical exchange between Italy and Germany, there are still characteristics that give the music and its performance style an Italian or German "accent."

Most of the defining characteristics of national singing derive from language.[4] As Andrea von Ramm has observed,

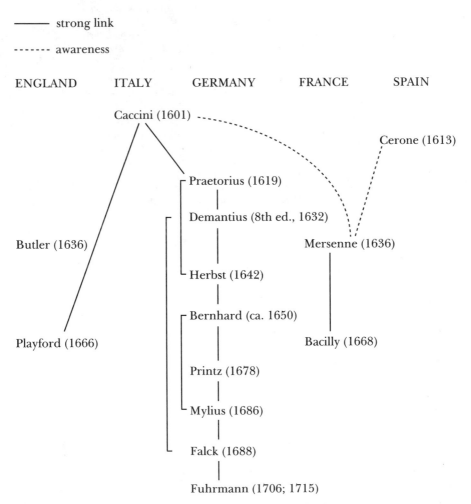

——— strong link

------- awareness

ENGLAND	ITALY	GERMANY	FRANCE	SPAIN

Caccini (1601)

Cerone (1613)

Praetorius (1619)

Demantius (8th ed., 1632)

Butler (1636)

Mersenne (1636)

Herbst (1642)

Bernhard (ca. 1650)

Playford (1666)

Bacilly (1668)

Printz (1678)

Mylius (1686)

Falck (1688)

Fuhrmann (1706; 1715)

FIGURE 1.1 Linkage of selected seventeenth-century singing treatises.

The characteristic sound of a language can be imitated as a typical sequence of vowels and consonants, as a melody, as a phrasing. There is an established rhythmical impulse of a language and a specific area of resonance involved for this particular character of a language or a dialect. In German one can say instead of 'Dialekt' also 'Mundart.' . . . This causes a different sound, a different resonance, and a different singing voice, depending on the language sung.[5]

Seventeenth-century writers on singing also recognized the importance of language. Christoph Bernhard discusses *Mundart* at some length in *Von der Singe-Kunst oder Manier*.

The first [aspect of a singer's observation of the text] consists in the correct pronunciation of the words . . . such that a singer not rattle [*schnarren*], lisp or otherwise exhibit bad diction. On the contrary, he ought to take pains to use a graceful and irreproachable pronunciation. And to be sure in his mother tongue, he should have the most elegant *Mund-Arth*, so that a German would not speak Swabian, Pomeranian, etc, but rather Misnian or a speech close to it, and an Italian would not speak Bolognese, Venetian or Lombard, but Florentine or Roman. If he must sing in something other than his mother tongue, however, then he must read that language at least as fluently [*fertig*] and correctly as someone born to it. As far as Latin is concerned, because it is pronounced differently in different countries, the singer is free to pronounce it as is customary in the place where he is singing.[6]

The importance of *Mundart* makes it essential to open the Pandora's box of historical pronunciations, which in their specifics are beyond the scope of this chapter. While Italian (a language full of dialects) has changed little in its pronunciation in the last four centuries, French and English have changed profoundly. As a literary language, German was in its infancy in the seventeenth century; it did not achieve a standardized pronunciation for the theater until the late nineteenth century. Even the same language, such as Latin, was pronounced differently in different places (and still is). Research in historical pronunciations yields many revelations in the poetry and expands the palette of sounds available to the aural imagination.[7]

The singer's art was closely aligned with the orator's during the Baroque period. The clear and expressive delivery of a text involved not only proper diction and pronunciation, but also an understanding of the rhetorical structure of the text and an ability to communicate the passion and meaning of the words. How this was achieved differed according to the particular characteristics of the language and culture as well as the musical style. The swing of the pendulum between the primacy of the words and the primacy of the music that occurred during the seventeenth century is important to bear in mind as we survey singing in Italy, France, Germany, England, and Spain.

Italy, ca. 1600–80

During the 1580s and '90s, florid singing in Italy reached a zenith with singers who excelled in the *gorgia* style of embellishments. These singers included women, boys, castrati, high and low natural male voices, and falsettists. The term *gorgia* (= throat) identified the locus of this technique, involving an intricate neuromuscular coordination of the glottis, which rapidly opens and closes while changing pitch or reiterating a single pitch—an action that is apparently innate to the human voice.[8] A basic threshold of speed is required in order for throat articulation to work easily. The glottal action can be harder or softer depending on the degree of clarity desired[9]; the Italians apparently used a harder articulation than the French. In 1639 André Maugars observed that the Italians "perform their passages with more roughness, but today they are beginning to correct that."[10] Throat articulation works best when the vocal tract is relaxed and there is not excessive breath pressure.[11]

Ludovico Zacconi described *gorgia* singers as follows:

> These persons, who have such quickness and ability to deliver a quantity of figures in tempo with such velocity, have so enhanced and made beautiful the songs that now whosoever does not sing like those singers gives little pleasure to his hearer, and few of such singers are held in esteem. This manner of singing, and these ornaments are called by the common people *gorgia*; this is nothing other than an aggregation or collection of many eighths and sixteenths gathered in any one measure. And it is of such nature that, because of the velocity into which so many notes are compressed, it is much better to learn by hearing it than by written examples.[12]

In Italy throat-articulation technique was often referred to as *dispositione*.[13] There is ample evidence that it was carried over with the advent of monody and the new, more declamatory styles of singing, in spite of changes in ornamentation style and vocal technique. We find ornaments, such as the *ribattuta di gola* ("re-beating of the throat"), for example, whose very name suggests its performance technique. Caccini described the *trillo*, a repercussion on one pitch, as a "beating in the throat."[14]

Learning a repercussion ornament was recognized as a good way to master throat articulation. Caccini remarks that the *trillo* and *gruppo* are "a step necessary unto many things."[15] It is in this context that we should understand Zacconi's remark that "the *tremolo*, that is, the trembling voice, is the true gate to enter the *passaggi* and to become proficient in the *gorgia*."[16] Equating Zacconi's *tremolo* with pitch-fluctuation vibrato, as some scholars have done, contradicts the nature of throat articulation technique.[17] I understand his reference to the continuous motion of the voice to refer to the rapid opening and closing of the glottis, which in the *trillo* is done continuously on one note. Learning this glottal action independent of changing pitch is enormously helpful as a first step, before advancing to *passaggi* and other ornaments involving rapid changes of pitch. As Zacconi says, it indeed "admirably facilitates the beginnings of the passages."[18] It is impossible to use throat articulation and continuous vibrato simultaneously, because the two vocal mechanisms are in laryngeal conflict with each other. Because Zacconi's remarks so clearly refer to the *gorgia* style, it is highly unlikely that his *tremolo* signifies either pitch-fluctuation vibrato or intensity vibrato.[19]

The declamatory style of singing developed by singer-composers such as Peri and Caccini extended speech into song. It most likely involved a laryngeal setup known today as "speech mode," in which the larynx is in a neutral position, with a relaxed vocal tract and without support from extrinsic muscles. Speech mode would have easily accommodated the continued use of throat articulation. What was new, compared to Renaissance practice, was the role (and style) of ornamentation in expressing the text and the use of a more flexible breathstream to reflect the increasing exploitation of the qualitative nature of the Italian language. This flexible breathstream would have ebbed and flowed with the accentuation of the text.[20]

The increased interest in the qualitative nature of Italian is tied to the development of the *stile rappresentativo*. Musical rhythms evolved from the characteristic rhythms associated with different poetic line lengths and poetic feet. Singers were highly sensitive to the different dynamic stresses for the *verso piano, verso tronco*, and *verso sdrucciolo*.[21] As Ottavio Durante says in the preface to his *Arie Devote* (1608), "You must pay attention to observe the feet of the verses; that is to stay on the long syllables and to get off the short ones; for otherwise you will create barbarisms."[22] G. B. Doni in his *Trattato della musica scenica* (1633–35) defined three levels of speech in the *stile recitativo*: narrative, expressive recitative, and special recitative (a style in between the other two), each of which had its own subtly different characteristic style of speech, compositional style, and manner of singing.

Consistent with the extension of speech into singing was the relatively narrow vocal compass of much of the music in the new style in the early decades of the century and the general preference for "natural" register rather than falsetto. Caccini was quite explicit: "From a feigned voice can come no noble manner of singing, which only proceeds from a natural voice."[23] Bellerofonte Castaldi wrote:

And because they treat either love or the scorn which a lover has for his beloved, they are represented in the tenor clef, whose intervals are proper and natural for masculine speech; it seems laughable to the Author that a man should declare himself to his beloved with a feminine voice and demand pity from her in falsetto.[24]

Falsettists certainly were common in church choirs[25] and were preferred to less skilled boys for solo parts.[26] The overriding conclusion to make from Caccini's comment is not to switch registers within the same piece and to transpose, if necessary, to avoid doing so. This is basically a one-register concept. For the new style of the early seventeenth century, the falsettist was not yet the operatic *voce mezzana*.[27]

Different voice registers had been recognized as early as the Middle Ages. In the *Lucidarium*, for example, Marchettus mentions three registers: *vox pulminis*, *vox gutturus*, and *vox capitis*.[28] Jerome of Moravia in the *Tractatus de Musica* identifies *vox pectoris*, *vox gutturis*, and *vox capitis*.[29] Yet many questions persist regarding the concept of register in the seventeenth century, namely: (1) Were different voice registers used or mixed within the same piece? (2) If so, how many registers were recognized? (3) What was the nature of the transition from one register to another? (4) What was the quality of each register? and (5) How do these early terms relate to modern concepts of register?

Most seventeenth-century writers discuss only two registers, natural and falsetto; Zacconi, however, discusses three: *voce di testa*, *voce di petto*, and a mixture of the two, called *voce obtuse*. He generally prefers the *voce di petto* to the *voce di testa*.[30] The need to develop a smooth passage between registers is not addressed in Italian sources before Tosi's *Opinioni* (1723). Of primary importance to early-seventeenth-century Italians was the distinction between "natural" register and "falsetto."

Another aspect of the new style of Italian singing involved greater attention to subtle dynamic shadings and colorings of the voice to express the text. The new flexible airstream facilitated the greater use of dynamics, especially in ornaments such as the *messa di voce* (a gradual crescendo and dimenuendo) and *esclamatione* (the inverse shape). The crescendo was not necessarily correlated with pitch-fluctuation vibrato, as is often the case today. Durante tells us to make a crescendo on the dot and in ascending chromatic prgressions.[31]

In the absence of dynamic indications in the music, the rhetorical structure of the text and the qualitative ebb and flow of the Italian language provide a dynamic *chiaroscuro* from which one can shape a flexible dynamic plan. However, it is important to bear in mind the underlying dynamic shape of the voice, which I call the "vocal pyramid," a concept for multiple voices that dates back as far as Conrad von Zabern (*De modo ben cantandi*, 1474).[32] In this "pyramid" the lowest voices are fuller and heavier, the highest voices softer and finer. This is a balance somewhat different from what we often hear today, when choirs are somewhat "top heavy." Hermann Finck articulated this concept in a polyphonic context in his *Practica musica* (1556): "A discant singer sings with a tender and soothing voice, but a bass with a sharper and heavier one; the middle voices sing their melody with a uniform sound and pleasantly and skillfully strive to adapt themselves to the outer voices."[33]

As solo singing developed, Italian singers incorporated this sound-concept into one voice. Singers today are taught to phrase to the highest point of the musical line, whereas in text-centered music of the early Baroque the rhetorical stress customarily takes advantage of the greater strength of the lower range. This became more fully developed later in the century as the range of vocal writing expanded. The "pyramid" has enormous implications both for dynamics in general and for the dynamic shape and direction of each phrase.

Another important characteristic of the new style was a certain rhythmic freedom, called *sprezzatura*. The singer was relatively free to depart from a regular tempo and/or from the notated musical rhythms in order to inflect the text. Rodolfo Celletti describes *sprezzatura* quite aptly: "It signifies a kind of singing liberated from the rhythmic inflexibility of polyphonic performance and allowing the interpreter, by slowing down or speeding up the tempo to 'adjust the value of the note to fit the concept of the words' and hence to make the phrasing more expressive."[34]

Modern singers trained to sing with absolute rhythmic precision need time to become comfortable with the concept of *sprezzatura*. The easiest way to incorporate it into singing is by first declaiming the text in an impassioned way as an orator or actor might. When I am not singing from memory, I often use a small prompt book with the texts set out according to the poetic lines, so that I can see the text as poetry freed from the musical notation. *Sprezzatura* can be equally daunting to a continuo player used to counting measures. In Ensemble Chanterelle, a group with which I perform regularly, theorbist Catherine Liddell has developed a notation system for works in *stile recitativo*, shown in Example 1.1, which reproduces only the singer's text and the bass pitches corresponding to the correct syllables, without any durational values (plus any necessary figures and some shorthand reminders about chord arpeggiation). This allows me total rhythmic freedom, frees her from unnecessary visual information, and enables both of us to make each performance responsive to the inspiration of the moment.

Perhaps the overriding characteristic of Italian singing in the first part of the century was the passionate engagement of the singer with the music, which in turn engaged the audience. Marco de Gagliano described hearing Jacopo Peri: "No one can fully appreciate the sweetness and the power of his airs who has not heard them sung by Peri himself, because he gave them such grace and style that he so impressed in others the emotion of the words that one was forced to weep or rejoice as the singer wished."[35] This passionate engagement becomes all the more important today when performing for an audience (mostly) unfamiliar with the language, the poetry, the music, and the style.

The changes in Italian singing that took place in the generation after Caccini and Peri are closely tied to the rise and influence of the castrati and to the stylistic developments in the opera and the cantata that altered the balance between text and music. These changes did not happen overnight and were no means complete by 1680, but were well established

EXAMPLE 1.1. Excerpt from Sigismondo d'India, *Laamento di Didone* (1623), illustrating notation system devised by Catherine Liddell for works in *stile recitativo*.

This notational system was devised by a skilled continuo player for her own use. It presupposes familiarity with the piece and assumes that some rehearsal with a more complete score has taken place. It reflects performance decisions made in rehearsal. This is most apparent with respect to tied and untied notes in the bass that depart slightly from the original notation, and with respect to words that are subject to elision and have been deliberately separated by the singer for dramatic reasons.

Some explanations of the markings used in the score:

( ) around figured bass signs indicates that the pitches in parentheses are covered in the vocal part.

− is used in the text (1) to indicate when a bar line or a bass note occurs in the middle of a syllable, (2) to indicate a long(er) note in the vocal part, (3) to provide a visual cue to signal a chord with a special affect, or (4) to provide a visual signal for a consonantal cue by the singer.

⌣ alerts the continuo player to (1) an *anticipazione della syllaba* at cadential points and (2) to places of elision in the text.

by musical developments in Rome and Venice. They involved greater divisions between recitative, arioso, and aria; greater pictorialization of ornamentation to depict or idealize particular words; changes in the shapes, ranges, and character of the vocal lines; and more generalized (and less nuanced) emotional states portrayed in the aria. In the process, speech gave way in the aria to lyricism and spectacle; subtlety gave some ground to sonority; and singers became *virtuosi* of the highest order. Venetian opera in particular glorified the art of singing.[36]

The Teatro dei Barberini and the Venetian public theaters were larger than the halls of noble palaces where opera had its first performances,[37] but still significantly smaller and with smaller orchestral forces than we normally find today. The Venetian opera "orchestra" often consisted of only two violins and a large continuo group, thus putting more focus on the singers.[38] Castrati with their penetrating sound quality, wide ranges, large breath capacity, and extensive musical training were ideal voices for the theater.[39] The hermaphroditic quality of their voices gave them the ability to play both male and female roles.

There are characteristics of the castrato voice that we will never be able to duplictate in our time, even though the last castrato, Allesandro Moreschi (d. 1922), sang in the Sistine Chapel until 1913. Modern technology has enabled us to hear an electronic synthesis of the voices of soprano Ewa Mallas-Godlewska and countertenor Derek Lee Ragin, used in the 1995 movie *Farinelli*, in an attempt to approximate a castrato voice. Whatever one thinks of the results, this is obviously not a viable solution for live performance. The question of what voice type is the best substitute for a castrato—a male falsettist, a female mezzo-soprano, or a female soprano—is still open to debate.[40]

Composers capitalized on the wide ranges of the castrati, which in turn led to an expansion of range in every voice type. At the top of their ranges, castrati rarely went higher than a".[41] Lyric, low coloratura bass voices, such as the Demon in Landi's *Sant'Alessio*, traversed C up to f". While the tessituras on the whole seem to us now to be generally low, range became an important aspect of character delineation. Although higher voices of castrati and females were generally preferred, bass voices were also given important roles, while the tenor voice was largely neglected.

In the absence of a mid-century Italian source on singing as comprehensive as Tosi's *Opinioni*, the music itself can provide clues to the evolution of vocal technique. In order to accommodate the wider ranges, singers likely used more than one vocal register. Falsetto and head voice would have been necessary to achieve the upper extension of the range. For female singers, head voice alone may have sufficed, though there is nothing from a laryngeal point of view to have precluded the use of falsetto at any point in the range.[42] Tosi is the first source to discuss this issue though it is unclear whether his equation of *voce di testo* with falsetto extends to all voice types.[43] We can only surmise how smoothly blended was the transition between registers before ca. 1680. It was certainly of utmost importance to Tosi, who preferred head voice for executing *passaggi* and other ornaments.

The predominance of speech mode that characterized the *stile rappresentativo* began to reach its limitations with the need for more sound and the development of a more lyrical aria style; it continued, of course, as the technique for recitative. Recitative style evolved into a more rapid, *parlando* character, though vestiges of the older *stile rappresentativo* can be heard in Cesti's *Orontea*, for example, alongside the newer arioso and *parlando* styles. Throat articulation also continued into the eighteenth century. There is no reason to think that the flexible airstream would have changed either, as the qualitative aspect of the words did not lose its importance altogether. Singers added to these resources a more cantabile style of singing, capable of a wide variety of colors and dramatic characterizations. If their breath technique and laryngeal position were not fundamentally changed—in order to execute the glottal action of throat articulation and to project the qualitative aspect of the Italian language— then this style of singing would have involved increased use of subtle adjustments of the vocal tract itself to achieve greater intensity of sound and more variety of sound qualities.

This cantabile style continued to allow singers extremely fine pitch control. Any increase in sonority would not have been so great as to lead to pitch distortion or to constant pitch-fluctuation vibrato. While singers then and now might agree that it is important to sing in tune, the definition of "in tune" has changed considerably. For those of us raised in a predominantly equal-tempered sound world, unequal temperaments can be a revelation. Modern computer technology and tuning boxes now make it possible to access exactly all sorts of different tuning systems with precision. Of chief importance for singers is not only developing the ear to match the pitches of the continuo and obbligato instruments, but also recognizing the implications of accurate pitch and temperament for how one sings and how one responds to the music.

Chromaticism was an important expressive device, used by many Italian composers. In the seventeenth century the major and minor semitone, such as D♯ and E♭, were distinctly different pitches, as Maugars indicates in describing the singing of Leonora Baroni: "When she passes from one note to another she sometimes makes you feel the divisions between the enharmonic and the chromatic modes with such artistry that there is no one who is not greatly pleased by this beautiful and difficult method of singing."[44]

The distinction between the major and minor semitone has strong implications for the amplitude of pitch-fluctuation vibrato.[45] In order to preserve the distinction between the major and minor semitone, the total amplitude of pitch fluctuation could not have exceeded a quarter tone— substantially smaller than what we hear today. In comparison to modern operatic singing, this involves a completely different vocal aesthetic, a different technique, and a different way of conceiving of vocal sound altogether. One cannot sing this repertory successfully using a technique that requires suppression of vibrato in the vocal tract to "straighten" the sound, which causes tension and fatigue. In order to maintain pitch control, one must use much less air pressure than in modern operatic singing. Any "straightening" of the sound must be done at the point of imaging the sound before one sings, not after it has been initiated.

As opera developed, a singer's skill in acting became increasingly important. Maugars observed that Italian singers "are almost all actors by nature."[46] The anonymous author of the acting treatise *Il corago* (ca. 1630) reminds us that "above all, to be a good singing actor, one must also be a good speaking actor."[47]

France

We are fortunate in having several detailed sources on French singing from the seventeenth century, the most important of which are Bacilly's *Remarques curieuses sur l'art de bien chanter* (1668) and Mersenne's *Harmonie universelle* (1636).[48]

French singing did not undergo the radical changes seen in the Italian school at the turn of the century,[49] though the French were certainly aware of developments in Italy. Mersenne, for example, mentions Caccini, who performed at court in 1604/5. There were notable champions of the Italian style of singing in France, as demonstrated by various efforts (ultimately unsuccessful) to establish Italian opera there. One of Louis XIII's favorite singers, Pierre de Nyert, the teacher of Bacilly and Lambert, studied briefly in Rome, and a handful of castrati sang at the court of Louis XIV prior to 1700.[50] Although Italianisms became increasingly present in French music toward the end of the century, in the main the style and technique of French singers differed considerably from those of their Italian counterparts.

Early-seventeenth-century French singing retained many aspects of sixteenth-century technique, particularly with respect to breathing. I have described the French approach to breathing as a "steady-state" system, where air pressure, speed, and volume remain virtually constant.[51] Such a system is perfectly suited to the quantitative nature of seventeenth-century French language and to the *chanson mesuré* and *air de cour*. Throat articulation, known in France as *disposition de la gorge* or simply *disposition*, was also used in the elaborate *doubles* (ornamented second verses of *airs*) as well as for *agréments*.

Airs de cour were published in great numbers throughout the century and served as the model for the operatic *airs* of Lully. They were often performed in the salons of the *precieux*, for an elite audience as preoccupied with the refinement of language as with dress and manners. Singers had to be as concerned with pronunciation as with any other aspect of their art. The French took the concept of *Mundart* very seriously.

Pronunciation meant more to the French than just the accurate delivery of the sounds of speech. It involved (1) proper execution of the sounds of the language without foreign accent; (2) clear delivery of those sounds so that the words could be understood in a room of any size; (3) the proper observance of syllabic quantity; and (4) inflection of the words in a way that facilitated perception both of their meaning and their underlying passion. French actors were highly skilled in these aspects of pronunciation. We know that Lully developed his style of recitative in part by hearing the declamation of the actress La Champmeslé. Singing required a more heightened and exaggerated declamation than speech, one that conveyed both the character of the words and the passion they expressed. Perhaps it is the spirit of Cartesian rationalism that explains why French writers on singing—Mersenne and Bacilly in particular—codified and preserved the art of French singing in detail.

Any thorough investigation of French singing diction must confront the differences between the seventeenth-century and modern versions of the language, as well as the differences between the quantitive character of French at this time and other qualitative European languages. Because of its defining importance to French vocal style and technique, one can make a strong argument for using historical pronunciation in performances of seventeenth-century French vocal music. The details of pronuncation with respect to both vowels and consonants are available in the primary sources. Bacilly also discusses syllabic quantity in great detail. The most striking difference between seventeenth-century court pronunciation and modern French vowel sounds is the -oi vowel, which was pronounced *oé* or *oué* until the Revolution.[52]

Even before the publication of Descartes's *Passions de l'âme* (1649), Mersenne (Descartes's schoolmate and correspondent) had observed that "each passion and affection has its proper accent."[53] Mersenne outlines three primary passions, each with varying degrees of intensity: anger, joy, and sadness. Anger, for example, is best conveyed by abruptly cutting off end syllables of words and by reinforcing final notes.

The projection of a particular passion was chiefly achieved by the degree of emphasis given to the *consonants*—either through duration or forcefulness of articulation. Bacilly outlines a technique of prolonging or suspending consonants, later called "consonant doubling" by Bérard.[54] The Italians, by comparison, centered their expression in the *vowels*, which could bloom and color with the qualitative inflection of the words.[55] If we regard Italian singing as "singing on the vowel," then we can view French singing as "singing on the consonant."[56]

Bacilly devotes a chapter to the technique of consonant inflection to express the passion of the words. Consonants that are to be prolonged can be sung (i.e., given pitch, in the case of voiced consonants) and sustained (for voiced consonants and fricatives) longer or shorter and articulated harder or softer, depending on the passion being expressed. The force of the consonant articulation would not alter the *dynamic level* of the subsequent vowel(s), which was governed by the steady-state airstream onto which the consonants were placed. The prolongation of the consonants would affect, however, both the *duration* of the subsequent vowel(s) and the relationship of the vowels and consonants with respect to the *rhythm*. Prolonged consonants can bleed over into the beat, rather than coming slightly ahead of the beat as is normally done in singing Italian. This technique, which is similar to some styles of pop singing today, should not be confused with the plosive, aspirated consonants associated with some schools of modern choral diction or with the German approach to consonants discussed below.

Because consonants contain much greater expressive information in the French school, the interaction between singer and accompanist(s) is different. The accompanist must listen in a different way to coordinate with the consonants—both in time and character—more than with the vowels. The resulting articulation matches quite well with the *stile brisé* of plucked instruments, which is perhaps why Bacilly preferred the theorbo for accompanying the voice.

The French found a way of compensating for most singers' tendency to spend less time on consonants in singing than in speaking. They intuitively understood what we now know scientifically, that to reach a threshold of intelligibility, a brief acoustic event such as a consonant needs to be higher in amplitude or longer in time. They also understood the expressive parameters in amplitude and duration to convey meaning and feeling. With consonants voiced on a precise pitch, we can be virtually certain that subvocal "scooping" was not a general feature of French singing at this time.

Both Mersenne and Bacilly describe a quality of the ideal singing voice that is related to *harmonie*, a certain quality of body or focus in the sound that was independent of the overall size of the voice. Mersenne describes this quality as being like "a canal which is always full of water" as opposed to a "thin trickle,"[57] while Bacilly describes it as the "amount of tone or *harmonie* present in the voice" that "nourishes the ear."[58]

Because of the degree to which consonants were "sung" in the French school, proper pitch control was of great importance. Mersenne's comments on intonation and evenness make it clear that vibrato was an ornament in the French school. He indicates that there should be no fluctuation in pitch when sustaining a tone, even when there is a crescendo or decrescendo.[59]

By the early eighteenth century we can document several types of ornamental vibrato used by the French. One type, produced in the throat, Montéclair termed the *tremblement feint*, in which the beating was "almost imperceptible."[60] The *flaté* was a breath vibrato appropriate for long notes, in which the amplitude was so small that it did not "raise or lower the pitch." This is perhaps more akin to what we would regard as intensity vibrato today. Montéclair describes a third type of vibrato: "The *balancement* which the Italians call *tremolo* produces the effect of the organ tremolo. To execute it well, it is necessary that the voice make several little aspirations more marked and slower than those of the *flaté*."[61] Montéclair also describes a nonvibrato tone appropriate for long notes: "The *son filé* is executed on a note of long duration . . . without any vacillation at all. The voice should be, so to speak, smooth like ice, during the entire duration of the note."[62]

Delicatesse was a quality highly prized by the French, especially in the execution of ornaments, as Mersenne indicates in describing the trill:

> And if one wishes to do this trill with all its perfection, one must even more redouble the trill on the note marked with a fermata [*d'un point dessus*], with such a *delicatesse* that this redoubling is accompanied by an extraordinary lightening [*adoucissment*] that contains the greatest charms of the singing proposed.[63]

Mersenne is describing a kind of singing so delicate that the finest nuances of throat articulation could be executed. This is chamber singing at its most subtle. The visual analog to the delicate filigree of French ornamentation style is the lacelike decoration of the silver furniture at Versailles (most of which was melted down to pay for Louis XIV's aggressive wars).

Perhaps the most important charactersisic in an ideal French singing voice was *douceur*, a quality that Bacilly felt came naturally to a *belle voix* and that could be cultivated in others. Mersenne writes,

> But our singers imagine that the *esclamationi* and the *accenti* which the Italians use in singing smack too much of Tragedy or Comedy, which is why they don't want to do them, though they ought to imitate what is good and excellent in them, because it is easy to temper the *esclamationi* and to accommodate them to the *douceur Française*, in order to add what they have more of in the Pathetic to the beauty, clarity and sweetness of trills, which our musicians do with such good grace, when having a good voice they have learned the method of proper singing from good masters.[64]

There is no extended discussion of vocal registers in French sources until the late eighteenth century.[65] One possible conclusion is that they used primarily only one register, at least for a given piece. The French, who favored equality over variety, apparently did not employ a vocal concept similar to the Italian "pyramid."

The French did recognize the existence of natural and falsetto registers. Bacilly observes that natural-voiced singers scorned falsettists and that the falsetto voice tended to be more brilliant (*éclatante*), the natural voice more in tune. Bacilly preferred small voices and high voices and generally felt that female voices (and falsettists) were at an advantage over male voices, though not entirely. He writes,

> It is established that feminine voices would have the advantage over masculine ones were it not for the fact that the latter have more vigor and strength for executing runs and more talent for expressing the passions than the former. For the same reason, falsetto voices bring out much more clearly what they sing than natural voices. However, they are somewhat harsh and often lack intonation, so that instead of being well cultivated they seem to be faded [*passé*] in nature. In addition I cannot avoid mentioning in passing an error all too common in the world concerning certain falsetto voices . . . whether because one is set awry in spirit or perhaps because these sorts of voices are in some fashion against Nature, it is easy to scorn them and to speak ill of those who possess such voices. Although upon reflexion one must observe that they owe everything in their vocal art to their voices thus elevated in falsetto, which renders certain *ports de voix*, certain intervals and other charms of singing quite differently than the tenor voice.[66]

Bacilly distinguished different qualities of voices: pretty, good, light, big, expressive, brilliant, but viewed them as qualities in different singers, not incorporated in one voice. The French recognized the individual variety in the human voice and felt that not every singer was equally suited to every type of expression.

Bacilly considered the following to be vocal faults: singing in the nose, poor voice projection, poor trills and *accents*, placing ornaments incorrectly such as at the end of a song, executing runs with the tongue and with unevenness and rushing (*avec certaine inégalité & précipitation*), poor pronunciation, and confusing long and short syllables. Bacilly preferred to hear the musical talents of a singer rather than the vocal quality in and of itself.[67]

Both Mersenne and Bacilly identified four general voice types: *basse* (or *basse-taille*), *taille*, *haute-contre*, and *dessus*.[68] Of these four, the *haute-contre* has been the least well understood and was for Lully perhaps the most important, for he wrote many title roles for this voice type, reflecting the French preference for higher voices for both sexes.[69] It is generally accepted today that the French *haute-contre* was not a falsetto voice, but a very high natural one with a range from g to a', extending occasionally to b'.[70]

The French stressed the qualities of intonation, evenness, clarity, flexibility, sweetness, sonority, and body in the ideal singing voice. French singing was expressive in the small, highly nuanced details of text delivery—especially in the consonants—and ornamentation. There was a clear demarcation between principal notes and notes of ornamentation. This is a vocal aesthetic substantially different from that cultivated by modern singing methods.

Germany

German sources on singing from the seventeenth century outnumber both Italian and French. As the chart in Figure 1.1 indicates, there are strong links among the German sources. The Socratic model established by Praetorius in *Syntagma musicum* III (1619) was imitated throughout the century by writers who tried to convey what they understood of the Italian style of ornamented singing. Though there was increasing impact of Italian musical developments in Germany as the century progressed, the vocal aesthetic that emerges from German treatises changed relatively little, except in its attitude toward falsetto.

Praetorius called attention to the close connection between singing and oratory. It was important for a singer not only to have a good voice, but also an understanding and knowledge of music, skill in ornamentation (which required throat articulation), good diction, and proper pronunciation. We can establish from Praetorius that the Germans ca. 1620, like the Italians ca. 1600, used throat articulation, prized the development of good breath control, and did not favor using falsetto. Praetorius's description of the requisites of a good singing voice has been quoted frequently, in modern times often as a defense for using continuous vibrato[71]:

> The requisites are these: that a Singer first have a beautiful, lovely, agile [*zittern*] and vibrating [*bebende*] voice . . . and a smooth [*glatten*], round throat for diminutions; secondly, the ability to hold a continuous long breath without many inhalations; thirdly, in addition, a voice . . . which he can hold with a full and bright [*hellem*] sound without Falsetto (which is a half and forced voice).[72]

In the above quotation, Praetorius's term *zittern* probably signifies more than its literal meaning of "trembling." Considered in light of Zacconi's discussion of the importance of the *tremolo* for learning the *gorgia* technique and singing *passaggi* (see above), it is likely that Praetorius (who learned much from Italian theorists) refers not to continuous pitch-fluctuation vibrato, but to that "trembling" of the voice that is the essence of throat-articulation technique, and hence the source of vocal agility.

Demantius outlined six important elements in proper singing in his influential *Isagoge artis musicae* (8th ed., 1632): (1) accurate pronunciation of vowels; (2) careful attention to semitones; (3) matching the tone of voice to the affect of the text; (4) correct intonation and proper awareness of the harmony; (5) avoidance of shouting, and (6) proper attention to the text and avoidance of breath articulation or "ha-ha-ha" in coloratura passages. Though he makes no direct reference to throat articulation, Demantius's admonition against breath articulation or aspiration is quite clear and was closely quoted by Georg Falck.[73] Demantius does not mention vibrato.

Christoph Bernhard outlined nine elements of good singing, the first of which he called *fermo*, which was keeping the voice steady on all notes except when doing a *trillo* (single-note repercussion) or an *ardire*, an ornamental type of vibrato for passionate expression. In any other context, polished singers, according to Bernhard, did not use pitch-fluctuation vibrato, which he termed *tremolo*, with the exception of basses, who used it seldom and only on short notes.[74]

Bernhard's student Wolfgang Mylius follows Praetorius's model in his *Rudimenta musices* (1686), except that he omits the word *zittern* and uses *belebende*, meaning "lively," where Praetorius uses *bebende*: "First a youth or singer must have by nature a beautiful, lovely, lively [*belebende*] voice well-disposed to a trill and a smooth, round throat."[75]

Praetorius, Printz, and Falck all use the term *zittern* in connection with what we would call a trill today, but that they called *tremolo*.[76] Mylius also uses *zittern* to refer to the two-note trill, while Printz and Falck use it in conjunction with the single-note *trillo*.[77] *Zittern* thus seems to refer to vocal agility, implying throat articulation, akin to the Italian term *dispositione*. Printz uses the term *Bebung* to describe the *trilletto*, probably an intensity vibrato: "*Trilletto* is only a vibrating [*Bebung*] of the voice so much gentler than the *trillo* that it is almost not struck [with the throat]."[78] Intensity vibrato or "shimmer" gives vitality to a tone while keeping the pitch steady. Printz's description of his *trilletto* seems to have been the basis for Fuhrmann's *tremoletto*, which he describes in terms not unlike Printz's: "*Tremoletto* is a vibrating [*bebung*] of the voice, almost not struck at all, and happens on one note or in one Clave, as is best to show on the violin, when one lets the finger remain on the string and as with the shake, slightly moves and makes the tone shimmer [*schwebend*]."[79] Fuhrmann also gives a musical example, shown in Figure 1.2.

EXAMPLE 1.2. "Tremoletto" (from Fuhrmann—*Musicalischer Trichter*, 66).

Printz gives a very detailed description of the lightness and rapidity of throat articulation, which was the principal technique for executing ornaments. He recommends keeping the mouth in an average opening, the cheeks in a natural position (*not* raised, as in a "smile" position), the tongue relaxed, the jaw still.[80] Printz's comments should dispel any notion that a single-note *trillo* sounded like a bleating of a goat: "Throat articulation (the beating in the throat) happens very gently, so that the voice is not at all constricted [*geschliesset*]."[81]

In the second half of the century, the Germans seem to have followed an evolution similar to the Italian school, though a bit later, in mixing the falsetto with the natural voice. With the greater cultivation of different voice registers, the Germans also followed the Italians in applying the "pyramid" shape of the voice. Printz articulates the concept quite explicitly: "The more a voice ascends and the higher it is, the more subtle and softer it should sing, and the lower a voice gets, the greater strength should be given to it."[82]

The German vocal ideal then was one of a lovely, light, well-supported voice that accorded itself to the meaning of the words, was agile, shimmering, and unforced, using falsetto only when absolutely necessary at the top of the range, and in the second half of the century, following the "pyramid" shape of the Italian school.

Printz, like Bacilly and Mersenne, understood the need for greater clarity in singing consonants, especially in larger spaces. His solution was to make the consonants higher in amplitude (not longer in duration as discussed above for French singing), with a forceful, hard pronunciation:

> The consonants should be very strongly pronounced, especially in large rooms or in open spaces. Vowels are easy to do, on account of their sounds, but not consonants. So that one can understand the consonants from far away, they must be pronounced harder than in normal speech, yea almost excessively hard.[83]

The German language, like Italian, is qualitative. German writers recognized the dynamic ebb and flow of the language in good oratory and in good singing.[84] It is likely then that German singers used a flexible breathstream similar to the Italians, whose style and technique of singing they so frequently tried to emulate.

England

We have few English sources on singing from the seventeenth century, though there is a considerable body of material on oratory, rhetoric, and acting.[85] The evolution from the lute songs of Dowland to the continuo songs of the Lawes family to the late songs of Purcell shows remarkable developments in both declamatory style and vocal technique. Part of this evolution, of course, involves a synthesis of an indigenous English style with Italian and, to a lesser extent, French influences, and the gradual development of professional singing.

The migration of Italian music and musicians to England in the early decades of the century involved the madrigal more than monody. Before about 1625, English solo singing largely perpetuated sixteenth-century practice.[86] Only two court musicians arrived from Italy in the years between 1603 and 1618.[87] A very few English musicians—notably Dowland, Lanier, and possibly Coprario—traveled to Italy. Robert Dowland published a lute-song version of Caccini's *Amarilli, mia bella* in 1610, and other versions of this song (some quite florid) were circulated in manuscripts, but few Italian monodies were exported to England.

The English Renaissance style of singing is outlined in William Bathe's *Briefe Introduction to the Skill of Song* (ca. 1587). Bathe stresses the importance of (1) singing the vowels and consonants distinctly, according to local pronunciation; (2) having a breath technique to sing long phrases and a tongue capable of clear enunciation at a fast tempo; (3) a knowledge of musical notation and the proper proportion of note values; and (4) maintaining a clear voice for proper intonation.[88]

Lanier introduced the Italian *stylo recitativo* to England ca. 1613 in Campion's *Squires Masque*. Lanier's *Hero and Leander* (ca. 1628) is a direct imitation of Monteverdi's recitative-lament style, though it is hampered a bit by the greater profusion of consonants and the different accentual patterns of the English language.

Charles Butler's *Principles of Musick* (1636) is one of the earliest seventeenth-century sources to discuss singing in detail. He calls attention to the importance of the text, as the element that sets singing apart: "Good voices alonᵉ, sounding onᵉly the notᵉs, are sufficient, by their Melodi and Harmoni, to delight the ear; but beeing furnished with soom laudable *Ditti* they becoom yet morᵉ excellent."[89]

Butler further indicates that the punctuation of the text should provide the punctuation of the music. A singer's observation of textual and musical punctuation is important in shaping the rhetorical and dramatic structure of any vocal piece. Early-seventeenth-century English composers often amplify the text through different rhetorical means of word repetition.[90] Declaiming the text, both for diction and rhetorical emphasis, is extremely important in this repertory. Pronouncing the words distinctly was an important consideration for an English singer, particularly in an age in which the quality of the poetry often exceeded that of the music. Butler seems to describe the use of speech mode in advocating that singers sing "as plainly as they would speak."

He also understood the importance of proper posture when singing:

Concerning the Singers, their first carᵉ shouldᵉ bee to sit with a decent erect posturᵉ of the Bodi, without all rediculous and uncoomly gesticulations, of Hed, or Hands, or any oder Partᵉ; then ((that the Ditti (which is half the gracᵉ of the Song) may be known and understood)) to sing as plainly as they would speak; pronouncing every Syllable and letter (specially the Vouels) distinctly and treatably. And in their great varieti of Tonᵉs, to keep still an equal Sound: . . . dat onᵉ voice droun not an other.[91]

One possible interpretation of "equal" in this context is that the English in the first third of the century did not use "pyramid" registration (at least in a polyphonic context) and favored an equal balance of all the voices. However, this interpretation is possibly contradicted by

Butler's observation, again in a polyphonic context, that "The Bass is so called, because it is the *bassis* or foundation of the Song, unto wie all oder Parts bee sete: and it is to be sung wit a deep^e, ful, and pleasing Voic^e. . . . The Treble . . . is to bee sung with a big cleer^e sweet^e voic^e."[92]

Butler's concept of "equality" in this case might have meant equal within the parameters of the pyramid—a balance different from the modern norm. His description of the countertenor voice is also puzzling: "De Countertenor or *Contratenor*, is so called, becaus it answeret de Tenor; dow commonly in higer keyz: and ther^{e}for^e is fittest for a man of a sweet shrill voic^e." What Butler means by "shrill" is unclear; it may simply be an indication of falsetto. Edward Huws Jones has argued that the English countertenor voice is equivalent to the modern tenor, the English "tenor" to the modern baritone.[93] René Jacobs regards the low Purcellian countertenor and the French *haute-contre* as having "very much in common."[94] By the time of Purcell the countertenor voice used both natural and falsetto registers.

Playford's translation of Caccini's preface to *Le Nuove Musiche* was not published until the 1664 edition of *A Breefe Introduction*.[95] Playford's glosses on Caccini are of considerable interest, particularly with respect to the *trillo*. Playford indicates that one can approximate the sound of the *trillo* by shaking the finger upon the throat, and also that it could be done by imitating the "breaking of a sound in the throat which men use when they lure their hawks."[96]

Playford's "Directions for Singing after the Italian Manner" lasted through the twelfth edition of *A Breefe Introduction* (1694). It seems that the early Italian methods persisted in England until at least ca. 1680, considerably longer than in Italy. According to Ian Spink, the *trillo* had become obsolete in England by 1697.[97]

During the Restoration there was a resurgence of interest in Italian music. The king had his own group of Italian musicians, and castrati and other Italian performers arrived bringing the music of Carissimi and Stradella, among others, to the awareness of the English. Although Pietro Reggio's treatise *The Art of Singing* (1678) unfortunately does not survive, it suggests that in the last quarter of the century the English used an Italian singing technique, though one that accommodated the English language and the mixed musical style of the period.

Pronunciation of English changed considerably during the seventeenth century: Restoration English, for example, is even further removed from modern "BBC" English than seventeenth-century French is from its modern counterpart. There was some interest in England in establishing a standardized orthography during this period, and as a result there are some very useful sources for historical pronunciation. Among the most detailed is Christopher Cooper's *The English Teacher or the Discovery of the Art of Teaching and Learning the English Tongue* (1687).[98]

Seventeenth-century English was regarded as problematic for setting to music in comparison to Italian. Playford writes,

The Author hereof [i.e., Caccini] having set most of his Examples and Grace to *Italian words*, it cannot be denyed, but the *Italian* language is more smooth and better vowell'd than the *English* by which it has the advantage in *Musick*, yet of late years our language is much refined, and so is our Musick to a more smooth and delightful way and manner of singing after this new method by *Trills, Grups and Exclamations*, and have been wed to our English *Ayres*, above this 40 years and Taught here in *England*; by our late Eminent Professors of *Musick*, Mr. *Nicholas Laneare*, Mr. *Henry Lawes*, Dr. *Wilson and* Dr. *Coleman*, and Mr. *Walter Porter*, who 30 years since published in Print Ayres of 3, 4, and 5 Voyces, with the *Trills* and other Graces to the same. And such as desire to be Taught to sing after this way, need not to seek after *Italian* or *French* masters, for our own Nation was never better furnished with able and skilful Artists in Musick, then it is at this time, though few of them have the Encouragement they deserve, nor must Musick expect it as yet, when all other Arts and Sciences are at so low an Ebb.[99]

Playford refers to a quality of smoothness in singing the text, reflecting the Italianate "singing on the vowel." Depending on the style in a late-seventeenth-century English piece, I sometimes slant my text delivery to include aspects of both the Italian and French schools.

Vibrato was a vocal ornament in English singing as it was elsewhere in Europe.[100]

Spain

Spanish contributions to musical developments in Italy were significant: the Spanish may have given Italy the castrato voice.[101] Many elements from Spanish spoken theater (such as *buffo* parts, the character of the servant-confidant, and the mixture of different elements of social class) were incorporated into Italian opera. While these elements sparked many musical developments in Italy, they did not lead to the same degree of innovation in Spain, where the Baroque arrived much later than elsewhere in Europe. The court of Philip IV (1622–50) was conservative, the musical life of the chapel heavily steeped in the Renaissance Flemish tradition. Foreign influences on Spanish musical life in the second half of the century were also limited, though this was not for lack of exposure.[102]

The principal treatise we have for Spanish singing is Domenico Pietro Cerone's *El Melopeo*, published in Naples in 1613 and written in Spanish (not Cerone's native language), possibly in order to curry favor with Philip III and the Spanish viceroy in Naples. A very conservative work, *El Melopeo* nonetheless exerted a profound influence in Spain that lasted into the late eighteenth century. An enormous volume, it is the earliest musical treatise still surviving that was brought to the New World.[103]

Book 8 of *El Melopeo* deals with *glosas*, which we might call in English "running divisions," and with *garganta* technique, the throat articulation technique that singers used to execute them. One can view this section as Cerone's diminution manual in the sixteenth-century tradition of Diego Ortiz and Tómas de Santa Maria, from whom Cerone borrows some examples.

Cerone says little about vocal technique and claims that his aim is to aid the beginning *glossador*; yet he does tell us that *cantar de garganta* means the same thing as *cantar de gorgia* in Italian. The *glosas* require agility (*destreza*), lightness (*ligereza*), clarity (*claridad*), and time (*tiempo*). These descriptive words are strikingly similar to the words used by the French in outlining the ideal singing voice. Cerone makes it clear that the number of notes in a division do not need to add up metrically, but that perfection consists more in maintaining the time and the measure than in running with lightness, because if one reaches the end too late or too soon, everything else is worthless. He also recommends, unlike the Italians, doing the division in one breath. Execution of divisions for Cerone requires primarily (1) strength of the chest (*fuerça de pecho*), by which I think he means breath capacity rather than strong air pressure— since he goes on to say he means by this being able to sing to the end of the line, and (2) the disposition of the throat.

Spanish singers used a fundamentally Renaissance vocal style and technique until very late in the seventeenth century. Many of the texts of later seventeenth-century *tonos* and *tonadas* are of a narrative or descriptive nature, not expressive in the manner of Italian monody. Their general style is restrained and simple, though they may have been ornamented in the *garganta* style. Louise Stein has pointed out that most of the actress-singers active on the Spanish stage were not well educated and were trained by rote in a traditional, popular style,[104] in marked contrast to the training of the Italian castrati.

One of the challenges in performing Spanish vocal music of this period lies in finding a balance between the accentuation of the text and the (often complex) musical rhythms. *Sprezzatura* does not seem to have been adopted by the Spanish. Although one might occasionally apply "corrective" word accentuation, the overriding rhythmic vitality of the music seems to take precedence as a general rule over accentual matters of the text. This creates a typically Spanish dynamism between the words and the music.

Conclusion

The pan-European approach that has characterized many performance-practice surveys dealing with singing and the widespread availability of recordings in our own time have led to a regrettable homogenization of performance styles in present-day performances of seventeenth-century music. As we have shown, significant differences existed among the various national schools of singing during the seventeenth century. There are also aspects of the singing of Jacopo Peri, Caterina Martinelli, Barbara Strozzi, Anna Renzi, John Pate, John Gosling, Antoine de Boesset, Michel Lambert—to name but a handful of great singers from the seventeenth century—that were probably as distinctive and unique to each of them as is the case in the singing of Placido Domingo, Kathleen Battle, Barbra Streisand, Bobby McFerrin, and Frank Sinatra today. In performing seventeenth-century vocal music (or any vocal music, for that matter) one must match technique and style not only to the time period, region, physical setting, genre, voice type and range required, accompanying instrument(s), pitch standard and tuning system being used, and the particular piece of music at hand, but also to the unique characteristics of one's own voice and musical personality.

Exploring historical vocal techniques and the culture(s) in which they were developed connects us to the music more directly and enriches our understanding of it. *It also makes it easier to sing.*

Notes

1. Dowland–*Ornithoparcus*: 88.
2. Translated in MacClintock–*Readings*, 173.
3. For a comparison of these two schools, including audio examples, see Sanford–Comparison.
4. See Sanford–Comparison, pars. 1.1 and 1.2.
5. von Ramm–Singing Early Music, 14.
6. "Das erste bestehet in rechter Aussprache der Worte, die er singend fürbringen soll, dannenhero ein Sänger nic' t schnarren, lispeln, oder sonst ein böse Ausrede haben, sodern sich einer zierlichen und untadelhaften Aussprache befleissen soll. Und zwar in seiner Muttersprache soll er die zierlichste Mund-Arth haben, so dass ein Teutscher nicht Schwäbish, Pommersich [etc.], sondern Meissnisch oder der Red-Arth zum nächsten rede, und ein Italiener nicht *Bolognessich, Venedisch, Lombardisch*, sondern *Florentinisch* oder *Römisch* spreche. Soll er aber anders als in seiner Muttersprache singen, so muss er dieselbe Sprache zum aller wenigsten so fertig und richtig lesen, alss diejenigen, welchen solche Sprache angebohren ist. Was die Lateinische Sprache anbelanget, weil dieselbige in unterschiedenen Ländern unterschiedlich ausgesprochen wird, so steht dem Sänger frey, dieselbe so, wie sie an dem Orthe, wo er singt, üblich ist, auszusprechen." Bernhard–*Von der Singe-Kunst*, 36. Bernhard goes on to say that is it also prudent to pronounce Latin in an Italian manner.
7. For further information on historical pronunciations, see Copeman–*Singing in Latin*; and Sanford–Guide.
8. The first writer to identify the locus of this technique was Maffei–*Discorso*, 30. For a more physiological and scientific description of this technique, see Sherman/ Brown–Singing Passaggi.
9. This is my empirical observation. Sherman/Brown did not address this issue.
10. Maugars–*Response*, translated in MacClintock–*Readings*, 122.
11. See Sanford–Comparison, par. 2.2. Sherman/Brown (Singing Passaggi, 36, n.24) have observed that "increasing the subglottal breath pressure has the following effect: . . . it makes the execution of florid passages difficult or impossible."
12. Zacconi–*Prattica*; translated in MacClintock–*Readings*, 69.

13. For more detailed discussion see Sanford–Comparison, par. 7.1 and audio examples 15, 16. See also Sanford–Vocal Style, 51ff; and Greenlee–Dispositione, 47–55.

14. "Cioè il cominciarsi dalla prima semiminima, e ribattere ciascuna nota con la gola." Caccini–*Nuove musiche*, preface.

15. Strunk–*Source Readings–Baroque*, 25.

16. Zacconi–*Prattica*; translated in MacClintock–*Readings*, 73.

17. See, for example, Harris–Voices, 105.

18. Zacconi–*Prattica*; translated in MacClintock–*Readings*, 73.

19. Gable suggests this in Observations, 94. Intensity vibrato is produced with a different vocal mechanism than the *trillo*, so the former would not lead directly into the latter.

20. See Sanford–Comparison, pars. 2.2, 2.6, and audio examples 4, 8.

21. See *New Grove Dictionary of Opera*, s.v. "*Stille rapprensentativo.*"

22. "Bisogna avvertire di osservare i piedi de i versi, cioé di trattenersi nelle sillabe lunghe, e sfuggir nelle brevi, perche altrimeni si faranno de barbarismi." See also Sanders–Vocal Ornaments, 70–71.

23. "Ma dalle voce finta non può nascere nobilità di buon canto: che nascer à da una voce naturale comoda per tuta le corde." Strunk–*Source Readings–Baroque*, 31–32. Praetorius also reiterated Caccini's point of view. See below.

24. "E perche trattano o d'Amore, or di sdegno che tiene l'Amante con la cosa amata, si rappresentano sotto Chiave di Tenore, cui intervalli sono propri, e natural del parlar mascolino, parendo pure al Autor sudetto cosa da ridere che un huomo con voce Feminina si metta a dir le sue ragioni, e dimandar pietà in Falsetto ala sua innamorata." Castaldi–*Primo Mazzetto di fiori*, preface.

25. See Kurtzman–*Vespers*, ch. 15.

26. Viadana remarks in the preface to *Concerti ecclesiastici* (1605), for example, "Che in questi Concerti saranno miglior effeto i Falsetti, che i Soprani naturali, si perche per lo piu Putti cantano trascuramente, e con poca gratia come anco perche si è atteso alla Lontananza, per tender piu vaghezza, no vi è peró dubbio, che non si si puo pagare condenari un buon Soprano naturale: ma se ne trovano pochi." ("In these concertos, falsettos will have a better effect than natural sopranos; because boys, for the most part, sing carelessly, and with little grace, likewise because we have reckoned on distance to give greater charm; there is, however, no doubt that no money can pay a good natural soprano; but there are few of them.") Translated in Strunk–*Source Readings–Baroque*, 62.

27. For a discussion of the *voce mezzana*, see R. Jacobs–Controversy, 289.

28. See Gerbert–*Scriptores* 3: 120.

29. [When chant is sung by two or more singers] "Tertium est, ut voces dissimiles in tali cantu no misceant, cum non naturaliter, sed vulgariter loquendo, quedam voces sint pectoris, quedam gutturis, quedam vero sint ipsius capitis." Coussemaker–*Scriptorum* 1: 93b.

30. Zacconi–*Prattica*, 77r.

31. Sanders–Vocal Ornaments, 73.

32. See R. Jacobs–Controversy, 289.

33. MacClintock–*Readings*, 62.

34. Celletti–*Bel Canto*, 16.

35. MacClintock–*Readings*, 189.

36. See Rosand–*Opera*, esp. ch. 8.

37. Celletti–*Bel Canto*, 19.

38. Rosand–*Opera*, 24.

39. The Sistine Chapel had begun replacing falsettists with castratos in the late sixteenth century. See Kurtzman–*Vespers*, ch. 15.

40. For more detailed discussion of the castrato voice, see Heriot–*Castrati; New Grove*— Castrato; Habock–*Kastraten*; Sawkins–For and Against.

41. Celletti–*Bel Canto*, 39. Burney recounts that the castrato Matteo Berselli, who was active in the 1720s, could go from c' to f''' with "the greatest of ease." Quantz gives

Farinelli's range as from a to d''' in 1726, adding several notes a few years later. See Sanford–*Vocal Style*, 23.

42. I use my falsetto for special effects. Many female popular singers do as well.
43. Many writers after Tosi equated head voice and falsetto.
44. MacClintock–*Readings*, 122.
45. See Moens-Haenen–*Vibrato*.
46. MacClintock–*Readings*, 122.
47. Translated in Termini–Baroque Acting, 149.
48. Other sources include Jean Millet (1666), Jean Rousseau (1683), François Raguenet (1702), and Jean-Laurent Le Cerf de la Vieville (1704).
49. Anthony (*French Baroque*, 45) has discussed the musical conservatism of France in the seventeenth century.
50. See Sawkins–For and Against.
51. See Sanford–Comparison, par. 2.5.
52. For a discussion and examples of seventeenth-century French pronunciation, see Sanford–Comparison, pars. 5.1, 6.1–6.4, and audio examples 5, 13, 16. See also Sanford–Guide, and Gérold–*L'Art*, 215ff.
53. Mersenne–*Harmonie universelle* 2: 367.
54. Bacilly–*Remarques*, 307ff.
55. To hear examples of this Italian approach, see Sanford–Comparison, audio examples 4, 6, 8, 15.
56. Ibid., audio examples 5, 9, 13, 16.
57. Mersenne–*Harmonie universelle* 2: 354.
58. "Il y a encore une Remarque à faire dans la difference des Voix, par le plus ou le moins de son & d'harmonie qu'elle produisent, c'est à dire qu'il en est qui remplissent, ou pour parler dans les terms de l'Art, qui nourissent mieux l'oreille que d'autres plus deliées, & que dans le language ordinarie on nomme des Filets de Voix, bien qu'elles se fassent entendre d'aussi loin, qu'elles ayent autant ou plus d'étendué que les premières." Bacilly–*Remarques*, 47.
59. "La justesse consiste à prendre le tone proposé, sans qu'il soit permis d'aller plus haut, ou plus bas que la chorde, ou la note au'il faut toucher, & entonner. L'égalité est la tenue ferme, & stable de la voix sur une mesme chorde, sans qu'il soit permis de la varier en la haussant ou en la baissant, mais on peut l'affoiblir, & l'augmenter tandis que l'on demeure sur une mesme chorde." Mersenne–*Harmonie universelle* 2: 353.
60. Montéclair–*Principes*, 83.
61. "Le Balancement que les Italiens appellent Tremolo produit l'effet du tremblant de l'Orgue. Pour ke bien executer, il faut que la voix fasse plusieurs petites aspirations plus marquées et plus lentes que celles du Flaté." Ibid., 85.
62. Ibid., 88.
63. "Et si l'on veut faire cette cadence avec toute sa perfection, il faut encore redoubler la cadence sur la note marquée d'un point dessus, avec une telle delicatesse, que ce redoublement soit accompagné d'un adoucissement extraordinaire, qui côtienne les plus grands charmes du Chant proposé." Mersenne–*Harmonie universelle* 2: 355.
64. "Mais nos Chantres s'imaginent que les exclamations & les accents dont les Italiens usent en Chanant, tiennent trop de la Tragedie, ou de la Comedie, c'est pourquoy ils ne veulent pas les faire, quoy qu'ils deussent imiter ce qu'ils ont de bon & d'excellent, car il aisé de temperer les exclamations & de les accommoder à la douceur Françoise, afin d'ajoûter ce qu'ils ont de plus pathetique à la beauté, à la netteté, & à l'adoucissement des cadences, que nos Musiciens font avec bonne grace, lors qu'ayant une bonne voix ils ont appris la methode de bien chanter des bons Maistres." Mersenne–*Harmonie universelle* 2: 357.
65. See, for example, J.-P. Martini–*Melopée*.
66. "Il est constant que les Voix Feminines avoient bien de l'avantage par dessus les Masculines, si celles-cy n'avoient plus de vigeur & de fermeté pour executer les traits

du Chant, & plus de Talent pour exprimer les passions que les autres. Par la mesme raison les Voix de Fausset font bien plus paroistre ce qu'elles chantent que les Voix naturelles; mais d'ailleurs elles ont de l'aigreur, & manquent souvent de justesse, à moins que d'estre si bien cultivées, qu'elles semblent estre passées en nature. Au reste je ne puis m'empescher de faire mention en passant d'une erreur fort commune dans le Monde, touchant certaines Voix de Fausset . . . parce que l'on se l'est mis mal à propos dans l'Esprit, soit peut-estre parce que ces sortes de Voix estant en quelque façon contre Nature, on se porte plus facilement à les mépriser, & dire mal à propos de ceux qui les possedent, qu'ils n'en ont point, quoy que si l'on y faissant bien reflexion, on remarqueroit qu'ils doivent tout ce qu'ils ont de particulier dans la Maniere de Chanter à leur Voix ainsi élevée en Fausset, qui fait paroistre certains Ports de Voix, certains Intervales, & autres Charmes du Chant, tout autrement que dans la Voix de Taille." Bacilly–*Remarques*, 46–47.

67. Ibid. 89–90.

68. These terms are not easily translated into English. *Basse* and *taille* are more or less equivalent to bass and tenor, respectively, while the term *dessus* refers to "the highest voice part, sung by children, women or girls, castratos, and all those whose voices have not . . . changed . . ." (René Ouvrard [1624–94], *La Musique rétablie depuis son origine* [Ms, Bibliothèque de Tours; cited in Benoit–*Dictionaire*, s.v. "Dessus," by J. Duron). A description of the *haute-contre* follows in the main text.

69. Bacilly–*Remarques*, 45.

70. For more discussion see Cyr–Haute-Contre.

71. See, for example, Henahan–Listening.

72. "Die *Requisita* sinde diese: dass ein Sänger erstlich eine schöne liebliche zittern=und bebende Stimme (doch nicht also/wie etliche in Schulen gewohnet sein/sodern mit besondere *moderation*) und einen glatten runden Hals zu *diminuiren* habe: zum Andern/einen stetten langen Athem/ohn viel *respiren*, halten können: zum dritten auch eine Stimme als *Cantum*, *Altum* oder *Tenor* &c. erwehlen/welche er mit vollem und hellem laut/ohne Falsetten/ (das ist halbe und erzwungene Stimme) halten könne" (Praetorius–*Syntagma* III: 231). Herbst quotes this verbatim in *Musica Practica*, 3. Falck (*Idea*, 90) also quotes this closely, but interestingly with the words *zittern* and *bebende* omitted.

73. Falck–*Idea*, 92.

74. See Bernhard–*Singe-Kunst*, 31–32. Note that Bernhard differs from other sources that regarded vibrato as appropriate for long notes.

75. "Erstlich soll ein Knabe oder Sänger von Natur eine schöne/liebliche/belebende und zum <u>trillo</u> bequeme Stimme und glatten runden Hals haben." Mylius–*Rudimenta musices*, sec. 5. Mylius uses the term *trillo* for a two-note trill, not a repercussion.

76. "*Tremolo*: Ist nicht ander/als ein Zittern der Stimme über einer *Noten*: die Organisten nennen es *Mordanten*." Praetorius–*Syntagma* III: 235. "*Tremolo* ist ein scharffes Zittern der Stimme über einer grössern *Noten*/so die nechste *Clavem* mit berühret. Er steiget entweder auf oder ab/und ist entweder verkürsset oder verlängert." Printz–*Musica modulatoria*, 46.

77. "Trillo is ein Zittern der Stimme in einer *Clave* über einer grössern *Noten* mit einem etwas scharffen doch lieblichen und manierlichen Anschlagen." Printz–*Musica modulatoria*, 57. "Trillo is ein liebliches sauffen/und ein Zittern der Stimme über einer Notà." Falck–*Idea*, 102.

78. "Trilletto is nur eine Bebung der Stimme/so viel linder als Trillo/oder fast gar nicht angeschlagen wird." Printzl–*Musica modulatoria*, 58.

79. "*Tremoletto* ist eine Bebung der Stimme, so gar nicht angeschlagen wird/und in Unisono oder einem Clave nur geschiehet/wie auf der Geige am besten zu zeigen/wenn man den Finger auff der Seite stehen lässet/und solchen doch mit Schitteln etwas beweget und den Thon schwebend macht." Fuhrmann–*Musicalisher Trichter*, 66.

80. "Hier erinnern wir ins gemein/dass ein jede Figur ihren manierlichen *Apulsum gutturalem* haben müsse/das ist/ein Angehlagen/welches in der Kehle gemacht werden

soll mit einer natürlichen Geschickligkeit/nicht mit einmen garstigen Drücken/hartn Stossen/Meckern/oder Wiehern/so/dass der Sänger den Mund mittel mässig eröffne/die Backen nicht hohl mache/sondern sie bleiben lasse/wie sie die Natur gegeben/und die Zunge nicht in die Höhe hebe/noch Krümme/sodern gerade und niedrig liegen lasse/damit sie den Schalle nicht den freyen Durchgang verhindere; auch das Maul anbeweglich still halte/und nicht käue." Printz–*Musica modulatoria*, 43.

81. "Das Anschlagen in der Kehle geschieht sehr linde/jedoch so/dass die Stimme nicht gar geschliesset werde." Printz–*Musica modulatoria*, 45.

82. "Je mehr eine Stimme aufsteiget/und je höher sie ist/je subtiler und linder sol sie gesungen werden/und je tiefer eine Stimme wird/je grössere Stärke sol ihr gegeben werden." Printz–*Musica modulatoria*, 21.

83. "Die Consonantes sollen sonderlich in grossen Gebäuen oder offenen Orten sehr Scharf ausgesprochen werden. Den die Vocales sind wegen ihres Lauts leicht zu fassen/nicht aber die Consonantes. Dannen hero/so man auch die Consonantes in die Ferne verstehen sol/müssen sie schärfer als im gemeiner Rede/ja fast übermässig scharf ausgesprochen werden." Printz–*Musica modulatoria*, 41.

84. See Praetorius–*Syntagma* III: 229.

85. For a detailed discussion of these sources, see Toft–*Tune*.

86. See Duckles–Florid Embellishment, 332.

87. They were Giovanni Maria Lugario and Angelo Notari. See Spink–Cavalier Songs, 62.

88. Bathe–*Introduction*.

89. Butler–*Principles*, 95.

90. For a detailed discussion of rhetorical devices in text setting see Toft–*Tune*, 127ff.

91. Butler–*Principles*, 97.

92. Ibid., 41.

93. See Huws Jones–*English Song*, 41ff.

94. R. Jacobs–Controversy, 288.

95. See Playford–*Breefe Introduction*, 39ff.

96. Ibid., 55. In a master class I gave some years ago at UCLA, there was a singer who had studied falconry and was able to imitate a modern luring call that was not too dissimilar from a *trillo*. Nowadays the image of a silent machine gun or silent laughter is likely an equivalent teaching aid.

97. Spink–Playford's Directions, 134.

98. Facs. rep. Scolar Press, 1969.

99. Playford–*Breefe Introduction*, 57.

100. Viz. Roger North's drawing of pitch fluctuations in a long note in *Notes of Me* (ca.1695), reproduced in Moens-Haenen–*Vibrato*, 171. See also Gable–Observations, 91–92.

101. See *New Grove*–Castrato.

102. See Stein–*Songs*, 190, 329.

103. Stevenson–Cerone, 31.

104. Stein–*Songs*, 190.

2

Solo Singing 2:
The *Bel canto* Style

Julianne Baird

Of the various national styles of singing in the Baroque era, the Italian style was the mainstream. There has been a more or less unbroken tradition of *bel canto* singing ever since Caccini wrote about it in his *Nuove musiche* (1601). The classical *bel canto* style crystallized in the late seventeenth century, when musical considerations triumphed over the text-dominated style of the early part of the century. By that time Italian opera had become something of a commodity, and Italian singers were in demand throughout Europe. Unfortunately, for about the last three-quarters of the century there are essentially no Italian treatises on singing. There are, to be sure, numerous treatises from German writers of this period,[1] but while they were enthusiastic admirers of the Italian style, few of them had direct association with *bel canto* singers. Pierfrancesco Tosi (ca.1646–1732), a castrato singer and actor of some note, was, however, thoroughly conversant with the *bel canto* style. His *Opinioni de' cantori antichi, e moderni* was published in 1723, chronologically beyond the limits of this *Guide,* but by that time Tosi was well into his seventies. His ideas about singing were formed during the closing decades of the seventeenth century, when he was at the height of his career. Moreover, the title of his book clearly indicates Tosi's awareness of the "ancient"—by which he means the style of his own heyday as a singer—and the "modern" styles of singing, and it is clearly the former that he prefers.

Tosi's treatise was translated into English by J. E. Galliard (1743), and into German by J. F. Agricola (1757).[2] The latter's copious annotations are often quite illuminating, even for seventeenth-century practice, in spite of their late date.

Articulation

Articulation is perhaps the key element that distinguishes early Baroque from modern vocal style. The incredibly facile technique of the finest

Italian singers of the era can be seen in the florid written-out divisions that survive. These singers employed a rapid glottal articulation known as the "disposition of the voice" (*dispositione di voce*). Rather like a high laugh or giggle, with the air striking the soft palate, this technique facilitated rapid movement of the voice, though it is frowned on in modern vocal pedagogy. Later in the Baroque, when singers had to fill large performing spaces such as opera houses, this style of articulation fell out of favor. Glottal articulation is quite effective in intimate performance venues, but it is virtually inaudible in the far reaches of a large hall.

By the late seventeenth century, according to Tosi, there were two principal manners of articulating divisions—the *battuto* (detached, which replaced the glottal style) and the *scivolato* (slurred). Regarding the former, Agricola offers an interesting explanation:

> When practicing, imagine that the vowel sound of the division is gently repeated with each note; for example, one must pronounce as many **a**'s in rapid succession as there are notes in the division-just as with a stringed instrument, [where] a short bow stroke belongs to each note of the division; and in the transverse flute and some other wind instruments [where] each note receives its own gentle impetus by the correct tongue stroke, whether single or double."[3]

For the slurred divisions, Agricola suggests that the singer pronounce only *one* vowel, which is not rearticulated, and over which the entire division is sung.[4] For Tosi the *battuto* style of articulation is far more common than the *scivolato*: he allows only a descending or ascending four-note group to be slurred.[5]

In addition to the two common types of articulation for divisions, Tosi discusses two other special types. The first of these is the *sgagateata* [lit., cackling], a pejorative term used in Italy to describe the glottal articulation.[6] It was regarded as a fault because it is usually too feeble to be heard adequately. Tosi further disparages glottal technique for the reiteration of one tone. He writes,

> What would he [the good teacher] say about those who have invented the astounding trick of singing like crickets? Who could ever have dreamed that it would become fashionable to take ten or twelve consecutive eighth notes and break them up into small pieces by a certain shaking of the voice? . . . He will have even greater reason, however, to abhor the invention by which one sings in a laughing manner or sings in the manner of hens that have just laid an egg.[7]

Singing Instruction

The quick glottal articulation, *dispositione di voce*, was an important element of singing instruction in the early part of the seventeenth century.

It had not entirely disappeared by the last decades of the century, though Tosi disparages it. Agility, however, was extremely important. The trill was stressed as not only the hallmark of agility, but also as the foundation of the agility; the fast notes must be practiced in order to make the trill more even. This was contrasted with long notes, called *fermar la voce* by Tosi. Italian singing teachers probably started with long notes as their first exercise.

Tosi rebukes the many singers of his day who, in their rejection of "old-fashioned" style, neglect to practice the *messa di voce,* a crescendo-decrescendo over a long note. He recommends that it be used sparingly and only on a bright vowel. *Messa di voce* was an important aspect of singing instruction, and when Roger North suggested that one begin on the viol by playing long-held notes with a *messa di voce,* he probably was imitating singing instruction.

Tosi thus specifies two types of sustaining of the voice. The function of the *fermar* is to steady the voice on a long, sustained note without crescendo and make it capable of singing sustained tones evenly and without vibrato, whereas the *messa di voce* entails a crescendo-decrescendo and often the introduction of vibrato at the highest point of the crescendo.

Tosi's observations for music students may be compared with descriptions of training regimens of the castrati in the papal schools and in Naples. Common to all are (1) emphasis on the practice of agility (ability to execute fast passages), (2) emphasis on exercises for long, sustained notes, (3) the study of composition, (4) work in front of the mirror, and (5) the study of literature and languages.

At the Papal Chapel school in Rome, students were required to devote themselves during the first hour of the morning to the practice of difficult divisions. A second hour was spent practicing the trill, and a third was devoted to developing correct and clear intonation—all this in the presence of the master and in front of a mirror, in order to watch the position of the tongue and the mouth. The morning regimen ended with two hours devoted to the study of expression, taste, and literature. In the afternoon, one half hour was devoted to the theory of sound, another half hour to simple counterpoint, and an hour to composition. The remaining time was spent practicing the keyboard and composing motets or psalms.[8]

Diction

Tosi has a great deal to say about diction, and much of it pertains to the singing of divisions.

> Every teacher knows that the divisions sound unpleasant on the third and the fifth vowels (the **i** or the **u**).[9] But not everyone knows that, in good schools, they are not permitted even on the **e** and **o**[10] if these two vowels are

pronounced closed. . . . Even more ridiculous [it] is when a singer articulates too loudly and with such forceful aspiration that, for example, when we should hear a division on the **a**, he seems to be saying **ga ga ga**. This applies also to the other vowels.[11]

Some earlier Italian writers, such as Camillo Maffei, said that the **u** vowel sounded like howling, especially since the Italian word for howling is *ululando*. The **i** was rejected because it was thought to produce the sounds made by small animals.[12] Agricola is critical of basses who, when singing divisions, "put an **h** in front of every note, which they then aspirate with such force that, besides producing an unpleasant sound, it causes them unnecessarily to expend so much air that they are forced to breathe almost every half measure."[13]

Ornamentation

Divisions

Tosi indicates that ornaments should be performed with proper concern for the affect of the text, and that attention be paid to the preferred vowels (**a** and **o**) and to the type of articulation—slurred in the pathetic arias and detached in the lively ones. While sounding easy, the ornamentation should, in fact, really be difficult, though it should never sound studied. Dynamic colors are important, and the use of the *piano* in the pathetic adagio is especially effective, as is also a type of "terrace dynamics" (use of *piano* and *forte* without intermediate shadings) in the allegro. Choosing the appropriate place for an ornament is important; therefore, the singer should take care not to overcrowd it. It should never be repeated in the same theater because the connoisseurs would take notice. Tosi advises the singer to practice divisions that contain leaps after learning those that move by step.[14]

Tosi uses the following five adjectives to describe the "whole beauty" of divisions: *perfettamente intonato, battuto, eguale, rotto,* and *veloce.*[15] The first and last adjectives, "perfectly in tune" and "fast," need no explanation. The term *battuto*, discussed above under the section on "Articulation," refers to the vocal technique involving the motion of the entire larynx that was essential to the basic agility of the voice. *Eguale* means that the notes within the division should be "equal" in volume. *Rotto* (lit., broken) means "distinct." Simply put, *battuto* refers to the specific technique the singer is to use, while *rotto* refers to the effect perceived by the listener.

Cercar la nota

Tosi advises the teacher to "teach his students to sing all of the leaps within the scale with perfectly pure intonation, confidently, and skillfully."[16]

Agricola warns of a fault noticed in many Italian singers, whereby

> with a leap, even a small one, they sing, before they get to the higher note, one or even two or three lower notes. These are indistinct and may even be sung with a sharp aspiration. They even introduce *ad nauseum* this *cercar la nota* (searching for the note) to interval leaps larger than a third—which was not common practice among the ancients.[17]

One of the first theorists to describe the *cercar della nota* is Giovanni Battista Bovicelli, who speaks of it as "beginning from the third or fourth below the main note depending on the harmony of the other parts."[18] Christoph Bernhard specifies that it is the "note directly below the initial note," employed either at the beginning or during the course of a phrase and performed in a gliding manner very imperceptibly to the initial note.[19] Besides its function as an ornament, the *cercar della nota* is also a vocal technique used in the twentieth century to enable the singer to reach a high note more easily.

Messa di voce, messa di voce crescente, *and* strascino

We have observed that the *messa di voce* was a critical element of a singer's training. First seen merely as a device or ornament, the *messa di voce* is obviously intended by Guilio Caccini in *Le Nuove Musiche* (1602) when he speaks of *il crescere e scemare della voce* (the crescendo and decrescendo of the voice) as one single grace, which is performed on a whole note. One of the first writers to use the term, Tosi defines the *messa di voce* as "beginning the tone very gently and softly and letting it swell little by little to the loudest forte and thereafter letting it recede with the same artistry from loud to soft."[20]

A special effect that can be used instead of the appoggiatura in making an ascent is the *messa di voce crescente*. The adjective *crescente* simply means "rising." The effect is applied to a long-held note with a swell that gradually rises by a semitone.[21]

The *strascino*, or "drag," was like a glissando or slide. Tosi uses the term not only to denote an extremely slurred manner of singing but also to indicate a special ornament consisting of a slowly descending glissando scalar passage, considered especially effective in the pathetic style. He also says it involves an alternation of loud and soft, and it also seems to entail a *tempo rubato* over a steady bass.[22] The drag is distinguished from the *messa di voce crescente* primarily in that the latter encompasses only the interval of a rising half step, whereas the the drag can ascend or descend, and may have a wider compass. It is found in the works of Monteverdi and D'India, where on very affective words one sometimes finds an ascent of a chromatic half step, accompanied by a slur (see Ex. 2.1).

EXAMPLE 2.1. Sigismondo d'India, *O dolcezz'amarissime d'amore* (1609).

The Appoggiatura

Tosi devotes an entire chapter to the appoggiatura and recommends practicing this ornament in scalar passages, with an appoggiatura on each step of the scale. Agricola, strongly favoring on-beat execution of the appoggiatura, is careful to stress that the location of the syllable or word of the text underlay should occur on the appoggiatura itself rather than on the main note under which it is habitually written: ". . . when a syllable falls on a main note, which itself is notated with an appoggiatura or any other ornament, then it [the syllable] must be pronounced on the appoggiatura."[23] Agricola's rule referring to the on-beat performance of the appoggiatura must be understood in the context of earlier Baroque practice, in which the phrase *anticipatione della syllaba* referred to a situation in which an appoggiatura or a one-note grace similar to it actually *preceded* the beat and bore the syllable.[24]

The Trill

For Tosi the "perfect" trill is *eguale* (lit., equal), *battuto* (lit., beaten),[25] *granito* (lit., distinct), *facile* (lit., flexible), and *moderamente veloce* (lit., moderately quick). Some of these terms have already been encountered in relation to divisions. *Eguale* refers to the volume level of the two notes in relation to each other. When the two notes of the trill are not sounded equally, the resultant defective trill is often described as "lame."

Battuto refers to a specific vocal technique (essential to the trill) that involves the up-and-down movement of the larynx—that "light motion of the throat" that occurs simultaneously with the "sustaining of the breath" in executing the trill. When this "beating" movement of the larynx is not present or cannot be maintained, the trill of two notes collapses into a smaller interval or makes a bleating sound on one note alone; conversely, the larger the interval of the trill, the bigger the movement must be. Various Italian writers, including Tosi, use either or both of the terms *caprino* or *cavallino* to describe this sort of trill, in which the intended interval (major or minor second) cannot be maintained and which collapses unintentionally into a single pitch (or an interval smaller than a half-step).[26]

When the interval of the trill is smaller than a half step, or when the two tones of which it consists are beaten with unequal speed and strength, or quiveringly, the trill sounds like the bleating of a goat. The precise place for production of a good trill is at the opening of the head of the windpipe (larynx). The movement can be felt from the outside when the fingers are placed there. If no movement or beating is felt, this is a sure indication that one is bleating out the trill only by means of the vibration of air on the palate.[27]

An insufficiently open trill also might yield the comic effect with which the following Venetian poem described the trill of Pistocchi, the famous castrato and voice teacher:

> *Pistocco col fa un trill' se puto equagliare*
> *A quel rumor che'é solito de fare*
> *Quande se scossa un gran sacco di nose*[28]
>
> *(What sound did the trill of the great Pistocco make?*
> *The sound of a sack of nuts when given a shake.)*
> Translation by Lawrence Rosenwald

The eight types of trills that Tosi enumerates are the *trillo maggiore*[29] (trill of a whole step; Ex. 2.2a); the *trillo minore* (trill of a half step; Ex. 2.2b); the *mezzotrillo* (short and fast trill; Ex. 2.2c); the *trillo cresciuto* and the *trillo calato* (trilled slow glissandi—the first ascending and the second descending), the *trillo lento* (slow trill); the *trillo raddoppiato*[30] (which involves inserting a few auxiliary tones in the middle of a longer trill; Exx. 2.2d and 2.2e); and the *trillo mordente* (a very short and fast trill that is effective in divisions and after an appoggiatura; Ex. 2.2f).[31] Of these, only the *trillo cresciuto,* the *trillo calato,* and the *trillo lento* were obsolete in Tosi's time; the rest were prominent in current performance practice.

Also popular was the chain of trills, which places a trill on each note of a scale passage (Ex. 2.3).

Vibrato

There are several mechanisms in the human voice for producing vibrato. One of these occurs in the same manner as the trill, that is, by the up-and-down movement of the larynx in a manner less exaggerated than the trill. Vibrato was considered an inseparable feature of the human voice in the seventeenth century. It is very difficult, for example, for a singer to execute a *messa di voce* or crescendo totally without vibrato. An important clue regarding this phenomenon is the *vox humana* stop in Spanish and Italian

EXAMPLE 2.2. Tosi's trills (as realized by Agricola): (a) *trillo maggiore*; (b) *trillo minore*; (c) *mezzotrillo*; (d) *trillo raddoppiato*; (e) *trillo raddoppiato*; (f) *trillo mordente*

EXAMPLE 2.3. Chain of trills (Agricola)

organs, which was always a trembling stop, as early as the 1500s. Yet this does not necessarily mean that vibrato was constant. In the twentieth century a concept of singing as a string of "beautiful pearls" has developed. This is very different from the seventeenth-century aesthetic, in which the finest singers could alter their technique and their sound in order to adapt to the musical or dramatic context. Singers today are taught never to compromise their technique; thus they can produce those "beautiful pearls," the textual or dramatic context notwithstanding. There are certain situations in which a seventeenth-century singer would have sung without vibrato—perhaps on a dissonance, a leading tone, a tone aproached by chromatic half step, or a particularly expressive interval such as a tritone. Vibrato makes the note more like our "beautiful pearl," but often this weakens the effect, both musically and expressively. Seventeenth-century singers used a narrower vibrato than modern singers do, but they also sang with less volume. Because of their ability to execute rapid *passaggi*, these early singers could produce a very rapid vibrato when they wanted; the two skills were inseparable.

Rubato

Tosi, one of the first writers to discuss *tempo rubato,* mentions two types. In the first, time that is lost is later regained, while in the second, that which is gained is subsequently lost. It is difficult to accomplish, yet according to Tosi its mastery is the mark of an outstanding performer. He does not allow for the slowing down of a section with a subsequent return to the original tempo; the bass was generally expected to maintain a firm beat. Tosi recommends the use of rubato in the varied repetition of the A section of a *da capo* aria and praises the virtuoso castrato Pistocchi for his mastery of it.[32]

Registration

For the Italians the two vocal registers, *voce di testa* ("head voice") and *voce di petto* ("chest voice"), were to be united. The falsetto, which Tosi considers essential for beautiful singing, is apparently included with the former. For Tosi the falsetto must be completely blended with the natural voice.[33] In vocal music of virtually every style or era it is essential for the singer to be able to blend the two registers in the vicinity of the break—to be able to produce certain notes in either register, and to move easily into the head voice as the musical line ascends. A singer who lacks this ability will be unable to produce high notes gracefully, but forced to take the chest voice to its upper extreme, will sound as though shouting—much like the "belting" of a Broadway singer. Seventeenth-century singers were encouraged to sing the high notes lightly, rather than blast them out in the chest register.

In literature on the human voice one sees a great deal of confusion even today regarding the matter of registration.[34] In untrained voices a sharp "register break" can be easily identified by a change in tone quality and pitch as the voice moves up the scale, as for example in the contrast between the natural chest voice of the male and the head voice; there is a similar phenomenon in the female voice. Tosi says that one sometimes hears a female soprano singing entirely in chest voice.[35]

It is now commonly accepted that the vocal mechanism itself, not the head or chest, is the origin of the register.[36] The terms "chest voice" and "head voice" are at best vague and metaphoric terms, coined in an age "when people apparently thought that the voice left the larynx and was "directed" into these regions."[37] Early writers—extending as far back as Hieronymus of Moravia, and including more recent Italians such as Zacconi, Caccini, and Tosi—distinguished the registers according to the perception of sound. They made little or no mention of unifying the registers, which makes the voice sound more homogeneous, corrects problems of intonation, and increases the singer's range—matters that became more and more essential with the changing styles in singing and the increased expectations of the voice. While an early-seventeenth-century solo motet for soprano by Monteverdi or Luigi Rossi might have a range of an octave and a fifth (from c' to g'), contemporaries of Tosi such as Stradella used much wider and more demanding ranges. It therefore became essential in the *bel canto* style to blend the chest and head registers.[38]

The Appearance of the Singer

Tosi's directions regarding the singer's presence continue and refine the tradition expressed earlier in the seventeenth century by Italian writers and commentators on the subject. These include Durante, Da Gagliano, Diruta, Cerone, Scaletta, Doni, and Donati, whose caveats were directed largely against bodily and facial contortions and mannerisms that would detract from the singing.[39] Tosi advocates a noble bearing (graceful posture) and an agreeable appearance; he insists on the standing position because it permits a freer use of the voice and warns against bodily contortions and facial grimaces, which may be eliminated, he says, by periodic practice in front of a mirror. He recommends that if the sense of the words permit, the mouth should incline "more toward the sweetness of a smile than toward grave seriousness."[40] In short, Tosi recommends the *bocca ridente,* which requires not only a smiling mouth, but also a positioning of the vocal apparatus critical to the *bel canto* style.

Mauro Uberti has called attention to a late-fifteenth-century sculpture by Luca della Robbia in the Museo di S. Maria del Fiore, a marble relief that depicts a group of singers whose mouths are open in such a way, he believes, as to produce an agile voice and make easy the ornamentation characteristic of early Italian singing.[41] In studying the photograph of the sculpture on page 487 of Uberti's article, one can see that one of the singers has a very pleasant, relaxed, almost beatific expression on his face. The mouth, while not smiling, looks as if it is just ready to break into a smile. The heads of two others are lowered somewhat so that the smiling effect is not visible and their mouths are open wide enough but not too wide, apparently about the width of the little finger. A third, turned almost to profile, shows clearly, and even in a rather exaggerated way, the mouth position and facial expression that is common to all of the singing figures. The face is relaxed and natural looking: the lower jaw juts greatly forward. All the figures give the impression that the singing is done easily and without strain. These mouth positions are commonly found in early Italian representations of singing, according to Uberti, who distinguishes between Italian vocal techniques prior to the early nineteenth century and Romantic techniques.

Uberti also compares the position of the larynx in the Romantic style with that of the early style:

> In both the older and the more modern techniques the Adam's apple is tipped forward by muscles outside the larynx and thereby stretches the vocal cords. In the older techniques this is achieved by pulling forward the upper horns at the back of the Adam's apple . . . whereas in Romantic techniques the Adam's apple is pulled down . . . [and] the muscles attached to it from above react by tugging upward (just as they do when we yawn); the vocal cords join in the fray, as it were, and so reach that more vigorous contraction which is needed for the very powerful, stentorian high notes of modern operatic singing.[42]

In the *bel canto* technique, the mouth is opened only very moderately with the *bocca ridente* position. Uberti explains that the shield cartilage rocks or is tilted forward, moving on the fulcrum of its connection with the cricoid; the hyoid bone remains almost horizontal, the ligament between it and the thyroid or shield cartilage remaining flexible and relaxed; the muscle under the chin is short and relaxed; and the jaw is pressed moderately downward and somewhat forward. The singer has the sensation that "while the front wall of the throat is also drawn forward, the jaw itself remains free to move vertically." Also, as Uberti explains, "for the less energetic mechanism of the older techniques, the forward tipping of the Adam's apple can be facilitated by using a rather forward position of the jaw. We can see this position of the jaw in many Renaissance and Baroque depictions of singing . . . and to this day Neapolitans use it both in singing and in speaking."[43]

Conclusion

For singers seeking advice on performance in the late-seventeenth-century *bel canto* style today, there are many generalities, but few specifics. We can be reasonably certain that singing then was more articulated, less loud, and had less vibrato, but we do not know, for example, precisely when *bel canto* singers did and did not use vibrato, nor exactly how wide it was. Theorists of the time did not have a vocabulary that could adequately describe vibrato—nor do we. Such is the limitation of treatises on musical performance in any period.

Obviously, we do not have recordings of the great singers of the late seventeenth century, but we do have recordings made in the early years of this century. Listening to singers such as Galli-Curci, Adelina Patti, and Jenny Lind (a student of Manuel García), one is struck by the light, facile tone production, not unlike that of early-music specialists today. And Patti's "tone sounds absolutely straight . . . except for occasional ornamental vibrato."[44] These early recordings postdate Tosi and Pistocchi by some two centuries, yet perhaps they offer us at least a shadow of the original *bel canto* style.

NOTES

1. See, for example, Bernhard–*Singe-Kunst,* Baumgarten–*Rudimenta,* Fuhrmann–*Trichter,* Gibelius–*Bericht,* Printz–*Anweisung,* Printz–*Modulatoria,* and Printz–*Phrynis.*
2. Galliard–*Observations;* Agricola–*Anleitung.* See also Agricola/Baird–*Introduction,* which contains an English translation of the latter, as well as extensive commentary. There is also a Dutch translation by J. A[lencon], *Korte Aanmerkingen over de Zangkonst* (Leyden, 1731).
3. Agricola–*Anleitung,* 124; Agricola/Baird–*Introduction,* 151–52.
4. Agricola–*Anleitung,* 126; Agricola/Baird–*Introduction,* 153.
5. Tosi–*Opinioni,* 31; Agricola/Baird–*Introduction,* 153.
6. According to Agricola–*Anleitung,* 124; Agricola/Baird–*Introduction,* 152–53.
7. Tosi–*Opinioni,* 106; Agricola/Baird–*Introduction,* 152–53.
8. Bontempi–*Storia,* as reported in Haböck–*Kastraten.*
9. The vowel **i** as in the vowel sound in English "beet"; **u** as in English "food."
10. The vowel **e** as in the vowel sound in English "hay"; **o** as in English "go."
11. Tosi–*Opinioni,* ch. 4; Agricola/Baird–*Introduction,* 157.
12. Maffei–"Lettere," as translated in McClintock–*Readings,* 53.
13. Agricola–*Anleitung;* Agricola/Baird–*Introduction,* 157.
14. Tosi–*Opinioni;* Agricola/Baird–*Introduction,* 66.
15. Tosi–*Opinioni,* 30–31, 35. See Agricola–*Anleitung,* 123 (Agricola/Baird–*Introduction,* 151).
16. Tosi–*Opinioni,* 13; Agricola/Baird–*Introduction,* 66.
17. Agricola/Baird–*Introduction,* 67.
18. Bovicelli–*Regole,* 11 (trans. Baird).
19. In Bernhard–*Singe-Kunst,* par. 20.
20. Agricola/Baird–*Introduction,* 84.
21. Tosi–*Opinioni,* 22. Tosi recommends this effect particularly where one ascends from a major to a minor semitone, in which case, he says, the appoggiatura is inappropriate. See Agricola/Baird–*Introduction,* 14.
22. Tosi–*Opinioni,* 114. See also Agricola/Baird–*Introduction,* 23, 86.
23. Agricola/Baird–*Introduction,* 93.
24. See Bernhard–*Singe-Kunst.*
25. If the trill were not beaten (*battuto*), it often resulted in the goat bleat or *caprino* described elsewhere in Tosi's chapter.
26. See Agricola/Baird–*Introduction,* 18, 75, 126, 152. *Caprino* refers to the bleat of a goat, *cavallino,* to the whinny of a horse. They are treated as defects and are not identical with the repeated-note *trillo* found in the music of Monteverdi and Caccini. In describing the *trillo,* Christoph Bernhard specifies that "one should take great care not to change the quality of the voice in striking the trillo, lest a bleating sound result." Bernhard–*Singe-Kunst,* 15.
27. Agricola–*Anleitung,* 105; Agricola/Baird–*Introduction,* 18, 135.

28. Haböck–*Kastraten*, 335.
29. Tosi–*Opinioni*, ch. 8. See also Neumann–*Ornamentation*, 345–46. Neumann's interpretation of Tosi's description of this trill is part of his argument in favor of the main-note-dominated trill.
30. The extra notes that Agricola adds in his interpretation are at the beginning, and not in the middle as Tosi specifies. See Agricola/Baird–*Introduction*, 131.
31. Agricola interprets this trill as a mordent.
32. Tosi–*Opinioni*, 65, 82; Agricola/Baird–*Introduction*, 193.
33. Ibid., 14. See Agricola/Baird–*Introduction*, 67–68.
34. For a sketch of the history of ideas regarding registration, including modern views, see Agricola/Baird–*Introduction*, 9–10.
35. Tosi–*Opinioni*, ch.1, pars. 18 and 21; Agricola/Baird–*Introduction*, 68.
36. See *New Grove*–Acoustics.
37. Vennard–*Singing*, 66.
38. See Agricola/Baird–*Introduction*, 10.
39. See Duey–*Bel canto*, 61–62.
40. *Opinioni*, ch. 1, pars. 25-26. Agricola–*Anleitung*, 44; Agricola/Baird–*Introduction*, 82.
41. Uberti–Vocal, 486–87.
42. Ibid., 488. In the Romantic technique the vocal cords actively tense themselves continuously in an "isometric contraction"; they are less "nimble" than they are in the older method and thus "it takes a greater effort to negotiate *passaggi*" and other ornaments. Uberti (488) also reminds us of the well-known fact that the tension of the vocal cords can also be manipulated in ways other than the tensing described above—for example, by lateral movement of the arytenoid cartilages to which the vocal processes are attached. With this added adjustment the self-contraction of the vocal cords can then be concentrated largely upon control of intonation. This adjustment together with the earlier "technique for changing in the upper register" causes the vocal cords generally to be increased in length and flexibility, "but they are still capable of contracting somewhat in order to colour the vocal timbre for fine nuances of expression. This technique must have been used by Renaissance *camera* singers, otherwise they could never have improvised the elaborate graces and *passaggi* prescribed in so many treatises of the day."
43. Ibid.
44. Bernard D. Sherman in Baird–Beyond, 252, n.20.

BIBLIOGRAPHY

Agricola–*Anleitung*; Agricola/Baird–*Introduction*; Baird–Beyond; Baumgarten–*Rudimenta*; Bernhard–*Singe-Kunst*; Bontempi–*Storia*; Bowman–Castrati; Caccini–*Nuove musiche*; Crüger–*Kurtzer*; Duey–*Bel canto*; Fuhrmann–*Musicalischer Trichter*; Galliard–*Observations*; Gibelius–*Kurtzer . . . Bericht*; Greenlee–*Dispositione*; Haböck–*Gesangkunst*; Haböck–*Kastraten*; Heriot–*Castrati in Opera*; McClintock–*Readings*; New Grove–*Acoustics*; Printz–*Anweisung*; Printz–*Musica modulatoria*; Printz–*Phyrnis*; Reid–*Bel canto*; Tosi–*Opinioni*; Uberti–Vocal Techniques; Vennard–*Singing*.

Suggested Listening

Musica Dolce. Julianne Baird, soprano. Dorian 90123.
Songs of Love and War: Italian Dramatic Songs of the 17th and 18th Centuries. Julianne Baird, soprano, with Colin Tilney, harpsichord, and Myron Lutzke, violoncello. Dorian DOR 90104.

3

Vocal Ensembles and Choral Music 1: France and England

Anne Harrington Heider

The primary focus of this chapter is the performance of sung ensemble music, that is, music with several texted parts. Today the term "choral music" commonly implies that there is more than one performer on each part, while "ensemble music" commonly implies only one performer to a part. However, as we shall see, music of the seventeenth century that we customarily consider choral—polyphonic masses, motets, anthems, and the like—was very often performed as ensemble music. France and England are grouped together in this chapter partly for convenience, and partly because there are similarities in the uses to which choral music was put, and indeed in the kinds of choral music preferred, despite the obvious difference that one was a Catholic country and the other Protestant.

Choirs or choruses were to be found in churches, opera houses, and public theaters—places where both the sheer size of the venue and the desire for impressive pageantry mandated larger numbers of singers. On both sides of the Channel (or La Manche), the most up-to-date, stylish music made dramatic use of the contrasting sounds of choral singing, solo singing, and obbligato instruments. In the English verse anthem and the French *grand motet,* the choral sections tended to be homophonic, with strong dancelike rhythms maximizing the contrast between choral-orchestral tutti and solo singing or playing.

Ensemble Size and Vocal Types in England

Cathedral and chapel choirs in England used men and boys only. The English Chapel Royal of the earlier Stuart period typically included approximately twelve boys and twenty men, augmented by a variable

43

number of unpaid "extraordinary" members.[1] For quotidian purposes they sang in smaller numbers on a rotating basis, accompanied by a wind consort (cornetts and sackbuts) and organ. In the period immediately following the Restoration, cornetts substituted for boy trebles: "Above a Year after the Opening of His Majesties Chappel, the Orderers of the Musick there, were necessitated to supply the superiour Parts of their Musick with Cornets and Mens feigned Voices, there being not one Lad, for all that time, capable of singing his Part readily."[2]

The countertenor (male alto) enjoyed a great vogue in secular as well as sacred music in the later seventeenth century, and its role as the uppermost voice type of a male trio or chorus survived until the nineteenth century in innumerable anthems and glees.[3] However, there can be no justification for trying to make women sound like boys or falsettists, in the name of historically informed performance. A lean choral tone with a minimum of vibrato and meticulous attention to intonation will serve the music admirably and has excellent precedent in the work of such historically oriented ensembles as Les Arts Florissants and the Tallis Scholars, where women sing soprano and both men and women sing alto.

The designation "verse" for a section of an English anthem or canticle setting traditionally means that the section is sung by solo voices. However, Bruce Wood found "unambiguous evidence" in manuscript sources that verse sections of several Chapel Royal anthems could be sung by at least two singers on a part.[4] Generalizing from a small number of anthems to an entire repertory is risky. Nevertheless, if it is more practical for you to have two voices on each line in verse sections, the important thing will be to maintain the distinction between verse and "full" by having three or four voices on each part in full sections.

Performance space was limited in the small chapels at Whitehall and Windsor. Peter Holman suggests that spatial separation of groups of players and singers was a feature of music for the Chapel Royal at Whitehall, with singers positioned in the organ loft and instrumentalists in the "musick room"—part of a gallery that opened into the chapel at first-floor (United States' second-floor) level.[5] Fashionable visitors were also seated in the organ loft, at what inconvenience to the musicians we can only imagine. State occasions—for example, royal weddings, coronations, a Te Deum in celebration of a military victory—normally occurred in larger venues such as Westminster Abbey, and it was then that the whole Chapel performed together, augmented by the Abbey choir and organ.[6]

The violin band eventually replaced the wind consort as the usual accompaniment for Chapel Royal anthems. This did not happen overnight, but gradually during the period 1661–70.[7] If there were no obbligato parts, strings generally doubled voices in all passages for full choir, or perhaps only in the final chorus.[8] As late as 1676 the theorbo was frequently used to support the continuo in sacred music and consorts, though it disappeared soon thereafter.[9] "After the accession of William and Mary, the instrumental accompaniment of anthems was abandoned and the Chapel repertory became virtually indistinguishable from that of the cathedrals."[10]

Ensemble music for domestic use, such as madrigals, canzonets, *Psalms, Songs, and Sonnets* (the title of a collection by William Byrd), balletts, consort songs, and so forth, might be sung or played by any family members, male or female, adult or child. Since part music was usually published in sets of partbooks, each part in a separate small volume typically measuring about 5" x 8", one or two persons at most could sing or play from the same book. Even more limiting were books that displayed all four parts in one opening, positioned so that when the book lay flat in the middle of the table, each part faced a side of the table. The present-day director of an early-music ensemble can confidently arrange a wide variety of mixed one-on-a-part ensembles for this repertory, even omitting a voice if necessary, as long as instruments are used one on a part, and for a setting of a preexisting melody such as a psalm or hymn, the voice with the familiar tune is not omitted.

Ensemble Size and Vocal Types in France

The king's musicians consisted of three distinct entities. The *Musique de la Chambre* was made up of soloists: singers, lutenists, and players of other soft instruments, responsible for music for the entertainment of the court. The famous *24 Violons du Roi* evolved from the *Chambre* but became virtually autonomous because of their prestige. The *Musique de la Grande Écurie* employed players of sackbuts, oboes, cornetts, fifes, drums, and trumpets, who provided music for the battlefield, the hunt, and the public processional. In 1645 the *Musique de la Chapelle Royale* consisted of a *maître* (an honorary appointment given to a highly placed ecclesiastic rather than a musician), two *sous-maîtres* (one was *Compositeur de la Chapelle*, responsible for training the choir as well as choosing and composing music for the king's Mass), two cornettists, twenty-six singers, eight chaplains, four clerks, and two grammar instructors for the children. In 1682 a new royal chapel was inaugurated at Versailles; by 1708 it listed ninety singers: eleven sopranos, eighteen *haute-contres*, twenty-three tenors, twenty-four baritones, and fourteen basses. In *grands motets* the normal texture was five voices, the added part usually a baritone, hence the large number of low voices. There was a mixed ensemble of instrumentalists attached to the chapel, including strings, woodwinds, a theorbo, and a bass *cromorne*.[11]

Lionel Sawkins (1987) points out exceptional instances of women singing in the *Chapelle Royale*: there is a "Mlle. Delalande" mentioned on motet scores from around 1689, and Delalande's two daughters are known to have sung in the chapel after 1703. The *dessus* (soprano) part was more typically sung by boys (pages or *petits clercs*), falsettists (*faussets*), or castrati. Cardinal Mazarin imported castrati from Italy around 1660. There were eleven *dessus italiens* (*sopranistes, castrats, châtres*) active in the late 1600s in chapel choirs and operas.

Members of the *Chambre,* the *Écurie,* and the *Chapelle* passed freely from one group to another, and performances by combined groups were common, especially for such ceremonies as coronations, royal births and deaths, and the celebrations surrounding royal marriages.

The Sainte-Chapelle and Notre-Dame Cathedral were two of the largest and most prestigious musical establishments in Paris outside the royal purview. In the late seventeenth century, the choir school of the Sainte-Chapelle numbered five to eight chaplains, six to twelve clerics, and eight choirboys. Extra singers and instrumentalists were engaged for exceptional occasions; the musicians were grouped on two opposite sides of the upper chapel, on platforms specially erected.[12]

The French opera chorus from Lully to Rameau divided into a *petit choeur,* composed only of solo voices, and a *grand choeur* of many voices. Women sang soprano; men sang *haute-contre,* tenor, and bass. In the 1670s, the earliest days of the Académie d'Opéra, the chorus numbered fifteen; by 1713 the chorus of the Académie Royale de Musique included twenty-two men and twelve women.[13] The French *haute-contre* was not a falsetto voice, but a high, light tenor.[14] If even one of your tenors is comfortable at the high end of the range, you can have him sing *haute-contre* with your female altos and his voice will add a bit of "ping" to the sound of the section.

Part music for domestic use and simple music for private devotions, such as Huguenot metrical psalms, might be sung or played by any family members on a variety of soft chamber instruments. (Calvin's proscription of musical instruments in public worship did not apply to music in the home; as early as 1554 Louis Bourgeois, Calvin's own choirmaster, published settings of Genevan psalms "bien consonante aux instrumentz musicaulx.")

Conducting

It was exceptional for the leader of a seventeenth-century musical ensemble to do nothing but beat time, because it was exceptional to deploy such large numbers of performers that a centrally placed, highly visible conductor was necessary. (On the infamous occasion when Lully dealt himself a fatal wound while beating time, he was conducting more than 150 musicians in his Te Deum.[15]) For ordinary purposes, keeping the ensemble together could readily be accomplished by any reliable and experienced member whose vocal or instrumental role positioned him so that all could see him. A duple division of the pulse was signaled by a simple down and up; for a triple division, the downstroke occupied twice as much time as the upstroke. A singer used his hand, a stick (token of the ancient precentor's staff), or a roll of paper or parchment. Instrumentalists used the same body language they do today: the player of a bowed stringed instrument used the bow; a theorbo or archlute player moved the neck of the instrument down and up; continuo keyboard players could free one hand when needed or use eyebrows, shoulders, or torso to emphasize the pulse. Whether the choirmaster performed the task himself or delegated it undoubtedly varied with the familiarity of the music, the day of the week, the expected presence of important guests in the audience or congregation, and a host of other imponderables. The present-day early-music director is ideally situated to delegate the leading (while retaining the artistic direction) of some ensembles, which will tend to raise everyone's commitment to the artistic success of the performance.

Principal Seventeenth-Century English and French Singing Treatises

Bénigne de Bacilly's *Rémarques curieuses sur l'art de bien chanter* (1668) provides a window on singing and vocal pedagogy in seventeenth-century France. Though the author's expressed main purpose was to deal with the esoterica of applying quantitative rhythm to French poetry, over half the book is devoted to general principles of good singing.

John Playford's *An Introduction to the Skill of Musick* contains, in editions of 1664 and later, a "brief Discourse of the Italian manner of Singing," much of it lifted from Caccini's *Le nuove musiche* (1602). Playford's handbook went through nineteen editions, many thoroughly revised, spanning the years 1654 to 1730, so we may surmise that Caccini's advice on singing—attributed by Playford to "an English Gentleman who had lived long in Italy"—remained pertinent as the decades and the editions passed.

Pier Francesco Tosi's *Opinioni de' cantori* (1723) distilled a lifetime of experience as a successful professional singer and teacher. It was translated into several languages; the English translation, John Galliard's *Observations on the Florid Song* (1743), adds explanatory annotations and examples. Though Galliard was German, both his translation and his footnotes are in clearer English than Playford's.[16]

Healthy Singing

Good singing is an athletic pursuit. Just as with sports, aerobics, or jogging, the muscles that support the activity need to be methodically conditioned; once good condition is reached, it needs to be maintained. Then as now, the fit or well-conditioned singer can control pitch, manage the breath on long phrases, support a diminuendo as well as a crescendo, control vibrato, deliver rapid passagework articulately—in short, can handle the purely technical skills that Baroque music demands.

Bacilly, Playford, and Galliard all agree on the fundamentals: good posture, good breathing, and plenty of hours of practice, beginning with simple exercises and progressing to more challenging ones. You, as the director of a choir or vocal ensemble, need to know enough about vocal fitness to spot unhealthy singing and suggest ways to correct it, as well as to teach the fundamentals of good singing right along with the notes and the pronunciation. The best way to learn about good singing is to study with a good teacher. The early-music director who comes to his or her position from an instrumental background should take very seriously the obligation to handle young singers' voices intelligently. Often you only need one or two lessons yourself from a sympathetic colleague to get you started on a visceral—as opposed to a merely aural—understanding of good singing. Or you might have a "guest coach" for one or two rehearsals with your singers, concentrating on basic technique, with you singing right along with your students.

Bacilly says that while no teacher can make a beautiful voice out of thin air, nevertheless,

> What *can* be accomplished is in the realm of vocal corrections: The voice can be brought out more, where it previously was muffled. Continuous practice can make a rough voice delicate, correct bad intonation, and make a coarse voice sweet. . . . A *good* voice . . . is effective because of its vigor, strength, and its capacity to sing with expression, which is the soul of vocal art.[17]

Vocalizing in the falsetto voice is a useful practice for all singers, and you will not harm the voices of men in your ensemble by having them do easy vocal exercises in falsetto in the octave above middle C. Descending scales that bring the falsetto down into the mid-tenor range are useful not only for exercising the falsetto but also for developing more ease and more resonance in the high end of the chest voice. In the process, you might discover a particularly beautiful falsetto tone in one or another of the men, a potential countertenor for English repertory.

Importance of Text

Good singing is also an artistic pursuit. The technical skills of the singer need to be brought to bear on the expression of the text ("the soul of the vocal art") in ways that complement and enhance the mere notes on the page.

Vocal and choral music in the seventeenth century is text centered. This may seem obvious, but it bears repeating. The ensemble director should understand the literal meaning of every word of text in the program, as well as any metaphoric or symbolic baggage carried by the text. The singers should learn the meaning of every word they are singing from the very start. The director should know the correct pronunciation of every word, so that rehearsal time is not wasted. And he or she should provide the audience with both the original text and the translation in parallel.

Beyond good pronunciation, all subtleties of expressive singing—dynamic contrast, phrasing, variety of articulation, added embellishment—should be rooted in the performers' comprehension of the text.

Thomas Morley grumbled that "Most of our churchmen, so they can cry louder in the choir than their fellows, care for no more; whereas by the contrary they ought to study how to vowel and sing clean, expressing their words with devotion and passion."[18]

Mersenne agreed: "One of the great perfections of song consists of good pronunciation of the words and rendering them so distinctly that the auditors do not lose a single syllable. . . . The voice should be softened or reinforced on certain syllables to express the passions of the subject."[19]

Bacilly, Playford, and Dowland, translating Ornithoparcus,[20] all make similar statements, telling us explicitly that the text was paramount in the seventeenth century and implicitly that performers needed frequent reminders of this basic truth.

Historical Pronunciations

There have been some recent investigations into historical national pronunciations.[21] There are also recordings—-the Hilliard Ensemble's recording of Tallis's *Lamentations of Jeremiah*,[22] for example, or Les Arts Florissants' recording of Charpentier's *Le Reniement de St. Pierre*[23]—that provide aural models. Indeed, this is an area of performance-practice research that is far better communicated by sound media than on the printed page. Historical pronunciations can make startling differences in vowel sound and line articulation. They may help us achieve a closer approximation to the sounds the composer expected to hear—if we can correctly calculate regional variants, variants over time, and the wild-card effects of, say, a French choirmaster's having studied in Italy. While historical pronunciations can add distinction to a performance, they should have a lower priority in your budgeting of rehearsal time than well-matched vowels and clean, precise consonants.

Ornamentation

Ornamentation has two functions in Baroque singing: to enhance the affect of the text, and to display the accomplishments—the good taste and the virtuosity—of the singer. Bacilly, Playford, and Galliard all devote considerable attention to ornamentation. The myriad embellishments (Bacilly spends nearly eighteen pages on *ports de voix* alone) and the conflicting nomenclature in different traditions can be overwhelming at first; it is a good idea to use ornaments sparingly until you have spent some time familiarizing yourself with the examples and practicing them. Ornaments should be used in ensemble singing, especially in an opera scene or dialogue where distinct characters join in song. But if your singers do not yet have the technique—if they cannot handily deliver an extended trill or rapid diminutions—don't require it. The result will be the opposite of stylish Baroque ornamentation, labored instead of apparently effortless, planned instead of extemporized, worrisome instead of joyful. In time, with good models to emulate (recordings, if not you yourself), those singers with an improvisatory bent will emerge as leaders in the game and others will be emboldened to follow them.

Where there are several singers on the same part, added embellishment is rarely appropriate—excepting routine cadential ornaments that lend themselves to group execution (appoggiaturas, for example, are easier than trills to coordinate). Galliard goes so far as to say, "All Compositions for more than one Voice ought to be sung strictly as they are written; nor do they require any other Art but a noble Simplicity."[24]

There is a useful rule of thumb for Baroque music that says that one never does anything exactly the same way twice in a row. If a musical phrase is repeated exactly, with the same text, the second appearance should be louder, or softer, or more embellished, or less embellished (*senza* vibrato the first time and *con* vibrato the second is an effective contrast), or more emphatic, or more reflective—and the director's interpretation of the text will determine those choices. In ensemble singing, variation on repetition can also be achieved simply by allowing a different voice to emerge in the foreground.

This rule of thumb has a corollary that says that second and successive stanzas in strophic works, and reprises in *da capo* arias, should be embellished, not sung exactly the same way over again.

The two most popular styles of Baroque ornamentation, Italian and French, are described elsewhere in this volume. English music was mainly under Italian influence in the first half of the seventeenth century; the Restoration of the monarchy (1660) brought a wave of French influence, since Charles II had spent his exile at the French court; then toward the end of the century (beginning in the 1680s) the French vogue was tempered by a return of Italian influence. Decisions about ornamentation must take this into account.

Vibrato, One Kind of Ornament

Vibrato was viewed as an embellishment in Baroque music. Its use and misuse in early music has become a highly charged topic, still capable of eliciting raised voices in otherwise polite discussions. Suffice it to say that for vocal music of the seventeenth century, an unvarying straight tone is as inappropriate as an unvarying vibrato.

One needs to remember that the rich vibrato now cultivated in most vocal studios and heard in most concert-hall singing is a direct result of the need for loudness, to stand out against large orchestras of modern instruments and to fill large halls. Contrast in your imagination the singing of a professional "Classical" singer with the singing of a professional jazz vocalist. Why is the jazz voice so much more agile and flexible; how does it produce such an array of vocal colors? Quite simply, because the microphone takes care of loudness, leaving the singer free to explore a wider palette of expression. Jazz singing also provides examples of the use of vibrato as an expressive device, to say nothing of examples of improvised embellishment on reprises and second stanzas.

Encourage your singers to experiment with focused, well-supported singing that is not loud. Be clear on the fact that a straight tone requires more support, not less. Try to find performance venues for chamber music that are appropriately intimate. In small ensembles, where each singer is expected to display some individuality as well as some subordination to the artistic whole, vibrato is out of place only if (1) it interferes with intonation, (2) contradicts the affect of the text, or (3) never goes away.

Disposition, or the Execution of Rapid Passagework

Bacilly says that the art of good singing depends on three gifts of nature, each distinct from the others: the voice, the disposition, and the ear or the intelligence.[25] Present-day teachers will readily recognize the first and third of these gifts, and they might assume that the second refers to the singer's emotional health. But that is not what Bacilly had in mind, nor did Galliard, when he counseled the would-be teacher to listen "with a disinterested Ear, whether the Person desirous to learn hath a Voice, and a Disposition."[26]

Dispositione di voce in fact refers quite specifically to a particular method of performing rapid passagework, and despite Bacilly's opinion that it is a gift of nature, earlier writers on vocal technique describe it as a skill that can be learned. It is a skill that choral singers and solo singers alike need to master; and because the technique used in the seventeenth century differs from that taught today, a few references to this topic follow. Galiver (Cantare) explored late-sixteenth-century descriptions of *modo di cantare con la gorga* (the method of singing with the throat). Robert Greenlee (Dispositione) gathered descriptive references from nearly a dozen writers, from Maffei (1562) to Mersenne (1636), indicating that *buona dispositione* refers to the proficient use of some kind of throat articulation to produce extremely rapid diminutions or *passaggi* without any sacrifice of pitch accuracy.

Sherman and Brown (Singing Passaggi) conducted controlled observations of four different methods for rapid articulation, using microphone and electroglottographic waveforms, airflow waveforms, and video laryngoscopy. Their conclusion is that glottal articulation better reproduces the speed, clarity, and separation of notes admired by Renaissance and Baroque writers than any of the other three methods (mentally reproducing the vowel, abdominal/diaphragmatic pulsation, or adjusting the vibrato rate to coincide with the tempo of the diminutions). They address the distinction between glottal attack, which can be damaging to the voice, and glottal articulation, in which "the breath flow must be gentle and steady, and abdominal musculature should remain relatively relaxed."[27]

Playford, admiring the ability of a particular singer in executing trills very exactly, inquired of him how he practiced. The singer replied, "I used at my first learning the Trill, to imitate that breaking of a Sound in the Throat which Men use when they Lure their Hawks, as 'He-he-he-he-he'; which he used slow at first, and after more swift on several Notes, higher and lower in sound, till he became perfect therein."[28] Similarly, Sherman used laughter as a springboard in teaching glottal articulation (lecture-demonstration, 10 March 1995, Washington, DC) and found that even inexperienced amateur singers rapidly improved in their ability to sing long runs of allegro sixteenth notes cleanly.

Conclusion

All modern performances of early music represent a series of compromises. Even the most historically informed, scholarly, and dedicated choral director is unlikely to hide his or her performers behind a screen, for example, or require singers to learn all their music by solmization in the old hexachord system, or forego certain repertory altogether for lack of boy trebles. Musicians who are committed to historically informed performance must strike a balance between historical accuracy and an artistically satisfying performance, and the balance may shift with every piece of music on the program. Directors of student ensembles, understandably, will also place a priority on the education of the performers themselves, which introduces yet another set of compromises. To be conscious of the compromises you make and to articulate them clearly for your students and your audiences is one of the most important aspects of the art of the ensemble director.

NOTES

1. Holman–*Four and Twenty*, 389; Burney–*History* 2: 347.
2. Matthew Locke, *The Present Practice of Music Vindicated*, 19; quoted in Holman–*Four and Twenty*, 394.
3. Caldwell–*Oxford History* 1: 515.
4. *Music Brittanica*, vol. 64, xxix.
5. Holman–*Four and Twenty*, 389–99.

6. More detailed and comprehensive information about numbers and kinds of musicians can be found in Ashbee–*Records,* of which volumes 1–5 cover the reigns of the Stuart dynasty (James I through the death of Queen Anne in 1714).
7. Holman–*Four and Twenty,* 395–98.
8. Woodfill–*Musicians,* xxix.
9. Caldwell–*Oxford History* 1: 553.
10. Ibid., 565.
11. The bass *cromorne* is not a crumhorn, but an instrument related to the bassoon. See Herbert Myers's chapter on woodwinds in this volume.
12. Cessac–*Charpentier,* 364–69.
13. Anthony–*French Baroque,* 90–91.
14. Zaslaw–Enigma.
15. *New Grove*–Lully.
16. Tosi's ideas on singing are described in Julianne Baird's chapter on solo vocal style in this volume.
17. Bacilly–*Remarques* (trans. Caswell), 20.
18. Morley–*Plaine and Easie,* 20.
19. MacClintock–*Readings,* 173–74.
20. Ibid., 160–61.
21. Duffin–National Pronunciations; Copeman–*Singing in Latin.* McGee–*Singing* covers Latin and other languages and includes a CD recording, but it does not go beyond the very early years of the seventeenth century.
22. ECM Germany CD 833308-2.
23. Harmonia Mundi C 5151.
24. Galliard–*Observations,* 150.
25. Bacilly–*Remarques* (trans. Caswell), 18.
26. Galliard–*Observations,* 14.
27. Sherman/Brown–Singing Passaggi, 33.
28. Playford–*Briefe Introduction,* 94.

BIBLIOGRAPHY

Anthony–*French Baroque*; Ashbee–*Records*; Bacilly–*Commentary*; Benoit–*Versailles*; Bianconi–*Seventeenth Century*; Blow–*Anthems*; Brown and Sadie–*Performance Practice*; Burney–*History*; Caccini–*Nuove musiche*; Caldwell–*Oxford History* 1; Carter–Shape; Cessac–*Charpentier*; Copeman–*Singing in Latin*; Duffin–National Pronunciations; Gable–Some Observations; Galiver–Cantare; Greenlee–Dispositione; Holman–*Fiddlers*; MacClintock–*Readings*; McGee–*Singing*; Mersenne–*Harmonie universelle*; Monson–*Voices*; Morehen–English Consort; Morley–*Introduction*; Playford–*Introduction*; Rosow–Performing; Sawkins–For and Against; Sherman/Brown–Singing *Passaggi*; Spink–*English Song*; Tosi–*Opinioni*; Woodfill–*Musicians*; Zaslaw–Enigma.

4

Vocal Ensembles and Choral Music 2: Italy and the Germanic Lands

Gary Towne

Music was constantly changing in the seventeenth century. Yet even those who acknowledge this evolutionary condition often overlook the sources and inspirations for Baroque musical style. There is little that is unprecedented: practically every feature of the style evolved directly from some sixteenth-century musical practice. The *stile antico* did not expire operatically with the development of monody, continuo playing, and the highly figured Baroque style; rather, all lived on side by side, and composers of the seventeenth century—Claudio Monteverdi, Heinrich Schütz, and others—wrote music in both styles with equal fluency.[1] The opposition of the two styles in larger works enriched the new aesthetic of contrasting affects, and these contrasts contributed further stylistic freedom to already well-defined national and regional styles. Baroque innovations particularly reinforced traditional bonds of musical influence between Italy and Germany.

Geographical proximity, ancient political ties, and continuing intellectual exchange had always bestowed common features on music in Italy and the German-speaking countries. In the seventeenth century, expanding cities, exhibitionistic churches, profligate nobility, and burgeoning numbers of middle-class amateurs supported a rich profusion of new musical styles in both sacred and secular music. The stabilization of Protestantism in the north added further diversity. These groups demanded a rich menu of vocal ensemble works to display their standing. Such works ranged from large-scale festival works for major churches and the ruling class to smaller works for private gatherings, school choirs, and the day-to-day celebrations of city churches throughout Italy and the north. The variety of genres and styles obliges a performer to investigate a work's musical construction in its original context.

The resolution of both stylistic and contextual issues addresses many questions: size and constitution of ensembles, vocal type and production, ornamentation and improvisation, tuning and pitch, tempos and rhythm, to name only the musical factors. Architectural venue, liturgical interactions, and dramatic or social contexts add further elements for consideration that can only be alluded to here. Modern performance practice thus depends on the model emulated as much as on the type of music or the apparent size of the ensemble indicated in the score. We are most familiar with large and celebrated ensembles of the sixteenth and seventeenth centuries: the Sistine Chapel, the chapel of Saint Mark's in Venice, Michael Praetorius's ensemble specifications, the cathedral of Salzburg, the Habsburg Court, and performances at Hamburg's Gertrudenkapelle.[2] But smaller ensembles were much more common, and the ubiquity of part-singing meant that the music had to be very adaptable.[3]

Jerome Roche estimated that in the Po valley alone there were at least seventy-three institutions employing a church composer as *maestro di cappella,* a significant indicator of the widespread use of polyphony.[4] A city's reputation rested partly on its church music, but these musical institutions were only the most visible ones in a culture well enriched by private music-making and patronage among noble and wealthy citizens. The plethora of performing organizations explains the frenetic activity of Venetian (and other) music publishers required to supply them.[5] Catholic areas of Germanic countries had similar social and ecclesiastical structures, and in Protestant areas, school music supplemented burgeoning civic, ecclesiastical, and private musical patronage. Considering all of these situations, we can postulate hundreds, perhaps thousands of singing organizations. The presence of so many models implies considerable variation in local practice and context within certain general parameters.

One key general principle is *concertato* practice. This principle arose from two significant developments of the sixteenth century: the advent of monody in the Florentine *camerata,* and the use of *cori spezzati* in Venice and other Italian cities.[6] The monodic style enshrines a wide range of emotional contrast, while the works of Giovanni Gabrieli and other polychoral composers manifest contrasts of musical textures, timbres, dynamics, and spatial placement. Often, Gabrieli's large works include choirs marked *voce* and *cappella.* The former were intended for a soloist on each line, the latter for a larger group of singers.[7] A clear example of this practice, in which the two clearly labeled vocal choirs have dramatically different musical styles, is Gabrieli's *In ecclesiis.* This principle of a choir of soloists (*favoriti*) versus a *ripieno* (full) choir became fundamental to seventeenth-century music throughout Italy and Germany, but it was influenced locally by the size of the available ensemble. At Saint Mark's, where the number of singers grew from about twenty to forty in the first half of the century, alternation could still involve two choirs totaling only four and eight singers apiece, and even the normal maximum would have contrasted two solo quartets with two *ripieno* choirs of only sixteen voices each. Thus, the normal *ripieno* would have used between two and four voices on a part.[8] In Rome, for dedicatory celebrations in Saint Peter's in 1600, multiple choirs included from three to six adults on a part, with more boys on the soprano and numerous instrumentalists, whose roles are unspecified.[9]

The relatively large, opulent performances just described were exceptions to general practice. The Sistine Chapel's thirty-odd members did not always perform together, and performances by extracted solo quartets may have been quite common.[10] Even more common were small-to-middle-sized churches, like the basilica of Santa Maria Maggiore in Bergamo, the chapel of the city. In the first decade of the seventeenth century, regular singers generally numbered around eighteen, with twelve to fourteen instrumentalists. Others were occasionally brought in, up to a total of twenty-five singers. This fell off in the second quarter of the century to under ten singers, with about six instrumentalists. Part music was required on non-Lenten Sundays, some forty-six Saints' days, special occasions in Lent, and various vigils and processions.[11] Similarly, at the beginning of the century, at the basilica of San Antonio in Padua, there were three adults on each lower part, with unspecified numbers of boy sopranos.[12] In the third quarter of the century, the numbers at Santa Maria di Campagna in Piacenza were even smaller, with eight to ten singers and six instrumentalists. In this case, the addition of a second singer on each part constituted the *ripieno*.[13] By the end of the century, the cathedral of Messina had nineteen singers and ten instrumentalists.[14] Thus, after subtracting four *favoriti*, the *ripieno* choirs normally used only two to four singers on a part.

When even smaller churches cultivated part music, they went so far as to use singers on some parts and organ on the rest, as described by Viadana.[15] Monasteries and convents used polyphony, too, often with performance practices that astonish us. Practically any sacred polyphony was judged accessible to choirs of either gender. In male establishments, the presence of falsettists and occasionally boys and castrati permitted the use of the full vocal range in performance of virtually any liturgical polyphony. But female houses got around the physical vocal limitations we might allow to limit repertory by adopting expedients that would raise eyebrows today, but that permitted them wide flexibility. They did not hesitate to perform much polyphony not specifically composed for women, as well as occasional solo works. It was usually possible to find women who could sing in the normal tenor range, and rarely one who could sing bass. Otherwise the problem of the bass part was solved by singing it up an octave and/or playing it at pitch on a bass instrument or the organ, or by transposition of the work upward by a fourth, fifth, or more. Yet even such tortured adaptations retained the distinction between *favoriti* and *ripieno* so characteristic of the Baroque *concertato* style.[16]

This distinction also obtained in Germany. Praetorius (1619) said that the numbers following the title of a piece indicate the most essential voices first (*favoriti*), and that the remaining numbers indicate *ripieno* choirs that can be omitted.[17] He also described a wide variety of alternative performance arrangements.[18] Aside from his own works, music similar to his most opulent prescriptions was also heard at the cathedral of Salzburg and at the Habsburg court.[19] At the former, the episcopal court supported over forty singers and thirty to forty musicians, who performed concerted music with as many as ten different spatially separated groups or as many as thirty-two separate parts.[20] The imperial court's musical establishment was of comparable size and supported performance of the grandest post-Venetian works, as well as more intimate motets and masses in the *stile antico*.[21] Such grand works cannot be discussed individually, but their rich textural variety displayed the usual contrast between *favoriti* and *ripieno*, with rich flourishes of contrasting vocal and instrumental timbres in every choir. Nevertheless, in the Germanic countries, as in Italy, such grandiosity represents only the most elaborate manifestation of a part-singing performance tradition that, in a simpler medium, was widespread in households, cities, and churches.

The smaller city church was more like that of Dietrich Buxtehude. Most of his surviving "choral" works seem to have been for a choir of soloists, although a few works employ *ripieno* voices, beyond the ten to fourteen musicians on strings and winds.[22] But the presence of Latin school choirboys should not deceive us into imagining a large *ripieno* here any more than in Italy. In many German cities, the Latin school's obligations required dividing its choristers among three or four churches, so the number of choristers employed in any one church was between four and twelve.[23] And a substantial increase in the use of polyphony in the seventeenth century, from as seldom as six times a year to weekly, put further strain on available vocal resources.[24] Solo ensembles represented a universal practice in sacred choral music of the seventeenth century, with *ripieno* doubling of voices employed only where performance forces permitted.

Thus, even in large performances, it is very clear that nothing like our modern "concert choir" of fifty to eighty voices on four parts ever existed. Even six voices on a part would have been extraordinary, and the contrast between *favoriti* and *ripieno* was usually between soloists and a choir of two to three on a part, often with instrumental doubling. When larger forces were available, the number of parts and spatially separated choirs grew, rather than the number of performers on any one part. The disposition of these forces was most variable.

The fame of Saint Mark's in Venice arose from the erroneous belief that its choir balconies inspired spatially separated choirs in music for *cori spezzati*. The musical style itself seems to have originated in Padua, although Venetian documentary and iconographic evidence supports its renown soon afterward as a center for multiple-choir music.[25] But Venetian and other evidence also supports performance of double-choir works with both groups in the same place next to each other.[26] Even though cities, bishops, and lords undoubtedly enjoyed the self-congratulatory opulence of music with singers and musicians scattered all about, it is unlikely that a restricted performing space ever prevented the performance of a major work. Flexibility of placement was merely one more part of the repertoire of expedients for adapting works, like the elimination of *ripieno* parts doubling the *favoriti,* or their replacement by instruments.[27] Such adaptation according to the group's particular needs, although an imprecise rendering of the composer's fullest intentions, was and remains a permissible approach to works by Gabrieli, Praetorius, Biber, Schütz, and others with otherwise daunting scoring.

Instruments generally mingled with the voices in three guises, continuo, *obbligato,* and *colla parte.* The use of continuo was ubiquitous throughout the seventeenth century, even when it was not specifically called for. Right from the beginning of the century, the presence of even a simple *basso seguente* line (an unfigured bass line for organ made up of the lowest sounding pitches from each chord) should be interpreted as some sort of continuo part.[28] Although church continuo instrumentation usually included the organ, combinations involving regal, harpsichord, theorbo, bassoon, *violone,* or even greatbass *Pommer* (shawm) were not unknown, and any effective combination of the above is suitable for both sacred and secular music, as long as some kind of continuo is used, for Praetorius awards continuo a nearly universal role in leading a performance.[29]

Obbligato instrumental parts can be divided into three types: the first, like some choirs[30] in Gabrieli's music, has instrumental lines similar to the vocal lines, that is, a second choir of contrasting timbre (and perhaps location) but similar musical characteristics. The second type is a variation on this, namely, accompanying instrumental parts in a choir having one solo vocal part. The third type of *obbligato* instrumental part has an independent figuration or a *ritornello* function that makes it more distinctive from the parts around it, exemplified by duets for treble instruments in the works of Monteverdi, Schütz, and others. Clearly, *obbligato* parts of the third type are much more essential than those of the first or second, which can be replaced by a keyboard part or sometimes even omitted.

Colla parte doubling of vocal parts is less universally documented, but it was probably very common. In some Italian churches, the practice of doubling some or all voices of sacred polyphony appears to have continued at least into the seventeenth century.[31] In German-speaking countries, it remained common throughout the century, as is documented at the

Habsburg court, the cathedral of Salzburg, and in Buxtehude's works.[32] A common combination for such doubling was cornett and trombones, even up to Bach's time, although string doubling seems to have been preferred by Buxtehude.[33] The actual indication of such doubling was less common than was the practice itself.[34] It is unclear whether a similar ensemble might have supported congregational singing in Protestant worship.

Performance practices such as those mentioned above are discussed mainly for large-scale works. Small-scale works, like sacred concertos and secular madrigals, lieder, and the like, would seem to require only one singer to a part, especially in light of the choir of *favoriti* as the most universal ensemble, even in larger works. The use of solo ensembles was probably standard as late as the madrigals of Alessandro Scarlatti.[35] Solo performance is certainly indicated where a singer represents a particular character, for example, a shepherd in a pastoral drama or one of the characters in a biblical representation—like Schütz's *Christmas Story* or the cantatas performed for papal Christmas entertainments, in which closing choruses were probably sung by the collected characters, as in *opera seria*.[36]

Even beyond such clearly dramatic works, the quest for a historical performance practice should also take into consideration other possible liturgical or dramatic contexts. In Catholic sacred works, this includes the place of Gregorian chant, or organ versets in appropriate alternation with liturgical polyphony. In Lutheran works, it suggests the alternation of chorale verses between organ and choir, and perhaps with a large congregation singing the tune monophonically.[37] In some cases, reconstruction of an entire liturgical service or secular festival offers a thrilling performance montage. Research can uncover equivalent contexts for secular works as well, for interpolation of musical numbers in dramas as *intermedii*, set pieces, or melodramas. Such an expanded performance context can be further enriched by architectural investigation in order to locate musical forces as they might have been in a period performance for the best aural effect.[38]

The music's sound also depends very much on the types of voices used. At no other time prior to the present has there been such an array of different voice types, vocal productions, and vocal techniques. And now, all vocal types prevalent in the seventeenth century except the castrato have been rediscovered and revived, including female tenors as well as male altos and sopranos, both boys and adults. Most of the vocal techniques used by these voices have also been rediscovered. Different voices were associated with different contexts, however. Choir schools in both Germany and Italy trained boys. When they grew older and their voices changed, they provided tenors and basses. Adult males also sang alto, or occasionally soprano, in falsetto. But neither boys nor adult falsettists could surpass the expertise, technical ability, and power of the great castrati.

Castrato voices became more common in Italy in the first part of the seventeenth century, but diminished in number toward the century's end.[39] Female voices, while accepted in secular music, were not permitted to sing with men in Catholic churches, although they may have sung occasional special solos in aristocratic chapels.[40] The reverse was true in Italian female convents, as previously discussed, where women sang all parts, through transposition of the works, instrumental doubling of lower voices, or the use of rare female basses and tenors. Such flexibility extended to the selection of voices for various parts of any vocal music, which was based less on fixed classifications (i.e., castrato versus falsettist versus boy soprano) than on the ranges needed, the voices available, and their ability and training.

The training of voices seems to have been largely by private lessons, even in the choir schools. This is documented in sixteenth-century Bergamo by the trial of Pietro Pontio, who was indicted for, among other things, teaching the boys in groups.[41] As music became more challenging and soloistic, solo instruction remained the method of choice in the seventeenth century.[42] That the same type of instruction was the rule in female convents might explain the continual controversy over their use of male music teachers when no sister was sufficiently competent.[43] The training of women's voices outside the convent had no such problems, though. Although performance opportunities were more restricted than for men, in the Mantuan ducal chapel, female *virtuose* took their places among men, boys, and the finest castrati money could hire.[44] This practice can already be seen in the performances of the *concerto delle donne* in Ferrara. Documentation of vocal training is sparse, however, perhaps because patrons preferred to hire singers already trained.

The type of vocal production taught has been controversial, at least partly due to the modern entrenchment of nineteenth-century operatic technique in which vibrato provides the only safety valve for loud, high-pressure tone production.[45] Since most seventeenth-century vocal training began in choir schools, with Gregorian chant, the singers' technical basis was quite different. Modern "historically correct" singers have rediscovered how to produce a clear, beautiful tone that is fully relaxed but has minimal vibrato. But such tone production does not imply the perfectly blended half voice cultivated by many modern choirs. Since seventeenth-century vocal ensembles were collections of little more than a few singers, there could be little or no difference in volume between *favoriti* and *ripieno* singers, even when lack of independent parts indicates that the former doubled the latter in tutti sections. Singers of either type would utilize a tone production centered around a solid *forte* in any sacred or spectacle music designed for public performance.

Nevertheless, within such a well-supported tone production, good interpretation demands shaping each individual note, as well as the larger phrasing of the melodic line, and a clear understanding, enunciation, and projection of the text. Modern singers may also wish to research historical pronunciation of the text as well.[46] For nonsoloists, these skills, plus good intonation, would have been much more essential than complex ornamentation.[47] But the final interpretive layer for soloists must also include improvisatory ornamentation using throat articulation, which demands a relaxed but vibrato-free technique (although vibrato can itself be used within the repertory of ornaments).[48] Soloists who have fully mastered this technique can improvise using elaborate *passaggi* and diminutions like those described by the theorists dalla Casa, Rognoni, Bovicelli, Bassano, and others described elsewhere in this volume.[49] Such ornamentation is essential for soloists among the *favoriti*, even if *ripieno* singers should avoid it to concentrate on enunciation, shaping, phrasing, and intonation.[50]

Intonation is one of the most critical aspects of this style; florid lines require harmonic clarity that only good intonation can give. Nevertheless, intonation and tuning would themselves have varied with the performance context. When singers were unaccompanied, they would likely have sung simultaneous octaves, fifths, and thirds as close to pure as possible. But when they performed with instruments, we must assume that they adopted the instruments' tuning. This is of particular concern with regard to the fretted strings and keyboard instruments, especially the organ, on continuo parts. Fretted strings such as lutes and viols can make some concessions to perfect intonation through the use of double fretting or variable finger placement and pressure around the frets, but keyboard instruments are completely inflexible, and any instruments or voices performing with them must match their pitches.

In the early seventeenth century, matching keyboard pitches often meant performing in quarter-comma meantone, which provides perfectly lovely just intonation as long as one keeps to the right keys. By the time of Buxtehude, however, the use of well-tempered tuning was coming into vogue in Germany, especially the temperaments of Andreas Werckmeister.[51] The greater chromatic flexibility permitted by these temperaments was balanced by the fact that more chords were slightly out of tune, although not as badly as the wolf chords of the meantone system. Although singing frequently with such instruments may have affected singers' tuning ability, nevertheless, seventeenth-century singers probably had an excellent sense of just intonation, which we should try to duplicate in our performances of this music. Pitch, however, is another question.

There was no single pitch standard in the seventeenth century, but by a very ancient tradition, many organs in Germany and Italy were built higher than today's standard pitch; the usual *Chorton* in Germany was about a semitone higher than a=440, and north Italian organs were quite variable, anywhere from slightly to a third higher.[52] The reason for this is the considerable savings in metal derived from exchanging one or two of the instrument's longest pipes with two of the shortest ones at the other end of the keyboard. This made more difference in the performance of works than we might suppose, since organists playing a meantone-tuned instrument had a limited range of transposition possibilities. As the century progressed, the widening ranges of written voice parts may have required more frequent transposition by the organist, which undoubtedly spurred the adoption of more equal temperaments.

In addition to pitch and tuning, the seventeenth century saw the advent of the new considerations of tempo, dynamics, and sectionalization. By the end of the sixteenth century, the old mensural system, which had defined both tempo and meter for centuries, was breaking down. The 2:1 relationship between C and cut-C had ceased to exist, and the two mensurations were roughly equivalent, with C slightly slower.[53] A triple proportion or triple time signature could signify either a 3:2 or 1:1 relationship with a preceding duple meter, depending on context.[54] The presence of characteristic dance rhythms can also indicate the tempo, even where no verbal marking appears.[55] Toward the end of the century, verbal tempo markings did begin to appear. But these merely confirm the tempo suggested by the prevalent note values in the music, just as dynamic markings of the period merely signal to players the size of the ensemble playing at any given moment.[56] Overinterpretation of either of these types of signs should be avoided.

Tempo, dynamics, rhythmic variety, and melodic invention combined with timbral and spatial contrasts to provide seventeenth-century music with unprecedented sumptuousness. The rich variety of musical effects provided essential vehicles for the abundant emotional affections so central to seventeenth-century aesthetics. The expressive means inherent in the notes themselves—rhythm, melody, and harmony—provided the most essential components. Augmented by clever dynamic and tempo contrasts, these primary elements acquired more expressiveness, even in a relatively small performance. But in a musical institution that was richly endowed, infinite timbral variations and enveloping reverberations over, under, and around must have provided an experience closer to the ninth circle of paradise than anyone in the seventeenth century (or now) would have any reason to expect. Whether our ensemble is a modest chamber group or the large, imperial size, whether we perform this music from modern editions, original parts, or something in between, the electrifying contrasts of seventeenth-century music in all their richness, variety, and affect must be the final aim of all our interpretive skills.

NOTES

1. I am deeply grateful to Jeffrey Kurtzmann for providing draft material from his book in progress, *The Monteverdi Vespers of 1610: Music, Context, Performance.*
2. Lionnet–Performance Practice, with essential background in Sherr–Performance Practice; and Sherr–Competence and Incompetence; Moore–*Vespers at Saint Mark's*; Praetorius–*Syntagma* III: 102–39 (119 *recte*), 169–97 (see also the translation of this volume, Lampl–*Syntagma*); Gable–Saint Gertrude's; Chafe–*Biber,* Saunders–*Cross.* I am also very grateful for the guidance of Charles Brewer, who generously shared his pro-

found knowledge of seventeenth-century music in the Austro-Hungarian Empire, as well as providing a superb and widely varied discography.

3. I translate as "part-singing" or "part music" the term *cantus figuratus,* or figured song, which can indicate mensural polyphony, monody, or homophonic *falsobordone.*
4. Roche–*North Italian,* 16.
5. Ibid., 15.
6. The root of the description of monodic works as *concerti* seems to be in Viadana–*Cento concerti ecclesiastici,* 419–23. Indeed, the term concerto was deemed appropriate for any work in the continuo style. The characteristic that merits such description is more difficult to pin down. Caccini–*Nuove musiche,* 45–47, emphasizes the superiority of the new style for interpretation of affect. In Caccini–*Nuove . . . scriverle,* [xxxiii], he advocates affective contrasts. (Pages are cited from the Hitchcock edition.)
7. Charteris–Performance–336–38. See also Bryant–Cori Spezzati, 169; Moore–*Vespero,* 275–76, and Moore–*Vespers at Saint Mark's,* 97–99.
8. Moore–*Vespers at Saint Mark's,* 85–110.
9. Rostirolla–Policoralità, 36–42.
10. Lionnet–*Performance Practice,* 3–15. Sherr–*Competence* clarifies factors that reduced the number of paid singers who were singing at a given moment.
11. For Bergamo, see Padouan–*Santa Maria Maggiore,* 73–85, 91–94; Padouan–Modello, 137–39.
12. Billio d'Arpa–Freddi, 245–47.
13. Mischiati–*L'organo,* 91–93.
14. Donato–Policoralità, 147.
15. Viadana–*Cento concerti ecclesiastici,* 419–20. This practice parallels that in works by Giovanni Gabrieli, noted in Charteris–Performance, 343–44.
16. Kendrick–*Genres,* 332–58. For documentation of such practices in the eighteenth century, see Talbot–Tenors.
17. Praetorius–*Syntagma* III: 196, translated in Snyder–*Buxtehude,* 361 ff.
18. Praetorius–*Syntagma* III: 166–97, referred to in Chafe–*Biber,* 55.
19. Chafe–*Biber,* 31–69; Saunders–*Cross,* 18–57, with discussion of particular groups of works following.
20. Chafe–*Biber,* 37–51.
21. Saunders–*Cross,* 18–22, 61–151.
22. Snyder–*Buxtehude,* 90–93, 361–66.
23. Butt–*Music Education,* 110–11; David/Mendel–*Bach Reader,* 116–24.
24. Butt–*Music Education,* 16–23.
25. D'Alessi–Precursors, 210, notes that Treviso, Verona, and Bergamo shared with Venice the distinction of being the first performance sites of music for *cori spezzati* after Padua. Regarding the spatially separated performance practice, see Bryant–Cori Spezzati, 181–85; Moore–*Vespers at Saint Mark's,* 106–10.
26. Bryant–Cori Spezzati, 170–72; Moore–*Vespers at Saint Mark's,* 103–6. My own research in Bergamo suggests similar closely spaced choirs there, at least in the sixteenth century. Spatial experimentation may have increased after the construction of new organ balconies above the choir in the 1590s.
27. Charteris–Performance, 343–44, describes scoring like this. Even so, it is probably wise to research the work's context. Publication of works (like Praetorius's) often included explicit statements about their adaptability in the composer's view. Nevertheless, exercise of some discretion seems advisable.
28. Charteris–Performance, 339–43. See also Bartlett/Holman–Gabrieli, 27–28.
29. Moore–*Vespers at Saint Mark's,* 84–110; Snyder–*Buxtehude,* 371, 377–82; Praetorius–*Syntagma* III: 144–45 (*recte* 124–25).
30. In the seventeenth century the word "choir" can refer to a group consisting of voices, instruments, or a mixture of the two.

31. Bartlett/Holman–Gabrieli, 27, advocate caution. See also Moore–*Vespers at Saint Mark's*, 100–01. The list in Rostirolla–Policoralità, 40–41, indicates instruments in at least one choir, but does not discuss doubling or independent parts.
32. Saunders–*Cross*, 28–29; Chafe–*Biber*, 49, 54; Snyder–*Buxtehude*, 364–66, 382–84.
33. Snyder–*Buxtehude*, 364–66; Chafe–*Biber*, 49; Saunders–*Cross*, 29.
34. Saunders–*Cross*, 28.
35. Jürgens–Madrigale.
36. Gianturco–Cantate, 6.
37. *Alternatim* practice in Catholic liturgy is fairly well known and understood. See Higginbottom–Alternatim and –Organ Mass. Bonta–Uses discusses the substitution of instrumental music for portions of the organ mass in the seventeenth and eighteenth centuries. Chorale verse alternation in Lutheran services is discussed in Gotsch–Organ, 10; as cited in Kazarow–Lutheran. Snyder–*Buxtehude*, 98, observes that *alternatim* practice existed in Lübeck from the fifteenth century, that later it may have included organ chorale interludes, and that organ chorale accompaniment appears in documentation of 1703.
38. Gable–Gertrudenmusik.
39. Hucke–Besetzung, 386–92, discusses the replacement of soprano falsettists by castrati in the Sistine Chapel, beginning in the late sixteenth century and continuing through the seventeenth. See also Rosselli–Castrati, 156–58.
40. Talbot–Tenors, 129–30, discusses the prohibition of mixed choirs. Parisi–Ducal Patronage, 21–36, 64–68, 129–35, 233, 288, discusses the hiring of female singers for the Ducal chapel. It is not clear whether they actually participated in sacred music.
41. Murray–Teaching Duties, 118–22.
42. Padouan–Santa Maria Maggiore, 42–43.
43. Several allusions in Kendrick–*Genres*.
44. Parisi–Ducal Patronage, 21–36, 64–68, 129–35, 233, 288.
45. Gable–Observations, 93–94. See also Uberti–Vocal Techniques, 486.
46. Caccini–*Nuove musiche*, 46–48; Sanford–French Language, 1–3; Hilse–Treatises, 20–21; Praetorius–*Syntagma* III: 126 (*recte* 106), 196, translated in Butt–*Music Education*, 96–97, 108. Reconstruction of archaic and regional pronunciations is becoming a common performance practice. For vernaculars, consultation of a local college's foreign language department may be helpful. See also Duffin–Pronunciation Guides and McGee–*Singing Early Music*. For Latin variants, begin with Duffin–National Pronunciation and Copeman–*Singing*.
47. Sanford–Seventeenth-Century, 64–68, discusses the essential nature of good intonation.
48. Ibid., 56–61, 71–78.
49. Ibid., 56–59.
50. Butt–*Music Education*, 110–12, 138–41, discusses the problem of simultaneous ornamentation by more than one singer on a part, and its contribution to retarding the adoption of multiple singers to a part in some areas of Germany. He also notes the intense opposition to all musical ornamentation associated with the Pietist movement.
51. Snyder–*Buxtehude*, 85, postulates 1683 as the date Buxtehude's organ was retuned to Werckmeister's temperament.
52. Ibid. The variability of Italian organs in the sixteenth century is well documented in Mischiati–Documenti, 42–43.
53. Boal–Purcell's Clock Tempos, 32–34. See also Boal–Timepieces.
54. Boal–Purcell's Tempo Indications; *New Grove*–Tempo.
55. *New Grove*–Tempo.
56. Ibid.

SUGGESTED LISTENING
(Graciously contributed by Charles E. Brewer)

Italian Traditions

Giacomo Carissimi: Judicium Extremum / Jonas / Jephthe. His Majesties Sagbutts and Cornetts, Monteverdi Choir, Members of the English Baroque Soloists; John Eliot Gardner. Erato 2292-45466-2.

Claudio Monteverdi: Vespri di S. Giovanni Battista. Netherlands Chamber Choir, Chorus Viennensis, Monteverdi Ensemble Amsterdam; Gustav Leonhardt. Philips 422 074-2.

Giacomo Antonio Perti: Messa a otto voci per soli, ripieni e strumenti. New College Choir di Oxford, Cappella Musicale di San Petronio: Sergio Vartolo. BonGiovanni GB 2039-2.

Vespri Concertati della Scuola Bolognese di P. Franceschini, G. Torelli, D. Gabrielli. Coro e Orchestra della Cappella Musicale di S. Petronio, Tölzer Knabenchor, Ensemble Vocal d'Avignon: Sergio Vartolo. Tactus TC 650001.

A Venetian Coronation, 1595: Andrea & Giovanni Gabrieli. Gabrieli Consort and Players; Paul McCreesh. Virgin Classics VC 7 91110-2.

Venetian Vespers: Monteverdi, Rigatti, Grandi, Cavalli. Gabrieli Consort and Players; Paul McCreesh. DGG Archiv Produktion 437 552-2.

Central and East Central European Traditions

Heinrich Ignaz Franz Biber (attributed): Missa Salisburgensis. Escolania de Montserrat, Tölzer Knabenchor, Collegium Aureum; P. Ireneu Segarra, O.S.B. EMI deutsche harmonia mundi CDC 7 49236 2.

Heinrich Ignaz Franz Biber: Requiem in F minor / String Sonatas. New London Consort; Philip Pickett. Editions de L'Oiseau-Lyre 436-460-2.

Heinrich Ignaz Franz Biber: Vêpres. Choeur et Orchestre Studio de Musique Ancienne de Montreal; Christopher Jackson. REM Éditions REM 311207.

Festal Mass at the Imperial Court of Vienna, 1648. Yorkshire Bach Choir, Yorkshire Baroque Soloists, Baroque Brass of London: Peter Seymour. Novello Records NVLCD 105 (includes Christoph Straus's *Missa Veni sponsa Christi*, and works by Andreas Rauch, Girolamo Fantini, Antonio Bertali, and Giovanni Priuli).

Johann Heinrich Schmelzer: Vesperae sollennes, Heinrich Ignaz Franz Biber: Missa Alleluya à 36. Gradus ad Parnasum; Konrad Junghänel. BMG / deutsch harmonia mundi 05472 77326 2.

Northern European Traditions

Dietrich Buxtehude, "Ein Starken Music . . ." Six Cantatas. Orchestra Anima Eterna, Collegium Vocale; Joos van Immerseel. Channel Classics CCS 7895-1.

Dieterich [sic] Buxtehude: Membra Jesu Nostri (BuxWV 75). The Monteverdi Choir, The English Baroque Soloists, Fretwork; John Eliot Gardiner. DGG Archiv Produktion 427 680-2.

Palestrina/Bach–Missa sine nomine / Kuhnau, Pezel, Reiche. Concerto Palatino. EMI Classics CDC 7 54455 2.

Michael Praetorius, Mass for Christmas Morning. Gabrieli Consort and Players; Paul McCreesh. DGG Archiv 439 250-2 (also includes works by Samuel Scheidt and Johann Hermann Schein).

Heinrich Schütz, Psalmen Davids SWV 22-47. Kammerchor Stuttgart & Soloists, Musica Fiata Köln; Frieder Bernius. Sony Vivarte S2K 48042.

Thomaskantoren vor Bach: Knüpfer, Schelle, Kuhnau. Cantus Cölln; Konrad Junghänel. BMG / deutsch harmonia mundi 05472 77203 2.

BIBLIOGRAPHY

Bartlett and Holman–Gabrieli; Boal–Purcell's Clock Tempos; Boal–Purcell's Tempo Indications; Boal–Timepieces; Bonta–Uses; Billio D'Arpa–Freddi; Bryant–Cori Spezzati; Butt–*Music Education*; Caccini–*Nuove musiche*; Caccini–*Nuove . . . scriverle*; Chafe–Biber; Charteris–Performance; Copeman–*Singing*; D'Alessi–Precursors; David and Mendel–*Bach Reader*; Donato–Policoralità; Duffin–National Pronunciations; Duffin–Pronunciation Guides; Gable–Saint Gertrude's; Gable–Some Observations; Gianturco–Cantate spirituali; Gotsch–Organ; Hilse–Bernhard; Hucke–Besetzung; Jürgens–Scarlatti; Lampl–*Syntagma*; Lionnet–Performance Practice; Kazarow–Luther; Kendrick–*Genres*; McGee–*Singing*; Mischiati–Documenti; Mischiati–*L'Organo*; Moens-Haenen–*Vibrato*; Moore–Vespero; Moore–*Vespers at Saint Mark's*; Murray–Teaching Duties; *New Grove*, s.v. "Alternatim," "Organ Mass," "Tempo"; Padouan–Modello; Padouan–Santa Maria Maggiore; Parisi–Ducal; Praetorius–*Syntagma* III; Roche–*North Italian*; Rosselli–Castrati; Rostirolla–Policoralità; Saunders–*Cross*; Sherr–Competence; Sherr–Performance Practice; Snyder–*Buxtehude*; Talbot–Tenors; Uberti–Vocal Techniques; Viadana–*Cento concerti ecclesiastici*.

II

INSTRUMENTAL ISSUES

5

Woodwinds

Herbert W. Myers

Of all the centuries in the recorded history of Western music, the seventeenth witnessed the most thoroughgoing and decisive changes in the nature of woodwind instruments. While the sixteenth century had produced some remarkable developments, resulting in the rich and varied instrumentarium of the late Renaissance, these can be viewed as essentially evolutionary in spirit; they consisted of expansions of existing families and the invention of complementary types intended to serve with them and round out the palette of instrumental colors. The developments of the mid-to-late seventeenth century were, by comparison, nothing short of revolutionary, consisting of complete remodelings of a limited number of Renaissance winds—flute, recorder, shawm, and curtal—to produce radically new types that ultimately eclipsed their progenitors (not to mention their few remaining rivals, such as the cornett). The affinity between these new forms (Baroque flute, oboe, and bassoon in particular, the recorder representing something of a special case) and our own seems clear; we recognize them more as youthful versions than ancestors of our modern designs despite the tremendous technological gulf between them.

Unfortunately from our own point of view, those responsible for the remodelings left virtually no written record of the process. It has been left to more recent scholars to piece together the story, relying on extant instruments, iconography, and recollections of eighteenth-century writers, along with a few scattered seventeenth-century documents. It is fairly clear, of course, *what* changes were made; it is harder to determine when, where, by whom, and (perhaps most important of all) why. France, under the musical domination of Lully, has long been hailed as the cradle of the new designs; more recent scholarship, however, has begun to recognize the contributions of makers from other countries. In addition, several scholars have begun to question the traditional dating of the innovations, suggesting for some a period closer to the death of Lully (1687) than to the middle of his career. (For instance, the long-accepted date of 1657 for the debut of the oboe—in Lully's *Ballet de l'Amour Malade*—has recently been shown to have been based on some mistranslations and groundless assumptions.[1] On the other hand, the developments leading to the bassoon may have started considerably earlier and involved builders from Italy, Spain, and Holland as well as France.[2] Work in this area continues; while it is unlikely that a large body of documentation—written or iconographic—lies in wait, yet to be discovered, the evidence of musical sources (particularly manuscript scores and parts) has yet to be exploited to the full in solving some remaining puzzles.

Despite the subsequent importance of the remodeled woodwinds, we should not regard what came before as a mere prelude. This kind of bias would be especially inappropriate here, in a book concerned with the seventeenth century as a whole. However, the earlier forms of woodwinds have been covered in considerable depth in a previous volume in this series (see relevant articles in *A Performer's Guide to Renaissance Music*, Jeffery Kite-Powell, ed., 1994); moreover, most of the authors contributing to that volume have allowed their definition of "Renaissance" to encompass at least part of the seventeenth century. Rather than repeating basic information, this survey will attempt to present a summary. In recounting historical developments in instrument design it will pay particular attention to some of the causes: changes in musical aesthetics and practice. These have often been ignored by scholars researching instrument history, who have tended instead to concentrate on morphology— how many joints, how many keys, what style of ornamental turnery. In fact, an instrument is defined at least as much by its use as its shape; form *follows* function. Of particular importance to both use and design is the question of pitch; to Quantz writing in the eighteenth century, for instance, the remodeled woodwinds owed their very existence to their adoption of low (French) pitch.[3] All the winds are affected by the choice of pitch standard, of course, but for flutes and recorders there is an additional pitch-related question: when and where does their traditional Renaissance employment at 4-foot pitch give way to use at 8-foot pitch? At what point did alto and tenor instruments become accepted as sopranos? This is not an easy question to answer, as we shall see.

Late-Renaissance Winds

The Sources

We owe much of what we know about instruments of the early seventeenth century—and, indeed, about Renaissance instruments in general—to two remarkable writers, Michael Praetorius and Marin Mersenne. Each produced a comprehensive treatise on musical theory and practice: Praetorius's *Syntagma musicum* (in three volumes, 1614–20[4]) and

Mersenne's *Harmonie universelle* (1636–37[5]). The two authors are often lumped together, but despite their shared thoroughness they could hardly be more different in style and approach. Praetorius—Lutheran composer, organist, and kapellmeister—is always the more pragmatic; Mersenne—Jesuit priest, mathematician, philosopher, and scientist—the more speculative. Praetorius's information appears to flow from his own practical experience, while Mersenne's often seems a secondhand acquisition (which he does not always understand in depth). Rare is the page in Mersenne's instrument descriptions without some inexplicable ambiguity or frustrating lack of clarity. (Not that Praetorius himself is without errors or inconsistencies, but his usually have some simple explanation.) Mersenne treats verbally of matters (such as instrument dimensions) that Praetorius entrusts to the carefully drafted plates of the *Theatrum instrumentorum* (the appendix to the *Syntagma* II) to communicate; such verbal descriptions are naturally prone to error. Perhaps it should be mentioned in Mersenne's defense, however, that his text simply has more information about instruments than Praetorius's (including fingering charts and musical examples), providing more places for things to go wrong.

Perhaps an example will show how we have to second-guess Mersenne's information, taking him for what he means—or his informants meant—rather than for what he says. In his description of the *fluste à trois trous* (three-holed tabor pipe), Mersenne explains the tablature system he intends to use for fingering charts for all of the woodwinds.[6] Circles (or zeros) are used here, he says, to indicate "all fingers off." However, in the chart for *flageollet* that follows,[7] he then uses zeros not only in this way (as indicators of "all-open" notes), but also to mark the thumbhole in fingerings for overblown notes. Although he reiterates that zeros mean open holes, he also suggests (three pages later) that the thumb should actually half-hole in the upper octave![8] This statement is followed almost immediately by the chart for *fluste à six trois* (six-holed pipe—what we might call a pennywhistle), which makes sense only if zeros are allowed to have yet another meaning: they can indicate overblowing on instruments without a thumbhole, in which case they signify the first *closed* hole. (Were they to signify an *open* hole, there would be no difference between the fingering for b″—one zero—and that for c‴—six zeros.) This would also appear to be their import in his second chart for the *fluste d'Allemande* (transverse flute[9]) and chart for *fifre* (fife[10]); in any case, these fingerings work on actual instruments only if the holes marked with zeros are left closed, not open.[11] However, in the intervening charts for *fluste à neuf trous* (recorder[12]) the zeros marking the thumbhole in second-octave fingerings should probably be taken to indicate half-holing (or "pinching"), even though Mersenne once again mentions that they mean open holes.

Thus it appears that whoever made up the charts must have been making a distinction between a "stack" of zeros (to mean "all off") and a single zero heading a fingering (to indicate overblowing in general—and "pinching" specifically, when there is a thumbhole); furthermore, it seems that this distinction was lost on Mersenne himself. Whatever the answer, this is just a small sample of the kind of confusion we may encounter in what purport to be simple and straightforward explanations.

Besides the differences in style between Mersenne and Praetorius are also the obvious temporal and geographic differences; when they present divergent pictures we are often left to guess whether these reflect changes over time or different national uses. Sometimes other written sources can provide clues. Another primary source is represented by the instruments themselves, a goodly number of which survive from this period; however, they are rarely dated, and their provenance is also often in doubt. Then, too, fate has been kinder to some instruments than others, and we do not necessarily have either the best or most representative samples. We are fortunate, therefore, to have both written and physical evidence, since each is able to complement the other.

Recorders and Flutes

Praetorius begins his discussion of woodwinds with the recorder. By his time the original set of three sizes (ones we would now call alto, tenor, and bass) had expanded considerably; he lists eight sizes: *klein Flötlein* or *exilent* in (seven-fingers) g", *discant* in d", *discant* in c", *alt* in g', *tenor* in c', *basset* in f, *bass* in B♭, and *grossbass* in F.[13] Such a complete set—presumably with some duplications of certain sizes, following his earlier recommendations[14]—was available from Venice for about 80 thalers, he says, and indeed those illustrated[15] resemble surviving examples of Venetian manufacture. These are characterized by a plain, robust, one-piece construction, a comparatively wide bore, and a voicing that favors the low register; sizes larger than a tenor are fitted with a key (for the bottom note), which is covered by a protective barrel or "fontanelle." Surviving examples have what has been called a "choke" bore: the top end is basically cylindrical, but begins to contract near the upper fingerholes and then widens out again at the bottom. The contraction itself is what makes the larger recorders feasible, for without it, the fingerholes have to be impractically large and finger stretches become impossible.

It is the flaring "foot" section that distinguishes this bore profile from that of the Baroque and modern recorder, whose foot-joint bore continues instead to contract. This terminal contraction is responsible for the success of the Baroque high-note fingerings, which generally do not work on Renaissance-style recorders (except on some of the smaller ones, provided they have comparatively large fingerholes; see for instance the modern instruments based on the late-seventeenth-century "transitional" set by H. F. Kynseker of Nuremberg). In fact, Praetorius mentions that the larger recorders—those with keys, it would seem from the chart of ranges[16]—are ordinarily limited in range to a thirteenth, while the smaller ones can generally reach a fourteenth; certain extraordinary players, however, can force another four to seven tones beyond the standard range. (Has he been reading Ganassi about this?)

We should note that most of the members of Praetorius's recorder set are separated by fifths, in contrast with the alternating fourths and fifths typical of later families. The exceptions come at the outer edges of the set; there is a *discant* in c" (in addition to the one in d"), but no *alt* in f'. He explains[17] the reason for this alignment in fifths (typical of all the winds): a quartet can be made up of any three adjacent sizes, using two of the middle size (as alto and tenor). This works out particularly well for recorders when the music is written in the standard "low clefs" of vocal music (see the discussion of *chiavette* in the chapter on "Pitch and Transposition," this *Guide*). In fact, in the *Syntagma* III[18] Praetorius lists recorders among the instruments best suited to pieces in these clefs. It is when the music moves outside these restricted traditional ranges that problems arise, since four (and possibly even five) sizes must be used together, necessitating transpositions (up a second and down a fourth in particular) to accommodate the bias of the smaller instruments toward sharps. For shawms the ideal solution, he suggests, would be for makers to build *discant* and *alt* instruments in c' and f (as alternatives to the traditional d' and g pitches); although he does not mention this idea in connection with recorders, we see it beginning to be realized in the case of the *discant* in c".

Surviving instruments present a slightly more varied picture of the recorder in this period. Assuming a reference pitch of about a'=460 (about a semitone above modern; see "Pitch and Transposition," this *Guide*), there are a number of *bass, basset,* and *tenor* recorders built a tone above the pitches Praetorius gives; they are thus an octave (rather than a ninth) below the corresponding *tenor, alt,* and *discant* instruments in c', g" and d". These actually outnumber the corresponding "standard" sizes— as defined by Praetorius—in at least one museum collection (in Vienna).[19] Practorius also seems unaware of two other phenomena of Renaissance recorders: the so-called "extended" and "columnar" versions. The former are instruments (primarily of *bass* and *grossbass* size) provided with lower extension keys, adding three diatonic notes below the normal bottom note; the latter are instruments built in a curious columnar shape and adorned with brass "seives" covering the voicing windows and with other ornamental work.[20] While extant examples of both seem to come from the sixteenth century (being associated with the builders Schratt and Schrattenbach of Hamburg[21]), columnar recorders still show up in the iconography of the seventeenth. They are also significant in being some of the few Renaissance recorders built to a low pitch standard (in this case about a'=392, a tone below modern).

In his recorder chapter Praetorius mentions some acoustically related instruments, which need not long detain us here: *stamientienpfeiff* or *schwägel* (tabor pipe) and *gar kleine Plockflötlein*. The former came in three sizes (he illustrates two, along with their associated tabor); the latter was a tiny (three- to four-inch-long) pipe with three fingerholes and a thumbhole, which nonetheless was capable of almost a two-octave range![22] Praetorius's next (and very short) chapter concerns *querpfeiffen* (transverse flutes), under which he also includes *doltzflöten* (flutes with recorder-like tone generator, of which no examples survive) and military fifes. The consort of flutes illustrated is comprised of three sizes: *discant* in (six-fingers) a', *alt-tenor* in d', and *bass* in g. In contrast with the recorders, the pitch of the flutes is quite low—about a minor third below modern, judging by their lengths.[23] This pitch is near the low end of the spectrum for surviving flutes; the majority of these cluster about two centers: a'=435 and a'=410 (the latter about a semitone below a'=440).[24]

It should be noted that Praetorius's pitch designations for both recorders and flutes are an octave higher than those given in the sixteenth century. He has the credit for first mentioning in print the aural illusion whereby flutes and recorders can appear to sound an octave below their actual pitch; thus a *tenor* recorder or flute is actually at *discant* pitch and can serve in either role. This statement has often been taken as a blanket sanction for the use of recorders and flutes at 8-foot pitch for music of that period (as well as earlier). However, other evidence (including from Praetorius himself) suggests that this 8-foot-pitch use was exceptional. For instance, in discussing instrumentation in the *Syntagma* III, Praetorius quite clearly assumes that flutes will be playing at 4-foot pitch; in fact, he reverts here to the traditional pitch notation for them (referring to d" and f" as high notes for [tenor] flute when d'" and f'"—sounding pitch—are obviously meant).[25] For recorders it would appear that he assumes 8-foot pitch only for the large set, which—he indicates—is effective only when playing by itself, not mixed with other instruments.[26]

The use of both flutes and recorders at 4-foot pitch remained the norm for quite some time; this is clear from the notation of seventeenth-century pieces that specify these instruments. Examples for flutes include works by Monteverdi, Schein, and Schütz[27]; ones for recorder include works by Bertali, Schmelzer (his famous *Sonata à 7 Flauti*), and H. I. F. Biber (his *Sonata pro Tabula à 10*).[28] The *Fluyten Lust-hof* of Jacob van Eyck (Amsterdam, 1646), though now associated primarily with recorder, seems to be intended for either instrument; prefatory instructions bound with some copies show both. The most likely candidates are a recorder in c" and a flute in g', once again putting the notation an octave below the sounding pitch.[29] As late as 1677 Bartolomeo Bismantova shows the written scale of an alto recorder in (sounding) g' as beginning an octave lower, on g.[30] This late survival of the "Renaissance" notational practice is all the more remarkable because the instrument illustrated by Bismantova is of the three-piece, Baroque format; he is, in fact, the first to document the new design.[31] The first works to notate recorder and flute music consistently and unequivocally at its actual pitch seem to come from late-seventeenth-century France (from the pens of Lully and Charpentier in particular[32]) and England (under French musical influence at that time).[33] It is natural to look to Mersenne for the roots of this "Baroque" practice; as usual, however, his presentation leaves us with as many puzzles as answers.

Mersenne's set of recorders is—on the surface, at least—not all that different from Praetorius's. Unlike Praetorius, however, he divides them into two groups, a *petit jeu* and a *grand jeu,* which, he says, can be "tuned" (i.e., played) together, just as are the small and large stops (*jeux*) of the organ. The *petit jeu* consists, he tells us, of three sizes, separated by fifths: *dessus, taille* (which also serves for the *haute-contre*), and *basse.*This information is thus in accord with standard Renaissance practice, as explained (for example) by Jambe de Fer almost a century earlier.[34] Mersenne gives no specific pitches for any of his recorders; we can only assume a continuance of the traditional f, c', and g' (sounding) pitches for the instruments of the *petit jeu.* The problem comes when we consider their physical measurements. His length for the *basse* (two and three-quarters *pieds,* or about 893 mm) is reasonable enough, being in the neighborhood of the length of Praetorius's *basset.* (Unfortunately, Mersenne fails to clarify whether his measurements are of total lengths or sounding lengths, making exact comparisons impossible.) But his *taille* measurement of one *pied* five *pouces* (460 mm) is far too short; it is midway between what we should expect for *taille* and *dessus* proportioned to such a *basse.* However, the worst is yet to come; he claims that the *dessus* is but eleven *lignes* (less than an inch!) in length. This is of course ridiculous, but even at eleven *pouces* (298 mm) it is too short to stand at a ninth above the *basse.* It is close, however, to the length of Praetorius's *discant* in c", suggesting that there was (unbeknownst to Mersenne) a fourth size of recorder in the *petit jeu* in France—not surprising, given developments elsewhere. Confirmation of this notion is to be found in Mersenne's fingering chart for recorder. This is for an instrument in (seven-fingers) c', written pitch; no physical size is specified. However, the high-note fingerings given are those of the standard Baroque (and modern) instrument, which (as pointed out above) do not generally work on Renaissance recorders—particularly the larger ones. Thus a small instrument (and one with a "Renaissance" exterior but a "Baroque" bore, rather like that needed for van Eyck) is implied; the notation would then still be an octave below the sounding pitch. Such an instrument would be handy for playing the top part of Mersenne's musical example, which goes up to written f"—a high (though not impossible) note for his *dessus* in g'.

The *basse* of the *petit jeu* serves as the *dessus* of the *grande jeu,* according to Mersenne. Below this instrument are a large *taille* and *basse,* ones Praetorius would have called *bass* and *grossbass* (but unlike his, possessing lower extensions, as described above). If the carefully rendered engraving of this set can be trusted, the seven-finger note of the *taille* would seem to be a fourth (and that of the *basse,* an octave) below the *dessus* of the *grand jeu.*[35] It is not at all certain that the recorders of the *grand jeu* were in common use in Mersenne's France. The ones he is describing, he says, were a gift from England to one of France's kings; he is rendering their key mechanism in such detail "so that our [French] builders can make some similar."[36] In any case, the *grand jeu* as he describes it is poorly suited to performing his musical example; one needs to add a *taille* (tenor) from the *petit jeu* in order to play the top part, since the normal limit of a Renaissance *basse* (Praetorius's *basset*) is d".

Mersenne's information about flutes leaves even more room for interpretation. He begins by describing "one of the best flutes in the world," providing *almost* enough measurements for a reconstruction. Though a few details are lacking, it is clear that (acoustically speaking) this is a Renaissance-style tenor flute with a bottom note somewhere around d'.[37] For this he gives two fingering charts, one starting on g and the other on d'. One is not merely a transposition of the other, since the fingerings themselves differ significantly. The chart on g is, in fact, unique among early charts for Renaissance-style flutes in that all the notes of the second octave are simple overblown octaves of the fundamental register; all other charts switch to overblown twelfths, beginning with the twelfth note itself. It has been suggested that behind the g-chart lurks a "proto-Baroque" flute (with some sort of tapering bore to improve the octaves)[38]; while this is an intriguing idea, it is corroborated neither by Mersenne (who claims the bore is cylindrical) nor by any other evidence from that period. It seems more likely that a small flute is indicated (one in g', a tone lower than Praetorius's *discant*), since it is on smaller instruments that the cylindrical flute's tendency to overblow flat can better be overcome; for one thing, the holes can be made proportionately larger on a smaller flute. As we have seen, it appears that just such an instrument is the one called for as an alternative to the recorder in certain prefaces to van Eyck's *Fluyten Lust-Hof*; although no fingerings are given in the Dutch source, the range is exactly the same as Mersenne's (nineteen notes, the traditional range of the Renaissance flute). In all of this only one thing is certain, however: the g-chart is *not* for a Renaissance bass flute, since the latter is incapable of a range larger than two octaves.

Mersenne's d'-chart is also unique; it is the only one to specify the actual sounding pitches of the d'-flute. This fact has led Raymond Meylan, for one, to suggest that Mersenne's musical example for flutes is meant to be played at 8-foot pitch, using a g-bass for the tenor part and an instrument from some other family for the bass.[39] (Mersenne mentions that sackbut, serpent, or "some other bass" is used with flutes, since the bass flute cannot descend so low.[40]) This is certainly the most straightforward and probable explanation, but unfortunately one other possibility cannot be ruled out: that one is expected to use the g-chart on the d'-flute, thus effecting a transposition. (In this transposition all three upper parts can be played on d'-flutes, as had been the normal Renaissance practice.) Several objections might be raised to this notion, however, not the least of which is that it supposes that the g-chart might actually work on the d'-flute as Mersenne has described it—highly improbable, as we have seen. It seems far more likely that Mersenne obtained two charts for flute and merely assumed that both applied to the same instrument; he implies that their differences arise merely from personal differences among players.[41]

Thus, after sorting through Mersenne's ambiguities and inconsistencies, we are left with evidence of a mixture of notational practices for recorders and flutes: *petit jeu* of recorders (as well as g'-flute) at 4-foot pitch, *grand jeu* of recorders (and probably the larger flutes) at 8-foot pitch.

Developments of the Late Seventeenth Century

At some as yet undetermined point after Mersenne's writing, the recorder and flute underwent the radical alterations that produced the forms we now call "Baroque." Both were given three joints: a cylindrical head, a tapering body, and a foot (tapering on the recorder, generally cylindrical on the flute). The flute was given a closed-standing key for D♯ (a difficult half-hole fingering on the keyless Renaissance flute), and both instruments were graced with ornate exterior turnery. Along with these changes in morphology came changes in pitch, nomenclature, and intervals between sizes—changes that represented especially radical departures for the family of recorders. (It is meaningless, in fact, to speak of a "family" of flutes in this period, since most of the evidence—sparse at best—concerns one size, the one we would now call the "concert flute," or simply "flute."[42]) As mentioned above, the Renaissance habit of separating family members by fifths was given up in favor of alternating fourths and fifths (as with most modern orchestral woodwind families); the result is the "C and F" alignment of recorders with which we are still familiar. In France itself—still thought to be the origin of the new designs—the pitch standard to which recorders and flutes were now made was very low (a'=392 to 415 or so, judging by extant examples). Such a low pitch was already quite normal for Renaissance flutes, as we have seen, but it was unusual for recorders. The change in both nominal pitch and pitch standard had a particularly drastic effect on the alto recorder, now the dominant solo member of the family. The real pitch difference between an old *alt* in g' at high Venetian pitch (a'=460 or so) and an alto in f' at a'=392 is a fourth; the new instrument is actually closer in pitch to the old tenor.

The reasons for these changes (and for the parallel changes to reed instruments, to be discussed below) can probably be boiled down to one word: the violin. In France the violin family had achieved dominance over other instruments, particularly in the theater.[43] Quite obviously, it was necessary for wind instruments to match violins in range, pitch, and volume in order to play with them (or act as substitutes for them). Expressiveness as such seems not to have been as important an issue at first as it later became, since the recorder clearly had the advantage over the more dynamically flexible flute through the end of the century; the flute can be said to have come into its own only in the eighteenth. The new forms of woodwind were quickly adopted in other countries and proved to be remarkably adaptable, remaining fundamentally unaltered for more than a century—a real tribute to their designers.

It appears that in France the word *flûte*, unqualified, generally refers to the recorder in this period; the specific terms for the recorder are *flûte douce*, *flûte à bec*, and *flûte d'Angleterre*, while that for the transverse flute is *flûte d'Allemagne* (or *flûte allemande*).[44] The new French nomenclature for the members of the recorder family seems to have been derived from the part names of Lully's string band: *dessus*, *haute-contre*, *taille*, *quinte*, and *basse*, signifying what we would now call sopranino, soprano, alto, tenor, and bass recorders, respectively. This terminology obviously represents a real break from that of the Renaissance, in which *haute-contre* and *taille* were the same physical size in most families; it reflects the differentiation in size of the French orchestral strings. (In Lully's orchestra the three "parts of the middle" were played on violas of three different sizes—albeit with one tuning—specializing in three different registers.) While it is only in eighteenth-century sources that we find this recorder terminology used in its entirety,[45] its seventeenth-century origin is confirmed by Lully's own use of the labels *taille* and *quinte de flûtes* for alto and tenor recorders, respectively. As rational as this new terminology may be, it still leaves room for misunderstanding, since the *taille* recorder generally has the function of a *dessus*. Thus one cannot be certain when *dessus de flûte* is called for (as, for instance, in Charpentier's *Médée* of 1694, or in the 1677 *livret* of Lully's *Isis*) whether sopranino or alto is actually meant. In any case, the use of a sopranino would be exceptional for the seventeenth century; the craze for the *petites flûtes* began in the eighteenth.[46]

Concerning the *basse*, Lully himself makes a distinction between *petite basse* and *grande basse*. The former would seem to be the normal f-bass, which Lully assigns to an inner part, notated at sounding pitch. The *grande basse* is, however, a mystery, since no Baroque-style recorders larger than f-basses seem to have survived. The only documented type of recorder capable of playing Lully's *grande basse* recorder part at 8-foot pitch is an extended *grossbass*—Mersenne's largest; indeed, one writer has pointed to his example as the obvious candidate.[47] However, this solution ignores the difference in pitch standard between Mersenne's recorders and Lully's orchestra; a remodeled, "Baroque" version of the instrument would be required. Such a contraption would seem both clumsy and ineffectual in a theater orchestra. Perhaps the most likely solution is a c-bass (a type known to exist in the late seventeenth century, even if none sur-vives[48]), adapting the part, which it shares with the continuo, to its own range. Such a c-bass, sounding at pitch, would also seem to be called for in certain works of Charpentier (who in other instances requires an f-bass, sounding an octave higher than notated).[49]

These appearances of bass recorders are, in any event, exceptional; by far the most usual use of *flûtes* in French theater of the period is to play the paired *dessus* parts of a trio texture.[50] Whole consorts of recorders belong in the category of theatrical "special effects." Recorders had long had this role in English drama, having been associated with scenes of love, death, and supernatural visitations, as well as with pastoral sub-jects.[51] This role seems to have survived the interregnum; it was appar-ently a recorder consort in a performance of Massinger's play *The Virgin Martyr* that so affected Samuel Pepys in 1667/8 that he was moved to pur-chase a recorder, "the sound of it being, of all sounds in the world, most pleasing to me."[52] Previously Pepys and his wife had been devotees of the flageolet—the first of the French woodwinds to have been adopted by the English. The flageolet is in many ways the perfect amateur wind: small and easily carried, it has but six fingerholes, which are regulated by the most easily controlled digits (thumb and first two fingers) of each hand.[53] Though it came in more than one size, its principal seventeenth-century employment seems to have been as a solo instrument.[54] To be sure, it is with a repertory intended for amateurs (the "lessons"—i.e., tunes—con-tained in Thomas Greeting's *The Pleasant Companion*[55]) that the instru-ment is now associated. However, in the seventeenth century it led a pro-fessional life as well. John Banister (along with Greeting a member of the royal violin band) was a noted exponent, his specialties having been the playing of the flageolet to the accompaniment of a throughbass and "in consort" (that is, mixed with other instruments).[56] In France, too, the fla-geolet was not thought unworthy of a professional player; for instance, the ravishing flageolet playing of "Osteterre" (presumably Jean Hotteterre, grandfather of Jacques Hotteterre le Romain) is included in a short list of the musical marvels of the era in the *Memoires* of the Abbé Michel de Marolles (1656).[57]

Also surviving the interregnum in England was the name "recorder," even though the new form of the instrument was greeted by some as a newcomer and not as part of a continuing tradition. For instance, John Hudgebut in his preface to *A Vade Mecum* (the first tutor for the Baroque-style recorder, published in 1679) says, "Though the *Flagilet* like *Esau* hath got the start, as being of a more Antient Standing, The *Rechorder* like Jakob hath got the Birthright. . . ." Soon the name "recorder" begins to disappear, being replaced by "flute douce," "flute a bec," or simply "flute"—the name it would carry through most of the eighteenth centu-ry.[58] Thus, in the few years between the working careers of Locke (one of the last, it would appear, to use the Renaissance-style flute consort[59]) and

Purcell, the word "flute" had taken on an entirely new meaning. It is quite certain that for Purcell "flute" meant recorder; he did not know (or in any case employ) the transverse flute at all.[60] In its limited seventeenth-century appearance in England (notably—perhaps exclusively—in James Talbot's notes on instruments, ca. 1695) the latter is called by its French name "flute d'Allemagne," suggesting that it was not quite yet a natural-ized citizen.[61]

Concerning the introduction of the new flute and recorder into other countries, we know considerably less, particularly since there is no dedi-cated seventeenth-century repertory of the sort we have from England. For Germany, at least, surviving instruments can provide some clues. The recorder seems to have experienced a development in Germany paral-leling that in France, as shown by the set, mentioned above, by Hieronymus Franziskus Kynseker (1636–86) of Nuremberg.[62] These recorders, which predate the adoption of the French designs, are super-ficially closer in style to Renaissance than Baroque models. However, we should not be misled by their comparatively plain exterior. Besides their obvious jointed construction, they exhibit two other Baroque innova-tions: contracting bottom bore and separation of sizes by alternating fifths and fourths.[63] (This set has often been said to be in "G and D," but it seems more likely to have been considered as being in "C and F" at a high *Chorton* standard—about a'=477—at the time.) We should not be too surprised at these innovations having taken place in Germany; it was, after all, a German—Praetorius—who first suggested in print both the building of recorders with jointed construction[64] and the "C-and-F" alignment of woodwind families.[65]

It is the next generation of German builders—Johann Christoph Denner (1655–1707) and his colleagues Johann Schell (1660–1732), Nikolaus Staub (1664–1734), and Johann Benedikt Gahn (1674–1711)—whose instruments first show the direct influence of the new French designs; these were presumably introduced by French oboists in about 1680 as they had been to England a few years earlier.[66] In England, how-ever, the older-style woodwinds had all but died out, except in certain cir-cles; in Germany there was still a thriving tradition of wind music, which survived the incursion of French orchestral winds and their associated practices and continued to coexist with them for a long time. The indige-nous tradition is shown, for instance, in the *Grundrichtiger Unterricht der musikalischen Kunst* of Daniel Speer (Ulm, 1697),[67] who represents the recorder by a chart[68] for the soprano in c" (*quartflöte*) rather than the f-alto that had become the standard in French practice. We see these coex-isting musical fashions reflected in the recorders of Denner and his cir-cle; not only are there among them a few of "Renaissance" or "transi-tional" type, but those of the new French pattern are built to high German pitch standards (*Chorton*) as well as to low French ones. Significantly, no transverse flutes survive from these seventeenth-century makers; the first German ones we know about come from the workshop of Jakob Denner (1681–1735), J. C. Denner's son.

Of the same generation as J. C. Denner was Richard Haka (1646–1705), who was born in London but spent his working life (from about 1660 until his death) in Amsterdam. An interesting three-piece Baroque flute by Haka has recently come to light; because of its obviously early date and backward-looking outward form,[69] the question of possible Dutch leadership (or at least participation) in the development of the Baroque flute has been raised.[70] Pure speculation at this point, this idea deserves further research. Similarly, Italian leadership (or perhaps primacy) in the development of the Baroque recorder has been suggested on the basis of Bismantova's primacy in illustrating the new design.[71] However, there is no independent corroboration of this notion; the first indigenous Italian recorders of Baroque design that survive date from the next century. Moreover, 1677 (the date of Bismantova's treatise) is not really all that early in the development of the Baroque recorder as it is now understood, as we have seen.

Reeds

It is now time to return to the early seventeenth century and pick up the story of the reeds. The late Renaissance is often characterized by the variety of its reed instruments, a variety made evident in the *Syntagma* II of Praetorius. Of course, the full panoply of instruments was not available in all geographic areas or to those in all social strata. As students of performance practice, it should be our focus to determine the limitations of the use of these instruments as well as their possibilities. Fortunately, there have been some excellent modern studies that have addressed these issues in detail, combining archival and iconographic information with that provided by the treatises and the existing instruments themselves.

The seventeenth-century reed instrument with the longest history is certainly the shawm. One of the biggest problems in discussing it nowadays is terminology, particularly since the English names now used by players for the various members differ from the traditional English usage of the period; we will try to make the best of a confusing situation. Praetorius illustrates six basic sizes, whose seven-finger notes are separated by fifths: from the top down these are a', d', g, c, F, and BBb. Although he treats them as a family, the nouns change after the first two (called *schalmeyen*), the rest being called *pommern*. As he explains, the distinction rests on the presence or absence of keys (*pommern* having one or more, *schalmeyen* having none); this habit reflects medieval French terminology, which distinguished between the original, keyless, soprano-pitched *chalemie* and the keyed *bombarde* that had been developed to play lower parts. (The etymological relationship of *bombarde* to *pommer* is perhaps less obvious than that between *chalemie* and *schalmey*—except maybe to a linguist.) About 1500 the French began to use the word *hautbois* to refer to the whole family; this word, of course, is the origin of the English term "hoboys" (likewise applied to the whole family, as was the term "waits" or "waits' pipes," as well as "shawms"). Praetorius's three largest sizes were provided with four keys, like those of the "extended" forms of recorder discussed above; these he calls *basset-* or *tenor pommer, bass pommer,* and *grossbass pommer.* The smallest *pommer* is the *alt* (with but one key); it and the *discant schalmey* were, taken together, the "type form" instruments of the shawm family and those the most in use, in all countries and all periods. These two shawms were known in England as "tenor" and "treble," respectively; the modern term "alto shawm" (a more-or-less direct translation of Praetorius's *alt pommer*) did not exist in English. Of the rest, the *bass* was probably the next most common, at least in the seventeenth century, while the *exilent* or *gar klein discant schalmey* was the rarest of all.

Besides these standard sizes, Praetorius mentions three others: the *nicolo* (a tenor without extensions, having but one key), a *discant* in c', and an *alt* in f. The latter two are, in fact, hypothetical—ones he would *like* to see made, in order to make it easier to combine instruments of the whole family. He suggests using a choir of shawms to participate with other instruments and with voices in sacred motets and concerti. For this purpose he suggests that one omit the "screaming" *discant schalmey*—probably the most characteristic voice of the family—and use only the *pommern,* transposing the music down a fourth at the same time.[72] Though Praetorius's models were generally Italian, this use of a choir of shawms seems to have no precedent in Italy itself. There the appearance of shawms, small or large, in church was rare.[73] Just how common the larger *pommern* were within Germany is difficult to determine. They are specified occasionally (under the name *bombardon*) in the works of some German composers; for instance, J. H. Schein's *Hosianna, dem Sohne David* (1623) requires three—two *basset* and one *bass,* as indicated by the ranges. Nearer the end of the century the *bass* is still being called for in some of the works of Buxtehude. A *grossbass pommer* is illustrated in the hands of the Nuremberg musician Nikol Rosenkron in 1679,[74] and six years later St. Mary's Church of Lübeck (where Buxtehude was organist) purchased a similar instrument.[75] These latter were probably used to double continuo lines at 16-foot pitch.

Praetorius's suggested use of a low shawm choir lies somewhat outside the main tradition of the shawm band, which was based on the ability of the higher shawms to make their presence known in less than ideal acoustical surroundings—outdoors or competing with the noise of crowds. In its capacity as a band instrument the shawm was alive and well in most European countries through most of the seventeenth century. Its repertory, however, remains something of a mystery, being only infrequently written down. Some of the few examples that were are the result of the band's participation in extraordinary events, such as coronations.[76] Pictorial and other evidence makes it clear that sackbuts—certainly more portable than the larger *pommern*—were generally used to play the lower interior parts, as well (one would presume) as the bass when no reed bass was available. A bass curtal (proto-bassoon; see below) seems to have substituted for the necessarily stationary *bass pommer* when the band needed to be mobile. Another instrument that could find its way into the shawm band was the cornett, apparently as a second treble—a role found uncomfortable by many modern cornettists who have tried it! Given these common mixtures of brass and reeds, Praetorius's remark[77] that "as to pitch, most shawms are a tone higher than cornetts and sackbuts" is rather puzzling—the more so since this statement is not borne out by his own evidence. (The scaled representations of instruments in his plates allow us to compare their dimensions with those of actual instruments; surviving shawms of the sizes he illustrates produce his nominal pitches at about a'=460, as do the cornetts and sackbuts. Obviously one cannot expect this sort of analysis to be absolutely accurate; however, the margin of error has to be less than the whole tone mentioned by Praetorius.) Perhaps he means that shawms as a group generally transpose their music up a step (something he suggests they should do, just a few sentences later), while the cornetts and sackbuts usually play at pitch. If so, he has chosen an odd way to put it!

Mersenne's shawm band is more traditional than Praetorius's, both in function and makeup. He explains[78] that shawms are the loudest instruments, except for trumpets; they are used for large assemblies, such as ballets (though violins have replaced them there), weddings, village festivals, and other public celebrations. His musical example,[79] in six parts, calls for two trebles, two tenors (i.e., *alt pommern*), sackbut, and bass. His specification of nominal pitches is neither clear nor consistent, but the interpretation with the fewest difficulties would put the treble (*dessus*) in c', seven fingers, and the tenor (*taille*– also called *haute-contre*) in f. The *basse* is clearly in (seven-fingers) F, with extensions down to C; this puts its basic fingering an octave below that of the *taille*, in contrast with the ninth between Praetorius's corresponding *bass* and *alt*. This octave relationship is confirmed by a comparison of dimensions; those Mersenne supplies for the *dessus* and *taille* conform basically to Praetorius's illustrations of the *discant schalmey* and *alt pommer,* while the length given by Mersenne[80] for the *basse* is about 12 percent shorter than that of Praetorius's *bass pommer*—an appropriate difference in size for the interval of a whole tone. Thus the French shawm family must have been conceptually in "C and F," just like the ensuing oboe/bassoon family but at a much higher pitch (about a'=512, in effect).[81] For the higher shawms the practical consequences *for fingering* are the same whether one thinks of the instruments as being in d' and g, transposing up a tone (as by Praetorius) or in c' and f (as by Mersenne), but for the bass the French system (with an instrument built up a tone from Praetorius's) has a clear advantage.

One of the distinguishing characteristics of the smaller shawms is the so-called *pirouette* (Mersenne's term; Talbot calls it the "fliew")—a small piece of turnery that surrounds the base of the reed and presents a flat surface to support the lips. Most extant shawms lack their original pirouettes (and, of course, reeds), but enough information survives from Mersenne, Talbot, and iconographic sources to allow accurate reconstruction.[82] It is clear that early shawm reeds and pirouettes resembled closely those still in use on modern Catalan shawms. Here the pirouette provides support for the lips while in no way impeding their control of the short, wide reed. Dynamic flexibility is not only feasible but indulged in to the fullest, though at an overall greater volume than with orchestral reeds. Despite the early efforts of Anthony Baines in making this point,[83] scholars often still assume that the presence of a pirouette implies tonal inflexibility. Thus, much importance has been ascribed to the lack of a pirouette in one of Mersenne's illustrations of a treble shawm.[84] This depiction has sometimes been seen as representing a milestone in the development of the expressive oboe, when it may be merely a schematic view with the pirouette left off for clarity. (The pirouette is, in any case, present in Mersenne's other, more elegant and more accurate illustration of a treble shawm.[85])

Acoustically related to the shawm is the curtal (pronounced "curt'l"), in which a conical bore like that of the shawm is doubled back on itself to produce a long sounding length in a short—that is, "curt"—package. (It is still often called the "dulcian"—one of its German names—because the first suppliers of copies in this century were Germans, who called it that on their price lists. But "curtal" is its traditional English name.) Praetorius illustrates a whole family of them, in sizes corresponding to those of the shawms. However, he says that the *doppel-fagott* (the curtal corresponding to the *grossbass pommer*) is available in two different pitches, one a fourth and one a fifth below the bass curtal or *chorist-fagott*; these are known as the *quart-fagott* and *quint-fagott*, respectively. (However, no representatives of the *quint-fagott* appear to survive.) In addition, curtals were made in two styles, *offen* (open) and *gedact* (covered); in the latter the bell opening is provided with a sieve-like cover, somewhat damping the sound. Praetorius says that the *fagotten* are softer and sweeter in sound than the *pommern* (hence the alternative name *dolzianen*) due to the folded bore and—when present—the bell cover. (On the other hand, as we have seen, an *offen chorist-fagott* could substitute for a *bass pommer* in a shawm band, so the difference was not necessarily extreme.)

As in the case of the shawms, not all sizes of curtal were in common use throughout Europe. The bass (bottom note C) had by far the greatest currency in all countries. In England it was known as the "double curtal" (since pitches in the octave below G or *gamma ut* were called "double notes"); the next size smaller—the "single curtal," with G as its bottom note—was known there as well. (The terms "bass curtal" and "tenor curtal" for these are modernisms, again based on a partial adoption of German terminology.) The use of other sizes seems to have been confined to Germany and Spain, although it has been suggested (based on Mersenne) that the *quart-fagott* was known in France.[86] In Spain families of curtals (called *bajónes*) were used in church to accompany the choir; this practice continued well into the nineteenth century.[87] The Spanish penchant for shawms in church is well documented, and it is often assumed that they doubled or substituted for choral voices.[88] However, it is quite possible that the shawm band's participation was mostly (or even exclusively) *in alternatim* with the choir, and that the only reed instrument actually mixing with voices in the sixteenth and seventeenth centuries was the *bajón*.[89]

Other conically bored reed instruments in use at the outset of the seventeenth century were *bassanelli* (a family of soft-toned, low-pitched "oboes"[90]) and—at the other end of the tonal spectrum—windcap shawms. The latter were known in modern times as *rauschpfeiffen,* until Barra Boydell connected the name *schreierpfeiffen* (literally "screaming pipes") with extant examples; Praetorius must be somehow in error regarding the instruments he illustrates under that name.[91] The rest of the reeds of the era—crumhorns and their derivatives—were cylindrically bored. Praetorius mentions *cornamuse* (like crumhorns but straight, with sieve-like opening to damp the sound), *sordunen* (with doubled-back bore and mouth-held reed, like curtals), one size of *kortholt* (like *sordunen,* but with a windcap), and *racketten* (the *extensio ad absurdum* of the doubled-back-bore principle). Few of these, conical or cylindrical, were known outside Germany and northern Italy, and even there they were rapidly falling into disuse. (Even the crumhorn—certainly the instrument among them with the widest distribution—hardly survived Praetorius himself; after his death it is cited in inventories more often than performances.[92]) The simple reason, once again, seems to be the violin, whose domination of instrumental music was more complete in Italy and Germany than yet in France. Crumhorns and their ilk are in their element playing Renaissance-style vocal polyphony; few instruments are as good at making clear the inner parts of close-voiced counterpoint. In Italy especially, however, the new emphasis in both vocal and instrumental writing was in expression of emotion, not counterpoint for its own sake, and Germany was very much under Italy's musical influence throughout the century. The instruments of choice were clearly those of the violin family and those winds with similar capabilities: cornetts, sackbuts, and curtals. The rest of the winds were found deficient in either range or expressive power (or, in the case of the shawm, civility) and became literally "voices from the past."

In France, however—far from Italian influence—several of the Renaissance reeds lived on. Besides the crumhorn (which he calls *tornebout*), Mersenne describes the *courtaut* (similar to the *sordun*), the *cervelat* (*rackett*),[93] and the *hautbois de Poi[c]tou* (historically a detached bagpipe chanter fitted with a windcap, but similar in principle to the *schreierpfeiff*). We would hardly be considering this last an art instrument at all, of course, but for the royal favor it enjoyed as part of the *Hautbois et musettes de Poitou* of the *Grande Écurie*. (Just to what extent, or how long, the names of such official court ensembles reflected reality is somewhat uncertain—for instance, the *fifres* of the *Joueurs de fifres et tambours* were, by the end of the seventeenth century, an oboe band![94]—but we can be sure the titles at least started out having some element of truth to them.[95]) On the other hand, Mersenne's inclusion of the *tornebout* and *cervelat* may be more a result of his own fascination with their mechanical and acoustical properties than a reflection of actual use in this period. In any case, his *tornebout*—the traditional Renaissance crumhorn—is *not* to be identified with the French *cromorne* of the second half of the century; the latter has been shown to have more similarity to the bassoon.[96]

Mersenne says that the *courtaut* can serve as a bass to *musettes*; whether by *musette* he means here the complete bagpipe with its bag and drones or merely a detached chanter fitted with a windcap—the form he prefers—is unclear. But it is clear from his description of the musette that it was not quite yet the fully developed and standardized instrument of the treatises of Borjon de Scellery (1672)[97] and Hotteterre le Romain (1738).[98] Though the main physical characteristics of the musette—bellows, cylindrically bored chanter, and so-called "shuttle drone"[99]—were already in place (and had been as early as Praetorius), there is no mention by Mersenne of the peculiar technique described by Borjon and Hotteterre whereby a semblance of articulation is achieved on an instrument actually incapable of stopping between notes. This technique is referred to as "covered playing" by Borjon; it depends on leaving most of the fingers *on* their respective holes and raising them only *one at a time* for the notes of a melody—not the normal woodwind practice, to be sure! The six-finger note on the chanter is treated as the "default" position; it tends to sound, however briefly, between the other notes. But since it has the same pitch (g') as the top note of the complex drone, it seems to disappear; it is perceived as a space—and thus an articulation. However, with this "covered" approach to fingering, cross-fingering becomes unavailable as a method of producing chromatic alterations; for this reason multiple closed-standing side keys were adopted on the musette long before they were even considered for other woodwinds.

The Oboe and Bassoon

Almost half a century has passed since Joseph Marx suggested that the oboe was invented in the 1650s and first used in Lully's *Ballet de l'Amour Malade* of 1657.[100] Scholars have generally accepted his reasoning; recently, however, Bruce Haynes has shown that the iconographic record supports a later dating of the emergence of the true oboe (i.e., somewhere in the 1680s),[101] and Rebecca Harris-Warrick has questioned some of Marx's readings of the written evidence and thus some of his conclusions.[102] Together these researchers have furthered the view that the change from shawm to oboe was a gradual and evolutionary one, perhaps over a few decades, rather than a sudden and decisive one. While it is true that not all the characteristics we associate with the Baroque oboe had to have been present at the outset, two were absolutely essential to its acceptance as an orchestral instrument: in order to be mixed with violins, it had to play at an acceptable volume *and* at a compatible pitch. Historians have paid more attention to the matter of volume, even though pitch is actually the more crucial consideration from the standpoint of instrument design. (Volume is at least as much a question of reeds.)

As pointed out by Bruce Haynes,[103] the actual interval between a typical Renaissance treble shawm and an oboe at low French pitch is a perfect fourth—just as we have found in comparing typical Renaissance and Baroque alto recorders; the new treble instrument is once again closer in pitch to the old tenor. This pitch difference does not manifest itself so obviously as a size difference in the case of the oboe and shawm, however; the treble shawm is already rather long for its pitch, having a considerable bell extension past the fingered holes. This bell extension is not "just for show"; its proportions (and the positions of its resonance holes) are carefully engineered to stabilize crucial notes in the scale. (In particular, the half-holed notes a minor third and minor tenth above the seven-finger note—$E\flat$s on an instrument considered in c'—are rendered stable by this extension.) Making a proportional expansion to bring a treble shawm down a fourth would result in an instrument almost a yard long—obviously a clumsy and inelegant solution; clearly a complete remodeling was in order. Jointed construction was "in," as was ornamental turnery. In keeping with the more elegant design was a reduced wall thickness, which in turn dictated smaller fingerholes. The lowered seventh hole was now out of reach, requiring a key for the bottom c'. The loss of an effective half-hole fingering ultimately necessitated a key for $e\flat$ and its octave, and the similar loss of some cross-fingerings necessitated the double holes typical of Baroque oboes. Thus, while many of the details of the new instrument might have remained in flux for some time, most of its basic features were a direct consequence of lowering the pitch and must have been present as soon as it moved indoors and joined the orchestra.[104] Marx may have been hasty in assuming that the *hautbois* took part in the *Concert champestre de l'Espoux* of Lully's *Ballet de l'Amour Malade* (it is not called for by name in the *livret*), but it was definitely sharing the stage with violins just a few years later in his ballet *Les Nopces de Village* (1663).[105] However, the first incontrovertible evidence of the doubling of violin lines by the *hautbois* dates from some years later, so that the question of the debut of the "virtual oboe" may be debated for some time to come.

Steps toward the development of the bassoon seem to have come much earlier than those documented for the oboe. By comparison to curtals of standard design, for instance, Mersenne's examples (referred to variously—possibly indiscriminately—as *fagots* and *bassons*) have further extensions of range in the bass, although the additional keys and their covers are still of "Renaissance" design. An early seventeenth-century curtal of Italian provenance (now in Vienna) has jointed construction. (In fact, hints of both extensions of range and jointed construction can be found even earlier, in evidence from Spain and even Peru![106]) What appears to be the first iconographic evidence of the four-jointed bassoon (a painting from somewhere in the 1660s, attributed to Harmen Hals) comes from Holland, as does one of the first surviving examples (a bassoon by Richard Haka)[107]; as in the case of the Haka *traverso* mentioned above, this information has led to speculation about possible Dutch leadership in the development of the new design.[108] Ultimately, however, all this non-French evidence will probably represent only a minor embarrassment to those upholding the traditional view that the bassoon, like the oboe, Baroque flute, and Baroque recorder, was a French invention. (The very name "bassoon" in English bespeaks a French origin, of course; Talbot calls it the "French basson."[109]) Once again the real issue is musical practice and the attendant question of pitch; as soon as we have a bass reed instrument capable of orchestral doubling—at low French pitch—we can regard it as effectively a bassoon regardless of the number of its joints or the layout of its thumb keys. One survey of extant curtals claims that all surviving basses are at "high" pitch (i.e., above modern).[110] By contrast, the pitch typical of bassoons is low (although there are a few exceptions); in fact, in Germany (where both curtal and bassoon continued to overlap in use long into the next century) pitch remained one of the important distinctions between the two.[111]

The bassoon was immediately accepted as the bass of the oboe family; it is generally subsumed under the name *hautbois* and only occasionally singled out for special mention. Completing the family is the *taille de hautbois*—traditionally called the "tenor" oboe in English but now sometimes referred to as an "alto." This instrument, like its descendant, the modern English horn, is built in (seven-fingers) f, a fifth below the oboe proper. Two different late-seventeenth-century oboe band configurations have been identified, one French, the other English; these apparently reflect the different orchestral practices of the two nations. The typical layout of Lully's orchestra was in five parts: violin, three violas, and bass; Purcell's was in four: two violins, viola, and bass (like a modern string quartet). The latter translates directly into an oboe band consisting of two oboes, tenor, and bassoon. Oddly enough, the French oboe band texture was also four part, but it seems to have differed in its choice of instrument for the second part (labeled *haute-contre* by Lully); this part occasionally descends below the range of the oboe.[112] (Note that in neither type of oboe band is the sackbut welcome, as it had been in the shawm band.) One of the current "hot issues" among researchers and players concerns the possible existence of a special instrument (pitched midway between oboe and *taille*) for the *haute-contre* part. Proponents of this *"haute-contre* theory" have cited as evidence the existence of some high-pitched *tailles*, the cleffing of parts, and the analogy of the differentiation in size of French violas. Much of this evidence is inconclusive; the viola analogy itself "cuts both ways," since the tuning of the French violas is the same even though their physical size differs.[113] Whatever the solution, it must rest on evidence from the era of the oboe itself; the earlier tradition (through the time of Mersenne) assumed an equivalence between *haute-contre* and *taille* for most instrument families, as we have seen.[114]

Technique

In this review of seventeenth-century woodwinds and their use we have concentrated on the questions of what, when, where, and why; it seems appropriate in closing to think about how. When early treatises and tutors examine matters of technique, they are concerned primarily with two aspects: fingering and articulation. To both of these issues the early approaches were quite different from the modern ones. Details obviously vary from instrument to instrument, time to time, and place to place; the specialist performer of a historical instrument has no choice but to become familiar in depth with the relevant sources. The following survey is not intended as a substitute for such personal research, but only as a guide to some of the general principles.

Modern recorders, as we have seen, are based on Baroque ones; so are their fingerings. It is in the very efficient high-register fingerings that both differ from their Renaissance predecessors. However, certain features of Baroque recorder fingering seem closer in spirit to Renaissance principles than to modern. The standard fingerings for the modern recorder (as for most modern winds) avoid the "shading" or partial covering of holes; such shadings (particularly for the ring finger of the lower hand) were still very much a part of Baroque recorder fingering. (It should be pointed out that the "double holes" commonly provided for the bottom two fingers on the modern recorder were rare on early ones, although they are mentioned as a possibility by both Loulié and Hotteterre in the early eighteenth century.[115]) The major ramification of this shading technique is for the fourth and eleventh notes of the scale— *B♭*s on the alto—which are too flat on antiques when the modern fingerings are used; thus ●●●●/●○●○ and ø●●●/●○ø○ were used instead of ●●●●/●○●● and ø●●●/●○●○. Another note that is often flat on antiques with the standard modern fingering is c‴♯; solutions to this problem (using partial coverings) are suggested by Freillon-Poncein (1700) and Loulié.[116] (Hotteterre, however, gives the modern fingering.) A peculiarity of the English recorder tutors of Hudgebut, Banister, and Salter is the differentiation between enharmonic pairs (particularly d″♯ and e″♭); following the principles of just intonation (as well as meantone temperament) the sharp is given a flatter sounding fingering than the flat.[117] Such differentiation is a nicety clearly of no interest to Freillon-Poncein, Loulié, and Hotteterre (although the last of these does suggest making this kind of distinction on the transverse flute, sometimes with fingering but more often with embouchure adjustment). Characteristic of the French sources (beginning with Mersenne) as well as the English is the use of so-called "buttress-finger technique," according to which the ring finger of the lower hand is left down for most of the notes of the low register (where it makes little difference to pitch) in order to provide physical support. There is, however, no sign of this practice in Bismantova.

It is, however, in the fingering of trills that we find the greatest difference in principle between Baroque and modern practice. On an instrument such as the recorder that involves cross-fingerings, one often finds it virtually impossible to alternate smoothly and rapidly between adjacent notes using standard fingerings; the problem arises in particular when the upper note of the pair is cross-fingered. Players have long resorted to "trick" fingerings to avoid simultaneous closing and opening of holes; it is in the nature of the trick itself that the modern and early practices differ. The usual modern solution is to find an alternate fingering for the lower note that produces the right pitch, so that one can trill by merely adding a finger (or fingers) to the fingering of the upper note. The Baroque solution (first documented in the English recorder tutors of Hudgebut, Banister, and Salter, but apparently a French invention) was to begin and end the trill with the standard fingerings, but to make the trill itself with a finger involved in playing the lower note. A specific example will make this difference clear. In playing a trill from f″ to e″ on the alto the modern player will usually trill with the ring finger of the upper hand: •°•≈/°°°o. This works because •°••/°°°o is usually in tune as an alternate fingering for e″ on the modern instrument. (It is rarely so on antiques, by the way.) The Baroque player, however, would first play the f″ (•°•⁄/°°°o) and then switch to the normal fingering for e″ (•°°⁄/°°°o), making the trill itself with the forefinger of the upper hand. The success of this expedient depends on the prolongation of the upper note as an *appui* or appoggiatura, as well as the suppression of the pitch during the actual trill (through abating the breath and trilling quickly and close to the hole). Modern commentators have often stressed the "out of tune" quality of the early trill fingerings, but it seems likely that early players worked hard to make the listener unaware of any intonation difficulty. Loulié's directives to "trill quickly and diminish the breath" when performing such "irregular or defective" trills imply as much.[118] It should also be mentioned here that trilling across the register break—avoided in modern playing by the use of alternate fingerings—seems to have been enjoyed by early players; this trill with its curious warbling effect was called a "double shake" in the English tutors.

The same principles also apply to the transverse flute and to the oboe.[119] In charts for the flute, however, there are even more of these "irregular" trills than for the recorder—apparently because cross-fingering is inherently less efficient on the flute, making its scale less even than the recorder's. Thus, where the recorder will use "normal" fingerings in trilling from a plain-fingered note to a cross-fingering (such as d″ to c″♯), the flute will substitute an "irregular" fingering in the analogous situation (a′ to g′♯, in this case; trilling with the middle finger of the upper hand rather than the fingers of the lower hand avoids the rapid alternation of the "solid," plain-fingered a′ with the "woolier" sounding, cross-fingered g′♯). The flute's trill fingerings, though logical, are contraintuitive for many modern players; again, there is no substitute for a careful study of the sources. One final matter of fingering concerns the reeds—oboe, bassoon, and curtal: charts from the seventeenth and early eighteenth centuries show simple octave fingerings as much as possible throughout the upper register; there is little evidence for the so-called "long fingerings" favored later for high notes, in which the simple octaves of the upper-hand notes are stabilized through addition of lower-hand fingers. While it has been suggested that these earlier charts might reflect the ideal more than actuality, it does seem that the better the instrument, the more closely it is able to conform to their straightforward fingerings.

Modern woodwind articulation generally depends on the broad contrast between tonguing and slurring—matters that can be simply specified by musical notation. It is assumed that separate notes (and those at the beginning of a slur) begin with the tip of the tongue. When repetitions become too fast to be executed easily and cleanly with the tip of the tongue, flutists join their brass-playing colleagues in employing "double tonguing," alternating "t" and "k"; practice is expected to make the two consonants as equal in effect as possible. (Such double tonguing is not an option for reed players, with the occasional exception of bassoonists; they must work to achieve a fast single tonguing.) Seventeenth-century players of flute, recorder, and cornett inherited a range of different double tonguings, which offer possibilities between the effects of single tonguing and slurring. The articulations given by Bismantova in 1677 for recorder and cornett are essentially the same as those given by Ganassi and Dalla Casa in the sixteenth century (although the classification differs somewhat). Bismantova's *lingue dritte* are single tonguings, serving for notes from breves to eighths: "t" for cornetto, "d" (implying a softer attack) for recorder. His *lingua roversa* ("reversed tonguing") applies to eighths and smaller values and involves "r"s and "l"s: "te-re-le-re" (or "de-re-le-re," for recorder). He also recognizes two other possibilities, which he says, however, are not in use, at least in the cantabile style then in vogue. These are "te-che-te-che" (essentially modern double tonguing; Italian "ch" is equivalent to English "k") and "ter-ler-ter-ler" (in which each note appears to be "clipped" with an "r"). The French Baroque sources bring in a new element: the placement of the "r" in a position of comparative rhythmic stress, at least in certain situations.[120] Modern commentators have sometimes talked about the relative *strength* of the "t" and "r" (there are no "l"s in the French practice), but more important is the matter of *connection*: the "r" always represents a point of comparative elision, regardless of its rhythmic position. It is always part of a two-note tonguing group initiated by a "t"; it cannot itself initiate such a group. A relationship between the use of "r" in a position of comparative stress and the practice of *notes inégales* seems obvious, although it is not made explicit by Freillon-Poncein, Loulié, or Hotteterre.

NOTES

1. See Harris-Warrick–Lully's *hautbois*, 97–106.
2. Kopp–Bassoon, 85–114.
3. Quantz–*Versuch debouché*, 242.
4. Praetorius–*Syntagma* I, II, and III. The first volume is in Latin, the second and third in German (mostly, with a few lapses into Latin). The sections of *Syntagma* II dealing with instruments are translated into English in Praetorius/Blumenfeld–*Organographia* and Praetorius/Crookes–*Organographia*.
5. Mersenne–*Harmonie universelle*. The books on instruments are translated into English in Mersenne/Chapman–*Harmonie universelle*.
6. Mersenne–*Harmonie universelle* 3: 231, Mersenne/Chapman–*Harmonie universelle,* 301.
7. Ibid., 233; 302 of translation.
8. Ibid., 236; 305 of translation. Chapman adds to the confusion by mistranslating *debouché* as "closed."
9. Ibid., 242; 313 of translation.
10. Ibid., 244; 314 of translation.
11. Thus Mersenne's second- and third-octave fingerings for d'-flute reported by Anne Smith in her composite charts, though strictly correct in interpreting his zeros as open holes, probably misrepresent the intent of the original compiler of his tablature. See A. Smith—Renaissancequerflöte, 61–63; and A. Smith–Renaissance Flute, 30–33.
12. Mersenne–*Harmonie universelle* 3: 238; 309 of translation.
13. Praetorius–*Syntagma* II: 34.
14. Ibid., 13.
15. Praetorius–*Syntagma, Theatrum instrumentorum,* pl. 9.
16. Praetorius–*Syntagma* II: [21].
17. Ibid., 37.
18. Ibid., III, 157.
19. See Marvin–Recorders, 30–57.
20. See Baines–*European and American,* illustrations 425–29.
21. See Lambrechts-Douillez–Blokfluit, 907–19.
22. The modern "garklein" offered by some makers is usually, in fact, a tiny recorder—a "supersopranino" in c‴—which is so small as to be barely playable by most adults.

23. Of all the early woodwinds, Renaissance flutes, being cylindrical in bore, have the most consistent relationship between outer dimensions and pitch.
24. See Puglisi–Renaissance Flutes.
25. Praetorius–*Syntagma* III: 156.
26. Ibid., 158. Just how common the large recorders might have been is difficult to determine. However, it is hard to believe that they were available to any but the most affluent persons and institutions, and still harder to believe that their use would have continued to grow in the period after Praetorius; their limitations would have been perceived as more and more of an impediment.
27. Discussed in A. Smith–Renaissancequerflöte, which provides clefs, ranges, and other pertinent information. Two additional works (by Leipzig cantors Johann Schelle and Sebastian Knüpfer) are cited by Raymond Meylan, *The Flute* (Portland, OR: Amadeus, 1988), 100–01. (This work is a translation—by Alfred Clayton—of *Die Flöte* [Bern: Hallwag AG, 1974], which in turn is a translation from the French.)
28. See Hunt–*Recorder*, which cites the original clefs for the Schmelzer.
29. See van Baak Griffioen–*van Eyck*, 377–90, for a discussion of the recorder proper to this repertoire, and A. Smith–Renaissancequerflöte, 24, regarding the flute.
30. Bismantova–*Compendio*, [91]. Bismantova also provides a chart "per suonare alla quarta," treating the instrument as though it were in d'; this results in a transposition of a fifth from the previous notation, but a fourth from the actual sounding pitch.
31. See Castellani–*Bismantova*, 79.
32. See Eppelsheim–*Orchester*, 64–97, for a discussion of the flute and recorder as employed by Lully.
33. The first published music for the redesigned Baroque recorder are the English tutors of John Hudgebut (*A Vade Mecum*, 1679), John Banister (*The Most Pleasant Companion*, 1681), and Humphrey Salter (*The Genteel Companion*, 1683). See H. Myers–Recorder Tutors, 3–6.
34. Jambe de Fer–*Épitome musical*. Mersenne was undoubtedly acquainted with Jambe de Fer's treatise, since he reprints the latter's illustration of a viol (*Harmonie universelle* 3: 191).
35. See Eppelsheim–*Orchester*, 81–88, for an analysis of Mersenne's rendition of the recorders of the *grand jeu*. Eppelsheim has been ingenious in explaining the mechanism of the foot-operated lower extensions—a contrivance that has seemed implausible to many.
36. Mersenne–*Harmonie universelle* 3: 239; 308 of translation. Just when this set of recorders came to France is a matter of some debate. Hunt–*Recorder* (39) assumes they were given by Henry VIII to Louis XII; Lasocki–Recorder Consort (132), following the reasoning of Patricia M. Ranum, proposes a date closer to Mersenne's own time. The fact that Mersenne himself seems not to know to which king they were sent would seem to support an earlier dating. That he does not appear to consider them "out of date" (as pointed out by Lasocki) is not necessarily meaningful; he is often more interested in what is acoustically or mechanically feasible than in actual practice.
37. See Robinson–Reconstruction, 84–85. Robinson's reconstruction of Mersenne's flute plays in d' at about a'=440. If this pitch should seem anomalous for France at that period, it should be noted that one surviving French instrument from just a few decades later—the two-piece, cylindrically bored flute by Lissieu, now in Vienna—also plays at about modern pitch. (Regarding the dating of this instrument see J. Bowers–New Light, 8–9; regarding its dimensions, see Puglisi–Survey, 80.) On the other hand, Mersenne himself says (3: 243; 312 of trans.) that flutes in general "are placed at chapel pitch to perform concerts"; the French *ton de chapelle* was usually quite low (a'=392 or so). Thus Mersenne has left us yet another puzzle!
38. See Meylan–*Flute*, 94–95.
39. Ibid., 101.
40. Mersenne–*Harmonie universelle* 3: 243; 312 of translation.
41. Ibid., 242; 312 of translation.

42. The first documented appearance of the new flute seems to be in Lully's *Le Triomph de l'Amour* (1681); in addition to being called for to play the upper two parts of a trio texture in the "Ritournelle pour Diane," it is suggested as an alternative to the recorder for the highest part of four in the "Prélude pour lAmour." Significantly, the three lower parts would remain on recorders in either case, there being no lower flutes to replace them. A facsimile of the "Prélude pour lAmour" is to be found in the article "Lully" in *New Grove*. See also Eppelsheim–*Orchester*, 65–66, 72.

43. Mersenne called the violin "king of the instruments" (*Harmonie universelle* 3: 177; 235 of translation); according to him, violins had already replaced the shawms for ballets (303; 378).

44. The term *flûte traversière* becomes common only in the eighteenth century, beginning apparently with Jacques Hotteterre le Romain's *Principes de la flute traversiere, ou flute d'allemagne, de la flute a bec, ou flute douce, et du haut-bois* (Paris, 1707).

45. Specifically, in Montéclair's *Jepthé* (1732) and later in the *Encyclopédie* of Diderot; see Eppelsheim–*Orchester*, 72–80.

46. See Ibid., 93–94.

47. Ibid., 88–89.

48. James Talbot (writing ca. 1695) calls it a "double bass"; see Baines–Talbot, 18.

49. Eppelsheim–*Orchester*, 90–93.

50. In some of Lully's works the lower of the two *flûte* parts goes below the range of an alto recorder and thus requires a tenor; in some cases, too, the upper part requires half-holing of the bottom notes of the alto. (See Eppelsheim–*Orchester*, 71, 79–80.) Such parts would seem much better suited to performance on transverse flutes; in fact, these instruments cannot be absolutely ruled out just because *flûte* generally means recorder. Marin Marais, for instance, would seem to be using the word *flûtes* in a generic sense in the title to his *Pièces en trio pour les flûtes* [note the plural form], *violon, & dessus de viole* (Paris, 1692), since the engraving (by Charles Simonneau) surrounding this title depicts both recorders and transverse flutes. (See Bowers–New Light, 10–11; she has identified this title page as the first as yet discovered iconographic evidence of the Baroque flute.)

51. See Lasocki–Elizabethan, 3–10.

52. See Hunt–*Recorder*, 57. That Pepys heard a recorder consort in the play is, of course, informed conjecture; his own words mention only "the wind-musique when the angel comes down." If it *was* a recorder consort (as seems probable), it is still uncertain whether it would have been made up of Renaissance- or Baroque-style instruments. There is some evidence that the older style wind consorts were still in use (notably in Matthew Locke's music to Thomas Shadwell's *Psyche* of 1675, as well as John Banister's *Musick, or A Parley of Instruments* of the following year), while the remodeled recorder (along with the new oboe) would appear to have been introduced into England by French players brought there by the composer Robert Cambert in 1673; see Holman–*Fiddlers*, 343–53, and Lasocki–French hautboy, 339–40.

53. See Mersenne–*Harmonie universelle* 3: 232; 301 of translation. Later writers (Bismantova and Freillon-Poncein) specify thumb and three fingers of the upper hand, plus thumb and forefinger of the lower; Greeting (*The Pleasant Companion*) gives both dispositions but prefers the former.

54. Mersenne (*Harmonie universelle* 3: 237; 306 of trans.) gives an example in four parts, requiring flageolets of three different sizes. This consort would seem best suited for canine delectation: the instrument Mersenne describes for the *dessus* is only 120 mm (about 5 inches) in length, putting the ensemble at approximately 2-foot pitch!

55. London, 1661; further editions in 1666, 1672, 1675, 1680, 1682, 1683, and 1688.

56. See Holman–*Fiddlers*, 352–53.

57. See Hunt–*Recorder*, 50–51: "According to this writer [the Abbé de Marolles] the music-lovers of his day 'etoient ravis de la Poche et du violon de Constantin et de Bocan, de la viole d'Otman et de Maugars, de la musette de Poitevin, de la flute doûce de La

Pierre et du flageolet d'Otteterre.'" (The spelling "Osteterre" cited in the main text comes from the article "Hotteterre" in *New Grove*.)

58. When it was then necessary to distinguish it from the "German flute" (the usual eighteenth-century English term for the transverse flute), it was often called the "common flute."

59. See Holman–*Fiddlers*, 348–49.

60 See Bergman–Purcell, 227–33 for a list and discussion of Purcell's works employing recorder.

61. See Baines–*Talbot*, 6–17. For examples ca. 1700 of English employment of the transverse flute (still with French forms of the name), see Holman–*Fiddlers*, 349.

62. Nuremberg, Germanisches Nationalmuseum MI 98–104; see Kirnbauer–*Verzeichnis*.

63. Actually, it is only the alto and tenor members of this set whose bores continue to contract at the bottom; the soprano and bass members have the traditional Renaissance "choke" bore (with a terminal flare). This apparent anomaly can easily be explained: the alto and tenor instruments are the ones that can benefit the most from the effect of the lower constriction in improving high notes. The soprano achieves the same effect through larger holes, while the bass was probably not expected to have much of a high register anyway.

64. Praetorius–*Syntagma* II: 34–35.

65. Ibid., 37; see also [22].

66. See Haynes–Bach's Pitch, 62–63 for a list of French oboists active in Germany at this period.

67. Facs. repr. by Edition Peters, Leipzig, 1974.

68. Found between pages 256 and 257.

69. It bears a striking resemblance to the two-piece cylindrical flute by Lissieu, ca. 1660-1675 (mentioned above, n.37).

70. See Solum–*Early Flute*, 36–37.

71. See Castellani–Bismantova, 9–80.

72. Praetorius–*Syntagma* III: 66–68. He had already mentioned the large *pommern* as substitutes for equivalently pitched trombones or curtals (II: 159–64).

73. For a discussion of the instruments commonly used in at least one Italian church—the influential San Marco of Venice—see Bartlett/Holman–Gabrieli; and Selfridge-Field–Bassano. Klitz–Composition has argued that a part labeled *dolzaina* in a canzona (1636) by G. B. Buonamente is intended for bass *pommer*—without, however, establishing that the larger *pommern* were actually in use in seventeenth-century Italy. Klitz has ruled out the curtal (since Buonamente elsewhere specifies *fagotto*); however, not ruled out is some alternative form of curtal (perhaps one with a dampening bell cover, like Praetorius's *gedact chorist-fagott*). Certainly a quieter form of curtal is more in keeping with the word *dolzaina* (which, confusingly, predates both the invention of the curtal and the development of the larger shawms) than is the more raucous *bass pommer.*

74. See Langwill–*Bassoon*, 3 [pl. 3].

75. See Snyder–*Buxtehude*, 375. *Schalmeyen* and *quartflöten* (probably soprano recorders, not tenors as posited by Snyder) were also purchased for Buxtehude's use at St. Mary's; see 373–74.

76. For instance, the pavan played at the coronation of Louis XIII in 1610 (reprinted in Baines–*Woodwind*, 272) and the two fantasies for shawm band by Louis Couperin, possibly for the coronation of Louis XIV in 1654 (discussed in Oldham–Two Pieces, and reproduced in facsimile in plates 97–100 of that source).

77. Praetorius–*Syntagma* II: 37.

78. Mersenne–*Harmonie universelle* 3: 303; 378 of translation.

79. Ibid., 304; 378–79 of translation.

80. Five *pieds du roy*. Ibid., 297; 371 of translation.

81. The same scheme must have been used in England; Talbot's "English hautbois or waits treble" is in (seven-finger) c' and his "waits tenor" is in f. (He mentions no bass.)

Again the dimensions given resemble those of Praetorius's *discant schalmey* and *alt pommer.* See Baines–*Talbot,* 11–12, 21.

82. See Myers–*Practical Acoustics,* 104–17.

83. See Baines–Shawms.

84. Mersenne–*Harmonie universelle* 3: 295; 370 of translation.

85. Ibid., 302; 377 of translation.

86. Once again, Mersenne's information is internally inconsistent. He says on page 300 of *Harmonie universelle* (374 of trans.) that the *basson* (curtal) that he has depicted on that page descends a fourth lower than "the ordinary ones," yet he gives its overall bore length as five and one-half *pieds de roy*—about right for a normal bass curtal, as pointed out in Kopp–Bassoon, 90. Elsewhere (299; 373 of trans.) Mersenne notes that curtals differ in pitch, some going "lower than others by a third or fourth"—thus at least confirming the existence of different sizes in France. For a survey of surviving pieces specifying curtals, see Klitz–Bassoon in Chamber Music.

87. See Kenyon de Pascual–Brief Survey.

88. See Kreitner–Minstrels.

89. For instance, a distinction in roles between a player of the *bajón en los cantos de órgano* and a member of the *capilla de los ministriles* (shawm band) is implicit in the 1592 document from Palencia quoted in ibid., 536.

90. See Foster–Bassanelli for an inventive approach to a reconstruction according to Praetorius's illustration—*Theatrum instrumentorum,* pl. 12.

91. See Boydell–*Crumhorn,* 325–41.

92. See both Boydell–*Crumhorn* and K. T. Meyer–*Crumhorn* for archival information regarding the distribution and demise of the crumhorn and related winds.

93. It should be mentioned that this is still the cylindrically bored *rackett* of the Renaissance and not yet the conically bored version—actually a bassoon in compact form—whose invention near the end of the century has been credited to J. C. Denner.

94. See Sandman–Wind Band, esp. 30.

95. See Anthony–*French Baroque,* 12–14, for a short history of the *Grand Écurie.*

96. See Boydell–*Crumhorn,* ch. 6, 183–95.

97. Scellery–*Traité de la musette.*

98. J.-M. Hotteterre–*Méthode.*

99. This is, in fact, a multiple drone in a very compact package, resembling a *rackett.*

100. Marx–Baroque Oboe, 3–19.

101. Haynes–Lully, 324–38.

102. Harris-Warrick–Thoughts.

103. Haynes–Lully, n.22.

104. Much work still needs to be done in analyzing surviving so-called "transitional" oboes and other variants. If they play at shawm pitch, they were likely to have been considered shawms; if at oboe pitch, oboes.

105. Harris-Warrick–Thoughts, 105, Harris-Warrick–Score, 356–59.

106. See Kopp–Notes, 95–99; Kenyon de Pascual–Wind-Instrument Maker, 26; and Kenyon de Pascual–Jointed Dulcian, 150–53.

107. See Waterhouse–17th-century bassoon, 407–10.

108. See Kopp–Notes, 109–11.

109. See Baines–*Talbot,* 19.

110. See Stanley and Lyndon-Jones–*Curtal,* 3. However, curtals at lower pitches may have existed; the acoustical length of Praetorius's *gedact chorist-fagott (Theatrum instrumentorum,* pl. 10) is about 12 percent greater than that of the *offen* form, suggesting a pitch difference of a whole tone between them. (Praetorius himself seems unaware of this pitch difference, it should be noted.) See also "Pitch and Transposition," this *Guide,* 339, n.18.

111. Fuhrmann–*Musicalischer Trichter,* 92. See Dreyfus–*Bach's Continuo Group,* 111.

112. When a five-part string score was adapted to the four-part oboe band, the common practice seems to have been to leave out the *quinte* (i.e., third viola) part, as argued in Harris-Warrick–A Few Thoughts, 102–05.

113. This fact has led Harris-Warrick to suggest as an alternative possibility that the oboes for *taille* and *haute-contre* might have differed some way in construction rather than tuning, as befitted specialists in different registers; see ibid., 105.

114. The only wind family discussed by Mersenne in which there is a distinction in pitch between *haute-contre* and *taille* seems to be the cornetts, although once again there is some confusion. His musical example (*Harmonie universelle* 3: 277; 347 of trans.) demands an *haute-contre* built a tone lower than the *dessus* in (six-fingers) a and a *taille* a fifth lower than the *dessus*. In the text, however, he twice says (273 and 278; 343 and 348 of trans.) that the only difference between *dessus* and *taille* is that the latter has a key—impossible if they are to be a fifth apart. It seems the musical example is more likely to be correct, if only because it may have a more direct line to a practicing musician!

115. See Semmens–Translation, 136; Ranum–Problems; and Hotteterre–*Principes*, 36–37; 78 of translation.

116. See Freillon-Poncein–*Manière*, [19]; and Semmens–Translation, 138.

117. See H. Myers–Recorder Tutors, 4.

118. Loulié defines a trill as "irregular or defective" when the fingering for the *appui* is not retained in the trill itself; see Semmens–Translation, 138–39 [ff. 176r to 177r]. Loulié's directives find an echo half a century later in the flute method of J. J. Quantz, who is even more specific about the technique of suppressing the pitch during such trills in order to correct their intonation; see Quantz–*Versuch*, 104–08 (86–89 of orig.).

119. See, in addition to Freillon-Poncein and Hotteterre, J[ohn] B[anister], *The Sprightly Companion* (London, 1695), the first tutor for the oboe.

120. The "r" itself is almost certainly still a dental one, rather than the uvular "r" that has now become standard in Parisian French; for evidence regarding this question see David Lasocki's introduction to his translation of Hotteterre–*Principes*, 19–20.

For Further Reading

Besides the instrument histories cited in the footnotes, the following may be of interest: Montagu–*Medieval and Renaissance*; Montagu–*Baroque and Classical*; Remnant–*Musical Instruments*; van der Meer–*Musikinstrumente*; and Young–*Look of Music*.

6

Cornett and Sackbut

Bruce Dickey

The Cornett and Sackbut Ensemble

The cornett is a lip-vibrated, wooden, finger-hole horn, usually curved and of octagonal cross section, which went out of use in the early nineteenth century. The sackbut is the ancestor of the modern trombone, made of thinner brass and with a narrower bore and bell than its descendant. The histories of these two instruments, differing so greatly in physical characteristics, nevertheless became inextricably intertwined in the course of the sixteenth century, remained so throughout the seventeenth, and gradually diverged in the eighteenth as the cornett fell into obsolescence. The story of this "marriage" is unique in the history of musical instruments and largely determined the destinies of both instruments for two hundred years.

The cornett, developed through the addition of finger holes to the animal horns widely used for signaling in the Middle Ages, evolved around the turn of the sixteenth century into the most important soprano voice of the Renaissance instrumentarium. The sackbut, derived from the medieval natural trumpet through the application, in the late fifteenth century, of a U-slide mechanism, developed quickly into the most important tenor and bass wind instrument of the sixteenth century. Each of these instruments needed the other to provide the homogeneous consort typical of Renaissance tastes; each complemented the other perfectly. The sackbut generally lacked the agility necessary for intricate ornamentation required of soprano lines[1]; the cornett family lacked middle and low voices. (Tenor and bass cornetts were eventually developed, but were never as popular as sackbuts on lower parts.)

It was first and foremost in Italy where ensembles of cornetts and sackbuts took hold, eventually replacing the late-medieval mixed wind band of shawms and slide trumpet.[2] By the beginning of the seventeenth century, the cornett reigned as the virtuoso solo instrument par excellence, and the *concerto di cornetti e tromboni*, usually known as the *piffari*, was an essential feature of the musical landscape of virtually every city of any importance in Italy. Outside Venice, the center of cornett and sackbut playing, extensive documentation exists for such groups in cities such as Bologna, Genoa, Brescia, Udine, Florence, Rome, and Naples. Virtuosi of the cornett were extravagantly praised by local chroniclers (and often correspondingly remunerated by their patrons). Their numbers included highly trained composers (Giovanni Bassano in Venice, Ascanio Trombetti "detto del Cornetto" in Bologna, "il Cavaliere" Nicolò Rubini del Cornetto in Modena), at least one famous artist (Benvenuto Cellini), as well as several cloistered nuns (most notably at the convent of San Vito in Ferrara).

The duties of the *piffari* centered on ceremonial civic functions: daily "performances" in the public square, accompanying the entrances and exits of prominent officials as well as providing entertainment for their meals and playing for processions and at public celebrations. In addition, these groups often provided music for Mass or other church functions, either as an official unit or, more often, as a pool of players to be called on when needed to augment the salaried musicians of the *cappella*. Not all theorists agreed (nor did the church, at least officially, since the Council of Trent) that these instruments were appropriate in the church. In disparaging their use in sacred or refined circumstances, though, Vincenzo Galilei clearly expresses a personal bias:

[Cornetts and trombones] are often heard in masquerades, on stage, on the balconies of public squares for the satisfaction of the citizens and common people, and, contrary to all that is proper, in the choirs and with the organs of sacred temples on solemn feast days . . . these instruments are never heard in the private chambers of judicious gentlemen, lords and princes, where only those [musicians] take part whose judgement, taste and hearing are unsullied; for from such rooms [these instruments] are totally prohibited.[3]

Ensembles of cornetts and sackbuts were heard in Italy right through the seventeenth century, and in some cases through the eighteenth century. The *Concerto Palatino della Signoria di Bologna,* one of the most renowned of these ensembles, existed for more than 250 years, usually in a formation of four cornetts and four trombones, and was not disbanded until 1779. By this time standards on the cornett had sunk so low that the city fathers voted to silence the *Concerto Palatino,* stating that

either the great difficulty of adapting the said cornetts, very imperfect in their structure, to the harmonious expression of that kind of music which corresponds to the genius of the present time, or the scarceness of subjects in possession of the natural disposition necessary to take on and cultivate the sound of this instrument, actually out of use, has made manifestly clear the absolute necessity of substituting the cornetts with some other instrument more grateful to the ear and which might remove the unpleasantness which results from hearing, in the public functions and, above all, in the churches, a very disagreeable dissonance, from which derives a manifest scandal.[4]

The Concerto Capitolino in Rome, with six cornetts and six sackbuts, was not disbanded until 1798, when, on the arrival of Napoleon, it was replaced with a military band.[5]

North of the Alps, most German civic authorities maintained a wind band by the fifteenth century. Its principal instruments were (by the sixteenth century) the cornett and the sackbut, although the players each mastered many instruments. This instrumental versatility appears to represent one of the principal differences between the German *Stadtpfeifer* and the Italian *piffari*. To be sure, many Italian cornettists and trombonists played other instruments as well, but the practice seems to have been neither as widespread nor as officially sanctioned as in Germany, where wind players often began their careers among the string players (*Kunstgeiger*) and only later were promoted to the more prestigious wind instruments.

As in Italy the duties of the *Stadtpfeifer* included functions both civic (including the famous "tower music") and sacred. A truly enormous quantity of German sacred music from the seventeenth century includes parts for cornetts and sackbuts, sometimes in obbligato roles, but more often doubling voices in the *ripieno* choir. This practice was virtually universal in the performance of music in the *stile antico*, the classical sixteenth-century polyphonic style still much used in German Lutheran churches as late as the eighteenth century. A manuscript in the Berlin Staatsbibliothek that preserves, partly in the hand of J. S. Bach, a group of instrumental and vocal parts to Palestrina's *Missa sine nomine à 6* bears witness to the prevalence and persistence of this practice in Leipzig. Bach's instrumentation of this Mass includes two cornetts and four trombones, as well as a continuo group of organ, harpsichord, and violone.

Bach's famous complaint in 1730 that the Leipzig *Stadtpfeifer* were "partly retired, and partly not at all in such practice as they should be" undoubtedly reflects a decline in this famous group that took place after 1720. Nevertheless, the *Stadtpfeifer* continued to play cornetts and sackbuts into the nineteenth century in some places. The French composer and musicologist Jean Georges Kastner heard them in Stuttgart in 1840, though he was little impressed with their skill.

Farther south, at the Catholic courts of Munich, Innsbruck, and Vienna, cornetts and sackbuts were cultivated at a level rivaling Venice. Indeed there was a constant exchange of musicians across the Alps, often involving cornett and trombone players (e.g., cornettist Girolamo Dalla Casa and his trombone-playing brothers, who were employed for a time at the Bavarian court). Music for the Imperial Court at Vienna, in particular, often included brilliantly virtuosic parts for these instruments. Moreover, literally hundreds, if not thousands, of sacred works in manuscript of composers such as Fux, Biber, Anerio, Sances, and Bertali call for cornetts and sackbuts *colla parte* or in modestly obbligato roles. Characteristically, these pieces call for an ensemble of one cornett, two trombones, and a curtal (*fagotto*) instead of a cornett and three trombones.

We are much less well informed about the use of cornett and sackbut ensembles in England, France, and Spain, partly because the lack of a flourishing music publishing industry in the seventeenth century in these countries means that there is much less surviving music. What is certain is that these instruments were used frequently and widely to double voices in church choirs.

In England the use of these instruments at the Court, in the Chapel Royal, and in provincial and collegiate churches was widespread at least to the time of the Commonwealth. Although a definitive history of the royal wind music remains to be written, a look at the incomplete archival records reveals that in the first three decades of the seventeenth century a wind ensemble of three cornetts and three sackbuts came increasingly to dominate over the more varied groups of recorders, flutes, and shawms more prevalent in the previous century. In the Chapel Royal as well as in the cathedrals at such places as Canterbury, York, and Durham, the cornetts and sackbuts were used principally to double the voices of the choir. Roger North describes the practice at Durham:

> They have the ordinary wind instruments in the Quires, as the cornet, sackbut, double curtaile and others, which supply the want of voices, very notorious there; and nothing can so well reconcile the upper parts in a Quire, since wee can have none but boys and those none of the best, as the cornet (being well sounded) doth; one might mistake it for a choice eunuch. . . .[6]

As widespread and popular as this practice may have been, it was ultimately new tastes imported from the French court that spelled disaster for players of these instruments. John Evelyn's diary contains the following entry for December 21, 1662:

> [one] of his Majesties Chaplains preached: after which, instead of the antient grave and solemn wind musique accompanying the Organ was introduced a Consort of 24 Violins . . . after the French fantastical light way, better suiting a Tavern or Play-house than a Church: This was the first time of change, & now we heard no more the Cornet, which gave life to the organ, for that instrument quite left off in which the English were so skillfull.[7]

Eventually even the town Waits, civic instrumental ensembles similar to the German *Stadtpfeifer*, succumbed to French fashion. The *Edinburgh Town Council Register* of 1696 reports that the cornetts there were to be replaced by the "French hautboye and double curtal, instruments far more proper than the instruments they now have to play upon."

The Cornett

When we speak of the cornett in the seventeenth century, we must speak of a family of instruments differing in size and tonal characteristics. Each of these instrument types had specific functions and patterns of use (often differing from country to country or region to region).

Curved Cornetts

The cornett family may be divided into two main groups: curved and straight. The principal group was that comprised of the curved cornetts, also sometimes called "black cornetts" (*cornetti neri*) since they were nearly always made of two pieces of wood glued together down the length of the instrument and covered with black-dyed leather or parchment to insure the integrity of the joint. Curved cornetts came in the following sizes.

CORNETT (*CHORZINK, DESSUS DES CORNETS*)
The standard cornett was pitched in A (cornett pitches always refer to the note that sounds when all finger holes are covered), and in the hands of a skillful player could ascend to d" or, according to Praetorius, as high as g". Because pitches in the seventeenth century were not standardized, it is impossible to fix this A with any precision in absolute terms. Surviving instruments, however, tend to be high with respect to the modern pitch standard of a=440. In general it could be said that they range from approximately a=440 to a=500, with an average close to a=466 (a halftone above a=440). For this reason modern cornett makers have tended to standardize cornett pitches at a=440 (usually referred to as "modern pitch") and a=466 (usually called "high pitch" or sometimes *Chorton*).[8]

CORNO TORTO (*GROSSER ZINK, TENOR CORNETT, TAILLE DES CORNETS*)
Large cornetts pitched in D (a fifth lower than the standard cornett) are described in a number of historical sources, but the terminology they employ has led to considerable confusion. The name *corno torto* (crooked horn) is first found in Zacconi (1592) and probably refers to the fact they these cornetts were usually made with a double curve resembling an "S." They were made both with and without a key mechanism that added an additional finger hole and a low C to the instrument's range. Despite Praetorius's disparaging remark that their sound resembled that of a cow horn and that they were better replaced with trombones, more than thirty-five such instruments survive in museum collections, many of them finely made. They seem to have been widely used both in Italy and in Germany if we are to judge by the large number of parts marked "cornetto" written in tenor clef or descending below the range of the standard cornett.

CORNETTINO (*KLEINZINK*)

Despite the Italian form of its usual name, the small cornett in d or in e seems to have been primarily a German instrument. Although Praetorius describes it as a *Quintzink,* a fifth above the standard cornett, other theorists describe it as a *Quartzink,* and indeed most surviving examples are in d. The cornettino was used extensively in the second half of the seventeenth century in Germany (particularly northern Germany) and Poland. Most cornettino parts are playable on the standard cornett, the preference for the smaller instrument in these cases presumably being one of timbre rather than of technical facility.

ALTO CORNETT (*HAUTE CONTRE DES CORNETS*)

Although Mersenne mentions an *haute contre des cornets* pitched in G a step below the *dessus,* the existence of alto cornetts outside of France is largely conjectural. They are described by no other theorist, but *contralto di cornetto* is found as one of the regular positions in Bologna's *Concerto Palatino* alongside the *soprano di cornetto.* Indeed, the alto parts of much of the canzona and motet repertory known to have been played by such groups would be unplayable on the standard cornett in A.

BASS CORNETT (*BASSE DU CORNET*)

As with alto cornetts, there is some doubt that bass cornetts existed outside of France (although a few large instruments survive in museum collections). Mersenne describes an instrument in G, one octave below the *haute contre.* This bass cornett is distinct from the serpent, which Mersenne indicates descends to E and which he calls "le vraie basse des cornetts." The serpent was unknown outside of France until the eighteenth century.

Straight Cornetts

The second major group of cornetts includes the straight cornetts, sometimes known as *cornetti bianchi* because of the absence of (black) leather covering. These instruments, turned in one piece, came in two types.

THE CORNETTO DIRITTO (*GERADER ZINK*)

This was equivalent to the curved cornett except that it was fashioned from one piece of wood turned on a lathe. Its detachable mouthpiece was identical to that of the curved cornetts and thus its sound was similar.

THE MUTE CORNETT (*CORNETTO MUTO, STILLER ZINK*)

This was made like the *cornetto diritto* except that its mouthpiece was fashioned from the upper end of the bore. This integrated mouthpiece, tending to be deep and wide and lacking the narrowed back-bore of the separable mouthpiece, gave the mute cornetts a highly distinctive, soft tone quality. Mute cornetts were widely used in the sixteenth century in mixed consorts, but their use in the seventeenth century was mostly restricted to Germany and Austria, where they were effectively used by such composers as Schütz, Praetorius, and Sances, often as an alternative to the transverse flute (*cornetto muto o fiffaro*).

Outside the cornett and sackbut ensemble the principal roles of the cornett were substituting for or playing with the violin and supporting or substituting soprano voices. In addition, toward the end of the seventeenth century the cornett was sometimes used as a substitute for the trumpet, both in Germany and in Italy, and it was a regular member of the *bande des hautbois* at the French court, doubling the top part.

Up until about 1650 it is extremely common in Italian printed music to find the indication *per violino overo cornetto* (for violin or cornett). Indeed, it is rare to find a printed work with the simple indication *per cornetto*. The cornett was the preeminent virtuoso soprano instrument in the sixteenth century, but after 1600 it began to lose ground to the more modern and fashionable violin. The alternative instrumentations found with great frequency in the early part of the seventeenth century reflect both a musical practice and a commercial reality. In many respects—range, agility, and dynamic flexibility—the cornett and violin were musically equivalent and were often considered interchangeable. This flexibility of instrumentation had its commercial side as well, however, as publishers tried to sell their printed music to players of both the older and the newer instruments.

After 1650 it became commercially unattractive to associate new music with the old-fashioned and difficult cornett. This does not mean, however, that the cornett went out of use at this time. Manuscript sources demonstrate that professional cornettists of a high level continued to be active in at least some centers such as Venice, Bologna, and Ferrara. While writing for the cornett before 1650 tended to emphasize agility, particularly through the use of rapid linear divisions, writing after 1650 tended to imitate the natural trumpet, sometimes, though not always, being restricted to the notes available in the natural harmonic series of the trumpet, and frequently exploiting the extreme high range of the instrument (up to d" and even e"!).

Evidence from Bologna indicates that while it was the violin that initially led to the cornett's decline, it was sometimes the oboe that directly replaced it. There exist in the archives of San Petronio instrumental parts with the indication *cornetto* scratched out and *obois* written over it in a later hand.

Even where virtuosi were unknown, the cornett was widely used to support human voices, or to substitute for them where boy sopranos were scarce. This was true wherever the cornett was played, from Italy to Germany, from England to France and Spain. In Germany the ways in which the cornett was used with voices are better documented both because writers like Praetorius described them in detail and because both printed and manuscript music tended to be more specific about this function. Most typically we find a pair of cornetts or mute cornetts playing obbligato parts (often in alternation with a pair of violins or recorders, probably played by the same *Stadtpfeifer*) and one or two cornetts doubling the soprano lines of the *ripieno* choir. In some cases the cornett takes this soprano part alone, replacing the soprano voice. An example of this practice in a small-scale piece is provided by Schütz's *Benedicam Dominum* from the first book of *Symphoniae sacrae,* where the cornett provides the soprano to a "vocal" quartet.

In the third volume of his *Syntagma musicum,* Michael Praetorius gives detailed information on the instrumentation of polychoral works. After describing the use of the cornett to double the soprano line of the vocal choir, he suggests two characteristic uses of the cornett. In a choir with high clefs, cornetts may take the top three parts or may be mixed with violins (either two violins and a cornett, or two cornetts and a violin), with a trombone playing the bass. In addition, in a string choir with normal clefs, a cornett, particularly a mute cornett, may play the alto line an octave higher. Precisely this practice is described in the preface to a collection of motets published by Bernardino Borlasca in 1616, the year in which he was also appointed *Hofkapellmeister* of the Bavarian court in Munich:

> The first choir is to consist of four principal parts with a soprano, castrato or pleasant falsetto, accompanied by a body of diverse [stringed] instruments such as viole da braccio or da gamba, a large harp, a lirone, or other similar instruments as are common today, especially at the Bavarian court [...] The second choir should, like the first, also consist of the same voices, but of different instruments. For if in the first are found plucked instruments or strings, in the second should be placed wind instruments, such as cornetts and trombones, and pleasingly tempered by a violin playing the contralto part an octave above. In the same way in the first choir, a cornett playing the same part if it is a choir of viols is such a different instrument that by following these instructions one will be assured of obtaining lovely and delightful harmony.[9]

Moreover, a collection of polychoral motets from 1613 by the Viennese composer Christoph Strauss has many parts in alto clef marked *cornetto muto.* These are probably meant to be played an octave higher in the manner described by Praetorius.

The Sackbut

Like the cornett, the sackbut was made in several sizes. Praetorius, always teutonically thorough, describes four sizes: (1) *Alt* or *Discant Posaun,* an alto pitched in D or E; (2) *Gemeine rechte Posaun,* a tenor pitched in A; (3) *Quart-* or *Quint-Posaun,* bass instruments pitched in E or D; and (4) *Octav-*

Posaun, a contrabass pitched an octave below the tenor. It is unlikely that the alto sackbut was much used in Italy, if it was known at all. Virgiliano gives only two sizes, tenor and bass, and Italian printed music nearly always has only the indications *trombone* and *trombone grande.* Even Praetorius admits that the alto, due to its small size, does not sound as good as the tenor, which, with practice can play just as high.

A note is in order here about slide positions and pitch terminology. Slide positions (called in German *Züge,* literally "pulls") were conceived diatonically, chromatic notes being produced by modifications of the diatonic positions. Thus the second *zug* produces a harmonic series a whole tone below the first *zug.* Because of the pitch flexibility required in playing in situations without fixed pitch standards and in unequal temperaments, first position was played with the slide slightly extended (about the width of two fingers). The harmonic series produced in this position, which generally corresponds to approximately a Bb at modern pitch, was named the series on A. This must be understood with reference to the discussion above about high pitch standards. A modern trombonist coming to the sackbut will normally apply the pitch terminology he has learned on the modern trombone, and will thus play the sackbut at a=440. If, on the other hand, on the same instrument he learns the historical pitch denominations, he will be playing at a=466 or what is sometimes called *Chorton.*

When played by a virtuoso, the sackbut was a remarkably agile instrument. Like cornettists and violinists, trombonists played divisions on vocal pieces of which a few examples survive: the divisions for *trombone bastarda* of Francesco Rognoni Taeggio cover an astonishing range and require great agility.[10] Ensemble canzonas and sonatas of the first three decades of the seventeenth century frequently draw on this division technique and display frequent *passaggi* in sixteenth and thirty-second notes. Just as the cornett was frequently considered an alternative to the violin, the trombone was typically the alternative to the *viola* (meaning usually the *viola da braccio*) in the case of tenor parts, or to the *violone, fagotto* (curtal) or *theorbo* for bass parts. While there are very few solo compositions written expressly for the trombone, soprano-bass and soprano-soprano-bass sonatas frequently employ the instrument in a florid manner, and occasionally offer brief solo passages.

In Germany and Austria trombone virtuosity tended to stress aspects of the instrument's technique different from the rapid *passaggi* of the Italians. In Austria, composers like Schmelzer made ample use of arpeggiation and rapid register changes. The trombone was frequently used with the curtal, often in a quartet including a violin and a cornett as well. Works for an ensemble of this sort include sonatas of Fux, Valentini, Ferro, Marini (written during his German sojourn), Weckmann, and Schmelzer, as well as concertato vocal works by Albrici, Pohle, Konwalynka, and Schulze. At the Bavarian Court in Munich the Italian cornettist from Udine, Giovanni Martino Cesare, wrote a collection of sonatas for cornetts and sackbuts that contains one of the only solo sonatas for trombone. Like Schmelzer, Cesare exploits rapid register changes rather than extensive divisions. Cesare also included a motet for one voice and three trombones. The small-scale *geistliches Konzert* with an ensemble of three or four trombones was used to great effect by Schütz, Buxtehude, and others.

Apart from its soloistic role, the sackbut, like the cornett, was widely used to supplement and support *ripieno* voices. An interesting and little-known sidelight to this function was the widespread use of trombones in Italian convents. Since the end of the Council of Trent in 1563, all female monasteries were placed under strict *clausura*. Many convents were famed for their music, and for them this presented a serious dilemma, since under no circumstances could men perform together with the nuns. For the performance of polyphonic music, one obvious solution was the use of trombones for bass and tenor parts. Despite the fact that church authorities continued to forbid the use of most musical instruments in the convents, many nuns were renowned for their ability not only on cornetts but also on tenor and bass trombones. Foremost among the musical convents was S. Vito in Ferrara at which, according to Bottrigari, the nuns played both cornetts and sackbuts "so gracefully and with such a sweet manner, and with such just and sonorous intonation of the notes, that even those who are judged excellent in that profession confessed that it is a thing incredible to those who hear and see it."[11]

Historical Playing Techniques

In many ways, the techniques required in playing the cornett and the sackbut are the same as those used in playing modern brass instruments. Since most beginning players do not have access to teachers of historical instruments, it can be extremely helpful to get some basic advice from a good modern brass teacher, particularly regarding breathing and embouchure development. The beginning cornett or sackbut player should be aware from the beginning, however, that certain techniques do differ. Rather than repeating here the general advice that can be found elsewhere, I will restrict myself to dealing with what is distinctive about the old instruments.

The cornett and the sackbut were considered the most capable of all the musical instruments in imitating the human voice. This was and should be today the most profound goal of the player. In the search for an appropriate tone quality, articulation, and dynamic range, the human voice is the principal model (and not the modern trumpet or trombone!).

Holding the cornett: perhaps the greatest difficulty in the initial stages of learning the cornett is finding a way of holding the instrument comfortably. Most cornett players will find that the large stretch required to reach the finger holes can best be accommodated by adopting a finger position closer to that of the transverse flute (oblique to the instrument) than to that of the recorder. This position will bring the inside of the left hand at the base of the first finger into contact with the cornett above the first finger hole and provide stability to the instrument. Similarly with the right hand the instrument will be supported at the base of the first finger and by the little finger, which will remain on the instrument at all times.

Cornett embouchure: cornett players, including those who play the trumpet, will be best advised to use a small (so-called "acorn") mouthpiece such as the ones provided by the best cornett makers (in the case of the Christopher Monk Workshop, ask for the acorn type). This small mouthpiece can be placed either in the center (though most players place it slightly off-center) or in the corner of the mouth. The corner position was adopted by many, if not most, early players for reasons that are not yet entirely clear. If the corner position is adopted, the muscles of the embouchure must work in an asymmetrical fashion—that is, the muscles in the corner of the mouth in which the mouthpiece is placed must be relaxed enough to allow the lip tissue to vibrate, while the opposite corner must be kept firm.[12] The center embouchure functions basically as does any brass embouchure, except that the center of the lips should be kept more relaxed than in trumpet playing, in order to allow a maximum vibrating surface within the extremely small mouthpiece. It is important, however, that the corners of the mouth be kept firm at all times and in all registers, as they supply stability to the embouchure.

Cornett fingering: the tuning of any cornett is an imperfect compromise. This is not to say, however, that it need be played out of tune. A good player learns the adjustments that must be made to certain notes along with the fingerings for those notes. If these adjustments are made by changing the shape of the embouchure and not by relaxing and tensing it, they can be extremely accurate. For example, bringing the corners of the mouth toward the center (as if pronouncing the vowel "oo") will lower the pitch, and pulling them back away from the center will raise it. It is a good idea to practice this procedure on long tones, bending the pitch downward by half steps.

The goal of a cornett player should be to play perfectly in tune in meantone temperament, or, more accurately, to play pure intervals above a stable bass instrument playing in meantone. This will require playing all sharped notes lower than their equivalents in equal temperament, and in some cases much lower than they can be tuned by adjusting the finger holes of any cornett. Thus C♯, G♯ (except for fingering ♯1, which tends to be low), and D♯ must always be played with the lip position mentioned above. On the other hand, notes with flats must be played relatively high. This may often be aided by using a different fingering from that used on the enharmonically "equivalent" sharp note. The central B♭, however, is nearly always low and must be lipped up.

Fingerings, particularly for some accidentals, vary somewhat from instrument to instrument. For this reason I have given several alternate fingerings for certain notes in the fingering chart in Figure 6.1. These fingerings are based on personal experience with the modern instruments most generally available. Historical fingering charts and museum instruments sometimes require slightly different fingerings. In particular c and c' often require forked fingerings (0 123 46), and the fork is also preferred on f'. Modern instruments are seldom constructed with these forked fingerings in mind, however, and consequently they seldom sound well or play in tune.

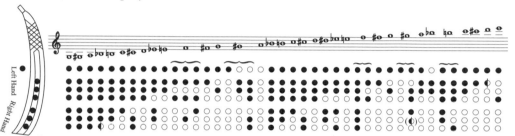

FIGURE 6.1. Fingering chart for cornett in g.

Historical articulation on cornett and sackbut: articulation is perhaps the area in which modern and historical playing techniques differ the most. Historical wind articulation was based on the alternation of pairs of unequal syllables: a kind of double tonguing. In modern wind playing, however, double tonguing is seen as an aid to velocity, and the greatest possible equality of the two syllables is assiduously strived for. In the music of the sixteenth and seventeenth centuries, the aim of double tonguing was not equality, but rather inequality. This inequality was a reflection of the doctrine of "good" and "bad" notes: good notes, which fell on metrically strong beats and were consonant, were slightly stressed; bad notes, metrically weak and dissonant (passing), were correspondingly unstressed. The application of a compound tonguing that alternated a hard consonant with a softer one (*te re*), or one close to the teeth with one further back in the mouth (*te che*), provided an ideal means of realizing this desired inequality.

The system of articulations was comprised of three kinds of double tonguings: (1) *te che te che*, (2) *te re te re*, and (3) *le re le re*. The first of these tonguings was described as hard and sharp, the third as smooth and pleasing, the second as intermediate. In fact, the first tonguing, which corresponds to modern double tonguing, was little used as it was considered too unvocal. The third tonguing, since it could best imitate the throat articulations of the singers' divisions, was the favorite for playing rapid divisions, and was given the special name *lingua riversa* ("reverse tonguing"). The reason for this name is unclear, but has to do with the fact that the written syllables actually stand for a slightly different movement of the tongue than that produced by pronouncing them clearly. The closest approximation to this movement for English speaking players is "diddle diddle."[13] Since this tonguing can be used only on very fast notes, the most useful tonguing for passages at moderate speeds is *te re te re*. It is important, however, that these two syllables be pronounced in a way that results in a double-tongue movement. The Italian *re* is pronounced with a rolled *r* in which the tongue makes a single stroke against the ridge behind the upper teeth. The closest approximation in English is the soft "t" in the relaxed American pronunciation of "water."

Generally speaking, all notes of the speed of eighth notes or faster should be tongued with one of the compound tonguings described above. Exceptions include repeated notes and leaping notes, which should be single tongued.

Despite the fact that the seventeenth-century Bolognese theorist Artusi claimed that the trombone differed from the cornett in that it had only one tonguing, we may safely presume, on the basis of the music if nothing else, that the best trombonists of the time also used these compound tonguings. Modern trombonists experienced in jazz will recognize in the *lingua riversa* a tonguing commonly used among jazz players. They should be encouraged to experiment with the connections between these articulations.

Repertory

Obviously, the repertory for cornetts and sackbuts, and for these instruments in other instrumental combinations, is vast. It will be impossible here to survey this literature in any depth. The best I can attempt to do is to point out certain parts of the repertory that are of particular interest, or that are especially accessible. Those interested in pursuing this music in greater detail are referred to the bibliographic listings at the end of this chapter. In particular, I should mention that, together with Michael Collver, I have published *A Catalog of Music for the Cornett* (Bloomington: Indiana University Press, 1996), a listing of the entire cornett repertory.

Italy

Many of the most important early-seventeenth-century collections of Italian sonatas and canzonas for one to four instruments have been published in inexpensive facsimile editions by the Studio per Edizioni

Scelte (known as SPES) in Florence. Particularly recommended in this series are the collections of Girolamo Frescobaldi, Giovanni Picchi, Gio. Battista Riccio, Dario Castello (Books 1 and 2), Biagio Marini (*Affetti Musicali*), Gio. Battista Fontana, and Florentino Maschera. Students can learn very quickly to read from seventeenth-century facsimile notation and the skill thus learned vastly increases the amount of repertory available. The above-mentioned collections contain pieces in a variety of textures including soprano solo, SS, SSB, B, BB, SSBB, SSTB, and SATB. The collections by Castello and Fontana contain the most difficult music (the bass parts of Fontana are not generally suitable for the sackbut), and those by Riccio and Maschera (all four-part SATB canzonas) the easiest. A large number of canzonas of Frescobaldi, Riccio, and others are also available in good modern editions from London Pro Musica Editions.

Undoubtedly the most important Italian composer for cornetts and sackbuts was Giovanni Gabrieli. His canzonas (mostly contained in two Venetian prints of 1597 and 1615) range in scale from four parts (one cornett and three sackbuts) to twenty-two parts. Most of the canzonas are available in score and parts from King's Music in London. From the same publisher may be had a great deal of Venetian concerted music for voices and instruments, much of it including cornetts and sackbuts. Of particular interest are such large-scale Gabrieli motets as *In ecclesiis à 14* (3 cornetts, viola, 2 trombones, SATT soli, SATB *ripieno*, B.c.), *Quem vidistis pastores à 14* (6 voices, 2 cornetts, 3 trombones, 3 unspecified instruments, B.c.), and *Surrexit Christus à 16* (3 voices, 2 cornetts, 2 violins, 4 trombones, B.c.)

A great deal of four- to eight-part canzona repertory is being made available in modern score in Garland Publishing's ambitious "Italian Instrumental Music" series, edited by James Ladewig. In addition to the Venetian repertory, this series contains music of many of the lesser-known composers of the Lombard school, such as Ottavio Bariolla, Gio. Domenico Rognoni Taeggio, Agosto Soderino, Francesco Rovigo, and Ruggier Trofeo. All of this repertory is suitable to cornetts and sackbuts, and often of moderate difficulty. In addition, London Pro Musica Editions has published a great deal of Italian instrumental ensemble music, including all of the ensemble canzonas of Frescobaldi.

A certain amount of mid-seventeenth-century Italian concerted music has parts for two violins (some of it suitable for cornetts) and three trombones, including motets of such composers as Monteverdi, Rovetta, Grandi, Usper, Fontei, and Cavalli. Some of this music is available from King's Music (request a catalogue). Anyone interested in pursuing this repertory in depth is referred to Jerome Roche's excellent book *North Italian Church Music in the Age of Monteverdi* (Oxford: Clarendon Press, 1984).

Germany

A large of amount of German music with cornetts and trombones, both instrumental and concerted with voices, is included among the volumes of the *Denkmäler deutscher Tonkunst* (DDT), *Denkmäler der Tonkunst in Oesterreich* (DTÖ), and *Das Erbe deutscher Musik* (EDM).

The principal volumes with instrumental music are:

DDT:
  Vol. 63: Johann Christoph Pezel

DTÖ:
  Vol. 19: J. J. Fux
  Vols. 111-112: Johann Heinrich Schmelzer

EDM:
  1. Reihe, 14: Daniel Speer, J. G. C. Störl, and Matthias Spiegler
  2. Reihe (Kurhessen): Moritz v. Hessen
  2. Reihe, Schleswig-Holstein, 4: Matthias Weckmann

In addition to instrumental music, the German *Denkmäler* volumes include vocal works with parts for cornetts and trombones by Ahle (DDT 5), Bernhard (DDT 6 & EDM 90), Buxtehude (DDT 14), Capricornus and Krieger (DDT 53), Knüpfer (DDT 58-59), Bildstein (DTÖ 122), Draghi (DTÖ 46), Fux (DTÖ 3), Kerll (DTÖ 49), Herbst (EDM), Meder (EDM 68), and others.

In addition, the Syracuse University Library has a microfilm collection of the entire Liechtenstein Music Collection from Krómĕříz, Czechoslovakia. This collection, of which a catalogue is available from Syracuse, contains hundreds of instrumental and sacred vocal works, a large part of which have parts for cornetts and trombones (including composers Biber, Bertali, Bernardi, Capricornus, Carissimi, Draghi, Kerll, Kern, Merula, Poglietti, Sances, Schmelzer, Vejvanovský, and many others).

The collected works of Heinrich Schütz, Johann Hermann Schein, Michael Praetorius, and Samuel Scheidt are further important sources of cornett and sackbut repertory. For Schütz, whose *Psalmen Davids* and *Symphoniae sacrae* (books I & III) contain the most important works for brass instruments, the reader is advised to consult the old *Gesamtausgabe*, which is more faithful to the original sources with regard to clefs, keys, and instrumental indications than the new edition. For Praetorius, the most important works are to be found in *Polyhymnia Caduceatrix et Panegyrica* (1619).[14]

England

Very little music specifically for cornetts and sackbuts has survived from England. This is undoubtedly due in part to the fact that the cornett began its road to obsolescence about the time that it became common to specify instrumentations in that country. Thus a good deal of music that would have been played on these instruments probably survives in sources lacking instrumental indications. One of the most important of such sources, but one that can at least in part be identified with the cornett and sackbut ensemble, is the set of five manuscript partbooks at the Fitzwilliam Museum now known as Fitzwilliam Mus. MSS 24. D.13-17. This set of books, originally a set of six of which the tenor book is now missing, has been convincingly demonstrated to represent part of the repertory of the royal wind music under King James I. The partbooks contain music of various sorts: untexted madrigals and motets by late-sixteenth-century Italian composers (Ferrabosco, Marenzio, Lasso, Anerio, Rovigo, Vecchi, etc.), a variety of Pavanes and "Almandes" and miscellaneous other pieces partly attributed with initials, but without instrumentations, and finally (read from the back of the volumes upside-down) a series of dances by Matthew Locke, Charles Coleman, and Nicholas Lanier labeled "5 partt things ffor the Cornetts." (Some of the Locke pieces are also found in the British Library in an autograph score headed "for His Majesty's Sagbutts and Cornets." While the entire Fitzwilliam manuscript undoubtedly represents repertory of the royal wind music, the earlier parts of it (principally the Italian madrigals and motets) probably were intended for the diverse sorts of wind bands popular during Elizabethan times. Some of them would certainly have been played on cornetts and sackbuts, but it is the later dances that would have been their special province. The pieces of Locke, Coleman, and Lanier have been edited by Anthony Baines and published by Oxford University Press.

Notes

1. Notwithstanding the admittedly astonishing efforts of some virtuosi (see discussion of Rognoni's divisions for *trombone bastarda* below).
2. The question of when cornetts were introduced into the Italian wind bands and when the shawms ceased to be used is a complex one, and one that had much to do with local traditions. We know from an exchange of correspondence between Giovanni Alvise Trombon (member of the Venetian *piffari*) and Francesco Gonzaga (see Prizer Piffaro, 160–62) that by 1505 both cornetts and shawms were played by the *piffari* of Venice and of Mantua. In Bologna the term *piffari* continued to be applied to the wind band of shawms and trombones up until 1546, though cornetts appear in the ensemble before that (in the *Statuti* of 1637 the eight *piffari* are defined as four cornetts and four trombones). In 1546 the name *piffari* is changed to *musici* in view of the replacement, by now total, of the shawms by cornetts (Gambassi–*Concerto Palatino*, 9). Though this development followed its own course in each musical center, by the

113

beginning of the seventeenth century the transition must have been complete almost everywhere. By 1600 most such groups were called *concerti di cornetti e tromboni,* the older designation *piffari* having gradually disappeared along with the reed instrument to which it originally referred.

3. Galilei–*Dialogo.*
4. Gambassi–*Concerto Palatino.*
5. See Cametti–Musici, 95–135.
6. Wilson–*North,* 286.
7. Evelyn–*Diary,* 449; cited in Holman–*Four and Twenty,* 395–97.
8. For an explanation of the confusing issue of pitch standards in the seventeenth century, see Herbert W. Myers's chapter "Pitch and Transposition" in this volume.
9. Borlasca–*Scala Iacob,* preface.
10. Rognoni–*Selva,* 61.
11. Bottrigari–*Il desiderio,* 49.
12. For a practical discussion of the corner embouchure see "The Side Embouchure" by Yoshimichi Hamada in the *Historic Brass Society Newsletter* 5 (Summer 1993): 29–30.
13. In fact several writers, in describing the *lingua riversa,* rather mysteriously say that when pronounced quickly the *le re le re* becomes *ler ler.* If we substitute for the Italian alveolar *r* the English *d* (its nearest equivalent) and then replace the missing e above with an apostrophe, the similarity to *diddle* (or *did'll*) becomes apparent:

Dalla Casa's:	*dere lere lere lere*
becomes:	*der ler ler ler*
which becomes:	*ded'led'led'led'l*
very close to:	*did'll did'll did'll did'll*

The *did'll* tonguing consists of alternating the vowel *i* with the consonant *l,* playing the first note on the vowel and the second on the consonant (possible on *l* since air escapes around the sides of the tongue). This alternation is not apparent in the *lingua riversa* when spelled in the form *lere lere lere.* In order to make the alternation evident, we must remove the *e* between the *r* and the *l* (*ler'ler'*) and place one note on the *e* and one on the *r'l.* If we pronounce a series of such syllables we notice that the first note of each pair is always played on the vowel and the second on the *l.* Beginning with a model *dere lere lere* where each syllable pair (after the first) begins with *l,* we have come to a pronunciation where the second note of each pair is the one played with the *l;* the tonguing has become reversed.

14. Volumes 17a and b of the Praetorius *Gesamtausgabe.*

BIBLIOGRAPHY

Alsop–'*Trio' Sonata*; Apel–*Violin*; Baines–*Brass*; Besseler–*Bourdon*; Besseler–Posaune; Carse–*Wind Instruments*; Carter–Sackbut; Collver/Dickey–*Catalog*; Fasman–*Bibliography*; Galpin–Sackbut; Gambassi–*Concerto Palatino*; Guion–*Trombone*; Herbert–Sackbut; Kämper–*Ensemblemusik*; Karstädt–*Zinken*; Kirk–Cornett; McGowan–Sackbut; Newman–*Sonata*; Polk–*Instrumental Music*; Prizer–Piffaro; Roche–*Church Music*; Selfridge-Field–*Venetian Instrumental Music*; Wigness–*Performance Project*; Winkler–*Posaune*; *Das Zinkbuch.*

Selected Listening

Giovanni Gabrieli, Canzonas, Sonatas, Motets. Taverner Choir, Consort and Players, Andrew Parrott, director. EMI CDC 7-54265-2.

Il Concerto Palatino. North Italian Music for Cornetts and Trombones 1580–1650. Accent ACC 8861 D.

Il Cornetto. Works of Italian and English composers of the 16th and 17th centuries for Cornetto. Jeremy West, cornetto. Edition Open Window OW 004.

"Il vero modo di diminuir." Virtuoso Music from 16th-century Italy for cornett, organ, and harpsichord. Doron David Sherwin, cornett; Andrea Marcon, organ and harpsichord. Giulia GS 201010.

Claudio Monteverdi: *Vespro della Beata Vergine.* The Taverner Consort and Players, Andrew Parrott, director. EMI DSB 3963.

Palestrina/Bach. *Missa sine nomine* and music of the Leipzig *Stadtpfeiffer.* EMI Classics CDC 7 54455 2.

"Quel lascivissimo cornetto. . . ." Virtuoso solo music for cornetto. Accent ACC 9173 D.

Johann Hermann Schein. *Opella Nova II.* Musica Fiata, Roland Wilson, director. Deutsche Harmonia Mundi RD 77036.

Schütz. *Christmas Story* and Praetorius Motets from *Polyhymnia Caduceatrix et Panegyrica.* Taverner Choir, Consort and Players, Andrew Parrott, director. EMI CDC 7-47633-2.

Heinrich Schütz. *Symphoniae Sacrae I.* Accent ACC 9178/78 D.

Sonate Concertate. Virtuoso instrumental music of Castello and Scarani. Accent ACC 9058 D.

A Venetian Coronation 1595. The Gabrieli Consort and Players, Paul McCreesh, director. Virgin VC 91110-2.

Venetian Music at the Hapsburg Court. Musica Fiata, Roland Wilson, director. Deutsche Harmonia Mundi RD 77086.

Venice Preserved: Bassano, Gabrieli, Monteverdi. Gentlemen of the Chappell; His Majesties Sagbutts and Cornetts; Peter Bassano, director.

7

Trumpet and Horn

Steven E. Plank

Historical Introduction

In writing about seventeenth-century music, commentators have often underscored its foundations in the idea of affective response. This central goal of arousing the passions of the soul brought into play a large vocabulary of musical figures, keys, and instrumental timbres, each powerfully evocative of particular emotional concepts. Few, if any, instruments were as closely tied to associative meanings as the trumpet, whose sound, sight, and number were invariably manifestations of majesty, heroism, and kingly might. At the court of Louis XIV, for instance, where the external displays of pomp were unrivaled (though often imitated), thirty-six trumpets (four *trompettes ordinaires,* eight *trompettes non servants,* and twenty-four *trompettes de la garde du corp*) were employed to herald and represent the king's majesty.

The link between the trumpet and majesty is a direct outgrowth of the trumpet's highly practical military use as a signal instrument. Standard trumpet calls of "saddle up," "to horse," "to watch," "gather up the tents," and the like often guided troop action.[1] Moreover, the field trumpeter, assuming some of the rights of an ambassador, could be sent behind enemy lines as an emissary, a dangerous function that J. E. Altenburg in the eighteenth century called the field trumpeter's "most important duty."[2] The calls themselves could also be used "strategically." Altenburg again notes how on one occasion the enemy was tricked into thinking reinforcements were on the way by having trumpets sound from various directions.[3]

As a rich symbol of noble prowess, the field trumpeter claimed a number of exclusive privileges that, at least in the Holy Roman Empire, were protected through the establishment in 1623 of an imperial guild of trumpeters and kettledrummers. The articles of privilege were reconfirmed and expanded at various times over the next century and a half, and were held valid in some places until well into the nineteenth century.[4] The guild articles promoted a few basic ideas, namely that the number of players should be few, their training rigorous, and the use of the instrument exclusive, or nearly so. For instance, a teacher could have only one pupil at a time, although the teacher's son might also be included as a second student. The pupil's apprenticeship ran for two years, leading to an examination on important military signals and some clarino playing. Following this, the trumpeter, now released from the apprenticeship, had to wait for seven years and must have participated in at least one military campaign before he himself could take on pupils. Moreover, in order to prevent the demeaning of this jealously guarded, aristocratic instrument, the guild privilege closely restricted "who played what," and where they did so. Municipal musicians, for example, might play in church and on the town tower; student trumpeters might play at university occasions. Not unexpectedly, conflict and abuse were frequent as the guild attempted to preserve the noble aura surrounding the instrument and its associations.

The ceremonial aspects of the trumpet were indeed rooted in the military, but its sound obviously graced important public occasions of all dignified sorts. And though its basic meaning of majesty and stateliness remained constant, the usage of that symbolism varied with the context. An interesting example emerges in the descriptions of the Venetian celebration of the end of its plague in 1631. Documents record that a minister of health ceremonially declared the end of the plague from a pulpit in the Piazza San Marco to the "accompaniment" of twelve trumpets, drums, artillery, and bells. After this impressive proclamation, the public official, trumpeters and drummers preceding him, went into the basilica of Saint Mark's for a Mass of Thanksgiving. Two of the trumpeters, from the evidence of the pay records, played during the Mass in a Gloria and Credo by Monteverdi. What they played is uncertain, as the score leaves no evidence of their participation. Scholar James Moore has suggested that they played fanfares in conjunction with the warlike reiterations of certain violin passages. In other words, the tones that earlier heralded the majesty of the Venetian state (and its minister) might easily have transferred to the majesty of the Church's "King of Kings"; the idiom remained the same, though setting and function altered.[5]

When the Venetian trumpets moved from the piazza into the Basilica they moved into the world of "art" music, although to be sure in this particular case we do not know what they played—it may have been little different from what they played outside—but the artistic distance from field and piazza to church and court was *potentially* great. The trumpet's dual nature, explicit in the Baroque repertory and in contemporary treatises, was long characteristic. Altenburg, for instance, likens the distinction between field and clarino playing to the biblical duality of "blowing" and "sounding an alarm."[6] Girolamo Fantini, the celebrated Tuscan trumpeter, tellingly entitled his trumpet tutor a *Method for Learning to Play the Trumpet in a Warlike Way as well as Musically*. . . . (1638), clearly acknowledging the dual nature of the instrument. Moreover, the idea is poetically echoed in anonymous verse at the beginning of his treatise:

> *This one [Fantini]—who with the sound of [his] bellicose instrument*
> *At his will made helmets vacillate,*
> *Spears shatter, and chargers,*
> *Fiercer than lightning or the wind, shiver—*
>
> *Now see how he, in a musical ensemble,*
> *Sweetening his proudest sounds,*
> *Makes knights and ladies [alike] languish with joy,*
> *His martial talent put to Love's use.*[7]

Much as the usage of the instrument varied, so too did the social identity and musical sophistication of its practitioners. Though the field trumpeter bedecked with ostrich plume and clad in livery represents the mainstream, others practiced the art with skill. Municipal musicians in cities like Leipzig, adept at a variety of instruments, boasted accomplished trumpeters among them such as Johann Pezel or later, Gottfried Reiche. Interestingly, the survival of a large number of trumpet sources in German and Austrian monasteries suggests, as Smithers has pointed out, the likely existence of monastic trumpeters.[8] And if their social identity was diverse, so too was their musical breadth. Some trumpeters were musically illiterate. Michael Praetorius, for example, tellingly requires that only three trumpeters in the standard multiregister trumpet ensemble (see below) be able to read music.[9] On the other hand, trumpeters such as Alessandro Orologio at the imperial court of Rudolf II were impressively wide-ranging in their musical accomplishments. Orologio was active as a composer of vocal music, and rose to the prestigious post of *vice-Kapellmeister* in 1603.[10]

The Instruments

What sort of instruments did these trumpeters play? In the main, the trumpet of the seventeenth century was an elongated, twice-folded instrument, common in iconography and surviving examples (see Fig. 7.1). The majority of the surviving instruments are from Nuremberg. The instruments of Nuremberg makers were widely disseminated in their own day and were the product of a specialized guild of craftsmen, an offshoot of the Guild of Coppersmiths. The families of Haas, Ehe, and Hainlein, among others, were important makers, active over several generations. In their work we see that although much in the construction and form of the instrument remained the same, important changes in the bell occurred. A "shallow-flare" bell, encouraging a dark sound, is found on instruments to

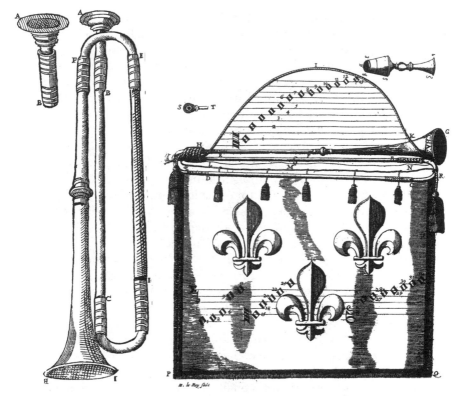

FIGURE 7.1. Two illustrations of a twice-folded, elongated trumpet, as depicted in Marin Mersenne, *Harmonie universelle* (1636).

ca. 1650. From that time, however, the bell flare increased while the bell throat narrowed. Brightness and clarity of tone as well as an ease in the high register resulted. This important constructive change complements new or future directions in the repertory that would favor a higher tessitura for the trumpet. Perhaps the makers were responding to compositional trends, though it seems equally likely they were influencing them.[11] Other variables influencing the sound are the metal itself and its thickness. Sometimes, for instance, ceremonial instruments were made of silver instead of the more customary brass, and lavishly decorated. And though they made a striking visual impression, their sound was held by some— notably Altenburg—to be inferior. Altenburg also observes the usefulness of strong and thick metal for *principale* playing, and the ease of the high register associated with thin and weak metal.[12]

Doubtless of great influence on the sound of the instrument was the mouthpiece, which in the Baroque era featured a hemispherical cup and a sharp-edged angle where the throat meets the cup. Unsurprisingly, dimensions vary considerably,[13] and the width of both cup diameter and flat rim can be quite large by present-day standards. Modern thinking about the relationship of mouthpiece size and range would lead us to think that the large dimensions of some mouthpieces were for low-register *principale* playing. Some individuals have suggested the contrary. Jeremy Montagu, for example, asserts with daunting confidence that "only with this [large] size is range, tone and quietness possible."[14] Similarly, Eric Halfpenny states that "wide, big-bored mouthpieces in no way inhibit the fourth octave, for the sharp inner edge of the rim appears to give greater support for the lips when playing in the clarino register than . . . a more modern type of mouthpiece." He continues, suggesting that the great breadth of the flat rim reduces lip fatigue.[15] Altenburg suggests avoiding mouthpieces with narrow cup and small throat because, even though the high register is made easier, the tone quality suffers in low and high registers alike. Interestingly, he gives an illustration of his father's mouthpiece—strikingly large by modern standards, but one "upon which he could, without forcing, reach high C, D, and E."[16]

Trumpets in the seventeenth century were generally pitched in C or D. Praetorius, writing in the early seventeenth century, notes that D *Cammerton* (approximately a half step higher than modern pitch)[17] was common until "a short time ago it became the practice in many court orchestras either to use the trumpet in a lengthened form or to attach crook tubes to its front, such that the fundamental tone of the instrument was brought a tone lower, to the C *ad modum hypoionicum*. . . ."[18] The D pitch after Praetorius continued to be common in the field and in some art repertories, where it occasionally merited special comment. For example, D trumpet parts by the Bohemian composer P. J. Vejvanovský bear the label *trombae breves,* the "brevity" referring to overall tube length of the D trumpet. The seventeenth-century repertory confirms that both pitches were in use. In Italy, C predominates until around 1680, after which time Italian composers favor D. In France and England, composers called for both keys. Unusually, Henry Purcell on occasion even requires both keys within a single work (e.g., *Dioclesian, Fairy Queen,* and *Indian Queen*). Some contemporary writers proposed strong national distinctions of trumpet pitch. Christoph Weigel, in his *Abbildung der gemeinnützlichen Haupt-Stände* (1698), places French trumpet pitch a step above the German, and English trumpet pitch a step above the French; this presages a similar hierarchy that appears later in Altenburg's treatise.[19]

The elongated, twice-folded shape was the principal, though not the only shape in which trumpets were made. For example, the author of the earliest trumpet method, Cesare Bendinelli, owned a trumpet made by Anton Schnitzer in 1585 that he later gave to the Accademia Filarmonica in his native city of Verona. It and another surviving instrument from 1598 in the Kunsthistoriches Museum in Vienna have a rare and faintly exotic figure eight, pretzel shape. Another form, the horn-shaped, coiled trumpet, has received perhaps a disproportionate amount of attention owing to its depiction in the hands of Bach's trumpeter, Gottfried Reiche, in a splendid portrait by Elias Haussmann. Earlier, Praetorius observed that "some persons prefer trumpets fashioned in the form of a post-horn and wound round like a snake. But such trumpets are not as good in tone as the other trumpets."[20] He includes an illustration of one such instrument in his well-known *Theatrum instrumentorum* (1620) with the label *Jägertrommet* (hunting trumpet). Other writers associated this form with Italy. Weigel writes, "One finds also a class of coiled trumpets, and [these] are the Italian or Welsh [i.e., "foreign"] trumpets, which are six-coiled."[21] In a similar vein, though contradicting Praetorius's remarks about tone quality, Altenburg states:

> [H]ere the so-called invention or Italian trumpet presumably merits first mention, since the construction [of this instrument], with its more frequent coils, [makes it] comfortable [to hold]. It is used mainly in Italy, has the same trumpet sound as the above-mentioned [elongated trumpets], and comes in various sizes.[22]

Its low rate of survival suggests that its usage was a special case.[23]

The Repertory

The repertory of the trumpet in the seventeenth century is extensive and encompasses concerted compositions, sonatas with basso continuo, and improvised or quasi-improvised trumpet ensembles. These latter pieces feature upper-register passagework over slow-moving reiterations of an open-fifth drone in the bass. The wide range of the single timbre as well as the imposing sturdiness of the drone makes for an immense sound that was surely one of the glories of the day.[24] A six-voice texture is typical, with each voice distinctive in range. Thus[25]

Part or Register Name	Range
Clarino	c"–a"
Principal, Quinta, Sonata	c'–c"
Alter Bass (Alto e basso)	g–e'
Volgan (vulgano), Faulstimme	g
Grob, Basso, il groso	c
Fladder-Grob	C

The leading, foundational voice of the ensemble was the middle-register "Principal." Improvisation was in relation to its simple outline, and early sources such as Bendinelli and the Danish trumpet books of Lübeck and Thomsen[26] preserve hundreds of single-line examples, that is, "principal" parts that would serve as the basis for ensemble realization. The simplicity and generic similarity of many of the lines in the early sources has prompted Smithers to question how such meager material could engender distinctive ensemble parts at all.[27] Smithers's musical point is well taken; however, Bendinelli's trumpet method, with over 300 "monophonic" lines specifically shows how *clarino* and *alto e basso* lines are derived from them, a clear confirmation of intention. Sometimes the principal part put forth familiar melodies. Bendinelli, for example, includes the familiar Christmas lied *Josef lieber, Josef mein* as well as melodies entitled "Hungarian Dance," "Hens Clucking," and "Fox Don't Bite Me."

Atop this principal voice, the clarino player improvised free, upper-register figuration. Beneath the principal voice, the *alto e basso* "shadowed" by playing whatever the principal played, but one harmonic lower in the overtone series. This is all rooted within the sonic space of the low-register drone, played by the *Volgan* and the *Grob,* the latter sometimes doubled down an octave by the *Fladdergrob.*[28] Timpani would also participate as a matter of course. Bendinelli suggests that each player in the ensemble enter in turn, from bottom to top, and further suggests the option of antiphonal performance by two groups of trumpeters. The gradual buildup that the single entries afford is echoed on a much more dramatic scale by the acceleration of the figuration in the course of the works.

The ceremonial use of this kind of ensemble practice seems self-evident. But it was not only within the confines of ceremonial function that the trumpet ensemble found an outlet. Concerted church music by early-seventeenth-century German composers used the trumpet ensemble as well. Heinrich Schütz's expansive psalm motet *Danket dem Herren* (*Psalmen Davids,* 1619) provides only one notated trumpet part, though it bears the plural heading *Parte per le Trombette. à 13. Mit Trommeten und Heerpaucken,* with the implication that the traditional ensemble participates.[29] Similarly, Praetorius's popular *In dulci jubilo* from the *Polyhymnia caduceatrix et panegyrica* (1619) includes among its performance options two versions with multiple trumpets, one the traditional multiregister trumpet ensemble.[30] Other examples include the earliest such usage, Reimundo Ballestra's *Missa con le trombe* (before 1616), as well as psalm settings from the now lost *Gaudium Christianum* (1617) by Michael Altenburg and Christoph Straus's *Missa Veni Sponsa Christi.*[31]

The use of solo trumpet(s) in the seventeenth century was impressively large and is well documented by modern writers.[32] Surprisingly few examples, however, are for trumpet and continuo alone. Fantini's celebrated treatise of 1638 contains over fifty short dance movements, often in varied sections, and eight more substantial sonatas for trumpet and organ. These pieces comprise the trumpet's first substantial solo entry into the realm of "art" music. Fantini's solo sonatas find an echo in the more developed two sonatas for trumpet and continuo by G. B. Viviani (1678). In our own day, the combination of solo trumpet and organ has proved to be very popular, but given the paucity of seventeenth-century examples—Fantini, Viviani, and only a few others—it seems historically a much less favored combination. Prior to Fantini, the trumpet was occasionally called for in small concerted ensembles. Schütz, under the influence of his Venetian study with Monteverdi, wrote collections of

Symphoniae sacrae for several voices and obbligato instruments. The concerto *Buccinate in neomenia tuba* (Bk I, 1629), taking its lead from the opening psalm verse ("Blow up the trumpet in the new moon," Ps. 81/3), is scored for cornett, trumpet (or cornett), two tenors and bass, with basso continuo. The scoring is unusual for the time, though indeed strongly suggested by its text, and documents that the trumpet's ability to achieve a chamber-music intimacy was present from early in the century.

The trumpet's role in concerted music richly blossomed at Bologna in music associated with the vast basilica of San Petronio. The trumpet not only ensured a measure of ceremonial splendor within the basilical liturgy, but also offered a workable timbre within the very resonant acoustic of the building. The first published Bolognese trumpet works are three sonatas by Maurizio Cazzati (Op. 35, 1665), *maestro di cappella* at San Petronio from 1657 to 1671. Numerous compositions followed by composers such as Domenico Gabrielli, Giuseppe Maria Iacchini, Petronio Franceschini, and a particularly large number by Giuseppe Torelli.[33] These works are important not only in context of the growth of the trumpet repertory, but also in solidifying the structural principles of the concerto. The trumpet idiom, owing to its associative meanings and its melodic constraints, was well defined: triadic figures and vigorous dactylic rhythms in the spirit of fanfares were typical (see Ex. 7.1). However, the string ensemble obviously commanded a

EXAMPLE 7.1a. Petronio Franceschini: Sonata in D, mvt. 2

EXAMPLE 7.1b. Maurizio Cazzati: Sonata 5, *La Caprara* Op. 35, no. 10, mvt. 1

EXAMPLE 7.1c. Cazzati: *La Caprara,* mvt. 4

more diverse vocabulary. Accordingly, it is not surprising that here in the Baroque trumpet concerto the ritornello principle, with its characteristic thematic distinctions between tutti and soli, receives important formation. The trumpet fanfare idiom, though characteristic, by no means gives the full range of the trumpet's expression. In Franceschini's Sonata, for example, the opening movement finds the solo trumpets exchanging elegant melodic arches; the third movement is a lamentative cantabile in the unusual minor dominant[34] (see Ex. 7.2).

EXAMPLE 7.2. Petronio Franceschini: Sonata in D: (a) mvt. 1; (b) mvt. 3.

A proper survey of the seventeenth-century repertory—well beyond the scope of this chapter—would note at length the rich Austro-Bohemian school including works by Heinrich Biber and P. J. Vejvanovský, the wide use of the trumpet in England, especially by Henry Purcell in both church and theater, and also in several imaginative trumpet songs with solo voice, and the highly emblematic use of the trumpet in French ceremonial music by Jean-Baptiste Lully and Marc-Antoine Charpentier, among others.

Playing Techniques

Seventeenth-century playing techniques differ considerably from those of the modern player. And while the absence of valves is a dramatically visible difference, concerns of articulation, dynamics, ornamentation, intonation, and nonharmonic tones invited and continue to invite comment.

Articulation

Trumpet articulation, like that of other wind instruments of the day, favored a hierarchical system of alternating syllables with different stress and weight. Fantini, for example, offers a number of patterns in which generally *l* and *t* are strong, *r* syllables weak. His patterns include the equivalent of both the modern slur (*tia tia*) and double-tonguing (*teghe teghe*). Interesting, too, is the importance of vowels in shaping the articulation.

le	ra	le	ra	li	ru	li
ta	te	ta	ta	ti	ta	ta
ti	ri	ti	ri	ti	ri	di
la	le	ra	la	la	la	la
te	ghe	te	ghe	te	ghe	di
lal	de	ra	de	ra	de	ra

ti	a	ti	a	da
la	la	le	ra	la
di	a	di	a	da
ta	ra	te	re	da
le	ra	le	ra	la
ti	ri	ti	ri	da[35]

These patterns are reserved for faster-moving, diatonic motion. Once again, they are common to all wind instruments of the day and are based on an important inequality of attack through which the hierarchy of strong and weak beat is conveyed. The association of the syllables with the trumpet is underscored by Praetorius's nomenclative reference to the trumpet as "in vulgar Latin, taratantara."[36] Similarly, in the famous sixteenth-century program chanson by Janequin, *La Guerre: Escoutez tous gentilz,* the sounds of battle are vocally imitated, replete with "Ta ri ra ri ra ri ra ri" for the vocal "trumpets."[37]

Dynamics

The subtle vocal quality of many of the tonguing patterns above is well served by a soft dynamic, fully within the purview of the Baroque trumpeter. The French music encyclopedist Marin Mersenne observes that:

> [T]hose who know how to sound them [trumpets] perfectly decrease the sound as much as they wish by simply moderating the wind, which they disperse with so much variety that they imitate the softest echo and take away boredom and the desire to hear the softness of the lute and other instruments in those who love harmony.[38]

Similarly, in a 1691/2 description of St. Cecilia's Day festivities in London, John Shore is praised for his soft playing: "While the company is at table the hautboys and trumpets play successively. Mr Showers hath taught the latter of late years to sound with all the softness imaginable. . . ."[39] And Altenburg, with undisguised pride, describes his trumpeter father, Johann Caspar:

His tone in clarion playing and the various modulations thereof, which he was able to join skillfully with a singing, flowing character, his ease in the high and low [registers], his expression of the manifold ornaments, and his execution were, without false praise, something ingeneous and outstanding. Clarino playing was not at all difficult for him, and he was capable of delivering it so softly that it could scarcely be heard, yet each individual tone was clearly audible.[40]

The ability to play softly is an important component of solo clarino playing. The trumpet ensemble, on the other hand, was perhaps less given to soft extremes. In *Syntagma musicum* III, Praetorius tellingly advises conductors to speed up the tempo when the trumpets play, because the breath requirements, presumably from loud playing, make them rush. More telling is his suggestion that the trumpet ensemble be placed *nahe bey der Kirche* for purposes of balance. The phrase *nahe bey der Kirche* in its most straightforward reading suggests that the trumpeters are placed outside the church. Hans Lampl has suggested, however, that *Kirche* here may refer not to the church itself, but rather to the *Hauptkirche* or nave, in which case the trumpeters would remain within the building, but removed from the choir.[41]

Ornamentation

The trumpeter, like other musicians in the seventeenth century, sought elegance and grace through ornamentation. Among trumpet sources, Fantini is particularly explicit about the rendition of three ornaments: the *groppo*, the *trillo*, and the here unnamed *messa di voce*. The *groppo* and *trillo* are both commonly cadential ornaments, the former a rapid alternation of two pitches, the latter quick reiterations of a single pitch. (The *trillo* was extensively employed in early monodic singing, and its presence in Fantini reminds us of the degree to which instrumental practice followed vocal models.) Fantini writes: "Finding a *groppo*, one should articulate it with a pointed tongue, whereas the *trillo* is performed with the strength of the chest and articulated with the throat, and can be executed on all the notes of said instrument."[42] Also borrowed from vocal practice is the *messa di voce*. Applied to long notes, it offers a dynamic swell and decay that gracefully shapes the sound. On cadential resolutions it provides a satisfying, rounded "sinking in"—in feel perhaps not unlike the balletic *plié*. Fantini describes it thus:

[W]herever notes of one, of two, or of four beats length are found, they should be held in a singing fashion, by starting softly, making a crescendo until the middle of the note, and [then] making a diminuendo on the second half [of the note] until the end of the beat, so that it may hardly be heard; and in doing this, one will render perfect harmony.[43]

The gracing of long notes is obscurely discussed by Bendinelli, who advises the trumpeter to "learn then to lead his chin [together] with the notes of each register. This is called 'accenting the trumpet,' which gives it elegance."[44] He indicates this with dots placed under whole notes and breves throughout the trumpet range. Tarr has suggested that this "leading the chin" involves "the slight alteration of the vowel sound on a given note by means of chin motion."[45] Perhaps Bendinelli is describing a kind of chin vibrato, and the dots underneath the notes represent the vibrato's pulsations.

Intonation and Nonharmonic Tones

The natural trumpet of the seventeenth century, because of its reliance on the overtone series, presents a number of challenges to the player in terms of intonation and in playing notes outside of the overtone series. The seventh, eleventh, thirteenth, and fourteenth partials (b♭', f", a", and b♭") are problematic in varying degrees: the b♭s are slightly low, the f" very sharp, the a" very flat. The problems of the eleventh and the thirteenth partials were well known. Charles Burney, for instance, in commenting on an oratorio by Alessandro Scarlatti, writes:

> Among the songs of a different cast, there is one, accompanied by a trumpet, in which the beauties and true genius of that instrument have been studied, and all its defects avoided, by using only the key-note, the second, third, and fifth of the key, all which are sustained so long, that if the fourth and sixth [i.e., the eleventh and thirteenth partials] had been equally employed, the harmony would have been intolerable.[46]

Although these pitches were obviously problematic, the f and the a are demonstrably "lippable" in tune, as is the f to f♯, and we may assume that this was a mainstream technique. As Altenburg puts it, "One must necessarily try to correct them [the out-of-tune pitches] by using a skilled embouchure and a proper amount of exertion, if one wishes rightfully to deserve [to be called] artistic and expert."[47]

The same technique of "lipping" comes into play in rendering notes outside the harmonic series. Such notes occur generally in quick passing contexts, as the illustrations from Fantini's sonatas show (see Ex. 7.3). Fantini's ability to play between the overtones is now well known, thanks to its description by Mersenne. Mersenne relied on the evidence of a

EXAMPLE 7.3. Girolamo Fantini: Sonata No. 5, *detta dell'Adimari*.

French physician, Pierre Bourdelot, who heard Fantini and the great Roman organist Girolamo Frescobaldi play together in Rome. French trumpeters in Rome at the time described the nonharmonic tones played by Fantini as "false, confused, and entirely disordered."[48]

The difficulties of lipping have prompted modern trumpet makers to introduce antinodal finger holes that, when opened, place the trumpet in a different overtone series, one in which the problem notes of f and a are in tune and secure. Moreover, to counteract the general precariousness of the natural trumpet, other finger holes are often supplied that eliminate alternately the even or odd partials, thus dramatically reducing the risk of the intended note being replaced by a too-near neighbor.[49] The use of finger holes radically compromises the historicity of the instrument, for they have not been documented earlier than the late eighteenth century.[50]

The technical perfection of modern recordings and their influence on concert standards have nurtured this compromise, ironically while at the same time commodifying historical "authenticity." Given this context, few players dare the concert stage or recording studio with "fully natural" trumpets, despite their having developed a formidable technique that, one suspects, extends well enough to "lipping" in private. Historicity need not supplant musical goals, however, for us to suspect that a less compromised historical technique and instrument, as with other manifestations of historically informed performance, have much to offer our modern performances of seventeenth-century music.

In 1976 Jeremy Montagu wrote an article entitled "Choosing brass instruments" in the then relatively young journal *Early Music*. He advises that "those looking for accurate copies of old instruments [trumpets] . . . will find that only one firm is worth looking at. . . . Players seeking instruments for clarino playing can only go to Meinl und Lauber of Geretsried in Germany."[51] These instruments, made under the guidance of Edward Tarr, were the unrivaled choice and of enormous influence in the revival of the Baroque trumpet. In the over twenty years since Montagu wrote, many other makers of all stamps have joined the field, offering a wide array of instruments with varying degrees of historical detail. The American trumpeter Fred Holmgren gives a helpful survey of modern choices in his article "Stalking the Valveless Trumpet."[52]

The Horn

By 1700 the trumpet commanded a large and impressive repertory and was supported by a rich tradition of instrument making, especially from Nuremberg. The same was not true for the horn. In fact, it is only around 1700 that we glimpse the beginnings of the artful use of the horn and the development of its "concert" form in the Viennese *Waldhorn*.

Hunting horns in the sixteenth century took two shapes, namely the snail-like helical form[53]—what Mersenne calls the *cors à plusiers tours*—and the smaller crescent-shaped *trompe Dufouilloux,* with its characteristic small loop of tubing halfway between mouthpiece and bell.[54] This latter form served well the traditional monotonic hunting calls of the field and long remained in use in that context. Horace Fitzpatrick observes that in the first part of the seventeenth century, these two forms seem to have merged in an instrument that combines the "hoop of one and the long conical tube of the other," an instrument like those in mid-century tapestries at Fontainebleau and the Louvre.[55] This circular *trompe de chasse*[56] may well have been of French origin—significantly, an English advertisement for the trumpet maker William Bull from 1682 refers to the availability of "French Horns"[57]—and in the early 1680s it made a striking impression on Franz Anton, Count von Sporck, a nobleman zealous in his pursuits of music and hunting. The count was so taken with the sound that he had some of his own players trained in playing the *trompe de chasse* and transplanted the instrument and technique to his native Bohemia. There the sound of the hunt eventually became a refined, prized timbre in the orchestra. An important component in this transformation was the change the instrument undertook at the hands of builders Johannes and Michael Leichnamschneider in Vienna, ca. 1700. The Leichnamschneider *Waldhorn,* with its larger-bored tubing, wider-throated, more conical bell, and darker tone, set the standard for the eighteenth-century orchestral horn.[58]

The German-Bohemian affinity for the instrument may be seen in the early appearance of several horn works there in the last part of the seventeenth century, including a *Sonata da Caccia con un Cornu* from the Kremsier archives—dating from the 1670s, this sonata would importantly predate Count von Sporck's importation of the horn—and a *Concerto à 4* by Johann Beer.[59] Earlier in the century, the horn—perhaps in its helical form—was occasionally used in theatrical performances to establish a hunting theme through simple fanfares, as seen in Cavalli's *Le nozze di Tèti e di Peleo* (1639/54) and Lully's music for *La princesse d'Elide* (1664).[60] Early-eighteenth-century scoring for the horn was also in context of opera, as seen in Carlo Badia's *Diana rappacificata* (1700) and Reinhard Keiser's *Octavia* (1705).[61]

NOTES

1. Don L. Smithers reminds us that "military engagements during the seventeenth century were often won or lost depending on the ability of cavalry to manoeuver quickly according to orders relayed by trumpet calls. The trumpet has been likened in this respect to the use of the walkie-talkie in World War II." See Smithers–Baroque Trumpet after 1721, 358.
2. See Altenburg–*Essay*, 43. Altenburg urges the trumpeter to be alert in rendering this duty: he should not let the enemy learn anything damaging from him, but he should

keep his eyes open to discover something about the enemy (44–45)! Altenburg's treatise is one of the most important descriptive sources for the Baroque trumpet. Although its late date of 1795 would seem to remove it from the scope of this study, his essay is frequently a retrospective account of traditional practices.

3. Ibid, 26.
4. Tarr–*Trumpet*, 95–98. See also Smithers–Hapsburg, 84–95; and Altenburg–*Essay*, chapters 5 and 6.
5. Moore–Venezia, 323–24; 345–46.
6. Altenburg–*Essay*, 24.
7. See Fantini–*Method*, 2. For a facsimile edition, see Fantini–*Modo*. For a recent biographical study, see Conforzi–Fantini, 159–73.
8. See Smithers–*Baroque Trumpet*, 192.
9. See Lampl–Translation, 226. For a facsimile edition, see Praetorius–*Syntagma*.
10. See *New Grove*–Orologio, Alessandro, by Keith Polk. Cf. Smithers–*Baroque Trumpet*, 168, where Orologio appears as *Kapellmeister* from 1606.
11. The standard discussion of the Nuremberg brass makers is Wörthmüller–Nürnberger. Recently Barclay (*Trumpet-Maker*) has based his important discussion of the craft on their practice. Regarding the development of bell profiles, see ibid., 22–24, and Tarr–*Trumpet*, 101–02. Altenburg–*Essay* states that "those [trumpets] made by J. W. Haas in Nuremberg and set with angel-heads are commonly held to be the best" (10).
12. Ibid., 9–10.
13. See, for example, the interesting chart in Baines–*Brass*, 125.
14. Montagu–*Instruments*, 31.
15. Halfpenny–William Bull, 20–21. See also his Trumpet Mouthpieces, 78. In the latter source, Halfpenny suggests that distinctions between high- and low-register mouthpieces, if they can be made at all, might exist in tubular shanks versus tapered backbores, the latter favoring the high register (80).
16. Altenburg–*Essay*, 80. The issue of mouthpieces has on occasion prompted considerable discussion, a notable example of which is "Mouthpieces for Historical 'Brass' Instruments," *Cornett and Sackbut*, no. 1 (February 1979): 4–23. This article brings together the sometimes strong views of scholars and players, including Montagu, Tarr, and Smithers. I am grateful to my colleague Timothy Collins for bringing this interesting example to my attention.
17. The term *Cammerton* takes on different meanings at different times and places. For a review of this issue, see the chapter "Pitch and Transposition" by Herbert Myers, in this volume.
18. Praetorius–*Syntagma* II–Blumenfeld, 33. He later states that some favor tunings a half step or whole step lower than C.
19. Dahlqvist–Pitches, 29–41, and *Bidrag*, 562–63. Significantly, owing to the vagaries of changing pitch standards, the seventeenth-century C *Cammerton* described by Praetorius would become the eighteenth-century D *Cammerton* or E♭ *tief Cammerton*. See Dahlqvist–Pitches, 32.
20. Praetorius–*Syntagma* III (trans. Blumenfeld): 33.
21. Quoted in Dahlqvist–Reiche's Instrument, 179.
22. Altenburg–*Essay*, 13–14.
23. For a defense of its employment, see Smithers–Baroque Trumpet after 1721. In response, see Dahlqvist–Corno, 40–42.
24. The earliest sources for this kind of trumpet ensemble—Bendinelli–*Trombetta* and notebooks by two German trumpeters at the Danish court, Magnus Thomsen and Hendrich Lübeck—derive from the end of the sixteenth century; shortly thereafter this type of ensemble was described in detail by Praetorius in *Syntagma* III; its most celebrated "composed" manifestation is the opening toccata to Monteverdi's *Orfeo* (1607). Despite this clustering of sources around the turn of the century, the practice

in all likelihood had been in existence for some time. See Downey–Correspondence, 325–29. For a survey of the musical sources, see Hiller–*Trumpets*.

25. Cf. D. Altenburg–*Untersuchungen*, 358–60.

26. For a facsimile edition of Bendinelli, see Bendinelli–*Trombetta*; for a modern edition of Thomsen and Lübeck, Schünemann–*Trompeterfanfaren*. For a discussion of this repertory, see Downey–Trumpet.

27. Smithers–*Music and History*, 344.

28. Daniel Speer suggests that this fundamental low C is best played with a trombone (*Quart-Posaune*) mouthpiece. Cited in Altenberg–*Untersuchungen*, 363.

29. See *Heinrich Schütz: Sämtliche Werke*, ed. Philip Spitta (Leipzig, 1885–94, 1909, 1927), 3: xv.

30. See Boudreaux–Praetorius, 223.

31. Tarr–*Trumpet*, 102, and Downey–*Trumpet and Its Role* 3: 1–63; 252–303.

32. For detailed discussion, see Smithers–*Baroque Trumpet*, and Tarr–*Trumpet*.

33. For detailed discussion of the Bolognese school, see Schnoebelen–San Petronio and Enrico–*San Petronio*. The soloistic use of the trumpet within the liturgy was earlier essayed at Vienna. See Riedel–*Kirchenmusik*.

34. The restriction of the trumpet to the overtone series not only restricted harmonic modulation but also discouraged minor tonalities. The minor dominant was enabled by the seventh partial of the overtone series. Tonic minor required moving outside the overtone series by the process of "lipping" (described below). Although tonic minor is rare, one of its more conspicuous appearances is in Purcell's "Hail, Bright Cecilia" (1692). In the aria "The Fife and All Harmony of War," Purcell requires the trumpets to "set up" the final cadence with a striking, strong-beat, minor-third scale degree.

35. Fantini–*Modo*, 10–11. For an instructive discussion of wind articulation, including a comparative table, see Dickey, Leonards, and Tarr–Bismantova, 172–77.

36. Praetorius–*Syntagma* II: 32.

37. Clement Janequin, *Chansons Polyphoniques* (Monaco, 1965) 1, 23–53.

38. Mersenne–*Harmonie universelle* (trans. Chapman), 330.

39. *The Gentleman's Journal* (January 1691/2) in Husk–*Account*, 28–29.

40. Altenburg–*Essay*, 62.

41. Praetorius, *Syntagma* III: 170.

42. Fantini–*Method*, 3. Fantini's fully articulated *groppo* forms an important contrast with the later normative slurred trill.

43. Ibid., 3.

44. See Bendinelli–*Trumpet*, 4.

45. Ibid., 10.

46. See Burney–*History of Music* 2: 585.

47. Altenburg–*Essay*, 72. Although tuning the eleventh and thirteenth partials are the major challenges of intonation, one should also be aware of the difficulties of playing the natural trumpet with equal-tempered instruments. This is especially noticeable in the conflicting size of major thirds.

48. See Conforzi–Fantini, 164. Regarding the lipping of nonharmonic tones in England, see Downey–Pepys, and in response, Pinnock/Wood–Counterblast, and Holman–English Trumpets, 443.

49. The German system associated with instruments made by Adolf Egger & Son of Basel and Meinl und Lauber of Geretsried (now Ewald Meinl), originally developed by Otto Steinkopf in 1960, is a three-hole system: a thumb vent transposes the harmonic series a fourth, thus tuning the problematic f and a; two additional finger holes eliminate the odd and even partials, respectively. The English, as seen on instruments by Stephen Keavy, have developed a four-hole system with a separate hole each for f, a, the odd partials, and the even partials. In some passages this may buy security at the high price of a complex finger technique.

50. A handsome silver trumpet by William Shaw of London, dated 1787, is the earliest example. See Halfpenny–Harmonic Trumpet. Halfpenny suggests that the vents were used here for a quick change to the dominant tonality or for ease of high notes.
51. Montagu–Choosing, 36.
52. Holmgren–Stalking, 5–8.
53. Two examples of helical horns from the late sixteenth/early seventeenth centuries were discovered in the Staatliches Historiches Museum in Dresden. Several art works depict them as well, including the famous *Allegoria dell' udito* by Jan Breughel. See Morley-Pegge–*French Horn*, 11–12.
54. So called because of its depiction in Jacques du Fouilloux's hunting treatise *La vénerie*.
55. Fitzpatrick–*Horn*, 3–4.
56. As Dahlqvist observes, the cognate Italian term *tromba da caccia* indicates the horn as well. See Dahlqvist–Corno, 40, and Reiche's Instrument, 181–82.
57. See Morley-Pegge–*French Horn*, 17.
58. Fitzpatrick–*Horn*, 11–44.
59. Hiebert–Horn, 4.
60. Transcribed in Morley-Pegge–*French Horn*, 80–81.
61. G. F. Handel's presence in Hamburg at the time of *Octavia*'s premiere is significant, as he would later introduce the horn in England in his *Water Music* (1717).

BIBLIOGRAPHY

Altenburg–*Essay*; Barclay–*Trumpet Maker*; Bendinelli–*Trombetta*; Fantini–*Modo*; Fitzpatrick–*Horn*; Morley-Pegge–*Horn*; Smithers–*Baroque Trumpet*; Tarr–*Trumpet*; Worthmüller–Nürnberger.

Suggested Listening

Baroque & Brass. Haarlem Trumpet Consort; Friedemann Immer, trumpet. Teldec 842977.

Baroque Masterpieces for Trumpet and Organ, vol 3. Edward H. Tarr, trumpet, and George Kent, organ. Nonesuch H-71358.

Giuseppe Torelli: The Complete Trumpet Works. Per-Olov Lindeke, David Staff, Edward Tarr, Gabriele Cassone, Stephen Keavy, and Robert Farley, trumpets; Capella Musicale di San Petronio (Sergio Vartolo). Bongiovanni BG 5523-24-25-2.

Italian Baroque Trumpet Music. Stephen Keavy and Crispian Steele-Perkins, trumpets; Parley of Instruments (Peter Holman). Hyperion CDA66255.

Italian Masterworks for Organ and Trumpet. Edward H. Tarr, trumpet and Irmtraud Krüger, organ. Christophorus CHR 77145.

Music for Trumpet & Orchestra. Crispian Steele-Perkins, trumpet; Tafelmusik (Jeanne Lamon). Sony Vivarte SK 53 365.

Trompetenkonzerte des italienischen Barock. Friedemann Immer and Graham Nicolson, trumpets; Concerto Köln. Musikproduktion Dabringhaus und Grimm MD+G L3271.

Trumpet Collection. Jonathan Impett, trumpet; The Clarion Ensemble. Amon Ra CD-SAR 30.

8

Percussion and Timpani

John Michael Cooper

The seventeenth century marks a curious period in the history of percussion instruments. On the one hand, the usage and performance techniques of most percussion instruments apparently remained quite stable during these years. By contrast, the kettledrums or timpani, virulently condemned by Sebastian Virdung in 1511 as "the ruination of all sweet melodies and of all music,"[1] were transformed from strictly outdoor, military instruments into an important component of concerted-music ensembles, particularly in sacred music. Because of these disparate evolutions we will consider the performance practices and musical styles associated with percussion instruments outside the kettledrum family only in general terms,[2] concentrating on the developments in musical style that shaped the literature and performance practices of the timpani.

Percussion

Seventeenth-century sources generally corroborate Benjamin Harms's assertion that the construction and performance practices of most percussion instruments have changed relatively little in the centuries since the instruments' first appearance.[3] Two of the most important seventeenth-century authors who discuss instruments outside the kettledrum family are French (Marin Mersenne, 1636, and Pierre Trichet, ca. 1640[4]), yet where percussion instruments and techniques are concerned these writers concur to a remarkable extent not only with previous treatises, but also with their German contemporary Michael Praetorius.[5] Indeed, the most important differences lie in the authors' views on the merits of individual instruments. The French authors devote considerable space to a variety of percussion instruments, whereas Praetorius states that there is no need to discuss what he considers the "ragamuffin instruments" (*lumpen-instrumenta*)—including cymbals, cowbells, strawfiddles, hand cymbals, handbells, tambourines, field drums, anvils, and various Turkish instruments—because they "do not really belong in music."[6]

This situation necessitates three important observations about perceptions and usages of the non-kettledrum percussion instruments in the seventeenth century. First, most verbal descriptions inevitably reflect French practices and tastes; concerning German opinions we have only Praetorius's dismissal and the fortunately detailed (and for the time, remarkably ethnomusicological) illustrations provided in the *Theatrum instrumentorum* at the end of his *De Organographia* (1619; see Figs. 8.1 and 8.2). Second, the fact that Praetorius's *lumpen-instrumenta,* with the exception of strawfiddles, were all traditionally used in military music suggests that the rhythms used in playing these instruments might well have reflected the performance traditions of military music, which Praetorius and other theorists clearly do not consider true music. Finally, the late seventeenth century seems to have witnessed the emergence of somewhat distinct national drumming styles in military music, and this development would have influenced percussion instrumentation employed in any given piece on a specific occasion.[7]

Frame Drums: Hand Drum and Tambourine

These instruments, generally consisting of a cylindrical frame with a skin stretched across one end or (more seldom) both, are discussed by Trichet and illustrated by Mersenne and Praetorius.[8] Information on the construction of the hand drums is limited to the explanation that the shell was usually made of wood and covered with some sort of skin; occasionally a snare was stretched across the bottom skin of the two-headed hand drum. These drums might be between two and five inches deep and six and fourteen inches across.[9]

Mersenne describes the tambourine as the *tambour de Bisquaye* and states that it consists of pairs of jingles (thin plates of metal or white iron) suspended on leather strings spanning slots cut into the shell; Trichet associates it with the Basques and their neighbors the Béarnois, and describes it as being about twelve inches across, shaped like a sieve or sifter.[10]

Hand drums and tambourines alike were played with the hand, not sticks or beaters. Hand drums probably made use of the same variety of techniques still employed today, using different parts of the hand and different types of finger strokes. Mersenne states only that the tambourine is played with the fingers; Trichet specifies that it is held in the left hand

FIGURE 8.1. Praetorius, *Syntagma musicum* II, *Theatrum instrumentarum*, plate 23: field timpani (1); field drums (2); Swiss fipple flute (3); anvil (4). From Michael Praetorius, *Syntagma musicum*, vol. 2, Bärenreiter edition. Bärenreiter Music Corporation, Englewood, NJ. Reprinted by permission.

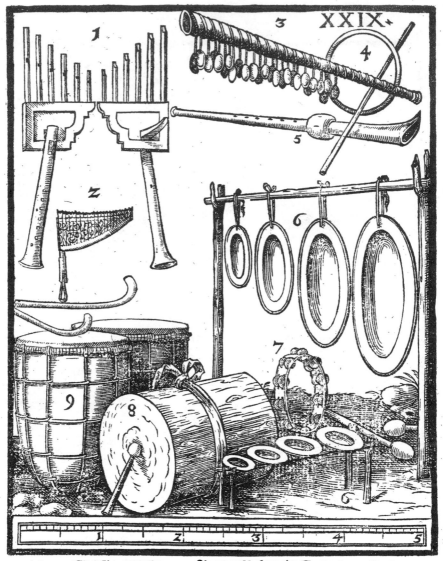

r. 2. Sind Satyri Pfeiffen . 3. Americanisch Horn oder Trommet. 4. Ein Ring so bey
den Americanern gleich wie ein Triangel geschlagen wird. 5. Americanische Schalmey. 6. Becken/
darauff die Americaner/ wie bey vns auff Glocken/spielen. 7. Ein Ring mit Schellen/ die sie in die hö.
uffwerffen vnd wiederfangen/ etc. 8. 9. Americanische Trummeln.

FIGURE 8.2. Praetorius, *Syntagma musicum* II, *Theatrum instrumentarum,* plate 29:
satyr pipes (1 and 2); American horn or trumpet (3); A ring, played by the
Americans in the way we [Germans] play the triangle (4); American shawm
(5); cymbals, upon which the Americans play in the way we play bells (6); A ring
with jingles, which they throw into the air and catch again (7); American drums
(8 and 9). From Michael Praetorius, *Syntagma musicum*, vol. 2, Bärenreiter edition. Bärenreiter Music Corporation, Englewood, NJ. Reprinted by permission.

and played with agile movements of the fingers of the right hand.[11] Though contemporary sources provide no clear indication of the musical contexts in which hand drums and tambourines were used, one might assume that both were employed in dance music (especially since there have evidently been no fundamental changes in performance technique such as those that might result from use of the instrument in a different stylistic context).

Two-headed Cylindrical Drums: Field Drum and Tabor

The principal differences between these drums and the hand drums were their dimensions, the manner in which they were struck, and their functions. In addition, there evidently was a substantial difference in function between the field drum and the tabor, though the construction was similar.

The most detailed description of the field drum is provided by Trichet, who states that it was normally used by the French in warfare as elsewhere and could be as much as two feet long and almost as wide. Each end was to be covered with a strong hide that was fastened near the rim by means of hoops, which in turn were bound to the hoops at the other end of the shell by means of cords. One head was to be spanned by a double string (snare), which preferably was made of gut, and the other head struck by two sticks, the size of which varied according to the dimensions of the drum.[12]

Mersenne illustrates two varieties of field drum. In the first, the tension on the rim of each head is adjusted by means of a counterhoop, whose suspension is controlled by tightening or loosening a node located on one side of the shell; a similar node on the other side of the shell was used to adjust the other head. The relatively precise tuning facilitated by this mechanism led Mersenne to discuss the use of field drums (not just timpani) in choirs of four or more, and to use this pitch differentiation in his sample rhythms for the drum (see Ex. 8.1).[13]

Mersenne's second variety of field drum (evidently corresponding to that discussed by Trichet) provides for no such flexibility in tuning the heads; they are attached directly to one another. Mersenne associates this drum with a pair of cymbals almost identical to modern ones and leaves no doubt as to his lack of respect for the two instruments, stating that the greatest pleasure they afforded consisted in the interest they held for artists and scientists.[14]

The tabor was generally used along with a pipe, the two instruments played by a single person. It was suspended from the elbow, forearm, or wrist of one person and played with a single stick; the other hand was used on the three finger holes of a fipple flute. Sebastian Virdung stated in 1511 that this combination was common among the French and the Dutch;

EXAMPLE 8.1. Mersenne, *Harmonie universelle,* drum rhythms.

Trichet stated only that it was common among the French.[15] Since Mersenne and Trichet prescribed that the dimensions of cylindrical drums corresponded to the sticks used, and since the tabor was played with only one stick, the tabor itself probably tended to be smaller than field drums.

Other Nonpitched Percussion Instruments: Cymbals, Triangles, Castanets, and Clappers

Mersenne's derogatory reference to cymbals marks the only appearance of platelike cymbals in seventeenth- and eighteenth-century writings on percussion.[16] By contrast, the seventeenth-century preference seems to have been for small, handheld cymbals, each shaped like a small bowl. To judge from the illustrations provided by Praetorius and Mersenne, the diameter of these cymbals was not much greater than the span of the hand—perhaps six to eight inches.[17]

Mersenne stated that triangles were held suspended in the left hand and struck with a beater held in the right; they could be made of silver, brass, and all other metals, but ordinarily steel was used because of its "more piercing, merry, and exciting sound." Around the bottom edge should be suspended a series of circular rings made of the same metal as the triangle itself.[18]

Mersenne and Trichet also mention castanets and clappers—groups of two or three pieces of metal or wood joined at one end and free to clap against one another at the ends. Both authors were impressed by the rapid diminutions possible on these instruments, stating that this effect "defied the imagination."[19] Trichet associated the castanets specifically with the Spanish, and Mersenne implied this association by stating that they were frequently used with the guitar; one might assume that they could also be used outside the context of music in the Spanish style, but no direct evidence to this effect seems to have survived.

Strawfiddle and Bells

The brittle tone of the strawfiddle or *Strohfiedel* (a xylophone with a single row of wooden bars resting on a wooden frame and supported by a bed of straw to keep the frame from damping the vibrations altogether) is aptly testified to by the instrument's appearance in Hans Holbein's terrifying sixteenth-century woodcut series *Bilder des Todes* (1532/1538).[20] Apparently, however, Holbein's feelings were not universally held in the seventeenth century: Praetorius illustrated a similar instrument with fifteen graduated bars, and Mersenne stated that it provided as much pleasure as any other musical instrument, illustrating and discussing a Flemish variety consisting of seventeen bars, the highest of which was tuned a seventeenth higher than the lowest. Mersenne also reports that the longest bars were about ten inches long and suggests that they should be made of a "resonant wood such as beech" (though any number of other materials could be used, including other woods as well as brass, silver, and stones).[21]

But for Mersenne, bells were the most excellent of all percussion instruments: to them are devoted fully forty-seven of the sixty pages on percussion in the Book on Instruments. These bells, however, are not a series of graduated metal bars arranged according to pitch (the modern glockenspiel or orchestral bells), but traditional bells suspended with the open end down and struck by a clapper. In addition, the Italians G. B. Ariosti (b. 1688) and G. Trioli (fl. 1695–1706) wrote compositions for the *sistro* or *timbale musicale,* a glockenspiel with twelve bars played with wooden hammers.

Timpani and Nakers

The Sources

The fundamental change in the role of the kettledrums in seventeenth-century musical life is reflected in their greater prominence in contemporary writings about music. In the sixteenth century and earlier, information concerning the instruments and their use in contemporary music was transmitted primarily through iconographic sources and passing remarks in contemporary accounts of festivals, processions, and the like. But the seventeenth century produced at least five substantial discussions of the drums in writings about music. These writings, together with iconographic evidence and the relatively few surviving specimens of seventeenth-century instruments, provide a clear and exciting view of the performance practices and literature of the drums during their crucial period of transition.

The implications of this improved source situation can be fully appreciated only against the backdrop of the role the drums played in earlier times. In general, the timpani had been ignored in treatises on music; the earliest substantial discussion was Sebastian Virdung's 1511 diatribe in *Musica getutscht*. Referring to the "tympanum of St. Jerome" discussed in the so-called "Dardanus letter" often cited in contemporary discussions of sacred music,[22] Virdung goes on to describe his contemporary timpani:

> Of this instrument [the tympanum of St. Jerome] I know absolutely nothing, for the thing one now calls "tympanum"—the large field kettledrum— is made of a copper kettle and covered with calfskin, and is struck with sticks in such a way that it thunders very loudly and brightly. . . . These drums . . . cause much unrest for the honorable, pious elders, for the infirm and the ailing, and for the worshippers in the monasteries who must read, study, and pray; and I believe and hold it for truth that the devil conceived and invented them, for there is nothing holy or even good about them; instead, they are the ruination and the oppression of all sweet melodies and of all music. Thus, I can be absolutely certain that this "tympanum" that was used in worshipping God must have been a completely different thing than the drums we use now, and that we are completely wrong to give the name to that devilish instrument, which is actually not worthy to be used in music . . . For if beating or rattling is to be music, then so must binders or coopers or those who make barrels also be musicians . . . [23]

The vehemence of Virdung's diatribe suggests that he was arguing against a practice that was gaining (or had already gained) some acceptance, as does the fact that he included the instruments at all. This impression seems to be corroborated by Michael Praetorius a century later. In volume 2 of *Syntagma musicum* (1619) the Wolfenbüttel Kapellmeister condemns the timpani in language strikingly similar to Virdung's discussion, but in volume 3 (published the same year) he suggests the drums' use, in the company of the trumpets, as a defining characteristic of the first of thirteen styles of arranging chorales and hymn tunes for polychoral ensembles. That Praetorius had so completely reversed his ideas on polychoral scoring techinques—an issue central to early-seventeenth-century musical style—within the space of a year seems unlikely; more probably, he was simply reluctant to contradict Virdung's authority directly in *De organographia*—a volume obviously conceived as a successor to *Musica getutscht*.[24]

After Praetorius we encounter two important French discussions of the drums: the "Livre des instruments" of Marin Mersenne's *Harmonie universelle* (1636) and Pierre Trichet's *Traité des instruments de musique* (ca. 1640). These are followed at century's end by Daniel Speer's important discussion of the timpani in his *Vierfaches musikalisches Kleeblatt* (1698).[25] In addition to providing information concerning the construction and design of the instruments and mallets themselves, these sources also reveal much about the way the drums were viewed in the seventeenth century and the musical contexts in which they were employed.

Finally, the seventeenth century provided a crucial source of information not available for the study of the drums during early periods: a multitude of actual scores and parts specifically designating the use of the timpani. The earliest known such work—Heinrich Schütz's setting of Psalm 136, performed in Dresden on 2 November 1617—was followed closely by Michael Praetorius's polychoral setting of the Christmas hymn *In dulci jubilo*, published in his *Polyhymnia caduceatrix et panegyrica* (Wolfenbüttel, 1618).[26] These works, both of which call for *ad libitum* realization of the timpani part, were followed in France at mid-century by a number of notated parts in the operas and ballets of Jean-Baptiste Lully. The 1680s witnessed the emergence of a number of notated parts in Austria—primarily Salzburg, where Andreas Hofer (1629–84) and H. I. F. Biber (1644–1704) composed numerous sacred works employing the drums, including Biber's so-called "Festival Mass" (1682), which was long misattributed to Orazio Benevoli (1605–72) and erroneously cited as the work used for the dedication of the Salzburg Cathedral in 1628.[27] In the closing decades of the century, notated timpani parts began to appear throughout Germany and Austria, thereby documenting the performance practices of the drums in the works of lesser-known composers such as Johann Philipp Krieger (1649–1725) and Philipp Heinrich Erlebach (1657–1714), as well as those of Sebastian Knüpfer (1633–76) and Johann Schelle (1648–1701). These notated parts, some of which are replete with annotations from the timpanists who performed them, supplement the vast number of references to occasions at which the timpani and trumpets were employed *ad libitum*, and they provide a luxuriously detailed outline of the drums' development.

Instruments and Mallets

Two commonly held misconceptions about the early timpani need to be corrected. First, the large kettledrums, with their screw-tightened heads and metal hemispherical kettles, are not (as is commonly believed) evolutionary descendants of the smaller nakers, whose heads were customarily lace-tightened and whose kettles, often as not, were made of wood or clay. Iconographic evidence clearly demonstrates that both varieties of drum—and a bewildering array of curious admixtures of their respective features—coexisted in both the East and West as far back as the thirteenth century. Moreover, small neck-laced kettledrums continued to be produced in what is now Western Europe up to the late nineteenth century—indicating, presumably, that they were still used in some musical contexts during that period. In other words, the timpani did not actually replace their supposed forebears; they merely occupied a more prominent position in the music that has been the subject of musicological and organological discussion (viz., orchestral music as opposed to, for example, dance-ensemble music).

More important for specific application in performance practice is the matter of the mallets used during the seventeenth century. Conventional wisdom has long held that the early timpani were played with wooden sticks, and that the idea for covered mallets was developed by Hector Berlioz—an assumption clearly reflected in numerous "original-instrument" recordings that reveal an unreasonably harsh timpani timbre. The assumption that the use of softer covered mallets was Berlioz's innovation may stem from Berlioz himself; like many of the composer's eminently quotable anecdotes, however, it is ultimately untenable.[28]

In fact, most seventeenth- and eighteenth-century writings concerned with the performance of concerted music discuss uncovered wooden sticks as the exception rather than the rule. Daniel Speer, for example, states that the heads of the mallets were "wrapped in the shape of a small wheel," and an anonymous author writing in Johann Adam Hiller's *Wöchentliche Nachrichten und Anmerkungen die Musik betreffend* in 1768 makes a similar remark, without indicating that the sound produced by such sticks was muffled rather than "usual."[29] The head of the mallet, according to these and other writers, could be either bead- or disc-shaped, but in most cases it was covered with leather, cloth, or wool. These possibilities seem to be corroborated by numerous illustrations that clearly suggest covered rather than unwrapped mallets.[30] Thus, the seventeenth- and eighteenth-century depictions of uncovered mallets in outdoor performance situations may well say more about the drums' use in those contexts than in the performance of concerted music.

Three aspects of the drums' construction merit discussion here. First, the modern timpanist uses heads of uniform texture and thickness, usually made from machine-honed aborted calfskin or (more commonly in the past twenty years) mylar or polyethylene terephthalate; the eighteenth-century timpanist, however, generally had to work with thicker, hand-scraped heads made from some variety of animal skin. Calfskin was probably the most common material for the heads (it is cited by both Virdung and Praetorius[31]), but other materials were used as well: Mersenne suggests sheepskin and advises against using muleskin, and the anonymous article in the 1768 *Nachrichten und Anmerkungen* states that muleskin and goatskin were also used.[32] Some sources (Speer and Eisel among them) suggest that the half-tanned heads were to be smeared with brandy or garlic and dried in the sun or at some distance from a small fire, but another anonymous eighteenth-century author quoted by Johann Ernst Altenburg in his *Versuch einer Anleitung zur heroisch-musikalischen Trompeter- und Pauker-Kunst* (Halle, 1770/1795) disagrees, suggesting that pure water could be used instead, without risk of corrosion.[33] Obviously, for modern performers the latter is more practical—a means of maintaining the humidity and tension of the head similar to the way calfskin bass-drum heads are rubbed down with water to prepare them for use in concerts.

Second, though early timpani were generally smaller than their modern counterparts, the variation in size was considerable, even if one sets aside the smallest drums as belonging to the family of nakers rather than timpani. In general, the diameter of the modern drums used for the range of pitches normally encountered in the Baroque timpani literature, G to d, ranges from twenty-five to thirty-two inches (a modern twenty-five-inch drum will reach the pitch of f—virtually unheard of in the Baroque literature). But Mersenne and Trichet speak of the largest early-seventeenth-century French drums as about twenty-four inches in diameter, and the scale provided in Praetorius's "Theatrum Instrumentarum" of *Syntagma musicum* II suggests diameters of approximately seventeen and twenty-four inches.[34] Even more interesting is that Mersenne, whose illustration reveals that his remarks concern neck-laced timpani apparently made of wood, prescribes that the pitch of the drums derived not so much from the tension on the heads as from the depths of the kettles.[35] The timpani were to be employed in choirs of anywhere from three to eight drums, the kettles of which were to be scaled according to Pythagorean pitch ratios. Thus, if the largest drum available had a diameter of twenty-four inches, a drum tuned a fourth higher would be eighteen inches in diameter and a drum tuned an octave higher would be twelve inches in diameter. This prescription reflects the continuation of an old tradition of using timpani choirs—a tradition that was first suggested in illustrations of Leonardo da Vinci and later developed into the use of multiple timpani in works by Johann Philipp Krieger (1649–1725), Christoph Graupner (1683–1756), Antonio Salieri (1750–1823), Antoine Reicha (1770–1836), and of course, Felix Mendelssohn (1809–47) and Hector Berlioz (1803–69).[36]

One final physical feature of the Baroque timpani merits description here: a device known as the *Schalltrichter* (literally, "sound-bell"), which was intended to increase the resonance of the drums. Similar in shape to the bell of a modern horn, the *Schalltrichter* was loosely mounted on the bottom inside of the kettle, extending upward into the interior of the drum from a small central hole at the bottom of the kettle. Surviving specimens clearly indicate that timpani continued to be made with the

143

Schalltrichter well into the nineteenth century, but since the device was first mentioned by Johann Philipp Eisel (who stated in 1738 that it was "currently in vogue"[37]), its use in the seventeenth century must remain a matter of conjecture. As we shall see, however, other aspects of early Baroque performance practice suggest that such a *Trichter* would have been useful already in the early seventeenth century.

Beating Spot

Equally profound differences were produced by one aspect of the Baroque timpanist's technique that has largely eluded scholarly attention: the different beating spot. The modern timpanist, whose drums for the Baroque repertoire range from twenty-five to thirty-two inches in diameter, typically strikes the head about one-fourth the distance from the edge to the center of the drum. This technique emphasizes the harmonically related modes of vibration and effects a relatively long decay time, thus providing maximum resonance and a rich harmonic spectrum for the nominal pitch. There is also one disadvantage, however: the fundamental is almost completely absent. The nominal, or perceived, pitch sounds one octave above the fundamental, with accompanying partials a fifth, an octave, and a tenth higher; in effect, then, the fundamental is suppressed by its longer-lasting and harmonically richer overtones.[38]

In contrast to modern practice, all available evidence indicates that the Baroque timpani were struck exactly in the center of the head or within a centimeter or two of the center—the only location at which the audible pitch is the fundamental. This beating spot produced a sound substantially different from that for which modern timpanists strive: the decay was virtually immediate, and the pitch was deprived of the clarifying effect provided by the upper partials.

The sound produced by beating in the center might seem extremely unmusical by modern standards. But when one considers that the timpani were first used only in outdoor military contexts (where the open air would render negligible any lengthier decay time produced by striking closer to the edge), and that the *Schalltrichter* was apparently introduced not long after it had become common to use the drums indoors (where a longer decay time and greater clarity of pitch would have made an appreciable difference in the musical effect of the drums), the different beating spot seems logical.

Further evidence makes the argument even more convincing. For example, it would have been infinitely easier for a horse-mounted timpanist to strike the center of the smaller drums than to place his strokes as prescribed by modern practice. Moreover, early iconographic evidence, which usually is notoriously fraught with contradictions and inconsistencies, almost without exception clearly shows the drums being struck at the center of the head. And finally, the *Schalltrichter* makes no discernible difference in the tone or pitch of the drums if one strikes in the modern beating spot; if the beating spot falls in the center of the head, however, the device makes an appreciable difference in tone and pitch. In other words, the peculiar "sound-bell" popular in the early eighteenth century was evidently introduced to compensate for the thuddy tone produced by striking at the center of the head—and it both corroborates the early beating spot and indicates that greater resonance became desirable as the drums were increasingly used indoors, in concerted music.[39]

For the modern timpanist using Baroque-style drums, this means that the heads should be much tighter than they would be if one were to play in the usual modern beating spot. Tuning should be done by striking the head just off center in order to produce the nominal pitch in the same octave as if one struck a modern drum closer to the edge. The *Schalltrichter* will increase the resonance and clarity of the pitches, but the tone will still have a substantially shorter decay time than the modern norm. This quicker decay in turn facilitates what is probably the most far-reaching difference between Baroque and modern performance techniques: the liberal embellishment of the notated parts.

Embellishments

Though contemporary documents show that timpani were a regular component of concerted-music ensembles whenever a festive, courtly, or military context was to be suggested, most composers seldom wrote out timpani parts. In France, however, a tradition of notated timpani parts arose around mid-century (initially in the works of Jean-Baptiste Lully, and then in the works of his successors at the royal court). These parts, in keeping with general French notational trends, are extremely detailed. Evidently, the drums were provided with a notated part whenever their use was desired,[40] and the specificity of the notation would have discouraged extensive *ad libitum* embellishment. Even the celebrated *Marche pour deux timballiers* (ca. 1685) by André Danican Philidor Sr. provides little room for embellishment, even though these pieces—surely designed as court entertainment—would have been a natural venue for virtuosic embellishment.

Outside France a different practice seems to have obtained. If any single trait can be identified as common to almost all seventeenth-century timpani parts notated outside Lully's domain, it is that these parts comprise mostly "white notes" or other notes of relatively long rhythmic duration, rather than the typically busy figurations of the French parts, or those of the remainder of the ensemble in the more florid textures in which the timpani commonly are used. But since even modern drums are incapable of projecting the full duration of a note through the activity of an entire ensemble without using a roll, one must conclude that the

Baroque timpanist was not expected to execute, for example, a notated whole note by simply striking the head and letting it ring. Instead, it was assumed that the timpanist would embellish the part as needed in order to maintain a sounding timpani presence throughout the duration of the notated rhythm.

Though there are exceptions to this general notational practice,[41] general avoidance of detailed figures in Baroque timpani parts left the way in which the notated rhythms were embellished to the imagination of the timpanist. After all, guild-trained players—whose training centered around the art of embellishment—generally laid claim to all performance opportunities, sacred as well as secular, and no experienced guild player would have been inclined simply to strike the drums and let the dry, unadorned note die away with a simple thud. What follows is a summary of the various types of embellishments and their appropriate usages.

SCHLAGMANIEREN

The term *schlagmanieren,* or "beating ornaments," is collectively applied to the ornaments employed in timpani performance practices of the seventeenth and eighteenth centuries.[42] The simplest of these figures are simply gestures commonly used in the eighteenth-century timpanist's vocabulary. A second group (known as *schläge,* or strokes) has to do more with visual effects than with sound. And a third, more complicated group comprises the *zungen,* or tonguings—specifically formulated rhythmic diminutions of different patterns of written notes. In general, these figures should be coordinated with those of the trumpets and employed liberally, according to the timpanist's discretion, in order to embellish timpani parts as other parts were embellished during the Baroque.

Virtually the only one of the first group of embellishments still generally used today is the roll. During the seventeenth and eighteenth centuries, two varieties of this figure existed. First, there was the *roulement,* a rapid, unmeasured series of strokes on a single drum. Marin Mersenne described this figure as follows in 1636: "[I]t is first necessary to note that some beat the drum so fast that the mind or the imagination cannot comprehend the multitude of blows that fall on the skin like a very violent hailstorm."[43] Whether the *roulement* was executed with single or bounced strokes is uncertain; the type of stick used may well have influenced the decision more than considerations of sound quality.

The second type of roll was called the *wirbel*—the usual modern German term for the unmeasured roll. Unlike the modern roll (and the Baroque *roulement*), the *wirbel* was a *definitely measured* series of strokes *between the two drums.* Moreover, the illustrations of this figure in Altenburg's treatise demonstrate that the *Wirbel* existed in two forms, the *einfacher wirbel* (simple *wirbel*) and the *doppel-wirbel* (double *wirbel*). As shown in Example 8.2, the only difference between these two was their different metrical structures.

EXAMPLE 8.2. *Wirbel* and *doppel-wirbel* (from Johann Ernst Altenburg, "Versuch einer Anleitung . . . ," 129). Deutscher Verlag Für Musik, Leipzig. Used by permission.

An important point concerning the use of the *roulement* and *Wirbel* must be addressed here. Generally, performances of early music and studies of timpani performance practices continue to regard the addition of a roll (*roulement*) on the final note of a composition as the most authentic manner of execution. Contemporary evidence suggests otherwise, however. Speer, for example, says of the *final-cadence*: "Before the final cadence, the timpanist must always play a good, long *wirbel*, and after this, just as the trumpets cut off, first play the last, and very strong, stoke on the drum tuned to c and placed to the right-hand side. . . ."[44]

In other words, the material immediately preceding the final cutoff must be definitely measured and may be played between the two drums—quite the opposite of the *roulement,* whose notes should be indistinguishable and (presumably) played on a single drum. Speer also provided a musical illustration of this sort of ending, which he dubbed the "final flourish," or *final-cadence* (Ex. 8.3).[45]

But the *roulement* and *wirbel* were not the only ways in which performers filled longer note values. If Altenburg's treatise is any indication, performers could also embellish a half note or whole note by means of any combination of quarter notes, eighth notes, or triplets. The only guideline seems to have been that the general contours of the passage should concur with those of the notated part (for example, a passage in which a notated whole-note C is followed by a notated whole-note G should include C and G on the respective downbeats).

The second family of embellishments, known as the *schläge* (strokes or beats), were characterized according to the idiomatically timpanistic

Paukenwirbel

Finalschläge

EXAMPLE 8.3. *Final-cadence* (from Speer, *Musikalisches Kleeblatt,* 219).

technique involved in their execution. Conceptually, the simplest of these are the *kreuzschläge* and *doppel-kreuzschläge* (cross-stickings and double cross-stickings). As shown in Example 8.4a, the cross-stickings are a clear counterpart to modern triplet cross-stickings.[46] The execution of the double cross-stickings, on the other hand, is more difficult: as shown in Example 8.4b, Altenburg's notation of two stems on the noteheads suggests that each note was to be played by striking the head simultaneously with both sticks—a notion that is born out by descriptions of the figures as late as the mid-nineteenth century.[47] In addition, the *achtel-* or *einfache schläge* (eighth-note or simple strokes, Ex. 8.4c) evidently were to be played by striking the drums simultaneously with both sticks, alternating the strokes of each stick from half height to full height (a visual effect known today in the snare-drum technique as "half-switching").

The *schläge* are telling indications both of the improvisatory nature of Baroque timpani performance practices and of the importance of visual—almost theatrical—techniques for realizing the parts authentically: since most involve techniques that in some way compromise the tone quality of the drums, intrinsically musical effects cannot be their raison d'être. Cross-stickings, though sometimes a musical necessity in the later repertory (as at the end of Beethoven's Eighth Symphony), are rarely necessary in the earlier literature; double cross-stickings are an even more explicitly visually conceived figure; and the *einfache schläge,* with their dramatic half-switching of the mallets, clearly were designed to please the eye at least as much as the ear.

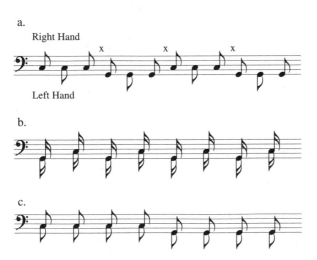

EXAMPLE 8.4. (a) Cross-stickings; b) Double cross-stickings; (c) Eighth-note or simple beatings.

A more intrinsically musical motive led to the codification of the final group of figures, the *zungen* (literally, "tonguings"), whose name obviously reflects the timpani's close affinities to the trumpets in terms of musical usages and performance practices. The *zungen* are in fact nothing more than diminutions employed by the players of the lower trumpet parts (those notated at g-g^1 and commonly designated *principal* or *quinta*) and the timpanist, whose part generally doubled that of the lower trumpet rhythmically and melodically.

Contemporary sources suggest that six different *zungen* were in use by the mid-eighteenth century. As shown in Example 8.5a–c, the *einfache zungen* (simple or single tonguings) were performed by adding a single note to the original notated part, and the *doppel-zungen* (double tonguings) by adding two strokes to the original figure; the *ganze doppel-zungen* (complete double tonguings) were an extension of the *doppel-zungen*. In addition, the figure common in timpani parts could be embellished by means of the *tragende zungen* (whose name presumably derived from the "carrying" motion created by moving the sticks rapidly between the drums without cross-sticking; see Ex. 8.5d). The timpanist's decision as to which of these diminutions should be employed was probably determined by factors such as tempo, rhythmic activity in the remainder of the ensemble, embellishments added by the trumpets or other instruments, and harmonic context— or simply his own invention.

EXAMPLE 8.5. (a) Simple tonguings as notated and realized; (b) Double tonguings as notated and realized; (c) Extended double tonguings as notated and realized; (d) Carrying tonguings as notated and realized.

Conclusions

The advent of notated percussion parts and the proliferation of treatises discussing percussion during the seventeenth century largely eliminated the first question that percussionists face in music of earlier centuries: when to play. Percussion instruments may occasionally have been used in the context of dance or other instrumental music;[48] timpani could be used whenever trumpets were present; and trumpets could be added whenever a piece was performed to suggest a courtly or festive occasion.

Rather than face this issue, the performer dealing with a notated or *ad libitum* part in a piece of seventeenth-century music faces issues that are at once more bewildering and more rewarding: *how* to realize the part in an historically authentic manner. The best response to this issue is to remember that there is no single best response. Variety and invention were as much the prerogative of the performer as they were of the composer, and aside from using instruments that had not yet come into existence, the only way to give an "inauthentic" performance was to perform strictly according to what was notated.

NOTES

1. Virdung–*Musica getutscht,* fol. 13r.
2. For further discussion of these issues, see Blades–*Percussion*; further, Blades and Montagu–*Early Percussion*; Montagu–*Making Early Percussion*; and especially Harms–Early Percussion in Kite-Powell–*Renaissance*.
3. Harms–Early Percussion, 161.
4. Mersenne–*Harmonie universelle* 3. Percussion instruments discussed in Book 7, one of the "Books on Instruments" (trans. Chapman). Trichet's *Traité des instruments de musique* was first published under the editorship of François Lesure, in *Annales musicologiques* 3 (1955): 283–87, and 4 (1956): 175–248. Though the work was begun around 1630, the section on percussion presumably dates from after 1636, since in it Trichet refers to "Mersenne's book on instruments" (i.e., book 7 of *Harmonie universelle*).
5. Praetorius–*Syntagma* II: esp. 4, 78–79. English translations by Harold Blumenfeld (New York, 1980) and David Z. Crookes (Oxford, 1986).
6. Ibid., 78–79.
7. For information concerning the emergence of national styles of playing field drums and tabors, see *Historic Percussion* (Austin, TX, 1994), esp. 118–25.
8. Trichet/Lesure–*Traité,* 238–39; Mersenne–*Harmonie universelle* 7: 53; Praetorius–*Syntagma* II, *Theatrum instrumentorum,* pl. 23, 29.
9. Harms–*Early Percussion,* 162.
10. Mersenne–*Harmonie universelle* 7: 53; Trichet/Lesure–*Traité,* 238–39.
11. Mersenne–*Harmonie universelle* 7: 53; Trichet/Lesure–*Traité,* 239.
12. Trichet/Lesure–*Traité,* 238.
13. Mersenne–*Harmonie universelle* 7, between pages 56 and 57.
14. Ibid., 7: 53.
15. Virdung–*Musica getutscht,* [24]; Trichet/Lesure–*Traité,* 238.
16. Praetorius's *Theatrum instrumentarum* includes in plate 29 a set of "cymbals [*Becken*] that the Americans play like we play the bells": a set of four graduated plate-shaped objects with indented bells, resting on a frame of long crossbars and suspended above

the ground. Unfortunately, Praetorius provides no further information about these instruments.

17. Mersenne–*Harmonie universelle* 7: 49; Praetorius–*Syntagma* II: *Theatrum*, plate 40.
18. Mersenne–*Harmonie universelle* 7: 49.
19. Trichet/Lesure–*Traité*, 247; Mersenne–*Harmonie universelle* 7:, 49. A rare notated example of castanet music may be found in Feuillet–*Choréographie*, 100–02.
20. For a reproduction, see Blades–*Percussion*, 204.
21. Mersenne–*Harmonie universelle* 3: 175–76.
22. The reference is to the instruments described in a letter to Dardanus supposedly written by St. Jerome. For a description of the letter and the instruments discussed in it, see Hammerstein–Instrumenta, 129–32.
23. Virdung–*Musica getutscht*, fol. 12v.
24. See Cooper—Realisation and Embellishment.
25. Speer–*Grundrichtiger Unterricht*. For a rather free translation of Speer's treatise, see Howey–*Speer*.
26. For a magnificent recording of this setting of *In dulci jubilo*—complete with an authentically realized timpani part, see the recording by Paul McCreesh under "Suggested Listening."
27. The misattribution of the Mass was originally made by W. A. Ambros in the second edition of his *Geschichte der Musik* (Leipzig, 1881), 144. The first discussion referring directly to the timpani appears to have been Kirby–Kettle-Drums. Kirby's article was in turn cited by several widely read studies of percussion, Titcomb–Kettledrums, 154; Gangware–Percussion, 138; Peters–*Drummer-Man*, 48; Blades–*Percussion*, 236. For a concise overview of the corrected attribution, see Ernst Hintermaier, "The *Missa Salisburgensis*," *The Musical Times* 116 (1975): 965–66.
28. In the *Traité de l'orchestration* (1844) Berlioz stated that most orchestras still used only wooden sticks and wooden sticks covered with leather, and then asserted that the "most musical" effect could be obtained by using sticks with sponge ends. Berlioz also notes that sponge-headed sticks should be used when the works of the "old masters" specified that the timpani were to be covered or muffled—thereby distinguishing "modern masters" (presumably including himself) from those older ones. See Hector Berlioz, *Treatise on Orchestration*, trans. Richard Strauss and Theodore Front (New York, 1948), 380, 385.
29. Howey–*Speer*, 171–72; "Von den Paucken, deren Gebrauch und Mißgebrauch in alten und neuen Zeiten," *Wöchentliche Nachrichten und Anmerkungen die Musik betreffend* 2 (1768): 216.
30. For an early example of these pictures, see the anonymous painting of trumpeters and timpani, ca. 1569, reproduced in Naylor–*Trumpet and Trombone*, pl. 155. The painting, held in the Badische Landesbibliothek, Karlsruhe, shows a timpanist using sticks covered with what clearly appears to be a soft, textured material.
31. Virdung–*Musica getutscht*, 25; Praetorius–*Syntagma* II: 25.
32. Mersenne–*Harmonie universelle*, 51; "Von den Paucken," 208.
33. Altenburg–*Versuch*, 123 [*recte* 132].
34. Praetorius, *Syntagma* II, *Theatrum instrumentarum*, pl. 23.
35. Mersenne–*Harmonie universelle* 7: 54.
36. On the use of multiple timpani in the Baroque repertoire, see Cooper–Performance Practices, 78–81. A little-known early-nineteenth-century example of a prominent solo for three timpani is found in the Piano Concerto in E♭ Major by Ignaz Moscheles, in which the timpani state the subject, *solo*, in the first movement. For a reproduction of this solo, see *Allgemeine Musik-Zeitung* 24 (1821): 550.
37. Eisel–*Musicus autodidacticus*, 66.
38. For a useful overview of the pitch differences effected by different beating spots, see Thomas D. Rossing, Craig A. Anderson, and Ronald I. Mills, "Acoustics of Timpani," *Percussionist* 19 (1982): 18–30, esp. 22, 25–26.

39. My own experience indicates that when one uses Baroque-sized timpani and beats in the center of the drum in a chamber made mostly of wood or stone—that is, the indoor acoustic context in which the timpani were usually employed through the high Baroque—the sound is more like that of a pizzicato cello or double bass than of a timpani struck at the normal beating spot.

40. Indeed, the centralization of French musical life that occurred under Lully in the latter part of the seventeenth century certainly would have fostered the specific notation of all desired parts—simply in order to ascertain that those parts were not omitted in performance.

41. A good example of this kind of exception is the introductory timpani solo of Sebastian Bach's *Christmas Oratorio*, which in its original version in BWV 214 would have lent itself to free improvisation. For a discussion of this part, see Cooper–Realisation and Embellishment.

42. The usual translation of this term, "manners of beating," is insufficient because it neglects that in eighteenth-century German, *Manieren* was the usual term for ornaments.

43. Mersenne–*Harmonie universelle* 7: 56.

44. Speer–*Kleeblatt,* 219ff. The mention of the c̲ drum standing on the right-hand side indicates that Speer was speaking from the viewer's perspective, not the timpanist's (who would have said that the c̲ drum was placed to the left). Speer's statement was echoed almost verbatim, but with the placement of the drums corrected, in Eisel–*Musicus autodidactus.*

45. Speer's decision to notate the part at C and g—a tuning never encountered in the actual Baroque literature—reflects the traditional treatment of the timpani as transposing instruments. This example would best be regarded as written for timpani in G, i.e., drums tuned to G and d.

46. Cross-sticking is necessary here because the timpani were positioned with the smaller drum (c) at the player's left hand and the larger one (G) to the right.

47. See, e.g., Eduard Bersdorf's article "Doppelkreuz-Schlag" in his *Neues Universal-Lexicon der Musik* (Dresden, 1856–57) 1: 712. Isolated examples of this technique occur at the beginning of the "March to the Scaffold" in Berlioz's *Symphonie fantastique* and the third movement (mm. 318–22) of Mahler's Fourth Symphony.

48. Berthold Neumann argues that percussion instruments were not widely used in polyphonic dance music. See Neumann–Kommt pfeift and responses to it by Ben Harms and Peggy Sexton in *Historical Performance* 5/1 (Spring 1992): 32–34.

BIBLIOGRAPHY

Avgerinos–*Handbuch*; Avgerinos–*Lexikon*; Beck–*Encyclopedia*; Blades and Montagu–*Early Percussion*; Blades–*Percussion*; Bowles–Double; Bowles–*Timpani*; Bowles–Using; Cooper–Performance Practices; Cooper–Realisation and Embellishment; Hardy and Ancell–Comparisons; Mersenne–*Harmonie universelle*; Montagu–*Making Early Percussion*; Powley–Little-Known; Trichet–*Traité*.

Suggested Listening

Michael Praetorius, *Mass for Christmas Morning,* Paul McCreesh and the Gabrieli Consort and Players, Deutsche Grammophon Archiv CD 439 250-2.

9

The Violin Family

Part 1: Technique and Style

David Douglass

The seventeenth century was a period in which profound changes in style bridged the musical aesthetics of the Renaissance and the Baroque. As a result, seventeenth-century styles include elements of both periods. The complex nature of seventeenth-century music offers a wealth of musical expression to violinists who attempt to understand it. Since an in-depth analysis of the numerous musical styles that developed during the seventeenth century is beyond the scope of this chapter, my intention is to identify the major stylistic trends that motivated the musicians of the era, and to explain how these trends affected both the violin and the violinist.

Any discussion of style will eventually address issues of technique. Inasmuch as the seventeenth century was a volatile period of stylistic change, techniques had to adapt rapidly in order to communicate those changes more effectively. I shall explain the stylistic connection to those changes in technique.

Throughout this chapter I shall refer to the violin and violinists, but it should be understood that my intention is to include (in the Renaissance sense) all sizes of violin and viola, just as the terms "recorder" or "viola da gamba" can imply all sizes of those instruments.

Style and Context

Many violinists, when first attempting to play in a historical style, are both confused and intimidated by the immensity of the subject. To start with a definition, one might say that style is that quality that imparts meaning to a performance—a meaning that can be appreciated through the context of the culture that gave it birth. In still simpler terms, style is the meaningful shapes we give to music. Notated pitches and rhythms, played without inflection, provide musical direction through harmonic and melodic rhythm, but that direction alone never fully expresses all that either the music or the performer has to offer. The shapes that we give those notes, through the manipulation of sound, articulation, dynamics, time, and the improvisational addition of notes can impart a special meaning to what we play. The vast number of possible combinations of shapes can allow for any piece of music to be performed in a tremendous range of styles, even within one cultural context (compare, for example, Jimi Hendrix's rendition of *The Star Spangled Banner* to anything you'll ever hear at the ballpark).

One could learn a particular style by assembling, piece by piece, all of the many shapes used in that style. And, indeed, many performers begin to learn to play stylistically by this method. But that process by itself is ultimately unsatisfying. It would be the same as learning to recite poetry with meaningful inflections and dramatic pauses, but in a language you didn't understand. It is far more useful and satisfying to have an understanding of the general background and framework of a particular musical style and how that framework changed over time. The task, then, is to establish the stylistic context of a repertory so that the special details of a particular place and time have meaning. Once the stylistic context of a piece of music is established, the specific stylistic details included in a performance of that music can be arrived at through intuition, as well as deduction.

At the most subtle level, the stylistic context of any repertory is closely linked to all of the social forces that shape human (and therefore musical) history, and a truly complete picture of a style can only be assembled through an interdisciplinary study that brings together as much information about a period as possible. It is hoped that your native curiosity will carry you on a lifelong pursuit of knowledge that will enhance your perception (and performance) of many styles.

The most important principle underlying all stylistic development is so simple that it is usually overlooked. That principle is that stylistic context is fully perceived only when it is examined with a forward-looking perspective as regards time. In other words, you will understand a style better if you know where it came from. Even though that seems obvious, it is difficult (and ultimately impossible) to accomplish. It is irresistible to bring our modern sensibilities back to whatever we play, and, in a sense, that bit of ourselves that we bring back is what makes it *our* music, our artistic expression, instead of a perfect historical recreation. Still, every attempt must be made to establish, for ourselves and the listener, the stylistic context of whatever we play, in order to invest a composition with some of the expressive shapes preferred by those who created it in the first place.

Seventeenth-century music, in particular, is performed too often (especially by violinists) from the more familiar perspective of the eighteenth century looking backward. The result is a performance that either sounds like crude or embryonic eighteenth-century music, or is merely incoherent. Within its correct stylistic context, a performance of seventeenth-century music can come to life. It can be heard as a culmination, or commentary on, that which precedes it. The same "historically informed" approach that unlocked our doors of perception into eighteenth-century music must be applied to any style to achieve the same results.

Technique

Violin Position and Bow Mechanics

For violin technique from any period, form follows function. As professional dance musicians, violinists of the early seventeenth century principally needed a technique that would provide the explosive articulations and relaxed sounds that would inspire their listeners to dance. The technique that is best suited to that function is one in which the violin is held low, cradled on the upper arm and drawn in toward the armpit (see Fig. 9.1). This low placement allows the bow-arm to work without having to hold it up as well. In this position, a down-bow is merely a sudden and absolute release of the weight of the arm. In fact, the weight of the arm can be thrown into the violin in very free, even reckless movements that produce, in addition to the necessary articulations and sounds, the sense of abandon that is appropriate for dance music. This position for holding the violin was important enough that seventeenth-century players used it for violins and violas of any size. Only when the instrument was too large for the left hand to reach was it played on the shoulder, and then it was held at a downward angle that kept the bow-arm in an orientation similar to the low-held position.

This is a radical change for violinists trained in modern techniques (i.e., virtually everyone), yet one that is essential in order to experience seventeenth-century music fully. The bow-arm is the single most important element of violin technique for the expression of style, since it produces the sound shapes that make a style meaningful. It is a change made even more difficult by the fact that modern violinists, through the process of learning to play with modern technique, generally have lost a sense of the weight of the bow-arm. (But most violinists can probably remember how much their bow-arm ached from the effort of continually holding it up when they first began!) As one begins to play while holding the violin in the lower position, it is difficult to break the habit of holding up the arm, even if one no longer needs to do so. In these initial efforts, a down-bow is usually the result of a controlled push rather than a sudden and absolute release of the weight of the

FIGURE 9.1.

arm. It is also common for beginners inadvertently to raise their right elbow in an effort to keep the bow-arm up. Eventually, though, it is possible to relinquish all unnecessary control of the right arm and experience the freedom of the lower position.

A small change in the bow-grip, effected by taking more of the stick in the hand, is also important for keeping the arm in a proper orientation to the instrument. It is best to keep the contact point of the index finger just inside the middle knuckle, while leaving the third and fourth fingers in their customary position. This grip will reestablish the smooth lines of hand, wrist, and forearm that were beneficial to higher-held positions. The grip also has the positive effect of eliminating some of the flexibility of the right hand (flexibility that is crucial to control in higher-held positions, since the larger muscles of the arm are busy supporting the arm), and moves most of the responsibility for the bow stroke to the forearm where, in the lower position, it belongs.

Learning this early violin technique can be made easier by playing as much dance music as possible. It is a technique that was inspired by—and is perfectly suited to—dance music, and when playing dance music one is inevitably drawn toward playing with the degree of physical freedom that does not allow for overcontrol of the bow-arm. Playing for dancers is even better: not only will you inspire them to dance, they will inspire you with the energy of their movements.

Just as dancing cannot be done while sitting, professional dancemasters (as they were called) never played while seated. Indeed, early violin technique is impossible to negotiate unless one stands, because in any other position the bow-arm will run into the right leg. Aside from this completely practical reason for standing, in the seventeenth century it was viewed as inappropriate to sit in the presence of your employers. Even bass violinists stood, placing their instrument on a stool, or hanging it from their neck with a strap attached to a ring embedded in the back of the instrument. Figure 9.2, an etching from the early seventeenth century, shows a violin band whose bass violinist plays with the instrument suspended in just such a manner.

Besides the fact that sitting makes the low-held technique impossible to use, standing allows you to play with the degree of physical freedom that is a joy to you as well as your audience. Period illustrations of violinists show them in poses we associate with rock and jazz musicians today, and it is no coincidence that violinists in the seventeenth century had a similar role to rock and jazz musicians in their popular culture. Once you become more comfortable with the low-held position for the violin, and can play with a loose bow-arm, your body will be able to make dance-like physical movements without distorting your playing. The bow-arm and the violin will trace circles that intersect at the contact point of the bow on the string.

There are also exercises that you can do in order to loosen the bow-arm and shorten the period of reorientation. One of these involves placing the

FIGURE 9.2.

bow on the A and D strings, near the frog, and then letting the arm fall, in an absolutely relaxed manner. When this is done properly the arm will drop completely to your side in one smooth movement, you will feel the elbow snap, and the bow will point straight to the floor. The resulting sound will be loud and rather harsh, but the bow will not totally overpower the string. I always urge my students to make bad sounds when they are first learning early violin technique, in order to encourage them to give up control of the bow-arm as quickly as possible. The control necessary for obtaining a good sound can be applied once the freedom of the bow-arm is well established, and that control involves simply allowing the arm to fall, but at a slower rate. This sounds much more complicated than it is. Those who have mastered violin playing in this position almost universally think of it as a much easier, less physically complicated way of playing.

The Bow Position's Primary Effect on Style

Beyond dance music, the simplicity of this early technique is perfectly suited to the entire repertory of the early seventeenth century. The natural, relaxed way the body approaches the instrument is mirrored in the straightforward character that is basic to all the forms enjoyed by seventeenth-century violinists. The simplicity of bowing in this position produces sounds that are resonant and uncomplicated, sounds that blend well in consort or enhance solo playing.

There is an additional stylistic advantage to the low-held position—apart from the benefits it imparts to sound and down-bow articulation—in the manner in which it alters the effect of the up-bow: without the weight of the arm to lift, the up-bow sounds more similar to the down-bow. Because of the physical nature of the up-bow, drawing the weak side of the hand and arm in toward the body, the up-bow will still feel like a gathering of energy to be released on the stroke of the down-bow (either suddenly, or gradually to produce more even strokes). It is important to be aware of the difference in sensations associated with the up-bow and down-bow strokes in order to perceive a cycle of motion, cause and effect, yin and yang, in the bow-arm, to meet the phrasing requirements of the music.

In general, though, the relaxed sounds that result from not holding up the bow-arm, combined with the natural similarity of bow strokes, allow one to perform the long phrases of seventeenth-century music in an appropriately flowing manner. By using a wide range of bow speeds and pressures, in conjunction with the quick-speaking, powerful articulations natural to the low-held position, dancemasters had a wide variety of expressive shapes at their disposal. It was necessary for them to have such an arsenal of expressive devices in order for them to give their music the same flexible expressivity that singers gave to vocal music—an important stylistic goal of the period for instrumentalists. With all of that expressive detail, even dance music can become eloquent, as well as exciting. Three recordings by the violin band that I direct, The King's Noyse (see "Recommended Listening," p. 175), provide examples that demonstrate many of the effects possible with a bow while the violin is in the low-held position (in both solo and ensemble music), as well as stylistic issues such as consort sound and blend, tuning and temperament, and the interpretation of different compositional styles.

Bowing Systems

For the first half of the seventeenth century, the most sought-after and influential violinists were Italians, or at least adherents to the Italian school of violin playing. The evidence that we have for bowing choices from Italian violinists—primarily Gasparo Zanetti's *Il scolaro*—indicates a relatively free use of the bow, compared to modern playing. The modern bowing conventions of beginning and ending with down-bows, and unifying bowings within an ensemble, were nonexistent. Once again, the effect of the low-held position on bowing obviated the need to organize the bowing so that strong beats received down-bows; an up-bow was practically the same. Instead, bowing could be organized so as to give certain strong notes within a phrase one of the special treatments possible for the bow in the low-held position. And the primary principal of equal-voiced polyphony demands that each part be true to the integrity of its own melody, so superimposing an arbitrary unification of bowings within an ensemble is too artificial an approach for the performance of consort repertories. Of course, straightforward dance music might produce both regular down-bows on strong beats and unified bowings within the ensemble, but then it is the music itself that produces the effect, not the performers who are superimposing an arbitrary system.

Experience has taught me that most of the consort repertory is best performed simply as it is written, beginning with up-bow or down-bow so that the first important note within a phrase receives a down-bow by means of the natural progression of bow strokes. After that first important down-bow, a vast majority of repertory continues with important notes falling naturally on down-bows without correcting the bow. This approach might involve bowing backward (in the modern sense) for an extended period of time, but it will feel unnatural only because it is unfamiliar, rather than because it is unnatural for the bow-arm. Sometimes it is necessary to correct the bow, but only to serve the needs of the phrase—to have a down-bow available when it is required. In general, when learning this use of the bow you should always challenge your feeling to need to correct the bow. Ask yourself whether the music really requires a down-bow, or whether you feel the need for a down-bow from habit.

There is one major exception to this approach to bowing seventeenth-century repertories and that is the so-called "French rule of down-bow," developed by Jean-Baptiste Lully during the last half of the seventeenth century and used by players of many nationalities for the performance of French-style orchestral music. After the restoration of the monarchy in England with the crowning of Charles II, for example, court violinists were required to learn and perform orchestral music according to this French approach to bowing. Much of the music from English composers of the late seventeenth century—Henry Purcell, for one—should be performed with French bowings.

The French system of bowing is an elaborate method that organizes the bowing so as to place a down-bow at the beginning of every measure. It is a utilitarian approach to bowing, rather than a musical one, that solves the problem of having many violinists play in unison without time-consuming discussions about bowing. There is, however, a distinctive musical effect that results from playing many consecutive down-bows, as often happens within this system. Repeatedly taking the bow off the string causes the sounds to be punctuated by silences, thereby producing a light, poised effect. The primary source of information about French bowings comes to us from the preface of Georg Muffat's *Florilegium Secundum,* a summary of which can be found in David Boyden's monumental *History of Violin Playing*. Muffat's examples of the bowings used in Lully's orchestra leave many questions about the use of the bow unanswered, but further clarifying information can be found in the writings of Michel Pignolet de Monteclair and Pierre Dupont. A summarization of Monteclair's and Dupont's work was assembled by Herbert Myers, and can be found in the preface to George Houle's edition of Pierre Beauchamps's *Ballet de Fâcheux* (Bloomington, 1991).

Violin Position and Left-Hand Mechanics

When the violin is held in the low early-seventeeth-century position, the left hand is required to hold the instrument as well as to finger the notes. The palm of the left hand should lie against the neck, and the heel of the hand will meet the body of the instrument. This is exactly what you were instructed not to do as a modern violinist, because when the violin is positioned on the shoulder, holding it in this manner creates angles that are detrimental to fluid playing. The low-held position dictates the opposite for the same reason: grasping the neck in the palm corrects the angles. There should be a smooth line from the back of the hand, through the wrist, and down the forearm to the elbow. In order to maximize the height of the fingers above the strings, it is best to have the neck nestled as low as possible in the crook between the thumb and first finger.

A short period of reorientation will be required in order to play in tune. Compared to the customary position of the left hand (with the instrument held on the shoulder), the first finger will lie sharp (and you will feel that it must be pulled back), while the third finger will lie flat (and when playing it tune, it will seem to require a stretch). There is a hidden benefit to changing the orientation of the fingers to the fingerboard and breaking the habits of left-hand finger position: your ear will have to become more involved in your playing. Many violinists stop hearing themselves once the physical habits of bowing and fingering become established, but the only way a violinist can ever play in an intonation system of unequal temperament, or play in an affective, stylistic manner, is to have the ear intimately involved in the process.

At first, the left hand will feel constrained by the requirements of its new role. In addition, beginners usually fear that the instrument will drop at any moment, and as a result they hold the instrument more tightly than necessary, thereby further restricting the flexibility of their fingers. In reality, the friction of the skin against the wood of the neck alone is sufficient to hold the instrument in place, and drawing the instrument in toward the body is probably the position in which it is least likely that the violin will drop. With a bit of practice, these feelings of insecurity soon disappear.

Once the left hand feels relaxed and comfortable in its new position, there is one more subtle function that should be learned. The left hand can also control the angle at which the instrument meets the bow. When playing on the upper three strings, the violin is best held flat, relatively parallel to the ground. When playing on the bottom string it is better to change the angle of the instrument, by rotating the neck slightly, rather than to raise the arm. A very small twist of the violin in the left hand, accomplished by rolling the neck between the thumb and first finger, can raise the bottom string to a position comparable to that of the middle and upper strings when the violin was held flat. This keeps the mechanics of the bow-arm consistent over the entire range of the instrument.

Shifting

The most common reaction to the low-held technique I have received from violinists has been to question its usefulness, based on the inability of the left hand to shift by the modern method. On that basis alone they often deduce that shoulder techniques are more advanced and therefore more serviceable for seventeenth-century repertory, and they are therefore hesitant to learn about the low-held position. My response to that reaction is to remind the student that there are many ways to shift, and none is superior to any other as long as it meets the requirements of the music. The truth of the matter is that the only thing that is important for the left hand is that the fingers be at the right place at the right time, and the advantages that the low-held technique impart to the bow-arm for playing stylistically far outweigh any perceived inconveniences to the left hand. It makes sense that once a person invests the time and energy to learn something as difficult as shifting with accuracy, the dread of going through that process all over again can make any alternate system seem nearly impossible, and therefore undesirable.

But shifting while holding the instrument low on the arm is simpler than when the instrument is held on the shoulder: one merely replaces fingers to assume a new position. For example, shifting from first to second position (one of the most common shifts, since the range of seventeenth-century repertory often ascends to c''' in the highest violin part, in patterns for which fourth-finger extensions are inadequate) is accomplished by replacing the third finger with the second, while the thumb remains back in first position. This slight forward movement of the fingers is much easier to perform accurately than when the entire hand and arm move forward as well. You have only to learn a new coordination for the fingers, so that they fall in the right place. It is possible to shift comfortably in this manner as high as third or fourth position, although if you must remain there for an extended period of time, it will be more comfortable to bring the thumb up as well. The shift down, then, is accomplished in two motions: first the thumb moves back, to be followed by downward finger replacement.

Practice shifting by repeatedly replacing fingers for any one pitch while being careful to maintain a consistent intonation. First work on moving only one position at a time. Slur, in long bow strokes on each string (but primarily the top string), a pattern of second finger, open string, first finger, open string, and so forth. Then slur a pattern of third finger, open string, second finger, open string, and so forth until you have completed a pattern of adjacent-finger replacement through to the fourth finger. Then practice a similar replacement exercise by interchanging fingers that are two positions apart: third and first, and fourth and second. Of course, this should be practiced only once the left hand is thoroughly comfortable and relaxed in first position; otherwise you will only add to the tension of the left hand.

The Transition to the Shoulder

When did violinists begin to play with the sort of technique that "Baroque" violinists use today? The transition to a shoulder-held position occurred slowly during the last half of the seventeenth century, but mostly toward the end of the century. Violin tutors from the early eighteenth century still instructed violinists to hold the instrument in the low position, but by then it was probably a conservative idea.

A more important question to ask is: *Why* did the violin move up to the shoulder? The reason the violin traveled to a higher position on the shoulder was that this, in turn, raised the bow-arm. The resultant sounds, created by bowing while carrying the weight of the arm, were then endowed with certain complexities that are appropriate for that repertory. Once you become comfortable with playing in the low-held position and can bow without holding up the weight of the arm, when you move the violin up to the shoulder the weight of the arm can be *perceived* and hence assimilated intelligently into the bow stroke. With more of your body incorporated into your playing, your body will actually help you to make interpretive decisions about style. This is the most important reason for learning the low-held technique, even if you primarily intend to play later repertories on the shoulder: you will have a unique and useful perspective that will improve your playing.

Once the instrument was in the shoulder position, the new orientation for the left hand allowed violinists to explore different melodic gymnastics that would have been difficult, or even impossible, with the instrument in the low-held position. Sometimes these melodic configurations can be an indication of whether a particular piece was intended for the low- or shoulder-held position, but not always, and it is unwise to let a few inconveniences of the left hand dictate the violin's position when the expressive needs of the bow arm should be the overriding concern. Furthermore, since both playing positions existed side by side at the end of the century, each composer (and often each piece) must be approached individually. The player should choose the position that allows the bow to express the music in the most natural and effective way.

Seventeenth-Century Style

Consort Music

At the beginning of the seventeenth century, most violinists were professional dance musicians who performed alone, or in ensembles often referred to as "violin bands." By this time the violinist's role as a dance musician embodied a tradition of almost a hundred years' duration. Violinists and violin bands were expected to improvise as soloists or even in groups, make rough arrangements of popular music for whatever number of players were involved, or, at the wealthiest courts and noble houses, play music written by such composers as John Dowland, Anthony Holborne, William Brade, and Michael Praetorius.

Improvised consort music was probably the most common repertory for the violin band, and is one of the more difficult (but rewarding!) styles to recreate. Group improvisation in the seventeenth century was accomplished in the same way that it is today: each musician, individually, plays a part that agrees with a unifying melody or chord progression. Also like musicians today, the more experience an ensemble has in doing this kind of playing, the more the players are able to discover roles that do not overlap, and what to play when, in order to add to the compositional creativity of the piece. For a more comprehensive discussion of the mechanics of group improvisation, consult my article in the November/December 1994 issue of *Strings* magazine.[1]

As for composed repertories, at the beginning of the seventeenth century music continued to be written and performed in the style of the Renaissance: all lines were of equal melodic importance in the polyphonic texture. Summarizing the style of instrumental music of the great composers from the early seventeenth century, one could say it is shaped much like language. In Renaissance vocal music each of the interweaving melodies is fashioned so that poetic phrases are expressed in complete musical phrases. To continue a linguistic analogy, these musical sentences are then linked together to form paragraphs, and the paragraphs are joined so that the composition tells one story from beginning to end. Sometimes words that have special significance to the text are given melodic gestures that describe those words (a compositional device known as "word painting"), but never in a way that distracts from the larger phrase. Instrumental music, with the possible exception of some dance music, was also composed in equal-voiced polyphony. Vocal forms were adapted for instrumental purposes, and vocal works were performed instrumentally.

For example, one collection of instrumental music written by John Dowland and published in 1604, *Lachrimae or Seaven Teares*, contains seven dances, called pavans, that are really variations on a song, also by Dowland, entitled "Flow my Tears." This collection, incidentally, was specifically designated for either the violin family or viols. Each pavan contains three sections, and each section vividly describes the meaning of the text. Since these pavans are best performed as though each of the five players is singing the text of the song, care must be taken to play in a manner that communicates the structure of the sentences of the text, as well as the eloquence of the individual words. Early-seventeenth-century violinists were well trained, from the experience they gained in their traditional role as dance musicians, to provide a tremendous variety of effects with the bow, and they were able to bring that eloquent detail to consort music without obscuring the phrasing. Even if no text is available to guide the performance of a piece of early-seventeenth-century consort music, it is best performed in this manner, as though it were texted.

Not all seventeenth-century consort music is specifically indicated to be performed on violin or by violin band. Rather, violin bands drew from a wide variety of musical sources and adapted the music for their purposes. One way the suitability of a polyphonic piece for performance by violin band can be determined is by the ranges of the parts. The most common configuration of a violin band included only one bass instrument, with violins and violas forming the remainder. Thus, in order for a composition to be playable by a violin band, all the parts other than the bass must stay on or above c (an octave below middle C). An astonishing amount of repertory conforms to this scoring and is available to violin bands for performance (or adaptation for performance). This is an easy, quick test for deciding which music might have been primarily intended for performance on a consort of viola da gambas, instead of violin band: the large range of the viola da gamba allows it to cover music that would require at least two bass violins.

With the continuing influence of treble-bass compositional forms, by the end of the seventeenth century, consort music began to take on the "orchestral" character that we are familiar with today: a compositional structure consisting of treble, bass, and a filler consisting of second violin and viola parts that have little melodic identity, and whose function is merely to fill out the harmonies. But this is the exception rather than the rule, and the safest (and most fulfilling) practice is to approach all seventeenth-century consort music as though each part is of equal melodic importance. The consort music of Heinrich Ignaz Franz von Biber, for example, is rich in the complexities of equal part-writing in spite of having been written during the last quarter of the century.

Consort Sound, Tuning, and Temperament

Sound is also an important component of style. The instruments used for the performance of early-seventeenth-century violin consort music ideally would have been constructed to blend as one sound, to enhance the effect of the equal-voiced polyphony. Furthermore, violins and violas were made in a variety of sizes so that parts in many ranges could be played with a more equal sound; for example, in order to provide a balanced sound throughout a five-part consort, one would play first-soprano parts on a small violin, second-soprano parts on a large violin, alto parts on a small viola, tenor parts on a large viola, and bass parts on a bass violin. Scoring the instruments so that all of the parts are equally balanced in sound also makes it easier for the players to shape their melodies so that they sound more similar. One must keep an open mind in assigning instruments to parts since sometimes they do not correspond to the usual ranges. In some extreme cases, an equal scoring will require only violas.

The intonation system used by violin bands was another intrinsic part of their sound. Consorts of instruments of unfixed pitch—such as violins, singers, and wind bands—had the ability to play pure intervals wherever they wanted. Fixed-pitch instruments without that ability, such as fretted instruments, harps, and keyboards, settled on meantone temperaments (most commonly, quarter-comma; see Tuning and Temperament in this volume), which favor only the major thirds. In a violin band performance the flavor of meantone temperament is heard melodically (through the use of large and small half steps), while the goal of intervalic purity can be extended to more intervals. Furthermore, a different tuning for the bass violin made this goal easier to accomplish. For most of the seventeenth century, the low string on the bass violin was tuned to B♭, one whole step lower than we are accustomed to tuning the cello today. With this tuning, bass violinists were able to tune their two bottom strings in perfect thirds (seventeenths, actually) to two violin strings (the bottom B♭ string to the violin D, and the F string to the violin A), thereby eliminating the problem that results from stacking perfect fifths down to low C. For more information on tuning and temperament, see Herbert Myers's chapter in this volume.

Practical experience with violin bands has taught me that the best results are obtained when everyone tunes as closely as possible to perfect intervals, and then, during a performance, uses a fingered note when the open strings are not appropriate for the chord. With the harmonic limitations of most early-seventeenth-century consort music, usually A and E are the only open-string notes that are troublesome for tuning. When A is the third of the F-chord, it is lower than when it is in either the D- or A-chords. The same is true for the E; as the third of the C-chord, it is lower than in either the A- or E-chords. A fourth finger can easily be used to avoid any problems caused by the tuning of the open strings, but by tuning the bass violin F string to the violin A, the F-chord and the C-chord are raised slightly, allowing the violinists and violists to play both thirds with open strings.

Extremely chromatic works often tax the violin band's ability to play in tune, and require a flexible orientation of the left hand to the fingerboard. Under those circumstances, the ear will often guide a player's fingers to unaccustomed placements. The best way to play convincingly and eloquently in any style is to have your ears and heart lead your technique, and then to make that technique as flexibly expressive as possible. This is a radical departure from current practice, and necessitates a particularly difficult reorientation for modern violinists who were taught a more pragmatic, systematic approach to technique.

Still another component of sound on the violin has to do with fingering choices. It is apparent from the evidence of seventeenth-century violin tablatures (a type of music notation that shows exactly where to place your fingers) that violinists preferred the sound of an open string to that of a fourth finger. Even measured trills to open-string pitches (as in cadences to D, A, or E) were done by a rapid alternation between the open string and a third finger a half-step lower, rather than by playing it all on one string with the third and fourth fingers. From this and other evidence concerning aspects of technique, it is obvious that seventeenth-century violinists valued sound over convenience.

Solo Music: Improvised Forms

At the beginning of the seventeenth century, violinists often played alone, for the entertainment of themselves and their audiences. This solo music was mostly improvised, in many forms that included unaccompanied preludes, divisions over ground basses, and Italian-style diminutions of vocal music (with or without the accompaniment of the original polyphony). Some composers—and a few violinists who were also accomplished composers, such as William Brade—wrote complicated divisions and ornamentations that were less spontaneously conceived, but for the most part, division playing was considered an improvised art. English violinists in particular enjoyed these improvised forms, using them (with only some stylistic changes) well into the eighteenth century. For example, one seventeenth-century book of English improvisations for violin, *The Division Violin,* was published in eighteen editions, well into the eighteenth century.[2]

The most important stylistic component common to all of these improvised solo forms is their melodic, vocal quality. This means that rather long phrases should be maintained, no matter how rapid the divisions become. As mentioned earlier, one of the primary advantages of the low-held technique used by violinists of the period is the equal sound of the bow strokes. It is no coincidence that both the low-held technique and this improvisational form of division playing have their roots in the sixteenth century, since they are such natural partners. By the last half of the seventeenth century, however, the same gradual changes affecting other styles of composition also crept into the world of division violin playing, and as a result, shoulder-held techniques became a more common way to play. For a more thorough analysis of the relationship between division style and the two playing positions, consult my article in the July/August 1990 issue of *Strings* magazine.[3] In that article I compare two divisions on the tune "John come kiss me now," respectively by violinists David Mell and Thomas Baltzer, which exist side by side in *The Division Violin,* and demonstrate the two quite different stylistic worlds (and their corresponding techniques) that coexisted in the last half of the century. Further discussed is how the different positions of the bow arm, in the low- and high-held positions, can be used to convey their respective styles with the same degree of physical naturalness.

To truly develop an understanding of seventeenth-century style and the cultural experience of the seventeenth-century violinist, it is necessary to learn how to improvise. Just as the techniques of the dancemaster allow a player the maximum amount of physical freedom, improvisation offers an equal degree of creative freedom. That sense of freedom can then carry over, in effect, into the interpretation of composed repertories. Ideally, when a listener hears a performance of a seventeenth-century composition, it should sound as though the performer is improvising. Ornamentation can certainly help to convey that sense of improvisation, but nothing really approaches the feeling of inspiration that comes from being totally involved in the creative process during a performance.

It is possible to learn to improvise your own divisions and diminutions by first becoming comfortable with technique and style (by performing a lot of repertory and practicing the exercises contained in seventeenth-century diminution treatises, all with the proper technique), and then putting away all music and beginning the slow process of rediscovering the pitches on the fingerboard. Start with ground basses (repeated harmonic patterns), simple ones at first, and then more complicated ones as you develop the ability to negotiate them with confidence and creativity. At first play just the chord tones (over the entire range of the fingerboard), and after those arpeggios become absolutely comfortable, add notes that fill in melodically, but proceeding slowly and methodically cannot be overemphasized. Keep your improvisations simple. This will allow you to learn to improvise coherently. It is also important to give to whatever you play a strong sense of melodic direction, even if you are playing only chord tones. After mastering grounds, you will have the ability to improvise variations of melodies that will surpass the effects of simple ornamentation, and those new melodies will form the basis for free unaccompanied prologues. These few sentences about learning to improvise sum up a process that will take many years to accomplish. But your efforts will pay huge dividends, not only to your playing, but to your appreciation of all music.

Solo Music: The Sonata

With the influence of monody, the new style of Italian vocal music that emerged at the beginning of the century, instrumental music began to explore new forms and find new avenues of expression. The two most important changes that this new style of vocal music brought to instrumental music were, first, a bass-treble compositional texture, and second, freer melodic writing that, in vocal music, allowed composers to set texts to melodies that served the meaning of the words more directly. Just as the melodic character of a piece of monody might change dramatically many times, in order to convey their texts in the most affecting way, instrumental music also began to incorporate melodies that, through dramatic contrast, described more complicated concepts. All solo and ensemble instrumental music was influenced, to some degree, by Italian monody, but the instrumental form that most closely approached the vocal model was the sonata.

If one examines an early-seventeenth-century sonata in isolation (as violinists often do) without the benefit of any other knowledge of seventeenth-century music, the early sonata can appear quirky or even senseless (or perhaps, in a generous assessment, playful), especially in comparison to later sonatas. Without any attempt to establish the correct technical or stylistic perspective, violinists tend to perform these sonatas in ways that maximize the qualities of quirkiness that they perceive. But an understanding of early Italian monody teaches us that all those dramatic chromaticisms, changes of character and meter, and so forth are mere details that are subservient to larger structures of the composition. With text, those dramatic musical devices amplify the meanings of the words, and sentence structure holds the piece together in larger, coherent units. In an instrumental composition, without the benefit of words, an extra effort must be made to link separate sections together into a coherent whole. In this way, the performance of an early-seventeenth-century sonata can be one dramatic journey, instead of a numbing laundry list of effects that at best demonstrate the left-hand skills of the performer.

The earliest sonatas, without question, are best performed with the low-held technique. Violinists today can benefit, just as seventeenth-century violinists did, from the range of articulations and sounds that are available when the instrument is held in that position. But for pieces written during the last quarter of the century, when the harmonic language was changing in ways that made the elevated arm an asset, a judgment must be made (as mentioned earlier, in discussing late division repertory) as to which position expresses the music in the manner most natural for the body. In my estimation the sonatas of Johann Heinrich Schmelzer, for example, retain enough of the early-seventeenth-century sense of melody and division-style melodic figuration that they are best performed in the low-held position, in spite of the demands that makes on the left hand. The sonatas of Biber, one generation later, contain a harmonic and melodic language that is most effectively played in the shoulder-held position.

It will be difficult not to make the decision on playing position on the basis of which is the most accommodating for the left hand. But giving, in general, primary importance to the expressive needs of the music will improve your ability to be an effective performer more than any amount of attention that you give to the technical difficulties. In the end, it will be your increased sensitivity to the expressive differences in music that will demand that you learn new techniques, search out new knowledge, and insist that you approach each piece as unique within a larger stylistic framework.

NOTES

1. Douglass–Play It, 32 ff.
2. Playford–*Division Violin*.
3. Douglass–Renaissance Violin, 24–27.

Part 2: Repertory

Kevin Mason

Modern string players who choose to play old music are faced with a daunting task. Whereas a violinist of the seventeenth century had but to master a few styles of playing and often composed or improvised his own music, violinists today must tackle a dizzying array of styles, play many different types of violins with many types of bows, and play almost exclusively music they did not compose. The modern response to this dilemma has been the development of historical performance practice—a scholarly discipline designed to give musicians a historically informed basis for making choices about performing old music. This chapter is based on a deep involvement with the historical performance movement, and its intent is to provide guidance of a practical nature to modern violinists who want to explore seventeenth-century violin music. Though this earliest phase of Baroque violin playing has received less attention than that of the eighteenth century, it is nevertheless too broad to treat in detail here. The overview that we provide is meant to stimulate interest in seventeenth-century violin playing, raise questions about its technique, and point out neglected but worthwhile repertories for performance.

Until recently, the usual approach of modern string players was to label as "early" violin all aspects of violin playing from its origins in the early sixteenth century to about 1750. As our awareness and subsequent experimentation with performance practices of all musical periods have grown, we have come to realize that such a simplistic generalization is no longer useful or satisfying as an artistic stance. For the most part, our interest in "early" violin has focused on the eighteenth century, when systematic treatises on style and technique began to appear with regularity. Moreover, the music of this era is familiar to us through performances on modern instruments. As a result, most modern performances of seventeenth-century violin music are accomplished through anachronistic means—the use of either modern or eighteenth-century instruments,

170

bows, ornamentation, phrasing rhetoric, and countless other components of style. Such a "rear-view-mirror" approach to performance has left most players (not to mention their audiences) with the impression that the earliest music for violin is simple, crude, and unorganized. As such, its only value is in its formative influence on later composers. This view is unfair to say the least. A more appropriate stance would be to view the world of the violin in the early seventeenth century as an outgrowth and culmination of styles, practices, and techniques of the Renaissance. As in the sixteenth century, a violinist's primary role in the seventeenth century was to play dance music—a function that tended to make the construction of the seventeenth-century instrument more like that of the Renaissance violin, rather than instruments of the eighteenth century, which were made for a different function. As a result, we can assume that the sound of a violin from Monteverdi's time may be as different from an instrument of Bach's time as it is from a modern violin. Also, the playing technique of the instrument, down on the arm instead of up on the shoulder, began in the sixteenth century as a response to the demands of playing Renaissance dance music—a technique that continued throughout most of the seventeenth century. The musical forms are either direct carryovers from the Renaissance, or are based on Renaissance forms. The "new" sonata, for instance, combines elements of virtually every form known in the sixteenth century: canzona, fantasia, toccata, ricercare, dance forms, ground-bass variation, and popular song. When one accepts the symbiotic relationship of musical function, style, and technique from a given period on its own terms, rather than blindly applying anachronistic practices of a later period, one can easily see how innovative, dynamic, and even shocking seventeenth-century violin music must have seemed in its original contexts. After all, this is our ultimate goal—to make the music we play sound as interesting, fresh, and alive as the day it was conceived.

"Orchestral" Playing

For modern musicians, instrumental music is neatly divided into two categories: orchestral music and chamber music. In the seventeenth century, however, there was no such clear distinction. The idea of music written specifically for a large, stable, string-based ensemble was just beginning to develop, and orchestras in the modern sense simply did not exist until at least the 1660s.[1] Throughout the seventeenth century, however, large numbers of instruments, including violins, played together on special occasions. The number and makeup of such ensembles were determined as much by the acoustical context as the political importance of the occasion.[2] Little music for such large ensembles survives, and the music that does makes little distinction between "orchestral" style and "chamber" style. The usual approach of composers given the task of creating large-scale music was to take new or preexisting music in typically three, four, or five parts and arrange it for whatever instruments happened to be available—a procedure that stems directly from Renaissance practice. Violins were often an important part of large ensembles, but as often as not it was a one-on-a-part violin band and the violins were far outnumbered by winds and/or continuo instruments. Organized and stable all-string orchestras began to appear in the 1660s when Jean-Baptiste Lully gained control of the famous *vingt-quatre violons du roy* at the French court. The success of this group led to the establishment of similar groups in Germany, Italy, and England around the same time.[3] Dance music was at the heart of the orchestral repertory, but there were also overtures, sinfonias, and other pieces that punctuated theater productions and also served to cover up the noise created by set and scenery changes. Virtually all of Lully's orchestral music was printed in the seventeenth century, and music in the French style for a German orchestra survives in a manuscript in Cassel, and in publications by Georg Muffat (*Florilegium* I [1695] and II [1698]).[4] Also, important English orchestral music from the seventeenth century includes Matthew Locke's music to *The Tempest*, John Blow's opera *Venus and Adonis*, and all the theater music of Henry Purcell.

Soloistic Violin Playing: The Sonata Repertory

To most modern violinists, the most familiar chamber music from the seventeenth century is the solo, duo, and particularly the trio-sonata repertory. Solo sonatas (*à 1*) were written for a single instrument (usually violin, but the cornett was an acceptable alternate), with continuo accompaniment usually provided by a keyboard instrument (harpsichord or organ), but sometimes by a lute, theorbo, or harp. Duo sonatas (*à 2*) could be either for a pair of violins and continuo or a violin with melodic bass (bass violin, cello, viola da gamba, bassoon, or trombone) and continuo. The trio sonata (*à 3*) required two violins (or violin and cornett), melodic bass, and continuo.[5] One important but misunderstood aspect of performance practice in early violin sonatas concerns the basso continuo. Unlike eighteenth-century practice, the continuo line should rarely be doubled by a bowed bass instrument. This is particularly true in the first half of the century and applies to all vocal and instrumental chamber music.[6]

While much work still remains to be done, particularly on sonatas by non-Italian composers, scholars and performers alike have been drawn to this music because this is where most of the rhetorical and technical innovations in violin playing occurred.[7] The sonata was developed by Italian musicians, and in its earliest guise was a free-form piece that moved quickly from episode to episode, exploring the affectual and technical capabilities of the violin. In these early sonatas, one can observe many idiomatic techniques for the violin, such as tremolo, pizzicato, *col legno*, double and triple stopping, use of the extreme ranges, echo effects, and playing loud and soft. Though the earliest sonatas included formal and stylistic elements from all other instrumental music, by the mid-seventeenth century composers began to distinguish between church sonatas (*sonate da chiesa*) and chamber sonatas (*sonate da camera*)—the former retaining many of the free-form aspects of the early sonata, and the latter being more or less a dance suite.

Among the most important Italian collections of early violin sonatas are those of Biagio Marini (1617, 1629, 1655), Dario Castello (1629), Giovanni Battista Fontana (1641), Marco Uccellini (1645), and Giovanni Legrenzi (1673). As Italian musicians moved north of the Alps, the sonata and the new styles of violin playing that were developed in conjunction with that form began to influence violinists all over Europe. Outside Italy, the most important contributions to the sonata repertory were made by German and Austrian musicians such as Johann Kindermann (1653), Johann Schmelzer (1659, 1664), and Heinrich Biber (ca. 1676). In England, the Italian sonata did not take hold until late in the century, but its style did influence the "fantasy-suites" of such composers as Matthew Locke. Virtuoso violin playing, however, was known in England throughout the century mainly through the Renaissance art of playing "divisions," or melodic ornamentations above a repeated chord progression known as a "ground." The culmination of this type of solo violin playing can be seen in *The Division Violin,* published by John Playford in 1684.[8]

One-on-a-Part Consort Playing: The Violin "Band"

The most important role of the violin in the seventeenth century is also the one most neglected by modern violinists—that of playing one-on-a-part consort music. Such music is known to us largely due to the revival of the viola da gamba, whose amateur devotees have spurred the publication of many scholarly and performing editions. Some of the repertory clearly is written for the viols (though less than most viola da gamba players would acknowledge), but most of it is either written specifically for or is appropriate for violin-family instruments. As gamba players will attest, seventeenth-century consort music is as rich and satisfying to play as it is broad in style and form. Though the repertory consists largely of dance music, there are also canzonas, sinfonias, fantasies, ground-bass variations, and arrangements of popular songs. If the sonata is predominantly soloistic in style, then consort music is decidedly unsoloistic, with each part assuming a more or less equal role. As a result, consort music is complete in and of itself and does not require a continuo instrument, although sometimes a basso continuo or a *basso seguente* part is provided, in which the player follows whichever line is lowest. It can involve as few as two instruments, or as many as eight or nine for double-choir pieces.

The most common makeup of a violin consort, or "violin band," however, is a four- or five-part ensemble of violin-family instruments. In general, the top part is played by a "treble" violin, with the middle parts played by "alto" and "tenor" violins (violas of various sizes), and the bass taken by a "bass" violin—similar to a cello, but larger and tuned to B♭.[9]

The four-part violin consort began in the sixteenth century as a true "Renaissance" ensemble in SATB format. The top part was usually taken by a violin with the lower parts played by violas (of different sizes sometimes) and bass violin. One of the most interesting pieces in this configuration is Carlo Farina's *Capriccio Stravagante* (1627), which incorporates many new string techniques, such as double and triple stops, tremolo,[10] *col legno*, and pizzicato. This early configuration with a single violin on top continued at least into the 1660s, where it appears in the music of Schmelzer (1662). A second configuration, with two violins on top, begins in the early seventeenth century as an expansion of the new trio texture through the addition of an optional viola part labeled *si placet*. By the 1620s this "string quartet" scoring was common: it is fully exploited in the music of Thomas Simpson (1621) and the later works of Marini (1655). One of the most important sources of seventeenth-century string quartet music is that of Gasparo Zanetti, whose *Scolaro* (1645) includes not only bowings, but also parallel versions of dances in regular notation and in violin tablature.

Likewise, the five-part consort could have either a single violin (largely an early configuration) or a pair of violins on top. In Italy the relatively little five-part music that survives is largely connected with the theater, as in Monteverdi's *Orfeo* (1609). North of the Alps, however, five-part consort music flourished. In England, five-part texture seems to have been the norm for the masque music of John Adson (1621).[11] English expatriate William Brade published five-part masque and other dance music in Germany (1609, 1617, 1621) as did German composers Michael Praetorius (1619), Samuel Scheidt (1621), Andreas Hammerschmidt (1636, 1639), and Johann Rosenmüller (1667). The German tradition of five-part consort music was continued in Austria by Schmelzer (1662) and Biber (1676, 1683).

The Concertato *Violin*

Perhaps the least familiar repertory for violin is *concertato* music—chamber works with voices and instruments "concerted" together.[12] There were basically two ways in which violins were combined with voices. In the first, the violin (or some other melodic instrument) is added to a preexisting vocal work, either doubling a voice part (with or without ornamentation) or improvising its own part based on the harmonic progression of the piece. Since this was largely an improvised art, or at least one of arrangement, we know little about it. In the second type of *concertato* music, the violin plays a composed part of its own, without which the composition would be incomplete. It is largely an Italianate phenomenon, with some of the best examples found in the works of Claudio Monteverdi (1610, 1619, 1638).[13] By the end of the century, *concertato* technique had become an integral part of cantata composition, as seen most notably in the cantatas of Alessandro Scarlatti. Early-seventeenth-century Italian musicians traveling north of the Alps influenced composers of chamber music most notably in Germany where *concertato* music was written by Heinrich Schütz (1629) and Andreas Hammerschmidt (1642, 1643).

NOTES

1. See Zaslaw–Orchestra.
2. See Spitzer–Orchestra.
3. The rise of the English court orchestra is recounted in Holman–*Fiddlers*.
4. The music is edited in Écorcheville, *Vingt suites d'orchestre du XVIIe siècle* (Paris, 1906; rpt. 1970).
5. Questions of instrumental substitutions in the seventeenth century are treated in Mangsen–*Ad libitum*.
6. See Jack Ashworth and Paul O'Dette's chapter "Basso Continuo" in this volume.
7. In particular, see Newman–*Baroque*; Boyden–*Violin*; Apel–*Violin Music*; and Allsop–'*Trio*' *Sonata*.
8. Playford–*Division Violin*; facs. rpt., New York: Performer's Facsimiles, 1995.
9. See Stephen Bonta–Bass Violin; Boyden–*Violini Piccoli*; and Boyden–Tenor Violin.
10. See Carter–Tremolo.
11. See also Sabol–*Stuart Masque*.
12. This is not to be confused with the "concerto" repertoire of the eighteenth century and later in which one or more solo instruments are "concerted" with an orchestra.
13. Monteverdi's *concertato* works involving violin as discussed in Holman–Monteverdi's String Writing.

BIBLIOGRAPHY

Allsop–'*Trio*' *Sonata*; Apel–*Violin Music*; Ashworth/O'Dette–Proto-Continuo; Bonta–Bass Violin; Boyden–Violini Piccoli; Boyden–Tenor Violin; Boyden–*Violin Playing*; Carter–Tremolo; Douglass–Play It; Douglass–Renaissance Violin; Holman–*Fiddlers*; Holman–Monteverdi; Mangsen–Ad libitum; Newman–*Baroque*; Selfridge-Field–*Venetian*; Spitzer–Orchestra; Zaslaw–Orchestra.

Recommended Listening

Canzonetta. The King's Noyse. HMU 907127.
The King's Delight. The King's Noyse. HMU 907101.
Stravagante. HMU 907159.

Editions of Music

Adson, John. *Courtly Masquing Ayres, Composed to 5 and 6 Parts, for Violins, Consorts, and Cornets*. London, 1621. Facs. ed. Amsterdam, 1977. Includes dance music in five and six parts suitable for violin band.
Biber, Heinrich. *Sonate tam aris*. Salzburg, 1676. Modern ed. *DTÖ*. Vols. 106–07 (1963). Sonatas in 5, 6, and 8 parts for violin band.

———. *Mystery (Rosary) Sonatas*. ca. 1676. Modern ed. *DTÖ*. Vol. 25 (1905). Sonatas for solo violin and continuo.

———. *Mensa sonora*. Salzburg, 1680. Modern ed. *DTÖ*. Vol. 96 (1960). Suites for string quartet and continuo.

———. *Fidicinium sacro-profanum*. Nuremberg, 1683. Modern ed. N. Harnoncourt (Vienna, 1977); and *DTÖ*. Vol. 97 (1960). Sonatas for four- and five-part violin band.

Blow, John. *Venus and Adonis*. Modern ed. by Clifford Bartlett (Wynton, 1984). Includes orchestral dance music for violins.

Brade, William. *Newe ausserlesene Paduanen*. Hamburg, 1609. Modern ed. by B. Thomas as *Pavans, Galliards, and Canzonas* (London, 1982). Includes dances and canzonas for unspecified five-part consort, but suitable for violin band.

———. *Pavans and Galliards*. Hamburg, 1614. Modern ed. by B. Thomas (London, 1986). Includes dance music for unspecified six-part consort, but suitable for violin band.

———. *Newe ausserlesene liebliche Branden*. Hamburg, 1617. Modern ed. in 3 vols. by B. Thomas (London, 1974). Includes dance music for unspecified five-part consort, but suitable for violin band.

———. *Newe lustige Volten, Couranten, Balletten, Padoanen, Galliarden, Masqueraden*. Hamburg, 1621. Modern ed. by B. Thomas (London, 1991). Includes dance music for unspecified five-part consort, but suitable for violin band.

Castello, Dario. *Sonate concertate in stil moderno*. Venice, 1629. Facs. ed. Florence, 1979. Includes duo and trio sonatas for violins.

———. *Sonate concertate . . . libro secondo*. Venice, 1629. Facs. ed. Florence, 1981. Includes sonatas á 1, 2, and 3 suitable for violins, plus two pieces á 4 for string quartet.

———. *Selected Ensemble Sonatas*. Modern. Ed. E. Selfridge-Field. Vols. 23 and 24 of *Recent Researches in the Music of the Baroque Era* (Madison, 1977).

Écorcheville, J., ed. *Vingt suites d'orchestre du XVIIe siècle français, publiées daprès un manuscrit de la Bibliothèque de Cassel*. Paris, 1906. Reprint 1970. String chamber orchestra music in the French style. Mostly four-part dances.

Falconiero, Andrea. *Il primo libro di Canzone, Sinfonie, Fantasie, Capricci, Brandi, Correnti, Gagliarde, Alemanne, Volte*. Naples, 1650. Facs. ed. Florence, 1980. Mostly dance music for two violins, unspecified bass instrument, and continuo.

Farina, Carlo. *Capriccio stravagante*. Included in *Ander Theil neuer Paduanen* (Dresden, 1627). Modern ed. by N. Harnoncourt (Wilhelmshaven, 1970). Extended free-form piece for four-part violin band with many special effects and techniques.

Fontana, Giovanni Battista. *Sonate a 1. 2. 3.* Venice, 1641. Facs. ed. Florence, 1981. Includes solo, duo, and trio sonatas for violins, and one sonata for three violins. All the solo and duo sonatas are edited by F. Cerha in vols. 13–15 of *Diletto Musicale* (Vienna, 1962).

Gabrieli, Giovanni. *Sonata a tre violini*. Included in *Canzoni et sonate* (Venice, 1615). The entire collection is edited as vol. 27 of *Le Pupitre* (Paris, 1971). Sonata for three violins and continuo (dated but serviceable modern edition in *Hortus musicus*).

Hammerschmidt, Andreas. *Weltlicher Oden oder Liebesgesänge*. Freiburg, 1642 and 1643. Modern ed. in *Das Erbe deutscher Musik*, 1st ser. Vol. 43 (1962). German secular songs for one and two voices concerted with solo violin and continuo.

———. *Erster Fleiss [& Ander Theil] neuer Paduanen, Galliarden, Balletten. . . .* Freiburg, 1636 and 1639. Modern ed. in *Das Erbe deutscher Musik*, 1st ser. Vol. 49 (1957). Dance music in five parts for violin band.

Kindermann, Johann. *Canzoni, sonatae*. Nuremberg, 1653. Modern ed. in *DTB*. Vol. 24 (1913). Sonatas and canzonas for one to three violins and continuo.

Legrenzi, Giovanni. *La Cetra. Libro quarto di sonate a due, tre e quattro stromenti. Opera decima*. Venice, 1673. Facs. ed. Bologna, 1970.

Locke, Matthew. *Chamber Music*. In *Musica Britannica*. Vols. 31 and 32 (London, 1971 and 1972). Consort music in two, three, and four parts, much of it suitable for violin family instruments.

———. *Music for* The Tempest. In *Musica Britannica*. Vol. 51.

Lully, Jean-Baptiste. *Oeuvres complètes*. Ed. H. Prunières. Paris, 1930–1939. *Les Ballets*. 2 vols. *Les Comédies-Ballets*. 3 vols. *Les Opéras*. 3 vols. Music for string orchestra.

Marini, Biagio. *Affetti musicali* [Opus 1]. Venice, 1617. Facs. ed. Florence, 1978. Modern ed. by Piperno (Milan, 1990). Includes sonatas, canzonas, sinfonias, and dance music in two and three parts for violins.

———. *Sonate, symphonie, canzoni* . . . Op. 8. Venice, 1629. Includes sonatas, canzonas, and dances *à 1, 2, 3, 4, 5*, and *6* for solo violin, two violins, and violin band.

———. *Sonate da chiesa, e da camera* . . . Op. 22. Venice, 1655. Facs. ed. Florence, 1979. Includes sonatas *à 2, 3*, and *4* for violins.

———. *String Sonatas* from Op. 1 and Op. 8. Ed. T. Dunn. Vol. 10 of *Collegium Musicum: Yale University* (Madison, 1981).

Monteverdi, Claudio. *L'Orfeo*. Venice, 1609. Reprint. 1615. Facs. ed. Farnborough, 1972. Modern ed. by Malipiero in Monteverdi, *Complete Works*. Vol. 11 (Vienna, 1968). Pairs of violins and the violin band are featured throughout this opera.

———. *Vespers*. Venice, 1610. Modern ed. by C. Bartlett (Huntingdon, 1991). Vocal music concerted with violin band.

———. *Settimo libro de madrigali*. Venice, 1619. Modern ed. by Malipiero, Monteverdi, *Works*. Vol. 7. Vocal music concerted with two violins up to six-part violin band.

———. *Madrigali guerrieri, et amorosi*. Venice, 1638. Modern ed. by Malipiero, Monteverdi, *Works*. Vol. 8. Reprint. New York, 1991. Vocal music concerted with two violins up to six-part violin band.

Playford, John. *The Division Violin*. London, 1684. Facs. rept. New York, 1995. Division variations on popular tunes for solo violin and continuo.

Praetorius, Michael. *Terpsichore*. Wolfenbüttel, 1612. Modern ed. (incomplete) in 6 vols. by B. Thomas (London, 1989). Includes dance music in four, five, and six parts for unspecified consort, but suitable for violin band.

Purcell, Henry. *The Works of Henry Purcell*. London, 1878–1965. Rev. ed. 1968– . *Dido and Aeneas*. Vol. 3. *Dioclesian*. Vol. 9. *Fairy Queen*. Vol. 12. *King Arthur*. Vol. 26. Orchestral music.

Rosenmüller, Johann. *Sonate da camera*. Venice, 1667. Reprint. 1670. Modern ed. in *Denkmäler deutscher Tonkunst*. Vol. 23 (1904). Dance suites for five-part violin band.

Sabol–*Stuart Masque*. Includes dance music in two-five parts suitable for violin band.

Scheidt, Samuel. *Paduana, galliarda, courante*. . . . Hamburg, 1621. Modern ed. S. Scheidt: *Werke*. Vols. 2–3 (Leipzig, 1971). Dances and canzonas for four- and five-part violin band.

Schmelzer, Johann. *Duodena selectarum sonatarum*. Nuremberg, 1659. Modern ed. in *DTÖ*. Vol. 105 (1963). Sonatas for one violin, viola da gamba, and continuo, and two violins and continuo.

———. *Sacro-profanus concentus musicus*. Nuremberg, 1662. Modern. ed. in *DTÖ*. Vols. 91-92 (1965). Sonatas for two-eight instruments and continuo.

———. *Sonatae unarum fidium*. Nuremberg, 1664. Modern ed. in *DTÖ*. Vol. 93 (1958). Six sonatas for solo violin and continuo.

Schütz, Heinrich. *Symphoniae sacrae I*. Venice, 1629. Modern ed. in *Neue Schütz Ausgabe*. Vols. 13 and 14. Includes vocal music concerted with two violins and continuo.

Simpson, Thomas. *Taffel-Consort*. Hamburg, 1621. Modern ed. B. Thomas (London, 1988). Includes dance music for unspecified four-part consort, but suitable for violin band.

Uccellini, Marco. *Sonate, correnti et arie* . . . Op. 4. Venice, 1645. Facs. ed. Florence, 1984. Sonatas and dances in two and three parts for violins.

Zanetti, Gasparo. *Il scolaro per imparar a suonare il violino, et altri stromenti*. Milan, 1645. Facs. rep., Florence, 1984. Modern ed. by J. Tyler (London, 1983 and 1985). Consists of dance music for four strings.

10

The Viola da
Gamba Family

Barbara Coeyman and Stuart Cheney

In many ways the seventeenth century marked the zenith of the viol in
Europe. Certainly we will never fully determine the scope of its use, but
the several hundred surviving instruments and thousands of compositions suggest that the viol may truly have been one of Europe's most popular art instruments ever.[1] While both the physical construction and
repertory of the viol in the seventeenth century contain many national
features evident since the Renaissance, certain other aspects of the viol
were common throughout Europe. We will summarize some of these
general features before examining the viol by national areas.

Repertory for the viol partakes of nearly all common compositional
approaches, instrumentations, and genres of the seventeenth century.
Imitative polyphony, inherited from the Renaissance, appeared in fantasies, ricercares, and other ensemble genres. Compositions based on
previously composed harmonies or melodies highlighted composers'
ingenuity at reworking and ornamenting known material as well as the
viol's capacity for sustained tones. The instrument also performed dance
music, often organized into suites and sonatas.

These compositional approaches parallel continent-wide trends in
instrumentation. All sizes of viols performed both uniform and mixed
ensemble music, most commonly composed in two to six parts, while divisions on grounds as well as unaccompanied music (usually for bass) test-
ed players' technical prowess in composed and improvised music. Viols,
particularly basses, performed not only soloistically but also assisted the
basso continuo by playing the bass line; they also accompanied voices in
what is called "lyra-way" playing. Viols of all sizes appeared in chamber
music, in combination with virtually all wind and string instruments then
in use; they were also used to complement voices.

During the seventeenth century, viols were built in several sizes and
shapes, showing only a slight reduction from the great variety seen dur-

ing the previous century.[2] Both iconography and surviving instruments suggest that the prevalence of relatively large instruments during the Renaissance carried through most of the first half of the seventeenth century. Most Italian and German treatises from 1590 to 1620 call for tunings a fourth or fifth lower than those used today—further evidence that larger instruments continued to prevail.[3] Some small English viols from early in the century may prove the exception and may also support Jean Rousseau's assertion in 1687 that it was the English who first reduced the standard sizes of viols. English instruments nearly the size of modern trebles are known from the first decades of the seventeenth century but small trebles from other countries are not known in this period. However, during the second half of the seventeenth century, smaller instruments analogous to modern sizes gradually became the norm throughout most of the continent. Division and lyra viols were slightly smaller than the contemporaneous basses, and the violone—usually a fourth or fifth below the bass viol—was also common.

Also underlining the viol's centrality in musical life, the instrument adapted features of playing technique from other instruments. Its distinctive resonance made it susceptible to influences from the lute and harpsichord in particular. Throughout the century, viol composition increasingly capitalized on this resonance, as in the *Pièces de viole* by Marin Marais. It is not surprising that these trends in composition parallel growing professionalism among players, builders, and teachers. Furthermore, throughout the century the instrument was the object of published discourse: treatises described construction of instruments, tuning, holding positions, right- and left-hand technique, and so forth.

The viol's popularity was due in part to the support of courts and upper-class patrons of music, many of whom played the instrument and also supported builders, composers, and professional performers. Iconographic evidence suggests that both women and men played, but research to date indicates that professional players and teachers were primarily men. Performance settings ranged from intimate, private locations in the context of other social activities where distinctions between performers and listeners and amateurs and professionals were minimal, to formal, public concerts featuring professional performers exclusively.[4] While throughout Europe the viol was virtually replaced by the louder, more dramatic violin by the mid-eighteenth century, this change of musical aesthetic was also a response to the larger physical settings that public concerts required. The timing of this transition from viols to violins varied. Viols fell from popularity in Italy and the Low Countries by the mid-seventeenth century; in England the instrument flourished until the end of the century, while in France and Germany the viol coexisted with the violin for at least the first few decades of the eighteenth century.[5]

The history of the seventeenth-century viol is so vast that we can address only some of its more prominent features, including principal repertory and composers, treatises and other writings concerned with playing technique, and builders and surviving instruments. We exclude issues such as construction, maintenance, and modern instruction books, discussed in an earlier volume in this series.[6] To fill the many *lacunae* we encourage the reader to explore references in our bibliography.[7]

The Viol in Italy

Repertory

Many traditions of viol playing and composing that flourished in sixteenth-century Italy continued in the early seventeenth century. In Italy the instrument served diverse musical functions, providing accompaniment in dramatic music, entertainment at social and academic gatherings of the upper classes and nobles, and virtuoso solo music.

Lower-range viols were primarily used in dramatic settings, beginning as early as the Florentine *intermedii* of 1565 and 1589. Among their gifts viols possessed special capacities to enhance personal vocal expressions such as lamenting or tender loving. It is for such affects, for example, that Monteverdi called for viols, from *Orfeo* of 1607 (*tre bassi da gamba* in Act 3) to his eighth book of madrigals in 1638. (*Altri canti d'Amor* includes two parts for *viola da gamba*.) His seventh book (1619) includes such specifications as *viola da braccio overo da gamba* and *basso de braccio overo da gamba*.[8] Monteverdi's own affinity for viols should not be surprising since his first professional post was as an instrumentalist at the Mantuan court, where he played viol and perhaps other bowed strings.[9] Additionally, throughout much of the century viols were commonly associated with church and oratorio productions, particularly in Venice.

The issue of terminology relating to the viol and violin families is too complex to be discussed in detail here, but several recent research studies have informed generalizations included in this chapter.[10]

It is ironic that it was in Italy, where the Renaissance viol thrived, that the instrument was first replaced by the violin family. If some observers prized the viol for its particular but subtle powers of expression, as described above, others began to see the violin as a more effective and obvious vehicle for moving the affections. Vincenzo Giustiniani, in his *Discorso sopra la musica* (after 1628), relished the passing of the era of viol and flute consorts, whose old-fashioned "unity of sound and of consonances became tiresome rather quickly."[11] From Rome in 1639, André Maugars, the French virtuoso player who had served Louis XIII of France and James I of England, commented: "As for the viol, there is no one in Italy now who excels at it; indeed it is very little played in Rome."[12] The Englishman Thomas Hill wrote from Lucca in 1657 that "the violin and organ they are masters of, but the bass viol they have not at all in use, and to supply its place they have the bass violin with four strings, and use it as we do the bass viol."[13]

In spite of the infiltration of violins, however, the viol continued to be used in Italy. Often the two instruments appeared side by side in instrumental ensembles at the beginning of the century. Viols are cited in instrumental ensemble music (sonatas and canzonas) at least through the 1670s, primarily in publications by Italian composers associated with Austrian or German courts: Biagio Marini (1626), G. B. Buonamente (1626, 1637), Carlo Farina (1628), Dario Castello (1629), Marco Uccellini (1639), Marco Antonio Ferro (1649), Gaspare Filippi (1649), and Antonio Bertali (1672). Specific rubrics in this repertory favor the bass instrument, for both melody and bass line, and sometimes include the viol in combination with violin, cornett, trombone, bassoon, flute or recorder, and a variety of plucked strings.

A few composers continued to write for homogeneous ensembles of viols. For example, Bartolomeo Montalbano's *Sinfonie* (Palermo, 1629) includes four movements for four viols, and a collection of five-part canzoni by Cherubino Waesich was published in Rome in 1632. Giovanni Legrenzi's *La Cetra* (Venice, 1673) contains two sonatas for four-part consort, the latest known works for viols to be published in Italy.[14]

A distinctive Italian repertory of Renaissance origin that continued in the seventeenth century was music for *viola bastarda*. This term indicates not a particular instrument, but instead a compositional and/or performance style, in which polyphonic vocal models—usually mid-sixteenth-century madrigals and chansons—were reduced to a single melodic line on the bass or contrabass viol.[15] Works firmly in the bastarda style range from the 1580s to the mid-seventeenth century.[16] Composers of this fascinating repertory consist primarily of viol virtuosos, some of whom also wrote treatises on the art of embellishment: Girolamo Dalla Casa, Richardo Rogniono, Francesco Rognoni, Aurelio Virgiliano, Orazio and Francesco Maria Bassani, and Vincenzo Bonizzi.[17] Particularly in its later stages, this Italian style of playing influenced English division viol technique. However, the *viola bastarda* should not be confused with the English lyra viol style.[18]

Instruments

The continued production of viols throughout the seventeenth and eighteenth centuries attests to at least a limited use of the instrument in Italy. While many Italian instruments were shipped out of the country, the foreign market alone cannot account for the entire output of Italian viols, including several by the finest Cremonese and Brescian builders.[19]

Another popular instrument in Italy was the *lirone* (or lyra da gamba), a viol with up to sixteen strings capable of playing sustained chords in continuo parts, either alone or in combination with other chordal instruments. It enjoyed widespread use in the accompaniment of dramatic monody. Originating in the sixteenth century as a bass version of the *lira da braccio,* the *lirone* was common throughout most of the seventeenth century. Maugars described hearing it in ensembles in Rome, and various inventories list the instrument well into the eighteenth century.

The Viol in England

Repertory

The greatest flowering of ensemble literature occurred in England, where the cultivation of consorts of viols lasted longer than in other nations.[20] The viol and its music were highly valued and cultivated in court, church, and domestic musical establishments during the reigns of James I and Charles I, the latter an ardent player. Even during the Commonwealth viols flourished except in public religious services. By the end of the century, however, only the bass viol sustained any notable popularity, the violins having taken over ensemble music in England as in Italy.

Most of William Byrd's viol consorts date from the Elizabethan period, ending in 1603. The most important precursors of the magnificent compositions for viols during the Jacobean and early Carolinian eras, Byrd's compositions established the three principal genres of English consort music for viol: fantasias, dance pieces, and contrapuntal works based on Taverner's popular *In nomine* cantus firmus.

The title of Anthony Holborne's *Pavans, Galliards, Almains . . .* (1599) mentions viols, along with violins and wind instruments, as appropriate for playing this charming repertory of dance music in five parts.[21] The dance music of Holborne reminds one also of early court masques, in which viols played a significant musical role. Though similarly based on dance music, John Dowland's *Lachrimae or Seaven Teares* (1604) contains ten "passionate" pavans, along with nine traditional galliards and two almands for five viols (or violins) with lute.[22] The first seven pavans, the *Teares,* are all based on *Lachrimae Antiquae,* also the theme of Dowland's lute song "Flow my tears."

Volume 9 of *Musica Brittanica,* entitled *Jacobean Consort Music,* includes other composers and repertory of the early seventeenth century, notably Orlando Gibbons, Alfonso Ferrabosco the Younger (also called Ferrabosco ii), and John Coprario (= Giovanni Coperario). Gibbons, who wrote masterfully in the "traditional" forms inherited from the generation of Byrd, sometimes designated the lowest part for double bass in G or A. Alfonso Ferrabosco was highly regarded for his forty fantasias and assorted dance pieces, *In nomines,* and "Lessons" for lyra viols (see below). Coprario distinguished himself in his fantasia-suites, which call for violins on the upper lines, supported by bass viol and organ, and his fine music for viol consort. Also noteworthy are the compositions of Thomas Tomkins, Richard Mico, William White, Thomas Lupo, and Michael East.[23]

William Lawes and John Jenkins are foremost among composers for the viol at mid-century. Although Lawes died at an early age in the Civil War, he left a large body of viol music, including suites for two bass viols with organ, for three lyra viols, and the masterful consort sets in five and six voices.[24] Lawes's fantasias are more expressive and idiomatic than those of earlier composers. His eleven "harp" consorts for violin, bass viol, harp, and theorbo are a distinctive and unusual contribution to the repertory.

Responding to Italian trends in instrumentation and genre, several of Jenkins's pieces employ violins with bass viol and organ. His supreme monuments for viols, however, are his sets of consorts for four, five, and six parts.[25] Their fascinating melodic, harmonic, and textural richness demonstrates why his music was probably the most widely circulated in England during his lifetime. The three-part fantasias show the trend toward shorter, sectionalized pieces; in these, the violin may be implied for the treble parts. Many of the bass parts in Jenkins's pieces involve virtuosic division writing so characteristic of English playing of the day.

Also from the middle of the century, the consort music of Matthew Locke and John Hingeston is associated with the brief heyday of the viol following the Restoration, before Charles II's explicit preference for violins (and for music to which he could tap his foot!). Hingeston wrote for standard combinations of viols, with and without violins, but his most imaginative pieces are those he composed for two and especially three bass viols.[26] The complex polyphony of Locke's *Consort of Fower Parts*, praised by North, is clearly for viol ensemble. The ten suites of the *Little Consort of Three Parts* works well on either viols, violins, or some combination of the two families. Locke also wrote the two-part consorts "ffor severall ffriends" (treble and bass), the three-part *Flatt Consort*, and the three-part *Broken Consort*.[27]

The fantasias and *In nomines* by Henry Purcell (1680) are the last in a tradition that spans nearly 150 years. Written when Purcell was in his early twenties, these works range from three to seven parts.[28] Since by this time treble and tenor viols had practically fallen out of fashion except in conservative amateur gatherings, Purcell may have intended that upper parts be played on violins and violas. Many compositional techniques, particularly the smooth counterpoint and shifting tonalities, pay homage to Jenkins and Locke.

The lyra viol was slightly smaller than a consort bass, with a flatter bridge to facilitate chordal playing, although its repertory is also playable on a consort bass.[29] Evidence suggests that the earliest lyra repertory was originally played on standard basses, with the smaller instrument developing at a later date. Therefore, it is accurate to speak of lyra viol, like *viola bastarda,* as a manner of playing. Notated in tablature, lyra viol music combines polyphonic, melodic, and chordal textures on a single self-sufficient instrument. Tablature allows the performer to adapt easily to the wide variety of tunings available, each contrived to exploit specific tonalities, open sonorities, and melodic and chordal finger patterns.[30]

Most surviving lyra music is for one viol, playing melody and accompaniment simultaneously, as in pieces for solo lute. A few works from early in the century are for two to three lyra viols, and from mid-century several compositions for one or two with other instruments are known. Lyra viol pieces by such composers as Coprario, Ferrabosco the Younger, Jenkins, Lawes, Dietrich Stoeffken, Simpson, and others were popular from the Jacobean period through the remainder of the century. From the first decade of the century we have Tobias Hume's *First Part of Ayres* (1605), *Captain Hume's Poeticall Musicke* (1607), and Ferrabosco the Younger's *Lessons for 1.2. and 3. Viols* (1609).[31] From 1651 on, John Playford published collections that included music for lyra viol, such as *A Musical Banquet* (1651) and *Musick's Recreation on the Viol, Lyra-Way* (1661, 1669, 1682).[32]

The division viol is another example of how a performing technique inspired the design of a new instrument: these were built smaller than basses in order to facilitate rapid passagework. Many composers wrote out divisions in solo and consort parts, while others left such embellishment to the discretion of a skilled interpreter. Entire sets of divisions were also composed on "grounds," or repeating bass patterns.[33] Simpson's *The Division-violist* (1659; subsequent editions are entitled *The Division-Viol*) provides the most thorough advice for this advanced playing technique.[34]

Throughout the period under consideration, viols took part regularly in ensembles with other instruments and with voices. Ensembles of viols, violins, and organ have already been mentioned. Additionally, Thomas Morley's *First Booke of Consort Lessons* (1599) calls for the standard "broken" consort of the turn of the century: transverse flute, treble viol or violin, cittern, lute, bandora, and bass viol.[35] Philip Rosseter's *Lessons for Consort* (1609) are similar to Morley's.[36] The bass viol is scored with cittern in Holborne's *The Cittharn Schoole* (1597), with keyboard in *Parthenia Inviolata or Mayden-Musicke* (ca. 1614), and with lutes and/or bandoras in Hume's *Poeticall Musicke* (1607).

In numerous secular and sacred contexts, viols provided accompaniment for voices. Between 1600 and 1622 the phrase "To Be Sung to the Lute and Base Violl" or some variant appears on title pages of many printed songbooks; from the 1620s to as late as 1695, wording such as "with a Thorow-Bass for the Theorbo or Bass-Viol" appears.[37] Additionally, title pages of vocal ensemble publications early in the century frequently include the phrase "apt for voices or viols." Viols also participated with voices in consort songs and verse anthems, both of which flourished up to the Commonwealth. In the latter genre, and often in the former as well, solo voices alternate with a choral ensemble, accompanied by viols and/or organ.[38]

Instruments

While one should be circumspect in using a few surviving instruments to draw conclusions about instrument design and practice of the past, the many extant seventeenth-century viols probably provide a relatively reliable picture of English viol building. Of the nearly 100 known extant instruments, almost two-thirds date from after 1650. Also, slightly more than two-thirds of these are basses, those from before 1633 on average slightly larger than later specimens. Principal English builders were Henry Jaye from the first half of the century, and Richard Meares and Barak Norman from the latter half. Although Mace cites Aldred, Jay, Smith, Bolles, and Ross (= John Rose?) as important makers during the early decades of the century, no instruments by either Aldred or Bolles are known to survive. Mace further advises that older instruments are preferable to newer ones. His recommended chest of instruments for a respectable musical household is a matched set of two trebles, two tenors, and two basses, plus two violins, two theorboes, and three lyra viols that could also serve as extra trebles if needed, or "likewise for Division-Viols very Properly."[39]

Treatises

During the first two-thirds of the century, English viol technique advanced beyond that of other nations. Based on his first-hand knowledge of English, French, and Italian practices, André Maugars declared in 1639 that although Italian musicians introduced the viol into England, English players "have since surpassed all other nations."[40] English musicians such as William Brade, Thomas Simpson, Daniel Norcombe, and William Young enjoyed success at various musical establishments on the continent during this period, and their presence influenced both repertory and technique in the Low Countries, Germany, and Eastern Europe.

That many of the published viol treatises in English contain a greater amount of practical information than those from other countries is no doubt due to the large number of amateur players seeking instruction. Principal English treatises that explain technique to beginning players include

1603	Thomas Robinson, *The Schoole of Musicke*
1652	John Playford, *Musick's Recreation on the Lyra Viol*
1654	Playford, *A Breefe Introduction to the Skill of Musick*
1655	Playford, *An Introduction to the Skill of Musick.* In two books
1659	Christopher Simpson, *The Division-violist*

1676   Thomas Mace, *Musick's Monument*
1699   Anonymous, *The Compleat Violist*
         (with pieces by Benjamin Hely)

Robinson's treatise is primarily a lute method, but it contains basic information on the viol such as the proper holding of instrument and bow, and instructs that "in all points, carrie your left hand upon it, as you doe upon the Lute." Playford's works of 1654 and 1655 contain information on tuning treble, tenor, and bass sizes and on mensural notation, but offer no information on holding either instrument or bow. *Musick's Recreation* explains only tuning methods and the reading of tablature. *The Division-violist* is the most thorough English treatise of the century. Starting with the second edition, the work was issued in Latin as well as English to accommodate the international market.

The Compleat Violist is comprehensive: it includes standard tunings, the correct manner of holding instrument and bow, and general principles for bowing (e.g., "to begin with a forward Bow, all even Numbers [of] prickt Notes & to draw backward ye first of all odd Numbers"). After fundamentals of notation, a graduated sequence of pieces moves the novice from single-line playing to complicated chords, sixteenth-note passages, and ornamentation.

Both Simpson and Mace advise that to hold a bass, one should sit comfortably and place the instrument between the calves "so that a Stander by, cannot easily take It Thence."[41] The viol should tilt slightly to the player's left, with the neck leaning back a little over but not touching the left shoulder and without the support of the left hand, which must be free to shift. Knees should be arranged to avoid impeding any bow motion, especially on the highest and lowest strings.

For the bow, Simpson advises holding the stick in the right hand near the frog (nut) between the thumb and the end of the index finger. The second finger curves inward below the stick, with the fingertip touching the hairs. Pressure is applied to the hair from the second finger while playing on the strings; this pressure is variable and helps to control the expressive qualities of the bowing, the articulation, and the dynamics. "If the second finger have not strength enough, you may joyn the third finger in assistance to it."[42] Mace adds that he (like most modern players) prefers a grip two to three inches from the frog.

For the left hand, both Simpson and Mace prescribe a position with the thumb behind the neck opposite the first finger, in the manner of lute technique, thus maintaining the ability to shift easily up and down the neck.[43] Both also strongly advise holding down fingers as long as possible to sustain both melody and harmony, a feature that players apparently had to be reminded of as frequently in the seventeenth century as today. Mace instructs the viol player to follow the same rules for left hand contained in his chapters on the lute.

Mace also admonishes the beginner to "Arm your self with Preparative Resolutions to gain a Handsom-Smooth-Sweet-Smart-Clear-Stroke; or else Play not at all." In bowing, Simpson allows for some movement of the right shoulder, but warns that in passages of "quick Notes" the wrist should come into play to avoid shaking the entire body. To accomplish this, either the forearm should lead the hand by means of a supple wrist, or the wrist alone should manage bow changes in very rapid passages. With regard to the flexibility of the elbow, he owns that there are opinions for both extremes (stiff and loose) and good players to affirm both methods. Simpson's own advice is for a stiff elbow "in Smooth and Swift Division," but a more flexible approach for "Cross and Skipping Division," in string crossings. Mace's best advice for arm motion is to produce a straight bow that remains parallel to the bridge from tip to frog. For bass viols, Simpson and Mace advise placing the bow two to three inches above the bridge. Mace also addresses other sizes of viols, advising bowing one and a half inches from the bridge for the treble "and so upon all Others, according to This Suitable Proportion."

The Viol in the Low Countries

Many paintings reflect the extent to which viol playing and other amateur music-making flourished in northern Europe. However, in the Low Countries political turmoil, social unrest, and Calvinist restrictions meant that public concert life was minimal, particularly in northern cities such as Amsterdam, Utrecht, Rotterdam, and the Hague.[44] However, music-making occurred in homes and in the numerous *collegia musica*. Although instrument building flourished in Brussels and Antwerp, few viols from the Netherlands survive.[45] Predictably, most of these are basses. Builders included Peeter Borbon of Brussels and Hendrick Jacobs, Jan Boumeester, and Pieter Rombouts of Amsterdam.

English influence was important in the north. The residence of the English court at the Hague starting in 1648 resulted in the publication of the *Konincklycke Fantasien,* twenty-nine three-part works specifying viols by English composers such as Lupo, Coprario, and Gibbons.[46] The correspondence and memoirs of statesman Constanijn Huygens (1596–1687) provide some of the most cogent insights into the Netherlands' contacts with other countries.[47] It is unfortunate that so few of his reported 800 compositions survive. Of several solos and trios for viols his single surviving instrumental work is an allemande for lyra viol.[48]

Viol music from the Low Countries parallels that from other parts of the continent and was inspired in part by music for other instruments. Viols performed dance music, often in combination with violins. Free types of imitative polyphonic compositions appeared under such classifications as *canzone* and *fantaisie* by little-known composers such as Peeter

Picart of Antwerp (1679); Charles Guillet (1610), who published one collection of twenty-four *fantaisie* in Paris; and Valerie Gonet (1613).[49] We know that the English style of playing lyra-way was cultivated in the Netherlands from Huygens's report of Stoeffken's visit to the Netherlands in 1646–49, when the two often played viol duets.[50] Important Belgian contributors to solo bass repertory at the end of the century include Carolus Hacquart (1649–1701) and Johann Schenck (1660–1712). Schenck's chief publications for viol date between 1688 and 1706 and include *Uitgevonende tyd en konst-oeffeningen* Op. 2, *Scherzi musicali* Op. 6, and *L'echo du Danube* Op. 9, all for one viol and basso continuo; and *Le nymphe di Rheno* Op. 8, for two bass viols alone.[51]

Political and religious unrest accounts for the dearth of music publishing in the Netherlands during the seventeenth century. A few anthologies intended for both recorders and viols, such as *Der Goden Fluit-hemel* (1644), were published at mid-century. Most works in this collection are songs or dance tunes for one to three treble instruments by native composers. Two anthologies, *t'Uitnement Kabinet . . . met 2. en 3. Fioolen . . .*, of 1646 and 1649, contain nearly 200 pieces for treble and bass instruments in up to three parts by Dutch, Italian, French, and English composers.[52]

The Viol in Germany

Contrary to a common view that German Baroque viol music was highly distinctive and original—an impression undoubtedly fostered by familiar but somewhat anomalous repertory by composers such as J. S. Bach and G. P. Telemann—German viol music in the seventeenth century was generally an absorber of other national styles rather than a definer of new attitudes. The Thirty Years War (1618–48) devastated many areas of Germany, reducing the size of ensembles and disabling music publishing in most cities except Nuremberg. Accompaniment of vocal music was perhaps the viol's most distinctive contribution to German musical style. On the other hand, German ensemble music for viols alone is generally less responsive to the idiomatic ringing quality of the instrument. This generic sound may in part explain the viol's adept participation in vocal and instrumental chamber music in Germany, and its longer coexistence with the cello well into the eighteenth century. While exact data on repertory may never be compiled, Germany may have been the most prolific country of all in terms of number of compositions for the viol.[53]

Repertory

German viol repertory is comparable to that in other areas of Europe: consort playing dominates the first half of the century, music for solo bass viols with and without basso continuo, the second half. As in the Low Countries, English style influenced German polyphonic ensemble music, for which instrumentation is usually not specified. Under pressure from Italian violin music early in the century, viol consort playing in southern Germany declined early in the century, but remained strong in the north. The Englishman William Brade worked at the court of Schleswig-Holstein and in Hamburg, where he published a collection of suites in 1607, predating collections by German composers such as Johann Hermann Schein's *Banchetto Musicale* of 1617. Thomas Simpson settled in Heidelberg.[54] Eventually English visitors were replaced by Italian artists, largely because of the importation of Italian opera.[55]

At the end of the century, numerous multimovement suites and sonatas for one, two, and sometimes three basses with or without basso continuo were composed by native German composers. Perhaps influenced by French solo viol music and opera, instrumental practice adopted many French characteristics, although German composers generally treated the viol more as a melodic than a harmonic instrument, using fewer chords and idiomatic ornaments than did the French. A set of fourteen sonatas by August Kühnel (1645–1700) that appeared at the end of the century (1698) evinces English style and pedagogical intent. Twelve sonatas and suites from 1695 by Konrad Höffler (1647–1705) are also worthy of mention.[56]

German chamber music may be the least known repertory for the viol. During the second half of the seventeenth century, chamber instrumentations commonly included one or two violins, bass viol, and continuo. In some repertory the viol does nothing more than embellish the continuo, but in others it displays the Italianate proclivity for improvisation and virtuosic display. The two dozen sonatas for violins and bass viol by Dietrich Buxtehude exemplify this repertory, and other contributors to this style include Johann Kaspar Kerll, Johann Heinrich Schmelzer, Johann Michael Nicolai, Johann Theile, Johann Adam Reincken, and Philipp Heinrich Erlebach.[57] Viols also appeared in German sacred and secular vocal music, presaging Bach's similar use of the instrument in the following century. Many German and Viennese seventeenth-century composers, in particular Buxtehude, incorporated the viol to highlight special affects, especially passion, lamenting, celestial love, and the voice of Christ.[58] This repertory adeptly blends English consort scoring with Italianate concertato principles.

Instruments

Collections of viols probably not unlike those illustrated by Michael Praetorius in 1618 are commonly documented in German upper-class homes and courts by the end of the sixteenth and the beginning of the seventeenth century.[59] Praetorius's drawings suggest that all sizes were in common use. Research indicates that surviving German viols outnumber those from other countries. Two-thirds of these are basses, but trebles, tenors, and *violoni* also remain. German viol builders include Joachim Tielke of Hamburg, Ernst Busch of Nuremburg, Jacob and Marcus Stainer, Martin Hoffman of Leipzig, and Gregorius Karp of Koenigsberg.[60]

The Viol in France

In France, viol repertory evolved from relatively generic use and easy technique to virtuosic solo music. As in many other aspects of cultural life during the richest decades of the reign of Louis XIV in the second half of the century, French writing for solo *basse de viole* established a pan-European standard and offered the principal challenge to the emerging Italianate violin practice. In the early eighteenth century solo repertory for treble and pardessus viols surpassed even that for bass in the hands of some composers.

It is clear that the viol paralleled certain practices found in other parts of Europe. It remained integral to the cultural life of the nobility at court as well as the upper classes in private homes, where it was used in the context of social entertainments. Many viol players received endorsements from nobles and held positions in court music institutions, especially under Louis XIV. Eventually the instrument moved into the opera orchestra and other mixed ensembles, events that coincided with growing professionalism among performers and teachers. Iconography suggests that the instrument was played by both men and women nobles, but apparently only males became professionals.

Repertory and Composers

Repertory for French viols in the seventeenth century parallels the other national styles: up to mid-century, polyphonic ensemble music predominated; music for unaccompanied bass appeared in mid-century; solo music, usually for bass, with basso continuo prevailed during the final decade. Additionally, the viol was an integral part of instrumental and vocal chamber music.

Many of the early ensemble works are *fantaisies*; dance music for viols, often arranged in suites, appeared in the 1640s. The influence of English consort music on French ensembles has not yet been explored in detail, but clearly there were connections in repertory and performers between the two countries As noted above, André Maugars worked at the court of James I (1620–24), and Mersenne's *Harmonie Universelle* (1636) includes music by Ferrabosco as an illustration of the *fantaisie*.[61] Most surviving early-seventeenth-century French ensemble music does not specify viols, nor does it exploit the distinctive timbres of the instrument in the way the English repertory does, although across the decades compositional style became more idiomatic. Approximately 150 compositions that viol ensembles may have played are known to survive. Most of this repertory is for two to six parts and is also playable by mixed consort or keyboard instruments alone, particularly organ. It includes works by Eustache DuCaurroy (1610), Guillet (1610), Claude LeJeune (posthumous collection of 1612), Etienne Moulinié (1639), Nicolas Métru (1642), Henri DuMont (1652, 1657, and 1668), and Louis Couperin (mss, ca. 1650).[62] The *Concert pour quatre parties de Violes* of 1680 by Marc-Antoine Charpentier is a last effort in France for this scoring.[63]

Inspired by increasingly idiomatic technique, similarities to lute and harpsichord, and the development of the dance suite, composers for the viol turned to unaccompanied solo pieces by mid-century. The full extent of this repertory is only now being clarified: some manuscripts designated for viol survive, but viol players may also have played music designated for lute, and certainly must have improvised.[64] At least several dozen pieces were composed by Nicolas Hotman (ca. 1613–63), treble viol player in Louis XIV's court.[65] Dubuisson (ca. 1622–ca. 1680) composed 116 movements, most grouped into the dance suites that formed the principal genre for the instrument in the second half of the seventeenth century.[66] Le Sieur de Ste. Colombe produced his collection of sixty-seven *concerts* for two bass viols sometime before 1680, and more than 170 additional works for solo bass viol by the composer have recently been discovered.[67] These pieces—idiomatic for viol, but with suggestions of the *stile brisé* (broken style) of plucked instruments—attest to Ste. Colombe's skill as a player. The eight suites for unaccompanied bass by Le Sieur De Machy (1685) are the only known published works of this type from France; half are in staff notation and half in tablature, lending credence to our belief that viols and lutes shared repertory.[68]

The peak of development for the French viol is the solo repertory with basso continuo, most of it arranged in suites of dances.[69] Between 1686 and 1725 Marin Marais published five books in all, containing almost 600 pieces for one or two bass viols and basso continuo, arranged in forty suites.[70] All five volumes contain extended prefaces explaining playing technique. Additionally, Marais's own performance skill and dramatic talent (he wrote four successful operas) are suggested in the virtuosic writing in many movements.

We also find the viol in French chamber music. François Couperin included it in several *concerts* of the 1690s, Charpentier used the viol in his *Sonata à 8* (ca. 1686), and Marais partnered it with the violin in several pieces such as six suites *en trio* of 1692 and the *Sonnérie de Sainte-Genevieve du Mont*.[71] Toward the end of the century, the viol also appeared as an obbligato instrument in French cantatas, such as those by Elizabeth Jacquet de la Guerre.

Builders

The most prolific French builder in the late seventeenth century was the Parisian Michel Colichon. Tourin's *Viollist* indicates that in the seventeenth century all sizes of viols were built in France. As in the rest of Europe, basses predominated by the second half of the century. Jean Rousseau asserted in 1687 that it was Ste. Colombe who added the low A string to the bass viol. By the end of the century, builders such as Colichon and Medard also built treble and pardessus viols, which offered some alternative to violins, whose increasing popularity nevertheless remained symbolic of Italianate performance.

Writings about the Viol

French writings on the viol variously discuss repertory, instrument construction, and playing style. Mersenne's description of the viol is the most complete statement from the first half of the century. Not coincidentally, several treatises appeared during the 1680s, the same decade that saw the first publication of a solo repertory. The theoretical writings of Danoville, *L'art de toucher le dessus et la basse de viole,* and Rousseau, *Traité de la viole,* both of 1687, offer comprehensive, analytical examinations of the instrument.[72] *Avertissements* to collections by DeMachy and Marais and pedagogical tracts by Dubuisson and Etienne Loulié are more practical in their orientation.[73] Not unexpectedly, the prefaces of publications often advance the personal viewpoint of their composers: apparently self-promotion in the music business was as important then as it is today. The relative difficulty of this repertory accounts for the need for such prefaces to explain symbols for fingering, bowing, ornaments, and others; and effects such as glissandos, vibratos, trills, mordents, and fingering are addressed. Modern performers may consult the prefaces of DeMachy and Marais for information about playing technique.

NOTES

1. Attention to the viol in general histories of Baroque music is disproportionately low compared to its popularity and repertory. While specific aspects of the viol have been studied recently, no comprehensive history of the instrument during the Baroque has appeared. Most of the information about existing viols and builders has been taken from Tourin–*Viollist,* 2d ed. in preparation by Dr. Thomas G. MacCracken. Special thanks to MacCracken for sending us information from this upcoming revised edition before publication.
2. Zacconi–*Prattica di musica*; Virgiliano–*Il Dolcimelo*; Banchieri–*Conclusioni*; Cerone–*El Melopeo*; Praetorius–*Syntagma* II.
3. The generalizations made here belie several issues of detail that remain to be solved. See Myers–Pitch and Transposition; Woodfield–*Early History*; Harwood–Double Standards (responses to this article are listed in the General Bibliography); Segerman–Praetorius . . . Viol; Catch–Talbot's Viols; Graham-Jones–Random Thoughts. Our thanks to Herbert Myers for shedding light on this subject.

4. Thomas Mace comments that consorts are "so Suitable, and Agreeing to the Inward, Secret and Intellectual Faculties of the Soul and Mind; that to set Them forth according to their True Praise there are no Words Sufficient in Language." Mace–*Musick's Monument*, 234.

5. See Linfield–Viol Consort, 163, where Roger North is cited for lamenting the passing of the old traditions as violins replace viols.

6. The viol is discussed in Gillespie–Bowed Strings in the *Renaissance* volume of this series.

7. Some of the principal sources of information about the viol include the *Journal of the Viola da Gamba Society of America*, *Chelys* (the journal of the Viola da Gamba Society of Great Britain), and the *New Grove Dictionary of Music and Musicians* with its several supplements. For scholarly and performing scores, a virtual explosion of modern editions for the viol include A-R Editions, Corda, Dove House, Faber, Fretwork, London Pro Musica, Nagels Musik-Archiv, Northwood, Scolar, Schott, Stainer & Bell, VdGSA Music, Hortus Musicus, and others. Series with facsimiles of viol music include those published by Caldwell of Oberlin, Minkoff, and Broude Bros. For practical information about the instrument, as well as instruction methods, see Gillespie–Bowed. See also method books by Grace Feldman, Alison Crum, and Martha Bishop. Many of the composers/performers mentioned here are described in more detail in individual entries in *New Grove*.

8. Holman–*Col nobilissimo*, 578–80.

9. Monteverdi's brother Giulio reports in the foreword to *The Fifth Book of Madrigals* that the composer has busied himself with his new duties as choirmaster as well as "the playing of the two *viole bastarde*," which may refer to the two primary sizes in use; thus he was still playing *viola bastarda* in 1605. This is further evidence that it was probably as a viol player that Monteverdi came to Mantua around 1590. See also Strunk–*Source Readings*, 406.

10. Not so controversial is the term *viola* (pl. *viole*), which is used in a general way for bowed string instruments, either *da braccio* (on the arm, the violin family) or *da gamba* (on the leg, the viol family). However, terms such as *basso*, *bassetto*, *basso di viola*, *contrabasso*, and *violone* have seen much ink spilled toward their clarification. The reader can find more details in major studies such as Bonta–Violone; Bonta–Terminology; Allsop–Role; Borgir–*Basso Continuo*; Peter Holman–*Col nobilissimo*.

11. Allsop–*Trio Sonata*, 26–27.

12. Maugars–*Response*, 17, 66. Apparently unknown to Maugars, the Barberini family enjoyed private viol consort performances in Rome throughout the 1630s, and as late as 1673 the Conservatorio dei Mendicanti in Venice purchased viols. See also Hammond–Decade, 105–09; and Bonta–Terminology, 40.

13. Hill–*Stradivari*, 110–111n.

14. Ed. in Bonta–*Legrenzi*. Bonta suggests that the occasion for this late, somewhat anomalous scoring was the acquisition by the Conservatorio dei Mendicanti, where Legrenzi was later employed, of a consort of several viols in the same year as the publication of the sonatas.

15. Paras–*Viola Bastarda*, xvii. This study not only examines the performance practice and sources of the music, but also contains fully notated examples of most of the known repertory.

16. Paras–*Viola bastarda* (36–49) traces sources up to 1626, 36–49. Saunders–Valentini has dated a piece written in Vienna or Kassel to c. 1650.

17. Besides Paras, London Pro Musica has published several *bastarda* settings in the series *Ricercate e Passaggi: Improvisation and Ornamentation*, 1580–1630.

18. Praetorius's often-repeated mistake was to assign several lyra viol tunings, designed for chordal playing, to the instrument he called the *viola bastarda*. See *Syntagma* II: 26, 47–48. See also Paras–*Viola Bastarda*, 11–13, 25.

19. The makers include Gasparo da Salò, Giovanni Paolo Maggini, Nicola Amati, Pietro Zenatto, Giuseppe Giovanni Battista Guarneri, Antonio Stradivari, Matteo Gofriller,

and Vincenzo Ruggieri. See Tourin/MacCracken–*Viollist*; Hill–*Stradivari*, 114. Information on instruments has also been provided by Ray Nurse, an instrument builder and researcher in Vancouver, B.C.

20. Viol music is included in editions of complete works of several of the more prominent composers, and the series *Musica Britannica* includes much English viol music.

21. Ed. Bernard Thomas (London, 1980).

22. John Dowland, *Complete Consort Music,* ed. Edgar Hunt (London, 1985).

23. Vols. 59 and 65 of *Musica Britannica* are devoted to Tomkins and Mico, respectively.

24. William Lawes, *Consort Sets in Five and Six Parts,* ed. David Pinto (London, 1979).

25. John Jenkins, *Consort Music for Viols in Four Parts,* ed. Andrew Ashbee (London, 1978); *Consort Music in Five Parts,* ed. Richard Nicholson (London: Faber, 1971); *Consort Music for Viols in Six Parts,* ed. R. Nicholson and A. Ashbee (London, 1976).

26. Hingeston's trios are published by Dove House Editions, Ottawa, Canada; the consort music by PRB Productions, Albany, CA.

27. Locke's repertory named here is edited in *Musica Britannica,* vols. 21 and 22. The *Flatt Consort* has also been edited by Nathalie Dolmetch in *Hortus Musicus,* no. 180.

28. Ed. Thurston Dart in *The Works of Henry Purcell*; also ed. Herbert Just for *Nagels Musik-Archiv,* nos. 58, 113.

29. See the articles on lyra viol sources by Frank Traficante listed in the bibliography. Besides the Hume and Ferrabosco publications for lyra viol(s) discussed below, see also *John Coprario: Twelve Fantasies for Two Bass Viols and Organ and Eleven Pieces for Three Lyra Viols,* ed. Richard Charteris in *Recent Researches in the Music of the Baroque Era,* vol. 41. For lyra viol in ensemble with other instruments, Traficante has edited *John Jenkins: The Lyra Viol Consorts* in *Recent Researches in the Music of the Baroque Era,* vols. 47 and 48.

30. Tunings for lyra viol were customarily expressed in terms of relative intervals between strings, rather than fixed pitches. They are given here in the tablature system, which refers to finger placement, with each letter representing a fret (i.e., a = open string, b = first fret, and so forth). The letters used to express tunings show where a finger would be placed on one string in order to match the next higher open string, working from the highest pair of strings to the lowest. Thus the letter "d" in any tuning system represents a minor third, "e" a major third, "f" a perfect fourth, and so on. Of the more than fifty tunings known to have been used in England and on the Continent, these nine predominated: f f e f h (violl way), d e f h f (harp way sharp), e d f h f (harp way flat), e f d e f (common tuning sharp, or French set), f d e f h (high harp way sharp), f e d f h (high harp way flat), f e f h f (lyra way, or bandora set), f f e f f (violl way, lute way, or plain way; also standard tuning), and f f h f h (Alfonso way–one of the tunings named for Ferrabosco). See Traficante–Lyra Viol Tunings.

31. Both Hume volumes are edited by Frank Traficante and published together in fascimile in *English Lute Songs* 1597–1632, vols. 24–25 (Menston, England, 1969). A facsimile edition of Ferrabosco's *Lessons* is published by Theatrum Orbis Terrarum, Amsterdam, and Da Capo Press, New York, 1973, in *The English Experience,* no. 514.

32. A facsimile of the 1682 edition, with introduction by Nathalie Dolmetsch, was published by Hinrichsen (London) in 1965. There are facsimile editions of the Marsh Lyra Viol Book (Boethius Press) and the Goess manuscripts (Tree Editions). Other modern editions of lyra viol music include Jonathan Dunford's edition of English and French repertory from Bibliothèque Nationale Rés. 1111, in *Pièces pour viole seule* (Strasbourg, 1992), no. 9219, and Martha Bishop's editions of *Tablature for One, Tablature for Two,* and *Tablature for Three* (for details on the latter, contact the Viola da Gamba Society of America).

33. Modern editions of divisions by Henry Butler are available in vol. 66 of *Recent Researches in the Music of the Baroque Era,* ed. Elizabeth V. Phillips and Jack Ashworth; divisions by Jenkins are published by Dove House and Fretwork.

34. The second edition of *The Division Viol, or The Art of Playing Ex tempore upon a Ground*

(London, 1665) is published in facsimile by J. Curwen, London, 1955.

35. Thomas Morley's *First Book of Consort Lessons,* ed. William Casey (Waco, TX, 1982). Also useful is Sydney Beck's edition (New York, 1959), although the lute, cittern, and pandora parts are transcribed. Mixed consort instrumentation seems to have often been used in Elizabethan and Jacobean theatrical productions.

36. Rosseter's collection as well as late-sixteenth-century pieces for mixed consort appear in *Musica Britannica,* vol. 40, ed. Warwick Edwards.

37. Ian Spink, *English Song: Dowland to Purcell* (New York, 1974), 261–69.

38. See Monson–Consort Song, 4–11; and Monson–*Viols and Voices* [no specific pp].

39. Mace–*Musick's Monument,* 245–46.

40. Maugars–*Response,* 17, 66.

41. Mace–*Musick's Monument,* 248.

42. Simpson–*Division-Viol,* 2.

43. Most modern players use the technique espoused by Jean Rousseau, in which the thumb is usually opposite the second finger.

44. The viol in the Low Countries has hardly been studied to date. The most recent information can be found in the research of Rudolph Rasch. See Crawford–Allemande, and Huygens; Cohen–*Evolution,* 87 ff; Rasch–*Konincklycke Fantasien,* Nogmaals, and Dutch Collections. Earlier work by Edmond van der Straeten (*History*) is noteworthy.

45. Tourin–*Viollist* includes only sixteen originating in Belgium, nine of these in the seventeenth century, and a similar number in Holland, six from the seventeenth century.

46. Modern edn. by Helmut Mönkmeyer, *XXIX Konincklycke Fantasien* as Band IV of *Monumenta Musicae ad Usum Practicum* (Celle, 1985); facs. ed. in partbooks in Rasch–*Konincklycke Fantasien.*

47. Huygens warrants greater study by music scholars. For information about his activities on the viol, see Crawford–Allemande, 176–77; and Crawford–Huygens. Also, see Huygen's correspondence about music in Huygens–*Musique* 2: 347ff.

48. A facsimile and transcription appear in Crawford–Allemande, 176–77.

49. Little is known about these composers. Picart and Gonet are discussed most extensively in Cohen–*Evolution,* 79–88, 123–29, 208–11, 260–69. Guillet's music is known in some editions in arrangements for organ.

50. See Crawford–Huygens, 46–50.

51. Karl Heinz Pauls has edited *Le nymphe di Rheno* in *Das Erbe deutscher Musick,* vol. 44, and *Echo du Danube* in vol. 67.

52. Rasch–Dutch Collections, 162–65. Much of this ensemble music is available in modern editions by Rasch and published by Saul Groen in Amsterdam.

53. Examination of the principal collected works of German music as in *Denkmäler der Tonkunst in Österreich, Denkmäler der Tonkunst in Bayern,* and *Das Erbe deutscher Musik* suggests that the viol was ubiquitous in German music-making in the seventeenth century.

54. There are many modern performing editions of the music of these composers. Among these, music by Brade has been released by Musica Rara and London Pro Musica; various combinations of movements from Schein's *Banchetto* are available from London Pro Musica, and Bärenreiter; and Simpson's music is also available from London Pro Musica.

55. Einstein–*Deutschen Literatur,* 29–44, discusses English influence; see bibliography for English translation. See also Linfield–Buxtehude, 176.

56. Kühnel's sonatas were published in 1928 by Schott, and by Alamire in 1984. Höffler's works are available in *Das Erbe deutscher Musik,* vol. 67, along with Schenk's *L'Echo du Danube.*

57. Editions of German music for viol are far too numerous to cite completely here: there are several editions of chamber music with viol by Dietrich Buxtehude; several German composers have been published by Dove House; sonatas by Gottfried Finger are available from Breitkopf; Philipp Heinrich Erlebach's trios sonatas are in the

Hortus Musicus series, vols. 117–18.

58. For more details, see Linfield–Buxtehude.

59. Praetorius–*Syntagma* II contains one of the earliest, yet quite extensive, discussions of viols in Germany.

60. See Tourin–*Viollist*.

61. Mersenne–*Harmonie universelle, Livre quatriesme des instrumens a chordes*, 190–204. The Ferrabosco *fantasie* appears on 200–01.

62. Modern editions of ensemble music by DuCaurroy, LeJeune, Guillet, and Moulinié are in progress, ed. B. Coeyman. See also Nicolas Métru, *Fantaisies a deux parties pour les violes*, ed. Paul Hooreman (Paris, 1973); Henri Dumont, Ensembles for Viol, ed. Barbara Coeyman (Ottawa, 1983); and Louis Couperin, *Pièces de Clavecin de Louis Couperin*, ed. Paul Brunold, rev. Davitt Moroney (Monaco, 1985).

63. The *Concert* has been edited several times, for example by Schott in 1958, but a new performing edition is needed.

64. Recent discoveries include sources of Marais and Ste. Colombe found in Edinburgh, Scotland; a manuscript of unaccompanied music by Young, Hotman, and Dubuisson in Warsaw; and music by Sainte Colombe in a manuscript in Tournus, France. Recent important research includes work by Jonathan Dunford, Stuart Cheney, François-Pierre Goy, and Donald Beecher.

65. Several of Hotman's pieces appear in Dunford–*Pièces*. A recent edition of fifteen Hotman works recently discovered in Warsaw has been published by Dove House Editions, ed. Ulrich Rappen. Hotman is mentioned in Mersenne's *Harmonicorum libri XII* (1635), 47.

66. Beecher and Cheney–*Dubuisson*; Cheney–Summary.

67. Sainte-Colombe, *Concerts a deux violes esgales*; facs. rpt., Geneva: Minkoff, forthcoming; modern edition by Paul Hooreman (Paris, 1973); new edition forthcoming by J. Dunford, to be published by Société française de musicologie, along with the first edition of the composer's unaccompanied works recently found in Edinburgh and Tournus.

68. DeMachy, *Pièces de Viole en Musique et en Tablature* (Paris, 1685); modern ed. Donald Beecher and Bryan Gillingham (Ottawa, 1982).

69. There is a good chronological listing of pieces for bass viol and continuo in the entry "Viole de gambe (répertoire)" in Benoit–*Dictionnaire*. A useful discussion of the French bass is Bol–*Basse de viole*.

70. The total count on Marais's works is actually higher than in these five books; for example, eighty-three additional works appear in the recently discovered manuscripts in Edinburgh. The five books of *pièces de viole* are available in two different facsimile editions, by Rudy Ebner of Basel, Switzerland, and Caldwell facsimiles of Oberlin, Ohio. Books 1 and 2 have been edited, with extended prefaces, by John Hsu and published by Broude Brothers. Several of Marais's pieces in the recently discovered Edinburgh manuscripts have been edited by J. Dunford, published by Les Cahiers du Tourdion, and Minkoff plans to publish three volumes of these Edinburgh manuscripts.

71. Couperin's *Concerts* are available in facsimile from Rudy Ebner of Basel, Switzerland, as well as Fuzeau Facsimiles of Paris. Couperin's *Complete Works* have recently appeared in a new edition from L'Oiseau Lyre, Monaco. Several editions or facsmiles of Marais's *La Gamme et autres morceaux de simphonie* and his 1692 *Trios* are available.

72. Danoville–*L'Art*; Jean Rousseau–*Traité* (both treatises are available in facsimile editions from Minkoff).

73. All of these writings are transcribed in Hans Bol–*La Basse de Viole*, 281–303. See also Kinney–Writings.

BIBLIOGRAPHY

General Resources

Chelys; Benoit–*Dictionnaire*; *New Grove*; *New Grove . . . Instruments*; *Journal of the Viola da Gamba Society of America*; Sandford–*Music*; Dodd–*Thematic Index*

Books and Articles

Allsop–*Trio Sonata*; Allsop–Role; Anthony–*French Baroque*; Bates–Early French Sonata; Beecher–Aesthetics; Beecher and Cheney–*Dubuisson*; Bellingham–Musical Circle; Benoit–*Musiques*; Benoit–Paris; Bol–*Basse de viole*; Bonta–*Legrenzi*; Bonta–Terminology; Bonta–Use of Instruments; Borgir–*Basso Continuo*; Bowles–*Musical Ensembles*; Brenet–*Concerts*; Buch–Texture; Buch–Influence; Caldwell–*Oxford History* 1; Cheney–Dubuisson; Coeyman–Viole de gambe; Cohen–Study; Cohen–*Evolution*; Cohen–Fantaisie; Crawford–Allemande; Cyr–Viol; Dalla Casa–*Il vero modo*; Dodd–*Warsaw*; Donington–*Interpretation*; Dunford–*Divers auteurs*; Einstein–*Deutschen Literatur*; Finlay–Musical Instruments; Gillespie–Bowed Strings; Graham-Jones–Random; Green–Rousseau; Gutmann–*Improvisation*; Hammond–Decade of Music; Holman–Col nobilissimo esercitio; Holman–*Fiddlers*; Holman–London; Hsu–*Handbook*; Hsu–Use; Hughes–Unaccompanied; Huygens—*Musique*; Kinney–Tempest; Kinney–Problems; Kinney–Writings; Krummel–*Music Printing*; Ledbetter–*Harpsichord*; Le Gallois–*Lettre*; Lesure–Terpsichore; Lesure–Le traité; Lesure–Une querelle; Linfield–Viol Consort; Mace–*Musick's Monument*; Massip–*La vie*; Massip–Paris; Maugars–*Response*; McDowell–*Marais and Forqueray*; Mersenne–*Harmonie Universelle*; Mirimonde–La musique; Monson–*Voices and Viols*; Moreno–*Music and Its Symbolism*; F. Neumann–*Ornamentation*; K. Neumann–Captain Hume; K. Neumann–Jean Rousseau; *New Grove*–Ornaments; Otterstedt–*Lyra-Viol*; Otterstedt–Spoon; Paras–*Viola Bastarda*; Payne–Provision; Pinto–Fantasy; Playford–*Briefe Introduction*; Playford–*Musick's Recreation*; Price–*Early Baroque*; Rasch–*Konincklycke Fantasien*; Rasch–Nogmaals; Rasch–Dutch Collections; J. Rousseau–*Traité*; Sadie–Bowed Continuo Instruments; J. Sadie–Charpentier; J. Sadie–*Bass Viol*; Saunders–Giovanni Valentini; Schneider–*Französische*; Schwendowius–*Solistische Gambenmusik*; Segerman–Praetorius and English Viol Pitches; Selfridge-Field–Instrumentation; Selfridge-Field–Italian Oratorio; Sicard–*L'école française*; Sicard–French Viol School Before 1650; Sicard–French Viol School . . . Repertory; Simpson–*Division-Viol*; D.A. Smith–Ebenthal; K. E. Smith–*Voices and Viols*; Spink–*Blackwell*; Strunk–*Source Readings*; Spink–*English Song*; Spitzer–Grammar; Teplow–Rhetoric; *Titon du Tillet–Vies*; Tourin–*Viollist*; Traficante–Lyra Viol Tunings; Traficante–Lyra Viol: Manuscript; Traficante: Lyra Viol: Printed; van der Stracten–*History*; Viles–New Grove Index; Walls–London; Woodfield–*Early History*; Woodfield–Viol; Woodfill–*Musicians*.

11

Keyboard Instruments

Mark Kroll

This chapter is written primarily for the keyboard player who wishes to explore the rich traditions of the seventeenth century, but who has had little or no experience with the instruments and their repertory. Such a player will be confronted with a bewildering array of choices and problems, and it is hoped that this will serve as a starting point from which to conduct further research and experimentation. Early-music specialists who play other instruments and who wish to know more about the keyboard literature may find it informative, and it could also be a reference source for experienced organists and harpsichordists.

After an initial philosophical statement, the chapter is divided into three sections. The first answers questions about early keyboard performance practice, including technical issues. Section two offers an overview of the most common forms and genres, and section three covers the national schools of seventeenth-century keyboard composition.

Steps to Parnassus

All music is ultimately vocal. Instruments are essentially mechanical extensions of the human voice and almost every aspect of musical expression uses song as a model. Ever since the first aulos was made, what student has not been urged by his teacher to "make it sing"?

However, making an instrument "sing" involves more than producing a beautiful sound and a sustained line. The player of early keyboard repertory would be well advised to keep in mind that music has its roots in speech, in rhetoric, and in the differentiation between vowels and consonants. The harpsichord, perhaps the most vocal of all the keyboard instruments, is ideally suited for this purpose. This intentionally provocative statement is offered here to underscore an aesthetic. The modern piano can easily and idiomatically produce vowels in a seamless legato texture, but the harpsichord—and to varying degrees the organ and clavichord—can reproduce *both* vowels and consonants, and by extension the subtle inflections, dynamics, and phrasing that are natural to a vocal line.

Performance Practice

Position of the Body and Hands

The first question for the player of an unfamiliar instrument is how physically to approach the hardware—in other words, hand and body position. The governing principles are relaxation and economy of motion; that is, the goal is to achieve the maximum musical result with the minimum of physical effort. This is of course true for all instruments, but it is particularly important for early keyboards.

The player should choose a chair that allows a straight line from the elbows to the knuckles when the hands are placed on the keyboard. The arms should hang loosely and naturally from the shoulders, assuming their normal position with elbows close to the body. Wrists should be neither lower nor higher than the hand. The body should remain erect, natural, quiet, and focused.

Simply stated, the harpsichord is played with the fingers. Contrary to the mechanics of modern piano playing, in which all parts of the body assume an important role in technique and sound production, playing the harpsichord only minimally involves the forearm, arm, and shoulders. The wrist is involved, but should always remain supple, flexible, and quiet. The fingers should be curved as much as possible without striking the keys with the nails, and should be poised at the edge of and also quite close to the surface of the keys. Little is achieved by striking the keys from a distance except inaccuracy, coarse articulation, and a harsh sound.

These principles are based on a large body of historical evidence, as well as this writer's extensive practical experience as a performer and teacher. They were clearly articulated by theorists and composers at the outset of this great period of keyboard composition. One of the first and most important sources is Girolamo Diruta's *Il Transilvano* (1593/1609), a most important and influential source of information on performance practice. Diruta's works are mentioned in the treatises of Costanzo Antegnati and Adriano Banchieri and received the recommendation of Claudio Merulo.

Regarding hand and body position, Diruta writes:

> To begin, the rules are founded on definite principles, the first of which demands that the organist seat himself so that he will be in the center of the keyboard; the second that he does not make bodily movements but should keep his head and body erect and graceful. Third, that he must remember

that the arm guides the hand, and that the hand always remains straight in respect to the arm, so that the hand shall not be higher than the arm. The wrist should be slightly raised, so that the hand and arm are on an even plane . . .[1]

The fingers should be placed evenly on the keys and somewhat curved; moreover, the hand must rest lightly on the keyboard, and in a relaxed manner; otherwise the fingers will not be able to move with agility. And finally, the fingers should press the key and not strike it . . .

This is probably more important than all else . . . You must keep the hand relaxed and light, as though you were caressing a child . . . And remember that the arm must guide the hand and must remain at the same angle as the key, and that the fingers must always articulate clearly, but never strike the keys; and lastly one finger should never be raised from the others. While one lowers the other must rise. As a final warning, do not lift the fingers too high, and above all, carry the hand lightly and with alertness.[2]

These principles, stated with such thoroughness and authority, became the standard for succeeding generations of keyboard players. Evidence of this can be found throughout the seventeenth and eighteenth centuries, and within every national style. For example, the French organist Nivers writes, "In order to play agreeably, you must play without effort. To play without effort, you must play comfortably. This is achieved by placing the fingers on the keyboard gracefully, comfortably, and evenly—curving the fingers, especially the longer ones, so their length is equal to the shorter ones."[3] In the next century F. Couperin, the sine qua non of harpsichord player/composers, writes in his *L'Art de Toucher le Clavecin*, "In order to be seated at the correct height, the underside of the elbows, wrists and the fingers must be all on one level: so one must choose a chair that agrees with this rule . . . Sweetness of touch depends, moreover, on holding the fingers as closely as possible to the keys."[4] Forkel, in recalling the playing style of J. S. Bach, has this to offer:

Seb. Bach is said to have played with so easy and small a motion of the fingers that it was hardly perceptible. Only the first joints of the fingers were in motion; the hand retained even in the most difficult passages its rounded form; the fingers rose very little from the keys . . . and when one was employed, the other remained quietly in its position. Still less did the other parts of his body take any share in his play, as happens with many whose hand is not light enough.[5]

Fingering

In the field of historical performance, a discussion of fingering is guaranteed to raise the blood pressure of keyboard players. It is beyond the scope of this chapter to provide an exhaustive study of this large and complex subject. The reader is urged to refer to the excellent work in the field by Lindley, Soderlund, Boxall, et al. However, an overview will prove useful.

The concept of "correct" fingering in the seventeenth century was derived from the theory of "good" and "bad" notes (indicating notes that were metrically strong and weak), which were to be played by "strong" and "weak" fingers respectively. However, there is a significant divergence of opinion even on this basic theory, and one can find a wide variety of applications of this principle.

In brief, right-hand scale passages were generally fingered 3434 . . . ascending and 2323 . . . descending; left-hand, 2323 . . . ascending, 3434 . . . or 2323 . . . descending. The thumb was usually avoided, but it would be a misrepresentation to assert that it was never used. For example, as early as 1555 the Spanish theorist Juan Bermudo offered as one possibility the fingering of right-hand ascending scales to be 1234   1234 and 4321   4321 descending.[6] His countryman Correa de Arauxo wrote in 1616 that it is better to use the right-hand fingering of 1234   1234 and in the left hand 4321   4321 for "extraordinary runs" ascending.[7]

Of primary importance is that the player should avoid falling into the trap of basing musical decisions on mechanical evidence. Certainly, important insights into the articulation and phrasing that might have been intended by the composers can be derived from a study of early fingering. To cite an obvious example, a skip of a fifth played with the same finger would preclude a legato interpretation. But a skilled player can just as easily play a passage fingered 3434 . . . legato as well as detached. The reader is firmly cautioned against deriving absolute and dogmatic rules of interpretation from historical evidence of finger placement. Use the fingering as an important guide, but as only one of many factors that determine musical interpretation.[8]

The problems of a simplistic and narrow approach were noted at the beginning of the century, even as the music was being written, and at its close. Praetorius wrote the following in *Syntagma musicum* II (1618):

Many think it is a matter of great importance and wish to despise such organists who are not accustomed to this or that particular fingering, but this in my opinion is not worth talking about. Let one run up and down the keyboard with his first, middle or last finger or even with his nose if that will help him, for as long as what he plays sounds fine and pure, and is correct and pleasant to the ear, it is not very important how one accomplishes it.[9]

In 1702 the admirable French theorist M. de Saint-Lambert wrote his excellent treatise on keyboard performance, *Les principes du clavecin*. Appearing at the midpoint of two centuries of keyboard music, Saint-Lambert shows both hindsight and foresight: "There is nothing in harpsichord playing that is more open to variations than fingering. The choice must depend entirely on 'commodité' [comfort] and 'bonne grace' [proper style], and will vary from player to player."[10]

Articulation

Questions of articulation and touch are as complex and elusive as those for fingering, and François Couperin's reservations about commenting on the subject are still valid: "As it would require a volume filled with remarks and varied passages to illustrate what I think and what I make my pupils practice, I will give only a general idea here."[11]

Turning again to Diruta, it appears that a legato style is advocated. He criticizes those organists who "take their hands off the keyboard so that they make the organ remain without sound for the space of half a beat, and often a whole beat, which makes it seem that they are playing plucked instruments."[12] Nevertheless, Diruta also acknowledges that a more detached approach is called for in dance music, where one can use "leaping to give grace and air to the dances." He adds, "The fingers must always articulate clearly, but never strike the keys; and lastly, one finger should never be raised from the others, but while one lowers the other must rise."[13]

Frescobaldi's well-known admonition "not to leave the instrument empty" also seems to indicate a legato-based approach, although he was referring particularly to arpeggiating suspensions and dissonances.[14]

Nivers supports an emphasis on vocal models:

A sign of good breeding in your performance is a distinct demarcation of all the notes and subtle slurring of some. This is learned best from singing. That is, for example, in playing a run of consecutive notes, lift each note promptly as you play the following one . . . To connect the notes, it is still necessary to distinguish them, but the notes are not released so promptly. This manner lies between confusion and distinction and partakes a little of each. It is generally practiced with the *ports de voix* . . . For all these matters consult the manner of singing, for the organ should imitate the voice in such things.[15]

It would therefore be difficult and potentially misleading to describe anything as a "basic" touch for seventeenth-century keyboard music. However, one can deduce a consensus for a "starting point" touch in which one releases the preceding note at the instant one strikes the next. From this "basic legato" emanate two ends of an infinite spectrum. In one, a variety of *detaché* or silences between the notes; on the other, a hyper-slurred "over-legato," in which many and occasionally all of the notes are sustained simultaneously (what I call a "digital damper pedal").[16] The subtle gradations in between are impossible to measure or catalogue. Their application is further modified by almost every possible variable: musical context, texture, harmonic and melodic implications, the instrument (i.e., organ, harpsichord, clavichord) and its national style, the vocal line (with real or imagined texts, and paying close attention to the natural rhythmic inflections of each native language), articulation symbols (e.g., slurs, aspirations), ornamental figures (e.g., *ports de voix*, acciaccaturas), rhetorical gestures, and so forth. Moreover, one must again be wary of seeking absolutes. Style is an organic and evolving phenomenon. What may have been suitable for a piece written in Naples in 1625 may no longer be appropriate for one written in the same city in 1692. Its fickle nature is succinctly descibed by J. Engramelle in 1775: "Lulli, Corelli, Couperin, and Rameau himself would be appalled if they could hear the way their music is performed today."[17]

Instruments: Organ, Harpsichord, or Clavichord

When we investigate the actual instruments of the seventeenth century, we are on firmer ground. Fortunately, a number of keyboard instruments from the period have survived, and many are still playable or have been restored to good condition. By nature and circumstance, keyboard instruments were built within the parameters of national and even local styles, and most (particularly organs) remained in the original location where they were used. We can therefore make reasonably certain connections between performer, composer, and instrument. These keyboards, then, provide invaluable and direct evidence about the actual sonorities for which the music was intended. Well-restored instruments from the period are valuable teachers. Playing them provides concrete, tactile information about the possibilities of touch, articulation, registration, pedal work, and other aspects of keyboard performance.

The question of which instrument to choose for a particular piece is not so easily answered. Many works of the seventeenth century were written to be played on any keyboard instrument, and today's performer should feel free to do just that. However, others indicate a particular instrument, or at least a preference. Title pages and prefaces are valuable sources of information. For example, Giovanni Trabaci writes that the works of his *Libro primo* (1603) might be performed on "any kind of instrument, but equally best on organ and harpsichord" ("sopra qualsivoglia stromento, ma piu proportionevolment ne gli Organi e ne i Cimbali"). The same remark is found in the second book, but here the cembalo is named first, perhaps implying the composer's preference. Trabaci further indicates his fondness for the harpsichord in his *Partite sopra Zefiro* (1615), where he advises that some variations are meant for harp, but the harpsichord could always play them because "the harpsichord is ruler of all the instruments in the world, and one can play everything on it with ease."[18]

Function is another important factor in deciding which instrument to use. Music intended for liturgical purposes indicates organ performance, and secular dance forms usually imply the harpsichord. For example, the Council of Trent outlawed dances, intabulations, variations, and other works based on secular sources in church, so for these a harpsichord

would be the first, but not the only choice. The Council did permit versets, intonations, toccatas, ricercares, fantasias, capriccios, canzonas, and
sonatas, thus supporting organ performance. The clavichord was a particularly useful practice instrument for organists, who could not always
count on the availability of an organ blower, or who wished to avoid the
uncomfortable conditions in churches. But it could also be a very expressive solo keyboard instrument, and many pieces were implicitly if not
explicitly intended for it.[19]

Some composers were unambiguous and specific. Scheidt indicates in
his *Tabulatura Nova* (1624) that these works were written for an organ
"with two manuals and a pedal, the melody being in the soprano or tenor
particularly on the *Ruckpositif* with a sharp stop so that one hears the
chorale melody more clearly."[20]

Johann Speth specified an unfretted clavichord for his *Ars magna consoni et dissoni* (1693): "For the correct execution of these toccatas, praeam-
bles, verses, etc., a good and well-tuned instrument or clavicordium is necessary, and that it should be prepared so that each *clavir* [key] has its own
string, so that two, three or four *clavir* do not have to play on one string."[21]
In the case of the French repertory the choice is unmistakable, since the
titles of pieces intended for organ were the registrations themselves.

Inventories can also be a valuable guide. For example, composers in
the employ of Don Cesare d'Este in 1600 would have had at their disposal ten organs of varying sizes, including an organ with paper pipes,
and twelve harpsichords, many with two registers.

Tuning and Temperament

Early keyboard instruments need to be tuned and in the case of harpsichords and clavichords, tuned often. This was an accepted fact early on,
as this charming understatement from the sixteenth-century English
Leckenfeld proverbs attests: "A slac strynge in a virgynall soundithe not
aright."[22] Pianists who are just becoming acquainted with early instruments might at first be surprised by the importance of tuning. Rather
than seeing it as an obligation, however, they will realize that it provides
a welcome opportunity to control two artistic variables: pitch and temperament. (See the chapter "Tuning and Temperament" in this volume.)

The choice of temperament can have a significant effect on the realization of the expressive potential of a composition and its affect. For example, the diminished fourths of Frescobaldi sound poignant in unequal
temperament, but lose that effect and become indistiguishable from major
thirds in a homogenous equal temperament. Likewise, certain keys take
on individual characters in nonequal tunings. This is not to say that equal
temperaments were unknown in the seventeenth century. Suggestions to
divide the octave into twelve equal parts can be found as far back as
Bermudo in 1555. In general, however, composers were well aware of fine

gradations in tuning, and of the effect of temperament on musical style. The final choice will depend on historical evidence, the nature of the instrument, the affect of the work, and the player's own ear.

Forms and Genres

The seventeenth-century keyboard repertory is rich in the number and variety of forms and genres. The antecedents of many can be found in the sixteenth century or earlier, but others were newly invented or represent transformations or combinations of older forms. Since these works often carry specific implications of tempo, character, and performance practice, it is important that the player be familiar with the nature and history of each. The following brief descriptions of some of the more commonly used terms will help the player get started.

Canzona

The roots of the canzona can be traced to the sixteenth-century French chanson, but it gradually became independent of vocal models or used them in elaborate transcription. The opening was usually in imitation, often with the characteristic rhythm ♩ ♪♪. Connections to the fugue are evident, and Praetorius in fact describes the canzona as a series of short fugues for ensembles of four or more parts. The canzona principle was carried to Germany by Froberger, and the emphasis on imitation and variation was adopted by Buxtehude, Muffat, and Kerll. It is in Germany where we find the closest relationship between the canzona and the fugue.

Ricercare

The term *ricercare* comes from the Latin "to seek" or "to find." The early ricercares were used as preludes for lute or keyboard (i.e., *ricercare le corde*—to try out the strings), and the most common texture was imitative. Further development of the ricercare in Germany placed emphasis on the variation principle, but the form gradually fell into disuse by the end of the century. J. S. Bach's eighteenth-century revival of the ricercare in the *Musical Offering* utilizes many of its stylistic characteristics, including the open-score format.

Fantasia

From the outset the term *fantasia* could appear interchangeably with ricercare, praeambulum, voluntary, capriccio, and canzona. Its origins are Spanish. The vihuelist Luis de Milán described the fantasia in 1535 as an instrumental composition whose form and invention spring "solely from the fantasy and skill of the author who created it"; fantasias were also good for "exercising the hands."[23] Independence from a written text is a hallmark of the genre.

The fantasia became highly imitative throughout the century, however, and Italian fantasias in particular featured a kaleidoscope of contrapuntal techniques. English composers also wrote contrapuntal fantasias but they soon placed greater emphasis on freedom and creativity. Thomas Morley wrote in 1597 that the fantasy is "the chiefest kind of musicke which is made without a dittie . . . when a musician taketh a point at his pleasure, and wresteth and turneth it as he list, making either much or little of it as shall seeme best in is own conceit.[24]

Toccata

Performers who have spent any time improvising at the keyboard will understand the impetus that created the toccata. The name is derived from *toccare* (to touch), and it is exactly this act that defines its nature. The most idiomatic and flexible of the early genres, it is found within all national schools and could appear as praeambulum, prelude, fancy, or intonation. A wide range of stylistic traits is evident. Some toccatas alternate fugal and chordal sections with brilliant passagework, while others might be full of rhapsodic figuration, and some are highly structured and monothematic.

Tiento

The term is Spanish and was used for several different types of compositions. The title comes from *tentar*—to try out or experiment—but from its original prelude-like character the *tiento* soon encompassed fantasias and ricercares as well. For example, the twenty-nine *tientos* written by the sixteenth-century master Antonio Cabezón include short pieces, rhapsodic works, and highly contrapuntal compositions.

Dances

Seventeenth-century keyboard repertory includes a large number of dance pieces. It is therefore incumbent on the player to understand the steps and movements of each dance in order to interpret properly its particular tempo, character, and style, and also to realize the subtle rhythmic inflections and articulations inherent in each dance movement. Better still, keyboard players are urged to learn and physically dance the dances themselves! The most common dances used by keyboard composers include *allemande, courante* and *corrente, sarabande, gigue, passacaglia* and *chaconne, pavane,* and *galliard.* The reader is directed to the chapter on dance in this volume for more information about this large and fascinating subject.

Repertory

Italy

Italy produced some of the most important keyboard literature in the seventeenth century. This is not surprising if one considers its rich Renaissance heritage, the central role of the church and its need for liturgical music, and the traditional support of music by noble families. The early keyboard player will find here an almost inexhaustible source of canzonas, ricercares, fantasias, toccatas, and variations.

One of the earliest major composers of ricercares was Giovanni Gabrieli; he streamlined the form, using fewer sections than his predecessors and expanding the role of augmentation, diminution, and counterpoint. Adriano Banchieri continued this tradition: his publications contain sonatas, capriccios, ricercares, canzonas, fantasias, and toccatas. Ercole Pasquini was Frescobaldi's predecessor as organist at St. Peter's in Rome until 1608. He and composers such as Giovanni de Macque used a bold, expressive harmonic language not unlike the madrigals of Gesualdo. Pieces in *durezze e ligatura* style were solemn compositions, distinguished by four- or five-part texture, slow harmonic rhythm, poignant suspensions, cross-relations, and dramatic dissonances. Regarding this practice, de Macque's student Ascanio Mayone explained in the preface to his *Secondo libro di diversi capricci per sonare* (1609) that some passages contained "wrong" notes, against the rules of counterpoint ("contra la regola del contrapunto"), but one should not be scandalized by them or think the author does not know the rules, since they are well observed in his ricercares. Pasquini's works include the earliest examples of the corrente in Italy, and de Macque was the first to use the *ruggiero* theme in his partitas. Trabaci was an important figure in the development of the ricercare and canzona, creating greater thematic unity in the ricercare form by using fewer subjects (e.g., ricercare *con una fughe, con due fughe,* etc.), which were then varied.

The Italian who towers above the rest is Girolamo Frescobaldi. A keyboard virtuoso and inspired composer, Frescobaldi became organist at St. Peter's at the age of twenty-five. It was said that his art was "at the ends of his fingers" and there is no doubt that as a keyboard player he was the greatest and most influential in Italy.[25] Frescobaldi's works represent some of the best ricercares, canzonas, variations, and toccatas in the literature, and the performer will do no better than to play and study them all.

One of the most important and enduring legacies that Frescobaldi has left us concerns performance practice. Possibly because his was such a new and daring style, or perhaps because no one could play quite like himself, Frescobaldi wrote extensively about the performance of his music. We are therefore fortunate to have explicit and detailed information about the realization of Frescobaldi's music as well as his aesthetic. By extension this information can serve as a general guide for seventeenth-century Italian keyboard music. The writings are found throughout his prefaces and in other sources. One of the most complete versions appears in the third edition of toccatas (1637). It is written in clear and practical terms, and the performer would be well advised to study and refer to them frequently when playing this repertory. Let the composer here speak for himself (italics are added by the author for emphasis):

To the reader:
1. This manner of playing must not follow the same meter; in this respect it is *similar to the performance of modern madrigals,* whose difficulty is eased by taking the beat slowly at times and fast at others, even by pausing . . . in accordance with the mood or the meaning of the words.
2. In the toccatas . . . one may play each section separately, so that the player can stop wherever he wishes . . .
3. *The beginning of the toccatas must be played slowly and arpeggiando . . .*
4. In trills as well as in runs, whether they move by skips or by steps, one must pause on the last note, even when it is an eighth or sixteenth note, or different from the next note [of the trill or run].
5. Cadenzas [i.e., cadential passages], even when notated as fast, must be well sustained, and *when one approaches the end of a run or* [cadential passage] *the tempo must be taken even more slowly.*
6. *Where a trill in one hand is played simultaneously with a running passage in the other, one must not play note against note, but try to play the trill fast and the run in a more sustained and expressive manner . . .*
7. When there is *a section with eighth notes in one hand and sixteenth notes in the other, it should not be executed too rapidly; and the hand that plays the sixteenth notes should dot them somewhat, not the first note, however, but the second one,* and so on throughout, not the first, but the second.[26]
8. Before executing parallel runs of sixteenth notes in both hands, one must pause on the preceding note, even when it is a black one; then one should attack the passage with determination, in order to exhibit the agility of the hands all the more.
9. In the variations that include both runs and expressive passages, it will be good to choose a broad tempo; one may well observe this in the toccatas also. Those variations that do not include runs one may play quite fast, and *it is left to the good taste and judgment of the players to choose the tempo correctly. Herein lie the spirit and perfection of this manner of playing and of this style.*[27]

Other Italian composers wrote about performance practice, and there is valuable information to be found in the works of Diruta, Banchieri, Antegnati, Trabaci, Mayone, Bottazzi, Grassi, Fasolo, Scipione Giovanni, and Bonini, and in the treatises on basso continuo practice by Viadana, Agazzari, and Cavalieri.[28] For example, we learn from Antegnati that canzonas were taken "in haste" and had "vivacity and *motivi allegri.*"[29] A slower tempo was preferred for ricercares. Banchieri wrote that repeated sections of *canzoni alla francese* "must be played adagio the first time *as in a ricercare* [italics mine], and in the repeat quickly."[30] Durante agreed with Frescobaldi that toccatas should begin *arpeggiando,* "with gravity and without *passaggi,* but not without *affetti.*"[31] Trabaci affirms that "the tempo is gradually slowed in approaching the end of *passaggi* or cadences."[32]

Composers of the generation after Frescobaldi do not reach his high artistic and technical level. Bernardo Pasquini was primarily a harpsichord composer. His suites consist of allemande, courante, and gigue, and their sweet, simple melodies presage the eighteenth-century galant style. Pasquini still felt the influence of Frescobaldi. He purchased *Il Primo Libro* (1628) in 1662, often quoted from it, and recommended Frescobaldi as a teacher. The music of Frescobaldi's students is not well known and deserves further study. They include Alessandro Costantini, who succeeded him at St. Peter's, and Francesco Mutii, his assistant and a recognized virtuoso himself ("in pulsandis organis in Romano solo nulli secundus"). Michelangelo Rossi is often claimed as a student of Frescobaldi, and his highly chromatic works are attractive, but records show that he was known primarily as a violinist. Alessandro Scarlatti wrote brilliant, if somewhat empty toccatas, and his harmonic language occasionally features surprising acciaccaturas that would later become a trademark in the works of his son Domenico.

Spain and Portugal

Because of geographical isolation, political history, and other factors, artistic developments in Spain and Portugal have always been somewhat set apart from the rest of Europe. The Spanish and Portuguese keyboard style also remained relatively constant throughout the seventeenth century, unlike the diverse schools of composition one would find in Naples, Rome, and Venice. Its roots lie deep in the sixteenth century, especially in the music of Antonio Cabezón; general characteristics are conservative contrapuntal textures, elaborate keyboard embellishment, and variation technique. The *tiento* was the predominant form.

There were several types of *tientos,* usually distinguished by organ registration. For example, the *tiento lleno* was to be played on one manual, full instrument. *Medio registro* implied a divided registration, and in a *tiento de medio registro de bajo* the left hand played solo figurations and the right hand played chords. The *ensalada* (lit., salad) consisted of four or five sections alternating duple and triple meters, in the style of the Neapolitan quilt canzona. A *tiento de falsas* would be written in slow quarter-note or half-note motion, relatively free of figuration, with a harmonic language reminiscent of the Italian *durezze e ligatura* style. Examples of this type can be found in the works of Correa de Arauxo, who would not hesitate to sound together e-natural and e♭, or c-natural and c♯. He described this type of intense dissonance as a *punto intenso contra remiso*.

Early composers of the period include Bernardo Clavijo, Francisco Peraza, and Sebastian Aguilera de Heredia, whose fame lasted into the eighteenth century. Aguilera's compositions are representative of the seventeenth-century keyboard style in Spain, including the use of uneven folklike rhythmic patterns such as 3+3+2 (♩ ♪♩ ♪♩), and *falsas*. Echo passages recalling Sweelinck are frequently used.

Manuel Rodriguez Coelho's *Flores de Musica* (1620) contains a huge repertory of over 133 works, among them *tientos, versos,* and kyries. Coelho's *tientos* are the longest of the century, some containing as many as 300 measures. He suggests in his versets that each is "for singing to the organ; this voice must not be played, the four below it must be played." This practice is also found in Italian sources. The use of the generic term *tecla* for keyboard in titles implies that the player in this period had a choice of instruments.

Correa de Arauxo is an important figure. Included with sixty-three masterful *tientos* in his *Libro de Tientos* (1626) is the *Facultad Organica*, a valuable source for seventeenth-century Spanish theory and performance practice. Correa advocates the use of inequality in triplets by suggesting that there are two ways to play them. The first is to play the three notes evenly, as written. In the second, the player dots the first of each group of three, creating the pattern ♩ ♪♩ (*como haziendo una semiminima y dos corcheas*). Correa shared with his Spanish contemporaries the love of complicated and uneven rhythms. In his works one not only finds the very Spanish 3 + 3 + 2 pattern but also groups of 5 and 7 against 2 or 3. He would describe such *tientos* as *muy dificultoso*.

Juan Cabanilles was the major figure in the second half of the seventeenth century. His fame reached France, and his student Joseph Elias wrote in 1722 that "the world may vanish before a second Cabanilles comes."[33] The output was enormous, and a projected complete edition of Cabanilles edition has been estimated to require 1,200 pages. His are some of the finest works in the seventeenth-century Spanish repertory, and they are unjustly neglected. Cabanilles wrote in every genre, including *tientos* and toccatas, and he was a master of variation technique. Prime examples are the *passacalles* and *paseos,* such as his magnificent ground-bass variations titled *Xácara*.

The Netherlands and Northern Germany

When we turn to the north, the climate changes dramatically. Here the Reformation and the Protestant church were the dominant forces behind musical expression and practice. Instead of the rhapsodic keyboard writing and wide range of affect in the South, northern composers used the

Protestant chorale and English variation technique as unifying principles. Fantasias tended to be tightly structured and monothematic. The keyboard writing in the toccatas usually featured sequential patterns over conservative harmonies, recalling the style of the early Venetian school rather than the emotional intensity of the composers of Rome and Naples.

The major early figure in the north was Jan Pieterszoon Sweelinck. Almost every genre that would be used in Germany throughout the century was established by Sweelinck, and his contributions to each reveal a masterful composer. Some of his most important works are based on the Protestant chorale. These assumed several styles, such as the *bicinium* (cantus firmus in one hand accompanied by left-hand figures), the *tricinium* (cantus firmus in inner voice with figuration in two outer voices), and the chorale motet. His ornamented chorale settings, in which the cantus firmus serves as the foundation for extensive melodic embellishment, were highly influential. From these works developed the great German organ tradition of chorale prelude and chorale variation. Much of Sweelinck's music was intended for organ performance, but there is also an excellent body of harpsichord music. His keyboard variations clearly fall under the sphere of the English virginalists. Sweelinck knew Peter Phillips and was a good friend of John Bull, who lived in the Netherlands for much of his life. Sweelinck's variations such as *Est-ce Mars* and *Mein junges Leben hat ein End'* are masterpieces in the literature.

Sweelinck had other Dutch contemporaries, such as Pieter Cornet and Henderick Speuy, but the true followers of Sweelinck were German. Sweelinck was in fact called "the teacher of German organists," and his students included such composers as Jacob Praetorius, Heinrich Scheidemann, and Samuel Scheidt. This generation of organist/composers continued the work of their Dutch master and firmly established the North German organ school—that is, a conservative style based on the Protestant chorale, but one of grandeur and power that expanded and exploited the full resources of the organ (e.g., virtuoso pedal technique and echo effects). Scheidt shared his teacher's penchant for variation technique, and also wrote partitas on popular secular melodies like *Est-ce Mars* and *Fortuna*. Scheidemann established Hamburg as the center of organ music from 1620 to 1645, and made major contributions to the setting of the chorale. Especially significant are his chorale preludes, chorale fantasias, and chorale variations or partitas. The next generation in northern Germany included composers such as Franz Tunder, Mathias Weckmann, George Böhm, and of course Dietrich Buxtehude. Tunder began to soften the severity of the style with displays of keyboard virtuosity. Works would often begin and end with dramatic sixteenth-note runs, and double-pedal writing and other virtuoso footwork was not uncommon. Interesting contributions were made by the others, but the major figure in this group was Buxtehude. His work represents the culmination of seventeenth-century German organ music. The chorale fantasias are rich in idiomatic keyboard effects, independent and virtuosic pedal parts, and the music can range from the strictly contrapuntal to giguelike. Buxtehude would gradually abandon the chorale-based compositional style in favor of freer forms, such as the praeambulum, in which he could use a wider range of tonalities and forms and have greater freedom for technical display. The influence of Italian opera and the French style was already being felt in Germany, and this is strongly reflected in the music of Böhm. His contributions to the organ chorale repertory are significant, but it his harpsichord music that commands greater interest. French characteristics, such as the use of *style brisé* (broken style) and French ornamentation, permeate these works.

Central and Southern Germany

Not surprisingly, the influence of Italy and France was more strongly felt in the central and southern parts of Germany, where there was less dependence on the Protestant chorale. To be sure, central German composers such as Johannes Kindermann and Johann Pachelbel wrote a large number of chorale settings, but their preludes and toccatas could resemble the rhapsodic style of Frescobaldi. Pachelbel contributed six variations based on secular and original themes in the *Hexachordum Apollinis* (1699), and three of his six chaconnes are for the harpsichord; the other three require organ pedals, although the pedal writing of these composers rarely approaches the virtuosity of the North. In the South we find early masters such as Johann Ulrich Steigleder, Christian Erbach, and in particular Hans Leo Hassler. Hassler studied with Andrea Gabrieli in Venice and became organist for the fabulously wealthy Fugger family. His ricercares are of great interest, and considerable length. Later generations include the francophile Georg Muffat, who studied with Lully in Paris. His *Apparatus musico-organisticus* (1690) contains twelve toccatas, a passacaglia, and a chaconne. The adventurous keyboard player with a sense of humor might well investigate the music of Alessandro Poglietti. He wrote some of the most bizarre and individual program music of the century, primarily for harpsichord. One such piece, the *Aria Allemagna* (1677), attempts to depict a "Bohemian Bagpipe," "French Hand-Kisses," and a "Polish Saber Joke."

The dominant figure in the second half of the century was Johann Jakob Froberger. A student of Frescobaldi in 1641, he created an inspired synthesis of Italian and German styles, particularly in his toccatas. Although he did not make as strong a distinction between the ricercare, canzona, and fantasia, here, too, his treatment of thematic development and keyboard figuration is masterful. Froberger traveled widely, living in Vienna and visiting Dresden, Brussels, Paris, and London. His connections with France were particularly strong, and he counted among his friends the lutentist Denis Gaultier and the *claveciniste* Louis Couperin. Froberger exerted a strong influence on the early French clavecin style, and he in turn was influenced by it. The musical bonds are nowhere more evident than in Louis Couperin's *Prélude à l'imitation de Mr. Froberger,* which pays homage to the German composer's free and expressive style (e.g., *Plainte faite à Londres . . .*). In a similar mood, each composer wrote a poignant *tombeau* on the death of their mutual friend Blancrocher. It is as a harpsichord composer that Froberger made his most significant contributions. Pieces such as his *Lamento sopra la dolorosa perdita della . . . Ferdinand IV* and the *Tombeau* plumb the depths of the expressive potential of the harpsichord. Froberger was responsible for the establishment of the harpsichord suite in Europe. His early works in this genre consisted of allemande, courante, and sarabande, but the gigue was soon included, appearing directly after the allemande.[34]

England

The great Elizabethan keyboard tradition as represented by composers such as Byrd, Gibbons, and Farnaby was not sustained during the first half of the seventeenth century. The establishment of the Commonwealth ultimately suppressed musical growth in England, particularly that of the organ, and this was admittedly not a rich period of keyboard composition. For example, Bull left his native country and ultimately settled in Antwerp in 1613, to the delight of Sweelinck but the detriment of the English. Some good keyboard pieces were written, including pavanes, galliards, variations, and especially the fantasia, which became a conservative, serious countrapuntal genre inspired by the English viol consort.

After the Restoration, keyboard music returned with thinner textures, simple melodies, and the inclusion of dances. For example, *Elizabeth Rogers' Virginal Book* (1656/7) contains no pavanes and galliards, but rather simple binary almans and corants. The French influence is now present. The music of the lutenist Denis Gaultier was well known and Jacques Gaultier and the renowned Richard family were in residence at the English court. Thus the suite begins to take prominence. Thomas Mace described the genre in 1676: "A Sett, or a Suit of Lessons, . . . may be of any Number. . . . The First always should begin (with) which we call a Praeludium or Praelude. . . . Then, Allmaine, Ayre, Coranto, Seraband, Toy, or what you please, provided They be all in the same Key. . . ."[35] A fine collection of suites by several different composers can be found in the publication *Melothesia* (1673).

The second part of *Musick's hand-maide* (1689) contains the first published keyboard music of John Blow and Henry Purcell. Blow, a major force in England as a composer and teacher, assimilated the German and French styles by copying music of Froberger, Fischer, Strungk, and others. Purcell is represented in this volume by thirteen pieces and a suite.

Eight more suites and six miscellaneous pieces were published posthumously in 1696 as *A Choice Collection of Lessons*. Although Purcell's genius and melodic gift are in evidence, his contributions to the keyboard repertory do not represent him at his most inspired or profound.

The *Choice Collection* does contain important guidelines about Purcell's performance practice. His "Instructions for Learners" explains ornamentation with a comprehensive "Rules for Graces," and he offers his thoughts on tempo:

> Common time . . . is distinguish'd by . . . **C**, . . . **¢**, . . . or **Ↄ**, ye first is a very slow movement, ye next a little faster, and ye last a brisk & airry time, & each of them has allways to ye length of one Semibrief in a barr. . . . Triple time consists of either three or six Crotchets in a barr, and is to be known by . . . $\frac{3}{2}$, . . . $\frac{3}{1}$, . . . **3**, . . . or $\frac{6}{4}$. . . . To the first there is three Minums in a barr, and is commonly pay'd very slow, the second has three Crotchets in a barr, and they are to be play'd slow, the third has ye same as ye former but is play'd faster, ye last has six Crotchets in a barr & is Commonly to brisk tunes as Jiggs and Paspys [passepieds].[36]

John Playford's *A breefe introduction to the skill of musick* (1654) has details about tempo, meter, modal theory and affect, and *Melothesia* includes a list of English ornaments.

Players of English keyboard music are often confused by the choice of instrument, and in particular the term "virginals." Reference to "a pair of virginallis" appears as early as 1517 in English documents. The title page of *Parthenia* (1612) and *Parthenia in-violata* (1625) refers only to "the virginalls," but that of *Musick's hand-maide* advertises "lessons for the virginalls or harpsycon." Many other names can be found. We read of "Espinettes," "Clarycordes," "Harpsicon," and "Harpsicalls"; and "Clavecymbal" is defined as "a pair of Virginals, or Claricords" by Blount in his *Glossographia* (1656).[37] Praetorius attempts to clarify things in 1619, writing that in England all instruments of the harpsichord type, large or small, were called "virginall."[38]

The spinet became common in middle-class England, and the term appears alongside harpsichord and virginals. Samuel Pepys confessed in his Diary on April 4, 1668, that he had decided to buy a spinet because "I had a mind to a small harpsichon, but this takes up less room, and will do my business as to finding out the chords."[39]

Foreign instruments were very popular in Engand, especially those built by the Flemish Ruckers family. For example, in 1710 it was reported that the Romer Tavern in Gerard Street housed "two matchless clavearis, which are considered the best in the whole of England . . . They are over 100 years old and were built by two of the most famous masters in Antwerp. The best was made by Hans Ruckers and the other by his son . . . Jean Rucker . . . Both have double-keyboards."[40]

France

ORGAN MUSIC

With regard to French keyboard music there is no difficulty in determining which work was written for organ and which for harpsichord. Composers in France made a clear and unambiguous distinction because almost every piece of the French organ literature carries the name of a specific organ registration (e.g., *Duo, Cromorne en taille, Dialogue sur les grand jeux, Plein jeu,* etc.). This tradition appears early on in France, the first example being a manuscript from 1610 with pieces titled *Pour le cornet* and *Pour les registres couplez.* The connection to Spanish organ music, with its emphasis on registration, should also be evident. Furthermore, each registration/title implied a specific compositional style and character. For example, a *plein jeu* piece called for the full organ registration (e.g., *grand orgue,* positif, and mixtures), and would be written in the dramatic *durezze et ligatura* style. A *petit plein jeu* would feature more figuration in sixteenth notes. A *récit de trompette* implied that the melody, often treated in fugal fashion, was played on the indicated stop and accompanied by flutes or other appropriate registrations. Its rhythm and character was usually that of a bourée or gigue. The French classical organ and the French classical style are thus intimately connected, and the player of this repertory would therefore be advised to become familiar with both the registration of the instrument and the genres that originated with it.

The earliest master of French organ music was J. Titelouze. His two published works, *Hymnes de l'Eglise* (1623) and *Le Magnificat* (1626), are generally conservative and dependent on Gregorian chant; the strict cantus firmus technique and a polyphonic texture recalls the Spanish style. Other followers of Titelouze include C. Racquet and E. Richard. F. Roberday attempted to introduce some Italian elements into French organ music, and even included works of Froberger, Frescobaldi, and Ebner in his *Fugues et Caprices* (1660). By mid-century the increasing popularity of opera, dance, and chamber music could not be ignored; organists gradually favored simple textures and elegantly ornamented melodies, while never completely leaving the older style. Some of the major publications of organ music include books by N. Gigault, who still wrote serious liturgical music but employed rapid manual changes and a high degree of ornamentation. N. Le Bègue wrote three *Livres d'Orgue,* consisting of Masses, *noëls* with variations, dances, and *simphonies.* A. Raison was Clérambault's teacher, and also a valuable commentator on style; the theme of his *Trio en Passacaille* bears a strong resemblance to Bach's Passacaglia in C minor. G. Nivers was said to have written with "detachment and easy grace" ("froideur et la grace facile") and contributed over a hundred compositions in the church modes. N. de Grigny wrote perhaps the last *Livre d'orgue* of the century in 1699, and several of these works were copied by Bach.

HARPSICHORD MUSIC

The music of the *clavecinistes* represents the most idiomatic and arguably the best pure harpsichord music of the seventeenth century. Its origins can be found in compositions by Dumas, la Grotte, Champion, and the *Joueurs d'épinette* of Louis XIII. Stylistic traits are shared with the French lutenists, such as an emphasis on dance movements, extensive ornamentation, and the improvisatory prelude.

In the clavecin style, a two-voice texture predominates, featuring an elegant, richly ornamented melodic line and a simple accompaniment. Intricate contrapuntal writing or choralelike homophony is avoided, and fugues, ricercares, fantasias, and sonatas are rare. The French harpsichord composer achieved maximum expressive effect by the resonant spacing of parts, a sensitivity to sonorities, and a rich harmonic language. Virtuoso keyboard displays were kept to a minimum.

Two of the most distinctive features of the style are its ornamentation and the *style brisé*. Players might at first be astonished by the number and variety of ornaments, and contemporary writers often expressed dismay at their profusion. However, this is not ornamentation in the sense of divisions or embellishments, and the manner in which it is used distinguishes it from all other Baroque keyboard music. The ornaments here are decorations of the melody like the additions to French furniture of the period. More important, they are meticulously notated and applied to create an astonishing range of nuance, color, and dynamics on the harpsichord. These *agréments* are not optional or improvisatory, but become an integral part of the composition. One need only play a French melody with ornaments removed to understand fully their crucial impact on the music, and it is advisable to learn a piece this way. Since most composers developed their personal system of notation, the player should carefully study the table of ornaments usually found at the beginning of the published work.

The *style brisé* or *style luthé* indicates arpeggiated writing that creates a kaleidoscopic palate of rich sonorities and implied polyphony. As the name implies, the *style luthé* recalls lute practice, and the technique is idiomatic to no other keyboard instrument but the harpsichord.

The ascent of Louis XIV to the throne in 1643 was a pivotal moment in the history of French music, and signaled a dramatic change in the society and culture. The lutentists and *jouers d'épinette* receded into the background, and their intimate, small-scale pleasures were replaced by grandeur and majesty. As Titelouze wrote to Mersenne, "I remember having seen in my youth everybody admiring and being delighted by a man playing lute, and badly enough at that . . . now I see many lutenists more skilled than he who are hardly listened to."[41] La Fontaine lamented in 1677 that "the time of Raymon and Hilaire is past, nothing pleases now but twenty harpsichords, a hundred violins. . . ."[42]

The *clavecinistes* attained the central place in the court of the Sun King, and produced some of the richest literature in the history of the harpsichord. The tradition remained fairly consistent for almost 200 years, reaching its culmination with F. Couperin and continuing into the last years of the eighteenth century.

Masterpieces of the seventeenth-century repertory were written by Jacques Chambonnières, Louis Couperin, and Jean Henry d'Anglebert, and many fine works will be found in the books of *Pièces de clavecin* by composers such as Dumont, Le Bégue, Hardel, Clérambault, and E. Jacquet de la Guerre.

Two aspects of French performance practice pose considerable challenges to the early keyboard player and deserve special mention here: *inégalité* and the improvisatory prélude.

INÉGALITÉ OR NOTES INÉGALES

There are numerous instances in the seventeenth-century keyboard repertory in which the performer is allowed and sometimes obligated to alter the notated rhythm. The practice of "overdotting" in overtures and the use of dotting in specific passages by Frescobaldi are two such examples. The principle of *inégalité* in French music, however, is unique to France and remains one of the most misunderstood concepts in all of performance practice.

Inégalité refers to the technique in which passages written with equal note values are performed in unequal rhythm. There is no disagreement that it was standard in the performance of French music. Numerous sources corroborate this fact. As François Couperin writes in *L'Art de toucher de clavecin*: "We notate otherwise than we perform, which is the reason why foreigners perform our music less well than we perform theirs."[43]

M. de Saint-Lambert states that "the equality of movement that we require in notes of the same value is not observed with eighth notes when there are several in a row. The practice is to make them alternately long and short, because this inequality gives them more grace."[44] The earliest account of French-style inequality is documented by Loys Bourgeois in 1550: "The manner of singing well the [quarter] notes is to sing them two by two dwelling some little bit of time longer on the first, than on the second . . ."[45]

Nivers advises in 1665 "to augment ever so slightly the aforementioned eighths, and to diminish ever so slightly in proportion those that follow . . . which is practiced according to discretion, and many other things which prudence and the ear have to govern."[46]

Bacilly wrote in 1668:

Although I say that in diminutions there are dots, alternate and assumed, which is to say that of two notes, one is ordinarily dotted, it has been deemed appropriate not to mark them, for fear that one one might accustom himself to execute them by jerks. [*Notes inégales* should be executed] so delicately that it is not apparent.[47]

Jean Rousseau warned in 1687 to "take care not to mark them [the *notes inégales*] too roughly."[48] Monteclair further cautions that "when the melody proceeds in disjunct intervals, the eighths are ordinarily equal."[49] In other words, the performer of French music must play a stepwise succession of apparently equal note values with some degree of inequality.

It is, however, not the existence but rather the degree of inequality that has led to such confusion and misinterpretation. The most common misconception is that inequality means the creation of uniform dotted rhythms. Although such dotting is, to be sure, a possible realization, it is only one of an infinite range of rhythmic interpretations. Composers were certainly able to notate such dotted rhythms clearly and without ambiguity, and they appear side by side with evenly notated passages.

To correctly understand *inégalité,* one must realize that it is really a highly refined rubato, an expressive device that must be applied with subtlety and artistry; its very nature is such that it cannot be notated. In one sense, *inégalité* is not a rhythmic concept at all, but rather one of articulation and phrasing. This becomes clear from the internal evidence of the music itself, and from the written sources as well. For example, Saint-Lambert writes: "It is a matter of taste to decide if they should be more or less unequal. There are some pieces in which it is appropriate to make them very unequal and others in which they should be less so. *Taste is the judge of this,* as of tempo" (italics mine).[50] Therefore, the use of *inégalité* defies a strict or simple mathematical realization, but demands of the performer the widest range of subtle expression, based on the character of the piece and on *bon gout.*

Inégalité remained within the borders of France. That is, composers of other nationalities were certainly aware of its existence, but there is no basis to assume that it should be applied to their music except when these composers were consciously writing in the French style.[51]

PRÉLUDE

Every nationality has a genre that is improvisatory in nature. For example, the Italian toccata, the German praeambulum, and the English prelude all allow the player considerable rhythmic and expressive freedom. However, the notation of French preludes is particularly difficult to decipher and interpret, and the inexperienced player might not know just where to begin. The French were aware that this practice might cause trouble. Le Bègue wrote:

> I have tried to present the preludes as simply as possible, with regard to both conformity of notation and harpsichord technique, which separates or repeats chords rather than holding them as units as is done on the organ; . . . I ask the intelligent gentleman to please supply what is wanting, con-

sidering the great difficulty of rendering this method of preluding intelligible enough for everybody.[52]

Almost every composer contributed works to this genre, and they used a wide variety of notational systems. Those of Louis Couperin are the most ambiguous, written entirely in whole notes with a forest of wavy lines. Other composers added occasional rhythmic figures, dotted lines to indicate simultaneous striking, and ornamental signs. The musical approach, however, is the same. The player should become familiar with the available information regarding performance practice and notation. He should make a thorough harmonic analysis of the piece, and it is often useful to write a figured bass for it whenever possible. A decision should be made as to which notes are melodic and which represent passing tones or keyboard figures. A familiarity with other improvisatory styles is advisable, and a comparison with Froberger's toccatas and pieces marked *à discretion* will be invaluable. On the surface, Froberger's notation in this style appears more regular, but the freedom of execution is no less than that which one would use for the French repertory.

F. Couperin speaks to the heart of the matter: "Those who would like to try these preludes should play them in a relaxed manner, not following the exact written values too precisely, unless I have expressly marked the word 'measured.' Thus, one may venture to say that, in many ways, music, as well as poetry, has its 'prose' and its 'verse.'"[53]

NOTES

1. Diruta refers here to the Spanish theorist Tomás de Santa Maria, who takes a diametrically opposed approach to hand position and playing technique. Santa Maria advocates "that the hands be placed hooked, like the paws of a cat, in such a manner that between the hand and the fingers there will in no way be any curvature; instead, the knuckles have to be very sunken, in such a manner that the fingers are higher than the hand [and] arched. And thus the fingers remain more pointed, so as to strike a greater blow" (Santa Maria–*Libro*, 37; trans. in Rodgers–*Early Keyboard*, 220). Santa Maria is an instructive and valuable source, but the reader should be cautioned that the early date of this treatise makes it more applicable to keyboard style in the middle of the sixteenth century rather than to the very different repertory of the seventeenth. It is interesting to note that the theorist was also thinking of the early clavichord: "The fifth thing is to press the keys down as far as they will go conveniently, so that if the instrument is a clavichord, the tangents will raise the strings properly; moreover, in such a way that the voices will not depart from their pitch by sharping" (Santa Maria–*Libro*, 32; trans. in Rodgers–*Early Keyboard*, 223).
2. Diruta–*Transilvano*; translated in Rodgers–*Early Keyboard*, 278–80; cited in Soderlund–*Organ Technique*, 34–35.
3. Nivers–*Livre d'orgue*; translated in Pruitt–*Nivers*, 158; cited in Soderlund–*Organ Technique*, 102.
4. F. Couperin–*L'Art* (trans. Halford), 29.
5. Forkel–*Bachs Leben*, Ch. 3; translated in David/Mendel–*Bach Reader*, 308.
6. Bermudo–*Declaración*, fol. lxix.
7. Correa de Arauxo–*Faculdad organica*, ff. 23–24. See also Lindley–Keyboard Fingering, 197.

8. The conscientious player who is committed to performing earlier repertory with historically informed principles would be well advised to avoid the use of the word "never" or "always." Musicians in earlier centuries were as accomplished musically and technically as today (if not more so), and were as diverse in the range of their strongly held approaches to playing and interpretation. Contemporary styles of performance would also often change, or be adapted to the particular exigencies of the situation or conditions of the performance (such as acoustics, nature of the instrument, social or religious context, etc.) To assume that there is one answer, one absolute "truth" to a musical question is not only incorrect, but antithetical to the very nature of artistic endeavor.

9. Praetorius–*Syntagma* II: 44; translated in Hammond–*Frescobaldi*, 235.

10. Saint-Lambert–*Principes* (trans. Harris-Warrick), 70.

11. F. Couperin–*L'Art* (trans. Halford), 31.

12. Diruta–*Transilvano* I, fol. 5v; translated in Hammond–*Frescobaldi*, 232.

13. Ibid.; translated in Rodgers–*Early Keyboard*, 298; cited in Soderlund–*Organ Technique*, 36. Once again Santa Maria–*Libro* (trans. in Rodgers–*Early Keyboard*, 225; cited in Soderlund–*Organ Technique*, 21) holds an opposing viewpoint: "The finger that strikes first is always raised before the one that immediately follows it strikes." In other words, détaché.

14. For an interesting article on the subject of "not leaving the instrument empty," see Tagliavini–Art.

15. Nivers–*Livre d'orgue*; translated in Pruitt–*Nivers*, 162; cited in Soderlund–*Organ Technique*, 104.

16. An excellent description of "overlegato" is provided by Saint-Lambert when explaining the execution of the *port de voix*: "The pen stroke drawn above the notes in the realization of the *port de voix* is a slur, which means it is necessary to run those notes together, that is to say that one must not raise the fingers while playing them, but wait until the second of the two notes is played before raising the finger that played the first one." Saint Lambert–*Principes* (trans. Harris-Warrick), 86. This technique should also be conservatively applied to the organ! Both Nivers–*Livre d'orgue* (preface) and Raison–*Seconde Livre d'Orgue* (preface) advocate it.

17. Engramelle–*Tonotechnie*; translated in Veilhan–*Regles*, Introduction.

18. Trabaci–*Secondo libro*, 117.

19. Some of the factors that would imply the use of the clavichord include written indications in the preface or title page, notated signs for *Bebung* (vibrato), idiomatic musical texture, and the purpose and location of the performance.

20. Scheidt–*Tabulatura nova*, preface.

21. Speth–*Ars magna*, "Vor-Bericht"; cited in Apel–*Keyboard*, 582.

22. Cited in Harley–*British Keyboard* 2, 151.

23. Milán–*El Maestro*, preface.

24. Morley–*Plaine and easie*, 180, cited in Apel–*Keyboard*, 209.

25. Frescobaldi was also not averse to blatant keyboard showmanship. Hammond–Frescobaldi, 232 (citing Antonio Libanori, *Ferrara d'oro imbrunito* [Ferrara, 1665–74], par. 3) describes how he would sometimes entertain his friends by playing compositions with the hands reversed, palms upward.

26. Other contemporary writers recommended playing eighths and sixteenths in this way in allegro movements, "as if they were half dotted," implying a generally accepted practice in the period. See for example Scipione Giovanni, *Intavolatura di Cembalo, et Organo* (Perugia, 1650; preface reproduced in Sartori–*Bibliografia*, 411–12).

27. Frescobaldi–*Toccate*, preface; translated in Apel–*Keyboard*, 456. The advice given here also appears in Frescobaldi's *Toccate e partite* of 1615.

28. Viadana–*Cento concerti*, preface; Agazzari–*Del sonare*; Cavalieri–*Rappresentatione*; preface.

29. Antegnati–*Arte organica*, cited in Hammond–*Frescobaldi*, 224.

30. Banchieri–*L'organo suonarino,* as cited in Sartori, *Bibliografia* 1: 184, and Hammond–*Frescobaldi,* 224.
31. Ottavio Durante, *Arie devote,* preface, cited in Hammond–*Frescobaldi,* 225.
32. Trabaci–*Secondo Libro.*
33. Cited in Apel–*Keyboard,* 771.
34. Froberger's gigues present an interesting performance practice problem. Several are notated in duple meter with dotted rhythms, rather than the expected groups of three in triple meter. Various solutions have been suggested, but the most probable performance is one suggested by Lucy Hallman-Russell (paper presented at the Acts of the International Froberger Colloquium, Monbeliard, France, 1992), in which the notated duple rhythms are played as triplets. A similar instance occurs in the gigue of Bach's "French" Suite in D minor.
35. Mace–*Musick's Monument,* 120; cited in Harley–*British Harpsichord* 2: 85.
36. Purcell–*Choice Lessons,* preface; cited in Donington–*Interpretation,* 344, 350. Purcell provides similar information in Playford–*Introduction* (1694), [75–78]. See also Harley–*British Harpsichord* 2: 219.
37. Cited in Harley–*British Harpsichord* 2: 153.
38. *Syntagma* II: 62.
39. Pepys–*Diary,* 149.
40. Z. C. von Uffenbach, *London in 1710, from the Travels of Zacharias Conrad von Uffenbach,* translated by W. H. Quarrell and Margaret Mare (London, 1934); cited in Harley–*British Harpsichord* 2: 165.
41. Mersenne–*Correspondence* 1: 75; cited in Ledbetter–*Harpsichord,* 8.
42. Jean de la Fontaine, "Epître à M. de Niert sur l'opéra" in *Oeuvres diverses,* vol. 2 (Paris, 1677; rpt., Paris, 1958), as cited in Ledbetter–*Harpsichord,* 13.
43. F. Couperin–*L'Art* (trans. Halford), 49.
44. Saint Lambert–*Principes* (trans. Harris-Warrick), 46.
45. Bourgeois–*Le droit chemin,* ch. 10; cited in Hefling–*Rhythmic Alteration,* 3.
46. Nivers–*Livre d'orgue,* 114; cited in Hefling–*Rhythmic Alteration,* 4.
47. Bacilly–*Remarques,* 232; cited in Hefling–*Rhythmic Alteration,* 6.
48. J. Rousseau–*Traité,* 114; cited in Hefling–*Rhythmic Alteration,* 12.
49. Monteclair–*Nouvelle méthode,* 15; cited in Hefling–*Rhythmic Alteration,* 15.
50. Saint Lambert–*Principes* (trans. Harris-Warrick), 46.
51. For a comprehensive and balanced approach to the question of inequality, see Hefling–*Rhythmic Alteration.*
52. LeBègue–*Pièces de clavecin,* introduction; cited in Apel–*Keyboard,* 714.
53. F. Couperin–*L'Art.*

BIBLIOGRAPHY

Antegnati–*L'Arte organica;* Arbeau–*Orchésographie;* Apel–*Keyboard Music;* Bacilly–*Remarques curieuses;* Banchieri–*L'organo suonarino;* Bermudo–*Déclaracion de instrumentos;* Blount–*Glossographia;* M. A. Bonino–*Bonini;* Boxhall and Lindley–*Early Keyboard Fingerings;* Boxall–Diruta; Brossard–*Dictionaire;* Butler–*Principles;* Brown and Sadie–*Performance Practice;* Correa de Arauxo–*Libro de tientos;* Couperin–*L'art de toucher;* Diruta–*Transilvano;* Dolmetsch–*Interpretation;* Doni–*Annotazioni sopra il Compendio;* Donington–*Performer's Guide;* Donington–*Interpretation;* Engramelle–*Tonotechnie;* Fasolo–*Annuale;* Forkel–*Bachs Leben;* Freillon-Poncein–*Veritable maniere;* Fuller–French Harpsichord; Gustafson–*French Harpsichord;* Hammond–*Frescobaldi;* Harley–*British Harpsichord;* Harnoncourt–*Musikalische Dialog;* Harnoncourt–*Klangrede;* Hawkins–*History;* Hefling–*Rhythmic Alteration;* Ledbetter–*Harpsichord;* Lindley–Keyboard temperaments; Lindley–Tuning; Mace–*Musick's Monument;* Mattheson–*Capellmeister;* Mersenne–*Correspondence;* Mersenne–*Harmonie universelle;* Montéclair–*Nouvelle méthode;* Morley–

MARK KROLL

Introduction; Neumann–*Ornamentation*; North–*Music*; Playford–*Introduction*; Perrine–*Livre*; Praetorius–*Syntagma* II; J. Rousseau–*Viole*; J.-J. Rousseau–*Dictionnaire*; Saint Lambert–*Principes*; Santa Maria–*Arte*; Silbiger–*Italian*; Silbiger–Roman; Simpson–*Division*; Soderlund–*Organ*; Tagliavini–Art; Tilney–*Unmeasured Prelude*; Veilhan–*Regles*.

12

Plucked String
Instruments

Paul O'Dette

The Lute

During the sixteenth century, the tuning, stringing, and construction of the lute remained remarkably consistent from one country to the next, with the exception of the vihuela in Spain with its waisted design. The basic six-course instrument, tuned fourth-fourth-third-fourth-fourth, was played all over Europe for most of the century with only subtle variations in stringing and construction practiced in different regions. In the seventeenth century, however, each country took its own approach to the instrument, resulting in new tunings, playing techniques, and types of lutes. In fact, the whole concept of how the lute should be used and what kind of music should be played upon it took radically different turns in different parts of Europe. To understand this development more easily, we will consider each country individually.

Italy

The trend in the late sixteenth century was to add bass strings to the lute to provide a more sonorous low register and to make playing in some keys easier. This trend continued in the seventeenth century, with the addition of an octave of diapasons to complement the original six courses, which were still tuned in the Renaissance fashion. The extra bass strings required changes in the construction of the instrument since they would have been too thick to make a satisfactory sound at the length of the fingered strings. Thick gut strings produce a dull, muddy tone, so that for gut-strung instruments, longer string lengths are preferable since thinner strings can be used. The process of wrapping strings with silver or copper wire was not invented until after 1650. This invention allowed

223

instrument makers to produce shorter instruments that had the same bright, clear tone in the middle and bass registers as the longer instruments of the first half of the century.[1] In order to use long, thin strings for the basses, a new design was necessary, involving two different string lengths, one short enough to facilitate easy reach of chords with the left hand, the other long enough for thinner strings to be tuned to the appropriate low pitches. Alessandro Piccinini had an instrument built in which the body was twice as long as that of a normal lute, with a second bridge on the soundboard to accommodate the bass strings.[2] He admitted that the two sets of strings produced quite different timbres since the basses were plucked in the middle of the string, while the trebles were plucked near the bridge.

The solution, Piccinini soon discovered, was to extend the neck, adding a second pegbox to accommodate the diapasons, which allowed all of the strings to be fastened to one bridge, thereby equalizing the resistance of the strings at the point of attack. This instrument, known as a *liuto attiorbato* (theorboed lute) or *arciliuto* (archlute), became the standard Italian lute of the seventeenth and eighteenth centuries. It was popular both as a solo and as a continuo instrument. The oft-quoted remark by Giustiniani in 1628, that the lute was no longer played in Italy, must refer to the old Renaissance lute, since the archlute figures very prominently in iconography, accounts of performances, and surviving music of the time—so much so, that it became unnecessary to specify "archlute" and the word *liuto* was used to refer to the extended-neck variety for most of the seventeenth and eighteenth centuries.

The other Italian lute of this period was the *chitarrone*, or *tiorba* (theorbo) as it was often called.[3] It was invented in the late sixteenth century as an instrument to accompany singers in the theater, a task that required more projection than most Renaissance lutes were capable of. This was accomplished by tuning the strings of a bass lute up a fifth, and replacing the first two strings, which broke at the higher pitch, with thicker strings tuned an octave lower. The octave displacement of these strings was not a problem since the instrument was invented to provide simple chordal accompaniments and the octave of the individual notes did not matter. At first simply a new way of tuning a bass lute, the chitarrone eventually had an extended neck added to it, providing an octave of bass strings for it as well.[4] Piccinini also claimed credit for this invention, adding that the *contrabassi*—strings of the 16-foot register—give the instrument its true character. Written continuo lines in seventeenth-century music rarely make use of these notes, but it is clear from surviving realizations and solo works that theorbists routinely dropped bass lines down an octave in order to make use of this most sonorous part of the instrument.[5] In Bologna, Maurizio Cazzati listed the *tiorba* as one of the instruments to play from his *contrabasso* partbook. As the examples on pages 277–78 show, the bass line may either be dropped an octave for several notes in a row, or the written bass note may be restruck an octave lower to provide greater sonority.

Praetorius and Piccinini mention the use of metal strings on the chitarrone, though gut seems to have been more common.[6] It is certainly more reliable and easier to control. The most common number of courses was fourteen, six on the fingerboard with eight diapasons. The diapasons were tuned diatonically according to key. Some early examples have only twelve courses, while Kapsberger used a fully chromatic nineteen-course instrument, an example of which may be found in a private collection in Mantua. Many modern players place seven or eight courses on the fingerboard—as was done in France—in order to access the low G♯ and F♯ so crucial for continuo playing. Surviving instruments and iconographic evidence indicate that some players used double courses over the fingerboard, while others preferred single strings. The latter are more convenient for articulating the long slurred passages—called *strascini*—so common in solo chitarrone music. Single strings can also be louder, as the player does not have to worry about hitting the double strings against each other. The diapasons were usually single.

In addition to the *strascini* mentioned above, theorbists took full advantage of the reentrant tuning of their instrument by playing scale passages across several strings, letting each of the notes ring as long as possible, rather than up and down one or two strings, where each note is stopped as soon as the next one is played. This technique is called *campanellas*, or "little bells" and was also employed on the Baroque guitar.[7] By playing some passages with *campanellas*, some with *strascini*, and some with individually articulated notes, a great deal of variety can be achieved. Because the third string is the highest in pitch, an unusual right-hand fingering pattern was devised—thumb, index, middle, index—in order to play arpeggios in the "correct" sequence from the lowest note to the highest (Ex. 12.1).[8] Not all chords can easily be arpeggiated in the normal sequence without using very complex right-hand fingerings, but the combination of chords in the "right" pitch sequence and those out of order gives the theorbo a special charm.[9]

To the casual observer, theorbos and archlutes look remarkably alike. The main difference is in the length of the fingered strings, which on the

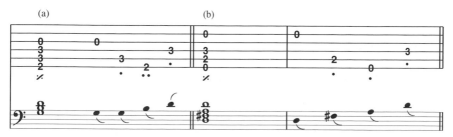

EXAMPLE 12.1.

225

theorbo is much longer, thus necessitating the top two strings to be tuned an octave lower. It is important to keep in mind that gut-strung instruments usually sound best when the highest-pitched string is very near its breaking point.[10] The length of the stopped strings on surviving theorbos is usually between 84 and 96 cm, while some Roman instruments are even longer. The largest instruments were probably tuned in G. Many of today's players perform on very small theorbos of around 76 cm, which, though easy to play, lack the brightness and sonority of full-sized instruments. Such short theorbos were probably originally tuned a third or fourth higher and used as *théorbe pour les pièces* (see section on French lutes below). Archlutes, on the other hand, tended to have string lengths of around 67 centimeters.[11]

Some observers may have used the terms "archlute" and "theorbo" generically in the seventeenth and eighteenth centuries, but experienced musicians clearly knew the difference since parts specifying one or the other are usually well conceived idiomatically. The theorbo has a very full tenor register, but lacks a true treble, while the archlute has a bright, clear treble but lacks the fullness of the theorbo. In addition, the basic pitch of the theorbo was usually a step higher than that of the archlute. For that reason, they were often chosen not only for their tonal characteristics but according to the keys they favored. The *tiorbino*, a small theorbo tuned an octave higher than the regular theorbo, is mentioned in accounts of some oratorio performances and chamber music, though just how common an instrument it was is not known. While the theorbo was preeminent in the early seventeenth century, the archlute seems to have overtaken its larger cousin by 1700, probably because its shorter string length makes for easier playability in a wider variety of keys. Archlutes are also more agile and seem to have often played florid, obbligato-style accompaniments, as opposed to the more sonorous approach used on the theorbo.

The use of the archlute and theorbo in seventeenth-century Italy may be summarized as follows:

1. Solo works for the theorbo were written by Kapsberger, Piccinini, and Castaldi; while for the archlute, composers include Kapsberger, Piccinini, Gianoncelli, Melii, and Zamboni.[12] Castaldi's 1622 collection includes nine duets for theorbo and tiorbino. One possible reason so little solo archlute music survives from the late seventeenth century is that lutenists made arrangements of violin sonatas (Corelli, Mascitti, etc.) for solo archlute. Sylvius Leopold Weiss is known to have played violin concertos on the lute right off the violin part—a practice he may have become acquainted with in Rome.

2. The theorbo was the favored instrument for accompanying singers and instrumental ensembles in the first half of the century, while the archlute became more popular in the second half of the century, especially in

Rome, where ensembles with two or three archlutes are common from the 1640s on.[13] Opera orchestras regularly featured two to four theorbos for most of the century, sometimes augmented with or replaced by archlutes.

France

The French approach to adapting the lute in the seventeenth century was quite different from that of the Italians. At first they, too, added extra bass strings to the standard six-course Renaissance lute, but were forced to stop at the tenth-course C, the lowest note satisfactorily produced by plain gut strings without increasing the string's length. At this point, according to Mersenne, experiments were undertaken to increase the resonance of the instrument. One player attached organ pipes to the neck of the lute, in the hope they would vibrate sympathetically with the strings of the lute. When that did not prove successful, a musette bellows was attached to the organ pipes, but this proved too cumbersome for the player, having to pump the bellows with his right arm while trying to pluck the strings at the same time.[14]

Others experimented with different tunings of the open strings in an effort to produce chords involving as many open strings as possible, thereby increasing the resonance of each chord, since gut is most resonant the longer the vibrating string length. In other words, open strings are more sonorous than stopped strings, chords in the first position are more sonorous than those in higher positions, and so on. The result was the adoption of more than a dozen scordatura tunings, many of which were given identifying names, "French flat tuning," "French sharp tuning," *ton de la harpe, à cordes avalées*, and the soon-to-become-standard French D-minor tuning.[15] After experimentation with Jacques Gautier's twelve-course lute with an extended pegbox, the French settled on eleven courses, all on one neck.[16]

The new French tunings produced more resonance than was possible with the old Renaissance tuning (*vieux ton*), but they did not increase the volume of sound, nor did the French show any particular interest in doing so. For that reason, the French lute of the second half of the seventeenth century was primarily a solo instrument, sometimes used to accompany solo singers or small groups of instruments. Its intimate quality was expressed by one writer in this way: "This instrument will suffer the company of but fewe hearers, and such as have a delicate ear. . . . It is a disgrace for the lute to play country dances, songs or corants of violins. . . . To make people dance with the lute it is improper. . . . It is neither proper to sing with the lute."[17] Earlier in the century more than a dozen lutes were used to play in court ballets, while the lute was the favorite instrument for accompanying the hundreds of *airs de cour* published during the first forty years of the century. Taste evidently changed along with the tuning and setup of the lute in the second half of the century.

Jacques Mauduit is said to have introduced the theorbo into France around 1610. It apparently did not become a prominent continuo instrument there until the 1640s, but eventually supplanted the lute in that capacity. Ensembles consisting of violins, flutes, theorbo, bass viol, and harpsichord are often mentioned in the 1670s and '80s. [18] The royal opera under Lully normally included several theorbos in the continuo section. The earliest solo French theorbo music is from the 1680s, with the finest repertory being that by Robert de Visée. James Talbot's tuning for a "lesser French Theorbo for Lessons" is a fourth higher than the standard continuo theorbo in A, suggesting solo pieces may have been played on the smaller instrument. This would certainly make some of the music brighter and easier to articulate; however, the key indications in the Saizeney manuscript correspond to A tuning. [19] Solos were probably played on both instruments. Whether the lesser French theorbo was also used to play continuo is not known, but it would certainly make sense that different sizes and tunings were employed in ensembles with multiple theorbos. The archlute does not seem to have been very common in France, though Dieupart calls for it in his *Six Suittes de Clavessin pour un violon ou flute avec une Basse de Viole ou un Archilut* (ca. 1705). It was so unfamiliar to Mersenne that he printed the wrong picture of it in his *Harmonie Universelle* (1636) and had to print a correction several hundred pages later in the book!

The use of the lute in seventeenth-century France may be summarized as follows:

1. Solos, duets, quartets, songs, and small ensemble music in Renaissance tuning for ten courses until about 1645; *ballet de cour* ensembles of up to forty lutes are recorded in various sources. [20]

2. Solos and duets in the new tunings for nine to eleven courses starting with Francisque in 1600, becoming commonplace by 1630. To my knowledge, the only examples of these tunings being used for continuo are two English sources, Oxford, Bodleian Library, MS Mus. Sch. E 410–414 and Nanki Ms. N-4/42.

3. The theorbo was the workhorse continuo instrument from about 1640 onward. A significant solo repertory for it emerged in the late seventeenth century.

England

In England, both Italian and French tunings and instruments were used. The Renaissance tuning persisted into the eighteenth century, while the French transitional tunings began to make an appearance as early as 1606. The ten-course lute was the standard English lute from 1610 until around 1645, when the double-headed twelve-course lute took over. [21] The transitional tunings were popular between 1620 and 1700, while the old tuning persisted on the archlute until late into the eighteenth century. The D-minor "Baroque lute" tuning is also represented in numerous sources, so it would seem all of the tunings were practiced in England during the seventeenth century.

The twelve-course lute in transitional tunings was used for some ensemble music (e.g., Oxford, Bodleian Library, MS Mus. Sch. E 410–14), but it was the "lusty theorbo" that became the standard English continuo instrument by the 1640s. The theorbo had been introduced into England by Inigo Jones as early as 1605, when his instrument was confiscated by a customs officer at Dover, concerned it may have been "some engine [of war] brought from Popish countries to destroy the King." The suspicion with which the instrument was regarded by that customs official seems to have remained unchanged over the centuries! Whether this episode slowed the acceptance of the theorbo, or whether the popularity of the lute delayed its ascendance is hard to determine.

Linda Sayce has recently made a compelling case that the term "theorbo-lute" referred to a twelve-course, double-headed lute in standard Renaissance tuning until the 1670s, despite the existence of large, re-entrant Italian theorbos in England as early as 1605![22] This means that the instrument used to accompany the songs and consorts of Lawes, Coleman, and Jenkins was not a large reentrant theorbo, but a Renaissance lute with extra bass strings.[23] In the 1670s the instrument was enlarged and the top string tuned down an octave, but the G tuning was maintained—an important point considering the English predilection for flat keys. Italian theorbos probably still existed in England at this time, but their tuning in A would have been awkward for playing in flat keys, while the often high-lying bass parts of Lawes, Locke, and Purcell would have been unsatisfying with b as the highest string. Talbot describes a large theorbo with double courses throughout and the basses strung in octaves, though whether this was typical of the "English Theorbo" is not known. It is certainly easier to be "lusty" on thick single courses than on double courses, which rattle easily, but this may not have been what English players had in mind. Recent experience has shown that English theorbos suit the music written for them better than do Italian instruments, though this causes a dilemma for today's players, who must decide how many different instruments to buy and how to travel with all of them! To make matters more complicated, some English sources suggest theorbos could also be strung with wire strings.[24] Such diversity is frustrating to the modern performer trying to get the "right" instrument for the music. It is typical, however, for a period in which there was no standardization, and individual builders and performers were constantly experimenting to develop the best instrument for the music.

According to Thomas Mace, an organ with "a lusty theorbo" was the preferred continuo team for string consorts. Title pages of songbooks throughout the seventeenth century list the "theorbo lute" as the first choice for accompanying singers until 1687, the earliest instance in which the organ and harpsichord are listed ahead of the theorbo. Whether "theorbo lute" always referred to the English theorbo proper, or whether it sometimes referred to any kind of theorboed lute—including the arch-lute—is not clear. Some scholars have suggested the archlute was not introduced into England until the arrival of Handel and the Italian opera in 1710, but a surviving obbligato accompaniment to Purcell's "How pleasant is this flow'ry plain"[25] strongly suggests the archlute. Not only is it written in a seventeenth-century hand, it is also mentioned in Matthew Locke's *Melothesia* of 1673.

The use of the lute in seventeenth-century England may be summarized as follows:

1. Renaissance tuning on eight- to ten-course instruments until mid-1640s for solo music, songs, and ensemble music in the English consort style; on twelve-course instruments until the eighteenth century.

2. Transitional tunings used on eight-course lutes as early as 1606, on ten- to twelve-course instruments into the eighteenth century for solo music, songs, and ensemble music in the French style.[26] Whether or not continuo playing in these tunings was commonplace, as suggested by the examples in the Nanki Ms., is not known at this time.

3. The D-minor tuning first appeared in the 1630s and continued into the eighteenth century. Most of the surviving repertory for it consists of arrangements of popular songs, dances, and division pieces, including the works of Purcell and Handel.

4. The English theorbo in G with the top string down the octave was the preferred continuo instrument for songs and consort music from about 1670 on. The Italian theorbists who played for Handel probably played Italian instruments.

5. The archlute was used as a continuo and obbligato instrument from about 1660 until at least the 1740s.

Germany

Germany and Bohemia also followed Italian and French currents throughout the seventeenth century. The ten-course lute in old tuning remained popular into mid-century both as a solo and as a consort instrument despite the introduction of the new French tunings in the 1630s. The vogue for these tunings lasted into the late seventeenth century in Germany as it had in France, but again the D-minor tuning took over as the most common one by 1650. The chitarrone was introduced into Germany in the 1610s and is frequently mentioned alongside the *liuto*—either an eight- or ten-course lute or an archlute—as a continuo instrument. It was used in Italianate music—concertos, cantatas, sonatas, operas—well into the eighteenth century. A theorbo part in tablature for Buxtehude's *Fürchte dich nicht* survives in a manuscript in Uppsala along with theorbo parts for several other late seventeenth-century German works (see p. 276). Another kind of theorbo using the D-minor tuning, sometimes minus the top f, is described by Ernst Gottlieb Baron in 1727.[27] Exactly when it came into use or whether its use was widespread is not known. Obbligato parts for the *tiorba* found in early eighteenth-century Viennese operas seem to have been written with the D-minor tuning in mind, not the old Italian reentrant tuning. However, the painting of Johann Joseph Fux (1660–1741) directing *Costanza e Fortezza* shows him playing an enormous theorbo that was probably tuned in the Italian manner. The eleven-course D-minor lute was widely used as a continuo and solo instrument in German and Bohemian chamber music of the time (Esaias Reussner [1636–79], F. I. Hinterleitner [1659–1710], etc.). The archlute was also common in German-speaking countries in the seventeenth century, as can be seen by the numerous obbligato parts in operas and oratorios of the time (Camilla de Rossi [fl. 1707–10], Antonio Draghi [ca. 1634–1700], Agostino Steffani [1654–1728]). The lute was so popular around 1700 that Balthasar Janowka claimed that one could "cover all of the roofs of Prague with lutes."[28]

A plucked instrument of this period that has not yet received much attention is the *gallichon*, also called *colascione*, *calizon*, or *calchedon*, not to be confused with the southern Italian *colascione*, a two- or three-stringed folk instrument that played mostly parallel fifths and octaves (e.g., Kapsberger's and Piccinini's parodies called *Colascione*). A large six-course lute tuned a tone lower than the modern guitar (D,G,C,f,a,d) or (F,G,C,f,a,d), the gallichon was used as a solo and continuo instrument. Parts for it survive in sacred vocal music by Giovanni Felice Sances (ca. 1600–76), Gleitsmann, and Georg Phillipp Telemann (1681–1767), while Bach's predecessor in Leipzig, Johann Kuhnau (1660–1722), used it in performances of his church music, without leaving a separate part for it. Presumably, it played from the continuo part together with the organ. Giuseppe Antonio Brescianello (ca. 1690–1758) left a collection of eighteen very fine solo partitas for it in a manuscript in Dresden.[29] Talbot describes a *gallichon* loaned to him by the Moravian composer Gottfried Finger (ca. 1660–1730), measuring "just over two feet long" with a string length of "17 inches."[30] It is unclear precisely when and where the instrument was invented and how widespread its use as a continuo instrument was, but the survival of numerous originals suggests it was not an insignificant instrument.

Another instrument mentioned in many sources but not yet revived in the twentieth century is the *angélique*, or angel lute. A gut-strung, extended-neck lute, it looks very much like a theorbo but has ten strings on the lower pegbox and six on the upper, tuned diatonically on "white" notes from D to e'. Talbot observed that it is "more proper for slow and grave lessons than for quick and brisk by reason of the continuance of sound when touched which may breed discord."[31] Jakob Kremberg's *Musikalische Gemüths-Ergötzung*, published in Dresden in 1689, contains charming arias with *angélique*, lute, and guitar accompaniments in tablature. Thurston Dart has suggested that the instrument was invented by the Parisian lutenist Paulet Angélique, but the handful of surviving *angéliques* are found in museums in Schwerin and Leipzig and were made by German builders.

Spain

In Spain, the word "vihuela" was still used in the seventeenth century, though it seems to have become synonymous with the guitar in many instances, and therefore no longer in the old Renaissance lute tuning it used in the previous century.[32] How common the Renaissance lute tuning remained in seventeenth-century Spain is still unclear. The theorbo was known by at least 1624 when a member of the Piccinini family brought one over from Rome. It is shown in several Spanish paintings of the time and is mentioned in a number of musical sources as well. The archlute is also called for in several works, though the extent of its use is unknown at this time. While theorbo and archlute were used in Spain in the seventeenth century, they were not as popular, as typical, or as necessary as the harp and the guitar. The latter two instruments shared repertory and were often played together in ensemble. The bright plucked sound of the Spanish cross-strung harp with the strummed guitar is a delightful combination for the rhythmic, dance-oriented music of the time. The Florentine stage engineer Baccio del Bianco, who worked on productions of the court plays in Madrid in the 1650s, wrote of performances in which *el cuatro,* a group of four guitars, accompanied singing and dancing in court theatrical productions.[33] The principal continuo player at court was the harpist and composer Juan Hidalgo, and it is clear from the documents that guitars and harps played together as the mainstay of the improvising continuo band. The combination was quite common for Spanish dance music of the time, as well as for accompanying singers.

Technique

The period around 1600 was a time of transition and experimentation in lute technique. The Renaissance thumb-under technique, which facilitated rapid articulation by using the whole arm to generate energy, was gradually replaced by the "thumb-out" position, which produced a brighter, more penetrating sound, appropriate for ensemble playing.[34] The arm movement of the thumb-under technique may have been considered visually inelegant in the early Baroque as well. In the Renaissance, the standard right-hand fingering was an alternation of the thumb with the index finger to produce the characteristic strong/weak pairing so important to the music of this period. The thumb/index alternation also produces the velocity required by sixteenth-century divisions. The thumb was also responsible for bass notes and would jump from the treble to the bass as needed. This articulation continued into the seventeenth century; however, with the increase in the number of courses at this time, coupled with the more active bass lines of the early Baroque, leaping with the thumb became less practical and was eventually dropped in favor of middle/index alternation. This is generally less agile and fluid than the thumb/index alternation, but it allowed the thumb to remain in the bass register, a necessity when dealing with the ten- to nineteen-course instruments of the seventeenth century. Details about this transition are discussed in Beier–Right Hand Position and O'Dette–Tone Production. Another essential technique used in this period involves the rest stroke with the thumb, that is, resting the thumb on the next highest string after playing each bass note. This is important not only for orientation, but also to provide a more solid sound.

Soloists generally preferred the sound of the lute when played without fingernails while ensemble lutenists often used long fingernails on their right hand fingers. Thomas Mace remarked,

> Strike not your Strings with your Nails, as some do, who maintain it the Best way of Play, but I do not; and for This Reason; because the Nail cannot draw so sweet a Sound from a Lute, as the nibble end of the Flesh can do. I confess in a Consort, it might do well enough, where the Mellowness (which is the most Excellent satisfaction from a Lute) is lost in the Crowd; but Alone, I could never receive so good Content from the Nail, as from the Flesh: However (This being my Opinion) let Others do, as seems Best to Themselves.[35]

Sylvius Leopold Weiss maintained that

> In chamber music, I assure you that a cantata à voce sola, next to the harpsichord, accompanied by the lute has a much better effect than with the archlute or even the theorbo, since these two latter instruments are ordinarily played with nails and produce in close proximity a coarse, harsh sound.[36]

This suggests that those who played in large ensembles used nails, while those who played solos or intimate chamber music preferred the sound produced by flesh. Many who played theorbo and archlute also played the guitar, which also appears to have been played with fingernails in many cases. Certainly the strummed *rasgueados* on the guitar are more exciting when played with fingernails. Obviously, each player must make his or her own decision regarding the nail question and decide when and how to compromise.

Guitar

The guitar played an extremely important role in the seventeenth century both as a solo and continuo instrument. It was an essential instrument in the dance music of the time, often combined with castanets in performances of sarabands and chaconnes. Guitars came in a wide variety of sizes with four or five courses, the latter being standard for most solo repertory. The standard instrument was tuned e' b g d a, with larger instruments tuned a tone lower in D; smaller instruments in a" and b" were used to add color to consorts. According to Giovanni Paolo Foscarini (fl. 1621–49), ensembles involving multiple guitars should employ instruments of different sizes and tunings to produce a fuller, richer sound. There were numerous ways of tuning the basic five courses with regard to octaves (see Tuning Charts, pp. 239–41). Finding the right tuning for the music is extremely important if one is to make sense of the voice-leading, especially in *campanellas* passages. *Campanellas* are scale passages in which each note is played on a different string, allowing the notes to ring over like "little bells." James Tyler has given a list of the tunings he believes apply to each composer in his book *The Early Guitar.* Recently many players have become convinced of the need for a high g" octave string on the third course for Santiago de Murcia (fl. 1714) and other Spanish composers.[37]

The two basic techniques employed on the guitar at this time were plucking (*punteado*) and strumming (*rasgueado*), often employed in the same pieces. The elaborate strumming techniques discussed in seventeenth-century sources are reminiscent of many Latin and South American folk traditions and provide the essential color and rhythm to much seventeenth-century music.[38] The guitar was the preferred instrument for accompanying vocal music in the popular vein (*canzonette, villanelle,* and *villancicos*) in Italy, France, Spain, and England, prompting Italian publishers to include chord symbols, known as the *alfabeto,* above the vocal parts in their prints of this repertory. The *alfabeto* was a system of notating chords by letters, relieving amateurs of the task of learning to realize unfigured bass lines.

Many chords sound in inversions on the Baroque guitar due to its reentrant tuning, giving the instrument a special charm. Some modern observers have expressed disdain for the guitar's inability to realize bass lines in the notated octave, but this "defect" provides a rustic character that enlivens the music in a way the theoretically "correct" harmonies cannot provide. Another characteristic of the Baroque guitar is the use of extra dissonances to simplify left-hand fingering and to facilitate strumming. If a chord were to require an awkward stretch, or if a regular note of the harmony is not easily reachable, guitarists simply added interesting dissonances (see Ex. 12.2). This aspect of Baroque guitar practice may

EXAMPLE **12.2.**

have inspired the *acciaccature* that add so much spice to the keyboard music of Domenico Scarlatti (1658–1757) and Antonio Soler (1729–83).

The guitar was extremely popular throughout Europe in the seventeenth century. Solo and ensemble music survives from Italy, Spain, Portugal, Mexico, England, France, and Germany. For a comprehensive list of sources, see Tyler–*Early Guitar.*

Cittern, Gittern, Orpharion, and Bandora

The cittern was popular from the Renaissance through the seventeenth century, especially in England, France, Holland, and Italy. It was strung with a combination of iron and brass strings arranged in pairs—some of the low courses were even triple strung with octaves—and plucked with a quill. Most English and French citterns had four courses, while Italian instruments had six. The cittern is a chordal instrument fulfilling much the same role as a rhythm guitar in a rock band. Like the Baroque guitar, the cittern lacks a real bass, and produces many chords in inversion. For this reason, it is best used in combination with another instrument that is able to provide the written bass line. The cittern was most commonly used in dance ensembles and to accompany broadside ballads. It is an essential member of the English broken consort, and survived in Italy as a continuo instrument. The Italians added bass strings to the cittern as they had to the lute, resulting in an instrument they called *ceterone* or archcittern. Monteverdi calls for *ceteroni* in *Orfeo,* though most modern performances ignore his suggestion. The parts were probably similar to the ones provided by Pietro Paolo Melii in his *Balletto* of 1616. English solo music for a fourteen-course archcittern was published by Thomas Robinson in his *New Citharen Lessons* of 1609.

In his 1666 *Musick's Delight on the Cithren,* John Playford advised,

> For your right hand, rest only your little finger on the belly of your Cithren, and so with your Thumb and first finger and sometimes the second strike your strings, as is used on the Gittar; that old Fashion of playing with a quil is not good, and therefore my advice is to lay it aside; and be sure you keep your Nails short on the right hand.[39]

He went on to explain that the cittern had fallen out of favor, but hoped that by adopting "the gittar way of playing" he could "revive and restore this Harmonious Instrument." This makes clear that the cittern was normally played with a quill, but in an attempt to bring it back into favor in the late seventeenth century, finger-plucking was advocated. Besides Playford there is only one other late source that seems to require the cittern to be played with the fingertips.

Gittern was the name given to the Renaissance four-course guitar in sixteenth- and seventeenth-century England, though in the latter era it sometimes referred to a small cittern in guitar tuning, strung with wire strings and played with a quill. This may have been an attempt to enable guitarists to make "sprightly and Cheerful Musick" on wire strings without having to learn a new tuning.[40] Music for the gittern was published by Playford in 1652 and survives in a few manuscripts.

The bandora, or pandora as it is called in some sources, was devised "in the fourth year of Queen Elizabeth" (i.e., 1561) by the viol maker John Rose. It is essentially a wire-strung bass lute with a scalloped shape, slightly vaulted back, and often a slanted bridge and nut to increase the length of the bass strings. The surviving music for bandora includes a small but rewarding solo literature, a number a song accompaniments, and several lute duet grounds[41]; it is, however, in the broken consort repertory that the bandora really shines. It is an irreplaceable member of that ensemble, filling a double role as continuo and double bass. Together with the cittern, the bandora provides a continuo with the dynamic flexibility required in such a delicately balanced ensemble. The bandora is mentioned as a continuo instrument on the title page of numerous seventeenth-century collections—including several published in Germany—but it seems to have gradually fallen out of favor after about 1640. There is, however, one fascinating account by Roger North (ca. 1651–1734) of bandoras strummed with quills accompanying oboes and violins in late seventeenth-century consort music, suggesting that the instrument was played in some circles throughout the century.

The orpharion is a wire-strung instrument with a scalloped outline and a flat, or slightly vaulted back, tuned like a lute. (Robert Spencer has suggested the name is a combination of Orpheus and Arion.[42]) It was played almost exclusively in England and in some parts of Holland and northern Germany. Because of its tuning and due to the fact that it is mentioned as an alternative to the lute on the title pages of many books of lute songs, the orpharion can be used to play any English lute music. In fact, in thirty-two household inventories made between 1565 and 1648 the bandora and orpharion occur as frequently as the lute. While music published specifically for the orpharion mostly requires a seven-course instrument, the finest surviving example, made by Francis Palmer in 1617, has nine courses. In his *New Booke of Tabliture* of 1596, William Barley explains that on the orpharion, the fingers must be "easily drawn over the strings, and not suddenly gripped, or sharply stroken as the lute is: for if ye should do so, then the wire strings would clash or jarre together the one against the other. . . . Therefore it is meet that you observe the difference of the stroke."[43]

Mandore, Mandola, and Mandolino

Very small members of the lute family became popular in France, England, Germany, and Italy in the seventeenth century. The mandore was, according to Praetorius,

> like a very little lute with four strings tuned thus: g d' g' d". Some are also strung with five strings or courses and go easily under a cloak. It is used very much in France where some are so practised on them that they play courants, other similar French dances and songs as well as passamezzi, fugues, and fantasias either with a feather quill as on the cittern or they can play with a single finger so rapidly, evenly, and purely as if three or four fingers were used. However, some use two or more fingers according to their own use.[44]

In 1623 Alessandro Piccinini observed, "In France they are used to playing a very small instrument of four single strings called the Mandolla, and they play it with the index finger alone. I have heard some players play very well."[45] A quill may have been used for ensemble performances while the fingers were used for solo playing. Praetorius gives three more tunings, the first of which seems to have been the most common in France: (1) g" c" g' c' (2) c" g' c' g c (3) c" f' c' f' c.[46] Solo music for the first tuning survives in France (Chancy's *Tablature de mandore*) and in several Scottish manuscripts.[47]

In Italy the instrument was called the mandora, or later mandolino, and used the tuning g" d" a' e'. By 1657 a fifth and sixth course had been added providing a b and g below the e' string. Surviving four-, five-, and six-course instruments are mostly double-strung except for the first course, which, as on the lute, was often single. A substantial repertory of solo and ensemble music survives for this instrument, a detailed list of which can be found in Tyler and Sparks's *The Early Mandolin*.[48] The modern four-course metal-strung mandolin with violin tuning was invented in Naples in the mid-eighteenth century, and had its own independent repertory.

NOTES

1. Nurse–Development, 102–07.
2. See picture in Kinsky–Piccinini, 103–18.
3. Spencer–Chitarrone, 408–11; Mason–*Chitarrone*, 3–7.
4. Mason–*Chitarrone*, 1–10, 15–16.
5. North–*Continuo*, 63–65.
6. Mason–*Chitarrone*, 10–14.
7. See North–*Continuo*, 168.

8. Ibid., 164–67.
9. Ibid., 164–65.
10. Nurse–Development, 102–07.
11. See Spencer–Chitarrone, 416.
12. See North–*Continuo Playing*, 160, 294–96; and Mason–*Chitarrone*, 84–88.
13. See Maugars–*Response*, p. 9 of translation.
14. See Bailes–Introduction for more details.
15. See ibid. and accompanying examples.
16. Lowe–Historical Development; Bailes–Introduction, 218.
17. *Mary Burwell's Lute Book*, ca. 1670 (based on the teaching of Jacques Gautier), preface.
18. See J. A. Sadie–*Bass Viol*, 24–5, 33, 41, 66.
19. James Talbot, Oxford, Christ Church Mus MS 1187; Besançon, Bilbliothèque de la Ville, Vaudry de Saizeney MS 279152.
20. See Anthony–*French Baroque*, illustrations 2 and 4.
21. Spring–*Lute in England*; Lowe–Historical Development, 11–25.
22. Sayce–Continuo Lutes, 667 ff.
23. Henry Lawes's theorbo, which had survived intact in Oxford, was burned in a bonfire of "unnecessary artifacts" in the nineteenth century.
24. Mason–*Chitarrone*, 10–14.
25. Spink–*English Song*, 216; Holman–*Continuo*; recorded on *Hark, How the Wild Musicians Sing: Symphony Songs of Henry Purcell*, Redbird/The Parley of Instruments, Hyperion CDA 66750.
26. See Sayce, article forthcoming; Lowe–Historical Development.
27. Spencer–Chitarrone, 414, 419.
28. Janowka–*Clavis*.
29. Modern editions of nos. 6, 7, and 16 by Ruggero Chiesa (Milan: Edizioni Suvine Zerboni, 1976–77).
30. Prynne–Talbot's Manuscript, 52 ff.
31. Talbot–Ms 1187; see Baines–Talbot's Manuscript.
32. See O'Dette–Plucked Instruments, 147.
33. Stein–*Songs*, 149.
34. Beier–Right Hand Position, 5–24.
35. Mace–*Musick's Monument*, 73.
36. Cited in D. A. Smith–Baron and Weiss, 61.
37. See Lorimer–*Saldivar Codex*, xix.
38. Weidlich–Battuto, 63–86; Tyler–*Early Guitar*, 77–86.
39. Playford–*Cithren*, preface.
40. See Ward–Sprightly.
41. See Norstrom–*Bandora*.
42. Spencer–Chitarrone.
43. Barley–*Tabliture*, preface.
44. Praetorius–*Syntamga* II: 53; translated in Tyler/Sparks–*Early Mandolin*, 8.
45. Piccinini–*Intavolatura*, preface.
46. Praetorius–*Syntagma* II: 28.
47. See McFarlane recording, cited in the discography at the end of this chapter.
48. Tyler/Sparks–*Early Mandolin*, appendix 3.

BIBLIOGRAPHY

Bailes–French Lute Music; Beier–Right Hand Position; Bocquet–*Approche*; Bocquet–'Perfect' instruments; Kinsky–Piccinini; Lorimer–*Saldívar Codex No. 4*; Lowe–Historical Development; Lowe–Renaissance and Baroque; Lundgren–*New Method*; Mace–*Musick's Monument*; Mason–*Chitarrone*; Maugars–*Response*; Ness–Lute

Sources; Nordstrom–*Bandora*; North–*Continuo Playing*; Nurse–Development; O'Brien and O'Dette–*Lute Made Easie*; O'Dette–Observations; O'Dette–Plucked Instruments in the Renaissance; Poulton–*Tutor*; Poulton–*Lute Playing*; Radke–Beiträge; Russell–*Santiago de Murcia*; *New Grove . . . Instruments*; Satoh–*Method*; Sayce–Continuo Lutes; D. A. Smith–Baron and Weiss; Spencer–Chitarrone; Spring–*Lute in England*; Stein–*Songs*; Tyler–*Brief Tutor*; Tyler–*Early Guitar*; Tyler–Mandore; Tyler–Italian Mandolin; Tyler/Sparks–*Early Mandolin*; Ward–Sprightly; Weidlich–Battuto.

Discography

The Complete Lute Music of John Dowland. Paul O'Dette, lute. Harmonia Mundi HMU 907160-4 (5 volumes).
Lord Herbert of Cherbury's Lutebook. Paul O'Dette, lute. Harmonia Mundi HMU 907068.
Il Tedesco della Tiorba: Kapsberger–Pieces for Lute. Paul O'Dette, lute & chitarrrone. Harmonia Mundi HMU 907020.
Ancient Airs and Dances. Paul O'Dette, lute, archlute, and Baroque guitar. Hyperion CDA66228 (cassette KA66228).
Henry Lawes: Go Lovely Rose–Songs of an English Cavalier. Nigel Rogers, tenor; Paul O'Dette, lute, theorbo, and guitar. Virgin Classics VC 5 45004 2.
Sigismondo D'India: Lamento d'Orfeo. Nigel Rogers, tenor; Paul O'Dette, lute and chitarrrone; Andrew Lawrence-King harp, harpsichord, and organ. Virgin Classics VC 7 907392.
Alessandro Piccinini: Intavolature di liuto et chitarrone, libro primo. Nigel North, lute. Arcana A6.
Piéces de luth: French Lute Music of the Seventeenth Century. Nigel North, lute. University of East Anglia.
Piéces de luth. Anthony Bailes, lute. EMI 1C 063 30938.
The Scottish Lute. Ronn McFarlane, lute. Dorian DOR 90129.
Denis Gaultier: La rhetorique des dieux. Hopkinson Smith, lute. Astrée AS 6.
William Lawes: The Royal Consorts. The Purcell Quartet with Paul O'Dette and Nigel North, theorbos. Chandos CHAN 0584/5.
Luz y Norte (Released in the U.S. as *Spanish Dances*). The Harp Consort, Andrew Lawrence-King, director. Deutsche Harmonia Mundi.
John Jenkins: Late Consort Music. The Parley of Instruments. Hyperion CDA 66604.
Henry Purcell: Hark, How the Wild Musicians Sing. Redbird/The Parley of Instruments. Hyperion CDA 66750.
Matthew Locke: The Broken Consort–Part 1. The Parley of Instruments. Hyperion CDA 66727.
Henry Purcell: Complete Ayres for the Theatre. The Parley of Instruments, directed by Roy Goodman. Hyperion CDA67001/3.
The King's Delight. The King's Noyse. Harmonia Mundi CD HMU 907101.
The Queen's Delight. The King's Noyse. Harmonia Mundi CD HMU 907180.

Tuning Charts

14-course archlute

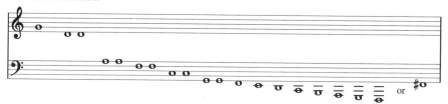

EXAMPLE 12a

14-course theorbo

EXAMPLE **12b**

10-course lute in Renaissance tuning *(vieux ton)*

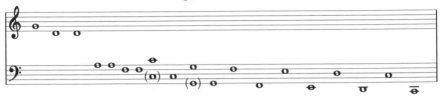

EXAMPLE **12c**

11-course lute in D minor tuning

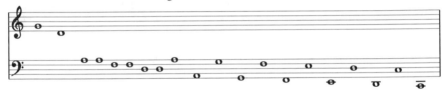

EXAMPLE **12d**

à cordes avalées

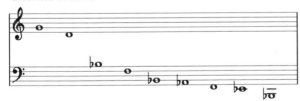

EXAMPLE **12e**

French flat tuning

EXAMPLE **12f**

French sharp tuning

EXAMPLE 12g

gallichon

EXAMPLE 12h

Angélique

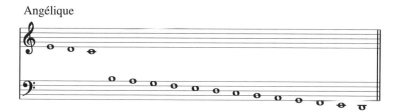

EXAMPLE 12i

Baroque guitar tunings

EXAMPLE 12j

Mandore

EXAMPLE 12k

Mandolino

EXAMPLE 12l

III

PERFORMANCE PRACTICE AND RELATED ISSUES

13

Ornamentation in Early-Seventeenth-Century Italian Music

Bruce Dickey

The seventeenth century was a period of Italian dominance in musical matters over much of Europe. Italian singers and instrumentalists were in great demand in Germany, Austria, Eastern Europe, and in England, and they brought with them their styles of ornamented singing and playing. A discussion of Italian ornamentation practice in the seventeenth century thus is relevant to the performance of much of the music produced outside of Italy as well. In addition, seventeenth-century ornamentation practice is a blending of traditional practices bequeathed from the sixteenth century and innovative techniques developed in connection with the new monodic singing style fashionable after the turn of the century.

The revolution in musical style around 1600 that led to the birth of monody and opera was as much a radical change in the art of singing as it was in the art of composition. One of the pioneers of the new style, Giulio Caccini, was first and foremost a virtuoso singer; he committed his "new way of singing" to paper only to prevent other singers from spoiling his songs by their "improper way of singing them." The new style of singing involved principally three aspects: (1) greater attention to the sentiments of the text, (2) a particular kind of rhythmic freedom (known as *sprezzatura*) that gave precedence to natural speech rhythms and created a kind of "speech in song" (*recitar cantando*), and (3) the use of a whole range of ornamental devices that were either new or used in new ways. We can get a sense of the novelty of these devices by listening to a description of contemporary singers by the Roman nobleman Pietro della Valle, himself present in 1600 at the first performance of Cavalieri's *Rappresentatione di anima e di corpo*:

However, all of these [singers of the old school], beyond the *trilli, passaggi* and a good putting forth of the voice, had in singing nearly no other art, such as the piano and forte, gradually increasing the voice, diminishing it with grace, expressing the *affetti,* supporting with judgement the words and their sense, cheering the voice or saddening it, making it merciful or bold when necessary, and other similar gallantries which nowadays are done by singers excellently well. At that time no one spoke about it, nor at least in Rome was news of it ever heard, until Sig. Emilio de' Cavalieri in his last years brought it to us from the good school of Florence, giving a good example of it before anyone else in a small representation at the Oratorio della Chiesa Nuova, at which I, quite young, was present.[1]

Perhaps della Valle exaggerates, yet he makes a distinction that seems valid: divisions belong essentially to the old style of singing, affective devices to the new. To be sure, divisions continued to be used (and sometimes written into the music) to a varying degree throughout the first half of the seventeenth century. Even Caccini, who protests so vehemently against the misuse of *passaggi,* includes many in his own pieces. We will see, however, that many of these *passaggi* consist of a succession of smaller, more or less formalized ornaments.

Any singer or instrumentalist who sets out to perform seventeenth-century music with stylistic awareness must understand the function of ornamentation. Too often, ornaments are treated as optional extras: small notes to be added to the music at will but with no intrinsic expressive connection to the written notes. To the seventeenth-century musician, however, ornaments were seen in a very different light. Their use was obligatory because they represented an essential means of expressing the sentiments of the text and of displaying grace.

The Renaissance concept of "grace" is fundamental to an understanding of the function of vocal ornamentation in the seventeenth century. Lodovico Zacconi, theorist and singing teacher, takes pains, in his *Prattica di musica* (1592), to demonstrate the relationship between ornamentation and "grace":

In all human actions, of whatever sort they may be or by whomever they may be executed, grace and aptitude are needed. By grace I do not mean that sort of privilege which is granted to certain subjects under kings and emperors, but rather that grace possessed by men who, in performing an action, show that they do it effortlessly, supplementing agility with beauty and charm.

In this one realizes how different it is to see on horseback a cavalier, a captain, a farmer, or a porter; and one notes with what poise the expert and skillful standard-bearer holds, unfurls, and moves his banner, while upon seeing it in the hands of a cobbler it is clear that he not only does not know how to unfold and move it, but not even how to hold it [. . .]

It is not, therefore, irrelevant that a singer, finding himself from time to time among different people and performing a public action, should show them how it is done with grace; for it is not enough to be correct and moderate in all those actions which might distort one's appearance, but rather one must seek to accompany one's acts and actions with beauty and charm. Now, the singer accompanies the actions with grace when, while singing, in addition to the things stated at length in the preceding chapter, he accompanies the voice with delightful *accenti*.[2]

Thus ornamentation is essential to the singer in demonstrating the same "grace" that distinguishes the horsemanship of a cavalier from that of a farmer. It is his means of showing that which he does, he does not just properly, but with supreme ease. It is part of the subtle and complicated courtly art of *sprezzatura*: using complicated artifice to make what is difficult appear to be so easy that it is done without thinking (while not, at the same time, letting it be seen that one is thinking about not thinking).[3] Tasteful singing was conceivable without divisions (in fact it was sometimes preferable), but never without ornaments.

The Division Style

The process of diminution consists of "dividing" the long notes of an unornamented melodic line into many smaller ones. Though denigrated by some of the proponents of the "new style," divisions were still very much a part of vocal and instrumental practice after 1600. Indeed, the period from 1590 to 1630 was one of the most fertile for the production of division manuals. These manuals typically presented a series of intervals (ascending second, ascending third, etc.) with sample divisions followed by ornamented cadences and often by entire madrigals, chansons, and motets in which the soprano, sometimes the bass, and occasionally all of the parts were provided with elaborate divisions, usually known as *passaggi* or *gorgie*. One of the most appealing and useful of the manuals, by Giovanni Luca Conforto, even claims to be a method for learning in a month's time the art of division.[4] Figure 13.1 shows the first page of Conforto's manual with divisions on the ascending second.

Not all singers, to be sure, were capable of singing *passaggi*, and this inability could have been the result either of a lack of understanding of harmony and counterpoint or a lack of natural agility of the voice (known as *dispositione*). There was general agreement that *dispositione* was a gift from God and that little could be done to develop it in a singer who lacked it. Such singers could still merit praise, however, provided they were "content to sing the part as it stands, with polish, gracefully adding a few *accenti*,[5] for this will be sufficient and will be a pleasure to hear."[6] In an attempt to make his music useful to the largest possible number of singers, Bartolomeo Barbarino presents a series of sacred monodies with unornamented and ornamented versions appearing side by side.[7] In that way, the author claims, they will be useful to (1) singers who have no *disposizione*, for they can be content to sing the plain versions, (2) singers

247

FIGURE 13.1.

who have *disposizione* but no knowledge of counterpoint, for they can sing the divisions as written out, and (3) singers who have both *disposizione* and a knowledge of counterpoint, for they can sing from the unornamented versions, improvising their own divisions.

Of the division manuals published after 1590, two are of particular interest because they provide a series of ground rules for the construction and employment of divisions. One of them (an undated manuscript called *Il dolcimelo,* produced about 1590 under the pseudonym Aurelio Virgiliano) gives rules for building divisions, and another (the *Prattica di musica* of Lodovico Zacconi) provides guidelines for the improvisation of *passaggi* in ensemble singing.

Virgiliano's rules for making divisions, shown in facsimile in Figure 13.2, are the most complete ones provided in any source and are a good point of departure for anyone wanting to learn the art of improvising *passaggi*. They may be paraphrased as follows:

1. The diminutions should move by step as much as possible.
2. The notes of the division will be alternately good and bad notes.[8]
3. All the division notes that leap must be good (i.e., consonant).
4. The original note must be sounded at the beginning, in the middle, and at the end of the measure[9] and if it is not convenient to return to the original note in the middle, then at least a consonance and never a dissonance (except for the upper fourth) must be sounded.
5. When the subject goes up, the last note of the division must also go up; the contrary is also true.
6. It makes a nice effect to run to the octave either above or below, when it is convenient.

1. La Diminutione caminar deue per grado il piu che sia possibile.
2. Tutte le Minute debbono essere una buona, e l'altra cattiua
3. Quelle Minute, che saltano, debbono essere tutte buone.
4. La nota del soggetto vuole esser sempre toccata nel principio, nel mezzo, e nel fine della battuta. E quando nel mezzo non tornasse commodo; si deue almeno toccar vicino in luogo, che gli sia consonante, e non mai dissonante; eccetto nella Quarta di sopra.
5. Quando il Soggetto camina in su; l'ultima nota delle minute deue ancor ella caminar di giu in su: e cosi per continuo.
6. Sarà bella maniera currere un'ottaua di lungo ò in giu, o in su; quando torni commodo.
7. Quando si salta un'ottaua; si deue fare in quella di sopra, e non in quella di sotto; per non incontrar l'altre parti.
8. Non deue la Diminutione discostarsi mai dal soggetto piu d'una Quinta sotto, ò sopra.
9. Solo in questi due, sol, di mezzo [music] si può la Diminutione discostare dal soggetto sette [music] gradi di sopra, e sette di sotto: Ma si concederà solo in una furia di semicrome.
10. Quando si trouano le due Terze di sopra: come [music] si concederà di potersi seruire della Quarta di sotto, perche sarà l'ottaua dell'ultima Terza come [music] Cosi per contrario, quando si trouerranno le due terze di sotto, far si potrà lo stesso: come [music]

FIGURE 13.2.

7. When you leap an octave, it must be upward and not downward, in order not to clash with the other voices.
8. The division must never move away from the subject by more than a fifth below or above.
9. Only on the two Gs in the middle may the division move away from the subject seven degrees above and seven below, but this is conceded only in a fury of sixteenth notes.[10]
10. When you find two thirds going upwards (g-b-d) you may use the fourth below [the first note] because it will be the octave of the final note. The same is true of descending thirds.

Virgiliano's rules describe quite accurately the division practice as it appears in written-out examples between 1580 and 1620. To be sure, stepwise motion is more consistently observed in vocal divisions than in instrumental ones. Yet even in instrumental divisions where triadic figuration is more frequently employed, the predominant melodic movement is stepwise.

Virgiliano's fourth rule lays down the cardinal principle of divisions, which serves to maintain contrapuntal integrity and proper voice leading. The original note must be sounded at the beginning of the division, exactly in the middle and again just before moving to the next note (with the possible substitution of another consonance in the middle). Example 13.1 shows one of Virgiliano's divisions on the descending second that follows his fourth rule strictly, and one that substitutes the upper third in the middle.

EXAMPLE **13.1.**

This rule gives a two-part structure to the division: a formula for departing from and returning to the same note, and a formula for moving to the next note. Awareness of this bipartite structure can be extremely helpful to the beginning improviser since it aids both in remembering division formulas and in constructing them. A few basic beginning figures can be combined with ending formulas for each of the different intervals to create a virtual infinity of complete divisions.

An examination of Virgiliano's examples reveals the fifth rule to be a corollary to the fourth. If the model moves by an interval larger than the second, the interval may be filled in with division notes, but they must approach the next note of the model from the same direction as the original interval, as shown in Example 13.2.

EXAMPLE **13.2.**

On casual reading, Virgiliano's sixth rule may seem to be contradicted by the eighth. Once again a careful examination of the musical examples provides an explanation. In the sixth rule, Virgiliano allows octave substitutions for the notes of the model. In the course of a division, however, one should not stray from the note one is ornamenting by more than a fifth (see Ex. 13.3). Exceptions to this rule are in fact rare, though they do occur, in the examples of Virgiliano.

EXAMPLE 13.3.

By studying rules such as these, and by playing examples of divisions on intervals, melodic patterns, and cadences, instrumentalists and singers became remarkably proficient at ornamenting single lines. Such divisions were cultivated both as a solo practice, with the other parts normally played on a lute or keyboard, and as an ensemble practice, with all the singers or instrumentalists tossing ornaments back and forth in a virtuoso exchange. The latter practice was clearly open to abuse and consequently was regularly condemned by theorists—so often, in fact, that we can be sure of its popularity among musicians. For practical advice on ensemble ornamentation we can find no better teacher than Lodovico Zacconi. From his treatise we can extract the following advice on employing the *gorgie* in ensemble singing:

1. In beginning a contrapuntal piece, when the other voices are silent, do not begin with *gorgie* until the other voices have entered.

2. Spread the divisions in a balanced way throughout the piece. At the end of a piece, do not let loose with an enormous ornament after having left the middle bare and dry.

3. The longer the note the more suitable it will be for divisions. Do not make *passaggi* on quarter notes, especially if they have text. If they are melismatic they may have a few divisions. On half notes some *passaggi* may be sung as long as they do not obscure the text. On semibreves and breves one may make as many ornaments as one wishes.

4. *Passaggi* may be used in all the voices though bass divisions will require special caution. Zacconi provides a series of special divisions for bass parts, the most noteworthy characteristic of which is the avoidance of filling in the descending fifth movement at cadences. Bass divisions were generally regarded differently from divisions in the other parts, and indeed some theorists prohibited them altogether. Singers tended to be more indulgent, though even they had some reservations: "It would please me greatly if whoever sings the bass would sing it firmly, sweetly, with *affetto* and with a few *accenti*, but of divisions, to tell the truth, I would want very few, and never at the cadences, because the bass is properly the

251

basis and foundation of all the parts. Therefore, he must always be firm, without ever wavering."[11]

5. *Passaggi* may be sung on all the vowels, though some will require special practice.[12]

Finally, Zacconi is eloquent on the nature of divisions as formulas in which repetition plays an essential part:

> The art of the *gorgie* does not so much consist in variation or in the diversity of the *passaggi* as it does in a just and measured quantity of figures, the great speed of which does not permit one to perceive whether that which one hears has already been said and is being repeated. On the contrary, a small number of figures can be reused many times in the manner of a circle or a crown, because the listener hears with great delight the sweet and rapid movement of the voice and does not perceive the multiple repetitions through the very sweetness and rapidity of the movements. It is incomparably better to do one thing often and well than, doing many things, to do them poorly in many ways.[13]

Here Zacconi is particularly perceptive, since one of the most common errors of beginning improvisers is that of trying to be too creative with each ornament. The repetition of formulas, as Zacconi points out, is fundamental to a fluid division style.

The division practice described by Virgiliano and Zacconi is that which had been in use for the last half of the sixteenth century. It is best exemplified by the manuals of Giovanni Bassano, Girolamo Dalla Casa, and Giovanni Luca Conforto. The divisions tend to flow smoothly with little rhythmic variety and extensive use of sequences. Around 1600 this division practice quickly began to be modified. Rhythms became more varied through the application of *radoppiate* (sudden bursts of notes in "redoubled" speed) and dotting, rendering the divisions less predictable and less sequential.

According to the sensibilities of the new singing style around 1600, melismatic eighth-note figures (and occasionally sixteenths as well) were lacking in grace if sung in a rhythmically literal way. As Caccini, Brunelli, Puliaschi, and others point out, they could be made more graceful by the use of dotting, back-dotting (the so-called "Lombard rhythm" or "Scotch snap"), and combinations of both of these. In Caccini's example, shown in Example 13.4, the rhythmic variants labeled "2" are all considered to have more grace than those labeled "1."

Brunelli, who borrows some of Caccini's examples in the preface to his *Varii esercitii* (1614), claims that *all* eighth notes, in contrast to sixteenth notes, must be dotted. His examples show a much more rigid dotting scheme in which normal dotting is considered better than no dotting, but back-dotting is "best" (see Ex. 13.5). The way in which Brunelli applied

EXAMPLE **13.4.**

EXAMPLE **13.5.**

these dottings in practice is unclear, since the divisions elsewhere in his book are written entirely in undotted eighth and sixteenth notes. If he intended for entire passages to be played with one type of dotting then his point of view is exceptionally rigid. It was the diversity and contrast of rhythms that seemed to interest the proponents of the new style. Giovanni Bovicelli makes just this point in his *Regole, passaggi di musica.* (1594):

> In order to avoid, as the saying goes, always repeating the same old song, often to the great tedium of the listener, [one may make use of] what seems to be an excellent ornamental device, that is, the varying of *passaggi* frequently, using indeed the same notes, but breaking them up differently. Because just as in writing or in speaking, it is extremely tedious for the listener or the reader if the discourse drags along without any colorful figures of speech, so also the *passaggi* in singing, if not made in different ways, almost as though brought to life with colors, will bring annoyance instead of delight. I mean to say that the *passaggi* must sometimes be a series of notes of the same value, and at other times the same notes must be varied in other guises, in such a way that even if the notes are the same, they will appear different, nonetheless, due to the different way they are put forth [see Ex. 13.6].[14]

The frequent varying of rhythms from one bar to the next, or even from one beat to the next, combined with an increasing concern with intelligibility and expression of the text, led to a profound change in the

EXAMPLE 13.6.

nature of ornamentation practice. The "tickling of the ear" created by "the sweet and rapid movement of the voice" was no longer sufficient for a time in which singing was to be "speech in song," expressing all the passions of the soul. One still finds divisions in compositions in the new style, but most often these "divisions" can be seen as a succession of individual ornaments, altogether more expressive and varied than the *passaggi* of the old style.

The Devices (*Maniere*)

The specific ornamental devices that were a part of the seventeenth-century Italian singing style can be divided into three categories: melodic devices, dynamic effects, and ornaments of fluctuation. By melodic devices we mean those ornaments that actually modify the melodic shape of the original by adding notes to it. In this they are similar to divisions, but briefer and more formulaic. Dynamic effects comprise a series of devices that involve the willful and expressive manipulation of the intensity of a note or a small group of notes. Into the category of ornaments of fluctuation we place those ornaments that consists of a regular and periodic fluctuation of pitch, intensity, or both.

Melodic Devices

THE GROPPO

Among the most frequent of all ornaments were the various kinds of cadential figures known as *groppi* (*groppo* is an old form of the modern Italian *gruppo* = "group"). The *groppo* is really a type of cadential division that became so common at the end of the sixteenth century that it took on a life of its own: it became an ornamental formula. In its basic form, as in Example 13.7, the *groppo* involves a repeated alternation between the leading tone and the tonic in which the final movement to the tonic is accomplished by means of a descent to the third below.

In practice the *groppo* was frequently performed *radoppiato* (redoubled) in sixteenth or even thirty-second notes, with many more repetitions of the half-tone step. Zacconi says that many singers like to fill an entire

EXAMPLE 13.7.

measure with sixteenth notes in this way, a practice to which he has no objection as long as the rising third figure at the end is done with grace and without violence.

Bovicelli is also concerned with the gracefulness required of singers in terminating the *groppo,* particularly with regard to placing the final syllable of the text at the end of the ornament:

> Where the *passaggi* are of many notes, and especially in finishing the *grop-petti,* which always end with sixteenth or thirty-second notes, one must, as much as one can, avoid pronouncing a new syllable on that note which immediately follows the *groppetto*; rather he must go on, slowing down with notes of a bit more value.[15]

Actually, as can be seen in Example 13.8, Bovicelli's solution involves finishing the *groppo* without changing syllables, then adding (after the final note of the cadence) an additional leading-tone movement in quarter notes (in this case ornamented with two eighth notes) upon which the syllable change is effected. This solution, which he adopts many times in his complete sets of divisions on motets and madrigals, creates a rather strange effect, not without an exotic appeal, but which appears to be uniquely his own.

Al - le - - - - lu - ia.

EXAMPLE 13.8.

The *groppo* is sometimes found with more elaborate terminations. Bovicelli gives a formula (Ex. 13.9), called the *groppo rafrenato* in which the sixteenth notes of the *groppo* are "braked" (*rafrenato*) before the final note. Another elaborate termination is given by Zacconi (Ex. 13.10) who refers to it as a "double *accento.*"

Al - le - lu - ia.

EXAMPLE 13.9.

EXAMPLE **13.10.**

While the *groppo* normally alternates the leading tone with the tonic, another version is sometimes encountered for use in the descending cadence. Conforto gives the version seen in Example 13.11, calling it the *groppo di sotto*.

EXAMPLE **13.11.**

A number of writers also describe *groppi* that incorporate *tremoli* or *trilli*. These will be discussed below together with other ornaments of fluctuation.

THE *INTONATIO*

The *intonatio* is an ornament done on the first note of a piece or of any phrase and consists of attacking the note a third (or sometimes a fourth) below and then rising to the written note with a dotted figure, as shown in Example 13.12, taken from Bovicelli.

O   son   fe -   ri - to   las -   so

EXAMPLE **13.12.**

The *intonatio* seems to have been done with great frequency. Caccini says quite simply that there are two ways of beginning a note: on the written note with a crescendo, or on the third below. His pieces as well as those of many others, including Monteverdi, have frequent written-out *intonatii*. In the excerpt of *Audi coelum* from Monteverdi's 1610 Vespers in Example13.13, the tenor intones the word *Dic* with a clear *intonatio*.

THE *ACCENTO*

Probably the singer's most important ornament in the first half of the seventeenth century was the *accento*. For Zacconi it was the ornament that most aptly demonstrated courtly grace. For Scaletta it was synonymous with "singing elegantly" and was especially useful to the singer not gifted with *dispositione* (the agility of the throat required in quick divisions).[16]

Accenti were generally done in places where divisions were considered inappropriate. These include:

EXAMPLE 13.13

- moments of strong affect, particularly involving expression of sadness, grief, or pain (thus Zacconi points out that certain kinds of texts particularly require *accenti* as, for example, *Dolorum meum, misericordia mea,* and *affanni e morte*)

- the beginnings of imitative pieces where one part sings alone

On the other hand *accenti* were particularly to be avoided, according to Zacconi:

- in some sorts of fugal entries and fantasies in order not to destroy the imitation

- with declamatory or imperative texts such as *Intonuit de celo Dominus, Clamavit, Fuor fuori Cavalieri uscite,* and *Al arme al arme*

The actual form of the *accento* is somewhat elusive. This is true in part because the use of the term varies in its specificity: at times it seems to refer to a single ornament with an exact melodic and rhythmic shape while at other times it appears to be a generic term for any ornament of few notes applied to a single melodic interval. Even when used in this generic sense, though, certain common identifiable characteristics recur.

The clearest (and one of the earliest) descriptions of the *accento* is that of Lodovico Zacconi from his *Prattica di musica* of 1592. The composer, Zacconi tells us, is concerned only with placing the musical figures in accordance with the rules of harmony, but the singer has the obligation of "accompanying them with the voice and making them resound according to the nature and the properties of the words." In particular, he continues, when one has intervals larger than the second to sing, one should make use of some "beautiful *accenti*." Zacconi illustrates the *accento* as applied to ascending and descending thirds with the examples in Example 13.14.[17]

This written example, however, only approximates the considerably more subtle art of singing the *accento,*[18] as Zacconi's description makes

EXAMPLE 13.14.

clear. In order to make an *accento* on the ascending third, for example, the singer must hold the first whole note a little into the value of the second. This lingering, however, must not exceed the value of a quarter note. One must then ascend to the second whole note, but, in passing, make heard "something like a sixteenth note." Thus, if we insist on fixing in objective rhythmic notation something which Zacconi clearly intends to be rhythmically vague and subjective, an *accento* on the ascending third would have the form illustrated in Example 13.15.

EXAMPLE 13.15.

Zacconi's example for the falling third in Example 13.14 introduces another common characteristic of the *accento* to be found in many later sources: the use of a rising second to ornament descending intervals. Indeed, *accenti* on ascending and descending intervals were often looked on quite differently and had sometimes very dissimilar forms. In its most usual occurrence, the rising second is used to ornament the descending second. This sort of descending *accento* is called the "true *accento*" by Francesco Rognoni in his *Selva de varii passaggi* (1620), who claims that there is another one used in ascending which can sometimes be pleasing as well.[19] His ascending and descending *accenti* are illustrated in Example 13.16.

EXAMPLE 13.16.

For the ascending and descending second (see Ex. 13.17), Zacconi's *accento* retains the approach to the second note from the third below. This approach, always using a dotted rhythm, is clearly related to the *intonatio*. In fact, Zacconi's *accento* on the second is essentially an *intonatio* used between two neighboring notes.

EXAMPLE **13.17.**

In view of the explicit function of the *accento* of helping to "carry the voice" (*portar la voce*) from one note to the next on larger intervals, it is rather more difficult to understand many of Zacconi's *accenti* for ascending fourths and fifths. Here he retains the dotted rhythm, but instead of filling in the interval melodically, as we might expect, in all but two of his examples he retains the leap as seen in Example 13.18.

EXAMPLE **13.18.**

To understand this rather odd form of *accento*, we must bear in mind that the purpose of the *accento* is to help the singer accompany not only the notes, but also the words, with grace. By adopting this form of the *accento* for a leap of an ascending fourth where there is a change of syllable on the second note, the singer avoids changing syllables on the leap. Instead, he changes syllable on the same note, but slightly after the beat (thus aiding the listener in hearing the consonant) and then produces the melodic interval melismatically.

The *accento* is described or at least mentioned in a great number of other seventeenth-century Italian sources on singing. Indeed, it is a rare discussion of singing in this period that does not at least mention it. There is, however, some disagreement among these authors as to whether *accenti* are properly made on ascending or descending intervals, or on both. While Rognoni claims, as we have seen, that the "true *accento*" is made only in descending, Scaletta maintains that they may only be made on ascending intervals, and indeed goes on to say that in a series of ascending intervals, "they are only done when the part ascends to the highest note . . . if there were four notes ascending by step, the *accento* would be done on the last and not on the others."[20]

The *RIBATTUTA DI GOLA*

Caccini gives the name *ribattuta di gola* (literally, "beating of the throat") to the ornament in Example 13.19. Although the name seems not to have been in general use—indeed the same ornament appears in the table of ornaments supplied by the editor to the first edition of Cavalieri's *Rappresentatione di anima e di corpo* carrying the name *Zimbelo*—the ornament is encountered frequently in monodies and ornamented pieces of the early seventeenth century.

EXAMPLE **13.19.**

A striking occurrence of the *ribattuta di gola* is seen in the setting of *Duo seraphim* from Monteverdi's 1610 Vespers (Ex. 13.20), where it is combined with a *trillo* in a series of virtuoso exchanges.

sanc - - - - - - - tus.

EXAMPLE **13.20**

Dynamic Effects

Without question, dynamics have always been a part of musical expression, at least in singing. Sylvestro Ganassi writes in 1535 that just as the painter imitates the effects of nature with different colors, so the singer varies his sound with more or less force according to that which he wishes to express.[21] The use of the natural dynamics of the human voice in expressing the text was not new in 1600. What was new was an intentional and self-conscious use of dynamics to create effects and the codification of these effects into ornamental devices. While we do not normally consider dynamics to be ornaments, the seventeenth-century concept of ornamentation went beyond our idea of embellishments to embrace any deliberately employed expressive device.

Beginning around 1600 one occasionally finds dynamics indicated in the music by the use of such terms as *piano, forte,* and *ecco.* Usually, these words are associated with echo effects. The *seicento* was interested nearly to the point of obsession in the echo as a natural phenomenon. Natural science was concerned with the physical properties of echoes (an investigation not without interest to the practicing musician, who was urged to seek out a grotto or valley with a clear echo to use as a practice place). The echo fashion filtered into literature in the form of wordplay in which an echo repeats incompletely the final word of a phrase, thus changing its meaning in unexpected and dramatic ways (e.g., *clamore . . . amore . . . more . . . re . . . e*). Poems based on wordplay echoes were obvious candidates for a musical setting and helped to increase the popularity of echo effects in both vocal and instrumental music as well.

Occasionally *piano* and *forte* appear as indications to the continuo player who was instructed to play loudly (with fuller registration) in *tutti* or *ripieno* sections, and more softly in concerted solo sections. Paradoxically, this situation was reversed for singers, who were instructed to sing more strongly in solo passages than in *ripieni*.

In addition to these "block" dynamics that applied to entire phrases or sections, singers used several devices to give dynamic shape to individual notes or small groups of notes.

The swelling and diminishing of a tone, widely known as *messa di voce,* was in use from the beginning of the seventeenth century, though it was not known by this term until at least the 1630s. Caccini calls it simply *il crescere e scemare della voce* ("increasing and diminishing of the voice"), though he mentions it mostly to state his preference for a contrary effect called *esclamatione* (see below). Della Valle, in the passage cited above, uses a similar expression in relating that it was one of the devices brought to Rome by Emilio de' Cavalieri in 1600. Mazzocchi appears to be the first to use the term *messa di voce* in 1638, but the ornament he describes involves increasing (and only increasing) both the volume and the pitch of a note. Ornaments involving the gradual sharpening of a note by a diesis (half of a small semitone) or by a small (enharmonic) semitone are described by other writers from the 1640s and were used in passing from one note to its enharmonic upper neighbor (e.g., f to f♯). Mazzocchi then describes the swelled note and indicates it in the music with the letter "C" (for *crescere*):

> When, however, one is to increase only the breath and the spirit of the voice, but not its pitch, this will be indicated by the letter "C," as was done in a few madrigals; and one should then observe that just as the size of the voice must first be sweetly increased, so must it subsequently be abated little by little, and so levelled off until it is reduced to the inaudible or to nothing, as from a well which thus responds to certain pitches.[22]

Interestingly, Mazzocchi applies the *crescere* almost exclusively to final notes.

More popular in the early decades of the seventeenth century than the swelled note was the *esclamatione*. Caccini describes it in detail, claiming that it is the principal means of moving the affections. It consists, he says, in beginning a note by diminishing it—that is, beginning strongly and immediately tapering—so that one can then strengthen it and give it liveliness. Thus the form of the *esclamatione* is opposite to the *messa di voce*: the *esclamatione* is typically done on downward-moving dotted figures, usually consisting of a dotted half note with falling quarter or dotted whole note with falling half. The voice is diminished little by little and then is given more liveliness "in the falling of the quarter note":

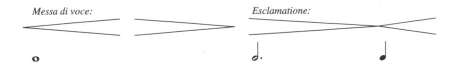

According to Caccini, a larger interval requires a more passionate *esclamatione,* as in his example in Example 13.21.

EXAMPLE 13.21.

Esclamazioni are mentioned by many other writers, but none of them provides much new information about it, with the exception of Francesco Rognoni in 1620. Rognoni's description varies little from that of Caccini, but he adds that "one gives spirit and liveliness to the voice on the quarter note with a little *tremolo.*"[23]

We will discuss later what is meant by the *tremolo* itself, but in writing out these *tremoli* rhythmically, Rognoni gives an indication, as can be seen in Example 13.22, of the exact point at which the crescendo is to begin. Both of Rognoni's examples indicate that the *tremolo,* and thus the crescendo of which it is a part, is to begin on the dot of the first note.

EXAMPLE 13.22.

Ornaments of Fluctuation

Numerous techniques have been used throughout history by both singers and instrumentalists to create fluctuations of pitch and intensity. These devices often represented part of an oral tradition (and thus remain frustratingly unelucidated in theoretical sources), but sometimes were personal and controversial. Being difficult to describe precisely, they frequently led to misunderstandings and terminological quagmires. In this the seventeenth century was no exception. Some of the techniques used around 1600 produce effects that we would normally call vibratos, others produce trills, note repetitions, and other effects strange to modern ears.

The term "vibrato" did not come into use until the nineteenth century, and the concept of vibrato as distinct from other kinds of fluctuations was foreign to the seventeenth-century musician. Thus an intensity variation produced by varying the bow pressure on a violin could share the same name as a whole-step trill on the organ: *tremolo*. To understand seventeenth-century ornaments it is best to give up the term "vibrato" and concentrate instead on the devices and the techniques used to produce all sorts of tone fluctuations.

Most devices of this sort in the seventeenth century went under the name *tremolo*. Sometimes it refers to the kind of unmeasured "quivering" or "trembling" that Praetorius and others ascribe to good voices, particularly those of boys. Zacconi's discussion is particularly interesting because he credits this *tremolo* with a role in the production of the *passaggi*:

> And in order not to leave out anything on this subject, for the great enthusiasm and desire that I have to aid the singer, I say in addition that the *tremolo*—that is, the trembling voice—is the true door for entering into the *passaggi* and for mastering the *gorgie*, because a ship sails more easily when it is already moving than when it is first set into motion, and a jumper jumps better if before he jumps he takes a running start.
>
> This *tremolo* must be brief and graceful, because the overwrought and the forced become tedious and wearying, and it is of such a nature that in using it, one must always use it, so that its use becomes a habit, because that continuous moving of the voice aids and readily propels the movement of the *gorgie* and admirably facilitates the beginnings of *passaggi*. This movement about which I speak must not be without the proper speed, but lively and sharp.[24]

Other descriptions of the *tremolo* appear to impute to it a more measured, rhythmic nature. Rognoni gives an example of the vocal *tremolo* (Ex. 13.23) and says that "for the most part the *tremolo* is done on the value of the dot of any note." Rognoni does not explain the technique used to produce the *tremolo,* but he does make a distinction between it and the *trillo,* saying that the latter is "beaten with the throat." Thus the

EXAMPLE 13.23.

tremolo is presumably a smooth and regular fluctuation of intensity and/or pitch.[25] It has, according to Rognoni, a special role in the production of the *esclamatione,* where a *tremoletto*[26] is used to give liveliness to the voice at the point where the voice is to increase in volume.

As opposed to the *tremolo,* which was unarticulated, the *trillo* is usually described as an *articulated* reiteration of a note "beaten in the throat"—that is, employing the same kind of throat articulation used for the execution of rapid *passaggi.*

The Roman falsettist Giovanni Luca Conforto was the first to notate it in his *Breve et facile maniera* of 1593. Conforto (see Ex. 13.24) uses a "3" to indicate that the repeated notes should be redoubled in speed (i.e., they should have three beams instead of the two that appear below them).

Trillo   Mezzo

EXAMPLE 13.24.

Conforto's *trilli* have terminations similar to the *groppo* and thus show some similarity to an ornament called the *tremolo groppizato* that appears four years earlier in Girolamo Dalla Casa's *Il vero modo di diminuir* (Ex. 13.25). Although

Essempio de tremoli groppizati de le tre sorti de figure per grado de semibreve.

Essempio de tremoli groppizati de minima.

EXAMPLE 13.25.

Dalla Casa uses the term *tremolo* instead of *trillo* it is tempting, given the speed of the ornament and its similarity to later *trilli*, to think that it represents an early example of the articulated reiteration.

Caccini's well-known example of how to learn the *trillo* shows a gradual increase in the speed of the reiterated notes. In his more extended musical examples (see Ex. 13.26), however, Caccini indicates *trilli* on notes as short as a quarter note and often includes figures with only two note repetitions. In view of Conforto's use of the number 3 to notate a faster *trillo* than those indicated by the notes, it could be that Caccini intends for the repeated notes to be redoubled in speed and number, the two written-out repeated notes being a kind of shorthand for note repetition. This hypothesis is supported by Ottavio Durante, who, in reference to the indication *t*, remarks that where it is found, "one must always trill with the voice, and when it is notated above a *trillo* or *groppetto* itself, one must then trill that much more."[27]

Despite the many descriptions of "beaten" *trilli*, the term was not exclusively used for a repeated-note ornament. In the preface to Cavalieri's *Rappresentatione di anima e di corpo* the table of ornaments gives a *trillo* that is nothing but a trill with the upper neighbor, and Bartolomeo Bismantova uses the term in the same way in 1677.[28]

EXAMPLE 13.26.

265

Conclusion

The ornamentation style discussed in this chapter was that used primarily by Italian singers from the last decades of the sixteenth century until roughly the mid-seventeenth century, when new influences, including those brought from the French court, began to modify vocal tastes and practices. Singers, however, were the model for instrumentalists as well, who were to imitate the human voice as much as possible. One of the most important ways of doing this was through the imitation and adaptation of vocal ornamentation. Thus Sylvestro Ganassi calls the tonguing used for division playing the *lingua di gorgia* after the throat articulations used by singers, and Francesco Rognoni says that his description of vocal ornaments is "something useful to instrumentalists as well for imitating the human voice."[29] Singing without ornaments can never have the required grace; instrumental playing without ornaments can never be truly vocal.

This ornamentation style was also exported, more or less intact, to Germany where Italian singers and Italian styles dominated in the seventeenth century. German writers like Praetorius, Herbst, and Crüger give examples of ornaments such as the *intonatio, accento, groppo, tremolo,* and *trillo* that are virtually identical to those of the Italians.

NOTES

1. della Valle–Della musica, 255–56 (page numbers refer to Doni–*Lyra Barberina*).
2. Zacconi–*Prattica* di musica, vol. 1, libro primo, cap. 63.
3. For a fascinating discussion of *sprezzatura* see Baldassare Castiglione, *Il libro del cortegiano,* Florence, 1528, *libro primo.*
4. It is interesting to note that Conforto was criticized by Pietro della Valle for his excesses in singing *passaggi.*
5. More about *accenti* below.
6. Scaletta–*Scala di musica.*
7. Barbarino–*Motetti.*
8. This is more a definition than a rule. An understanding of the concept of good and bad notes, the alternation of consonant notes on stressed beats with dissonant ones on unstressed beats, was fundamental to musical thinking in the sixteenth century, and is a prerequisite to Virgiliano's next rule.
9. As can be seen from his examples, Virgiliano is speaking here of the ornamentation of whole notes. His *battuta* thus refers to the entire value of the note being ornamented.
10. The reason for this exception and its restriction to g' is unclear to this writer. As an illustration of this point, Virgiliano has inserted in the text a musical staff with two semibreves, both on g'.
11. Scaletta–*Scala di musica.*
12. Opinions were mixed on the suitability of all the vowels for making *passaggi.* Durante takes the negative view: "[Singers] must [. . .] make use of those [*passaggi*] that are most appropriate and that work best for singing, guarding against doing them, however, in places that obscure the intelligibility of the words, [and] particularly on short syllables and on the odious vowels, which are *i* and *u*—for the one resembles neighing and the other howling" (Durante–*Arie devote,* preface).
13. Zacconi–*Prattica,* vol. 1, prima parte, cap. 66.

14. Bovicelli–*Regole,* Avvertimenti.
15. Ibid.
16. Scaletta–*Scala di musica* in the section entitled "Ultimo avertimento, utilissimo ancora per tutti quelli che desiderano cantar polito & bene."
17. Zacconi–*Prattica,* libro primo, cap. 63.
18. All ornamentation, of course, is difficult to fix into precise musical notation, but it seems to have been particularly true of the *accento* that its performance was meant to be free of a fixed rhythm. Words such as "lingering," "clinging," and "rather late" are frequently used to describe it, and we are frequently told that its exact nature can only be appreciated by hearing it done.
19. Rognoni–*Selva,* Avvertimenti.
20. Scaletta–*Scala di musica,* ch. 15.
21. Ganassi–*Fontegara,* ch. 1.
22. Domenico Mazzocchi, *Madrigali a cinque voci* (Rome, 1638), preface.
23. Rognoni–*Selva,* Avvertimenti. See Carter–Rognoni.
24. Zacconi–*Prattica di musica,* libro primo, cap. 66.
25. In instrumental music of the early seventeenth century, *tremoli* are often found written out in repeated eighth notes with or without slur marks (see Carter–String Tremolo). Such *tremoli* nearly always proceed continuously for the duration of an entire, brief section, often chromatic in character, and are quite clearly meant to imitate the organ tremulant. One sonata by Biagio Marini (*La Foscarina, sonata à 3* from the *Affetti musicali* of 1617) even has an indication in the organ part to "turn on the tremolo" (*metti il tremolo*), while the violins have the instruction "tremolo with the bow" (*tremolo con l'arco*) and the fagotto, "tremolo with the instrument" (*tremolo col strumento*).
26. Sometimes the term *tremoletto* (literally, "little tremolo") indicates a little trill of just two notes with the upper or lower neighbor.
27. Durante–*Arie devote,* preface.
28. Bismantova–*Compendio,* [23].
29. Rognoni–*Selva,* title page.

SELECTED READING LIST

The reading list below includes the most important Italian sources on singing between 1590 and 1680. Where facsimile editions or English translations are not available, the original texts of prefaces may often be found in the published catalogue of the Civico Museo Bibliografico in Bologna, which has original copies of most of these works. Some prefaces are also found in Claudio Sartori's *Bibliografia della musica strumentale italiana,* though Sartori is less generous with prefaces to the reader than with dedications. The list also includes several German sources that have extensive information on Italian singing style, as well as two invaluable German secondary sources which include extensive citations of sources in the original Italian.

Original Sources

1592. Zacconi, Lodovico. *Prattica di musica.* Venice. Partial German trans. by F. Chrysander, "Lodovico Zacconi als Lehrer des Kunstgesanges." *Vierteljahrschrift für Musikwissenschaft* 7 (1891): 337–96; 9 (1893): 249–310; 10 (1894): 531–67. Facsimile ed. Bologna, 1983.
1593. Conforto, Giovanni Luca. *Breve et facile maniera.* Rome. Facsimile ed. with German translation by Johannes Wolf. Berlin, 1922.

1594. Bovicelli, Giovanni Battista. *Regole, passaggi, di musica*. Venice. Facsimile by Nanie Bridgman, Documenta Musicologica. Kassel, 1957.

1598. Scaletta, Oratio. *Scala di musica*. Verona. Facsimile ed. of the 1626 edition. Bologna, n.d.

1600. Caccini, Giulio. *L'Euridice composta in musica*. Florence. Facsimile ed. Bologna, 1976.

1600. Cavalieri, Emilio de'. *Rappresentatione di anima e di corpo*. Rome. Facsimile ed. Farnborough, 1967.

1602. Caccini, Giulio. *Le nuove musiche*. Florence. Anon. English translation entitled "A Brief Discourse of the Italian Manner of Singing . . ." In J. Playford, *Introduction to the Skill of Music*. 10th ed. London. Rev. ed. of above in Strunk–*Source Readings-Baroque*. English trans. in Newton–*Nuove Musiche*. Modern musical ed. with English trans. in Hitchcock–*Nuove musiche*. Facsimile ed. by F. Mantica, preface by G. Barini. Rome, 1930. Facsimile ed. by F. Vatielli. Rome, 1934.

1608. Durante, Ottavio. *Arie devote, le quale contengono in se la maniera di cantar con gratia*. Rome.

1609. Banchieri, Adriano. *La Cartella*. Venice. Facsimile of 1614 ed. Bologna, n.d.

1612. Donati, Ignazio. *Sacri concentus*. Venice.

1614. Brunelli, Antonio. *Varii esercitii . . . per . . . aqquistare la dispositione per il cantare con passaggi*. Florence.

1614. Barbarino, Bartolomeo. *Il secondo libro delli motetti . . . da cantarsi à una voce sola ò in soprano, ò in tenore come più il cantante si piacerà*. Venice.

1615. Severi, Francesco. *Salmi passaggiati per tutte le voci nella maniera che si cantano in Roma*. Rome.

1618. Puliaschi, Giovanni Domenico. *Musiche varie a una voce*. Rome.

1619. Praetorius, Michael. *Syntagma musicum* III, *Termini Musici*. Wolfenbüttel. Facsimile ed. Kassel, 1958.

1620. Rognoni Taegio, Francesco. *Selva de varii passaggi*. Milan. Facsimile ed. with preface by G. Barblan. Bologna, 1970.

1638. Mazzocchi, Domenico. *Dialoghi, e sonetti*. Rome. Facsimile ed. Bologna, n.d.

1638. Mazzocchi, Domenico. *Partitura de' madrigali a cinque voci, e altri varii concerti*. Rome. Facsimile ed. Bologna, n.d.

1640. Della Valle, Pietro. "Discorso della musica dell'età nostra . . ." In G. B. Doni, *Lyra Barberina*, vol. 2. Florence, 1640. Facsimile ed. with commentary by C. Palisca. Bologna, 1981.

1642. Herbst, Johann Andreas. *Musica practica sive instructio*. Nuremberg.

1660. Crüger, Adam. *Musicae practicae praecepta . . . Der rechte Weg zur Singkunst*. Berlin.

1677. Bismantova, Bartolomeo. *Compendio musicale*. Ferrara. Facsimile ed. with preface by M. Castellani. Florence: S.P.E.S, 1978.

Secondary Sources

Brown–*Embellishing*; Gaspari–*Catalogo*; Goldschmidt–*Gesangsmethode*; Sartori–*Bibliografia*; Kuhn–*Verzierungs-Kunst*.

14

Basso Continuo

Jack Ashworth and Paul O'Dette

The term *basso continuo* designates a mode of accompaniment in use primarily between 1600 and 1750. Continuo practice embraces a wide spectrum of activities and styles, but all such accompaniment includes one thing in common: at least one player of any continuo part produces harmony, the choice of which the composer has designated or the music suggests, but the exact notes of which are left up to the performer. Thus a continuo part has two components: a bass line, which is provided by the composer and is generally to be performed as notated (except for possible octave displacements and restriking or tying of bass notes) and a set of harmonics, which may be specified by signs or implied by standard chord progressions within a given style; the notes that produce these harmonies are not written out, but are rather improvised by one or more players.

The idea of adding a chordal accompaniment to vocal or instrumental pieces had been practiced in one way or another for over a century, either by improvisation or by reading "short score" (meaning that the keyboard player or lutenist plays the notes sounded by the various parts, rather than an improvisatory realization), but the practice grew with special intensity in the declining years of the sixteenth century as musicians began writing—and publishing—such music in the convenient shorthand method of figured (and unfigured) basses. As the practice spread it was applied to older-style polyphonic textures, as well as to the newer ones of solo melody. Readers may consult *A Performer's Guide to Renaissance Music* (Schirmer Books, 1994), an earlier volume of this series, for a segment sketching the historical development of basso continuo.

Accompanying Soloists

When Vincenzo Galilei learned, at first to his horror, that Girolamo Mei's research into Greek music indicated that the texts were sung without accompaniment, he knew that modern songs could not be sung *literally* solo even if it was the surest way to achieve a proper affect. European ears were too used to harmony by this point; Pietro de' Bardi reports that Galilei himself set a passage from Dante, presumably to be sung in the new style and "precisely accompanied by a consort of viols."[1] It soon became clear that when working with singers the best way to provide flexible, expressive accompaniments was on a lute—or, more particularly, the chitarrone. Giulio Caccini (1546–1618), Sigismondo d'India (ca. 1582–1629), Jacopo Peri (1561–1633), Vittoria Archilei (1550–ca. 1620), and many others sang to their own accompaniment on the chitarrone, surely the most sensitive way to match accompaniment with solo. The early books of solo song, beginning with Caccini's *Nuove musiche* of 1602, recommend the chitarrone as the favored accompanying instrument, with harp and harpsichord as suitable alternatives.

Instrumental soloists had been accompanied in various contexts throughout the sixteenth century. In its last twenty years or so, a specific repertory developed for virtuoso players, especially of the cornett, recorder, and viola da gamba, who would play (or improvise) elaborate ornamental passages based on a polyphonic piece such as a madrigal, chanson, or motet. Diego Ortiz (ca. 1510–ca. 1570) gives instructions for this practice as early as 1553, and further examples are seen down through the end of the century. An entire style and repertory of viol music—that for *viola bastarda*—was built on this approach; it, too, is a style of instrumental solo playing with accompaniment, generally provided by a keyboard or lute player using the polyphonic piece as a model.

Organ Basses

In the choir loft, organists accompanied their choirs for sonority as well as to help them stay together—and in tune—more easily, especially in the multichoir pieces newly popular in Rome and Venice, where each choir might have a separate organ assigned to it. At first, these "accompaniments" simply doubled the singers' music, but in 1602 Lodovico Grossi da Viadana's *Cento concerti ecclesiastici* documented a newer practice in which the organist was given only a bass line over which harmonies were to be added, rather than simply doubling all of the vocal parts. This notational shorthand eventually freed continuo players from doubling the vocal parts and encouraged a simpler, chordal accompaniment that provided more rhythmic freedom to the singers as well, since their parts were no longer being doubled. The organ part thus became a separate, integral, and indispensable part of the music, where previously it had been used simply to enrich the sound and/or help the performers. It is for this reason that Viadana's work is generally cited as the first to use basso continuo.

Large Continuo Ensembles

Accompanimental textures were not limited to just a few instruments, however. We know from the recorded practice of the Florentine *inter-*

medii, the Ferrarese *concerto grande,* and from the writing of Agostino Agazzari (1578–1640) that it was popular to accompany large ensembles with a variety of instruments, each contributing its most interesting characteristics (e.g., the chitarrone's sonorous low bass strings, long drawn-out chords on the *lirone,* scales and ornaments gently plucked over the whole range of the harp, etc.). Agazzari explains that accompanying instruments are divided into two types: *instruments of foundation* (such as harpsichords, lutes, and organs) to provide the basic chordal harmonies, and *instruments of ornamentation* (such as violins and lutes, now playing melodically) to improvise ornaments based on the harmonies and general shape of the music.

Continuo batteries remained a basic and popular texture for most of the seventeenth century. In addition to specific examples, such as Claudio Monteverdi's *Orfeo* (1607) with its three chitarrone, *ceteroni,* harps, two harpsichords, organ, and regal, and Rossi's (1647) with four harpsichords, four theorboes, two lutes, and two guitars, we have generic combinations peculiar to specific countries, such as the organ and theorbo in England, or the harp and guitar in Spain. In fact, it would seem that continuo ensembles of five to ten players were not uncommon. In 1683 one observer remarked that in Venetian opera houses it was difficult to see the action on stage "because of the forest of theorbo necks."[2]

Performance

Continuo accompaniment requires one or more chordal instruments, the choice and number depending on the size of the performance space, how many people are being accompanied, and what they are doing. In addition, different repertories and musical styles sometimes entail the use of specific instrumental combinations, as suggested above. Incidentally, it should also be noted that not all "continuo parts" were necessarily intended for *players*: in his *Musicalische Exequien* (1636), Heinrich Schütz provides a figured bass part labeled for either the "violon or the director (*Dirigent*)." This would seem to be a part that could be used by the player of the lowest line, or, in lieu of a full score, by a leader to help keep track of the proper harmonies.

Doubling the Bass Line

It has long been thought that continuo in Baroque music involved two components, a chordal instrument (harpsichord, organ, lute, etc.) and a sustaining instrument (cello, viol, bassoon, trombone, etc.). While this classic "team" does appear to have been standard for later Baroque music, the use of a bowed bass instrument to double the written bass line has been challenged in recent years.[3] The situation is complicated and varies from repertory to repertory, but can be summarized as follows: secular solo song was originally conceived for voice and lute or chitarrone and does not require or benefit from the addition of a bowed bass in most cases up until the very active bass lines of the second half of the seventeenth century. There are several reasons for this: (1) the bass lines at this time are largely unmelodic and simply represent the lowest note of the harmony; (2) the decay of a plucked sound gives the singer a transparent texture over which to deliver the text clearly, and (3) the fewer performers involved the more flexible the performance can be, which is undoubtedly the reason Caccini and others considered self-accompaniment the ideal for the repertory. Bass-line doubling was practiced in special cases (e.g., Monteverdi's *Combattimento*) or used in the theater for more carrying power. In England many lute songbooks include a part for bass viol, but there is no evidence the practice continued after John Attey's collection of 1622, or that it was more than an option in the first place. In the sacred repertory, Viadana makes it clear that he assumes the organ to be used as standard accompaniment. No mention is made of a bowed bass, nor would its use have been assumed at this time. The organ was frequently doubled by a chitarrone, however, providing a clearer bass than the organ can produce on its own. The combination of organ and chitarrone was a very popular one, as may be seen in surviving church documents and accounts of performances.[4]

Archlutes and theorbos were considered melodic bass instruments as well as continuo instruments, and often doubled the bass line in addition to playing chords. This is important to keep in mind, since most of the discussion about bass-line doubling over the past ten or fifteen years has centered on the question of doubling by sustaining instruments, such as bass viol, cello, or bassoon. For much of the seventeenth century, doubling by a plucked instrument was preferred since it provided clarity without muddying the texture. Situations in which sustained instruments were used to double the bass line usually involved either highly active lines, or acoustical environments that required an especially strong bass, as in large churches (e.g., Heinrich Schütz [1585–1672], Michael Praetorius [1571–1621], Andreas Hammerschmidt [1612–75], the Roman oratorios, Maurizio Cazzati [ca. 1620–77], etc.) or in theater venues (English masques, Italian opera, etc.).

In fact, the whole idea of doubling seems to have arisen in situations either where the bass needed extra clarity or support, or where the music needs extra emphasis, as in the few bars of Monteverdi's *Orfeo* where it is specified. Nearly all of the evidence for doubling in the first half of the century is found in reference to large concerted music performed in churches; it seems to have been the exception rather than the rule. Concerted music with voices and strings (including Monteverdi's Eighth Book of madrigals; Johann Rosenmüller [1620–84], Giacomo Carissimi [1605–74], and many other German and Italian sources) make it clear that bowed bass instruments normally played with the strings but not with the voices. This sets up a clear antiphonal effect: voice(s) with continuo, contrasted with strings and continuo. When the bass is doubled throughout, this structure is lost. An interesting exception to this is the Italian practice of a string ensemble improvising a chordal accompaniment over the bass, as discussed by Agazzari and indicated by Domenico Mazzocchi (1592–1665), Pier Francesco Cavalli (1602–76), and others.[5]

Many modern performers of seventeenth-century music fail to recognize that bowed bass players of the period often had their own independent partbooks and did not automatically play from the "continuo" book; Monteverdi's *Vespers* (1610) and *Madrigals of Love and War* (1638) provide two well-known examples. Italian collections of sonatas (Biagio Marini [1595–1665], Castello [fl. 1621–29], Giovanni Battista Fontana [d. ca. 1630], etc.) included a partbook for bowed bass, which plays only when there is an independent part. In fact, the bowed bass partbook rarely includes the bass of the continuo until much later—indeed, as late as 1697 Bernardo Tonini suggests that a cello may double the bass line *ad libitum*.[6] The whole question of bass line doubling must be considered on a repertory-by-repertory basis.

Basses Figured and Unfigured

As the practice of providing accompanists with only a bass line caught on, composers and theorists used different ways to indicate the harmonies. Many basses were provided without any figures, on the assumption that players would be able to supply appropriate harmonies based on the line itself (and by listening to what was going on above); some theorists (e.g., Francesco Bianciardi, Alessandro Scarlatti, and Bernardo Pasquini[7]) devote a relatively large amount of space to teaching this skill.

In any event, the earliest use of figures (both numbers and signs) is sparse, and at no time can we assume that all figures are necessarily given, nor are octaves or rhythmic placement precisely specified. The figures are an aid to sensitive accompaniment, not a prescription of a keyboard part. In Italy, after bass lines had been published with figures for a few decades, players evidently developed this sensitivity to a high degree, for continuo lines began appearing there (again) with no figures.

So players must be aware that virtually *all* continuo parts, practically speaking, are only partially figured to a greater or lesser extent. Sometimes the missing figures are obvious but often more than one solution exists, lending the performer freedom to come up with expressively creative solutions. (A particularly interesting case is Matthew Locke's *How Doth the City*, for which John Blow [1649–1708] published a continuo part and for which we also have Locke's own performance copy, with additions in his own hand. Locke added harmonies the original could never be thought of as suggesting.[8]) Many writers give advice for handling figureless passages and/or single notes in characteristic positions—for example, a bass line rising a half step generally calls for placing a first-inversion triad on the first note; the penultimate note of a cadence, if it drops a fifth or rises a fourth to the final note, should by convention be figured in one of the ways shown in Example 14.1.

EXAMPLE 14.1. Conventional patterns for realizing a falling fifth at a cadence.

A solitary sharp or flat used alone, without a numeral, simply means to raise or lower the third above the bass note. Thus, in a part with one flat in the signature, a G with a sharp above it indicates a G-major chord. Also, note that continuo figures serve as *reporters* of the harmony as much as they indicate what to actually play: every figure does not need to be played even if present—especially when accompanying soloists.

Basso Seguente

A *basso seguente* is a composite line consisting of the lowest-*sounding* part at any given moment, whether the notes of the written bass line or not. If you are playing continuo from the bass line there may be passages where it rests—and therefore the accompanying ensemble rests as well (basso noncontinuo, as it were). Accompanists playing from a *basso seguente* part, on the other hand, continue playing at all times, for as a serial compilation of whatever is the lowest-sounding line, it never stops. Adriano Banchieri in 1607 mentions and describes this term, also calling it *barittono*.[9] When an upper line momentarily became the functional bass it was referred to as a *bassetto* and generally was to be played in its proper octave and not one octave down; the relevant measures appear in the basso continuo part, but in the "home" clef of the visitor. (Schütz provides an exception when he mentions in the *Musicalische Exequien* [1636] that if a part is in alto or tenor clef, such as a trio for two sopranos and alto, that the *Violon* may double the lowest-sounding part an octave down.)

Pointers on Style

There is no one package of stylistic advice that can accommodate all Baroque music; however, several basic principles surface consistently.

The essence of continuo playing is to provide harmony and rhythm, and to provide gestures that match or complement the solo part(s). Continuo players need to shape and inflect lines, using crescendos, diminuendos, *messe di voce,* and *esclamationi,* together with the voices and instruments being accompanied. The playing should be spontaneous, inventive, and interactive. Continuo playing that strives merely to stay out of the soloist's way actually makes it more difficult for singers and string players to create the kinds of affects required in early Baroque music, since a flat, neutral shape counteracts a highly inflected one. At the same time, hyperactive continuo playing diverts attention from the solo parts and usually works at cross purposes. As Benigne de Bacilly observed in 1668,

> If the theorbo isn't played with moderation—if the player adds too much confusing figuration (as do most accompanists more to demonstrate the dexterity of their fingers than to aid the person they are accompanying) it then becomes an accompaniment of the theorbo by the voice rather than the reverse. Be careful to recognize this, so that in this marriage the theorbo does not become an overpowering, chiding spouse, instead of one who flatters, cajoles, and covers up one's faults.[10]

Texture

Four parts is the norm, but to imitate the shape and gestures of the solo line(s), the texture of continuo chords needs to be as varied as possible—according to Bianciardi and Giovanni Domenico Puliaschi[11]—with full chords for strong beats, strong syllables, and dissonances, and thinner chords for weak beats, weak syllables, and resolutions. Constant four-part texture is useful as an exercise in voice-leading, but it creates a relentless texture and prevents dynamics or inflection on harpsichords, organs, lutes, or harps. The thickness and complexity of the accompaniment should also match the forces at hand—full ensembles generally require four-part harmony and more, but for soloists one must often reduce the number of notes in the right hand, a practice recommended by Agazzari (1607), Praetorius (1619), Wolfgang Ebner (1653), and Lorenzo Penna (1672).[12]

When using the organ, players must also be careful about registration. Schütz had specific suggestions for this, cautioning his players only to use a *still Orgelwerck* ("soft organ registration," suggesting flutes) in the *Musicalische Exequien* so that the words might be understood.[13] In the *Psalmen Davids* he also recommends using differing registrations (soft and loud) to underscore the differences between the small and large groups of singers (*Favorito* and *Capella,* respectively[14]; see also Schütz, *Psalmen Davids,* 1619[15]; this advice is echoed in Praetorius as well).[16] Viadana takes a different tack, noting that volume should be controlled by varying the thickness of keyboard texture, *not* by adding/subtracting stops.[17]

Doubling the Bass an Octave Down

Several writers suggest that the bass line can be played or doubled an octave lower to provide a richer sonority.[18] Alessandro Piccinini considered the *contrabassi* to be the soul of the chitarrone and the archlute, and recommended that they be used as much as possible.[19] Existing seventeenth-century realizations make extensive use of this 16-foot register (see Exx. 14.2 and 14.3).

EXAMPLE 14.2. Dieterich Buxtehude, *Fürchtet dich nicht,* BuxWV 30, Sonata, mm. 1–11. Reprinted with permission of Schirmer Books, an imprint of Simon & Schuster Macmillan from *Dieterich Buxtehude: Organist in Lubeck* by Kerala J. Snyder. Copyright © 1987 by Kerala J. Snyder.

EXAMPLE 14.3. Angelo Notari, *A la caccia*

Arpeggiation and Other Time-Fillers

If the sound dies away (as on a harpsichord or lute), restrike chords, or notes of chords, as necessary to keep some sort of presence.[20] Girolamo Frescobaldi and Penna both recommend to "spread the chords (*arpeggiare*), in order not to leave a void in the instrument."[21] Vary the speed and pattern of arpeggios, mixing them with block chords according to metric placement, rhythmic function, note values, and so forth. Use slower, fuller arpeggios to fill out long notes, and quicker rolls for shorter, more rhythmic chords. One common way to fill up a long note is to roll a chord on the downbeat and play the bass down the octave in the middle of the bar (see Ex. 14.4).

Place bass notes firmly on the beat, rolling the chord after the bass note.[22] Pianists and guitarists often learn to anticipate the beat with the bass in order to put the treble note on the beat. This approach is inappropriate in continuo playing as it puts the bass before the beat and creates serious ensemble problems. It is unfortunately a difficult habit to

EXAMPLE 14.4. Bellorofonte Castaldi, *Capricci a due stromenti cioe Tiorba e Tiorbina* (1622).

break. Arpeggios can go from the bottom up, from the top down (usually with the bass note played together with the top note in that case), or may start with the bass and then jump to a higher pitch and proceed down and back up again (see Ex. 14.5). In dance music, long cadential notes often require a rhythmic filler, as can be seen in the cadences of solo pavans or courantes, for instance (see Ex. 14.6). Another common method of expanding chords is through the addition of *acciaccature* or passing tones, which could either be used to enrich an arpeggio or add spice to a block chord[23] (see Ex. 14.7).

Register and Affect

Bianciardi recommends varying the register to suit the affect—for example, a low register for doleful music, a higher one for more animated passages. In essence, seventeenth-century sources advocate imitating the affect and inflection of the words as much as possible through varying the

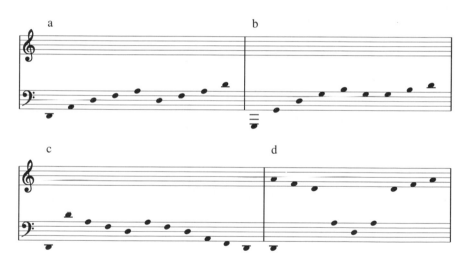

EXAMPLE 14.5. Sample arpeggio patterns for continuo realization.

EXAMPLE 14.6. Sample cadential patterns for continuo realization.

EXAMPLE 14.7. Continuo realization of an aria, ca. 1700, from Anonymous, *Regole . . . d'accompagnare* (Rome, Biblioteca Casanatense MS RI; reproduced in Borgir–*Performance*, 136). Reprinted by permission.

timbre, dynamics, register, chord-voicing, articulation, and shaping. Thus, harsh, bright colors may be used for "anguish," "pain," or "torment"; beautiful sounds for "sweetness" or "pleasure"; low earthy colors for "earth," "hell"; high celestial sounds for "heaven," "angelic."

Doubling the Soloist

Opinions vary on this. Many writers echo the opinion of Agazzari, who suggested in 1607 that one should "be careful to avoid, as far as possible, the same note which the soprano is singing, and not to make diminutions on it, so as not to double the voice part and obscure the goodness of the said voice . . . therefore it is good to play within quite a small compass and low down,"[24] while Penna (1672) suggests doubling a part if it is sung by a soprano or alto[25] and Johann Staden (1626) says that you should try to avoid doubling the soprano, but that it is not always possible.[26] The implication is that solo parts should not be doubled consistently, but that doubling the odd note is unavoidable, except in sacred vocal polyphony or English viol fantasias (William Lawes [1602–45], John Jenkins [1592–1678], etc.), in which the organ plays a short score of all the parts.

The question extends to dissonances and thirds as well. Andreas Werckmeister (1698) cautioned,

> It is also not advisable that one should always just blindly play, together with the vocalists and instrumentalists, the dissonances which are indicated in the Thorough-Bass, and double them: for when the singer expresses a pleasing emotion by means of the dissonance written, a thoughtless accompanist may, if he walk not warily, spoil all the beauty with the same dissonance: therefore the figures are not always put in order that one should just blindly join in with them; but one who understands composition can see by them what the composer's intention is, and how to avoid countering them with anything whereby the harmony might be injured.[27]

This passage is a reminder that figures are frequently "descriptive" of the harmonies in solo parts and not necessarily "prescriptive" of what the continuo player should play. However, beware of the "table-scraps" school of continuo playing, an approach that forbids the doubling of all dissonances and thirds and requires the accompanist to avoid all notes in the solo part(s), playing only what is left over. The problem with this manner of playing is that it forces the player to concentrate on what *not* to play, rather than on how best to make appropriate gestures. While exposed thirds and dissonances are often better left to the soloist, habitually avoiding them leaves the continuo player with the fewest notes to play at the moments of greatest tension, the opposite of what is musically required. It is both awkward and unnatural to avoid them rigorously; indeed, written-out parts of the period indicate that players often doubled thirds and dissonances in the interest of creating the most sonorous and inflected lines possible. (Thirds sound less obtrusive if doubled in a lower octave, rather than at the top of a chord. This also makes intonation less tricky.)

Dissonances may be doubled for more bite, even in octaves for extra emphasis, but resolutions are best left to the solo part(s) to lighten the moment of resolution. A full chord with the dissonances doubled can then be contrasted by thinner chords on the weaker beats to achieve an effective hierarchy between tension and relaxation. Dissonances cannot be convincingly conveyed when the continuo plays only a root and fifth because there is often not enough sound for the soloist to rub against. Such a texture is also too thin to give the dissonances the pungency they require. In meantone temperament bare fifths are quite sour, which is probably the reason they so rarely occur in solo lute and keyboard music of the period. In addition, written-out accompaniments usually double dissonances rather than avoid them. Some sources show continuo instruments playing a major triad against a 4-3 suspension in a solo part, or a 6 chord against a 7-6. This is another way to create a strong clash on the dissonances to add to the continuo player's bag of tricks.

At the same time, there is a recent fashion in Europe for doubling everything, using a predominantly thick texture with constant rhythmic subdivision and frequent use of high registers. While there is evidence of very full-textured playing in the eighteenth-century sources, mainstream seventeenth-century practice does not appear to have involved such extreme doubling and subdivision, which has the effect of straitjacketing the soloist(s), especially in recitative music.[28] In Italian monody, for instance, the continuo player needs to give the singer as much rhythmic freedom as possible, by not adding subdivisions or runs that force his or her hand. Runs are generally distracting in continuo playing except as a special effect (e.g., for flashes of lightning or a torrent of water), or as a link connecting one section of a piece with another, especially in dance music.

This brings up another crucial but rarely discussed feature of early Baroque continuo practice: it seems likely that continuo players generally played standard harmonic progressions for most of the seventeenth century, allowing composers to add extraordinary dissonances and "blue notes" in the solo parts to clash against the accompaniment (see Ex. 14.8, especially the downbeat of the third measure). Editors and scholars are often puzzled by these dissonances and sometimes try to realize extraordinary harmonies to take them into account. In fact, based on the figuring in original sources and surviving realizations, it seems clear that these blue notes were not to be realized, but that they represent a special kind of dissonance designed to clash against straightforward harmonies.

Cadences

Seventeenth-century cadences generally involve 4-3 or 7-6 suspensions; however, these were elaborated in a variety of interesting and often dar-

EXAMPLE **14.8.** Henry Lawes, *Sweet Stay Awhile* (figures editorial).

ing ways. While dominant-tonic movement in the bass was nearly always harmonized with a 4-3 suspension, a seventh could be added after the third, or a third before the fourth. This allows the possibility of playing a flatted sixth with the fourth, or even of adding a seventh to the first third (see Ex. 14.9). The English had a particular predilection for false relations in cadences, as may be seen in John Blow's examples for accompanying standard cadences that include flatted thirds and sixths on the downbeat of the penultimate bars, forming most telling dissonances with the "operative" notes of the passage called for by the figures.[29] A flatted sixth over a dominant can be harmonized with a major third going to a fourth in addition to the more usual six-four harmony (see Ex. 14.10).

Many writers mention that final cadences (or medial cadences of any importance) should be taken with a major third, whether called for by the figures or not. This advice spans the century from Agazzari (1607)[30] to Locke (1673).[31] The minor third was an imperfect interval and was generally avoided in cadences except in overlapping imitative entrances, and in France. Friedrich Niedt (1674–1708) explained, "I know very well, it is true, that French composers do the opposite, but everything is not good just because it comes from France."[32] In some situations, an open chord (without a third) is indicated in string or voice parts, providing the continuo player with an alternative to playing every cadence major. In Restoration England, cadences of all three varieties are found: major, minor, and open, giving the continuo player options according to the desired effect.

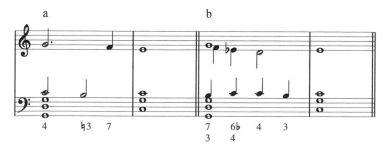

EXAMPLE **14.9.** Sample realizations for cadential suspensions.

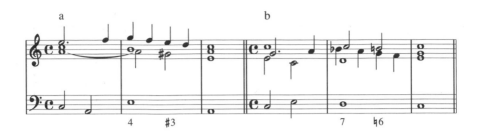

EXAMPLE 14.10. John Blow, sample realizations for cadential suspensions.

Contrary Motion

On a keyboard, the overall effect should be of the right hand playing in contrary motion to the left. Virtually all writers mention this; Penna (1672) adds that if it is not possible, then the right hand should play parallel tenths with the bass, certainly an easy way around many difficult passages.[33]

Parallel Motion

Many writers agree that while parallel fifths and octaves should be avoided in composed music, they are not particularly noticeable in continuo improvisations and shouldn't be worried about unduly. As Viadana writes, "The Organ part is never under any obligation to avoid two Fifths or two Octaves, but those parts which are sung by the voices are" (1602).[34] However, do be careful to avoid parallels between the outer voices or, slightly less problematically, between an inner voice and an outer one.

Bass Runs

When the bass line has diatonic runs, chords should be played on the first notes of groups (e.g., four or eight), depending on the speed of the piece and the note values. Locke (1673) adds that you may substitute parallel thirds or tenths in the right hand for chords, and that the theorbo player need not play chords at all.[35] Plucked instruments may strum the harmony in the rhythm of the bass line to produce more direction in the line if desired.

When the bass line moves by skip, each note may require its own chord, although in practice the speed of the piece determines how many chords can be played—the faster the speed, the fewer the chords. In any event, chords in the right hand of a keyboard part should be taken with as many common notes between them as possible. Werckmeister suggests that "when the Bass leaps, the other parts should some of them remain stationary, or only rise and fall by step with the leaping Bass."[36]

Added Ornamentation

Some specific suggestions about ornamentation as culled from period sources may be useful to help set the stage for a discussion of the nature of a good continuo part. Viadana (1602) and Girolamo Giaccobi (1609) suggest adding some passages, while Agazzari (1607) says to avoid inordinate scales and runs, but that some ornamentation is allowed[37]; he specifically mentions *gruppi*, trills, and *accenti*.[38] Banchieri (*Eclesiastiche sinfonie*, 1607) admonishes the player to not ornament the bass line,[39] while Francesco Gasparini encourages it.[40] An Italian theorbo manuscript in Modena provides pages of elaborately ornamented cadences,[41] while Thomas Mace's examples (1676) indicate a somewhat less florid approach. Praetorius (1619) recommends ornamentation on the organ if one is using a bright registration but to forego it when accompanying on the regal,[42] and Schütz writes in 1623 that the organist and/or violist should add runs and embellishments when a singer holds or repeats a note.[43] If the solo line is in the bass register, the continuo part will often be a less elaborate skeleton thereof and should not be ornamented. Penna (1672) mentions that "With a Bass, one may indulge in some little movement, but if the Bass has passages, it is not good to move at the same time"; nor should one make divisions at all if the soloist is a soprano, alto, or tenor.[44] Penna also gives detailed advice on the playing of cadential trills in either or both hands, which one presumes was a standard addition through the century—yet Penna's suggested trills are anything but standard.[45]

See also the section Independent Contribution of the Accompanist, below.

Imitative Entrances

Concerning imitative sections, writers agree that the accompanist should double the first voice entering without supplying chords. Heinrich Albert (1640) says that chords should begin with the second entrance[46]; Penna (1672)[47] and Bartolomeo Bismantova (1677)[48] declare that chords should not begin until all voices have had their entrance, with each line of counterpoint doubled by the keyboard player. Viadana notes that after doubling the first entrance without chords, it is up to the accompanist to decide whether to add them or not.[49] Schütz would literally underscore the bass entry in an imitative texture by having the *Violon* remain silent until the bass makes its entrance, and then doubling it.[50] Eighteenth-century writers confirm that all fugal entries should be doubled on the keyboard, without chords, and there is no reason to doubt that it was not fairly standard practice in seventeenth-century music as well. Fugal movements require a knowledge of counterpoint, so that the accompanist will be aware of those places where entrances in inner parts cannot be indicated in the continuo part but would have been expected.

Tasto Solo

One special effect in eighteenth-century music is to have the keyboard player play single notes in the bass line without supplying any harmonies. This effect, called tasto solo, is not found in seventeenth-century keyboard sources except in the case of imitative entries, although Galeazzo Sabbatini's system (1628) does include playing the odd individual note without chords.[51] Some theorbo accompaniments of Bellerofonte Castaldi (ca. 1580–1649) and Johann Hieronymus Kapsberger (ca. 1580–1651) also have such passages.

Independent Contribution of the Accompanist

Agazzari and Penna, writing at opposite ends of the century (1607 and 1672), both suggest that the accompanist might imitate something just heard in the soloist's part.[52] Taking advantage of opportunities to answer a motive introduced by a soloist increases interaction while avoiding distraction. In southern Italy this developed into a practice known as *partimento,* in which common figures in the bass were answered in kind in the treble, or vice versa. Neapolitan treatises included systematic exercises to familiarize students with the most common situations (see Ex. 14.11).[53]

Instrumentation in early Baroque opera grew out of the tradition of the sixteenth-century *intermedii* in which a great deal of symbolism was associated with various instruments. Thus, wind instruments accompanied Neptune and sea monsters, pastoral characters were accompanied by recorders, Bacchus with crumhorns, Orpheus with the harp or lute, and so forth. According to Emilio de' Cavalieri, in the preface to his *Rappresentatione di Anima, e di Corpo* (1600), continuo scoring should change according to the affect, not necessarily according to who is singing. Thus a monochromatic character such as Caronte, in Monteverdi's *Orfeo* (1607), is accompanied by the regal, while Orfeo, who goes through an enormous variety of emotions during the course of the opera, is accompanied by organ alone, organ and chitarrone, harp, strings, and so forth. According to scorings suggested in seventeenth-century sources as well as contemporary comments made about different instruments, the following summary is suggested:

EXAMPLE 14.11. Francesco Durante, solo partimento exercise (from *Partimenti, ossia intero studio di numerati* (Bologna, Museo Bibliografia Musicale, MS M.14-7; reproduced in Borgir—Performance, 143). Reprinted by permission.

Chitarrone. For expressive music, recitatives, laments, light dances, and the like. The theorbo was listed as the preferred instrument to accompany solo song in Italy and France for the first half of the century and in England until 1687, when the harpsichord is listed first on a title page for the first time. The chitarrone was also widely used to accompany dance music and *ritornelli* for one or two violins (e.g., Biagio Marini, *Scherzi*; Salomone Rossi, *Gagliarde,* etc.).

Harpsichord. For rhythmic music, moments of turbulence (*Orfeo*, Acts 2 and 4), martial music (Monteverdi's *Combattimento*), and neutral characters (such as the shepherds in *Orfeo*). This is not to say that harpsichords never accompanied expressive music; they clearly did. The harpsichord was usually listed as the second choice after the chitarrone on title pages of Italian monody collections and English songbooks until the last decade of the century. Sources suggest, however, that the dynamic and timbral variety of the chitarrone was preferred for delicate, expressive music. Seventeenth-century musicians tended to typecast instruments to a certain extent, especially in the theater, avoiding the weaknesses of each instrument as much as possible. Of course, performers strove to overcome these weaknesses in order to be able to express the greatest variety of affects on each instrument. It is insulting to harpsichordists to suggest that the dynamics they learn to create through varying the touch are not enough, or that guitars are incapable of playing slow, serious music. There will always be exceptions to the basic principles to create variety and character.

Guitar. For light vocal music, dances, and comic characters in the theater.

Organ. For serious and tranquil moments; often coupled with the chitarrone. The organ was widely used in operatic productions at court, as well as in secular chamber music as Monteverdi makes clear in a letter of June 2, 1611, describing the use of chitarroni and organ to accompany madrigals. To what extent organs were used in commercial theaters is not yet known. In England the combination of organ and theorbo was the standard continuo group in consort music.

Regal. For underworld figures, bizarre characters, bass voices.

Lirone. For laments, often with a bowed bass or chitarrone to supply the bass line.

Harp. For celestial music, music of the gods.

Strings realizing a chordal "accompagnato." Used to highlight moments of special importance (e.g., "Sol tu nobile Dio" from Monteverdi's *Orfeo*; Cupid's "Ho difeso" in *Poppea*; "Amico hai vinto" from the *Combattimento*; the first performance of *Lamento d'Arianna*).

Review of Sources

Continuo treatises are not of the greatest help when actually playing music, as there is very little that can really prepare one for the sensitive requirements of following a soloist and providing supportive accompaniment while improvising from a given bass line that may or may not have figures. Experience in both playing and watching others play is the only true teacher here. Although the sources do offer a few comments that are of help, they are at times amusingly contradictory. F. T. A. Arnold (*The Art of Accompaniment from a Thoroughbass* [1931, rept. 1965]) and Peter Williams (*Figured Bass Accompaniment* [1970]) have each organized discussion on the dos and don'ts of stylistic accompaniment with reference to period sources, so it is unnecessary to repeat this advice; readers are encouraged to refer to their work for further information. Instead, the following is a compilation of some seventeenth-century treatises either specifically devoted to or at least including basso continuo instruction, listed chronologically by date of first printing or appearance, with some indication of which instrument(s) was probably intended.

Lodovico Grossi da Viadana. *Cento concerti ecclesiastici.* Rome, 1603. Organ.

Agostino Agazzari. *Del sonare sopra il basso.* Siena, 1607. Many instruments.

Francesco Bianciardi. *Breve regola per imparar a sonare sopra il Basso con ogni sorte d' Instrumento.* Siena?, 1607. Many instruments.

Adriano Banchieri. "Dialogo Musicale." Printed in the 2d ed. of *L' Organo suonarino.* Venice, 1611. Organ.

Michael Praetorius. *Syntagma musicum* III. Wolfenbüttel, 1619. He quotes freely, with useful editorial comment, from both Viadana and Agazzari. Many instruments.

Johann Staden. *Kurzer und einfältiger Bericht für diejenigen, so im Basso ad Organum unerfahren, was bey demselben zum Theil in Acht zu nehmen* (appended to his *Kirchenmusik, Ander Theil*). Nuremberg, 1626. Organ.

Galeazzo Sabbatini. *Regola facile e breve per sonare sopra il Basso continuo nell' Organo, Manacordo, ò altro Simile Stromento.* Venice, 1628. Organ, harpsichord, "or other similar instrument."

Heinrich Albert. A set of nine rules without separate title, given in the preface to his *Arien.* Vol. 2. Königsberg, 1640. No instrument specified, but organ, harpsichord, and lute are all mentioned.

Wolfgang Ebner. A set of fifteen rules printed by Johann Andreas Herbst in his *Arte prattica et poetica.* Frankfurt, 1653. None mentioned, but he was an organist.

Nicolas Fleury. *Méthode pour apprendre facilement a toucher le théorbe sur la basse-continué.* Paris, 1660. Theorbo.

Lorenzo Penna. *Li primi albori musicali per li Principianti della Musica Figurata*, Libro 2. Bologna, 1672. "Organ or harpsichord" in title, but in the book he mentions only the organ.

Matthew Locke. *Melothesia, or Certain Rules for Playing Upon a Continued-Bass.* London, 1673. Harpsichord, organ.

John Blow. "Rules for playing of a Through Bass upon Organ & Harpsicon." London, BL Add. MS 34072; ca. 1674. Organ and harpsichord.

Gaspar Sanz. *Instruccion de musica sobre la Guitarra española.* Zaragoça, 1674. Guitar.

Bartolomeo Bismantova. *Compendio musicale.* Ms, Ferrara, 1677. Keyboard instrument.

Perrine [first name unknown]. *Table pour apprendre à toucher le luth sur la basse continué.* Paris, 1682. Lute.

Jean-Henri d'Anglebert. *Principes de l'Accompagnement*, printed in his *Pièces de Clavecin.* Vol. 1. Paris, 1689. Harpsichord.

Denis Delair. *Traité de l'Accompagnement pour le Théorbe et le Clavessin.* Paris, 1690. Theorbo and harpsichord.

Andreas Werckmeister. *Die nothwendigsten Anmerckungen und Regeln wie der Bassus continuus oder General-Bass wohl könne tractiret werden.* Ascherleben, 1698. Keyboard instrument.

Summary Guide to Seventeenth-Century Continuo Practice

The chart on pages 291–95 provides a rough overview of continuo practice in seventeenth-century Europe, arranged geographically, chronologically, and by genre. It may be used to amplify and confirm general observations in the text.

In the <u>chordal accompaniment</u> column we have listed instruments associated with continuo accompaniment for the given repertory either because they are mentioned on title pages, in performance parts, or in descriptions of performances. They represent the best and most probable choices, in rough priority order generally speaking.

The question of <u>whether to double the bass line</u> rarely lends itself to an unequivocal answer. Where we know period practice with some certainty, the word "no" or "yes" appears in the far right column. Other entries are given best-guess estimates, sometimes with elaboration, based both on recent scholarship and our own intuition. Indeed, one purpose of these explanations is to give a sense of the ambiguity surrounding the topic; players should make informed decisions accordingly.

We have not attempted to specify <u>which instrument should be used for doubling</u>. The choices are manifold; the terminology seldom clear. For example, "Violone" can mean a member of the viol family at either 8' or 16' pitch; it was also a synonym for "violoncello" in late seventeenth-century Italy (see Bonta–From Violone to Violoncello). Doubling at 16' pitch was practiced at times (e.g., early seventeenth-century Germany), but it is simply inadvisable to make categorical statements using the terms "always," "never," and "16' pitch" in the same sentence.

In consort or orchestral textures where all lines including the bass are played by string or wind instruments as a matter of course, this column is marked "n/a" since the question of doubling is irrelevant.

"SS" in the third column means "short score"-style accompaniment, meaning that the keyboard player (or lutenist) plays the notes the chorus is singing, not an improvisatory realization.

"AOD" in the last column stands for "as occasion demands"; see notes referenced to each.

<u>Bibliography</u>. This chart represents likely possibilities for continuo instrumentation with evidence to support these possibilities drawn from period title pages and/or surviving parts, of which only a few are detailed here. This cannot guarantee a complete or unified picture, but it is a starting point from which performers can elaborate and refine by working firsthand with original sources. Modern editions are often misleading in matters of instrumentation as they combine two similar parts into one line, or suggest doublings that are not indicated in the original. For some repertories, one or more secondary sources are especially important in accessing or interpreting this information; these are noted individually, with full entries found in the bibliography for this chapter.

Genre	Typical Composers	Representative Choices for Chordal Accompaniment	Double Bass Line?
ITALY, 1600–1635			
Sacred Polyphony	Monteverdi, Anerio	organ/SS (sometimes optional)	no
Sacred Concerto	Viadana, Gabrieli, Monteverdi	organ, organ/SS, often with theorbo	AOD

In Viadana's *Cento concerti ecclesiastici* (1602) the organ is surrogate for a vocal ensemble and should basically double the vocal polyphony or sound like vocal polyphony in its absence; the bass line should not be doubled as a matter of course. Agazzari, however, suggests the participation of a violone in large ensembles and adds that it makes a nice effect when "touching the octave below the bass" from time to time; his instruction is published with sacred music in 1607. Chitarrone, violone, etc. were sometimes included as part of a separate choir in polychoral music; their participation was with that choir and was not necessarily considered as "doubling." This is seen through mid-century.

Solo Song/Monody	Caccini, d'India	theorbo, harp, harpsichord	no
Villanelle, Canzonette	Kapsberger, d'India	guitar, theorbo, harpsichord	no
Sonatas & Canzonas	Fontana, Castello	organ, theorbo, harpsichord	no

Separate bass parts are provided for pieces with independent bass lines.

Concerted madrigal	Monteverdi	chitarrone, harpsichord, spinet, lute, harp, organ	no

An accompanying bowed string on the bass line is used only when other strings are playing; it thus becomes part of a string ensemble. It does not play in a polyphonic vocal texture unless violins are also playing.

Opera	Peri, Gagliano, Monteverdi	harpsichord, organ, theorbo	no

Peri and Cavalieri mention the participation of a "lira grande" (=lirone) in their prefaces. This instrument, because of its unusual tuning, is unable to perform the notated bass line, but provides a sustained chordal accompaniment (see p. 271). In *Orfeo* Monteverdi specifies a bass bowed string in only three short passages, apart from the five-part string band. All are at turbulent, highly charged emotional points, and would seem to be intended for special effect.

Bibliography: Borgir-*Basso Continuo*, Stubbs-*L'armonia*.

ITALY, 1635–1665			
All Liturgical Music	Monteverdi, Rovetta, Cazzati	organ, theorbo	AOD

In a collection of psalms published in 1660, Cazzati suggests "organs" or, if unavailable, violone, trombone, or some similar instrument (for reference pitch); this does not correspond to "doubling" the line. Also, some polychoral collections designate a part with one of the choirs as "violone o tiorba"; these are not <u>in addition</u> to organ parts for those choirs, and do not "double" anything. But doubling does seem to have been standard practice in especially large churches such as San Petronio in Bologna. Otherwise, the bass line cannot be heard with clarity.

Oratorio	Carissimi	organ, theorbo, harpsichord, lute, lirone	AOD
Opera, Cantata (Venice)	Monteverdi, Cavalli, Cesti	theorbo, harpsichord	AOD

Opera, Cantata (Rome)	Landi, Rossi, Marazzoli	theorbo, archlute, harp, lirone, guitar, harpsichord	AOD

Evidence from earlier operatic practice, coupled with indications in oratorio scores of the 1640s and '50s, suggests that bass lines were occasionally doubled depending on the desired effect. Certainly, it makes more sense to double moving bass lines in arioso sections than those in static recitative passages. Doubling is also less likely in lighter musical textures.

Sonatas	Uccellini, Matiani	organ, harpsichord, theorbo	no

Bibliography: Borgir-*Basso Continuo*, Murato-*Operas*, Dixon-Continuo Scoring, Mason-*Chitarrone*.

ITALY, 1665–1700

Mass	A. Scarlatti, Legrenzi	organ, theorbo	yes
Oratorio	A. Scarlatti, Legrenzi		
recitative		organ, theorbo, harpsichord	AOD
aria		organ, theorbo/archlute or harpsichord	AOD
Opera, Cantata	A. Scarlatti, Legrenzi	theorbo, harpsichord, archlute	AOD

Surviving parts (or lack of them) indicate that small ensembles (one or two solo voices + bc) were not performed with the bass line doubled, while larger groups were.

Sonata da Chiesa	Colista, Corelli	organ	no

An independent part for cello or archlute is provided in most cases.

Sonata da Camera	Corelli	harpsichord or cello	AOD

Bass-line doubling was becoming more common at this time, but was still optional. Trio sonata collections as late as 1697 still list cello doubling as *beneplacito*. In *sonate da camera* of Corelli and others, double the bass line only if it is melodically interesting.

Concerto	Corelli	harpsichord, theorbo, organ, archlute	n/a

Bibliography: Allsop-*Trio Sonata*, Borgir-*Basso Continuo*.

ENGLAND, 1600–1635

Service Music	Gibbons	organ/SS	no
Masque Song	Ferrabosco, W. Lawes	lute, theorbo, cittern, bandora, harpsichord	yes

Bass lines were probably doubled to make them clearer in large, resonant rooms such as the Banqueting Hall at Whitehall.

Solo Song	R. Johnson, Lanier	lute or theorbo	no
String Consort	W. Lawes	organ/SS, theorbo	n/a

ENGLAND, 1635–1665

Ayre & Dialogue	H. & W. Lawes	lute, theorbo, or bass viol	no
String Consort	Jenkins	organ/SS	n/a

Lighter dance music, such as Jenkins's lyra consorts, was often accompanied by a harpsichord doubling the upper parts.

ENGLAND, 1665–1700

Service Music	Purcell/Humfrey	organ, theorbo	yes

In anthems and services with string parts, the practice appears to have been to double the bass line only when the upper strings were playing. Holman also notes that bass viols were employed at times to double the bass singers.

Ayre	Purcell, Blow	"theorbo or bass viol"; "organ, harpsichord, or theorbo-lute"	no?

First wording found on title pages of Restoration collections (e.g., Plkayford's *Theatre of Music*); second in Purcell's 1698 publication and Blow's of 1700. Note the conjunction "or" in each case.

Theater Music (string band)	Locke, Purcell, Blow	harpsichord, guitar, theorbo	AOD

Some performance accounts list bass viols with the continuo group, apart from and in addition to the bass member of the string ensemble. Also, some English theatrical producers followed the French practice of including bass-line doubling to accompany singing, but not instrumental pieces (sinfonias, act tunes, dances, etc.).

Chamber Music	Purcell	organ, harpsichord	no

The continuo line is considered one of the "parts" in each of Purcell's publications (*Sonatas in III Parts; Sonatas in IV Parts*) and must be played by a bowed string, but this is not the same as "doubling" it. The 1683 publication ("III parts") lists "organ and harpsichord" on the title page; that from 1697 ("IV parts") lists "harpsichord or organ."

Bibliography: Holman-*Fiddlers*.

NORTH GERMANY, 1600–1635

Sacred Polyphony	Schütz	organ/SS or lute	no?
Religious Polychoral	Praetorius, Schütz	one organ or lute per choir	yes
Sacred Concerto	Scheidt, Schütz	organ, theorbo	optional
String Consort	Schein, Brade	lute, spinet—or none	n/a

Bibliography: Kirchner-*Generalbass*

NORTH GERMANY, 1635–1665

Sacred Concerto	Schütz, Hammerschmidt	organ, lute, harpsichord	optional

One set of parts of Schütz's *Weihnachtshistorie* (1664) shows that in that performance, anyway, the organ played all the time but the harpsichord only accompanied the Evangelist's recitatives and one other passage; it did not play during the choruses.

The second and third volumes of Schütz's *Symphoniae Sacrae* (1647 and 1650) include two partbooks for basso continuo, one each for organ and *violon*, while Hammerschmidt says that a bowed bass at 8' or 16' pitch may be added if desired. Rosenmüller's bass parts follow the Italian practice of doubling the bass only as a part of a string consort, not during vocal solo passages.

Sacred Polyphony	Schütz	organ/SS or lute	no?
String Consort	Hammerschmidt	lute, spinet, theorbo	n/a

Bibliography: Kirchner-*Generalbass*

NORTH GERMANY, 1665–1700

Church Cantata	Buxtehude	organ, theorbo	AOD

Continuo lines were doubled at 8' and 16' as necessitated by the acoustics.

String Consort	Rosenmüller	harpsichord, organ, theorbo,	n/a
Chamber Music	Buxtehude	harpsichord	no

Bibliography: Kirchner-*Generalbass*, Snyder-*Buxtehude*.

SOUTH GERMANY, 1600–1635

Mass	Priuli, Valentini	organ	AOD
Sacred Concerto	Staden, Valentini	organ, theorbo	AOD
String Consort	Valentini	organ, harpsichord, theorbo	n/a
Concerted Madrigal	Valentini	chitarrone	?

SOUTH GERMANY / AUSTRIA, 1635–1665

Mass	Schmelzer, Kerll, Bertali	organ, theorbo	yes

The rubric "organ and violone" seems standard in this repertory.

Oratorio	Bertali, Sances	organ, theorbo	yes
Opera	Cesti	harpsichord, theorbo	yes

No detailed account of the 1662 performance of *Il pomo d'oro* remains. Guido Adler quotes a 1662 Florentine account of a Cesti *serenata*, for which continuo was provided by a "grossen Spinet (mit zwei Registern), von der Theorbe und dem Contrabass . . . die vostimmigen Chöre sollen ausserdem noch einer Bassviola und dem klienem Spinett begleitet werden" (*Denkmäler der Tonkunst in Österreich* 6: xxiv). It is unclear what difference is intended between *Contrabass* and *Bassviola* in this context. This account does not indicate whether the bowed instruments played throughout; it is unlikely they did at this early date. The operas of Steffani in the early eighteenth century, for example, do not double the bass when the archlute plays.

Chamber Music	Nicolai, Schmelzer	harpsichord, organ	no

Schmelzer's instrumental pieces, which include bass with strings, specify organ continuo.

SOUTH GERMANY / AUSTRIA, 1665–1700

Mass	Draghi, Schmelzer, Kerll, Biber	organ	yes

Biber's scores (as well as those of other German composers) often specify *fagotto* on the continuo line.

Oratorio	Draghi, Pederzuoli	organ, theorbo, harpsichord (?)	yes
Theater Music	Draghi, Biber	harpsichord, theorbo	yes
Chamber Music	Biber, Schmelzer, Muffat	harpsichord (theorbo, organ)	yes

Manuscript sources of this repertory sometimes include as may as four copies of the continuo part, suggesting participation by a varied and colorful ensemble.

BASSO CONTINUO

FRANCE, 1600–1635: no basso continuo repertory

Prints with basso continuo do not appear in France until Huygens's *Pathodia Sacra et Profana* (1647), followed by du Mont's *Cantica sacra* of 1652. However, accounts of performances with lutes and theorbos from the 1610s and later suggest that the practice was not unknown in France in the early part of the century.

FRANCE, 1635–1665

Air de Cour	Huygens, Lambert	theorbo, lute, harpsichord	no
Motet	du Mont	organ, theorbo	?

FRANCE, 1665–1700

Opera, Ballet	Lully		
(solo vocal parts & choruses)		theorbo, harpsichord	yes
(instrumental ensembles)		no continuo used	n/a

Bass violins were the bottom of the 5-part string ensemble "house band," but viols were used to double the bass line in vocal sections, both solo and choral.

Mass, Motet	de Lalande, Lully	organ, theorbo	yes
Chamber Music	Charpentier, F. Couperin	theorbo, harpsichord	yes

Bibliography: Eppelsheim-*Orchester*, J. Sadie-*BassViol*, Sadler-*Role*.

SPAIN, 1635–1665

Theater Music	Hidalgo	guitar, harp, harpsichord, theorbo	?

Bibliography: Stein-*Songs*

NOTES

1. Strunk–*Source Readings*, 364.
2. Worsthorne–*Venetian*, 98; cited in Mason–*Chitarrone*, 116.
3. Borgir–*Basso Continuo*, Dixon–Continuo, O'Dette–Continuo.
4. See Dixon–Continuo.
5. See Rose–Agazzari.
6. Tonini, *Suonate da chiesa a tre* (Venice, 1697), preface.
7. Bianciardi–*Breve regola* (1607); A. Scarlatti, London, British Library Add MS 14244; B. Pasquini; Bologna, Biblioteca G. B. Martini MS D138 [ii].
8. Locke–*Anthems and Motets*, xviii.
9. Cited in Arnold–*Thoroughbass*, 899.
10. Bacilly–*Remarques*, trans. Caswell, 11.
11. Bianciardi–*Breve regole* (1607); Puliaschi–*Musiche* (1618), preface.
12. These four sources cited in Arnold–*Thoroughbass*, 70, 99, 131, and 153, respectively.
13. Kirchner–*Generalbass*, 30.
14. Ibid.
15. Preface, xii.
16. Praetorius–*Syntagma* III: 138–39.
17. Cited in Arnold–*Thoroughbass*, 15.
18. Agazzari, 1607, cited in Arnold–*Thoroughbass*, 70; Bianciardi, 1607, cited in Arnold–*Thoroughbass*, 78.

19. Piccinini–*Intavolatura*, preface.
20. Caccini–*Nuove musiche*, cited in Arnold–*Thoroughbass*, 42–43.
21. Cited in Arnold–*Thoroughbass*, 154; and Tagliavini–Art, 299–308.
22. Simpson–*Division Viol*, 9.
23. Penna–*Li primi albori*, 186–87; cited in Arnold–*Thoroughbass*, 146–47, n.41.
24. Cited in Arnold–*Thoroughbass*, 70.
25. Cited in ibid., 148.
26. Cited in ibid., 109.
27. Cited in ibid., 210.
28. Christiensen–Generalbass-praxis, 39–88.
29. Cited in Arnold–*Thoroughbass*, 170.
30. Cited in ibid., 69.
31. Cited in ibid., 156.
32. Cited in ibid., 228.
33. Cited in ibid., 136.
34. Cited in ibid., 18.
35. Cited in ibid., 157.
36. Cited in ibid., 207.
37. Cited in ibid., 70, 72.
38. Cited in ibid., 70.
39. Cited in Williams–*Figured Bass* 1: 30.
40. Gasparini–*L'armonico pratico*, 104–10 (90–94 of trans.).
41. See Caffagni–Modena, 25–42.
42. Cited in Kirchner–*Generalbass*, 33.
43. Cited in Williams–*Figured Bass* 1: 63.
44. Cited in Arnold–*Thoroughbass*, 153.
45. Penna–*Li primi albori*, 152–81; cited in Arnold–*Thoroughbass*, 138–46.
46. Cited in Arnold–*Thoroughbass*, 129.
47. Cited in ibid., 150.
48. Bismantova–*Compendio*, [83]–[84].
49. Cited in Arnold–*Thoroughbass*, 14.
50. Cited in Kirchner–*Generalbass*, 129.
51. Arnold–*Thoroughbass*, 115–20.
52. Ibid., 72 and 148, respectively.
53. Borgir–*Basso continuo*, 141–47.

BIBLIOGRAPHY OF SECONDARY SOURCES

Allsop–Role; Allsop–'*Trio*' *Sonata*; Arnold–*Thoroughbass*; Ashworth–Continuo Realization; Bonta–Violone to Violoncello; Bonta–Sacred Music; Borgir–*Basso continuo*; Burnett–Bowed String; Christensen–Generalbass-Praxis; Dixon–Continuo; Eppelsheim–*Orchester*; Fortune–Continuo Instruments; Fortune–Italian Secular Song; Garnsey–Hand-plucked; Gasparini–*L'armonico pratico*; Goldschmidt–Instrument-Begleitung; Hancock–General Rules; Hansell–Orchestral Practice; Heering–*Regeln*; Hill–Realized Continuo; Holman–Continuo Realizations; Holman–*Fiddlers*; Jander–Concerto Grosso; E. H. Jones–*English Song*; E. H. Jones–To Sing and Play; Kinkeldey–*Orgel und Klavier*; Kirchner–*Generalbaβ*; Kite-Powell–*Renaissance*; Locke–*Anthems and Motets*; Mason–*Chitarrone*; Murata–*Papal Court*; O'Dette–Continuo; North–*Continuo Playing*; Rose–Agazzari; Sadie–*Bass Viol*; Sadler–Keyboard Continuo; Schneider–*Anfänge*; Schütz–*Psalmen Davids*; Simpson–*Division-Viol*; Snyder–*Buxtehude*; Stein–*Songs*; Schnoebelen–Performance Practices at San Petronio; Schünemann–Hertel; Strizich–Chitarra barocca; Strunk–*Source Readings*; Stubbs–*L'armonia*; Tagliavini–Art; Walker–*German Sacred*; Williams–Basso Continuo; Williams–Continuo (*New Grove*); Williams–*Figured Bass*; Wilson–*Roger North*.

15

Meter and Tempo

George Houle

We call the musical style of the seventeenth century "Baroque" in order to acknowledge the extravagant, glorious, sometimes even bizarre quality of this brilliant and emotional music. Innovations in the notation of seventeenth-century music gradually changed Renaissance mensural notation to accommodate this expressive and dramatic style. Three significant aspects of mensural notation changed: (1) the *tactus,* a down-and-up gesture of the hand to which note values were tied, was increasingly described as having various speeds, and over the course of the seventeenth century it encompassed a longer period of time and became what we call the bar or measure; (2) note values smaller than those included in the mensural system were commonly used; (3) the proportions of mensural notation were still written in the course of a composition to change the relationship of notes to the *tactus,* but they also began to be free-standing signs, placed at the beginning of the composition and therefore not directly related to a normative *tactus* or note duration. Time signatures evolved from these proportion signs but indicate instead what notes are to be included in a measure or bar.

This discussion of seventeenth-century notation will center on that used for most genres of instrumental and vocal music: motets, Masses, madrigals, fantasias, sonatas, concertos, arias, and songs. In addition, three important genres of seventeenth-century music—dramatic recitative, compositions imitating improvisation, and dance music—required performers to interpret the notation of meter and tempo quite differently.[1]

Of these three genres, the first and most characteristic of a new style in the Baroque was the performance and notation of the recitative. This style, basic to the new opera, was sometimes called *recitar cantando* or *stile rappresentativo.* The notation uses the sign C and more or less requires the performer today to think of a beat equal to the quarter note, since the singer's part is written using half, quarter, eighth, and sixteenth notes while the bass mainly sustains whole notes, except at cadences when the harmony moves faster. Despite notation that seems mathematically correct, descriptions of performance stress that the singer must disregard precise notation in favor of declaiming the text in music according to the cadence and sense of the words. Because of the usefulness and popularity of dramatic declamation in opera, the recitative style was transplanted to other genres including sacred music and even instrumental music, where the performer would strive to give the effect of declamation in a free and emphatic delivery. The notation of Claudio Monteverdi's *Combattimento di Tancredi e Clorinda* (1624) is a characteristic example of *recitar cantando*.

Dance music, from the early seventeenth-century collection in Michael Praetorius's *Terpsichore* (1612), through Italian and French collections of dances, culminating in the dances of Louis Couperin (1626–61), Jean-Baptiste Lully (1632–87), and Marin Marais (1656–1728) later in the century, used the usual mensuration and meter signs of the period, with whatever tempo indications are found in lyrical music, but the performer was also guided by the dance itself, through knowing its tempo and metrical structure.

Compositions imitating improvisation were characteristic of much solo music for instruments, mainly as versions of preludes that might have titles such as *toccata, intonazione, intrada, praeambulum,* among many other names. The French devised a special notation for their *préludes non mesurés,* using whole notes throughout, to avoid specifying duration or metrical structure, which was left entirely up to the performer. The notation used for other improvisational imitations was usually "correct" in regard to its mathematical accuracy on the page, but was supplemented with verbal directions to interpret the notation freely in general as well as in specific instances. The genre itself became well enough known that freedom in performance, called *stylus phantasticus* by German writers, could be applied almost by rule to appropriate compositions.[2]

To turn to the mainstream of notation in the seventeenth century, let us first examine the historical notation from which it evolved.

Introduction to Mensural Notation

In the early seventeenth century (i.e., in the music of Monteverdi and Praetorius) and in the practice of some musicians well into the late seventeenth century (for instance, Marc-Antoine Charpentier, 1634–1704) we find mostly a continuation of sixteenth-century mensural notation, a brief summary of which must suffice here; the interested reader may wish to consult more complete studies.[3] In the late fifteenth century, treatises by Franchinus Gaffurius and Johannes Tinctoris described and reformed mensural notation practices that remained influential during the sixteenth century, although then as now, notation continued to evolve. The mensural notation system was similar to written language in having ambiguities and duplications of meaning that required the reader to consider the context in order to interpret the signs correctly.

In early-sixteenth-century practice the principal note values of mensural notation—the *longa, breve,* and *semibreve*—were divided in half or in thirds to make smaller notes (see Ex. 15.1). The term *modus* governed the subdivision of the longa—if perfect, into three breves; if imperfect, into two. *Tempus* governed the subdivision of the breve into three or two semibreves, and *prolatio,* major or minor, divided semibreves into three or two minims. A perfect breve was equal to three semibreves, and a perfect semibreve to three minims. In American English, these names have changed: a breve is now a "double-whole note," a semibreve is a "whole note," and a minim is a "half note."

The term "perfection" designated three equal units that in total corresponded to the next larger note value in both *tempus* and *prolatio.* If a single breve was notated it was equal to three semibreves. However, if a breve and a semibreve comprised the "perfection," the breve was "imperfected" by the semibreve and thus equaled only two semibreves, with the

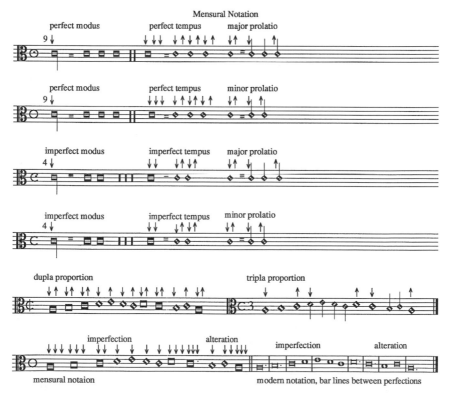

EXAMPLE **15.1.**

remaining one-third of the perfection made up by the semibreve. Another change in the duration of a note was caused by alteration. If a perfection had only two semibreves, the second was altered, and became twice as long so as to make up the three-thirds of the perfection. Both imperfection and alteration of note values became less frequent in the notation of the seventeenth century.

The performer was responsible for recognizing units equal to a "perfection," aided by rules (for instance, *similis ante similem perfecta est*—a note followed by its like is perfect) valid at various levels of note values. Where there might be doubt, a "dot of division" would be placed after the note value that completed the perfection to keep it from being reduced one-third in duration or to ensure the alteration of the second semibreve. A device adopted to enforce the reduction of note values by one-third was to fill in, or blacken, the note heads to be imperfected. If the notes were perfect, blackening them made them imperfect; if they were imperfect, blackening made them into "triplets."

The old sign for *tempus perfectum* was a circle and for tempus imperfectum, a half circle; *prolatio major* was indicated by a dot placed inside the circle or half circle, and *prolatio minor* by no dot. The speed of the various note values was normally linked to the human pulse by the down-and-up gesture of the *tactus,* the duration of which was equal to the semibreve.

Signs at the beginning of a part indicated whether *tempus* and prolation were perfect or imperfect, major or minor. This allowed notes that looked exactly alike to be either duple or triple subdivisions of the next larger note. The *modus* could be indicated by combinations of rests, but was usually of no practical significance to sixteenth-century musicians and even less to those of the seventeenth century.

Note values smaller than the *minim* (half note) always divided the next larger note duply unless their appearance was altered by adding a dot of augmentation. In other words, what we recognize as quarter notes, eighth notes, sixteenths, and even smaller notes were always just half of the next larger note value. They invariably indicated fast notes and were used to write ornamentation examples for learners in method books, and also when composers wished to specify ornamentation within their compositions.

In addition to these signs, mensural notation included proportions: mathematical fractions such as $\frac{2}{1}$, $\frac{3}{1}$ and $\frac{3}{2}$ that were placed after the mensuration sign at the beginning or where they were needed in the composition to change the meter, tempo, or both. Proportions changed the relation of notes to the *tactus.* $\frac{2}{1}$ indicates that two of the same notes replace one, $\frac{3}{1}$ indicates that three replace one, and $\frac{3}{2}$ means that three of the following equal two of the preceding. Duple proportion was more usually indicated by a vertical slash through the mensuration sign; C was changed to ¢ instead of using the fraction $\frac{2}{1}$.

Both C and ¢ indicated the same duple mensural subdivision on all levels of notation and were used interchangeably at the beginning of a composition. However, interpretations of proportions differed and led to confusion. If $\mathbf{C}$ in one voice were contrasted simultaneously with $\mathbf{\mathbb{C}}$ in another voice, the proportion was required to be exactly $\frac{2}{1}$; under $\mathbf{\mathbb{C}}$ the same notes would move twice as fast as under $\mathbf{C}$. In some instances $\mathbf{C}$ and $\mathbf{\mathbb{C}}$ were not intended to signify a difference of speed but reflected the genre of the composition. Some theorists defined $\mathbf{\mathbb{C}}$ as one and a half times faster than $\mathbf{C}$ rather than twice as fast, thereby introducing another uncertainty for performers.

Tempo was regulated with a steady gesture, called the *tactus*, usually given by one of the singers with a down-and-up motion of the hand. The tactus was considered to be equal to a person's resting pulse, and therefore generally moderately slow. The duration of the *tactus* was measured from the bottom of one downstroke to the bottom of the next and normally was equal to the semibreve, our whole note. Breves were equal to two *tactus* in imperfect tempus, and minims were equal to one half of the *tactus* in minor prolation. The *tactus* could be indicated by an equal down-and-up motion for all duple meters, or by a downstroke twice as long as the upstroke for triple meters.

Proportion signs could theoretically indicate tempo changes of almost infinite complexity, but only three proportions were commonly used: $\frac{2}{1}$ (*dupla*), $\frac{3}{1}$ (*tripla*), and $\frac{3}{2}$ (*sesquialtera*). After a change made by a proportion sign, a change back to the original relation of notes to the *tactus* could be indicated by the original mensuration sign or by reversing the numbers of the proportion fraction.

Theoretically—or rather pedagogically—the *tactus* was an unchanging beat, and consequently the note values proceeded (usually) faster in relation to the *tactus* by the proportion indicated. A proportion could bring a sharp tempo change, which a present-day musician might think would be the main goal of such notation, but this was sometimes not the case. Changes in note values often accompanied proportions, with the result that tempo changes were altered or even negated. For example, the proportion 2:1 made the breve equal to the *tactus* instead of the semibreve, but if the note values were doubled in size, only the appearance of the notation would change, not the tempo. This might signal a stylistic change or change of genre to a performer rather than a change of tempo.

Triple proportions often were reduced to a single number 3. The performer must rely on the context of the music to know whether this indicates *tripla* ($\frac{3}{1}$) or *sesquialtera* ($\frac{3}{2}$). If the music becomes unreasonably fast by supposing a *tripla* proportion, or too slow by supposing a *sesquialtera* proportion, the performer must adjust. Different signs could indicate the same proportion; for instance $\mathbf{\mathbb{C}}\frac{3}{2}$ is the same as $\mathbf{C}\frac{3}{1}$.

As far as was possible, the older notation was maintained by many seventeenth-century theorists and musicians writing conservative compositions. Monteverdi's notation for the Mass and Vespers of 1610, for instance, is old-fashioned and suitable for the seriousness of sacred vocal music. For the notation to be read correctly performers had to follow the mensural conventions quite closely and judge tempos by proportions in relation to the *tactus*. Editions that make changes in the notation to make it more easily read should still make it possible to reconstruct the original note values, tempos, and proportions so that the performer is aware of these aids to interpretation.

Mensural Notation of the
Early Seventeenth Century

The Tactus and the Beat

There are some important differences between our idea of the beat in music and the *tactus* of the early seventeenth century. Both are "beats" in the sense that the hand (or foot) can fall and rise to indicate a period of time that is equal to the duration of a note, but the *tactus* was taught to students as an unvarying pulsation against which note values could be performed: notes of large size were slow; smaller notes were faster, which served to give variety of tempo. The *tactus* was normally equal to the semibreve, our whole note, but its relationship to notes could be altered by mathematical proportions, indicating, for instance, that two notes should be performed in the time of one, or three in the time of two.

Our "beat" is entirely variable, and although it is usually identified with the quarter note, it can be equated with the half note or eighth note (or dotted half, dotted quarter, dotted eighth, or other note value) by the time signature. Then with the help of a multitude of tempo words, the performer forms a concept of how fast the beat is. The musical measure is another modern concept, signifying a group of beats to be performed in a manner to distinguish a hierarchical relationship among them, often described as "accented" and "unaccented."

The conductor of the *tactus* presumably was chosen because of an ability to execute a constant, steady, unvarying beat, like a clock. This ideal *tactus*-giver might have been something of a pedagogical myth in the early seventeenth century, but the image was retained, along with a normative tempo for the *tactus*, equal to the resting pulse, or *ca.* MM=60. The modern conductor does more than give the beat, of course, but giving the tempo is one of his or her most important functions. My experience is that there are practical limits to how slow or how fast a conductor may beat so as to be followed by an ensemble. If the beat is too slow, the conductor "subdivides," which doubles the speed of the beat and associates it with the next smaller note value. If the beat is too fast, then he or she consolidates two beats in one, halves the speed, and associates it with the next larger note value. In metronome indications, the beat seems to become too slow around MM 40, and too fast around MM 130–135. This provides a range of more than triple the speed of the slowest beat.

A subdivision or consolidation of the conductor's beat was recognized by some seventeenth-century musicians and theorists such as Andreas Ornithoparcus in John Dowland's translation of 1609:

Of the Division of tact

Tact is threefold, the greater, the lesser, and the proportionate. The greater is a Measure made by a slow, and as it were reciprocall motion. The writers call this tact the whole, or totall tact. And, because it is the true tact of all Songs, it comprehends in his motion a semibreefe not diminished: or a Breefe diminished in a duple.

The lesser Tact, is the half of the greater, which they call a Semitact. Because it measures by it [sic] motion a Semibreefe, diminished in a duple: This is allowed onely by the Unlearned.

The Proportionate is that, whereby three Semibreefes are uttered against one, (as in a Triple) or against two, as in a Sesquialtera.[4]

I believe that the choice between them depended on which note value was more conveniently associated with the *tactus* in performance. Generally, notation using mainly large note values such as the breve, whole note (semibreve), and half note (minim)—Praetorius's "motet style"—suggests the *tactus maior,* equal to the breve. Notation using smaller note values, including half notes, quarter notes, eighths, and sixteenths—"canzona style"—suggests the *tactus minor.*

The Speed of the Tactus in the Seventeenth Century

Recognizing the notational difference between motet style and canzona style gives rise to a seeming paradox in the speed of the *tactus*: when performing motet-style notation with mainly breves (double whole notes), whole, half, and quarter notes, the *tactus* (equal to the breve) generally was faster in order that these notes not proceed at a deadly slow pace; and in the canzona style, with half, quarter, eighth and sixteenth notes, the *tactus* (equal to the whole note), was slower so as not to rush the fast notes.

Other variations of tempo come from a performer's reaction to the meaning of the text. Marin Mersenne's 1636 discussion of the *tactus* advocates a normative speed, about MM=60, but he tells us that the ordinary practice of performers varied the speed and the way of indicating the beat, "to suit the custom of singing masters to beat the measure at whatever speed they wish." Mersenne discussed how the speed of the tactus was frequently quickened or slowed "following the characters, words, or the various emotions they evoke."[5]

Two seventeenth-century treatises by Agostino Pisa[6] and Pier Francesco Valentini[7] are entirely devoted to the *tactus* and suggest by implication that its normative speed was slower. The seventeenth-century *tactus* requires minute investigation because it so often included many small notes that necessarily slow it down. However, Valentini describes a *battuta veloce,* a "fast beat," as well as a *battuta larga,* a "slow beat," indicating that the *tactus* had become quite variable. Although neither Pisa nor Valentini specifically states that the normative *tactus* is slower than before, this might be deduced from the meticulous precision of their description of how to beat the *tactus.* Both writers describe the *tactus* gesture as beginning with the descent of the hand, rather than beginning at the bottom of the stroke, which, as Margaret Murata has seen, dissociates the *tactus* stroke from metrical accentuation. It is very hard to accent the beginning of the descent of the hand.[8]

Banchieri also wrote about the *tactus,*

> . . . diverse opinions are in print in volumes, folios, and discourses, some of which maintain that the *Battuta* begins with the falling of the hand and ends with its ascent; others maintain that it begins on the beat, and terminates on the upstroke; and others say that the motions are sung, and others that the stops [are sung, that is that one sings only when the hand moves or when the hand has come to a stop]. I have observed all these caprices, and I honor them all, leaving to everyone his own opinion. However, I also admire the virtuosi [i.e. the performers], with their fine grace; and forasmuch as actual practice has made it clear to me, I will say briefly that the musical Battuta has several actions, and wishing to describe it, it seems best to divide it into two motions and two stops; the motions we will call descending and ascending, and the stops the downbeat and the upbeat . . .

Banchieri's examples show that he thinks the *tactus* begins on the downbeat.[9] Does this also suggest that stress or accent may be associated with the gesture?

John Playford and Christopher Simpson in the mid-seventeenth century describe the "measure of the *tactus*" to musical beginners as quite slow:

> To which I answer (in case you have none to guide your Hand at the first measuring of Notes) I would have you pronounce these words (*one, two, three, four*) in an equal length, as you would (leisurely) read them: Then fancy those four words to be four *Crotchets,* which make up the quantity or length of a Semibreve, and consequently of a *Time* or *Measure*: In which, let these two words (*One, Two*) be pronounced with the Hand Down; and (*Three, Four*) with it up.[10]

Other descriptions of notation link the speed of the *tactus* to the size of notes used, to the mensuration signs, to proportion signs, or combinations of these in notation. Over the entire century there seems to be no question that the *tactus* came to indicate a longer and longer span of time.

Theorists in this instance were reacting to changes that had already taken place in notation and performance, illustrated by compositions in Joseph Wilhelm von Wasielewski's excellent *Anthology of Instrumental Music from the End of the Sixteenth to the End of the Seventeenth Century,* which faithfully reproduces the notation of the original sources.[11] Compositions from the early seventeenth century written in the mensuration sign ¢ can be guided by a *tactus* equal to the whole note: Canzonas *La Capriola* and No. 2 by Florentio Maschera (pp. 1 and 2), *Sonata con tre violini* by Giovanni Gabrieli (p. 13), and even the *Canzon à tre* by Tarquinio Merula (1639, p. 29) would possibly work with a whole-note *tactus*. The compositions early in the century written in ¢ seem reliably to work with a *tactus* equal to the double whole note: *Canzon per Sonar. Primi Toni* (p. 4) and the *Sonata pian e forte* by Giovanni Gabrieli (p. 7). The Sonata by Massimiliano Neri (1651, p. 34) has more contrasting note values as well as tempo words (Adagio, Allegro, piú Presto) to indicate tempo changes and quite possibly a slower *tactus,* perhaps even a subdivided beat equal to the half note. Another composition from the same composer in the same year on page 38 requires a quarter-note beat, as does the Sonata for Violin and Bass by Biagio Marini (1655, p. 40). Most of the later compositions written in ¢ in the collection require four quarter-note beats per bar: Giovanni Legrenzi (1655, 1663, pp. 42–43), Giovanni Battista Vitali (1667, 1668, pp. 47 and 49), Giovanni Battista Mazzaferrata (1674, p. 53), and so on.

The gradually increasing use of tempo words through the century is also striking in the Anthology, as is the number of compositions written with modern triple time signatures, which will be discussed later in this chapter.

Notation using a *tactus* sometimes subordinates the perceptible metrical structure of the music to metrically neutral notation in order to clarify tempo relationships. Marini's *Romanesca per Violino Solo e Basso* (1620, p. 18) is a prime example, in which the triple meter of the composition is written in ¢ through four *partes*. The reason for this seemingly obtuse notation is that the *tactus* implied no metrical structure through accentuation, unlike our concept of the beat and the measure, but it was taken as a reliable guide to tempo. The tempos of the subsequent *gagliarda* and *corente* are suggested through proportions and the durations of larger and smaller notes.

Seventeenth-Century Mensuration and Proportion Signs

Duple Meter Signs

The common, almost ubiquitous signs used to designate duple meters in the early seventeenth century are visually familiar to performers today: ¢ and ¢, which we call "common time" and equate with a quarter-note beat, four to the measure; and *alla breve* or "cut time," thought to indicate a half-note beat, two to the measure. Adriano Banchieri's *Cartella musica* of 1614 tells us how musicians interpreted ¢ and ¢ in the seventeenth century:

It is true that nowadays, by means of a misuse converted into a [common] usage, both [tempi] have come to be executed in the same way, [by] singing and resting according to the value of the semibreve, and beating the Major Perfect [¢] fast [presto] (since it has white notes) and the Minor Perfect [C] slow [adagio], since it has black notes. The one and the other turn out [to be] the same, except that there is a difference between the two in the proportions of equality, in sesquialtera of inequality, tripla and hemiolia.[12]

Praetorius's *Syntagma musicum* gives more details of this change as well as other changes in the practical use of mensural notation. His was an influential treatise for seventeenth-century musicians and is a valuable guide to us today, particularly for showing how much mensuration and proportion signs need the context of genre and style for a proper interpretation:

At the present time these two signs [C and ¢] are used; C usually in madrigals and ¢ in motets. Madrigals and other cantiones that abound in quarters and eighths under the sign C move with a faster motion; motets, on the other hand, that abound in breves and semibreves under the sign ¢ [move with a] slower [motion]; therefore the *tactus* in the latter is faster, and in the former is slower, by which a mean between two extremes is kept, lest too slow a speed produce displeasure in the ears of the listener, or too fast a speed lead to a precipice, just as the horses of the sun snatched away Phaeton, when the chariot obeyed no reins.

This indicates to me that motets and other sacred music written with many black notes and given the sign C must be performed with a *tactus* that is somewhat grave and slow. This can be seen in Orlando [di Lasso]'s four-voiced Magnificat and Marenzio's early sacred and other madrigals. Each person can consider these matters for himself and, considering the text and harmony, take the *tactus* more slowly or more quickly.

It is certain, and important to note, that choral concertos must be taken with a slow, grave *tactus*. Sometimes in such concertos, madrigal and motet styles are found mixed together and alternated, and these must be regulated through conducting the *tactus*. From this comes an important invention. Sometimes . . . the Italian words adagio and presto, meaning slow and fast, are written in the parts, since otherwise when the signs C and ¢ so often alternate, confusion and problems may arise.[13]

For Praetorius's contemporaries, the uncertainty of how to interpret this notation was sufficient to initiate the "important invention" of including a verbal description of tempo change. We may interpret from what he writes that the tempo words, the notation signs, and note values indicate an uncertain but moderate acceleration (*presto* or *velociter*) or deceleration (*adagio* or *tardè*) in the speed of the tactus; only much later do these words indicate extreme variations of tempo.

Étienne Darbellay's investigation of tempo and *tactus* in the notation of Frescobaldi shows that what Banchieri and Praetorius have written about C and ¢ applies to Girolamo Frescobaldi's music, particularly the *Capricci*

of 1624, with their lively and contrasting tempos.[14] Frescobaldi uses only
C as a duple mensuration sign in his *Capricci* of 1624, but employs note
sizes that contrast with one another to mark different styles. For instance,
notation using whole, half, and quarter notes can be equated with ¢ and
notation using quarters, eighths, and sixteenths imply **C**. Darbellay takes
Praetorius's description of the predominant note values of the two genres, madrigal and motet, as one of the major points to be observed in
assigning the different tempos of the *tactus,* using the term *Notenbild* or
"note picture." This clarifies an important point for instrumental music,
where there is no text to guide one as in the motet or madrigal, but
where the note values may be clearly differentiated. In duple meters, seventeenth-century performers read large note values to signify slow music,
and small notes fast music, although the *tactus* would be adjusted so as to
avoid the most extreme tempo differences implied by the notation alone.

Triple Meter Signs

Triple meter signs are a good deal more complex than duple signs. For
the first time in notational practice, "freestanding" proportional signs,
that is, triple proportions that do not refer to a previously established
integral value, are frequently found at the beginning of a composition.
Sometimes, later in the work, a sign might indicate a value to which the
proportion would have been related, had the sign come first, but some-
times the freestanding proportion is the only meter sign. $C\frac{3}{2}$, $\frac{3}{2}$, or plain
3 will usually introduce a composition with three half notes to the bar or
beat and $¢\frac{3}{2}$, $\phi\frac{3}{2}$, or plain **3** will indicate a bar or beat equal to three whole
notes. These freestanding signs, which may or may not deserve to be
called proportions, are found in place of the now obsolete signs of the
semicircle with a dot that indicated major prolation and the circle that
indicated *tempus perfectum* in sixteenth-century mensural notation. The
tempo significance of freestanding triple signs may be more subject to a
performer's interpretation than true proportions since they have no relation to a normative duple *tactus,* but only the suggestion of tempo that
note values alone give.

Examples of *proportio tripla* as freestanding signatures are found in
Praetorius's *Urania* of 1613, specifically parts 5 (*Surrexit Christus*), 8 (*Allein
Gott*), and 15 (*Erstanden ist der heilge Christ*), among other sections of the
work. *Proportio sesquialtera* as a freestanding signature is found in the last
three movements of Monteverdi's Vespers of 1610. Praetorius's *Musarum
Sioniarum Motectae et Psalmi Latini* of 1607 includes as part 34 a "Canticum
trium puerorum" of fourteen verses, with alternating verses that have
signatures of **C** and **3**, each a separate piece ending with a double bar. The
sections in **C** use eighth notes as their smallest value, with quarter and
half notes predominating, which implies that the *tactus* is *tardior,* slower.
The sections in **3** have three whole notes to the *tactus,* which probably is

celerior, faster. Another example is from Ludovico Grossi da Viadana's *Concerti ecclesiastici* of 1602: *Sanctorum Meritis* begins with the sign $\mathbf{\Phi}\frac{3}{2}$, and uses three whole notes to a *tactus*.

The use of triple meters within compositions beginning with **C** or **¢** is very frequent in the first half of the seventeenth century. For these the proportional meaning of the fractions $\frac{3}{1}$ and $\frac{3}{2}$ is exact and refers to the normative tempo of the *tactus* signified by **C** or **¢**, confirmed by the size of notes employed under these signs. One of the most celebrated pieces using these signs and proportions is Monteverdi's *Sonata sopra Sancta Maria* included in the Vespers of 1610, which has been thoroughly discussed by Roger Bowers, a scholar of medieval music, in a recent and important article.[15] There are seven changes to $\frac{3}{2}$ from **C**, all *sesquialtera* proportions that replace a duple *tactus* equal to a whole note with a *tactus* equal to three half notes. Of these changes, all are straightforward except the fifth return to **C** at *tactus* 130, p. 262 in the Malipiero edition. Monteverdi's notation here, while written in **C**, uses blackened minims (filled-in half notes, identical to quarter notes) with the number **3** written above to indicate that there are three to each *tactus*, half-note triplets, for all parts except for the treble "cantus firmus," which is notated in longer duple note values. The result of this unusual notation is precisely equal to the proportion of **C**$\frac{3}{2}$, used in the rest of the composition.

This has been changed in the Malipiero edition by halving the value of the blackened half notes so that they not only look like but have the value of triplet quarter notes, which also requires halving the value of the simultaneous quite ordinary notation of the "cantus firmus" that sings a repetition of the ostinato phrase "Sancta Maria, ora pro nobis." Malipiero's change of Monteverdi's notation has been incorporated into many if not all other modern editions, and Roger Bowers's correction of it has not been accepted by all. There is a question as to why Monteverdi used such unusual old-fashioned notation to indicate the same result as $\frac{3}{2}$ proportion. Bowers's answer, truly ingenious as well as thoroughly medieval in its reasoning, is that by using this notation Monteverdi preserved a setting in 147 (or 3 x 7 x 7) *tactus,* a number that reflects the Trinity multiplied by the Seven Joys and the Seven Sorrows of the Virgin. This seems to me not an impossible interpretation, but perhaps one not entirely typical of the thinking of seventeenth-century musicians.

Bowers asserts that Monteverdi's notation is medieval, and his view avoids emphasizing the changes that have altered aspects of it to fit the more modern practice of musicians of the early Baroque era. His main point is that this notation is according to mensural principles of long standing and in accord with the theorists of the early seventeenth century.

In Frescobaldi's *Capricci* of 1624, the first *Sopra Ut, Re, Mi, Fa, Sol, La* begins with the sign **C** with whole, half, and quarter notes, suggesting a *tactus celerior* equal to the breve. The first proportion (measure 33) with the sign **C** with a dot followed by **3** (**C·3**) equates three half notes to the former whole note—in other words, a $\frac{3}{2}$ or *sesquialtera* proportion. The music returns to **C** (measure 48) with some eighth and sixteenth notes as well as half and quarter notes. Perhaps the *tactus* would be given slightly more slowly. The next proportion is **O$\frac{3}{4}$** (measure 77), a *tripla* proportion with three whole notes to the *tactus,* which might be given a bit faster. The next **C** (measure 84) has mainly sixteenth notes, consequently one might use a *tactus* equal to the whole note, given more slowly. Further changes continue through the 196 measures of the piece.

Praetorius gives a thorough exposition of the *Signis proportionatis in Tactu Inaequali.*[16] He states that under triple signs the large notes are slower and the small notes faster than they would be in a strict proportion. Perhaps the most important element in Praetorius's explanation is that the sign itself signifies the speed of the *tactus,* although the genre of composition and the size of the notes must also be considered.

Praetorius adds another triple meter, the *Sextupla, seu Tactu Trochaico Diminuta,*[17] measured with an ordinary duple *tactus.* The term *sextupla,* Praetorius writes, means that there are six semiminims (quarter notes) in one *tactus.* These are sometimes written with the number **3** over each group of three notes. The *sextupla* can be notated in three ways: (1) in *hemiolia minore* (all black notes under the sign **¢**), there are three black minims or *semibreve cum Minima* on the downstroke, and three on the upstroke. If the sign **¶** is used for *hemiolia minore,* it indicates a proportion equating six semiminims or black minims with the *tactus.* (2) The second *sextupla* is used by the French and Italians in "Courranten, Sarabanden" and other similar pieces. Minims and semiminims are used in place of the black semibreves and black minims of the first *sextupla.* The sign $\frac{6}{4}$ indicates that six semiminims equal four of those before the sign. (3) The third way, Praetorius cautions, has proved so difficult for performers that he is uncertain whether it should be used. The sign *sesquialtera,* $\frac{3}{2}$, is used with semibreves and minims, but the *tactus* must be taken very fast, which often causes confusion, therefore he has written a retorted **Φ** before the $\frac{3}{2}$ proportion to indicate this fast speed. An example of this last notation is found in Praetorius's *Puericinium* of 1621, no. 4, *Singet und klinget,* on page 30 of volume 19 of the *Gesamtausgabe.* Praetorius is uncertain enough of the performer's familiarity with this to write a considerable preface in the score in explanation, and to mark the music with both *presto* and *celeriter.*

Frescobaldi's use of this *sextupla* (*sei per quatro*) meter can be seen in *Capriccio V, sopra la Bassa Fiamenga,* at measure 57, more or less in the first kind of notation described for *sextupla* by Praetorius.

The relationship of **C** and **¢** to the various kinds of triple proportions, while complex, can be rationally understood in most cases. The relationship is less clear when a triple meter follows a recitative-like section written in **C**, which must be performed freely according to the dramatic declamation of the words. Examples of this abound in the cantatas of

Barbara Strozzi, for example *Cieli, stelle, deitadi* from her Opus 8. The first of Heinrich Schütz's *Kleine geistliche Konzerte* of 1636 begins with a recitative-like section that is labeled *stylo oratorio* to warn the singer of its declamatory nature. A succeeding triple proportion cannot be calculated on the basis of a reliable steady *tactus*, but perhaps might be regarded as if it were a freestanding metrical sign.

At this point in our discussion of seventeenth-century notation the main principles of the conservative notation still widely used in the first half of the century have been considered.

The Advent of Time Signatures

The third major change in notation comes when freestanding triple mensural proportion signs were transformed into the fractional numbers of modern time signatures. Along with the invention and increasing use of these "new signs" used by "the Italians" (according to Jean Rousseau in 1683) comes a recognition that the measure (of the *tactus*) is no longer the duration of the musical beat, but rather a collection of beats organized by a different perception of meter.

An antique and conservative view of proportions is given by Pier Francesco Valentini in more than 150 pages of a closely written manuscript.[18] For Valentini, whatever number and size of notes replace those previous to the proportion, they occupy an equal amount of time. For instance, for him the proportions of $\frac{3}{2}$ and $\frac{3}{4}$ differ only in the size of the notes used, not in their speed.

Valentini gives examples of many numerical proportions, both duple and triple, and shows the value of every note in relation to the *tactus*. Each proportion is preceded by a mensuration sign that allows the performer to know the relationship of notes to the *tactus* both before and after the proportional change. Valentini explores every possible proportion regardless of its practical use, including superparticular proportions such as $\frac{5}{4}$, $\frac{7}{6}$, and $\frac{10}{9}$, multiple proportions such as $\frac{5}{1}$ and $\frac{7}{1}$, and submultiple proportions such as $\frac{1}{5}$ and $\frac{4}{7}$.[19] Among the plethora of fractions cited are those that subsequently became time signatures.

One interpretation of proportions is based on the equivalence of notes to one another; in $\frac{3}{2}$, three of any note value after the sign becomes equivalent to two before it. In ¢$\frac{3}{2}$, three semibreves become equivalent to two semibreves, and under C$\frac{3}{2}$, three minims to two minims. In another system, the *tactus* is the unit of equivalence: in $\frac{3}{2}$, the note values of three-thirds of a *tactus* become equivalent to two halves. The results are not altered, but Dahlhaus points out that the second system is closer to establishing the semibreve as the "whole note," the equivalent of a measure.[20]

Most theorists continued to hold that the speed of notes was relevant to the normative *tactus* of C and ¢, the signs governing mensural *tempus* (*tempo* in Italian), a word that evolved to mean the speed of notes. Proportion numbers were sometimes used alone, without a mensural sign to specify their relation to the *tactus*. This was not approved by most conservative theorists during the seventeenth century, including Giovanni Maria Bononcini, who wrote: "Finally it must be said that to use the proportions without mensural signs is (as Valerio Bona says in his *Regole di musica*) like sending soldiers on the field without a captain."[21]

It is in Bononcini's triple meter signatures and those of Lorenzo Penna (without mensural signs) that we begin to recognize the familiar time signatures of modern measures.

According to Bononcini they are[22]

tripla maggiore: O_1^3, C_1^3, Φ_2^3, $\mathbb{C}_2^3$ with three semibreves to the *tactus*, two on the downstroke, one on the upstroke

tripla minore: $\mathbb{C}_2^3$, O_1^3, C_1^3, $\mathbb{C}_2^3$, with two minims on the downstroke, one on the upstroke

C_4^3, *tripla di semiminime*

C_8^3, *tripla di crome*

C_4^6, *sestupla di semiminime*

C_8^6, *sestupla di crome*

C_8^{12}, *dodecupla di crome*

C_{16}^{12}, *dodecupla di semicrome*

Penna calls them signs of *tripola*, not proportions, and they are[23]

$\frac{3}{1}$, *tripola maggiore*, formerly indicated by Φ_2^3, three semibreves to the *tactus*, two on the downstroke, one on the upstroke

$\frac{3}{2}$, *tripola minore*, formerly indicated by O_2^3, three minims to the *tactus*, two on the downstroke, one on the upstroke

$\frac{3}{4}$, la *tripola picciola*, ó *quadrupla*, ó *semiminore*, ó *di semiminime*, semiminims and minims, two semiminims on the downstroke, one on the upstroke

$\frac{3}{8}$, la *tripola crometta*, ó *ottina*, ó *di crome*

$\frac{3}{16}$, la *semicrometta*

$\frac{6}{4}$, la *sestupla maggiore*

$\frac{6}{8}$, la *sestupla minore*

$\frac{12}{8}$, la *dosdupla*

Meter signatures with six in the numerator indicate three notes on the downstroke and three on the up; with twelve in the numerator, there are six on the downstroke and six on the upstroke.

The number of signs is small compared to those given by Valentini, but Penna mentions that he is explaining only those most frequently used. Penna includes a few additional proportions, the *hemiolia maggiore* and *minore,* that were "formerly used," and also the proportions $\frac{5}{2}$ and $\frac{7}{2}$, included as *tripola,* leftovers from Valentini's odd mensural proportions. Penna's explanation is brief, but he mentions that there "are others in other forms." He also explains some traditional uses of a proportional sign, for example, turning it upside-down signifies a return to the notation before the proportion was introduced.

Bononcini retains the mensural ₵ as a guide to his new signs. His general explanation of triple signs involves comparing the *tactus* and the notes before the proportion sign to those after it. "Of the others indicated, for greater brevity, they follow this general rule: the lower number indicates which note values went or were understood to go to the beat, and the upper number how many notes will go in the future (i.e. after the sign)."[24]

Penna gives no reason for the omission of a mensural sign (tempo) before the numerical proportion in his signatures, but in 1714 Printz comments on this:

> If the music begins with an irrational proportion [$\frac{3}{1}$, $\frac{3}{2}$, $\frac{3}{4}$, $\frac{3}{8}$] most of the new musicians omit the mensural sign, and use only the numbers that show the proportion. This is not without cause, as the denominator of the indicated proportion already has the ability to show the length of the *tactus*: therefore the mensural sign is superfluous, unnecessary, and should be abolished.[25]

Even in 1714 the fractional number of the time signature is explained as a proportion, but the omission of the mensural sign is explained as if it did not affect the proportional interpretation of the signature.

It seems that the proportion sign is still recognized in its traditional meaning by Bononcini, but he has this to say about the beat that regulates the speed of notes according to the various meter signs:

> It should be noted that all of the proportions corresponding to an equal beat are given by the same equal beat, and all the proportions of the unequal beat by the identical unequal beat. The motion does not vary except—occasionally—in speed, now an ordinary pace, now slow, and now fast, according to the wish of the composer, for this reason the parts of a composition are given different signs. Under these signs the same beat easily regulates [the music], as may be seen in the works of Frescobaldi and other learned composers, and in my own *opera sesta*.[26]

Bononcini does not explain what signs these are, and the first to come to mind today, tempo words such as *allegro* and *adagio,* may not have been in his mind. Frescobaldi was one of the first to specify that the "proportion" itself indicates the speed of the beat: "In the triplas, or sesquialteras, if they are major let them be played slowly, if minor somewhat more quickly, if of three semiminims more rapidly, if $\frac{6}{4}$, move the beat fast."[27]

Frescobaldi's interpretation of proportion signs is repeated by many performers and writers in the seventeenth century, including Bononcini.

Giacomo Carissimi amplifies this instruction and includes numerical signatures and the genre of the composition as determinants of the tempo. $\frac{3}{1}$, for example, is used in "slow compositions and serious works in the *Stylo Ecclesiastico*," $\frac{3}{2}$ is "used somewhat more briskly than the former, particularly in the serious style, and therefore the beat must be given somewhat faster." $\frac{3}{4}$ "requires a faster beat than the last as this tripla is used mostly in ariettes and happy pieces."[28]

Wolfgang Caspar Printz formulates a general rule to govern the speed of the *tactus* as indicated by proportional signatures: "The length of the trochaic beat is indicated by the lower number of the proportion, therefore this rule should be observed: the smaller the lower number of the proportion, the slower the beat; and the larger the number, the faster the beat."[29]

Étienne Loulié agrees with this formulation.[30]

Jean Rousseau derives the speed of some of his triple time signatures from individual note values that are equivalent before and after the fractional sign. He first explains that there are six varieties of ordinary signs, that is **C**, **¢**, **2**, **C3**, **3**, and $\frac{3}{2}$; then that there are four more, $\frac{3}{4}$, $\frac{3}{8}$, $\frac{6}{4}$, and $\frac{6}{8}$, that are "new signs used for only a certain time." Later, he mentions the origin of the "new signs" when he states that "the Italians" also used $\frac{12}{4}$, $\frac{12}{8}$, $\frac{9}{4}$, and $\frac{9}{8}$, signs that he does not discuss.[31] French music of this period that is written in imitation of the Italian style often uses Italian meter signs.

> Under the sign of $\frac{3}{4}$ (called thus because in place of the four quarter notes of **C** this measure has only three), the beat is given with three strokes, faster than under the triple simple **3**. As the quickness of these strokes makes them difficult to beat, each gesture is made by two unequal strokes, two quarter notes on the down, and one quarter on the up stroke. Under the sign of $\frac{3}{8}$, there are three eighth notes instead of eight in **C**. The beat is given as it is under the sign of $\frac{3}{4}$, but much faster.[32]

Jean Rousseau's explanation contradicts the concept that a measure is equated with the *tactus*; there are a number of beats in a measure, unless the speed is so fast that it is uncomfortable to give a full gesture to each "beat." He recognizes that the measure and the *tactus* are now seen to be quite different from one another.

A change in the meaning of the word *tact* also occurred in German late in the seventeenth century. Daniel Merck used it both in its traditional meaning of *tactus* and also in its modern German sense of "measure," which makes no sense at all unless the two meanings are understood appropriately and supplied by the reader. "*Tripla Major* wird diser genennet/ . . . in welchem drey gantze Tact erst einen Tact ausmachen." ("Tripla Major, as it is called, . . . is when three whole notes make one measure.")[33]

Perhaps Merck's meaning was clear to his contemporary readers, but it can now be understood only by using two terms for the word *tact*.

Two additional signs, **3** (triple simple) and **2** (*le binaire*) are frequently used in French tablatures to indicate a basic triple or duple metrical organization. **3** was conducted with two downbeats and one up for slow tempos, one downbeat of two pulses and an upbeat of one pulse for faster tempos, or one downbeat (or upbeat) of three pulses for very fast tempos.[34]

Loulié states that **3** is the same as $\frac{3}{4}$, while Rousseau indicates that it is conducted by three quick strokes (*trois temps légers*), in contrast to **C3**, which is conducted by three slow strokes. Regardless of the time signatures of French notation, the genre of the piece determines the speed of the music. Georg Muffat (writing about French music) remarks that "gigues and canaries need to be played the fastest of all, no matter what the time signature."[35]

There are still problems in indicating the tempo of music through time signatures. M. de Saint Lambert comments on the liberties taken by musicians contrary to the rules of tempo implied by signatures, and gives an example from the practice of the most eminent musician of the day:

> Often the same man marks two airs of completely differing tempo with the same time signature, as for example M. de Lully, who has the reprise of the overture to *Armide* played very fast and the air on page 93 of the same opera played very slowly, even though this air and the reprise of the overture are both marked with the time signature $\frac{6}{4}$, and both have six quarter notes per measure distributed in the same way.[36]

Saint Lambert gives a number of other examples of the confusion surrounding the tempo significance of time signatures and comments that "musicians who recognize this drawback often add one of the following words to the time signature of the pieces they compose: *Lentement, Gravement, Légèrement, Gayement, Vîte, Fort Vîte*, and the like, in order to compensate for the inability of the time signatures to express their intention."[37]

Note values and time signatures often needed the help of tempo words in order to transmit fully the composer's choice of tempo to performers, but these words were still only secondary indications in the late seventeenth century.

Notation of music from the later seventeenth century often seems so much like the music with which we are familiar that only in a few instances are we reminded that it is different. Sometimes editors rewrite the music, and of course they should inform the performer of what has been done. The most frequent changes made are to rebar the original notation, usually shortening what seem like excessively long measures; to substitute modern time signatures, for instance to replace **C** with $\frac{4}{4}$; and to halve the note values—for instance, to replace half notes and $\frac{3}{2}$ with quarter notes and $\frac{3}{4}$. Editors of music of the first half of the seventeenth century are more likely to have made these changes, and they are the cause of most of the confusion that can overtake a knowledgeable performer of this repertory. If you have to use a rewritten edition, the best solution is to try to reconstruct the original notation in order to understand what it implied. All good editions make it possible to reconstruct the original notation if changes have been made, and the very best editions reproduce the original notation, with explanations (if they are required) to enable modern performers to solve unfamiliar problems.

Much of the music of the seventeenth century is of such high quality and strong emotional force that the intuitions of good performers will lead to good performances even if only a full understanding of the notation will allow the music to shine forth as intended.

NOTES

1. In addition, an entirely different kind of notation called tablature was used for several instruments, notably for plucked string instruments such as lute, theorbo, and guitar, for the viola da gamba played as a lyra viol, and for keyboard music. Tablature notation was even invented for the recorder. Most tablature depicts finger position on the instrument rather than musical pitch and conveys technical information to the performer not included in standard notation. This notation is extremely useful to performers on the particular instruments, now as well as then, but cannot usefully be read by anyone else.

2. See the prefaces to Frescobaldi's *Toccate e partite d'intavolatura di cimbalo*, 1615, 1616, 1628, 1637 in the *Gesamtausgabe*, vol. 3, ed. P. Pidoux. A translation of Frescobaldi's preface is in MacClintock–*Readings*, 133. See also Hogwood–*Frescobaldi*. For French preludes, see Moroney–*Unmeasured Preludes*, 143.

3. Apel–*Notation* is widely available and still valuable. The most recent study is Busse-Berger–*Mensuration*. The articles "Notation" and "Proportions" in *New Grove* are also useful.

4. Ornithoparcus–*Micrologus*, Lib. 2, ch. 6, 46. In Ornithoparcus and Dowland–*Compendium*, 166.

5. Mersenne–*Harmonie universelle*, *Livre cinquiesme de la composition*, Proposition 11, 324.

6. Pisa–*Battuta*.

7. Valentini–*Trattato*, 34, par. 64, and 62, par. 129.

8. Murata–Valentini, 330.

9. Cranna–*Banchieri*, 472–73.

10. Simpson–*Compendium*, 18–19.

11. Wasielewski–*Anthology*. The first edition was published in 1874, and Da Capo Press, New York, reissued the *Anthology* in 1974, with notes by John G. Suess.

12. Cranna–*Banchieri*, 115.

13. Praetorius–*Syntagma* III: 52–54. "Jetzigerzeit aber werden diese beyde *Signa* meistentheils also *observiret*, dass das 𝄵 fürnehmlich in *Madrigalien*, das 𝄵 aber in *Motetten* gebraucht wird. Quia Madrigalia and alia Cantiones, quae sub signo 𝄵, Semiminimas & Fusis abundant, celeriori progrediuntur motu; Motectae autem, quae sub signo 𝄵 Brevibus and Semibrevibus abundant, tardiori: Ideo hîc celeriori, illic tardiori opus est Tactu, quò medium inter duo extrema servetur, ne tardior Progressus auditorum auribus pariat fastidium, aut celerior in Praecipitium ducat, veluti Solis equi Phaëtontem abripuerunt, ubi currus nullas audivit habenas.

"Darvmb deuchtet mich nicht vbel gethan seyn/ wenn man die *Motecten*, vnd andere geistliche Gesänge/ welche mit vielen schwarzen Noten gesetzt seyn/ mit

315

diesem *Signo* 𝄴 zeichnet; anzuzeigen/ dass alsdann der *Tact* etwas langsamer vnd gravitetischer müsse gehalten werden: Wie dann *Orlandus* in seinen *Magnificat 4 Vocum* vnd *Marentius* in vorgedachten *Spiritualibus* vnd andern *Madrigalibus* solches in acht genommen. Es kan aber ein jeder den Sachen selbsten nachdenken/ vnd *ex consideratione Textus & Harmoniae observiren,* wo ein langsamer oder geschwinder *Tact* gehalten werden müsse.

"Dann das ist einmal gewis vnd hochnötig/ das in *Concerten per Choros* ein gar langsamer gravitetischer *Tact* müsse gehalten werden. Weil aber in solchen *Concerten* bald Madrigalische/ bald *Motetten* Art vnter einander vermenget vnd vmbgewechselt befunden wird/ muss man sich auch im Tactiren darnach richten: Darvmb dann gar ein nötig *inventum,* das bisweilen/ (wie drunten im I Capittel des Dritten Theils) die Vocabula von den Wälschen *adagio, presto. h.e. tardè, Velociter,* in den Stimmen darbey *notiret* vnd vnterzeichnet werden/ denn es sonsten mit den beyden *Signis* 𝄴 vnd 𝄵 so offtmals vmbzuwechseln/ mehr Confusiones vnd verhinderungen geben vnd erregen möchte."

14. Darbellay–Tempo Relationships, 301–26.
15. Bowers–Reflections, 347–95. The music is in the Monteverdi *Opere,* ed. Malipiero, 14: 250–73.
16. Praetorius–*Syntagma* III: 52–54.
17. Ibid., 73–78.
18. Valentini–*Trattato,* 300–459.
19. This classification of proportions by antique mathematical terminology is explained in Morley–*Plaine and easie,* original edition, p. 17, vers. 18, and on pp. 127–28 in the modern edition.
20. Dahlhaus–Taktsystems, 230–36.
21. Bononcini–*Musico prattico,* 14. "Per ultimo si deue auuertire, che l'introdurre le proporzioni ne i canti, senza segno del Tempo e (come dice Valerio Bona nelle sue *Regole di musica*) come mettere i soldati in Campo senza Capitano."
22. Ibid., 20–23.
23. Penna–*Primi albori,* 36–40.
24. Bononcini–*Musico pratico,* 11. "De gli altri poi che seguono, per maggiore brevità si da questo regola generale, che il numero sotto posto denota quante figure andavano, ò s'intende, che andastero alla battuta, & il sopra posto, quante ne vadino per l'avenire."
25. Printz–*Compendium,* 16. "Wenn der Gesang mit einer *irrationalem Proportion* anfängt/ lassen die meisten neuen *Musici* das *Signum quantitatis mensuralis* weg/ und setzen unter die Zahlen/ so die *Proportion* andeuten/ allein: und zwar nicht ohne Ursache. Denn weil die untere Zahl der vorgeschriebenen *Irrationalen Proportion* schon die Krafft hat die Länge des Tactes anzudeuten/ so ist das *Signum quantitatis mensuralis* überflüssig/ unnöthig/ und also/ vermöge . . . abzuschaffen."
26. Bononcini–*Musico pratico,* 17–24. "Si deue auuertire, che tutte le proporzione di battuta eguale, si deuono constituire sotto l'istessa battuta eguale, e tutte le proporzione di battuta ineguale si deuono anch'esse constituire sotto la medesima battuta ineguale, non variandosi altro che alle volte il moto in questa maniera, cioè facendolo hora ordinario, hora adagio; & hora presto, secondo il voler del Compositore; per il che si possono far composizione, nelle quali le parti siano segnate diuersamente, purche i segni possano essere gouernate facilmente da una istesia battuta, come in diuerse Opere de Frescobaldi, e di molt' altri dotti Compositore si puï vedere, & eziando nella sesta mia opera.
27. Frescobaldi–*Il primi libro de capricci,* preface. "E nelle trippole, ò sesquialtere, se saranno maggiori, si portino adagio, se/ minori alquâto più allegre, se di tre semiminime, pió allegre se saranno sei per quattro si di/ a illor tempo con far caminare la battuta allegra." See also Hammond–*Frescobaldi,* 226–27.
28. Carissimi–*Ars cantandi,* 15.
29. Printz–*Compendium,* ch. 4, 17. "Die Länge des Trochaischen Tactes wird angedeutet durch die untere Zahl der vorgeschriebenen Proportion, davon diese Regul is Acht zu

nehmen: Je kleiner die untere Zahl der Proportion ist/ je langsamer soll der Tact geschlagen werden; und je grösser dieselbe Zahl ist/ je geschwinder soll der Tact geschlagen werden."

30. Loulié–*Élemens*, 29.
31. Rousseau–*Méthode . . . chanter*, 17.
32. Ibid., 36. "Au signe de Trois pour Quatre, ainsi nommé parce qu'au lieu que la Mesure au signe Majeur [**C**] est composé de quatre Noires, celle-cy n'en a que Trois, la Mesure se bat a trois temps plus vîtes que le Triple simple [**3**]; mais comme la vitesse de ces temps les rend difficiles a marquer, on le bat a deux temps inégaux; deux Noires pour le frappé & une Noire pour le levé. Au Signe de trois pour Huit composé de trois croches, au lieu que le Majeur en a Huit, la Mesure se bat comme au Trois pour Quatre, mais beaucoup plus Vîte."
33. Merck–*Compendium*, 11.
34. Loulié–*Élemens*, 29.
35. See Strunk–*Source Readings*, 444.
36. St. Lambert–*Principles*, 45.
37. Ibid.

BIBLIOGRAPHY

Aldrich–*Rhythm*. A study of seventeenth-century Italian theorists, prosody, and versification of song texts, with an anthology of solo song from the first half of the century.

Bank–*Tactus*.

Bowers–Reflections. A critical appraisal of this article by Jeffrey Kurtzman, with a reply from Roger Bowers, can be found in *Music and Letters* 74 (1993): 487–95.

Brainard–Proportional Notation. A thoughtful and meticulous investigation of proportional tempo relationships, with musical examples. Perhaps his conclusions indicate more precise gradations of tempo relationships than performers might be able or willing to realize in practice.

Darbellay–Tempo Relationships. A thorough understanding of the meaning of the notation and Frescobaldi's instructions may be gained by a careful reading of Darbellay's somewhat difficult writing.

Houle–*Meter*.

Murata–Valentini. An excellent and perceptive discussion of Valentini's prolix views on aspects of early-seventeenth-century notation.

16

Tuning and Temperament

Herbert W. Myers

Imagine a world in which the units used for linear measurement were not quite commensurate—one in which, by some quirky royal decree, let us say, twelve official inches did not quite make an official foot, or three feet exactly a yard. Most citizens, presumably, would be aware of a problem only rarely, but anyone whose profession depended on precise measurement would long since have become expert at making fine distinctions; we can be sure that architects and carpenters, for instance, would have come to distinguish unabashedly between "inches" and "twelfths of a foot." The units of our musical world—those we call "intervals"—are, in fact, of a similarly incommensurate nature, although unlike the units of our metaphorical example, their size is not determined arbitrarily; their mathematical ratios reflect basic acoustical phenomena. And unlike the professionals in our metaphor, musicians—those who must deal constantly with the problem—are for the most part unaccustomed to discussing it intellectually, generally preferring an intuitive approach. In fact, so out of favor is a "scientific" approach to intonation that to mention it may arouse suspicion among other musicians as to one's musical sensibilities.

It was not always so; in centuries before the nineteenth, a firm grasp of the mathematical foundations of music was considered to be one of the highest attainments of a good musician. But perhaps more relevant to the present discussion is the fact that different musical priorities in earlier times led to solutions different from the usual modern ones. (In our linear analogy above, our experts made a provisional redefinition of the inch in terms of the official foot; they might just as well have found reason to redefine the foot in terms of the official inch instead.) In order to appreciate these earlier solutions—and certainly in order to put them into practice ourselves—we have to have an understanding of both the underlying theory and terminology. Neither the conceptual basis nor the attendant math is really all that complicated, although the full ramifications of some intonation schemes can appear rather threatening. Fortunately, all the hard work, both theoretical and practical, has been done—over and over, in fact—and we are in a position to reap the benefit. It is the purpose of this chapter to introduce some of the basic concepts and terms, provide some historical context, and serve as a guide to the copious resources already available to the performer.

Central to tuning theory is the idea of ratio or proportion. Before the nineteenth century the intervalic ratios were understood in terms of string lengths on the monochord; more recently they have come to be understood in terms of vibration frequencies. Fortunately, the ratios themselves are the same, only inverted. Thus, the octave, produced by a 2:1 ratio of string lengths, is also produced by a 1:2 ratio of frequencies; the fifth can be thought of as either 3:2 or 2:3, and the fourth as 4:3 or 3:4. All that really matters is consistency: choose one form or the other and stay with it, at least in any one calculation. Remember, too, that in adding ratios, one multiplies; in subtracting, one divides. Thus, adding a fifth (3:2) to a fourth (4:3), we get a ratio of 12:6 (3 x 4 : 2 x 3), which reduces to 2:1—the ratio of an octave. Subtracting a fourth from a fifth should give us a major second; as with fractions, dividing by a ratio is the same as multiplying by its reciprocal (i.e., inversion), so that 3:2 multiplied by 3:4 (the reciprocal of the fourth, 4:3) gives us 9:8 as the ratio of a major second. (There is, incidentally, some research to suggest that this subtraction of a fourth from a fifth is pretty much what our brains are doing naturally and subconsciously to determine the size of a second.)

It was recognized from ancient times that a stack of six major seconds—a whole-tone scale, if you will—exceeds an octave by a fractional amount, equaling about an eighth of a tone. (This discrepancy is called a "comma"—a "ditonic" or "Pythagorean" comma to be exact.) This small interval can be divided up and distributed equally along the chain of ascending fifths and descending fourths comprising the octave, all without most listeners being any the wiser; this, of course, is exactly what is done to achieve our standard modern system, equal temperament. (It is customary in discussions like this, by the way, to treat of both fourths and fifths as "fifths," ignoring the octave displacements thus implied. For convenience this convention will be followed from here on.) One serious problem remains, however, which is a lot harder to eliminate or hide—that concerning the major third. To back up just a little: on our journey up the whole-tone scale, long before reaching the problem of the octave we find another discrepancy—another comma—this time between two 9:8 tones and a pure or "just" major third (with a ratio of 5:4). This "syntonic comma" is only slightly smaller than the ditonic comma we met above; it is still large enough to turn an otherwise sweet consonance into a comparative dissonance. (The ratio of the syntonic comma—that is, two tones less a pure major third—is 81:80; the math runs as follows: 9:8 x 9:8 = 81:64; multiplying by 4:5—the reciprocal of 5:4—results in 324:320, which reduces to 81:80.) If we substitute the slightly compressed major seconds of equal temperament for 9:8 (just) tones we are only a little better off; the major third of equal temperament is only slightly less dissonant than the Pythagorean ditone—the true technical name for the interval made up of two 9:8 tones. (Why musicians since about 1800 have been less disturbed than Renaissance and Baroque ones about the impurity of major thirds is a complex question. The answer has a lot to do with tone color—the impurities are more noticeable with certain timbres than others—as well as the changing role of the major third itself; it has come to be prized for its dynamic quality, which is even intensified when a "leading tone" or "tendency tone" is inflected toward its resolution.)

If we want to maintain the purity of the major third, we have only a few choices. One, called "just intonation," is to leave all but one of the intervening fifths pure, making that one bear the full brunt of the problem (and thus rendering it hopelessly dissonant, as well as producing a tone significantly smaller than 9:8—10:9, to be exact). On an instrument of fixed pitch (like a keyboard), no matter which of the fifths making up the third is made to be impure, it will be a bad choice for some chords, even within a single tonality. Thus, just intonation is really feasible only on flexible-pitched instruments (and the voice, of course), where the decisions can be continually renegotiated. Much more practical on keyboards is to distribute the comma equally over all four fifths, subtracting a quarter of it from each. The result, when extended to the complete octave, is the system called "quarter-comma meantone" temperament. ("Meantone" itself refers to the size of the major seconds, which represent a mean or average between the unequal-sized tones of just intonation.) Meantone temperament is far less restricted than just intonation, although it does impose some of its own limitations, particularly on a keyboard of normal design. Its limitations are due to its strong differentiation between enharmonically related notes, which is due in turn to the failure of three pure major thirds to add up to an octave. Thus, for instance, the note a♭—the octave of A♭—is higher than the g♯ three pure thirds above A♭ (i.e., top of the series A♭-c-e-g♯) by about a fifth of a tone. (The discrepancy this time is known as a "diesis.") Obviously both a♭ and g♯ cannot be obtained by the same key. On a normal keyboard with twelve notes to the octave, choices must be made; the usual "black-key" selections are C♯, E♭, F♯, G♯, and B♭. Another possibility is to provide "split" keys. Two usually suffice, giving an additional D♯ and A♭ (available from the raised rear halves of the E♭ and G♯ keys, respectively). Although meantone, like any temperament, is in the strictest sense achievable only on instruments of fixed pitch, its pure thirds and compressed fifths are basic to the tuning of many early woodwinds. Being somewhat flexible, however, the latter can in practice "untemper" the fifths and achieve something closer to just intonation.

Also often classed as forms of meantone temperament are those regular temperaments in which the major thirds are allowed to be somewhat larger than pure. (A "regular" temperament is one in which all usable fifths are of the same size; these include all twelve in equal temperament, but in meantone—in which the circle of fifths does not close—there is always one dissonant or "wolf" fifth.) These forms of meantone are named according to the amount by which the fifths are tempered: two-ninths comma, one-fifth comma, one-sixth comma, and so forth. There are also many "irregular" temperaments—ones that mix different sizes of fifth. These range from informal amendments to meantone (such as Praetorius's recommendation—*Syntagma* II: 155—that one slightly untemper some of the fifths of quarter-comma meantone in order to make G♯ usable as A♭ in a pinch) to various so-called "well-tempered" systems—"circulating" temperaments in which all keys are playable, but in which those nearer C-major (those more often used) are better in tune at the expense of the more distant. In discussing these systems some English-speaking theorists have painted themselves into something of a linguistic corner. Having made a rigorous distinction between "tunings" (in which the relationships can be described by ratios) and "temperaments" (which involve irrational numbers), they find the expression "well-tempered tuning" to be an oxymoron. (The distinction itself is ultimately more significant to theory than practice, by the way, since the irrational intervals can be approximated well enough by ratios that no one can tell the difference by ear.) Some resort to the somewhat odd-sounding expression "well temperaments," using "well" as an adjective; others call them "good" temperaments, keeping "good" in quotes to remind us of its special technical meaning. In any case, one of the most influential of these well-tempered systems is known as "Werckmeister III," being the third system offered by Andreas Werckmeister in his *Musicalische Temperatur* of 1691. (He had actually first published it a decade earlier in his *Orgel-Probe*.) Here the fifths C-G-D-A and B-F♯ are each made a quarter comma—ditonic, in this case—small; all the rest are pure.

These are the main types of tuning/temperament available to the seventeenth-century musician. There is no question as to the dominance of quarter-comma meantone temperament for keyboards throughout Europe during the first half of the century, and indeed in many places through the second half as well. This is not to say, however, that alternatives were unthinkable. Even some of the simplest transpositions strained at the limits of the system and were an acknowledged source of frustration for many. (For instance, when dorian on G is transposed down a tone to F, A♭s are required as notes of the basic scale, and D♭s may be needed as *ficta*; when instead it is transposed down a minor third to E, D♯s will certainly be needed as *ficta*. None of these accidentals is available on a normal, twelve-key keyboard tuned in the usual meantone configuration.) Retuning to suit the transposition (as detailed by Gian Paolo Cima [*Partito de ricercari, & canzoni alla francese,* Milan, 1606]) is possible for string keyboards, although the practice seems to have been unusual; it is impractical, of course, for organs. Split keys were quite a common solution (except, apparently, in France), but they are awkward at best and were unacceptable to many players. However, both the theory of equal temperament and its common use on fretted instruments had been recognized since the sixteenth century, and its use on keyboard instruments found some strong proponents in the seventeenth—albeit perhaps more among theorists (such as Mersenne) than performers. Notable among the latter, however, was Frescobaldi, famous for some daring modulations. But as an indication of the prevailing climate, his recommendation in 1640 to have the organs of Bernini's new apse in the Basilica of San Lorenzo in Domaso tuned to equal temperament was subverted; conservative attitudes prevailed, and the instruments were tuned to meantone.

The chief rivals to quarter-comma meantone in the latter part of the century were the less extreme versions of meantone (i.e., ones with thirds larger than pure) and certain irregular systems. Étienne Loulié (*Nouveau sistème de musique,* 1698) claimed that fifth-comma meantone was "better and more in use" than any other temperament, and his statement is echoed by some other writers. At the same time, however, the system known as *tempérament ordinaire* was an irregular one, in which the fifths *Eb-Bb-F* were made *larger* than pure. (It seems to have resulted from a fortuitous misunderstanding of Mersenne's unclear directions for tuning ordinary quarter-comma meantone!) In Germany, Buxtehude appears (from circumstantial evidence, at least) to have had the organs of St. Mary's, Lübeck tuned to Werckmeister III in 1683. Irregular circulating temperaments of this kind were praised in the early eighteenth century for the distinctive quality they brought to different keys, which are, of course, indistinguishable in equal temperament (as well as in meantone, for that matter, as long as its bounds are not overstepped). It might be argued, in fact, that well-tempered systems restored to tonality some of the variety of color lost with the passing of modality.

The seventeenth-century tuner would have had the choice between tuning completely by ear (counting beats) or by mechanical means— matching pitches with a monochord. The modern tuner has the same choice, except that the monochord has been superseded by the electronic tuning "box." There are numerous written sources giving instructions for tuning by ear. An excellent introduction is Mark Lindley's "Instructions for the Clavier Diversely Tempered" (*Early Music* 5/1 [1977]: 13–23). Much more detailed and thorough—dauntingly so—are the books by Owen Jorgensen: *Tuning the Historical Temperaments by Ear* (Marquette: Northern Michigan University Press, 1977) and *Tuning* (East Lansing: Michigan State University Press, 1991). The latter give exact beat rates for all intervals; these have been calculated for a pitch standard of a'=440 and have to be adjusted slightly for other standards. Also useful is Martin B. Tittle's *A Performer's Guide Through Historical Keyboard Tunings* (Ann Arbor, MI: Anderson, 1978; rev. ed. 1987).

Electronic aids also vary in thoroughness; the fanciest have several built-in tunings and can be programmed for a few more. But one can manage very well with the simplest ones that have a meter reading in "cents" (hundredths of an equal-tempered semitone). All one needs is a chart of the deviations (in cents) of each note from its equal-tempered value; these deviations can be extrapolated from sources such as J. Murray Barbour's classic *Tuning and Temperament: A Historical Survey* (East Lansing: Michigan State College Press, 1951; rev. ed. 1953, repr. 1961 and 1967; repr. New York: Da Capo, 1972). For instance, in Table 22, p. 26, specifying values for quarter-comma meantone, we find that *E* is 386 cents above *C*, or 14 cents shy of 400—its value in equal temperament. The meantone value for *F* is 503 cents, or 3 cents higher than in equal temperament. The only problem is that Barbour has centered his calculations on *C*; we need to center ours a little further to the right on the chain of fifths (on *D* or *A*, say) in order not to have too many of our notes come out flat. (This is easily accomplished by adding a constant positive number of cents to each deviation.) With *A* as our "ground zero," the deviations for quarter-comma meantone are as follows: *C*+10, *C*♯–14, *D*+3, *E*♭+20, *E*–4, *F*+13, *F*♯–11, *G*+7, *G*♯–17, *A*=0, *B*♭+17, *B*–7; if needed, *D*♯–21, *A*♭+24, *A*♯–24. The deviations for fifth-comma meantone (also centered on *A*) are instead *C*+7, *C*♯–10, *D*+2, *E*♭+14, *E*–3, *F*+9, *F*♯–7, *G*+5, *G*♯–14, *A*=0, *B*♭+12, *B*–5; *D*♯–14, *A*♭+17, *A*♯–17. Those for Werkmeister III (centered this time on *D*) are *C*+8, *C*♯–2, *D*=0, *E*♭+2, *E*–2, *F*+6, *F*♯–4, *G*+4, *G*♯=0, *A*–4, *B*♭+4, *B*=0.

One of the "hot issues" among early-music practitioners nowadays concerns the tuning of fretted instruments. These were assumed by most writers of the period to have been universally and inexorably in equal temperament. The reason has certainly been explained often enough: in order to produce the unequal semitones of other systems and at the same time offer the standard choice of accidentals, at least some frets would have to run "zigzag"—clearly impossible for the tied-on frets of normal lutes and gambas. However, just as some keyboardists sought alternatives to the prevailing meantone standard, some lutanists and gambists took pains to mollify the egregious major thirds of equal temperament, through both playing technique and adjustment of frets. Speaking directly to this question is Mark Lindley's *Lutes, Viols and Temperaments* (Cambridge: Cambridge University Press, 1984). As in much of his writing on tuning, Lindley here transcends the merely descriptive by making astute qualitative judgments about the musical effects of different systems on different parts of the repertory. (His article "Temperaments" in the *New Grove* remains one of the best introductions to the whole subject.)

See also "Tuning and Temperament" by Ross Duffin in the Renaissance volume of this series for many practical suggestions concerning this issue and others.

The importance of pure vertical relationships—and particularly the pure major third—to seventeenth-century musicians cannot be overemphasized. Clearly, any departures from purity would have been viewed, even by a Mersenne or a Frescobaldi, as a necessary evil, not the ideal. For modern musicians, used as we are to equal temperament—not to mention "tendency-tone" inflections—singing and playing using pure thirds definitely represents learned behavior. Of immense help here is practicing and performing to the accompaniment of a keyboard (particularly an organ) in quarter-comma meantone. Also helpful is listening to recordings of such instruments, concentrating on the serene consonances—the real raison d'être of this temperament—at least as much as on the melodic aspects that may first command one's attention. Woodwind players should be encouraged to obtain meantone versions of their instruments; rather than increasing one's burden (the usual fear), these actually predispose the instrument to better intonation. (One must, of course, help out a little bit by remembering to use the right fingerings—specifically those that differentiate between enharmonic pairs.) In the end, intonation is at least as important as timbre, if not more so, in recapturing the flavor of early music.

17

Pitch and Transposition

Herbert W. Myers

Interest in performing at historical pitches is a comparatively recent phenomenon. The acceptance of a'=415 as a standard for Baroque ensembles is barely twenty-five years old,[1] and of a'=430 for classical players, even younger. So well have these standards become established, however, that we easily forget the resistance they once met; the notion that we should forego the convenience of our hard-won modern standard was at first regarded as ridiculous by many leading specialists in early performance (as it still is by many traditionally trained musicians). But ultimately the profound effect of pitch on timbre was recognized, and adherence to low pitch has become something of a badge of honor among "serious" period-instrument ensembles for eighteenth- and late-seventeenth-century music.

Why, then, have performers of early-seventeenth-century music generally not demonstrated a similar interest in the historical pitches (particularly those higher than modern) of that era? There are various reasons, mostly practical. With one foot in the Renaissance, as it were, the early seventeenth century still depends somewhat on a Renaissance instrumentarium: families of instruments (particularly winds) whose pitch has to match and that collectively represent a large investment. Baroque and Classical music, by contrast, employ specialists on a small number of individual instruments, so that the economic commitment to a single pitch is not as great. Performances of early-seventeenth-century concerted works often involve church organs; they also often involve choirs, which are usually more willing to lower the pitch from accustomed levels than to raise it. (This observation is not meant as a denouncement of modern singers; as we shall see, aversion to singing too high was typical of many early singers as well.) But probably the chief impediment to the adoption of a special pitch standard for the early seventeenth century is the sheer complexity of the matter, making it difficult to come up with simple, practical, and universal solutions like those we have found for music of later eras. It has not helped that scholars have continued to wrangle over certain details, causing performers to give up and fall back on established modern conventions.

It is not that there is a dearth of information. Though there is nothing so absolute as modern electronic devices or even tuning forks (invented, it is generally thought, in the early eighteenth century), there exist many instruments from the period that are in good enough condition to give us a pretty accurate idea of their pitch. There are in addition numerous theoretical works and other documents that deal with pitch. But the instruments do not come with labels, so we do not know, for instance, whether a particular recorder was considered to be "in *C*" at one standard or "in *D*" at another; also, we cannot always know just how representative a particular instrument is of its time or place. Written records, on the other hand, treat primarily of relative standards, so that tying them down to specific pitches involves some detective work. The tendency to reason (or generalize) from small samples seems to have been as typical of humans then as now, accounting for some of the conflicting testimony among early sources (as well as conflicting modern accounts). It is thus necessary to examine as large a body of information as possible in order not to make the same kind of error. The most recent large-scale study of early pitch is a dissertation by Bruce Haynes: *Pitch Standards in the Baroque and Classical Periods* (University of Montréal, 1995). This is a thorough and intelligently reasoned work, whose scope encompasses both the seventeenth and eighteenth centuries. As Haynes points out, he has had an advantage over previous researchers, having benefited from the tremendous explosion of interest in—and practical experience with—historical instruments. Though scholars (including Haynes himself) will continue to work at details, his dissertation will undoubtedly be regarded for some time to come as the definitive word on early pitch. The present short summary of the seventeenth-century picture owes a great deal to Haynes's work.

Haynes has developed a clear and concise method of indicating pitch standards—one that will be adopted here. According to this system, standards near modern are labeled "~C" (the tilde meaning "about" or "circa"); those about a semitone above, "~C#"; those a semitone below, "~B"; and so forth. This system thus makes C the point of reference, rather than the more traditional a'. It is particularly apt when—as in the case of most Continental European standards—the pitch centers happen to fall near to notes of a chromatic scale at a'=440[2]; it breaks down when they are "in the cracks" (i.e., about halfway between those notes). Thus Haynes has adopted the use of a special symbol (β—Greek *beta*) to indicate a pitch standard between ~B♭ and ~B; this standard (at about a'=403) was a common and important one for woodwinds from the late seventeenth century through the eighteenth. (The entire "grid" of English standards seems similarly offset from most of the Continental ones, requiring a special nomenclature that will be explained below.)

This letter-based system helps one visualize transpositions (since it is similar in concept to our established nomenclature for transposing orchestral instruments). It also reflects appropriately the rather approximate nature of a lot of the data; when greater accuracy is demanded, vibration frequencies can still be used.

Pitch

Germany and Italy

Perhaps not surprisingly, it is Michael Praetorius who provides the most comprehensive discussion of pitch from the period. As he explains in a chapter devoted to the subject,[3] the mixing of all sorts of instruments together was a comparatively recent development, to which the disparity of instrumental pitch still represented a common and severe impediment. Nevertheless, he begins by acknowledging some of the reasons for having different standards for different media. First, as mentioned above, pitch affects timbre: "For the higher-pitched an instrument (within its class and type) is made, as with cornetts, shawms, and descant fiddles, the fresher they sound; conversely, the lower the trombones, curtals, bassanelli, bombards, and bass fiddles are tuned, the more solemnly and majestically they present themselves."[4] A second consideration is convenience: a low pitch is more comfortable for voices and stringed instruments, and a high one (although he does not mention this) may be better for certain wind instruments, since it eases finger stretches. A final consideration, implicit in his discussion of organ pitch, is economic: the shorter the pipes, the lower the cost (accounting, at least in part, for the trend in his day toward higher organ pitches).

Praetorius applauds the comparative standardization of organ pitch that has taken place in the princely chapels of (North) Germany. This pitch, known as *Chorton* (choir pitch), has risen over the years a whole step from its former level, and is now equivalent to those of Italy and England (although English pitch is just a fraction lower, as evidenced by the cornetts and shawms manufactured there). Some, he says, would like to raise the pitch yet another semitone; this is not a good idea, in his opinion, since the current pitch is already too high for voices and stringed instruments. Indeed, players commonly tune down a whole tone in order to avoid breaking strings, causing some inconvenience for other instrumentalists (who must then transpose) but making life easier for singers.

For this reason Praetorius likes the distinction, made "in Prague and some other Catholic choirs," between *Chorton* and *Kammerton* (chamber pitch). These pitches are a whole tone apart; the higher one— *Kammerton*—is equivalent to his North German standard *Chorton* and is

327

used only at table and for convivial and joyous occasions, being the most convenient for both wind and stringed instruments notwithstanding what he has just told us about its inconvenient height for strings). The lower one is called *Chorton* and is used only in churches, primarily for the sake of singers, who both strain less and sound better at the lower pitch. (Students of Baroque practice will notice that this usage of *Chorton* and *Kammerton* is the exact inverse of that of Bach's day, when the *higher* pitches of church organs were called *Chorton* and *lower* pitches were called *Kammerton*; see the studies by Bruce Haynes, listed below, for a detailed examination of pitch in Bach's era.) It would be good, he says, if organs could be tuned to this low version of *Chorton,* but he considers this to be impractical now that the high version (which he clearly intends to call *Kammerton* and to use as his reference pitch throughout his book) has become so well established in his German lands.

One other pitch standard figures in Praetorius's discussion, one a minor third below his *Kammerton* (and thus a semitone below the Prague *Chorton*). This, he says, is the pitch used in England formerly and in the Netherlands still for most wind instruments, and is the one used by the celebrated Antwerp maker Johannes Bossus for his harpsichords, spinets, and organs. While there is no denying that this is an advantageous pitch for harpsichords, flutes, and other instruments due to the lovely timbre it imparts, he says, it is nevertheless impractical to include instruments built at this pitch in concerted music, and one must stick by the afore-mentioned pitches, *Chorton* and *Kammerton.* However, the very low pitch (that is, the one a minor third lower than *Kammerton*) is much in use in Italy and in various Catholic choirs of Germany because of its suitability for voices. For this reason, music is often sung at this pitch through trans-position down a minor third, solely for the sake of the voices; to instru-mentalists such a transposition may seem offensive at first but is worth the trouble to learn to make.

The foregoing discussion treats of pitch standards in relative terms. However, Praetorius was not content to leave it at that, and he attempt-ed to specify pitch in absolute terms as well. Unfortunately, however, there is still some disagreement among scholars as to its exact level. This is certainly not the proper forum for an extensive continuation of the debate. Suffice it to say that there is a discrepancy of about a semitone between the two methods Praetorius chose to communicate his pitch standard: reconstructions of a set of little organ pipes according to dimensions he provided produce a pitch standard just a little below a'=440 (a'=430, say), while the pitch of a typical sackbut of Nuremberg make (with the slide extended by the width of two fingers, as he suggests) is just below modern B♭, or about a'=460. The latter pitch, it should be mentioned, is in better accord with the dimensions of most of the other wind instruments in his plates, which are carefully rendered to scale.[5] (Adding to the confusion are his occasional lapses in consistency; despite his best intentions he apparently sometimes reverts to local usage in calling his reference pitch *Chorton,* and he occasionally reports the pitch names of instruments according to lower standards instead of their "actual" pitches according to *Kammerton* as promised. One must sometimes take him for what he means rather than what he says, but getting two people to agree on the interpretation can be difficult. Still, however, the argument over a semitone represents real progress; forty years ago the interval at issue was a major third!)

The broad outlines of Praetorius's assessment are confirmed by surviving instruments and other evidence. Extant seventeenth-century German organs range in pitch from a'=450 to a'=501, averaging a'=474 (or ~C♯ according to Haynes's system, explained above). This range and average tend to corroborate both the comparative standardization at ~C♯ as well as the occasional push for ~D that his information implies. It appears that the majority of North Germans continued to refer to these high organ pitch standards as *Chorton,* although just a few seem to have adopted his terminology. On the other hand, South—that is, Catholic—Germans (such as Georg Muffat, writing near the end of the century) as well as Austrians refer to a *low* standard as *Chorton,* thus substantiating Praetorius's notion of the origins of his preferred system. (It is useful when contemplating this morass of conflicting terminology to bear in mind that *Kammerton* seems to carry no connotation of a low pitch in his day—nor indeed until after the advent of the redesigned French woodwinds that entered Germany in the 1680s. Praetorius was not merely inverting an established North German usage, as assumed by later writers; for him to have done so would have been both perverse and futile. Thus, even though his use of the term *Chorton* may be slippery, we can at least be sure about his meaning for *Kammerton.*)

Surviving German "ordinary" (i.e., curved) cornetts from the sixteenth and seventeenth centuries range in pitch from about a'=450 to 480, with the great majority falling between a'=460 and 470 (~C♯ in Haynes's system). Haynes has shown that in fact the one comparatively stable element throughout the period he studied is that of *Cornetton* (or *Cornettenton*—cornett pitch), apparently due to strong traditions of cornett building and playing. While *Chorton* in the North German sense might vacillate between ~C♯ and ~D (and even dip down—very rarely—to ~C in the early eighteenth century), *Cornetton* remained a relatively fixed standard at ~C♯.[6] At the same time, however, we have to recognize that the most common level for *Chorton* was also ~C♯, and that the majority of (North German) sources treat *Chorton* and *Cornetton* as equivalent rather than different. Praetorius himself once[7] equates *Cornettenton* with his *Kammerton*—further evidence that the level of the latter was ~C♯.

As we have seen, Praetorius also equates his North German standard with that of Italy, and indeed the preponderance of Venetian wind instruments from the period—surely his point of reference—are at pitches compatible with a standard at ~C♯ and thus bear him out.[8] However, a more thorough look reveals just a little more complicated picture. Northern Italian sources from his period and before speak of two pitches associated with the cornett, called *tuon del cornetto di mezzo punto* and *tuon del cornetto di tutto punto*. These terms might be Englished as "halfway (down) cornett pitch" and "all-the-way (down) cornett pitch" (or possibly "medium cornett pitch" and "total cornett pitch"). They differed, it seems, by a semitone; the higher of the two—*mezzo punto*—was by far the more common. Haynes has suggested, based on the pitches of extant Italian curved cornetts, that we can assume ~C♯ as the level of *mezzo punto*, putting *tutto punto* at ~C, or near modern pitch.[9] (Far more Italian than German cornetts survive. Italian ones of the curved variety tend to cluster around C and C♯, with scattered examples at ~D; those at ~C♯ represent the great majority.) The advantage to standards a semitone apart, as pointed out by Haynes, is that they can accommodate a wide range of performance pitches through simple transpositions of a whole tone. It is interesting to note that two different organs associated with Monteverdi before his tenure in Venice are said to have been at *tutto punto*: the organ at the cathedral of Cremona[10] (where his teacher Ingenieri was *maestro de capella*) and the one at the ducal basilica of Santa Barbara in Mantua[11] (where, it has been suggested, the *Vespers* of 1610 may first have been performed[12]).

Italian sources also use the term *tuono corista*—choir pitch—by which is meant a low standard, suitable for singers. (*Corista* by itself can also have the more neutral meaning of "pitch standard" or "starting place for tuning"; in modern Italian it has come to mean "standard pitch" or "tuning fork.") When a level for *tuono corista* is specified, it is most commonly "a tone below the pitch of cornetts" (meaning, presumably, a tone below *mezzo punto*), putting it at ~B, or about a'=415. This is very much the same level we have established for Praetorius's preferred *Chorton* (in the South-German sense); the similarity of both the names (*tuono corista*; *Chorton*) and their level is striking—and probably not coincidental, given the musical connections between Northern Italy and Southern Germany (as well as Austria) at that period. Where the pitch of organs was high (as, for instance, it was in Venice), *tuono corista* was achieved by organists through transposition. But organs were also often built to lower standards for the convenience of voices. Roman organs usually had credit for being the lowest.[13] That of St. Peter's (where Frescobaldi was organist, 1608–28 and 1634–43) was at about a'=484, or on the low side of ~B♭; several other organs are known to have been tuned to it. (Presumably Praetorius has Roman pitch in mind when he mentions that the standard a minor third below his *Kammerton* is "much in use in Italy.") One source[14] suggests that Roman organs were lowered to this pitch about 1600, having formerly been a semitone higher. In any case, an ecclesiastical standard at ~B♭ remained associated with Rome through the eighteenth century and into the nineteenth. The majority of Italian organs fall between the extremes of ~B♭ and ~C♯; in summing up the evidence of extant Italian organs, 1500–1680, Haynes writes, "Rome is the lowest at ~B♭, Naples and Florence both show ~B (Florence also shows ~C and ~C♯), and Lombardy and Venice show a similar range from ~C to ~C♯ (with Venice tending a little higher)."[15]

Though higher pitches were considered advantageous for instruments, at least some woodwinds were built to lower pitches, apparently for the convenience of voices—or, rather, for the convenience of the instrumentalists accompanying them, who would then not have to transpose. (Sackbuts could, of course, "crook" down, and strings could easily lower their pitch as well—although it is interesting to note that Antonio Barcotto, writing mid-century, specifically mentions violins as instruments that do better at high pitch than low![16]) Both mute cornetts and flutes are often cited as examples of such low-pitched woodwinds[17]; to these should be added Praetorius's *cornamuse* (tailless crumhorns, which were apparently of Italian provenance and which he says were at *Chorton*, a tone below *Kammerton*) and possibly some curtals.[18] In fact, however, rather few of the surviving mute cornetts are as low as ~B; the main cluster is around ~C—*tutto punto*, in other words.[19] Flutes, on the other hand, have large clusters at both ~B and ~C.[20]

It is tempting to see some direct connection between these earlier low-pitched winds and those of the later Baroque, but actually the evidence of low-pitched winds decreases as the seventeenth century progresses. The majority of both flutes and mute cornetts now extant come from sixteenth-century collections, and most of the archival references to winds at alternative pitches are similarly early. The popularity of the mute cornett itself seems to have waned drastically after the time of Praetorius; its rare appearances thereafter appear confined to Germany and Austria.[21] Both the *cornamuse* and low-pitched curtals were even more rare and short-lived. And evidence for pitch-changing crooks on sackbuts is meager after Praetorius. All in all, the trend seems to have been toward unanimity of pitch among the winds, as well as the strings performing with them in church. (Strings performing chamber music without winds would obviously have been free to choose any pitch they found convenient.) In Germany the standard remained some form of *Chorton* (in the higher, North German sense): usually ~C♯ but sometimes as high as ~D.[22] In Italy the instrumental standards associated with the traditional winds probably remained ~C and ~C♯; the former came to be known as *corista Veneto*—Venetian pitch—in the eighteenth century, and the latter, *corista di Lombardia*—Lombard pitch. Although the general lowering of Venetian church organs to ~C did not take place until the 1740s, positives—*portatili*—in Venice and other North Italian cities were already being built to vocal pitch nearly a century earlier according to Barcotto.[23] ~C may well have been the standard he had in mind as an excellent compromise, being "neither too high nor too low, so that every voice and instrument can adjust comfortably."[24]

England and France

Praetorius's knowledge of English pitch seems to have been based primarily on woodwinds imported from England, possibly augmented by information from itinerant English musicians in Germany. In any case, the actuality was once again rather more complicated than he realized. English church organs from the Tudor period through the early Restoration were often based on a bottom pipe of five- or ten-foot length, giving what was from the organist's point of view a C. This note, sounding between a modern G and A♭, was, however, used by the choir as an F. (The organist thus had to transpose when accompanying a choir, but played his own solo music "at pitch.") The choral standard thus established was known as "quire [i.e., choir] pitch" and stood at about a'=503, or midway between ~D and ~D♯. (The corresponding secular vocal standard—if there was one—would seem to have been about a minor third lower, based on a comparison of written ranges.) "Quire pitch" appears to have been a reference point for most English organs, for the majority of extant examples are at integral semitone relationships to it. Haynes uses the symbol "~Q" to represent it, with "~Q-½" then meaning "a semitone below ~Q," "Q-1" meaning "a tone below ~Q," and so forth. (As mentioned above, the pitches of this English "transposition grid" are offset from most of the Continental standards; the exception is ~Q-2, which—at about a'=401—is practically identical to ~β.) According to Praetorius, as we have seen, English winds were just a little lower than his *Kammerton* standard (~C♯), which puts them at ~Q-1, or about a'=448. As pointed out by Haynes, ~Q and ~Q-1 are compatible pitches, requiring a simple transposition of a major second to get from one to the other.[25]

Few if any English church organs escaped destruction during the Interregnum, but with the Restoration came a rebirth; in a ferment of organ building during the 1660s several examples of the traditional transposing instrument were produced, only to undergo replacement or extensive remodeling in the '70s and '80s. These changes, Haynes surmises, were occasioned by the adoption of the new French-style woodwinds. Surviving English winds from this period are mostly at ~Q-2 (=~β, the usual French standard at that time); the major third separating ~Q and ~Q-2 make for an awkward transposition. But most of the rebuilt or replacement organs were pitched at ~Q-½, a minor third above the winds; this is a much more practical interval for transposition.[26] Organs at ~Q-1 and ~Q-1½ were also common; the latter (at about a'=423) was identified at least once[27] as "chappell pitch" and became the dominant English organ pitch through the eighteenth century. Winds were eventually produced at this pitch (at which time it also became a common orchestral standard in England), but apparently not yet in the seventeenth century; ~Q–2 under the name "consort pitch" remained the principal instrumental standard well into Handel's time.[28] It may be possible to project this level for "consort pitch" backward into the earlier seventeenth century (before the French incursion), although direct evidence is lacking.[29]

Praetorius fails to mention French pitch standards, and unfortunately Mersenne—on whom we should be able to rely to fill in the gap—seems to have been more interested in pitch as an acoustical phenomenon than an issue among musicians and thus has little dependable information to impart. What can be learned from him must be gleaned in part by inference. He, along with other sources, mentions *ton de chapelle* (chapel pitch) as a standard associated with church organs.[30] The primary pitch of French organs from the seventeenth century into the nineteenth was ~Bb, except for a limited period (during the reign of Louis XIV) when, in court circles at least, it was raised somewhat. Mersenne also speaks of *ton de chapelle* as a possible instrumental standard, at least for the flute,[31] although the dimensions he gives for most winds (cornetts, shawms, curtals, recorders) suggest high pitch; in fact, most differ insignificantly from those of Praetorius. For instance, Mersenne's treble cornett (of the curved, "ordinary" variety) is just a little shorter than the corresponding one shown by Praetorius, and its size is consistent with the typical cornett pitch (~C♯) we have seen in Italy and Germany. Mersenne tells us[32] that the cornett was used "in vocal concerts and with the organ," and we know from other sources that it was often a regular member of French cathedral choirs despite the general ban on winds. It is thus perhaps significant that Mersenne's information on the cornett implies two different nominal pitches for the *dessus*: his chart showing the range[33] starts on c', while his musical example[34] specifies the more traditional a as the bottom, six-finger note.[35] An instrument in a at ~C♯ would indeed be in c' from the point of view of the organ (and voices) at ~Bb; perhaps Mr. Quiclet—Mersenne's informant about the cornett—found it more convenient to rename his pitches than to transpose down a minor third. (The effect on actual fingering would be the same in either case.) Mersenne's only comment on nominal pitch is to point out that the cornett in the hands of a skillful player is completely chromatic, and that its bottom note can thus be represented by any solmization syllable (i.e., the cornett can transpose at any interval).

Although the new woodwinds (Baroque flute, recorder, oboe, and bassoon) produced in the second half of the century are generally characterized by their low pitch, a few examples exist at ~C♯. Haynes reports the mention of a *ton d'écurie* (pitch of the [royal] stable) that might logically pertain to these; however, as he points out, a direct link is lacking. With the rise of French opera came a *ton d'opéra*, apparently quite stabilized at ~B♭—although the first real evidence of its level comes from the 1690s, after Lully's death. Slightly higher was *ton de chambre* (chamber pitch), the pitch to which *ton de chapelle* was raised temporarily during Louis XIV's reign (as mentioned above). The difference in pitch between *ton d'opéra* and *ton de chambre* was sometimes said to be a semitone. However, extant woodwinds of this early period generally cluster around ~B♭ and ~β; ~B is rare or nonexistent before about 1710. Haynes thus suggests that the level of *ton de chambre* was, in fact, ~β, and that the quarter tone separating ~B♭ and ~β might well have been *perceived* as a semitone.

As the new French winds found their way to other countries, they would naturally have brought with them their typical pitches. But the pitches that eventually took root were determined by local conditions. We have seen, for instance, how ~β became the dominant instrumental pitch in England apparently because of a serendipitous fit with established organ pitch. In Germany the first indigenous examples of the new French-style winds are at ~B♭ and ~β (as well as a few at ~C♯), but soon (probably by about 1700—and thus, apparently, earlier than in France itself) ones were being produced at ~B, too. The latter standard quickly became the "usual" *Kammerton* of the eighteenth century, having the advantage of a simple whole-tone relation to ~C♯, the prevailing organ standard. ~B♭, known variously as *Operathon, französischer Thon,* and eventually *tief Kammerton,* hung on for some time despite its less convenient relationship to the organ, probably because of its timbral superiority. ~ß might well have been found useful as a variant of both ~B and ~B♭ in a less stable pitch world than our own (as well as in concerts not tied to any organ pitch). The first indigenous Italian examples are at ~B and ~C—the latter a pitch not found in France until well into the eighteenth century. Being, like the earlier *mezzo punto* and *tutto punto,* a semitone apart, these woodwind pitches would have been similarly compatible with a wide range of organ standards.

Transposition

It should be clear by now that pitch and transposition are inseparable aspects—the yin and yang, as it were—of a single issue: to transpose is what you have someone do when you dislike the pitch! The mechanics of transposition are obviously the concern of the instrumentalist, even though the singer may have a greater stake in the result. The sixteenth century saw a radical change in the concept of instrumental pitch itself, for organ pitch—usually within one or two semitones of our own, as we have seen—became increasingly the standard by which the nominal pitches of instruments were measured. Gone by the early seventeenth century are most of the wildly disparate pitch standards (high by a fifth or more for shawms and rebecs; often low by a fourth or so for viols) implicit in treatises a century earlier.[36] Nevertheless, transposition for the sake of vocalists was still very much the norm, but the practice began to be phased out as the century progressed. The reason for this trend seems to be the changing nature of instrumental participation in vocal works. It is one thing to expect instrumentalists to transpose when doubling or substituting for vocal parts of limited range and technical difficulty; it is quite another when their parts are conceived with the specific capabilities and limitations of instruments in mind. In fact, transposition of *concertato* instrumental parts was comparatively rare. Most instructions regarding transposition—as found in both treatises and performance materials—concern the organist, who was often the sole instrumental participant.

The primary considerations were cleffing and mode.[37] The great majority of vocal polyphony of the sixteenth and early seventeenth centuries was written using only two combinations of clefs, one the "high clefs" (treble, mezzo-soprano, alto, and baritone clefs—G2, C2, C3, and F3) and the other the "low clefs" (soprano, alto, tenor, and bass clefs—C1, C3, C4, and F4). (Since the bass part in each case can have a larger range than the other parts, it is sometimes represented by a higher clef, that is, tenor clef—C4—in the high set, or baritone clef—F3—in the low one.) In the eighteenth century, long after the distinction had gone out of fashion, the high clefs were dubbed the *chiavette* (literally "little clefs" in Italian) by writers who correctly understood that earlier music written in these clefs needed to be transposed downward to fit vocal ranges; the low clefs were called the *chiavi naturali* ("natural clefs"). Theorists and composers from the period itself commonly call for transposition downward by either a fourth or a fifth, although other intervals are also mentioned. Among theorists the only holdout seems to be Thomas Morley, who recommends *against* transposing downward pieces in the "high keys" lest they lose the quality of liveliness that for him is their true nature. But even he implies that such transposition was the common practice.

Controversy has long attended the issue of the *chiavette*, but perhaps never so intensely as in the current dispute over their implications for parts of Monteverdi's *Vespers* of 1610. Here three movements—*Lauda Jerusalem* and the Magnificats *à* 6 and *à* 7—are notated in *chiavette*. About twenty years ago Andrew Parrott began conducting performances of the *Vespers* in which *Lauda Jerusalem* and the Magnificat *à* 7 were transposed down a fourth; about a decade later he published an article[38] explaining his reasons, pointing not only to the theoretical and practical sources calling for such transposition but also to the anomalies of range and tessitura that it resolves. For many performers and scholars his approach has been revelatory, but some have remained unconvinced. Stephen Bonta,[39] for instance, has shown that—as mentioned above—transposition of *concertato* instrumental parts of the type found in the Magnificat *à* 7 was, to say the least, abnormal.[40] In any case, it seems that the questions raised by anomalies of the *Vespers* cannot be answered absolutely for all time, but will remain as an impetus for further research and thought.[41]

A fourth is probably the only practical interval for transposition of the Magnificat *à 7*, given the virtuoso nature of some of the obbligati; however, transposition by other intervals was still commonly expected of instrumentalists at that time. Aurelio Virgiliano,[42] for example, provides charts for both viols and cornett-sackbut ensemble detailing transpositions over the range of an octave, from a second above written pitch to a seventh below. In both charts, playing a tone up, at pitch, a tone down and a third down is associated with music in the low clefs, while playing down a fourth, fifth, sixth, and seventh is associated with the high clefs. The exact interval might depend on various factors: the particular ranges of the parts (determined primarily by mode), the skill of instrumentalists in coping with additional sharps or flats occasioned by the transposition, and the temperament of keyboard instruments (which may demand retuning or leaving out certain notes in more remote keys). Praetorius, as we have seen, mentions transposing down both by a second and a minor third; the latter may turn out to be the more propitious interval for certain modes when one is dealing with the restrictions of a normal mean-tone tempered keyboard. For instance, his examples of downward transposition by minor third (ionian on *F* transposed to *D*; dorian on *G* transposed to *E*) are clearly preferable to transpositions down a tone; the latter would require *A*♭s—notes usually unavailable on a keyboard without split keys. (Dorian transposed to *E* would require *D*♯s—similarly unavailable—as *ficta*, but the lack of a leading tone can be better dealt with than the lack of a basic scale degree.) Nonkeyboard instruments are, of course, less restricted in this regard; nevertheless, it is interesting to note Virgiliano's annotation of the transposition down a tone for viols as *scommodissimo*—"most uncomfortable" (and that up a tone as *commodissimo*—"most comfortable").

In the *Syntagma* II Praetorius speaks of various transpositions associated specifically with woodwinds. The members of woodwind families were separated by fifths (except at the "outer edges" of some sets). He mentions one advantage of this arrangement: a quartet may be made up of any three adjacent sizes, doubling the middle member for alto and tenor parts; just by sliding down a size, as it were, a group could effect a transposition and produce a completely different timbre at the lower pitch. When a fourth size is mixed in, however, he suggests transposing either up a tone or down a fourth, as appropriate, in order to accommodate the bias of the higher instruments toward sharps. The real disadvantage of the system, however, comes when one combines instruments of five sizes, since the tonalities of the outer instruments are then separated by a major third, causing severe tuning difficulties. Thus, he suggests, makers should produce alternate versions of the upper members, built a tone lower; we see the beginnings of this practice in the *discant* recorder in c" he lists as an alternative to the one in d"♭, but it was later carried out in full in the "C and F" alignment of Baroque woodwind families. In the *Syntagma* III among suggestions for instrumentation of motets and other concerted pieces[43] Praetorius offers further recommendations for instrumental transposition. Many of these involve shifting the pitch down a fourth or fifth, making full use of the largest sizes of sackbuts, curtals, shawms, crumhorns, and viols then available. However, he reiterates his warning from the *Syntagma* II[44] against going too far in this quest for deep sonorities: some of the newly developed sub-bass instruments would allow transposition down a whole octave, but he has found that this produces an unpleasant throbbing sound from close intervals at such a low pitch. Better, he says, to stick with transpositions of only a fourth or fifth (or, in the case of the viols, to play the upper parts at pitch and put only the bass line down an octave).

Practical Considerations

Doubtless many readers will find all this information daunting in its implications for modern performance of seventeenth-century music, especially considering that the two pitches now most in vogue—a'=440 for Renaissance-style instruments, a'=415 for Baroque—appear to have been rare or in some countries nonexistent at the time. We need, however, to keep the question of pitch standard in perspective: important as it is, it is not the only—and certainly not the primary—consideration of a good performance. To be sure, the appropriate use of instruments at the now unusual pitches of ~C♯, ~B♭, and ~β should be encouraged, particularly among specialist performers. But many of the latter may find overriding practical reasons (as outlined at the outset of this discussion) for sticking with their accustomed equipment, at least for some performances. As in the past, the final performance pitch may be the result of a compromise among various conflicting needs. The most important lesson we may learn from consulting early writers may not always be the exact solutions they found, but instead the process by which these solutions were arrived at; we need to carry the same intelligence to finding our own answers. Above all, we must understand that no pitch standard is an end in itself, but rather the means to an end. It is silly, for instance, to try to replicate a particular historical pitch in the absence of the right equipment. For wind players, this would seem to go without saying, but it is an idea often not understood by string players. Among many modern players of the viol, for instance, playing at a'=415 has become *de rigueur*; few are aware that the sizes of modern viols have been chosen with modern pitch in mind, and even fewer are using instruments of the dimensions of typical seventeenth-century consort viols.[45] Playing at a'=415 on the smaller instruments demands the use of anachronistic overspun strings. By the same token, it is a misplaced priority to affect historical levels of vocal pitch without making use of historical types of voices. If we are really interested in getting it right, we have to go all the way!

NOTES

1. In this country, at least; it was instituted in Europe a few years earlier.
2. Haynes in fact centers his letter-based system on frequencies just slightly higher than those for notes at a'=440, using a'=470—an average for *Cornetton* throughout the period—as an anchor "less arbitrary than 440 Hz." The center for his "~C" is thus a'=443—a distinction insignificant for present purposes.
3. Praetorius–*Syntagma* II: 14–18. A recent article, Mitchell–Choral and Instrumental Pitch, has challenged Praetorius's assertions regarding the pitch of his day, the implications of which Mitchell finds inconvenient for a modern mixed choir. Mitchell is content to dismiss Praetorius in part because he finds him confusing, assuming that he is therefore confused as well. Needless to say, the present writer rejects Mitchell's thesis.
4. Praetorius–*Syntagma* II: 14.
5. See Myers–Praetorius's Pitch.
6. It is presumably unawareness of the differing Northern and Southern meanings of the term *Chorton* that has misled some scholars into placing *Cornettenton* a whole tone too high (i.e., ~D♯ instead of ~C♯), since South German and Austrian sources place *Cornettenton* a whole tone above *Chorton*; for example see Stradner–Cornetts and Trombones.
7. Praetorius–*Syntagma* II: 41.
8. He specifically refers to buying sets of recorders (like those he illustrates) from Venice; the majority of surviving examples are at ~C♯, though not always at the nominal pitches he specifies. (Among them, for example, are numerous c-basses, g-bassetts, and d-tenors—sizes he does not mention.) A much smaller number are compatible with ~C. Reed instruments, though somewhat less reliable witnesses, generally reflect pitches of ~C♯ or higher, with few (or none) at ~C.
9. See (in addition to his dissertation, Section 2) Haynes–Cornetts.
10. See ibid., 90–91, as well as Cesari and Pannain–*Istitutioni e monumenti* 6, xvi–xvii.
11. See Fenlon–*Mantua*, 104, 188. It might, however, be argued that the critical phrase *ha fornito l'organo di tutto punto* means merely "has furnished the complete organ" (since a modern Italian-English dictionary gives for *di tutto punto* "completely, thoroughly"). But the evidence regarding the Cremona organ refers unequivocally to pitch.
12. See Dixon–Vespers, 386–89.
13. Only one source mentions a still lower pitch: Doni (*Annotazioni*, 180–82) claims that the pitch of Naples was yet a semitone below that of Rome—an assertion not supported by surviving Neapolitan organs of Doni's era.
14. Ibid.
15. Haynes–*Pitch Standards*, 73.
16. Barcotto–*Regola*; translation and commentary in Picerno–*Organ Yearbook* 16: 47–70 (specifically ch. 16—p. 65 of trans.).
17. See R. Weber–Pitch, 8, and A. Smith–Renaissancequerflöte, 26. Having noticed the low pitch of several of the surviving examples, some authors and cataloguers have taken to stating their playing pitches in terms of lower nominal pitches (i.e., "mute cornett in [six fingers] g at a'=466," instead of ". . . in a at a'=415"). However, there is little evidence that the treble cornett, ordinary or mute, was ever *conceptually* in anything but a during the period, or that the tenor flute was conceptually other than in d' (after the early sixteenth century). Compounding the confusion, some have decided to give

nominal pitches in terms of a putative seven-fingered note, even though that note is lacking on flutes and most cornetts! One has to be careful in interpreting such reports.

18. Praetorius's *gedact chorist-fagott* (pl. 10, no. 4) is significantly longer in bore than his *offen chorist-fagott* (no. 3), suggesting that there may be the difference of a tone between them. Of surviving examples, only two (both *offen* and both in Vienna—nos. C200 and A194 in the Kunsthistorisches Museum) would appear from their dimensions to be at low pitch. (See Myers–Praetorius's Pitch, n. 38.)

19. Surviving examples range from ~B♭ to ~D, with well over half of them falling between a'=430 and 450. (This analysis differs just slightly from that of Haynes, who bases his on Tarr–Katalog; missing from Tarr's list are cornetts in Leipzig, which include four mute cornetts—two at ~C and two at ~B♭—that were once in the sixteenth-century instrumentarium of the Hofkapelle at Kassel. See Heyde–*Hörner*, 51–55, who curiously ascribes them to Bavarian workmanship despite brand marks generally accepted as belonging to members of the Bassano family of Venice.) These statistics thus do not support Weber's claim (Weber–Pitch) that "with few exceptions, [mute cornetts] stand a whole-tone lower than the 'normal' curved cornetts."

20. They range from ~A to ~C♯, with the largest cluster at a'=410 (on the low side of ~B) and a somewhat smaller one at a'=430 (on the low side of ~C). This assessment—by Haynes—is based on Puglisi–Survey; Haynes, however, has attempted to compensate for wood shrinkage, making his frequencies just a little lower than Puglisi's.

21. As pointed out by Bruce Dickey in private correspondence with Bruce Haynes, there are compositions calling for both mute and ordinary cornetts together (and thus suggesting an equality of pitch standard). See Haynes–Cornetts, n. 55 (100).

22. Buxtehude's organ in Lübeck, for instance, was (and is) at about a'=487 (Haynes–*Pitch Standards*, 274); it was described in the eighteenth century as being in *hoch Chorton*. That its pitch was exceptional is suggested by Buxtehude's purchases of various winds (and a special bocal for the great-bass shawm) "adjusted to the pitch of this organ." (See Snyder–*Buxtehude*, 373–75, 474, 476; Snyder mistranslates "Es oder Rohr" as "reed" [375].) Despite its high level, everyone seems to have been playing at the same pitch; there are no indications of transposition.

23. Barcotto–*Regole*; Haynes–*Pitch Standards*, 82.

24. Barcotto–*Regole*; Haynes–*Pitch Standards*, 86.

25. For the winds to play at ~Q they must play up a tone—an easy transposition. For the organist, who is already transposing up a fifth or down a fourth to play at ~Q, to play at ~Q–1 means transposing up a fourth or down a fifth instead—also simple transpositions.

26. Haynes treats of the interval between the "quire-pitch" organ and the winds at ~Q–2 as a major third; however, from the point of view of the organist, the transposition would be a minor third *upward* rather than a major third *downward*. Haynes's main point is still valid: given the usual choice of chromatic notes in meantone temperament (two flats and three sharps), a setup requiring transposition a minor third downward is still the better option, since it causes a tonal shift in the sharp rather than flat direction.

27. By James Talbot, writing ca. 1695.

28. There is little evidence if any to support the use of ~B♭ (the French *ton d'opéra*, about a quarter tone below ~Q–2) in England.

29. Haynes's main evidence for projecting ~Q–2 backward as the level for earlier seventeenth-century "consort pitch" is the continuity of terminology and probable continuity of viol-playing practice. As he points out, ~Q–2 is only a quarter tone above a'=392, the upper limit of Ephraim Segerman's estimate (based on the breaking tension of gut) of English viol pitch. (See Haynes–*Pitch Standards*, 340–42; Segerman–English Viol, 57; and Segerman–English Pitch, 14.)

30. Mersenne's confusion (or at least inconsistency) about pitch can be seen in his conflicting information regarding the level of *ton de chapelle*. In his discussion of organs

(*Harmonie universelle,* vol. 3, book 6, 325; 409 of trans.) he equates *ton de chapelle* with the pitch of an 8-foot open pipe; it is clear from the rest of his discussion that such a pipe was normally connected with the bottom C-key of the manual, just as we would expect. However, elsewhere (vol. 1, book 3, 169) he speaks of a 4-foot open pipe—which would, of course, sound at the octave of the 8-foot open pipe—*faisant le G re sol* ("producing G" [not c!]) at *ton de chapelle*. In yet another place (vol. 3, book 3, 143; 195 of trans.) he says that "those who sing the bass in a chamber" do not ordinarily go lower than a 4-foot open pipe, making this the effective sounding pitch of a written F (the lowest pitch of the piece he is discussing). Taken at face value, these last two statements imply a *ton de chapelle* about a minor third above modern pitch and possibly a chamber pitch a tone above that (although he does not go so far as to call it *ton de chambre*); they have been so interpreted by some, even though the implied pitch levels make little sense given what we know about voices.

31. He says (*Harmonie universelle,* vol. 3, book 5, 243; 312 of trans.) that flutes are placed at *ton de chapelle* for playing concerts; however, his exemplary flute was apparently at ~C rather than ~B♭; see "Woodwinds," this *Guide,* for a discussion of Mersenne's woodwind pitches.

32. *Harmonie universelle,* 274; 343 of translation.

33. Ibid., 273; 344 of translation.

34. Ibid., 277; 347 of translation.

35. In transmitting the musical example, the translation omits the references to fingering.

36. See Myers–Pitch and Transposition, 253–55. Although Praetorius was apparently the first to make organ pitch his explicit point of reference for all instrument pitches, almost a decade earlier Adriano Banchieri had given the tunings of gut-strung instruments in terms of keyboard ("organ or harpsichord") pitches in his *Conclusioni,* 52–55. Banchieri's repetitious insistence about his point of reference should perhaps serve as a reminder that it was not yet universal, and that there were still other ways of reckoning pitches. A case in point is the set of viol tunings given in Cereto–*Prattica musica*; these so-called "high" tunings, like those of the previous century, probably represent nominal pitches at a very low pitch standard (rather than what we—or Praetorius—would consider actual sounding pitches).

37. See A. Smith–Modus for an examination of this issue as discussed by early theorists. Although the article is in German, the detailed charts at the end (28 ff.) are perfectly understandable by anyone willing to look up a few key words.

38. Parrott–Transposition.

39. Bonta–Clef.

40. Parrott's answer to this and other objections to his performance solutions is to be found in Parrott–Getting It Right.

41. What is often forgotten in such discussions is the derivative aspect of some of Monteverdi's writing. It is well established, for instance, that the Magnificat *à 7* is based on that *à 6,* in which the only instrumental complement is the continuo organ. According to time-honored tradition, a parody remains at the notated pitch of the original; thus the notated pitch of the additional obbligato instruments of the Magnificat *à 7* results from a decision made long before their conception. By the same token, the few lowest notes of the cornett III part—sounding below the normal range of the treble cornett in the transposed version and thus regarded by some as a stumbling block for the whole transposition theory—are found in a *colla parte* doubling of a vocal line (in the final Amen). The instrument was probably assigned to the part as an afterthought, so that a few stray ill-fitting notes are not really all that relevant.

42. *Il Dolcimelo.*

43. Chapter 7, 152–68.

44. P. 46, concerning viols.

45. See Segerman–English Viols.

18

Dance

Dorothy Olsson

At all times and in each district, or Province, one has had a given dance, such as the English have measures and contredances. The Scottish have the Scotch Brawl, *the Germans the* Almain, *the Normans the* Bransles-de-villages, *the Bretons the* Triory, *or* Passepied. *The* Bransles de Poitou *come from the Poitevins, and the* Volta *from Provence. From the Italians come the* Gaillarde, *or* Romanesque. *From the Spaniards the* Sarabande *and* Pavane. *From the Moors the* Morisco. *From Paris, and some other places in France, we have a diversity of the* Bransles *and* Courantes.[1]

F. de Lauze enlightens us on the geographic diversity of dance styles, and his statement can also be applied chronologically, for this era saw exciting changes in dance technique. Based on surviving documents, two distinct periods present themselves, the late Renaissance (ca.1550–ca.1630) and the Baroque (ca.1670–ca.1725), with a transitional period in between (ca.1630–ca.1670).[2] That dance was an important element throughout this era is proved by the many literary references, costume and scene designs, and vast amount of music devoted to it. This chapter provides information to aid musicians and dancers in the performance of seventeenth-century dance and dance music, focusing on the late Renaissance and transitional periods. It should be remembered that what we know about dance in this era is highly colored by the fact that surviving manuals were written almost exclusively for use by the upper classes.

Courtiers and ladies were expected to be skilled in dance, as it played a prominent role at court: it helped to establish the formality of official occasions while ornamenting and glorifying the power of the nobility. On the social level, dance revealed the perceived strengths of the sexes—the power and dexterity of the male, the charms and beauty of the female. While courtiers and ladies honed their social graces (by flirting) and polished their dancing technique, the group dances were fun: they brought people together in an enjoyable way.

Dance in the theater was sometimes a political tool. Theatrical court entertainments were designed primarily to show off the wealth of the nobility. In English masques, Italian *intermedii,* and French *ballets de cour,*

FIGURE 18.1. Festivities for the aborted state visit to Rome of Prince Alexander Charles of Poland, 25 February 1634. (Illustration courtesy of Edmund H. Bowles; from Bowles–*Festival Books*, Fig. 122.) Spencer Collection. The New York Public Library. Astor, Lenox and Tilden Foundations. Used by permission.

dance played an integral role, and its importance to court society was enhanced by the fact that most of the dances were performed by courtiers themselves.[3] Courtiers continued to dance in theatrical productions until about the last quarter of the century, when professional dancers gradually gained prominence.[4]

A possible distinction between court and theatrical dance is that the latter included a choreographed entrance, while in social dances the dancers merely walked (after the customary honors) to their opening positions. Theatrical dances often presented designs that faced out toward the audience (and important dignitaries), whereas social dances offered patterns devised for the dancers themselves.[5] Theatrical dances were primarily group dances, either single-sex or mixed. Evidence for solo dances is scanty: Arbeau described the *morisque* (morris) dance for a solo man, and there is a reference to a solo in the Florentine *Intermedii* of 1589.[6]

Dance manuals principally describe social dance; precise information on theatrical dance is scarce. Among the few extant theatrical choreographies are four in Negri's book (see below) and Cavalieri's *ballo, O che nuovo miracolo,* for the Florentine *Intermedii* of 1589[7]; Arbeau's sword dance, *Les Bouffons* (see below), also has theatrical characteristics. For the later seventeenth century, the list of sources below identifies manuals that contain significant information on dance in the theater.

Sources

The sources that follow vary considerably in content. Some offer descriptions of dance steps, and a few provide complete choreographies. Some manuals also include music, illustrations, and rudimentary discussions of dance theory. Some of the manuals also offer advice on etiquette and fashion accessories—a reflection of the varied responsibilities of dancing masters. The manuals principally describe social dances for men and women dancing together. Most are couple dances, presumably performed by one couple at a time while others looked on; there are also several choreographies for three to six dancers. Processional-type dances such as the *pavan* were performed by several couples.

Sources are listed chronologically by country of origin. For complete citations, as well as information on reprints and translations, consult the General Bibliography.

France

THOINOT ARBEAU,[8] *ORCHÉSOGRAPHIE* (1588/89)

A cleric at Langres in eastern France, Arbeau wrote this treatise in dialogue format, nostalgically recalling dances popular in his youth. Arbeau's student Capriole[9] begs his master to teach him how to dance because as a young man, Arbeau had a "reputation for good dancing and dexterity in a thousand sprightly steps."[10] Arbeau favors his protégé with descriptions of the *bassedanse, pavan, galliard, tordion, la volta, coranto, alman, branles, Morris dance, canary, Spanish pavan,* and *Les Bouffons.* While these dance types were certainly performed at European courts, it is not known whether Arbeau was associated with any particular court, and therefore whether his choreographies are authentic court dances.

Arbeau's system of notation is unique: the music is printed vertically on the page and the steps are aligned with the corresponding note(s) of the music. While choreographic descriptions range from mere suggestions to some detail, *Orchésographie* remains an important treatise for the reconstruction of late Renaissance dance. It is the only known source for certain dances, such as the *pavan, alman,* and some *branles.* Arbeau also offers drum patterns for certain dances.

F. DE LAUZE, *APOLOGIE DE DANSE* (1623)

Although he gives no music and describes dances in a rather ornate fashion, de Lauze suggests several changes in technique: the use of turned-out feet, a gentleness of style, and deliberate upward and downward motions of the arms to accompany the steps. His steps are predecessors to those in eighteenth-century technique. De Lauze in fact shows contempt for some of the more intricate steps popular earlier in the century: he states that dancers "no longer like to mix among their compositions steps which look like those of a juggler, such as *fleurets, frisoteries,* or shakings of the feet; *pirouettes* (I mean several violent and forced turns), *caprioles,* nor even *demi-caprioles* if it not be in turning or finishing."[11]

De Lauze devotes considerable attention to the principles of dance and the procedures for the bow. He is probably the first dancing master to offer separate instructions for the lady; other manuals are primarily for gentlemen, with only cursory remarks for the ladies.[12] As the epigraph suggests, de Lauze was familiar with dances performed throughout Europe,[13] although he describes only the *courante, gaillarde,* and *branles* in any detail.

MARIN MERSENNE, *HARMONIE UNIVERSELLE* (1636)

Briefly describes the *allemande, branle, canary, courante, gaillard, gavotte, passamezzo, passepied, pavan, sarabande,* and *la volta,* but says that not all of these are in use in his day. Mersenne also provides some sketchy but interesting information on choreography.[14]

M. DE SAINT-HUBERT, *LA MANIÈRE DE COMPOSER ET FAIRE RÉUSSIR LES BALLETS* (1641)

Contains practical information on the structure, subject, airs (music) dancing, costumes, and machines of mid-seventeenth-century French ballets and *mascarades.* This concise source is unique in its description of the role of the "organizer" (stage director).

GUILLAUME DUMANOIR, *LE MARIAGE DE LA MUSIQUE AVEC LA DANSE* (1664)

A polemic against the Académie de la Danse, organized by dancers in disagreement with the prevailing performer's guild, the Confrère St. Julien. As head of this guild, Dumanoir rails against proponents of the Académie, who, he believed, were attempting to separate dance from music. Dumanoir asserts that dance cannot be separated from music.

CLAUDE-FRANÇOIS MÉNESTRIER, *DES BALLETS ANCIENS ET MODERNES SELON LES RÈGLES DU THÉÂTRE* (1682)

From his vast experience of producing numerous public spectacles (including equestrian ballets, pageants, triumphs, and other ceremonies), Ménestrier enlightens us on all aspects of these events, including structure, subject, poetry, costume, sets, machines, music, and dance. Known as the first history of ballet, this treatise offers many details about contemporary ballets, such as the *Balet comique de la reine* (1581) and *Le Triomphe de l'Amour* (1681).

ANDRÉ LORIN, *LIVRE DE CONTREDANCE PRESENTÉ AU ROI* (MS., 1685)

ANDRÉ LORIN, *LIVRE DE LA CONTREDANCE DU ROY* (MS., 1688)

These manuscripts present English *country dances* that had been introduced so successfully at Versailles in 1684. In an early version of Beauchamps-Feuillet notation, the dances are diagrammatically displayed and the tunes are correlated with the dance figures.[15]

MICHEL DE PURE, *IDÉE DES SPECTACLES ANCIENS ET NOUVEAUX* (1688)
Compares ancient spectacles (circus, theaters, triumphs) and "modern" entertainments (jousts, carousels, fireworks, *mascarades*, ballets). He discusses various elements of the ballet (subject, costumes, machines, music instrumentation, *entrées*, dance steps) and also mentions certain dance types (*courante, saraband, branle, gavotte, bourée, menuet*).

JEAN FAVIER, *LE MARIAGE DE LA GROSSE CATHOS* (MS., 1688)[16]
A significant source for late-seventeenth-century theatrical dance; provides both music and choreography (in notation unlike the Beauchamps-Feuillet system) for this stage production.

RAOUL-AUGER FEUILLET, *CHORÉGRAPHIE, OU L'ART DE DÉCRIRE LA DANCE* (1700)
An important manual on Baroque dance, the first known publication to describe "Beauchamps-Feuillet" dance notation. Feuillet also explains theory, steps (and variations), and arm motions. Two collections of notated dances are bound with *Chorégraphie*: fifteen theatrical dances by Feuillet, and nine ballroom dances by Louis Guillaume Pécour.

P[IERRE] RAMEAU, *LE MAÎTRE À DANSER* (1725)
Rameau provides detailed information about social and theatrical dance technique, the performance of steps, and their accompanying arm movements. No notation examples are given, but illustrations are supplied. Translated into English in 1728 by John Essex, *The Dancing Master.*

Italy

LUTIO COMPASSO, *BALLO DELLA GAGLIARDA* (1560)
An important source, the first known manual documenting the late-Renaissance dance style. No music is provided, but there are 166 *galliard* variations (ranging from simple to quite difficult) and instructions on performing certain steps used in the *galliard*.[17]

PROSPERO LUTIJ, *OPERA BELLISSIMA . . . DI GAGLIARDA* (1589)
Contains no music, but offers thirty-two variations (some of them virtuosic), as well as traveling passages, for the *galliard*. The technical vocabulary is quite similar to that of Compasso and Caroso.

FABRITIO CAROSO, *IL BALLARINO* (1581)

FABRITIO CAROSO, *NOBILTÀ DI DAME* (1600, 1605)
Caroso was a dancing master whose career probably centered around Sermoneta and Rome; many dances in *Il Ballarino* and *Nobiltà di dame* are dedicated to members of noble families in these cities. Presumably he was familiar with the social mores of the court, for he addressed many issues of etiquette and behaviour. Both of his books include prefatory material (dedicatory poems and a letter praising the nobility of dance), rules for etiquette and steps, and choreographies (seventy-seven in *Il Ballarino*,

forty-nine in *Nobiltà*).[18] The apparent dance types used by Caroso include: *alta, bassa, balletto, ballo, pavan, pavaniglia, passo e mezzo, galliard, tordiglione, saltarello, cascarda, spagnoletta,* and *canary.* Caroso offers social dances, mostly for couples, with a few dances for other combinations, such as three dancers, six dancers, and several couples.

Livio Lupi, *Mutanze di gagliarde, tordiglione, passo è mezzo, canari e passeggi* (1600)

Livio Lupi, *Libro di gagliarda, tordiglione, passo è mezzo, canari e passeggi* (1607)

Lupi's manuals, like Lutij's (see above), reveal a stylistic relationship with Caroso's, as the technical vocabulary is quite similar. The 1607 edition provides some music and his choreographic fare is more varied that Lutij's, encompassing variations for the *canary, passo e mezzo, galliard,* and *tordiglione.* The 1600 edition offers 150 variations and *passeggi* for the *galliard.*

Cesare Negri, *Le Gratie d'amore* (1602, 1604)

Closely follows Caroso's format. Negri's forty-three choreographies include *balletto, brando, ballo, bassa, canario, corrente, gagliarda, pavaniglia,* and *tordiglione.* His dances represent both social and theatrical types. Negri's dances are for solo couple, three, four, six, eight and as many as will, and he is the only Italian to include dances for two couples and for the *brando.*[19] This Milanese dancing master is more forthcoming than Caroso about the responsibilities of a dancing master, who in addition to teaching dance and choreographing might also teach fencing, and might accompany his master on military expeditions. Negri also provides us with important details regarding theatrical performances in which he was involved.

It is conceivable that the Italian dance style (through Negri and other Italian masters) was known in Spain. Negri's treatise was translated into Spanish in 1630, and Negri's patrons, the governors of Milan, were Spanish, as Milan was under Spanish rule at this time.

Ludovico Iacobilli, *Modo di ballare* (ms., ca. 1615–20)

A manuscript by a Jesuit priest that gives directions for certain dance steps and five dances, including a *gagliarda, spagnoletta,* and *canario.*[20]

Felippo de gli [sic] Alessandri, *Discorso sopra il ballo* (1620)

Alessandri mentions numerous dance types and hints of a newly developing dance style, echoing the view of de Lauze that intricate steps (such as those of Lutij, Caroso, and Negri) had fallen into disuse.[21]

Giulio Mancini, *Del origine et nobiltà del ballo* (ms., ca. 1623–30)

In this treatise, Pope Urban VIII's physician discusses the basic dance steps in use, popular dances, and the work of Caroso.[22]

England

"INNS OF COURT MANUSCRIPTS" (CA. 1570–CA. 1670)

So named because they were written by students from the various law schools. As they served only as aids to memory, they are deficient in technical information and only one includes music, yet they illuminate aspects of ballroom procedures.[23] Descriptions of steps are lacking, but there are choreographies (some quite abbreviated) for such couple dances as *pavan, galliard, alman,* and *measure.* The English dances have specific titles, as well as specific choreographies that differ from Arbeau's.[24]

JOHN PLAYFORD, *THE ENGLISH DANCING MASTER: OR, PLAINE AND EASIE RULES FOR THE DANCING OF COUNTRY DANCES, WITH THE TUNE TO EACH DANCE* (1651; LATER EDITIONS TO 1728)

The 1651 edition is the first major printed collection of English *country dances.*[25] As the subtitle suggests, the instructions for the 105 dances are set down in an abbreviated manner; each dance section is lined up underneath its corresponding musical section. A table briefly explains other symbols and three steps or step combinations.[26]

JOHN WEAVER, *ORCHESOGRAPHY OR THE ART OF DANCING, BY CHARACTERS AND DEMONSTRATIVE FIGURES* (1706)

A thoughtful and succinct translation of Feuillet's *Chorégraphie* (1700), describing theory, steps, and arm movements. No notated dances are included.

KELLOM TOMLINSON, *THE ART OF DANCING* (1735)

Tomlinson describes steps (including some theatrical steps) and their notation. Engravings show postures and positions of the arms and feet. He also mentions different dance types and their moods and tempos.

Spain

JUAN DE ESQUIVEL NAVARRO, *DISCURSOS SOBRA EL ARTE DEL DANÇADO* (1642)

Discusses the virtues of dance, its origins, performance of steps, dancing schools, requirements for a dancing master, and offers a listing of contemporary dancing masters. This treatise reflects the older Italian tradition: many of the steps—particularly some of the virtuosic ones—resemble Negri's. Yet in his call for a turning out of the legs, Esquivel Navarro indicates that dance style was changing, even in conservative Spain. He mentions several dances (such as *pavana, gallarda, folia, dos de Villano, chacona, canario, alemana*), but provides no music nor complete choreographies. He tells us that while certain dances (the *Españoleta, Bran de Inglaterra* [*English branle*], and *Turdion*) are no longer in fashion, it is still important for the dancing master to know them.

JUAN ANTONIO JACQUE, *LIBRO DE DANZAR DE BALTASAR DE
ROJAS PANTOIA* (LATE SEVENTEENTH CENTURY)[27]
Jacque briefly describes six dances (*pabana, gallarda, jácara, folias, billano*
[*villano*], *las Paradetas*), but provides no music and no explanation of steps
(which have the same names as Esquivel Navarro's).

Dance Style

While there certainly were regional differences, as de Lauze points out,
the late-Renaissance style generally maintained straight or natural positions of the feet and legs. There is a wide range of technique from simple flat-footed steps, to turns on one foot, to complex jumps and crossings of the feet in the air. The energetic and airy footwork found in many
of the dances reflects a characteristic joy and exuberance for dancing.
The upper body was held erect and few arm movements were used, save
for motions such as taking hands, clapping, and making arches; the arms
generally were not raised above shoulder level.

It is difficult to identify any particular national style of dance.
Distinctions can be made, however, on the basis of certain specific characteristics. English sources, for example, present dances that emphasize
floor patterns rather than steps. The Inns of Court dances are relatively
simple couple dances that move around the hall in processional formation with rudimentary figures.

It is tempting to believe that Arbeau offers "generic" choreographies
for the most typical dances of the late Renaissance, but as noted previously, we cannot be sure that his choreographies are valid for the French
court. This is not the case for the Italians, whose volumes are intended
for noble patrons. There are other key differences between Arbeau and
the Italians. Arbeau offers very few complete choreographies, while the
Italians provide approximately 150. Arbeau uses a unique notation system, correlating dance steps with notes of the music; Caroso and Negri
describe their dances in prose, usually correlating only the beginnings of
large sections of the dance with music. Arbeau's dances are rather simple,
even the *galliard* variations; the Italians present more difficult steps and
combinations. Complex *galliard* variations are presented in Negri, Lutij,
Compasso, and Lupi. Dance types in Arbeau are presented individually,
while the Italians often combine dance types into one *balletto* or suite.

That the latest dances traveled from court to court is confirmed by evidence that the treatises did so as well: Arbeau's treatise, for example, was
known in England.[28] The Italians, however, were perhaps the most successful at disseminating their dances. Negri lists Italian dancing masters
who taught at various courts throughout Europe. Italian books are found
in England and it is well known that Queen Elizabeth learned to "dance
high in the Italian manner."[29] Italian fencing masters, who may also have
been dancing masters, were in evidence in England ca. 1600.

During the mid-seventeenth century, clues for the transition between late Renaissance and Baroque styles are tantalizingly few and ambiguous, due to the lack of sources. The metamorphosis of dance technique was gradual, and embraced a marked alteration in the use of the limbs. By the end of the seventeenth century the feet and legs were turned out and the five positions of the feet, still used today in ballet, though with more fully rotated legs, were firmly established. While Baroque dance contains many springing steps, there was a decided softening of the motions (particularly in the prominent use of the bend and rise), masking a technique that requires considerable strength, balance, and control. Most of the nonspringing steps begin with a bend and rise (on one or two feet) and a gentle step, finishing in an elevated position on the ball of the foot. As in the earlier part of the century, theatrical dance borrowed from social dance technique but added more complicated movements such as leg beats, multiple *pirouettes* (turns), and other balancing feats that eventually surpassed the capability of the amateur dancer.

By century's end a well-defined system of arm motions based on the principle of opposition was in place. In its most fundamental form, the hand and arm on one side of the body circle up and arrive at their highest point as the opposite foot and leg finish the step. Thus the arm and hand balance the opposing foot and leg. This is essentially an elaboration on the opposition that occurs naturally when walking with freely swinging arms. Descriptions of this technique can be found in various sources, listed above.[30]

Interpretation of Dance Music

Interpreting dance music for performance can be challenging. For many musicians today, the most immediate concern is tempo, but understanding other considerations such as accents, mood, and movement characteristics is just as vital.[31] Knowledge of these characteristics is obviously helpful for instrumentalists when accompanying dancers, but can also be of use in interpreting dance music not intended to be danced. When a dance form is taken as a basis for elaboration or variations, the tempo may slow down. Knowledge of the strong and weak beats of the dance steps can help the musician place accents properly, as can an acquaintance with rhythmic tensions between the dance and the music, on a small level or at a larger phrase-length level. Naturally, recognizing the character of the dance aids in creating the emotional feeling of the music.

Many modern editions of these dances are available,[32] yet one must be wary: some editions misrepresent certain dances. The old edition of Susato's *Danserye* by F. J. Giesbert, for example, contains *galliards* that are incorrectly barred.[33] The reduction of note values from original to modern music notation can be misleading: transcriptions to $\frac{4}{2}$ or $\frac{6}{2}$ suggest that a dance is slow when this may not be the case.

Not all late-Renaissance dance music is regularly phrased; some pieces are intentionally irregular. The second section of Caroso's *balletto Nido d'amore,* for example, is five measures long and fits the choreography perfectly. Transcribed into modern notation, some of Arbeau's mixed *branles* result in mixed meters. One can even find examples of dances with both regular and irregular settings. Arbeau's *Branle de la guerre* contains what seems to be an extra beat near the end of the tune, but the choreography matches it exactly. Other settings of this piece found in Pierre Phalèse's *Löwener Tanzbuch* (1571) and Étienne du Tertre's *Septième Livre de Danseries* (1557) have not only regularized the ending by dropping the extra beat, but also altered the repetition scheme by beginning the second strain in the middle of a measure, thus shifting the accents and producing an entirely different feeling. Naturally, one cannot do Arbeau's choreography to these settings unless they are adapted.

Some dance sources have no music and some offer only monophonic tunes; others present complete lute tablatures, sometimes with the tune presented separately in mensural notation. Where no music is given in the dance source, one may substitute music of the same dance type. Generic dances such as *pavans, almans,* and *galliards* can be found in great number in period music sources. For pieces with only a single line of music, one may not always find polyphonic settings for them; indeed, a single-line tune may provide a welcome change on a program of otherwise polyphonic pieces. Sometimes a dance tune may be known under different names, as in the case of the *Spanish pavan* or *pavaniglia.* At other times, melodies may be similar but reveal diverse harmonizations in various arrangements. Although devoted to music before the seventeenth century, Howard Mayer Brown's *Instrumental Music Printed Before 1600* can be useful in locating dance tunes still current in the early seventeenth century.

Clues to instrumentation are also scattered among the dance sources. Arbeau mentions "violins, spinets, transverse flutes, and flutes with nine holes, hautboys and all sorts of instruments"[34] as suitable for the *pavan* and *bassedanse* of his youth. Although Arbeau discusses the use of a tabor for at least the *pavan* and *bassedanse,* there is some question as to the extent of drum accompaniment to late Renaissance dances. Other dance sources do not mention percussion, and iconographical sources rarely show percussion with dance bands,[35] but these instruments were certainly employed on ceremonial occasions and in some theatrical productions, for special effects.[36] Negri lists instrumental ensembles used in some of his theatrical dance pieces. For late-Renaissance dance, it appears that various instrumental ensembles were suitable, both wind and string, either one family of instruments or in broken consorts. By the middle of the seventeenth century, the emphasis seems to have shifted to the violin band; oboe consorts were also popular in France, and were employed primarily for ceremonial and theatrical productions.[37]

Obviously the tempo of a dance is governed to some extent by the dance type, but also by the physical limitations of the dance movements, so there can be a range of acceptable tempos. When meters change within a dance (as in the Italian *balletto*), setting a proportion between the different sections is a good idea (see "Meter and Tempo" in this volume). Musicians find it easier to accomplish a change of tempo when there is a specific relationship between the two sections, rather than an arbitrary indication such as "much faster."

Occasionally there are specific relationships between music and dance. For example, a recurrent musical phrase (or phrases) can be concomitant to a choreographic refrain or movement. In Negri's *balletto Bizzarria d'Amore*, the second and third musical sections accompany a dance refrain that returns after each of six dance figures. Choreography and music also have specific connections in the mixed *branle*.

The following is an annotated list of dance types popular through the seventeenth century.

Alman, allemande, tedesca.[38] While its name suggests that it may have originated as a German court dance, the earliest known use of the term for a dance is in an early sixteenth-century treatise from England.[39] A rhythmically uncomplicated dance, the *alman* is usually in duple meter, and frequently paired with an afterdance that transforms the melodic/harmonic material into triple meter.[40]

The only French choreography from the late Renaissance is Arbeau's. A line of couples dancing side by side, holding hands, progresses forward (or backward) around the room in what Arbeau describes as a "simple, rather sedate dance,"[41] performing easy walking steps that end with a leg lift. *Almans* are generally in a moderate tempo although they must be faster if, as Arbeau suggests, the dancers introduce little springs as in the *coranto*.[42] The few extant choreographies from around the turn of the eighteenth century bear no resemblance to the earlier form.

Ballo, balletto. In late-Renaissance Italian sources *ballo* and *balletto* seem to have been both a general term for "dance" and a heading for a specific dance. They were usually composed of two or more sections of different mensurations and dance types. Caroso's *Laura suave*,[43] for example, has an unlabeled duple-meter section followed by several sections in triple: *galliard*, *saltarello*, and *canary*. These dances probably developed directly from the fifteenth-century Italian *balli*, which also have unnamed sections.

Bourée, boree. The *bourée* may have originated as a folk dance and may have had connections with the *branle*; apparently it was danced at French court festivals in the sixteenth century. An early musical setting is found in Praetorius's *Terpsichore* (1612); interestingly, part of this piece, *La Bourée*, is concordant with an English *country dance* in Playford, *Parson's Farewell*.[44] Generally a simple homophonic piece in duple meter with a quarter- or eighth-note anacrusis (in $\frac{4}{4}$ time), the *bourée* was widely accepted in the seventeenth century and can be found in dance suites.[45] By the late seventeenth and early eighteenth centuries it became very popular as a discrete dance in moderate-to-quick duple meter with regular phrasing. There are no extant choreographies before the end of the seventeenth century, though there are twenty-four *bourées* from the early eighteenth century in Beauchamps-Feuillet notation.[46] The most prevalent step seems to have been the *pas de bourée*—a bend and a rise, followed by three steps.

Branle, brando, brawl. Originally a sideways step in the fifteenth-century *bassedanse*, the *branle* presumably adopted its name from the French *branler* (to sway), which describes the characteristic back-and-forth motion of the dance. As a discrete dance it came into its own around the beginning of the sixteenth century. In 1611 Randle Cotgrave defined the *branle* ("brawle") as a dance "wherein many (men, and women) holding by the hands sometimes in a ring, and otherwhiles at length, move all together."[47]

From the sixteenth century into the eighteenth, *branles* were grouped together in suites and used to open formal balls. Couples joined the line according to their rank, and this established the performance order of the subsequent couple dances (*danse à deux*). The components of the *branle* suite changed somewhat over time: according to Arbeau, it begins with double and single *branles*, followed by the *gay branle* and the *branles of Burgundy* (*Champagne*). By the early and mid-seventeenth century, the order seems to have been *simple, gay, poitou, double poitou, montirand*, and *gavotte*.[48]

We are fortunate to have choreographies and music for twenty-four *branles* in Arbeau. After de Lauze, whose descriptions are difficult to decipher, there are no known choreographies for group *branles*.[49] The *brando* may represent the Italianate form of the French *branle* in musical sources, but the only Italian choreographies (four in Negri) bear little resemblance, except that like the French *branle* suites they are group dances in several sections.[50]

Arbeau's mixed (*couppez*) *branles* are in mixed meters, created by the addition of choreographic and musical motifs. He cautions that the dancer know the mixed *branle* tunes well—helpful advice, for the music really does suggest choreographic changes. In Arbeau's *Pinagay branle*, for example, each time the musical motif of ¢♩♩♩ occurs, it corresponds to a jump and kick. Regional *branles* are named according to their place of origin, such as the *Poitou*, danced by the Poitevins, or the "Scottish," from Scotland. Mimed (*morguez*) or gestural versions such as the *Maltese branle* may have been originally devised for court masquerades.

Branles vary in tempo (sedate to very quick, according to Arbeau), and in meter (duple, triple, and mixed), and phrase lengths vary with the choreography. The *double branle* and *branles of Burgundy* (*Champagne*) are in duple meter, and have a strong first beat and a weak second beat. This coincides with the choreography of stepping in one direction and closing the step (or joining the feet together). While the *double branle* has "regular" phrases of four or eight measures, the simple *branle*, also in duple meter, has phrase lengths of three or six measures to accommodate the choreography. Music for the *Burgundian branle* occasionally has irregular phrase lengths, although no irregularities are suggested in the choreography. Generally in triple meter, the *branle gay* requires a lively tempo to facilitate jumped kicks. Arbeau implies that in this basic *branle* suite the dances progressively accelerate in tempo: the "elderly . . . dance the double and single *branle* sedately, the young married folk . . . dance the gay *branle* and the youngest of all . . . nimbly trip the *branles* of Burgundy."[51]

Canary, canario, canarie. A dance that according to Arbeau contained passages that are "strange and fantastic with a strong barbaric flavour,"[52] the *canary* first appeared in musical sources in the mid-sixteenth century. Although said to originate from the Canary Isles, Arbeau himself preferred to believe that it derived from a court masquerade in which dancers imitated the kings and queens of Mauretania. According to him, a young man and his lady partner take turns dancing before each other in variations—a form found also in Italian dances sources. Caroso, Negri, and Lupi provide variations for the *canary,* which could be a discrete dance but also formed a section in some *balletti.* The steps utilize many foot actions: scraping the foot along the floor and stamping the toes, heels, or entire foot. The lively *canary* persisted into the eighteenth century, primarily as a theatrical dance; extant choreographies reveal an intricate style with many springing steps.[53]

Canaries in duple or triple meter can be found in sixteenth- and early-seventeenth-century musical sources. The typical early form was a short tune of two phrases with fixed melody and harmony, reminiscent of an ostinato pattern. Later in the period, the *canary* was freer in melody and harmony; it is often found in compound duple meter, and occasionally appears in Baroque suites.

Chaconne, chacona, chacoon. First appearing at the beginning of the seventeenth century in Latin America and Spain as a ribald dance-song, the *chaconne*'s obscene character initially prevented its use at court. It was eventually toned down and accepted; Esquivel Navarro offers the first choreographic description, though it is not a complete dance. The musical structure, a set of continuous variations in triple meter played over a repeating harmonic scheme, resembles the *passacaglia.* In France the *chaconne* was tempered into a slow theatrical dance of noble character, slightly faster than the *passacaglia.* Most of the Baroque *chaconne* choreographies are lengthy solo dances.[54]

Coranto, corrente, courante. The *coranto* first appears in music prints in the mid-sixteenth century and continues through the middle of the eighteenth. The name (from It., *correre,* to run), signifies quickness; Arbeau characterizes it as "helter-skelter,"[55] and deemed it a jovial dance occasionally accompanied by a flirtatious game. The reconstruction of the *coranto* as given in Arbeau is unclear, but it is a quick, springing dance. Negri's *La Correnta* also uses steps with little jumps. The descriptions by Arbeau and Negri reflect the faster type of *corrente*.

The Italian *corrente* remained in fast triple meter, generally homophonic, with simple harmonies and rhythms,[56] but French composers began to explore the rhythmical and metrical ambiguities of the triple meter, ultimately creating a slower, more contrapuntal dance, the *courante*. De Lauze's description suggests that a change is taking place; although he characterizes the tempo as somewhat quick, its character is gentler. Mersenne (1636) claims that it was the most widely performed dance in France. Several decades later, King Louis XIV made the *courante* popular with his exquisite performances of this slow majestic dance; at his court, the *courante* was apparently danced following the *branles*.[57] From the mid-seventeenth century the *courante* became a part of the suite, falling between the *allemand* and the *saraband*.

Country dance, contredanse. The English *country dances* documented in Playford's *English Dancing Master* (1651) were probably adapted for court use from earlier peasant dances. Extremely popular in England throughout the seventeenth and eighteenth centuries, English *country dances* are usually in duple or compound meter[58] and have a range of tempos according to their choreographies and the dancers performing them. These were set dances for four or more people in forms such as a square for four, a circle for six, a square for eight, and a longways set for many couples. It is this latter form that retained popularity in England into the late seventeenth century and after.[59]

Steps are unimportant; it is the lovely figures (floor designs created by the paths of the dancers) and the social relationships of the dancers that made these dances so popular. When introduced at the French court in the 1680s, the dance form was eventually altered from its usual longways set into a square for eight. The French also added Baroque-style steps (which require a slower tempo) and called the new form *contredanse*.

Entrée, entrée grave. In mid-seventeenth century French ballet, an *entrée* was a group of dances related by subject. At century's end the *entrée* (*entrée grave*) was a slow duple-meter dance replete with dotted rhythms; it was a technically complex yet majestic dance, usually for a solo man.

Forlana, forlane. This may have been a folk dance associated with northern Italy, particularly the Friuli region.[60] An early musical example is the *Ballo furlano l'arboscello* in Phalèse (1583), a duple-meter setting.[61] No choreographies exist until the end of the late seventeenth and early eighteenth centuries, when it was quite popular as a moderately quick court dance in compound duple meter.[62]

Galliard, galliarde, gagliarda, cinque passi. The *galliard*, first mentioned in an essay by Vincenzo Calmeta from 1497–1500,[63] may also have originated in northern Italy. As a musical form it first appears in prints by Attaingnant about 1530, where it is one of several afterdances to the *pavan*[64]; later, it appears either as a discrete dance or paired with another dance such as the *pavan* or *passamezzo*. Often, it is derived melodically from a *pavan* as Morley explained in 1597.[65] The music of the sixteenth- and early seventeenth-century *galliard* is usually in a straightforward homophonic triple-meter setting with regular phrasing, sometimes with a hemiola just before the end of a phrase.

The *galliard* is a couple dance in which the gentleman and the lady entertain each other with variations, as found in Arbeau, Caroso, Negri, Lupi, and Lutij. Arbeau's basic *galliard* consists of a pattern of four kicks in the air and a cadence (a switch of feet in the air then landing on both feet); this sequence was called the "five steps" (*cinq pas, cinque passi*). One *galliard* pattern is performed in six counts with an emphasis on the fourth beat: **3** ♩♩♩|♩♩♩ Variations could range from one simple pattern of three or five steps (fitting into six beats) to complex sequences of twelve patterns; each variation ends with a cadence and is immediately executed again beginning on the opposite leg.

Tempos vary according to the choreography and the dancers; even Arbeau states that "it needs must be slower for a man of large stature than for a small man, inasmuch as the tall one takes longer to execute his steps and in moving his feet backwards and forwards."[66] The correct tempo is also crucial to a cousin of the *galliard, la volta*, in which the gentleman lifts and turns the lady in the air.[67] Musicians should defer to the dancers; once a tempo is determined, it must remain constant. A tempo that is too fast will not allow for a full, sweeping lift; conversely, a sluggish tempo provides the gentleman with the formidable challenge of keeping his lady aloft for long durations.

Through the seventeenth century the tempo gradually decelerated. De Lauze gives a fleeting indication of a softening of the style in this dance that may have slowed the tempo. By 1676 Thomas Mace regards the *galliard* as a sober dance in slow triple meter.[68] There are only a few examples of notated *galliards*[69] in the Baroque style and these often contain the *pas de gaillarde*, a step that in one version[70] comprises a soft jump, a plain step, a rise, and a fall.

Gavotte. As a French court dance and instrumental music form, the *gavotte* was popular from the late sixteenth through the late eighteenth centuries. Arbeau provides the first choreographic description of the dance, stating that *gavottes* are "a miscellany of double branles."[71] Arbeau's *gavotte* is a quick duple-meter dance with springing steps; passages from the *galliard* may be inserted as one pleases. While it is a group dance, Arbeau states that couples may take turns performing some passages in the center, followed by kissing all the dancers of the opposite sex. Kissing dances were also known in England.[72]

Most seventeenth-century *gavottes* are in duple meter, with a fairly simple homophonic texture. Although the *gavotte* is still mentioned in Arbeau and even at the end of the seventeenth century as closing *branle* suites, it also evolved into a separate court dance for a couple.[73] Still in duple meter, it now characteristically began with an upbeat in the middle of the measure.

Gigue, jig. The *gigue* may have originated in the British Isles, where it had been known as a popular dance from the fifteenth century; literary works describe the early *jig* as a lively bawdy dance with pantomime and complex footwork. In seventeenth-century England it was a song-and-dance number associated with improvised comedies, called *jiggs.* Musical examples through the seventeenth century generally exhibit straightforward homophonic textures in binary form. Most are in compound duple meter, although there are some duple-meter examples. Like the *coranto,* the *gigue* developed into two types by the end of the seventeenth century. In Italy the regular phrasing and homophonic texture of a lively dance in $\frac{12}{8}$ time was retained, while in France it took on a moderately fast tempo in $\frac{6}{4}$, $\frac{3}{8}$, or $\frac{6}{8}$ meter, the texture more imitative, sometimes fugal, with blurred phrasing. In the Baroque period it was a standard element in the dance suite, following the *allemande, courante,* and *saraband.* There are no extant choreographies from earlier than the end of the seventeenth century; notated *gigues* are lively dances with many springing steps.[74]

Hornpipe. A dance form of English origin. Musical examples and literary references date from the sixteenth century and there were several types: a solo dance, a rustic round dance, and a longways *country dance.* No choreographies exist prior to the late seventeenth century, with examples in the *country dance* and also in Baroque dance style. At this time the most common *hornpipe* was in $\frac{3}{2}$ meter with regular phrases and syncopated rhythms.

Loure. Also known as the slow *gigue,* the *loure* became popular in the late seventeenth century, predominantly as a virtuosic theater dance. It is either in a broad $\frac{3}{4}$ or $\frac{6}{4}$ meter and like the French-style *gigue* employs contrapuntal texture with irregular phrasing. *Loure* choreographies are extant only in Baroque dance sources.[75]

Matachin, morris, moresca. Popular throughout Europe between the sixteenth and eighteenth centuries, the *matachin* was a mock battle dance for a group of men. Arbeau's *Les Bouffons* remains the only known choreography for this skilled sword dance, yet another type was also current. Negri and others allude to grotesque elements in a *matachin* for fools; this type may have been related to the *morris dance* or *moresca.* The *moresca,* probably from Moorish sources, has an exotic quality. Arbeau recalls seeing *moresca* dancers with blackened faces, wearing bells attached to leggings; his choreography has heel-beating movements. Some elements are suggestive of the *morris dances* of England. Arbeau's music for the *moresca* is in duple meter; Mersenne's *moresque* in triple meter, but he provides no description.

Measure. The *measure* is known in England from the mid-sixteenth through the late seventeenth century. The term seems to have derived from the *mesure* or section of the fifteenth-century *bassedanse*.[76] Choreographies appear only in the Inns of Court manuscripts, where (in three of these sources) the term is applied to all the dances (including those called *alman* and *pavan*) described therein. These are relatively short couple dances with simple steps; most of them process around the room and some have floor patterns also found in the English *country dance*.[77] *Measures* employ duple or compound duple meter; some dances have hopped steps, requiring a quicker tempo.

Menuet, minuet, minuetto. The "queen" of court dances for over 150 years (from the mid-seventeenth century to the late eighteenth), the *menuet* is known primarily as a Baroque social dance. Its origins are difficult to ascertain: it may have derived from the early-seventeenth-century *branle à mener*.[78] As a court dance it appears to have been introduced in France in the 1660s; musical examples survive from this period as well. The *menuet* was an elegant, refined dance in moderate to lively triple time, with one couple at a time performing in the center of the room.[79] Choreographies begin to surface only late in the seventeenth century with the Favier manuscript and in Beauchamps-Feuillet notations.[80]

Musically, the *menuet* is characterized by a rather simple homophonic texture and binary form. From eighteenth-century dance sources we know that the *pas de menuet* took six beats, or two measures, of music. While the music is accented at the beginning of each measure, the basic *menuet* step[81] emphasizes beats one and three of its six-beat pattern, creating a wonderful cross-rhythm with the music. Another cross-rhythm occurs on a somewhat larger scale as dancers occasionally move in twelve-measure phrases against the eight-measure phrases of the music. The *menuet* was included in some Baroque dance suites.

Passacaglia, passacaille. The *passacaglia* was a lengthy Baroque theatrical dance in moderate triple meter.[82] The music for the *passacaglia*, like the *chaconne*, consists of continuous variations, usually on an ostinato bass.

Passo e mezzo, passamezzo, passing measures. Related to the *pavan*, the *passamezzo* is a duple-meter piece, played over a ground bass, most usually the *passamezzo antico* or *moderno*. Early examples exist in musical sources from the 1530s. Continuing in popularity into the seventeenth century, it was often paired with a triple-meter dance such as a *galliard* or *saltarello*. In dance sources it is a discrete dance in which a couple alternates between dancing together and performing variations for each other. Some of the variations presented by Caroso and Lupi are quite complex. Arbeau indicates that the *passamezzo* was quicker than the pavan.[83]

Passepied, paspy. The *passepied* may have begun as a *branle* from Brittany. Arbeau's *branle*, the *Triory de Bretagne*, was also called the *passepied*, a term that appears in other sixteenth-century sources.[84] In Arbeau and Mersenne it is a rapid duple-meter dance. But by the end of the seventeenth century it was in triple; by this time, it had evolved into a faster version of the *menuet*. It uses essentially the same steps as the *menuet*, but because of the faster tempo, the interest lies not so much in the steps and the cross-rhythms but in the floor patterns created by the dancers.[85]

Pavan, pavana, pavin. The term may be of either Italian or Spanish origin.[86] Musical examples appear early in the sixteenth century.[87] This slow duple-meter dance is usually followed by a triple-meter afterdance constructed from the same melodic and harmonic material[88]; the most common pairing ca. 1600 was the *pavan-galliard.* Ensemble *pavans* are generally in homophonic texture with two to four sections. Some early seventeenth-century *pavans* exhibit irregular phrase structure, and the profuse embellishment in one or more lines may point to the usage of the dance form as "art" music, no longer intended for the dance floor. As a social dance the *pavan* is found in German music sources until about 1620, but its use in the court setting was on the wane from the beginning of the century.

The first known choreography of the *pavan* is *Pavana Matthei,* from Caroso's *Il Ballarino* (1581); the *pavana* section is brief and untitled. Arbeau gives the choreography for the presumably "generic" *pavan,* a slow dance of noble character for couples processing around the room. Arbeau provides the accompanying drum beat: ¢ ♩ ♩♩

Although the *pavan* lost its popularity early in the seventeenth century, Favier makes use of the form in his 1688 *mascarade,* and two other notated *pavans* exist from the end of the period.[89]

Pavaniglia, Spanish pavan, Pavan d'Espagne. When most musicians are asked to play a *Spanish pavan* they respond with the same slow speed of a *pavan.* But Arbeau's choreography, which contains jumped kicks, requires a sprightly tempo. In both Caroso and Negri the choreographies for the *pavaniglia* are couple dances with often elaborate variations. Popular from the late sixteenth through the mid-seventeenth century, the duple-meter *pavaniglia* was based on the melodic and harmonic structure of a typical chordal scheme.

Rigaudon, rigadoon. The *rigaudon* was popular in the late seventeenth and eighteenth centuries, musically and choreographically very similar to the *bourée.* It was a moderately quick duple-meter piece with regular phrasing; examples in compound duple meter occasionally appear. In theatrical settings it was often associated with sailors or pastoral characters. A number of choreographies are extant, by Favier as well as in Beauchamps-Feuillet notation.[90]

Saltarello, saltarelle. The *saltarello* first appeared as an instrumental dance form in the late fourteenth century; in the fifteenth century it was related to the *bassedanse* and *ballo,* and also existed as a specific step pattern. In most sixteenth-century musical sources, the *saltarello* is a triple-meter afterdance to the *pavan* or *passamezzo.* Perhaps because of this pairing, and because musically the *saltarello* and the *galliard* are almost identical, the two dances have been regarded as identical,[91] but choreographically this is not the case. In Caroso's examples the *saltarello* is a discrete section succeeding the *galliard* section in *balletti.* In his *saltarelli* the couple dances together rather than perform alternating variations as in the *galliard,* and there are no *galliard* steps, but rather combinations of other steps.[92] As a court dance, the *saltarello* lost favor after the early part of the seventeenth century, although stylized music continued to appear; after a long hiatus, it returned at the end of the century as an adaptation of a popular folk dance.[93] The term is still used today for an Italian folk dance.

Saraband, zaravanda. The origins of this bawdy dance-song from Latin America and Spain have been well documented.[94] Even though performance of this lascivious dance was prohibited in late-sixteenth-century Spain, its practice continued and musical examples proliferated. Many examples were written for Spanish guitar, which along with castanets were linked to the performance of the dance. Seventeenth-century French composers such as Lully and Campra exploited its colorful character in theatrical works; a few early examples appear in Praetorius in 1612. Like the *coranto,* two distinct types of the *saraband* emerged over the course of the seventeenth century: a faster tempo version favored in Italy, Spain, and England and a slower version preferred in France and Germany. In Baroque dance suites it was usually the third movement, following the *allemande* and *courante.* Unfortunately, there are no choreographic descriptions of the dance until the end of the century.[95] As a social dance it is characterized by slow sustained steps although hops and leaps are occasionally found; theatrical *sarabands* are more technically demanding.

Spagnoletta, espagnolette. Numerous examples of this triple-meter tune and ground in musical sources from the mid-sixteenth century to the mid-seventeenth century attest to its popularity, yet there are only a few known choreographies, in Caroso and Negri.[96] These are pieces in which the dancers (two, three, or four) perform together with some solo passages. Apart from its name, there is insufficient evidence to suggest that the dance itself is of Spanish provenance.[97]

Tordion, tordiglione. The *tordion* is first mentioned in a late fifteenth-century literary source; in the early sixteenth century it was popular as an afterdance to the *bassedanse.* Compared musically to the *galliard,* it has two or three repeated eight-measure sections in triple time. Choreographically the *tordion* is equated with the *galliard* except that, as Arbeau states, the former is quicker and lighter, danced with steps closer to the ground. Examples of the *tordiglione* presented in Caroso and Negri bear a close association with the *galliard*; in these dances step patterns are virtually the same as those of the *galliard* and the form of alternating walking passages with variations is also followed.

Dance Reconstruction

The person reconstructing dances of the late Renaissance must have considerable training in both dance and music, as the two areas are so intricately connected. Dance training is essential for the interpretation of descriptions of steps and spatial patterns; musical training is necessary for working with mensural notation and lute tablature. Dance reconstruction also requires working with foreign languages as it is best to work with the original sources; errors in modern translations can lead to a complete misinterpretation of a dance.

For anyone interested in reconstructing late-Renaissance dance, the best place to begin is Arbeau's *Orchésographie*.[98] The dances are described both in prose and in a unique notation system in which the dance steps are aligned with the corresponding notes of the music. Illustrations for some of the individual steps supplement Arbeau's system. Although Arbeau's dances are considered to be easy to reconstruct, certain aspects are still open to interpretation.

The English sources are also relatively easy to use, but present their own problems, as there are few descriptions of steps. In one of the Inns of Court manuscripts, for example, the *galliard* is merely described as "One, two, three, foure & five," hardly enough information to reconstruct this dance were it not for Arbeau and the Italians.[99] Playford also uses unexplained terms and figures, for instance, "siding" and "arming."

Caroso and Negri generally include for each dance an illustration of the dancers' opening positions, followed by a prose description of the dance, and the music (in tablature and/or mensural notation). But while we have more detailed information here, these dances are difficult to reconstruct, for several reasons. Interpreting verbal descriptions of spatial patterns can be problematic when the text has several possible meanings, or seems to make no sense at all. Comparing different descriptions used within one source, and those in other contemporary sources, can be useful; a more practical solution is to try out different possibilities with live dancers. Descriptions of steps can be vague, and are often subject to a variety of interpretations. Although some of the steps are presented in terms of musical timing (i.e., breve, semibreve, etc.), fitting the dance steps to the music can still be frustrating, as the timings of the steps are not always given and these timings do not always seem to work with the music provided.

In late-Renaissance Italian dance, almost all steps can be used in different dance types and can be performed in duple or triple meter (with an alteration in timing). Steps are combined in various ways to make sequences. Most sequences begin with the left foot and there is a tendency after 1600—at least with Caroso's second publication—toward symmetry: once a sequence is executed on one side it is immediately repeated to the other side (beginning with the other foot), performed to the same amount of music. Sometimes it is not clear where the repetition of step sequences begins, and this relates directly to the pattern of musical phrases or sections. Sometimes one paragraph of dance description coincides with one or several sections of music. Negri gives rubrics above the music regarding the number of repetitions of the musical sections, but they are often inaccurate. They also do not indicate the correlation between musical and choreographic sections.[100]

The dance reconstructor can sometimes make semidramatic connections between a title of a dance and the dance itself; this can aid in determining the mood of the dance, and can also influence the tempo. In Negri's *La Battaglia* the dancers clap hands in mock battle, and make advances and retreats before an ultimate reconciliation. In other dances the connections are more subtle or there are none at all.

Besides the obvious applications of costuming, iconographical sources can aid in reconstructing period dances. We can gather information on possible instrumentation, the setting (indoor/outdoor, court/peasant, formal/informal), number of dancers, formation of group dances (line, circle, procession or other pattern) and the character or mood of the dance. Literary sources can likewise be illuminating in these areas.

Costumes

A crucial element for period dance is appropriate costuming. A costume can allow or enhance specific motions, but can also greatly restrict them. As the movements were originally conceived with specific garments in mind, the dance looks better in period clothing. In late Renaissance Italian dance, the overall shape of the costume—a narrowing of the bodice into the waist and accentuated hips (for men, a jacket skirt; for women, a bumroll or farthingale under a long, wide skirt)—was emphasized in sideways hip movements. The undulating effect of these movements cannot be replicated in modern attire!

Some dance movements are described with specific reference to costume parts; for example, in Arbeau's *la volta*, the gentleman turns the lady around in the air while lifting her under the busk (the bottom of the V-shaped bodice, snugly fitted over a stiff corset). While this lift can be accomplished without a corset, it is much easier when the lady wears one.

The sheer weight of the costume affects movement as do accessories such as the hat, cape, and ruff. Not only were heavy fabrics used, but there were several layers of clothing; a lady's costume could weigh upwards of sixty pounds. Because the ladies were so encumbered and their movements so hidden, it was natural that the gentlemen, whose legs were outfitted only as far down as the knees, were allowed greater freedom of movement, and thus were capable of performing more intricate steps.

Wearing a ruff, especially a tall one, encourages a long line of the head and neck for both men and women; a lady's corset greatly discourages slouching and makes it necessary for twentieth-century dancers to relearn how to sit. In some dances gentlemen wore hats, which were essential in the courtesies connected with the *reverence* or bow. Caroso and Negri both give suggestions on different ways to wrap the gentleman's cape for dancing.

FIGURE 18.2. *Ballet of Twelve Nations.* Festivities in Stuttgart surrounding the baptism of Prince Friedrich von Württemberg, 10–17 March 1616. (Illustration courtesy of Edmund H. Bowles; from Bowles–*Festival Books*, Fig. 94.) Spencer Collection. The New York Public Library. Astor, Lenox and Tilden Foundations. Used by permission.

Footwear is especially crucial to the kinds of steps performed and to the alignment of the body. The heeled shoe first appeared in the late sixteenth century, possibly coinciding with the emergence of the *canary*, a stamping dance that uses the heel in its movements. For late-Renaissance dance it is best to use a shoe with a very small heel (less than half an inch) and shoelace ties, such as the jazz or character shoes made by Bloch or Capezio. For the ladies, one might also experiment with *chopines*, elevated overshoes that protected delicate slippers and skirts from the mud in the streets; Caroso discusses the hazards they create in walking and dancing.[101] By the end of the seventeenth century, fashion dictated a taller heel, which facilitated the bends and rises of the Baroque technique.

Heavily draped arms in the early and mid-seventeenth century probably kept arm motions to a minimum. For example, the manner of taking arms and turning around, used especially in the English *country dance*, was probably done by the woman placing her forearm on top of the gentleman's forearm rather than the hooking of elbows popular in *country dance* today. As the cut of sleeves became shorter and lighter fabrics were used later in the century, the arms were freed to make more elaborate motions.

To have a properly costumed performance can be costly unless you have the recourse of borrowing already-made costumes from a theater group or school. Begin well in advance of the performance to get the costumes prepared, because even if you borrow garments, adjustments take time. Good costumers have clever and relatively inexpensive ways of designing costumes that will at least suggest the period.

Production Considerations

The design of the hall can play a significant role in the overall ambience of your performance, especially if the hall has a "historical" feel to it. Ballrooms of the Renaissance and Baroque were mostly long and narrow as opposed to the wide and often shallow shape of most modern stages. Adjustments may be necessary in some of the spatial patterns of the dances.

One also needs to determine the position of the original "audience." Social dances were probably performed in a ballroom with observers around all sides and at the same floor level; some dances, like the English *country dances,* definitely face the head of the room where the "presence" is located. The dance director needs to determine the best viewing angle for each dance, and decide whether to assign the role of the "presence" to the audience or to stage performers. Audiences for theatrical dance may have been on the same floor level or at a raised level, depending on the period and location; later in the century nascent proscenium stages were used with increasing frequency.

When looking for a performing space, keep in mind that dancers always appreciate a good-quality floor; a floor with a concrete base underneath is hard on dancers' feet and legs, and some surfaces (such as waxed floors) can be slippery. Certainly there are many factors that effect the choice of a performing space: type of floor, shape of performing space, cost, backstage facilities, and other considerations.

Just as one would aim for diversity in a music concert, so should one try to vary a program's dances, according to type, tempos, mood, number of dancers, and social setting. Do you intend to represent dances of the court, country, or theater? Be aware that the treatises of this time reflect court dances. Dances such as Arbeau's *branles* and the English *country dances* may have been modeled after genuine peasant dances, but it is nearly impossible to trace their origins. If the theme for a concert revolves around a certain country, it is not always necessary to restrict the program to dances or dance sources emanating from that country alone, as some manuals were known in other countries.[102]

Another issue facing the reconstructor pertains to the manner of presenting the social dances to a modern audience. As many of these dances were designed for a social ballroom setting rather than a theatrical presentation, they may seem rather dry. It is my opinion that it is possible to bring life to the dances while remaining true to the sources. One may add shoulder shading, devise variations (or substitute flashier ones), or enhance the dramatic quality (flirting, chasing, doing battle, etc.). It is most important to remember that these were recreational dances done by young people who were enjoying themselves.

The music may also be made more interesting by changing the instrumentation on repeats, or by adding ornamentation or improvised variations. One may also check various contemporary arrangements of a

FIGURE 18.3. Torch dance; part of celebrations surrounding the coronation of Matthias I as Holy Roman Emperor, Frankfurt-am-Main, 14 June 1612. (Illustration courtesy of Edmund H. Bowles; from Bowles–*Festival Books*, Fig. 82.) Spencer Collection. The New York Public Library. Astor, Lenox and Tilden Foundations. Used by permission.

piece; there are many interesting settings of the *passo e mezzo*, for example.

Improvisation was apparently an important element in the dance. The Italians—especially Negri, Lupi, and Lutij—treat it with some weight. Caroso, while not as explicit as the other Italians on the subject of improvisation, demonstrates that it was an important element in social dance by occasionally giving the performer a choice of sequences to do, especially in the *galliard* sections of his dances. Even Arbeau allows for some freedom in certain dances.

When beginning to plan a program that will include period dance, the director should locate a specialist in the historical dance field. Choreographers or dancers trained in ballet or modern dance are not automatically qualified. As indicated above, reconstructing these dances requires considerable and specific knowledge. Choreography in historical dance should also be done by someone familiar with the style. A few such specialists are identified in the resource checklist; one may also consult Stern's *Performing Arts Directory* or the *Register of Early Music America*. Attending a workshop to learn these dances firsthand is a valuable experience.[103]

Many historical dance specialists have a group of trained dancers, but if it is not financially feasible to bring in a troupe, there are alternatives. Depending on the repertory chosen, a group of local country dancers or the local college dance department may be willing to collaborate. Some of the simpler late-Renaissance dances and English *country dances* can be done quite easily by amateurs, but even with the English *country dances,* adequate rehearsals are required to be sure that the dancers attain the lovely flow that will bring out the figures of these dances. Some late-Renaissance Italian dances (especially certain *galliard* variations) can be quite challenging, and as one progresses to the late seventeenth century a dance background is necessary, for Baroque technique becomes difficult in footwork, balance, and coordination and grace of arm motions.

Well before the first rehearsal, the music director and dance director should discuss details of the music: overall program, tempos, proportional relationships of musical sections in different meters, number of repeats, instrumentation, and so forth. The musical group should make a rehearsal tape for the dancers so they can become accustomed to the distinctive sound of the ensemble with which they will be working.

Because of the lack of a standard notation system for these dances, the dancers need to be taught at rehearsal by the dance director, and this can take considerable time. In my experience with trained dancers, learning a new dance requires one hour of rehearsal for each minute of dance. In other words, if the program is to comprise twenty minutes of dancing, then one must allow at least twenty hours of rehearsal for the dancers alone, before getting together with the musicians. Amateurs or dancers not yet trained in the period style will require even more time. Dance rehearsals need to be conducted in an appropriate space. One may be lucky enough to have contact with a church or school that will lend space for free, but if not, the director should be aware of the costs involved when renting a dance rehearsal space. In New York, studio rental can cost between ten and twenty dollars per hour (or more).

While there are many considerations to take into account when preparing historical dances for performance, the result is gratifying for both musician and dancer and the work is well worth it. The visual excitement of costumed movement enhances a musical program greatly and musicians benefit in their performance in seeing the accompanying movements to the dances. From the dancers' standpoint nothing can compare to performing with live musicians. Ultimately our wish is to bring an appreciation of this wonderful material to our audience.

NOTES

1. De Lauze/Wildeblood–*Apologie,* 55.
2. The terms "Renaissance" and "Baroque" are used by music and dance scholars with slightly different time frames in mind. While musicians generally regard the turn of the seventeenth century as the beginning of the Baroque era, "Baroque" dance refers to the technique expounded in treatises of eighteenth-century dancing masters.
3. Certain dances, such as the antimasque dances of the English masque, which represented lowly or grotesque characters, were performed by professional actors.
4. In addition to the encouragement provided when Louis XIV permitted nonaristocratic dancers to assume noble roles after 1670, perhaps the ascendancy of professionalism can be partially attributed to the change in dance technique.

5. See Jones–*Relation*, 228 ff.
6. Single-sex dances such as Arbeau's *Les Bouffons* and several dances in Negri appear to have theatrical intention. See Sutton/Caroso–*Nobiltà*, 31. There is also evidence of solo dancing at other festive occasions, such as in the *Ballet of Twelve Nations*, a performance given during the festivities celebrating the baptism of Prince Friedrich von Württemberg. See Bowles–*Musical Ensembles*, 199–211.
7. For a transcription of this choreography, see D. P. Walker–*Intermèdes*.
8. "Thoinot Arbeau" is an anagram for Jehan Tabourot (1520–95).
9. "Capriole" is also the name of a step, a virtuosic jump or "caper" into the air while moving the legs and feet rapidly back and forth.
10. Arbeau–*Orchésographie* (1967), 14.
11. de Lauze/Wildeblood–*Apologie,* 99.
12. Lupi–*Libro,* however, presents several variations for women.
13. He states that the *canary* had become very popular.
14. See Mersenne–*Harmonie universelle* 2: 158–80, "Traitez de la voix et des chants," Livre second de chants, propositions 22–27.
15. See Harris-Warrick/Marsh–*Musica Theatre*, 85. A forthcoming of edition by Pendragon Press includes a facsimile of the 1685 ms., with commentary.
16. See the excellent examination of this manuscript in Harris-Warrick/ Marsh–*Musical Theatre*.
17. For further information see the introductory notes by Sparti in the facsimile edition of Compasso–*Ballo*.
18. With the publication of *Nobiltà,* Caroso became absorbed with the theory and practice of symmetry in the dance. See Feves–Changing Shape and Sutton/Caroso–*Nobiltà*.
19. Negri includes choreographies for four *brandi*; Caroso, Lupi, and Lutij have none.
20. See notes by Sparti in facsimile edition of Compasso–*Ballo*.
21. See Sutton/Caroso–*Nobiltà*, 19, 22–23.
22. See notes by Sparti in facsimile edition of Compasso–*Ballo*.
23. Some mss. describe events at a ball. Apparently there was an order for the dances that was adhered to throughout the time span of these mss.: *Quadran Pavan, Turky Lony, The Earl of Essex, Tinternell, The Old Alman, The Queen's Alman, Sicilia (Cecilia) Almain, Black Almain*.
24. For modern editions of these dances, see Cunningham–*Inns* and Pugliese/Casazza–*Practise*.
25. Descriptions of four *country dances* jotted down ca. 1648 are also extant, in British Library, Lansdowne no. 1115. See Cunningham–*Dancing,* 17.
26. Double, single, set and turne single.
27. Transcription in *Anuario musical. Barcelona.* 5 (1950): 190–98. For further information, see Gingell–Spanish Dance, and Stark–What Steps.
28. See Brainard–Renaissance Dance.
29. Maisse–*Journal,* 5.
30. For additional sources see the bibliography in Hilton–*Dance*.
31. See Donington–*Interpretation,* ch. 37, for information on tempos for specific dance types, drawn from original sources. For a discussion of late seventeenth- and early eighteenth-century dance tempos also see Harris-Warrick–Pendulum Markings.
32. Thomas/Gingell–*Renaissance Dance* contains an annotated list of sources of early dance music; modern editions are identified for some of these sources.
33. A new edition of the Susato work, with correctly barred galliards, has recently been published by London Pro Musica editions.
34. Arbeau–*Orchésographie* (1967), 67; he states also that these dances can be sung.
35. See Neumann/Myers–Percussion.
36. See Bowles–*Musical Ensembles* and Sabol–*Stuart Masque,* 19–21.
37. See Harris-Warrick/Marsh–*Musical Theatre,* 4–9, 68 ff.

38. For variant names of dance types, see Brown–*Instrumental Music,* and articles on these types in *New Grove.*

39. A *bassedanse* called *La allemande* appears in Coplande–*Maner.* Arbeau–*Orchésographie* (1967), 125 also suggests German origin.

40. For further information, see Hudson–*Allemande.*

41. Arbeau–*Orchésographie* (1967), 125.

42. The almans described in the Inns of Court mss. show processional dances like Arbeau, though with rudimentary figures added. Negri's *Alemana d'Amore* for four dancers is unlike Arbeau's; the tune (like two dances in Caroso) is similar to contemporary musical settings of the *ballo* or *balletto tedesco.* See Hudson–*Allemande,* vol. 1, ch. 3.

43. Caroso–*Nobiltà,* 109–20. For more information on the music, see Hudson–*Allemande.*

44. In Playford–*Dancing Master* (1651), 6. There are other versions of this tune throughout the seventeenth century: a six-part version called the *Bouree d'Avignonne* in the Philidor Collection; a five-part version labeled *Paduana soldat* in Georg Engelmann's *Fasciculus secundus* (1617); a texted setting in Valerius, *Neder-Landsche Gedenck-Clanck* (1626); settings for recorder in Jacob van Eyck, *Der Fluyten Lust-Hof* (1648); a version for violins and continuo in Johann Schmelzer, *Polish Bagpipes* (end of seventeenth century). See Bernard Thomas, ed., *Playford Dances,* vol. 1: *68 Dances* (LPM 102) (Brighton: London Pro Musica Edition, 1994). Also see Dean-Smith–*Playford.*

45. As in the Kassel Ms. dated ca. 1650–ca. 1670; see Écorcheville–*Vingt Suites.*

46. See Little/Marsh–*Danse Noble.*

47. Cotgrave–*Dictionarie.*

48. A chart showing the evolution of the branle suite from 1588–1660 can be found in R. Harris-Warrick/N. Lecomte–Branle, Benoit–*Dictionnaire.*

49. There are five branle-type dances for two or for four dancers in Beauchamps-Feuillet notation; see Little/Marsh–*Danse Noble.*

50. See Jones–*Relation,* 253ff.

51. Arbeau–*Orchésographie* (1967), 129.

52. Ibid., 180.

53. Most canaries are intended as theatrical dances. For Beauchamps-Feuillet notations, see Little/Marsh–*Danse Noble.*

54. Group chaconnes were often used as finales in *opéra-ballets* and *tragédies-lyriques,* but there are no extant choreographies. For other notations of chaconnes, see ibid.

55. Arbeau–*Orchésographie* (1967), 124.

56. Examples of the fast *coranto* are found in duple and in triple meter. Arbeau's *coranto* is in duple; Negri's *La Correnta* is in triple.

57. See Hilton–*Court and Theater,* 287. For extant Beauchamps-Feuillet notations of courantes, see Little/Marsh–*Danse Noble.*

58. Some dances change meters.

59. The longways dance is "progressive," a dance in which the top couple progresses down through the set (away from the "presence" or highest ranking noble at the head of the room), while the other couples progress up the set. Once a couple reaches the top, then it too begins the progression downward.

60. See Pressacco–*Sermone.*

61. Pierre Phalèse and Jean Bellère, *Chorearum Molliorum Collectanea . . . Recueil de Danseries* (1583). See Brown–*Instrumental Music.*

62. See Little/Marsh–*Danse Noble* for a list of notations.

63. Previously Matteo Maria Boiardo's poem *Orlando innamorato* (ca. 1490) has been cited as the earliest reference to the galliard. Sparti corrects this error and supplies new information in her introductory notes to Compasso–*Ballo,* 6–7.

64. Other afterdances were the *tordion, saltarello, hupfauff,* and *proportz.*

65. Morley–*Plaine and easie,* 296–97.

66. Arbeau–*Orchésographie* (1967), 78.

67. Most *la voltas* have regular phrasing and are musically similar to galliards; however, there are some interesting, irregular *la voltas*: see *Volte CCI* in Praetorius–*Terpsichore*.
68. Mace–*Musick's Monument*, 129.
69. See Little/Marsh–*Danse Noble* for a list of notations.
70. See Hilton–*Court and Theater*, 232–35.
71. Arbeau–*Orchésographie* (1967), 175.
72. There are several in Playford (1651), including *All in a Garden Green, Kemps Jegg*, and *Pauls Steeple*.
73. See Little/Marsh–*Danse Noble* for a list of notations.
74. Ibid.
75. Ibid.
76. Several scholars have attempted to unravel the mystery of the term "measure." Ward–English Measure; Mullally–Measures; Pugliese/Casazza–*Practise*; Cunningham–*Inns of Court*.
77. See Olsson–English Measures.
78. See *New Grove*, s.v. "Minuet."
79. There were two types of minuet, a "generic" one that followed a customary series of patterns, and a "figured" one that was a specifically choreographed dance. See Harris-Warrick/Marsh–*Musical Theatre*, 53.
80. See Little/Marsh–*Danse Noble*.
81. The *pas de menuet à deux mouvements*. There are also many variations. Favier's is distinctly different from other steps and may typify an earlier version. See Harris-Warrick/Marsh–*Musical Theatre*.
82. See Little/Marsh–*Danse Noble* for a list of notations.
83. See Sutton/Caroso–*Nobiltà*, 38–39, and Sutton's notes in Arbeau–*Orchésographie* (1967), 233.
84. See Sutton's notes in Arbeau–*Orchésographie* (1967), 236.
85. The passepied in the Favier manuscript begins with the dancers moving sideways to the left, the same direction in which Renaissance branles begin. See Harris-Warrick/Marsh–*Musical Theatre*, 162. For dances in Beauchamps-Feuillet notation, see Little/Marsh–*Danse Noble*.
86. Italian: "of Padua"; Spanish: from *pavon*, meaning "peacock."
87. Its earliest appearance is in Joan Ambrosio Dalza, *Intabulatura de Lauto* (1508).
88. Some pavans are in triple meter. See Sutton–Triple pavans.
89. See Harris-Warrick/Marsh–*Musical Theatre*; Little/Marsh–*Danse Noble*.
90. Ibid.
91. As Sutton (*Nobiltà*, 43) points out, this may be due to Morley's statement (*Introduction*) that the Italians call their *galliards* a *saltarello*.
92. Sutton/Caroso–*Nobiltà*, 43–44.
93. See Little/Marsh–*Danse Noble*.
94. See articles by Robert Stevenson and Richard Hudson listed in *New Grove*, s.v. "Sarabande."
95. See Little/Marsh–*Danse Noble*.
96. Caroso has four; two in *Il Ballarino* and two in *Nobiltà*. Negri offers only one, in duple meter, in *Le Gratie d'amore*.
97. See Sutton/Caroso–*Nobiltà*, 44.
98. The most accessible edition of *Orchésographie* is the 1948 translation by Mary Stewart Evans, reprinted in 1967 by Dover Publications, listed in the bibliography. One should be sure to read the notes given by Julia Sutton, and study the volume side by side with the original French edition. A facsimile edition of the 1596 edition of *Orchésographie* is available from Minkoff; see Bibliography.
99. See Cunningham–*Inns of Court*, 27.
100. See Jones–*Relation*, 196ff.

101. See Sutton/Caroso–*Nobiltà*, 140–41.
102. See Brainard–*Renaissance Dance,* 320. Also see Sutton/Caroso–*Nobiltà,* 2.
103. See listings in *Early Music America Bulletin.*

SELECT RESOURCES

Dr. Ingrid Brainard, 37 Princess Road, West Newton, MA 02165
  (617) 332-4064
Angene Feves, 70 Karol Lane, Pleasant Hill, CA 94523
  (510) 943-1356
Charles Garth, 31 Union Square W. #15D, New York, NY 10003
  (212) 255-5545
Dr. Rebecca Harris-Warrick, Dept. of Music, Lincoln Hall, Cornell University, Ithaca, NY 14853
  (607) 255-7141, Email: rh14@cornell.edu
Wendy Hilton, 330 W. 28th Street, Apt. 18-E, New York, NY 10001
  (212) 727-2098
Dr. Pamela Jones, 2355 Hingston, Montreal, P.Q., H4A2J3 Canada
Dr. Carol Marsh, School of Music, University of North Carolina, Greensboro, NC 27412
  (919) 334-5421, Email: c_marsh@hamlet.uncg.edu
Dr. Dorothy Olsson, 189 Claremont Avenue #63, New York, NY 10027
  (212) 865-7797, Email: olssond@is2.nyu.edu
Ken Pierce, 284 Harvard Street #71, Cambridge, MA 02139
  (617) 354-5191, Email: kpierce@mit.edu
Patricia Rader, 120 Bennett Avenue #3B, New York, NY 10033
  (212) 740-1131, Email: prader@nypl.org
Dr. Julia Sutton, 24 Graymore Road, Waltham, MA 02154
  (617) 893-0856, Email: jsutton@world.std.com
Catherine Turocy, Division of Dance, Meadows School of the Arts, Southern Methodist University, Dallas, TX 75275
  (214) 768-2951, fax (214) 768-3272

NOTE: The Internet (WorldWideWeb) can be a valuable resource. You can link to the Renaissance Dance sources page (which offers other links to source translations, bibliography, discography, and early music and dance resources) at the following address: http://www.ucs.mun.ca/~andrew/rendance.html

BIBLIOGRAPHY—SECONDARY SOURCES

Bowles–*Festival Books*; Brainard–Renaissance Dance; Brown–*Instrumental Music*; Buch–*Ballets de cour*; Christout–*Ballet de cour*; Christout–*Court Ballet*; Christout–Ballet de Cour au XVIIe siècle; Cunningham–*Inns of Court*; Dixon–*Nonsuch,* vol. 2; Donington–*Interpretation*; Ellis–*Lully*; Feves–Changing Shape; Feves–*Noble Gathering*; Fletcher, Cohen, and Lonsdale–*Famed*; Harris-Warrick–Pendulum Markings; Harris-Warrick/Marsh–*Musical Theatre*; Helwig/Barron–*Purcell*; Hilton–*Dance*; Hudson–*Allemande*; Inglehearn–*Ten Dances*; Jones–*Relation*; Lacroix–*Ballets*; Little/Marsh–*Danse Noble*; McGowan–*L'art*; Nagler–*Theatre Festivals*; Neumann/Myers–Percussion; *New Grove* (article on Dance, various articles about individual dance types, aspects of music and performance practice); Olsson–English Measures; Orgel–*Jonsonian Masque*; Payne–*Almain*; Pugliese/Casazza–*Practise*; Sabol–*Stuart Masque*; Schwartz/Schlundt–*French Court*;

Skeaping–Three Crowns; Sutton/Caroso–*Nobiltà*; Sutton–Minuet; Sutton–Triple pavans; Thomas/Gingell–*Renaissance Dance*; Ward–Measure.

Recordings

The Broadside Band, Jeremy Barlow, director. *Il Ballarino: Italian Dances, c. 1600.* Hyperion, compact disc A66244.

———. *English Country Dances From Playford's Dancing Master 1651–1703,* SayDisc, compact disc CD-SDL 393.

Feves, Angene. *Homage to Amor: Sixteenth Century Dances of Love from Fabritio Caroso's Il Ballarino (1581) and Nobiltà di Dame (1600).* Played by Les Verres Cassés. Copyright Angene Feves, 1987. Cassette tape only; booklet in preparation.

The Harp Consort, Andrew Lawrence-King, director. *Spanish Dances.* Deutsche Harmonia Mundi, CD 05472-77340-2.

Hespèrion XX, Jordi Savall, director. *William Brade: Hamburger Ratsmusik um 1600 (Consort Music c. 1600).* Deutsche Harmonia Mundi, compact disc 77168-2-RG.

New London Consort, Philip Pickett, director. *Tielman Susato: Danserye 1551.* L'Oiseau-Lyre, compact disc 436 131-2.

———. *Michael Praetorius: Dances from Terpsichore, 1612.* L'Oiseau-Lyre, compact disc 414 633-2.

New York Renaissance Band, Sally Logemann, director. *Country Capers: The Music of Playford's The English Dancing Master.* Arabesque Recordings, cassette tape NB 7520, compact disc Z6522.

———. *Praetorius: Excerpts from Terpsichore.* Arabesque Recordings, cassette tape NB 7531, compact disc Z6531.

———. *Washerwoman, War and Pease: The Music of Arbeau's Orchésographie.* Arabesque Recordings, cassette tape NB 7514, compact disc Z6514.

Piffaro, The Renaissance Wind Band (formerly The Philadelphia Renaissance Wind Band), Joan Kimball and Robert Wiemkin, directors. *Canzoni e Danze: Wind Music from Renaissance Italy.* Archiv, compact disc 445 883-2.

The Playford Consort. See Helwig/Barron–*Purcell* under Secondary Sources.

Les Talens Lyriques, C. Rousset, dir.; and La Simphonie du Marais, H. Reyne, dir.; Francine Lancelot, supervision. *Musiques à Danser la Cour et l'Opéra.* Erato, compact disc 0630-10702-2.

See also practice tapes accompanying published reconstructions, listed above in secondary sources: Dixon, Feves, Inglehearn, Pugliese/Casazza, Thomas and Gingell.

Dance Music Sources

This a very select list, citing only sources of ensemble music (in chronological order) that are available in reliable modern editions. For additional sources and listings of music for solo instruments (lute, keyboard, etc.), see Brown–*Instrumental Music* and Thomas/Gingell–*Renaissance Dance*; the latter volume includes an annotated list of printed and manuscript sources from 1530–1645. Collections of dance music not mentioned in the list below can be found in Thomas/Gingell–*Renaissance Dance*; B. Thomas–*Playford Dances*; Sabol–*Stuart Masque*; Helwig/Barron–*Purcell*; Nettl–*Wiener Tanzmusik*.

Abbreviations

ARS= American Recorder Society Editions
DM= Early Dance Music (LPM series)
EM= English Instrumental Music of the late Renaissance (LPM series)
EML= Early Music Library (LPM series)
LPM= London Pro Musica edition
MP = Musica Practica (LPM series)
TM= Thesaurus Musicus (LPM series)
TS = Thomas Simpson (LPM series)

1578. Giorgio Mainerio. *Il Primo Libro di Balli*. Venice. Dances included: *saltarello, pass'emez-zo, gagliarda, padoana, tedescha*. Modern ed. Selections in LPM TM13 (1979) and TM66 (1986); complete edition in *Musikalische Denkmäler*, vol. 5 (1960).

1582. Baltassar de Beaujoyeulx (Baldassare de Belgioioso). *Le Balet-Comique de la Royne*. Paris. Facs. rep.: (1) Binghamton, NY: Center for Medieval & Early Renaissance Studies, c1982. (2) Torino: Bottega d'Erasmo, 1965. Modern ed. American Institute of Musicology, Studies and Documents, no. 25 (1971).

1583. Pierre Phalèse. *Chorearum Molliorum Collectanea* . . . . Antwerp. Dances included: *paduanas, pass'emezos, alemandas, galliardas*. Facs. rep.: Peer, Belgium: Alamire, 1991. Modern ed. Celle: Moeck Verlag, 1965. *Der Bläserchor*, vol. 1, 5.

ca. 1590–1600. Murhardsche Bibliothek der Stadt Kassel und Landesbibliothek. Manuscript. MS 4o Mus 72. Dances included: *pavans* and *intradas*, 4–6 parts; includes seven pieces for specific (and varied) instrumentation. Modern ed. LPM RB11 (1994).

1599. Anthony Holborne. *Pavans, galliards, almains and other short aeirs*. London. Dances included: *pavan, galliard, almain*; 5 parts. Modern ed. LPM AH1 (1980).

ca. 1605. John Dowland. *Lachrimae, or Seaven Teares figured in Seaven Passionate Pavans, with divers other Pavans, Galiards, and Almands, set forth for the Lute, Viols, or Violons, in five parts*. London. Dances included: *pavan, galiard, almand*. Facs. rep.: Leeds: Boethius, 1974. Modern ed. Schott, ED 12141 (1985). Edition also includes Dowland pieces from other contemporary sources, including *pavan, galliard, courante, almand, volta*; pieces are arranged for viols or recorders; lute part also provided.

1609. William Brade. *Newe ausserlesene Paduanen, Galliarden, Cantzonen, Allman und Coranten*. Hamburg. Dances included: *pavan, galliard, allmand, coranta*; 5 parts. Modern ed.(s) LPM WB1 (1982).

1610. Thomas Simpson. *Opusculum Neuwer Pavanen, Gulliarden, Couranten unnd Volten*. Frankfurt-am-Main. Dances included: *pavan, galliard, courante, volte*; 5 parts. Modern ed. Selections in LPM TM60 (1992); selections in ARS No. 77 (19??) and ARS No. 89 (1981).

1611. Thomas Morley. *The first booke of consort lessons, made by divers exquisite authors, for sixe instruments to play together: viz: the treble lute, the pandora, the citterne, the base-violl, the flute, and the treble-violl*. London. Dances included: *pavin, galliard, maske, lavolto, coranto*; pieces are for six instruments: treble viol, flute, bass viol, lute, cittern, pandora. Composers include Richard Allison, John Dowland, Thomas Morley, Peter Philips [?], William Byrd [?]. Modern ed. New York: C. F. Peters, 1959.

1612. Michael Praetorius. *Terpsichore*. Wolfenbüttel. Dances included: over 300 dances, mostly French, *branle, galliard, pavan, passemezzo, ballet, courante, volta*. Modern ed. M. Praetorius, *Gesamtausgabe*. Vol. 15, Möseler Verlag, 1960; selections in LPM TM69 and LPM DM11–12.

1614. William Brade. *Newe ausserlesene Paduanen und Galliarden*. Hamburg. Dances included: *pavan, galliard, allemand*; 6 parts. Modern ed(s). Complete ed. in LPM MP3 (1992); Selections in LPM TM61.

1617. William Brade. *Newe Ausserlesene liebliche Branden, Intraden, Mascharaden, Balletten, All'manden, Couranten, Volten*. Hamburg. Dances included: *branle, intrada, mascarade, bal-*

let, allemande, courante, volta. Modern ed. Selections in LPM TM32 (1981) and TM43 (1984); selections in Musica Rara edition, London, 1974.

1617. Johann Hermann Schein, *Banchetto musicale.* Leipzig. Dances included: *padouanna, gagliarda, courente, allemande*; 4–5 parts. Modern ed. in LPM MP5 (1993); selections in LPM TM39 (1983), LPM TM44 (1984), LPM EML147 (1989).

1617. Thomas Simpson. *Opus newer Paduanen, Galliarden, Intraden, Canzonen, Ricercaren, Fantasien, Balleten, Allemanden, Couranten, Volten und Passamezen* . . . Hamburg. Dances included: *intrada, allemande, volta, courante, paduan, galliard, ballet, passamezzo*; five parts. Modern ed. Selections in LPM TM15 (1979); selections in Musica Rara edition (1972).

1621. John Adson. *Courtly Masquing Ayres.* London. Dances included: masque dances and other masque pieces. Modern ed. LPM EM3–5 (1976–1979); Musica Rara ed. (1975).

1621. William Brade. *Newe lustige Volten, Couranten, Balleten, Padoanen, Galliarden, Masqueraden auch allerley Arth, Newer Französisch Täntze.* Berlin. Dances included: *la volta, courante, ballet, padoane, galliard, mascarade.* Modern ed. In preparation, Bernard Thomas, LPM.

1621. Thomas Simpson. *Taffel-Consort.* Hamburg. Dances included: *ballet, paduan, courant, volta, mascarada, almand*; 4–5 parts. Modern ed. LPM TS1 (1988); selections in LPM TM34 (1983).

1625. Paul Peuerl. *Newe Padouan, Intrada, Dantz und Galliarda.* Nuremberg. Dances included: *padouan, courant, serenata, dantz, ballet*; 2–4 parts. Modern ed. Selections in LPM EML 266 (1994).

1645. Gasparo Zanetti, *Il Scolaro.* Milan. Dances included: *arie, passo e mezzo, saltarello, gagliarda, zoppa, balletto, alemana, corrente*; 4 parts. Facs. rep.: Firenze: Studio per edizioni scelte, 1984. Modern ed. LPM DM 5–6 (1983).

1651–1662. Uppsala University Library Instr.mus.hs 409. Dances included: *allemande, courante, sarabande, various branle, gavotte, bourre, pavane, galliard,* and a few nondance compositions; 213 pieces in 4–7 parts. Modern ed. Complete in *Seventeenth-Century Instrumental Dance Music in Uppsala University Library Instr.mus.hs 409 (Musica Svecica Saeculi XVII, 5,* in *Monumenta Musicae Svecicae,* 8). Stockholm: Edition Reimers, 1976.

1659. Maurizio Cazzati. *Correnti, Balletti, Galiarde.* Bologna. Dances included: *corrente, balletti, galliard*; 3–4 parts (2 violins, violone/viola, spinetta or chitarone. Facs. rep.: Bologna: Antiquae Musicae Italicae Monumenta Bononiensia, 1971.

Late seventeenth century. [Selection from "Philidor Collection"] Paris, Bibliothèque Nationale, Rés. F 496, 496, 497, 498. Dances included: *allemande,* ballet suites (including *gavotte, gaillarde, sarabande, allemande, entree*); 2, 4, 5 parts. Modern ed. Selections in Buch–*Dance Music.*

19

Theatrical Productions,

Or Aurora's Spicy Bed: Seventeenth-Century Opera Production for Those Not Normally Involved in Opera Production

James Middleton

"From Aurora's spicy bed / Phœbus rears his glorious head . . ."
Nahum Tate, *Dido and Æneas*, prologue

To many well-informed people in the English-speaking world, seventeenth-century opera *means Dido and Æneas,* the much-produced opera by Henry Purcell. We do not realize that the "spicy bed" harbors literally hundreds of little-known masterworks. *Dido* has become the "typical" Baroque opera for many people, when in fact no opera could be less so! A formally peculiar work that exists in near isolation as one of very few pre-nineteenth-century examples of all-sung theater in England, *Dido and Æneas* is typical only in that it has shared the fate of many of its more obscure continental cousins: shorn of its prologue and subjected to capricious editorial practice, it is *Dido*'s fate in our own century that makes it a representative example of a misunderstood genre.

Sooner or later, most college *collegia* and smaller professional early music ensembles end up doing Purcell's *Dido and Æneas.* This usually arises not out of any particular love for Purcell, but because the group has decided to *do an opera. Dido* is in English, it is short, it is available in a great multitude of fairly satisfactory (but equally unsatisfactory) editions. *Dido and Æneas* is not considered to be taxing, and it is without a doubt a highly effective piece of theater.

Almost immediately on beginning, problems start to rear their heads. For all its brevity, *Dido* is in fact an enormous work—it requires at least three complete changes of scene, more choral music than is found in most operas three times its length, more dance music than is found in most operas three times its length, and an elaborate plot requiring such props as a boar's head impaled on a spear. When all is said and done, *Tosca* is a much simpler work to bring off.

The *Dido* we know and love is in fact a fragment of a somewhat longer work. An allegorical prologue and a scene for the witches are missing. Then there is the matter of casting. *Dido* was long thought to have been premiered at "Mr. Josias Priest's boarding school for girls" outside London, which begs the question "Why these tenors and basses?" Recent controversies over a probable earlier performance at court solve no casting problems, but tend to open up entire new cans of worms. Approaching *Dido* shows us why we have to be cautious about approaching any early opera. There are many snares and pitfalls, both scholarly and practical, but these are dangerous only to the unwary.

Whence Could So Much Virtue Spring?

"Whence could so much virtue spring?
What storms, what battles did he sing?"

Tate, *Dido and Æneas*, Act 1

The term "seventeenth-century opera" encompasses a wide variety of types of music theater, from the earliest Florentine operas through the Venetian operas written for the public stage, Roman opera, and Neapolitan opera, to the French *tragédie lyrique,* English masque, English and Spanish semiopera, and Spanish *zarzuela*—in short a heterogeneous listing of types and styles of operas, or of the genres that coexisted as alternatives to opera in the Baroque period.

This is not the place for a discussion of the early development of opera (a list of useful publications appears at the end of this chapter). Suffice it to say that within the hundred-year span of the seventeenth century, opera changed from experimental theater of the most radical kind to an immensely popular entertainment genre. In the following discussion of the various strategies I use to bring these forgotten entertainments to twentieth-century audiences it will be useful to remember the sort of polar opposition of experimental theater and mass-market popular culture. The glory—or marketing genius—of early opera was that it uniquely blended these two opposed ideas. This is why late-twentieth-century audiences respond so strongly to early opera. Staging an early opera can be frustrating, challenging, exasperating, and richly rewarding. The most important thing about making a decision to do an old opera is to prepare oneself to make choices.

When you do *Tosca,* you need certain specific things—the banquet table, the knife, someplace for her to leap from. Furthermore, when dealing with the standard operatic repertory, there is a performing tradition (Tosca's red dress) that, whether it is observed or ignored, involves some level of expectation on the part of audience and performers. (She's not wearing the red dress!) There is no comparable level of expectation for early operas. Poppea may appear wearing only a bathtub or a full court gown. The dramaturgy of the early opera stage is so much more minimal than that of nineteenth-century opera that the array of choices appears infinite; for example, having decided to do *Dido and Æneas,* you must choose a setting. The given setting is ancient Carthage, but is this Carthage the mirror of a contemporary court, as imagined by the librettist Nahum Tate, or is it Carthage as imagined by a seventeenth-century visual artist—a romanticized archaeological recreation of classical antiquity? The Baroque artist's vision of a perfectly proportioned classical Carthage would have been based on Roman styles that date from about 1,500 years after the supposed action of the opera, which takes place immediately following the Trojan War. At this point you abandon history altogether and decide to stage *Dido* as a '50s sci-fi movie in which the queen of an exotic planet falls in love with a handsome astronaut!

What I hope to convey is that no choice is necessarily right or wrong, but that *any* choice you make needs to be consistent with itself and illuminate the story. The investigation of historic styles of playing and singing has become vitally important to late-twentieth-century music-making. Just so, it is equally important to find out enough about the performance conventions of a different time and place in order to make informed decisions about how to convey the same effect in a twentieth-century manner. A perfect example is the late Paul Echols's witty substitution of an onstage elevator for the *deus ex machina* effects in his production of John Eccles's *Semele.* Not to have brought the gods onstage in a "magical" way would have been a violation of the spirit of the piece, but his updated production sought and found an ingenious solution that preserved the work's intention. This is vital in staging old works—one must either do the thing (a flying chariot) or find its equivalent (an elevator). In a very basic sense, if he had not made that leap of equivalency, he would not really have been doing *Semele.* Most productions of old operas fall down at precisely this point—in assuming that the devices of the Baroque stage are too quaint for postmodern eyes, many directors fail to find any equivalent action, rendering long instrumental introductions and *ritornelli* awkward. By attempting to make things modern and "relevant" they undermine the pacing that is built into these works. It is a grave mistake to suppose that Monteverdi and Purcell did not know what they were doing.

I spoke above about how vitally important it is to consider the context in which it was first performed, and look at that context in relation to the circumstances of a twentieth-century performance. Although striking stagings can be achieved that have no relation to the original circumstances of a given work, it is always best to be aware of these circumstances before choosing to go in another direction. An archaeological recreation of the opening night of Monteverdi's *L'Orfeo* is not the only viable course—but when you discover that *L'Orfeo* had *three* opening

375

nights one is put in mind of a large range of historically informed choices that one might make in staging that piece: *L'Orfeo*'s first production was an extremely simple one given at the librettist's house, its second in the apartments of the Duke of Mantua's mother, "the most serene lady of Ferrara." The third production was a very fancy court production for a visiting prince for which Monteverdi wrote the rather equivocal happy ending now associated with the opera.

Above all, the stage action must proceed at the same pace as the music. Early operas are often overladen with stage business by well-meaning directors. The reason that Baroque operas are so often damned as static is that action and music are put hopelessly out of sync by attempts to fix the very static quality directors wish to avoid! Ultimately, this is a consequence of a lack of confidence in the material—but again I say it is a grave mistake to suppose that Monteverdi and Purcell did not know what they were doing. Baroque drama is a theater of ideas in which text is vitally important, action less so, and in many ways, Baroque opera embodies the purest expression of the ideals of Baroque drama. Indeed, such action as there is often resides only in music and text. This does not mean to suggest that nothing happens—but the things that occur tend to be interior rather than physical. To contrast *Dido* with *Tosca* is illuminating on this point: Floria Tosca's suicide is the climactic moment, dramatically and musically, of the opera. The death of Dido, although inevitable, comes after the musical climax of "When I am laid in earth," and her manner of death, either spontaneous by self-inflicted wound or by a dignified walk to her funeral pyre, is unimportant; I have seen each of these solutions used to good effect.

Too Dreadful a Practice

"In our deep vaulted cell the charm we'll prepare /
Too dreadful a practice for this open air!"

Tate, *Dido and Æneas*, Act 1, scene 2

Are the devices of the seventeenth-century stage too quaint? Are we really more sophisticated than Monteverdi's audience? Especially here in the context of a discussion of seventeenth-century music, I think it is relevant to suggest that the Baroque stage is, just like the harpsichord or viol, a period instrument. When you know that Monteverdi or Purcell put that instrumental interlude there to cover the noise of stage machinery, it tells you that something ought to happen on stage during that music.

The idea of a full period production is usually dismissed with the phrase "we can't do that" or "we don't want to do a museum piece." Yet this kind of thinking represents a basic lack of confidence in the work; neither statement is in fact an answer to the question "Well, why not?" A period staging avoids and solves many problems, such as that of having to brainstorm an effective substitute for ancient Carthage, and period staging also keeps us from having to match wits with long-dead librettists; to whom do we need to prove that we are cleverer than Nahum Tate? Historic staging becomes especially relevant in productions that incorporate period dance—indeed, how (or why) incorporate period dances in a nonperiod production? If the watchword is, as I have suggested, consistency, period staging gives one a clear and incontestably consistent point of departure and saves us from demanding a twentieth-century logic of an essentially illogical form.

Hand in hand with the physical concept, one needs to decide on a musical concept. With *Dido* this involves casting choices that I mentioned above—a thoroughly "period" approach to this problem would be to adapt the parts to the singers available: the original sorceress was likely a man, while the girls-school Æneas was probably female. Male sorceresses are fairly common in modern productions (the Kalmus score preserves ambiguous cleffing from an early source that makes this fairly easy to justify). In any early opera, it is best to give the part to the best available person who can sing it at the original pitch. The original pitch is important: the male soprano and alto heroes of the Baroque stage lose considerable punch in transposition—the lack of good falsettists a few years back led to numerous editions of old operas with these roles dropped an octave, so check sources whenever possible!

Speaking of editions, this is another important choice. There are very few early operas that are "orchestrated" in our sense of the word—Monteverdi's *Orfeo* is very unusual in that its instrumentation is specified. Most early opera manuscripts consist of a vocal line accompanied by a figured bass. Ideally, an early opera performance should start from this point, with a new performing edition made in process. This may not be practical, or even possible for your group, and not being able to realize a figured bass should not keep you from attempting a project, although it will limit your choices to editions which offer realized accompaniments—and further limit your options within the accompaniment itself.

A word on fashion: editions of early operas made from the 1920s through the '70s are still the most widely available versions of these works. If you have a band of period instruments and a skilled continuo group, you probably will not want to use these. But except for the fact that you will endure the tongue-clicking of purists, these unfashionable versions of old works are an excellent introduction to the style for general audiences. I believe that they do more good than harm, because they make an unfamiliar kind of theater available to a new audience. Besides, the purists of even a decade ago are now reviled by the new crop of purists, who somehow believe their work to be a true and accurate representation of "what they really did in 1687." It is best to realize and accept that any reconstruction is essentially of and for its own time. The goal ought to be a good production, rather than the definitive production, because any really good production is definitive on its own terms.

One area where these unfashionable versions are useful is in the area of cutting: most people think that Baroque operas are simply too long. The argument that most of them are shorter than *Götterdämmerung* will get you nowhere. This is where *Dido and Æneas* proves atypical—it is the one early opera that is routinely added to. If your audience is used to Wagner, you might try a hefty work uncut, but it helps to remember that few early operas (particularly Italian ones) existed as inviolable texts the way a late Wagner opera does: they were cut, rearranged, and otherwise messed with in ways that we would not dare to. So go ahead and do what you think your audience is ready for. Editions such as Raymond Leppard's of *L'Incoronazione di Poppea* or any of his versions of Cavalli operas are widely available, and provide solid models for how to trim an early opera without cutting out its heart.

How Shall This Be Done?

"Ruin'd ere the set of Sun? Tell us (tell us) how shall this be done?"
Tate, *Dido and Æneas*, Act 3, scene 1

For most ensembles choosing to do an opera for the first time, the question of whether to use a director (and where to find one) needs to be addressed quite early on. It is usually a mistake for the music director of the group to wear the additional hat of stage director—even though the ensemble director may be very good at "giving direction" in a musical context, the job is simply too big for one person. Inevitably, either the music or the drama will suffer.

A couple of words about the opera director's job: whether at the highest professional levels or in an undergrad collegium, the stage director's job is the same—he or she must take a handful of oddly assorted performers and make them all appear to be equally gifted actors! This is a difficult task, and one at which I have seen internationally famous "experts" fail miserably. Why is this so? Because opera performers are chosen primarily for their vocal skills, and only incidentally for their stage skills. This is so much the case that even people who ought to know better tend not to think of opera as theater, but as something rather different—no wonder people think opera is boring! Once exempted from the rules that govern public entertainment, opera is nothing but voices. Sad to say, many stage directors fall prey to this pernicious way of thinking, and because it is a hard job, we willingly forgive them—but opera is meant to be theater that is heightened by the addition of the musical component, not theater that presents music instead of drama.

It is very important not to do your opera in a vacuum! College or university ensembles will find their job made much easier by assistance from a theater department—indeed, unless you can afford to hire the whole staff from the outside, opera projects are usually unfeasible without interdepartmental collaboration. In the "real world" it is still a good idea to collaborate and pull as much expertise as possible from your local theater community—so it pays to familiarize yourself with what is available to you. (Early Music America maintains a list of specialist directors for referral.)

College and university ensembles can usually find a staff person to fill the stage director's role. Professional or semiprofessional ensembles need to do a bit more legwork to find stage directors. It helps to know something of a director's style before making a decision. It is also of crucial importance to make decisions about the direction a project is to take at the same time the search for a director is conducted. If you dislike a director's other work, it is unlikely that this person will make you happy as an opera director. If there is a lot of theatrical activity in your town, you should familiarize yourself with the people doing the work—all too frequently an opera production will be shot in the foot by music and stage directors who find themselves at cross-purposes! In a word, things really cannot be discussed too minutely beforehand. Finally, although your director need not be an early-music specialist, an opera stage director should be able to read music well enough to make the physical gestures of the staging complement the musical gestures of the work.

In the real world of small budgets and high stress, a choreographer often does double duty as "arranger of the stage picture" while the music director will coach dramatic intention. I have seen this solution work both very well and very badly. Of course, it presupposes the availability of a choreographer.

Besides the music director, stage director, and choreographer, it is very helpful to have a stage manager/director's assistant who can keep things running smoothly by arranging rehearsals and watching the score during rehearsals and all performances. If it is at all possible, an opera stage manager ought to be able to read music, as he or she needs to be able to follow a score in order to coordinate lighting cues and scene changes, as well as remind stage personnel of their cues (this can be done by watching text, but obviously a musically literate person will have an easier time of it). There is no person more valuable to a stage production than a good, experienced stage manager. A director may have access to stage managers that he or she likes to work with, or you can ask local producing organizations for referrals. (A stage manager ought to receive a fee equivalent to that of a lead singer. It is worth it.)

The stage manager is the person responsible for keeping things running according to schedule—a representative schedule is shown below:

Nine months or more from production: A work is chosen, basic concepts laid down, staff assembled. The busier your people are, the farther away from production time this work needs to be done. Very famous singers usually need to be scheduled more than a year in advance. (Often a project is generated because "We have famous singer X for October 1999—what can we do?")

<u>Six months from production</u>: Staff fully assembled, formal planning of specific producton details, casting ought to be underway.

<u>Three months from production</u>: Casting complete, scores to singers, design process underway.

<u>Six–eight weeks from production</u>: Rehearsals begin, costume and scenery construction commences. Rehearsals during this period should be at least one "full" (= large ensemble) rehearsal per week, plus scheduled individual coachings for principals with music and stage directors.

<u>Two–three weeks from opening night</u>: Daily or near daily runs-through with full cast and continuo. (It is often useful to do "act runs," that is, to run a single act twice in one session.)

<u>Ten days–one week from opening</u>: Full rehearsals begin. This is generally when the full instrumental ensemble is added, and when the show will move into the actual production venue. Here is a sample schedule for this final week:

<u>Ten, nine, eight days prior to opening</u>: Full run-through with continuo in rehearsal space.

<u>Seven days</u>: Move scenery into performance venue; run-through with continuo in evening.

<u>Six days</u>: Technical rehearsal, often stop and go—usually trying, but necessary to work out technical bugs.

<u>Five days</u>: First costume run, continuo.

<u>Four days</u>: Second costume run, continuo.

<u>Three days</u>: Third costume run.

<u>Two days</u>: First run with instruments. (Singers should be called about an hour earlier than instruments.)

<u>Day prior</u>: Final dress rehearsal, full run with instruments.

<u>Opening night</u>!

The production schedule above will look very idealistic to people who have done this sort of thing. Ideals are nevertheless good things to have.

Our Charms Have Sped

"Then since our charms have sped, a merry dance be led"
Tate, *Dido and Æneas*, Act 2, scene 3

There are a few early operas that do not incorporate dance as an essential part of the musical picture. *Dido and Æneas* is a perfect case in point: as it was performed at Mr. Priest's school, *Dido* was virtually a ballet with vocal interludes, calling for eleven dances in the prologue and opera proper. The most desirable solution is to have proper dances performed by good dancers—measured pacing by the chorus is usually pretty embarrassing because it tends to look like what it is, which is phony dancing. If no dancers are available, it is better to fill the dance music with stage business than to fake it. Teaching real dances to choral singers is very good experience for them, but may not be very satisfying to the audience.

I am a decided partisan of period dance: a sarabande looks better as a sarabande than as anything else. However, period dance is not the only kind of dancing that looks good in early opera—indeed, if you set your *Dido* in outer space, it is rather silly to do minuets. Interesting modern dance and ballet are perfectly good solutions, and may be more workable than attempting to do period dance. If what you do is consistent, it will be believable. For those wishing to do period dance, Early Music America maintains a list of choreographers for referral.

Great Minds Against Themselves Conspire

*"Great minds agains themselves conspire /
and shun the cure they most desire."*
Tate, *Dido and Æneas,* Act III, scene 2

There is hardly anything worse than a cheap-looking opera, the all-too-frequent result of trying to do too much with too few resources. The physical (visual) component of an opera production will ultimately be determined by the budget. A limited budget is not in itself a reason not to do an opera, although it is a good reason to be careful in your choices. I have found that it looks better to work well within one's means than to stretch things to the limit. When the budget is stretched to the last nickel, people can always tell. A spirited and well-paced concert or semistaged version can be very satisfying. Including dance can make a concert opera seem a lot more staged than it really is!

If you have the money, it is nice to use designers of scenery, costumes, and lighting who know their business and are used to providing these services. A director may have access to design professionals he or she likes to work with, or you may want to ask for recommendations from other local producing organizations, or conduct a search via the same want ad / bulletin board / word-of-mouth methods used to find a director (again, EMA may be able to help).

As with a director, you should not engage a design staff without a good idea of whether they will be able to make you happy.

On Thy Bosom Let Me Rest

"Thy hand, Belinda, darkness shades me—on thy bosom let me rest . . ."
Tate, *Dido and Æneas,* Act III, scene 2

There are no easy operas. People would not want to attend an easy opera. There are, however, good and bad choices. After long consideration, I have elected not to cite, except in a few special instances, specific editions. Such a list could only reflect my own prejudices and would in any case be outdated well before this volume goes to press! For those interested in finding available and accessible works, there is nothing that quite beats a crawl through a good music library. More expedient, however, may be a consultation with *The New Grove Dictionary of Music and Musicians,* which references under composer (though not under works) the various published editions of a given composer's works. Oddly enough, *The New Grove Encyclopedia of the Opera* does not provide this information. The key to *Grove's* system of abbreviations can be found at the front of each volume.

In the Baroque era, companies chose works (or commissioned them) based on their strengths. It's still a good idea. In this final section, I offer an overview of the seventeenth-century music-theater repertory as it relates to contemporary performance. If you are seriously looking for a work for staged performance, it is not necessary to limit yourself to stage works: the following list includes many masque-type entertainments as well as sacred oratorios in dramatic form that, although they were probably not originally staged, can be quite effective when mounted as stage pieces. Since so many of us do our work in churches, one might also consider recreating a liturgical event such as a Baroque wedding or funeral with all the trimmings.

The most "popular" composer of Baroque music theater is Henry Purcell (1659?–1695). Purcell is of course chiefly known for *Dido and Æneas,* his only "true opera," available in multitudinous editions (including one by Thurston Dart that reconstructs the lost prologue, and one by Benjamin Britten that replaces two lost scenes). In addition to *Dido,* it is worth mentioning *The Masque of Venus and Adonis,* written about 1683 by Purcell's teacher and successor, John Blow. Purcell's other dramatic music is well worth looking into: the semioperas (spoken dramas with operatic scenes), *The Fairy Queen* (1692), *The Indian Queen* (1695), and *King Arthur* (1691), can be done whole (expensive) or performed as musical excerpts. They are often performed with the plays replaced by narration done by a single actor. Another idea might be the presentation of scenes from the plays as *tableaux vivants* between the musical sections. *Dioclesian* (1690), *Timon of Athens,* and *The Tempest* (1695) include self-contained masques that, since they have nothing to do with the plays in which they are found, are eminently excerptable. Purcell's odes, such as *Come Ye Sons of Art,* are strongly theatrical in character; their frequent instrumental interludes are very danceable.

The masques that Purcell inserted into these dramatic works are part of an older tradition of courtly entertainment. The Stuart court presented these lavish variety shows for Twelfth Night and also for events such as the weddings of favored courtiers. Although none of the great masques of the Stuart court survives intact, a number of them, such as *Oberon, Lord*

Hays' Masque, and *The Squires' Masque* are considered reconstructible. Anthony J. Sabol's *Four-Hundred Songs and Dances from the Stuart Masque* (Brown University Press, 1982) makes this job easier. There are also later extant masques such as Matthew Locke's *Cupid and Death* (1654), written to get around the puritan prohibition against spoken drama.

The operas of Claudio Monteverdi run a close second to Purcell in English-speaking lands. *L'Incoronazione di Poppea* (1641/2) is available in a number of editions in English and in Italian. *L'Orfeo* (1607) is perhaps easier to bring off, but both require highly skilled singers and players, as does the nearly unapproachable *Ritorno d'Ulisse in Patria* (1640). Smaller groups and colleges might think of Monteverdi's many occasional pieces, such as *Il Combattimento di Tancredi e Clorinda* or *Il ballo delle ingrate* (1608), both small-scale works. There are smaller scale pieces yet, such as *Tirsi e Clori* (1619), perhaps the world's shortest opera, clocking in at about nine minutes. There has been a recent fashion for presenting an evening of shorter Monteverdi pieces, staged or semistaged, under titles such as "Love and War"—reflecting the title of Monteverdi's eighth book of madrigals, *Madrigali Guerrieri et Amorosi* (1638), in which several of these pieces were published. In the same vein, Marco da Gagliano's *La Dafne* (1608) requires modest forces and was written for the same Mantuan court festival as Monteverdi's *Ballo Delle Ingrate.*

All of the works of Francesco Cavalli (1602–76) were written for performance in the professional theater, and there are no smaller works that might appeal to smaller groups. Nevertheless, *L'Ormindo* and *La Calisto,* probably his best known works, are available in editions by Raymond Leppard, and others are beginning to be made available in less "edited" versions. Cavalli's *Il Giasone* (1649) was perhaps the most popular opera of the seventeenth century.[1]

Other Italian repertory worth looking into is the *intermedii* and madrigal comedies of the late sixteenth and early seventeenth centuries. *Intermedii,* such as *La Pellegrina* (1589, published in 1963 as *La Musique des Intermèdes*), were designed to be played between the acts of a play, or courses of a meal. The madrigal comedies of Adriano Banchieri such as *L'Amfiparnaso* (1597) and *La Pazzia senile* (1598) are staging challenges: they are suites of madrigals in which all voices sing all dramatic parts in polyphony. Some authorities think that they were performed in pantomime by *commedia dell'arte* actors while the singers sang their parts from the side. The *Delizie di Posilipo boscarecchie e maritime* (1620) is a Neapolitan court masque that mixes Italian and Spanish text with instrumental music and dance in praise of the rapacious Spanish Viceroy of Naples. I break my rule to tell you that it was published in Recent Researches in 1978 as *A Neapolitan Festa a Ballo.*[2] Emilio de' Cavalieri's *Il Rappresentatione de anima e corpo* (1600) is an early sacred opera requiring medium forces and minimal staging.

Francesca Caccini's *La Liberazione di Ruggiero* (1625) is an excellent piece requiring fairly modest forces, and it has the historical distinction of being the earliest extant opera by a woman. Finally, Jacopo Peri's *L'Euridice* (1600) is the first extant opera, and a tough nut to crack. Apparently it always was: Giulio Caccini (father of Francesca) set the *Euridice* libretto at the same time as Peri, because he did not want his students appearing in the production to have to sing Peri's music! I have always thought that reconstructing the big fight between Peri and Caccini would be the key to staging *L'Euridice*.

The French repertory does not consist entirely of immensely difficult *tragédies lyriques* by Lully. The great works of Lully and Charpentier are probably outside the realm of this discussion, as they require the resources of a *Roi Soleil* to be properly done. There are, however, lots of delightful small-scale pieces by Lully and Charpentier and their compatriots. Charpentier's *Acteon* (1683–5) makes a good companion piece to *Dido and Æneas*, and his *Les Plaisirs de Versailles* (ca. 1680), featuring a musical battle between the goddesses of *conversation* and *musique*, is absolutely hilarious. It makes a good pair with Lully's little-known *La Grotte de Versailles* (1668). An ambitious group might think of mounting one of the *comédies-ballet* of Molière with the original Lully or Charpentier music. Charpentier is also responsible for a number of delightful oratorios *de Noël*, which, although entirely dramatic in form, were probably not staged in the seventeenth century.

The German repertory of the seventeenth century (and most of the eighteenth) is almost entirely Italian and has not been sufficiently researched for me to have much to say about it. Heinrich Schütz composed a *Dafne* in 1627, which is still lost at this writing. In Spain, as in England, there was a long-standing tradition of spoken plays with songs performed in the busy public theaters in Madrid and in other urban centers, and this influenced the creation of partly sung genres for the court stages—the mythological semi-operas and pastoral *zarzuelas*. Useful editions of *zarzuelas* include those by Jack Sage of the music (by Juan Hidalgo) for Juan Vélez de Guevara's *Los celos hacen estrellas,* and Antonio Martën Moreno for Durón's *Salir el amor del mundo.* The extant music for the semi-opera *La estatua de Prometeo* (by Hidalgo and Calderón) is transcribed by Stein with the recent critical edition of the text of the play. A few all-sung operas are extant from this period in Spain, including Hidalgo's *Celos aun del aire matan* (1660) and Tomás de Torrejón's setting of *La Púrpura de la rosa*. Both of these have libretti by Pedro Calderón de la Barca, and both are forthcoming in performing editions by Louise K. Stein. Torrejón's *La Púrpura de la rosa,* written for Lima, Peru, in 1701 to celebrate the birthday of the new King of Spain, is an appropriate one with which to end this discussion—the first New World opera, it might well be called the last seventeenth-century opera.

NOTES

1. See Loewenberg–*Annals*, col. 25.
2. *Recent Researches in the Music of the Baroque Era,* vol. 25, ed. Roland Jackson.

FURTHER READING

The following reading list does not pretend to be comprehensive, and deliberately avoids foreign-language materials that may prove irrelevant to the general reader. All of the cited works have significant portions devoted to various aspects of seventeenth-century music theater.

Barnett–*Gesture*; Baur-Heinold–*Baroque Theater*; Bergmann–*Lighting*; Donington–*Opera*; Durón and Cañizares–*Salir*; Drummond–*Opera*; Grout–*Opera*; Hammond–*Music and Spectacle*; Laver–*Costume*; De Marly–*Costume*; Nagler–*Source Book*; Nagler–*Theater Festival*; *New Grove*; *New Grove Opera*; Nicoll–*Theater*; Nicoll–*Stuart Masques*; Orrey–*Opera*; Rosand–*Opera*; Sage–Hidalgo; Savage–Producing Dido; Stein–La Plática; Stein–*Songs*.

General Bibliography

Agazzari, Agostino. *Del sonare sopra il basso*. Siena, 1607.

Agricola, J. F. *Anleitung zur Singkunst*. A translation [with additions] of P. F. Tosi's *Opinioni de' cantori antichi e moderni*. Berlin, 1757. Facs. ed. Erwin R. Jacobi with preface and appendix. Celle: Hermann Moeck Verlag, 1966. Trans. Julianne Baird as *Introduction to the Art of Singing*. Cambridge: Cambridge University Press, 1995.

Albert, Heinrich. *Arien*. Vol. 2. Königsberg, 1640.

Aldrich, Putnam. *Rhythm in Italian Monody*. New York: Norton, 1966.

Alessandri, Felippo de gli. *Discorso sopra il ballo*. Terni, 1620.

Allsop, Peter. *The Italian 'Trio' Sonata: From Its Origins to Corelli*. New York: Oxford University Press, 1992.

———. "The Role of the Stringed Bass as a Continuo Instrument in Italian Seventeenth-Century Instrumental Music." *Chelys* 8 (1978–79): 31–37.

Altenberg, Detlef. *Untersuchungen zur Geschichte der Trompete im Zeitalter der Clarinblaskunst (1500–1800)*. Regensburg: Gustav Bosse, 1973.

Altenburg, Johann Ernst. *Versuch einer Anleitung zur heroisch-musikalischen Trompeter- und Pauker-Kunst*. Halle, 1770/1795. Trans. Edward H. Tarr as *Essay on an Introduction to the Heroic and Musical Trumpeters' and Kettledrummers' Art*. Nashville: Brass Press, 1974.

Antegnati, Costanzo. *L' Arte organica*. Brescia, 1608. Facs. rep. Bologna: Forni, 1971.

Anthony, James R. *French Baroque Music: From Beaujoyeulx to Rameau*. Rev. ed. New York: Norton, 1978.

Apel, Willi. *Italian Violin Music of the Seventeenth Century*. Ed. Thomas Binkley. Bloomington: Indiana University Press, 1990.

———. *The History of Keyboard Music to 1700*. Trans. and rev. Hans Tischler. Bloomington: Indiana University Press, 1972.

———. *The Notation of Polyphonic Music, 900–1600*. Cambridge, MA: Mediaeval Academy of America, 1942.

Arbeau, Thoinot (pseudonym for Jehan Tabourot). *Orchésographie*. Langres, 1589. Rep. with expanded title, 1596. Facs. rep. of 1596 edition. Geneva: Minkoff, 1972. Trans. Mary Stewart Evans. New York: Kamin Dance Publishers, 1948. Rep. with corrections, a new introduction, and notes by Julia Sutton; and representative steps and dances in Labanotation by Mireille Backer. New York: Dover, 1967.

Arnold, Franck T. *The Art of Accompaniment from a Thorough-Bass as Practised in the XVIIth & XVIIIth Centuries*. London: Oxford University Press, 1931. Facs. rep. in 2 vols. with intro. by Denis Stevens. New York: Dover, 1965.

Ashbee, Andrew. *Records of English Court Music*. Vols. 1–7. Aldershot: Scolar Press, 1991. (Vols. 8–9 forthcoming.)

Ashworth, Jack. "How to Improve a Continuo Realization." *The American Recorder* 27 (1985): 62–65.

———, and Paul O'Dette. "Proto-Continuo." In Kite-Powell–*Renaissance,* 203–13.

Avgerinos, Gerassimos. *Handbook der Schlag- und Effektinstrumenta*. Frankfurt/Main: Verlag der Musikinstrument, 1964.

———. *Lexikon der Pauke*. Frankfurt/Main: Verlag der Musikinstrument, 1964.

Bacilly, Benigne de. *Remarques curieuses sur l'art de bien chanter.* Paris, 1668. Facs. rep. of 1679 edition. Geneva: Minkoff, 1971. Trans. Austin B. Caswell as *A Commentary upon the Art of Proper Singing.* New York: Institute of Mediaeval Music, 1968.

Bailes, Anthony. "An Introduction to French Lute Music of the XVIIth Century." In *Le Luth et sa Musique.* Ed. Jean-Michel Vaccaro. Paris: Editions du Centre National de la Recherche Scientifique, 1984, II: 213–28.

Baines, Anthony. *Brass Instruments, their History and Development.* London: Faber & Faber, 1976.

Baines, Anthony. *European and American Musical Instruments.* London: Batsford, 1966.

———. "James Talbot's Manuscript." *Galpin Society Journal* 1 (1948): 9–26. Further install-ments in subsequent issues.

———. "Shawms of the Sardana Coblas." *Galpin Society Journal* 5 (1952): 9–16.

———. *Woodwind Instruments and their History.* Rev. ed. New York: Norton, 1963.

Baird, Julianne. "Beyond the Beautiful Pearl." In Sherman–*Inside.*

Banchieri, Adriano. "Dialogo Musicale." Printed in the 2d edition of *L' Organo suonarino.* Venice, 1611.

———. *L'organo suonarino.* Venice, 1605, 1611, 1622, 1638. Facs. rep. Bologna: Forni, 1969.

———. *La Cartella.* Venice, 1614. Facs. rep. Bologna: Forni, n.d.

Bank, J. A. *Tactus, Tempo and Notation in Mensural Music from the 13th to the 17th Century.* Amsterdam: Annie Bank, 1972.

Barbarino, Bartolomeo. *Il secondo libro delli motetti . . . da cantarsi à una voce sola ò in sopra-no, ò in tenore come più il cantante si piacerà.* Venice, 1614.

Barclay, Robert. *The Art of the Trumpet-Maker: The Materials, Tools, and Techniques of the Seventeenth and Eighteenth Centuries in Nuremberg.* Oxford: Oxford University Press, 1992.

Barcotto, Antonio. *Regola e breve raccordo.* Ms Bologna Cons C-80. 1652. Trans. and com-mentary by Peter V. Picerno. *Organ Yearbook* 16 (1985): 70.

Barley, William. *New Booke of Tabliture.* London, 1596.

Barnett, Dene. *The Art of Gesture.* Heidelberg: Carl Winter, 1987.

Baron, John, ed. *Spanish Art Song in the Seventeenth Century. Recent Researches in the Music of the Baroque Era.* Vol. 49. Madison, WI: A-R Editions, 1985.

Bartlett, Clifford, and Peter Holman. "Giovanni Gabrieli: A Guide to the Performance of his Instrumental Music." *Early Music* 3 (1975): 25–32.

Baryphonus, Henrichus. *Ars Canendi: aphorismis succinctis discripta & notis philosophicis, math-ematicis, physicis et historicis illustrata.* Leipzig, 1620.

Bates, Carol H. "The Early French Sonata for Solo Instruments: A Study in Diversity." *Recherches sur la musique française classique* 28 (1991–92): 71–98.

Bathe, William. *A Briefe Introduction to the Skill of Song.* London, 1587. Facs. rep. Kilkenny, Ireland: Boethius, 1982.

Baumgarten, Georg. *Rudimenta musices: Kurze, jedoch grundliche Anleitung zur Figuralmusick furnehmlich der studirenden Jugen au Landsberg an der Martha zum Bestern vorgeschrieben..* Berlin, 1673.

Beck, John, ed. *Encyclopedia of Percussion.* New York, Garland, 1995.

Baur-Heinold, Margarethe. *Baroque Theater.* New York: McGraw Hill, 1964.

Beecher, Donald, and Stuart Cheney. Introduction to Dubuisson, *Thirteen Suites for Solo Viola da Gamba.* Ottawa: Dove House, 1994.

———. "Aesthetics of the French Solo Viol Repertory, 1650–1680." *Journal of the Viola da Gamba Society of America* 24 (1987): 10–21.

Beier, Paul. "Right Hand Position in Renaissance Lute Technique." *Journal of the Lute Society of America* 12 (1979): 5–24.

Bellingham, Bruce. "The Musical Circle of Anthony Wood in Oxford During the Commonwealth and Restoration." *Journal of the Viola da Gamba Society of America* 19 (1982): 6–70.

Bendinelli, Cesare. *Tutta l'arte della Trombetta.* Ms, Verona, 1614. Facs. rep., ed. Edward H. Tarr. Kassel: Bärenreiter, 1975. Trans. and ed. Edward H. Tarr as *The Entire Art of Trumpet Playing.* Nashville: Brass Press, 1975.

GENERAL BIBLIOGRAPHY

Benoit, Marcelle. *Musiques de cour: Chapelle, Chambre, Écurie, 1661–1733*. Paris: Picard, 1971.
———. "Paris, 1661–87: The Age of Lully." In *Music and Society: The Early Baroque*. Ed. Curtis Price. Englewood Cliffs, NJ: Prentice-Hall, 1993.
———, ed. *Dictionnaire de la musique en France aux XVIIe et XVIIIe siècles*. Paris: Fayard, 1992.
Berger, Anna Maria Busse. *Mensuration and Proportion Signs: Origins and Evolution*. Oxford: Clarendon Press, 1993.
Bergman, Walter. "Henry Purcell's Use of the Recorder." *Hinrichsen's Eleventh Music Book: Music Libraries and Instruments*, 227–33. London: Hinrichsen, 1961.
Bergmann, Gösta M. *Lighting in the Theater*. Totowa, NJ: Rowman & Littlefield, 1977.
Bermudo, Juan. *El libro llamado declaración de instrumentos musicales*. Osuna, 1555. Facs. rep. Kassel: Bärenreiter, 1957.
Bernhard, Christoph. *Von der Singe-Kunst oder Manier*. Ms., ca. 1649. In *Die Kompositionslehre Heinrich Schützens in der Fassung seines Schulers Christoph Bernhard*. Ed. Joseph Maria Müller-Blattau, 31–39. Kassel: Bärenreiter, 1963. Trans. Walter Hilse as "On the Art of Singing: or, Manier." *The Music Forum* 3 (1973): 13–29.
Besseler, Heinrich. *Bourdon und Fauxbourdon*. Leipzig: Breitkopf & Härtel, 1974.
———. "Die Entstehung der Posaune." *Acta Musicologica* 22 (1950): 8–35.
Bianciardi, Francesco. *Breve regola per imparar a sonare sopra il Basso con ogni sorte d'Instrumento*. Siena?, 1607.
Bianconi, Lorenzo. *Music in the Seventeenth Century*. Trans. David Bryant. Cambridge: Cambridge University Press, 1987.
Billio D'Arpa, Nicoletta. "Amadio Freddi, musicista padovano." *Il Santo: Rivista antoniana di storia, dottrina ed arte* 27 (1987): 241–63.
Bismantova, Bartolomeo. *Compendio Musicale*. Ms., Ferrara, 1677. Facs. ed. Florence: Studio per Edizione Scelte, 1978.
Blachly, Alexander. "On Singing and the Vocal Ensemble I." In Kite-Powell–*Renaissance*, 3–12.
Blades, James. *Percussion Instruments and Their History*. London: Oxford University Press, 1970; ²1984.
———, and Jeremy Montagu. *Early Percussion Instruments: From the Middle Ages to the Baroque*. London: Oxford University Press, 1976.
Blount, Thomas. *Glossographia: or a dictionary interpreting all such hard words. . . .* London, 1656.
Blow, John. *Anthems with Orchestra 2 & 3*. Ed. Bruce Wood. *Musica Britannica*. Vols. 50 and 64. London: Stainer & Bell, 1984, 1993. (Notes on Performance 64, xxviii–xxxiii.)
———. "Rules for playing of a Through Bass upon Organ & Harpsicon." London, BL Add. MS 34072, ca. 1674.
Boal, Ellen TeSelle. "Purcell's Clock Tempos and the Fantasias." *Journal of the Viola da Gamba Society of America* 20 (1983): 24–39.
———. "Purcell's Tempo Indications in the Fantasias and Sonatas: Metronomic Indications before Mälzel." Paper presented at the College Music Society National Meeting, Portland, OR, 1995.
———. *Timepieces, Time and Musical Tempo before 1700*. Ph.D. dissertation, Washington University, 1983.
Bocquet, Pascale. *Approche du Luth Renaissance*. Self-published, 1988. Available through the Société Française de Luth, 48, rue Bargue, 75015 Paris, France.
Bol, Hans. *La basse de viole du temps de Marin Marais et d'Antoine Forqueray*. Bilthoven: Creyghton, 1973.
Bonino, Mary Ann. *Severo Bonini's Discorsi e Regole*. Provo, UT: Brigham Young University Press, 1979.
Bononcini, Giovanni Maria. *Musico prattico*. Bologna, 1673.
Bonta, Stephen. "Terminology for the Bass Violin in Seventeenth-Century Italy." *Journal of the American Musical Instrument Society* 4 (1978): 5–42.
———. "Clef, Mode, and Instruments in Italy, 1540–1650." Paper presented at the Fifth Biennial Conference on Baroque Music, Durham, NC, July 1992.

————. "From Violone to Violoncello: A Question of Strings?" *Journal of the American Musical Instrument Society* 3 (1977): 64–99.

————. Introduction to *The Instrumental Music of Giovanni Legrenzi: La Cetra . . . Opus 10, 1673*. Cambridge, MA: Harvard University Press, 1992, xiii–xvi.

————. "Terminology for the Bass Violin in Seventeenth-Century Italy." *Journal of the American Musical Instrument Society* 4 (1978): 5–42.

————. "The Use of Instruments in Sacred Music in Italy, 1560–1700." *Early Music* 18 (1990): 519–35.

————. "The Uses of the *Sonata da Chiesa*." *Journal of the American Musicological Society* 22 (1969): 54–84.

Bontempi, Giovanni. *Storia della musica*. Perugia, 1695.

Borgir, Tharald. *The Performance of the Basso Continuo in Italian Baroque Music*. Ann Arbor: UMI Research Press, 1987.

Borjon de Scellery, Charles-Emmanuel. *Traité de la musette*. Lyons, 1672.

Borlasca, Bernardino. *Scala Iacob, octonis vocibus, et varijs instrumentis omnibus anni solemnitatibus decantanda . . . opus sextum*. Venice, 1616.

Bottrigari, Ercole. *Il desiderio overo de' concerti di varij strumenti musicali*. Bologna, 1594. Facs. ed. Bologna: Forni, 1969.

Boudreaux, Margaret Anne. *Michael Praetorius's Polyhymnia Caduceatrix et Panegyrica (1619): An Annotated Translation*. D.M.A. dissertation, University of Colorado, 1989.

Bourgeois, Loys. *Le droit chemin de Musique*. Geneva, 1550.

Bovicelli, Giovanni Battista. *Regole, passaggi di musica*. Venice, 1594. Facs. rep., ed. Nanie Bridgman, Documenta Musicologica. Kassel: Bärenreiter, 1957.

Bowers, Jane. "New Light on the Development of the Transverse Flute between about 1650 and about 1770." *Journal of the American Musical Instrument Society* 3 (1977): 5–56.

Bowers, Roger. "Some Reflection upon Notation and Proportion in Monteverdi's Mass and Vespers of 1610." *Music and Letters* 73 (1992): 347–95. Critical appraisal of this article by Jeffrey Kurtzman, with a reply by Bowers, in *Music and Letters* 74 (1993): 487–95.

Bowles, Edmund A. "The Double, Double, Double Beat of the Thundering Drum: The Timpani in Early Music." *Early Music* 19 (1991): 419–35.

————. *Musical Ensembles in Festival Books, 1500–1800: An Iconographical & Documentary Survey*. Studies in Music 103. Ann Arbor: UMI Research Press, 1989.

————. "On Using the Proper Timpani in the Perofrmance of Baroque Music." *Journal of the Musical Instrument Society* 2 (1976): 56–68.

————. *The Timpani: A History in Pictures and Documents*. Stuyvesant, NY: forthcoming.

Bowman, Horace D. *The Castrati Singers and their Music*. Ph.D. dissertation, Indiana University, 1951.

Boxall, Maria. "Girolamo Diruta's 'Il Transilvano' and the Early Italian Keyboard Tradition." *English Harpsichord Magazine* 1 (1976): 168–72.

————, and Mark Lindley. *Early Keyboard Fingerings*. London: Schott, 1992.

Boydell, Barra. *The Crumhorn and Other Renaissance Windcap Instruments*. Buren: Fritz Knuf, 1982.

Boyden, David. "Monteverdi's *Violini Piccoli alla Francese* and *Viole da Brazzo*." *Annales Musicologiques* 6 (1958–63): 388–401.

————. "The Tenor Violin: Myth, Mystery, or Misnomer?" In W. Gerstenberg, J. La Rue, and W. Rehm, eds., *Festschrift Otto Erich Deutsch*, 273–79. Kassel: Bärenreiter, 1963.

————. *The History of Violin Playing from its Origins to 1761*. London: Oxford University Press, 1965.

Brainard, Ingrid. "Renaissance Dance." In Kite-Powell–*Renaissance*, 317–25.

Brainard, Paul. "Proportional Notation in the Music of Schütz and his Contemporaries." *Current Musicology* 50 (1992): 21–46.

Brenet, Michel [Marie Bobillier]. *Les Concerts en France sous l'Ancien Régime* Paris: Fischbacher, 1900.

Brossard, Sébastien de. *Dictionaire de musique contenant une explication des termes grecs, latins, italiens, & françois les plus usitez.* . . . Paris, 1703; ²1705. Facs. rep. of 1703 edition. Amsterdam: Antiqua, 1964.

Brown, Howard Mayer. *Embellishing 16th-Century Music.* London: Oxford University Press, 1976.

———. *Instrumental Music Printed Before 1600.* Cambridge, MA: Harvard University Press, 1965.

———, and Stanley Sadie, eds. *Performance Practice: Music after 1600.* New York: Norton, 1990.

Brunelli, Antonio. *Varii esercitii . . . per . . . aqquistare la dispositione per il cantare con passaggi.* Florence, 1614.

Bryant, David. "The 'Cori Spezzati' of Saint Mark's: Myth and Reality." *Early Music History* 1 (1981): 165–86.

Buch, David J. *Dance Music from the Ballets de cour, 1575–1651.* Stuyvesant, NY: Pendragon, 1993.

———. "Texture in French Baroque Lute Music and Related Ensemble Repertoires." *Journal of the Lute Society of America* 20–21 (1987–88): 120–54.

———. "The Influence of the ballet de cour in the Genesis of the French Baroque Suite." *Acta Musicologica* 62/1 (1985): 94–109.

Burnett, Henry. "The Bowed String Instruments of the Baroque Basso Continuo (c.1680–c.1752) in Italy and France." *Journal of the Viola da Gamba Society of America* 7 (1970): 65–91; and 8 (1971): 29–63.

Burney, Charles. *A General History of Music from the earliest ages to the present period (1789).* Rep. with critical and historical notes by Frank Mercer. New York: Dover, 1957.

Butler, Charles. *The Principles of Musik, in Singing and Setting.* London, 1636.

Butt, John. *Music Education and the Art of Performance in the German Baroque.* Cambridge: Cambridge University Press, 1994.

Caccini, Giulio. *L'Euridice composta in musica.* Florence, 1600. Facs. rep. Bologna: Forni, 1968.

———. *Le Nuove musiche e nuova maniera di scriverle (1614).* Ed. and trans. H. Wiley Hitchcock. *Recent Researches in the Music of the Baroque Era* 28. Madison, WI: A-R Editions, 1978.

———. *Le nuove musiche.* Florence, 1602. Facs. ed. by F. Mantica, preface by G. Barini. Rome, 1930. Trans. and ed. H. Wiley Hitchcock, *Recent Researches in the Music of the Baroque Era* 9. Madison, WI: A-R Editions, 1970. Anon. trans. entitled "A Brief Discourse of the Italian Manner of Singing . . ." in J. Playford, *Introduction to the Skill of Music.* 10th ed. London, 1683. Rev. ed. of the latter in Strunk–*Source Readings.* English trans. in Newton–Nuove Musiche.

Caffagni, Mirko. "The Modena Tiorba MS." *Journal of the Lute Society of America* 12 (1979): 25–42.

Caldwell, John. *Oxford History of English Music.* Vol. 1: *From the Beginning to c.1715.* Oxford: Clarendon Press, 1991.

Calvisius, Seth. *Compendium Musicae.* Leipzig, 1594.

Cametti, Alberto. "I musici di Campidoglio, ossia 'Il concerto di tromboni e cornetti del senato e inclito popolo romano' (1524–1818)." *Archivio della Società Romano di Storia Patria* 48 (1925): 95–135.

Carissimi, Giovan Giacomo. *Ars cantandi: Das ist richtiger und ausführlicher Weg / die Jugend aus dem rechten Grund in der Sing Kunst zu unterrichten.* Augsburg, 1696.

Caroso, Fabritio. *Il Ballarino.* Venice, 1581. Facs. rep. New York: Broude, 1967.

———. *Nobiltà dí Dame.* Venice, 1600, 1605. Facs. rep. Bologna: Forni, 1970. Ed. and trans. Julia Sutton as *A Treatise on Courtly Dance, Together with the Choreography and Music of 49 Dances.* Music ed. F. Marian Walker. New York: Oxford University Press, 1986.

———. *Raccolta di varij balli.* Reissue, with a new title page, of *Nobiltà di dame.* Rome, 1630.

Carse, Adam. *Musical Wind Instruments*. London: 1939. Reprint. New York: Da Capo, 1965.

Carter, Stewart. "Francesco Rognoni"s *"Selva di varii passaggi* (1620): Fresh Details Concerning Early Baroque Vocal Ornamentation." *Performance Practice Review* 2 (1989): 5–33.

————. "On the Shape of the Early Baroque Trill." *Historical Performance* 3/1 (1990): 9–17.

————. "Sackbut." In Kite-Powell–*Renaissance,* 97–108.

————. "The String Tremolo in the 17th Century." *Early Music* 19 (1991): 43–59.

————. "Trombone Obbligatos in Viennese Oratorios of the Baroque." *Historic Brass Society Journal* 2 (1990): 52–77.

Castaldi, Bellerofonte. *Primo Mazzetto di fiori*. Venice, 1623.

Castellani, Marcello. "The *Regola per suonare il Flauto Italiano* by Bartolomeo Bismantova (1677)." *Galpin Society Journal* 30 (1977): 77–85.

Castiglione, Baldassare. *Il libro del cortegiano,* Florence, 1528, *libro primo.* Trans. Virginia Cox as *The Book of the Courtier.* London: Everyman, 1994.

Catch, John R. "James Talbot's Viols." *Chelys* 17 (1988): 24–27.

Cavalieri, Emilio de'. *Rappresentatione di anima e di corpo.* Rome, 1600. Facs. rep. Farnborough: Gregg, 1967.

Celletti, Rodolfo. *A History of Bel Canto.* Trans. Frederick Fuller. Oxford: Clarendon Press, 1991.

Cerone. *El melopeo y maestro.* Naples, 1613.

Cesari, Gaetano, and Guido Pannain, eds. *La musica in Cremona nella seconda metá del secolo XVI.* . . . Vol. 6 of *Istitutioni e monumenti dell'arte musicale italiana.* Milan: Ricordi, 1939.

Cessac, Catherine. *Marc-Antoine Charpentier.* Trans. E. Thomas Glasow. Portland, OR: Amadeus, 1995.

Chafe, Eric. *The Church Music of Heinrich Biber.* Ann Arbor: UMI Research Press, 1987.

Charteris, Richard. "The Performance of Giovanni Gabrieli's Vocal Works: Indications in the Early Sources." *Music and Letters* 71 (1990): 336–51.

Cheney, Stuart G. "A Summary of Dubuisson's Life and Sources." *Journal of the Viola da Gamba Society of America* 27 (1990): 7–21.

Christensen, Jesper Joje. "Zur Generalbass-Praxis bei Händel und Bach." *Basler Jahrbuch für historische Musikpraxis* 9 (1985): 39–88.

Christout, Marie-Françoise. *Le Ballet de cour au XVIIe siècle.* Iconographie Musicale 8. Geneva: Minkoff, 1987.

————. *Le ballet de cour de Louis XIV (1643–1672).* Paris: Éditions A. et J. Picard et Cie., 1967.

————. "The Court Ballet in France, 1615–1641." *Dance Perspectives* 20 (1964): 4–25.

Coeyman, Barbara. "Viole de gambe (répertoire)." In Benoit–*Dictionnaire,* 717–19.

Cohen, Albert. "A Study of Instrumental Ensemble Practice in Seventeenth-Century France." *Galpin Society Journal* 15 (1963): 3–17.

————. "The 'Fantaisie' for Instrumental Ensemble in 17th-Century France: Its Origin and Significance." *Musical Quarterly* 48/2 (April, 1962): 234–43.

————. *The Evolution of the "Fantasia" and Works in Related Styles in the Seventeenth-Century Instrumental Ensemble Music of France and the Low Countries.* Ph.D. dissertation, New York University, 1958.

Collver, Michael, and Bruce Dickey. *A Catalog of Music for the Cornett.* Bloomington: Indiana Univeristy Press, 1996.

Compasso, Lutio. *Ballo della Gagliarda.* Florence, 1560. Facs. rep. with intro. by Barbara Sparti. Freiburg: fa-gisis Musik- und Tanzeditions, 1995.

Conforti, Giovanni Luca. *Breve et facile maniera.* Rome, 1593. Facs. rep. with German translation by J. Wolf. Berlin: M. Breslauer, 1922. Facs. rep., ed. Denis Stevens as *The Joy of Ornamentation.* White Plains, NY: Pro/Am Music Resources, 1989. Eng. trans. of preface by Stewart Carter in review of Stevens edition. *Historical Performance* 5/1 (1992): 50–54.

Conforzi, Igino. "Girolamo Fantini, 'Monarch of the Trumpet': Recent Additions to His Biography." *Historic Brass Society Journal* 5 (1993): 159–73.

Cooper, John Michael. "The Performance Practices and Literature of the Timpani in German Concerted Music of the Late Renaissance and the Baroque: Historical and Musical Perspectives." M.M. thesis, Florida State University, 1988.

Cooper, John Michael. "The Realisation and Embellishment of Timpani Parts in German Baroque Music: The *Schlagmanieren* Revisited." *Early Music*, forthcoming.

Copeman, Harold. *Singing in Latin*. Oxford: by the author, 1990.

Correa de Arauxo, Francesco. *Libro de tientos y discursos de musica practica, y theorica de organo intitulado Facultad organica*. Alcala, 1626.

Couperin, François. *L'art de toucher le clavecin*. Paris, 1716/1717. Trans. Margery Halford. [Van Nuys, CA]: Alfred, 1974.

Coussemaker, Edmund de. *Scriptorum de musica medii aevi*. Paris: Durand, 1864.

Cranna, Clifford A., Jr. *Adriano Banchieri's Cartella Musicale (1614): Translation and Commentary*. Ph.D. dissertation, Stanford University, 1981.

Crawford, Tim. "Allemande Mr. Zuilekom: Constantijn Huygens's Sole Surviving Instrumental Composition." *Tijdschrift van de Vereniging voor Nederlandse Muziekgeschiedenis* 37 (1987): 175–81.

———. "Constantijn Huygens and the 'Engelsche Viool.'" *Chelys* 18 (1989): 41–60.

Crüger, Johannes. *Kurtzer under verstendtlicher Unterrict recht und leichtlich singen zu lernen*. Berlin, 1625.

———. *Musicae practicae praecepta . . . Der rechte Weg zur Singkunst*. Berlin, 1660.

Cunningham, James B. *Dancing in the Inns of Court*. London: Jordan, 1965.

Cyr, Mary. "On Performing 18th-Century Haute-Contre Roles." *Musical Times* 118 (1977): 291–95.

Cyr, Mary. "The Viol in Baroque Paintings and Drawings." *Journal of the Viola da Gamba Society of America* 11 (1974): 5–16.

D'Alessi, Giovanni. "Precursors of Adriano Willaert in the Practice of *Coro Spezzato*." *Journal of the American Musicological Society* 5 (1952): 187–210.

d'Anglebert, Jean-Henri. *Principes de l'Accompagnement*, printed in his *Pièces de Clavecin*. Vol. 1. Paris, 1689.

Dahlhaus, Carl. "Zur Entstehung des modernen Taktsystems im 17. Jahrhundert." *Archiv für Musikwissenschaft* 18 (1961): 223–40.

———. "Zur Geschichte des Taktschlagens im frühen 17. Jahrhundert." In *Studies in Renaissance and Baroque Music in Honor of Arthur Mendel*. Ed. Robert Marshall, 117–23. Kassel: Bärenreiter, 1974.

Dahlqvist, Reine (with Edward H. Tarr). "Corno and Corno da Caccia: Horn Terminology, Horn Pitches, and High Horn Parts." *Basler Jahrbuch für historische Musikpraxis* 15 (1991): 40–42.

———. *Bidrag till trumpeten . . .* Ph.D. dissertation, University of Göteborg, 1988.

———. "Gottfried Reiche's Instrument: A Problem of Classification." *Historic Brass Society Journal* 5 (1993): 174–91.

———. "Pitches of German, French, and English Trumpets in the 17th and 18th Centuries." *Historic Brass Society Journal* 5 (1993): 29–41.

Dalla Casa, Girolamo. *Il vero modo di diminuir, con tutte le sorti di stromenti . . .* Venice, 1584. Facs. rep. Bologna: Forni, 1980.

Darbellay, Étienne. "Tempo Relationships in Frescobaldi's *Primo Libro di Capricci*." In *Frescobaldi Studies*. Ed. Alexander Silbiger, 301–26. Sources of Music and Their Interpretation: Duke Studies in Music. Durham, NC: Duke University Press, 1987.

Das Zinkbuch. Basler Jahrbuch für historische Musikpraxis 5 (1981). Includes articles by Bruce Dickey and Michael Collver, Edward Tarr, Petra Leonards, and Heinrich Thein.

David, Hans T., and Arthur Mendel. *The Bach Reader: A Life of Johann Sebastian Bach in Letters and Documents*. Rev. ed. New York: Norton, 1966.

De Marly, Diana. *Costume on the Stage, 1600–1940*. London: Batsford, 1982.

Delair, Denis. *Traité de l'Accompagnement pour le Théorbe et le Clavessin*. Paris, 1690.

Della Valle, Pietro. "Discorso della musica dell'età nostra . . . ." In G. B. Doni, *Lyra Barberina*. Vol. 2. Florence, 1640. Facs. rep. with commentary by Claude Palisca. Bologna: A.M.I.S., 1981.

Demantius, Christoph. *Isagoge artis musicae*. Freiburg, 1632.

Dickey, Bruce, and Michael Collver. "Musik für Zink: ein Quellenkatalog." *Basler Jahrbuch für historische Musikpraxis* 5 (1981): 263–313.

Dickey, Bruce, Petra Leonards, and Edward H. Tarr. "The Discussion of Wind Instruments in Bartolomeo Bismantova's *Compendio Musicale* (1677): Translation and Commentary." *Basler Jahrbuch für historische Musikpraxis* 2 (1978): 172–77.

Diruta, Girolamo. *Il transilvano dialogo sopra il vero modo di sonar organi, et istromenti da penna*. Venice, 1593. Vol. 2. Venice, 1609. Facs. rep. Bologna: Forni, 1969.

Dixon, Graham. "Continuo Scoring in the Early Baroque: The Role of Bowed Bass Instruments." *Chelys* 15 (1986): 38–53.

———. "Monteverdi's Vespers of 1610: 'della Beata Vergine'?" *Early Music* 15 (1987): 386–89.

Dixon, Peggy. *Nonsuch: Early Dance*. Vol. 2: *Quattrocentro Italian and Caroso and Negri Dances*. Glasgow: McKay, 1985. (Dance reconstruction and practice tape.)

Dodd, Gordon. Draft version of critical notes for *Warsaw, Biblioteka Warsawskiego Tomarzystwa Muzycznego, In. 377/No.221*. Facs. ed. Geneva: Minkoff, forthcoming.

Dolmetsch, Arnold. *The Interpretation of the Music of the 17th and 18th Centuries*. London: Novello, 1915.

Donati, Ignazio. *Sacri concentus*. Venice, 1612.

Donato, Giuseppe. "La policoralità a Messina nel XVI e XVII secolo." In *La policoralità in Italia nei secoli XVI e XVII*. Ed. Giuseppe Donato, 135–48. Miscellanea Musicologica 3. Rome: Edizioni Torre d'Orfeo, 1987.

Doni, Giovanni Battista. *Annotazioni sopra il compendio de' generi, e de' modi della musica*. Rome, 1640.

Donington, Robert. *The Interpretation of Early Music*. London: Faber & Faber, 1963. Rev. ed. New York: Norton, 1989.

———. *Opera and its Symbols*. New Haven: Yale University Press, 1990.

———. "Ornaments." In *New Grove*.

———. *A Performer's Guide to Baroque Music*. New York: Scribner's, 1973.

Douglass, David. "Play It." *Strings* 9/3 (November/December 1994): 32 ff.

———. "Renaissance Violin." *Strings* 5/1 (July/August 1990): 24–27.

———. "The Violin." In Kite-Powell–*Renaissance*, 125–38.

Dowland, John. *Andreas Ornithoparcus His Micrologus, or Introduction Containing the Art of Singing*. London, 1609. Facs. rep. Amsterdam, NY: Da Capo, 1969.

Downey, Peter. "A Renaissance Correspondence Concerning Trumpet Music." *Early Music* 9 (1981): 325–29.

———. *The Trumpet and Its Role in Music of the Renaissance and Early Baroque*. Ph.D. dissertation, University of Belfast, 1983.

———. "What Samuel Pepys Heard on 3 February 1661: English Trumpet Style Under the Later Stuart Monarchs." *Early Music* 18 (1990): 417–28.

Dreyfus, Laurence. *Bach's Continuo Group*. Cambridge, MA: Harvard University Press, 1987.

Drummond, John. *Opera in Perspective*. Minneapolis: University of Minnesota Press, 1980.

Duckles, Vincent. "Florid Embellishment in English Song of the late 16th and Early 17th Century." *Annales Musicologique* 5 (1957): 332–45.

Duey, Philip. *Bel Canto in its Golden Age*. New York: King's Crown, 1951. Reprint. New York: Da Capo, 1980.

Duffin, Ross. "National Pronunciations of Latin ca. 1490-1600." *Journal of Musicology* 4 (1985-86): 217–26.

———. "Pronunciation Guides." In Kite-Powell–*Renaissance*, 257–59.

———. "Shawm and Curtal." In Kite-Powell–*Renaissance*, 69–75.

———. "Tuning and Temperament." In Kite-Powell–*Renaissance*, 238–47.

Dumanoir, Guillaume. *Le mariage de la musique avec la dance.* Paris, 1664. Facs. rep. Bologna: Forni, 1985.

Dunford, Jonathan. Préface to *Divers auteurs du XVIIe siècle: Pièces pour viole seule.* Strasbourg: Cahiers de Tourdion, 1992.

Durante, Ottavio. *Arie devote, le quale contengono in se la maniera di cantar con gratia.* Rome, 1608. For a translation of the preface, see Saunders–Vocal Ornaments.

Durón, Sebastian, and José de Cañizares. *Salir el Amor de Mundo.* Ed. Antonio Martin Moreno. Malaga: Sociedad España de Musicología, 1979.

Ebner, Wolfgang. A set of fifteen rules on basso continuo printed by Johann Andreas Herbst in his *Arte prattica et poetica.* Frankfurt, 1653.

Einstein, Alfred. *Zur deutschen Literatur für Viola da Gamba im 16. und 17. Jahrhundert.* Leipzig: Breitkopf & Härtel, 1905. Trans. Richard D. Bodig as "German Literature for Viola da Gamba in the 16th and 17th Centuries." *Journal of the Viola da Gamba Society of America* 23 (1986): 81–92; 24 (1987): 51–64; 25 (1988): 29–52; 26 (1989): 7-82; 29 (1992): 27–64.

Eisel, Johann Philipp. *Musicus autodidacticus.* Erfurth, 1738; Augsburg, ²1762.

Ellis, H. Meredith. *The Dances of J.B. Lully.* Ph.D. dissertation, Stanford University, 1967.

Engramelle, Marie-Dominique-Joseph. *La Tonotechnie, ou l'art de noter les cylindres.* Paris, 1775. Facs. rep. Geneva: Minkoff, 1971.

Enrico, Eugene. *The Orchestra at San Petronio in the Baroque Era.* Washington, DC: Smithsonian Institution Press, 1976.

Eppelsheim, Jürgen. *Das Orchester in den Werken Jean-Baptiste Lullys.* Tutzing: Schneider, 1961.

Equivel Navarro, Juan de. *Discursos sobra el arte del Dançado.* Seville, 1642. Facs. rep. Madrid: Asociación de Libreros y Amigos del Libro, 1947. Trans. Lynn Matluck Brooks, in *Studies in Dance History,* forthcoming.

Evelyn, John. *The Diary of John Evelyn.* Ed. E. S. de Beer. London: Oxford University Press, 1959.

Falck, Georg. *Idea boni cantoris.* Nuremberg, 1688.

Fallows, David. "Tempo." In *New Grove.*

Fantini, Girolamo. *Modo per imparare a sonare di tromba . . .* Frankfurt, 1638. Facs. repr. Nashville: Brass Press, 1972. Trans. Edward H. Tarr as *Method for Learning to Play the Trumpet . . . .* Nashville: Brass Press, 1975.

Fasman, Mark J. *Brass Bibliography: Sources on the History, Literature, Pedagogy, Performance, and Acoustics of Brass Instruments.* Bloomington: Indiana University Press, 1990.

Fasolo, Fra Giovanbattista. *Annuale.* Venice, 1645.

Favier, Jean. *Le mariage de la Gros Cathos.* Ms., 1688. Facs. and commentary in Rebecca Harris-Warrick and Carol Marsh, *Musical Theater at the Court of Louis XIV: Le mariage de la Grosse Cathos.* Cambridge: Cambridge University Press, 1994.

Fenlon, Iain. *Music and Patronage in Sixteenth-Century Mantua.* Cambridge: Cambridge University Press, 1980.

Feuillet, Raoul-Auger. *Chorégraphie, ou l'art de décrire la dance par caractères, figures, et signes démonstratifs.* Paris, 1700; bound with *Recueil de dances composés par M. Feuillet,* and *Recueil de dances composées par M. [Louis Guillaume] Pécour.* Facs. rep. New York: Broude, 1968.

Feves, Angene. *Dances of a Noble Gathering: 16th-Century Italian Court Dances from Il Ballarino by Fabritio Caroso (1581).* Pleasant Hill, CA: Consortium Antiquum, 1985. (Dance reconstruction booklet plus cassette tape.)

———. "The Changing Shape of the Dance, 1550–1600 as Seen through the Works of Fabritio Caroso." Paper read at Dance History Scholars Conference, Harvard University, 1982.

Finlay, Ian F. "Musical Instruments in 17th-Century Dutch Paintings." *Galpin Society Journal* 6 (1953): 52–69.

Fitzpatrick, Horace. *The Horn and Horn-Playing and the Austro-Bohemian Tradition from 1680–1830.* London: Oxford University Press, 1970.

Fletcher, Ifan Kyrle, Selma Jeanne Cohen, and Roger Lonsdale. *Famed for Dance: Essays on the Theory and Practice of Theatrical Dancing in England, 1660–1740.* New York: The New York Public Library, 1960.

Fleury, Nicolas. *Méthode pour apprendre facilement a toucher le théorbe sur la basse-continue.* Paris, 1660.

Forkel, Johann Nicolaus. *Über Johann Sebastian Bachs Leben, Kunst und Kunstwerke.* Leipzig, 1802.

Fortune, Nigel. "Continuo Instruments in Italian Monodies." *Galpin Society Journal* 6 (1953): 10–13.

———. *Italian Secular Song from 1600 to 1635.* Ph.D. dissertation, Cambridge, 1953.

Foster, Charles. "The Bassanelli Reconstructed: A Radical Solution to an Enigma." *Early Music* 20 (1992): 417–25.

Freillon-Poncein, Jean-Pierre. *La Veritable Manière d'apprendre à jouer en perfection du Haut-Bois, de la Flute et du Flageolet.* Paris, 1700. Reprint. Geneva: Minkoff, 1974. Trans. Catherine Parsons Smith as *On Playing Oboe, Recorder, and Flageolet.* Bloomington: Indiana University Press, 1992.

Frescobaldi, Girolamo. *Li primi libro de capricci.* Rome, 1624.

———. *Toccate d'intavolatura di cembalo et organo.* Rome, 1637.

Fuhrmann, Martin Heinrich. *Musicalischer Trichter.* Franckfurt an der Spree, 1706.

———. *Musica vocalis in nuces, das ist: Richtige und vollige Unterweisung zur Singe-kunst.* Berlin, [1715].

Fuller, David. "French Harpsichord Playing in the 17th Century after *Le Gallois*." *Early Music* 4 (1976): 22–26.

Gable, Frederick. "Saint Gertrude's Chapel, Hamburg, and the Performance of Polychoral Music." *Early Music* 15 (1987): 229–41.

———. "Some Observations concerning Baroque and Modern Vibrato." *Performance Practice Review* 5 (1992): 90–102.

Galilei, Vincenzo. *Dialogo della musica antica, et della moderna.* Florence, 1581. Facs. rep. New York: Broude, 1967.

Galiver, David. "Cantare con la gorga." *Studies in Music* 7 (1973): 10–18.

Galliard, Mr. [=John Ernest]. *Observations on the Florid Song: or, Sentiments on the Ancient and Modern Singers.* London, 1743. Facs. rep. London: William Reeves Bookseller, 1976. (Trans. of Tosi—*Opinioni*.)

Galpin, Canon F. W. "The Sackbut, its Evolution and History." *Proceedings of the Royal Musical Association* 33 (1906–07): 2–25.

Gambassi, Osvaldo. *Il Concerto Palatino della signoria di Bologna.* Florence: Olschki, 1989.

Ganassi, Sylvestro. *Opera intitulata fontegara.* Venice, 1535. Reprint. Berlin-Lichterfelde: Lienau, 1959.

Gangware, Edgar B. *The History and Use of Percussion Instruments in Orchestration.* Ph.D. dissertation, Northwestern University, 1962.

Garnsey, Sylvia. "The Use of Hand-Plucked Instruments in the Continuo Body: Nicola Matteis." *Music and Letters* 47 (1966): 135–40.

Gaspari, Gaetano. *Catalogo della biblioteca musicale G.B. Martini di Bologna* Bologna: Forni, 1961.

Gasparini, Francesco. *L'armonico pratico al cimbalo.* Venice, 1708. Facs. rep. New York: Broude, 1967. Trans. Frank S. Stillings as *The Practical Harmonist at the Harpsichord.* Music Theory Translation Series 1. New Haven: Yale University Press, 1963.

Gerbert, Martin. *Scriptores Ecclesiastici de Musica.* Vol. 3. N.p., 1784. Facs. rep. Hildesheim: Olms, 1963.

Gérold, Théodore. *L'Art du Chant en France au XVIIe siècle.* Strasbourg: Commission des publications de la Faculté des lettres, 1921.

Gianturco, Carolyn. "*Cantate spirituali e morali,* with a Description of the Papal Sacred Cantata Tradition for Christmas, 1676–1740." *Music and Letters* 73 (1992): 1–22.

Gibelius, Otto. *Kurtzer, jedoch grundlicher Bericht von den Vocibus musicalibus.* Bremen, 1659.

Gillespie, Wendy. "Bowed Instruments." In Kite-Powell–*Renaissance*, 109–24.

Gingell, Jane. "Spanish Dance in the Golden Age: The Dance Text of Juan Antonio Jaque." *Proceedings of the Society of Dance History Scholars, Fourteenth Annual Conference (1991)*, 165–77. Riverside, CA: University of California, 1991.

Goldschmidt, Hugo. *Die italienische Gesangsmethode des 17. Jh. und ihre Bedeutung für die Gegenwart*. Breslau: Schlesische Buchdruckerei, 1890.

———. "Die Instrument-Begleitung der italienischen Musikdramen in der ersten Hälfte des 17. Jahrhunderts." *Monatshefte für Musikgeschichte* 27 (1895): 52ff.

Gotsch, Herbert. "The Organ in the Lutheran Service of the 16th Century." *Church Music* 1 (1967): 7–12.

Graham-Jones, Ian. "Some Random Thoughts on Pitch in English Viol Consort Music in the Seventeenth Century." *Chelys* 9 (1982): 20–23.

Green, Robert A. "Jean Rousseau and Ornamentation in French Viol Music." *Journal of the Viola da Gamba Society of America* 14 (1977): 4–41.

Greenlee, Robert. "*Dispositione di voce:* Passage to Florid Singing." *Early Music* 15 (1987): 47–55.

Grout, Donald J. *A Short History of Opera*. New York: Columbia University Press, 1988.

Guion, David. *The Trombone, Its History and Music, 1697–1811*. New York: Gordon and Breach, 1988.

Gustafson, Bruce. *French Harpsichord Music of the 17th Century: A Thematic Catalogue of the Sources with Commentary*. Ann Arbor: UMI Research Press, 1979.

Gutmann, Veronika. *Die Improvisation auf der Viola da Gamba in England im 17. Jahrhundert und ihre Wurzeln im 16. Jahrhundert*. Ph.D. dissertation, University of Vienna, 1975.

Haböck, Franz. *Die Kastraten und ihre Gesangskunst*. Stuttgart: Deutsche Verlags-anstalt, 1927.

Halfpenny, Eric. "Early British Trumpet Mouthpieces." *Galpin Society Journal* 20 (1967): 78.

———. "William Bull and the English Baroque Trumpet." *Galpin Society Journal* 15 (1962): 20–21.

———. "William Shaw's 'Harmonic Trumpet.'" *Galpin Society Journal* 13 (1960): 7–13.

Hammerstein, Reinhold. "Instrumenta Hieronymi." *Archiv für Musikwissenschaft* 16 (1959): 117–34.

Hammond, Frederick. "Girolamo Frescobaldi and a Decade of Music in Casa Barberini: 1634–1643." *Analecta Musicologica* 19 (1979): 94–124.

———. *Girolamo Frescobaldi*. Cambridge, MA: Harvard University Press, 1983.

———. *Music and Spectacle in Baroque Rome*. New Haven: Yale University Press, 1994.

Hancock, Wendy. "General Rules for Realising an Unfigured Bass in 17th-Century England." *Chelys* 7 (1977): 69–72.

Hansell, Sven. "Orchestral Practice at the Court of Cardinal Pietro Ottoboni." *Journal of the American Musicological Society* 19 (1966): 398–403.

Hardy, J., and J. E. Ancell. "Comparisons of the Acoustical Performance of Calfskin and Plastic Drumheads." *Journal of the Acoustical Society of America* 33 (1961): 1391–95.

Harley, John. *British Harpsichord Music*. Hants, England: Scolar, 1994.

Harms, Ben. "Early Percussion." In Kite-Powell–*Renaissance*, 161–71.

Harnoncourt, Nikolaus. *Der Musikalische Dialog: Gedanken zu Monteverdi, Bach und Mozart*. Salzburg and Vienna: Residenz Verlag, 1984. Trans. Mary O'Neill as *The Musical Dialogue: Thoughts on Monteverdi, Bach, and Mozart*. Portland, OR: Amadeus, 1989.

———. *Musik als Klangrede Wege zu einem neuen Musikverstandnis*. Salzburg and Vienna: Residenz Verlag, 1982. Trans. Mary O'Neill as *Baroque Music Today: Music as Speech, Ways to a New Understanding of Music*. Portland, OR: Amadeus, 1988.

Harris, Ellen. "Voices." In Brown/Sadie–*Performance Practice*.

Harris-Warrick, Rebecca. "A Few Thoughts on Lully's *hautbois*." *Early Music* 18 (1990): 97–106.

———. "From Score into Sound: Questions of Scoring in Lully's Ballets." *Early Music* 21 (1993): 355–62.

––––––. "Interpreting Pendulum Markings for French Baroque Dances." *Historical Performance* 6/1 (Spring 1993): 9–22.

––––––, and Carol G. Marsh. See under Favier.

Harwood, Ian. "A Case of Double Standards?: Instrumental Pitch in England c. 1600." *Early Music* 9 (1981): 470–85. Responses by Donald Gill, *Early Music* 10 (1982): 217–18; Herbert Myers, *Early Music* 10 (1982): 519–22; and Ian Harwood, *Early Music* 11 (1983): 76–77.

Hawkins, John. *A General History of the Science and Practice of Music.* London, 1776.

Haynes, Bruce." Cornetts and Historical Pitch Standards." *Historic Brass Society Journal* 6 (1994): 84–109.

––––––. "Johann Sebastian Bach's Pitch Standards: The Woodwind Perspective." *Journal of the American Musical Instrument Society* 11 (1985): 55–114.

––––––. "Lully and the Rise of the Oboe as Seen in Works of Art." *Early Music* 16 (1988): 324–338.

––––––. *Pitch Standards in the Baroque and Classical Periods.* Ph.D. dissertation, University of Montréal, 1995.

Heering. *Regeln des Generalbasses von dem Herr Musice Heering.* Berlin, Deutsche Staatsbibliothek, Mus MS theor. 348. Realizations of continuo parts for Corelli sonatas Op. 1. Cited in Williams–*Figured Bass* 1: 110.

Hefling, Stephen E. *Rhythmic Alteration in Seventeenth- and Eighteenth-Century Music:* Notes Inégales *and Overdotting.* New York: Schirmer Books, 1993.

Helwig, Christine, and Marshall Baron. *Purcell, Playford, and the English Court Dance.* 2 vols. New Haven: Playford Consort Publications, 1995. (Compact disc by the Playford Consort available.)

Henahan, Donald. "Listening for the Trill of it All." *New York Times.* 6 September 1987, "Arts & Leisure," 17.

Herbert, Trevor. "The Sackbut in England in the 17th and 18th Centuries." *Early Music* 18 (1990): 609–16.

Herbst, Johann Andreas. *Musica practica sive instruction pro symphoniacis.* Nuremberg, 1642.

Heriot, Angus. *The Castrati in Opera.* London, 1956. Reprint. New York: Da Capo, 1975.

Heyde, Herbert. *Hörner und Zinken.* Bd. 5 of *Katalog, Musikinstrumenten-Museum der Karl-Marx-Universität.* Leipzig: VEB Deutscher Verlag für Musik, 1982.

Hiebert, Thomas. *The Horn in Early Eighteenth-Century Dresden: The Players and their Repertory.* D.M.A. dissertation, University of Wisconsin, 1989.

Higginbottom, Edward. "Alternatim." In *New Grove.*

––––––. "Organ Mass." In *New Grove.*

Hill, John Walter. "Realized Continuo Accompaniments from Florence c.1600." *Early Music* 11 (1983): 194–208.

Hill, W. H., A. F., and A. E. *Antonio Stradivari: His Life and Work (1644–1737).* London, 1902. Reprint. New York: Dover, 1962.

Hiller, Albert. *Music for Trumpets from Three Centuries.* Cologne: Haas, 1993.

Hilse, Walter. "The Treatises of Christian Bernhard, [1] *Von der Singe-Kunst oder Manier.*" The *Music Forum* 3 (1973): 1–29.

Hilton, Wendy. *Dance of Court & Theater: The French Noble Style, 1690–1725.* Princeton: Princeton Book Co., 1981.

Hitzler, Daniel. *Extract aus neuen Musica oder Singkunst.* Nuremberg, 1623.

Hogwood, Christopher. "Frescobaldi on Performance." *Italian Music and the Fitzwilliam.* Cambridge: Fitzwilliam Museum, 1976.

Holman, Peter. "Continuo Realizations in a Playford Songbook." *Early Music* 6 (1978): 268–9.

––––––. "'Col nobilissimo esercitio della vivuola': Monteverdi's String Writing." *Early Music* 21 (1993): 576–90.

––––––. "English Trumpets–A Response." *Early Music* 19 (1991): 443.

––––––. *Four and Twenty Fiddlers: The Violin at the English Court, 1540–1690.* Oxford: Oxford University Press, 1993.

————. "London: Commonwealth and Restoration." In *Music and Society: The Early Baroque Era*. Ed. Curtis Price, 305–26. Englewood Cliffs, NJ: Prentice-Hall, 1993.

Holmgren, Fred. "Stalking the Valveless Trumpet." *Historic Brass Society Newsletter* 2 (1990): 5–8.

Hotteterre le Romain, Jacques (-Martin). *Principes de la flûte traversière, ou flûte d'allemagne, de la flûte à bec, ou flûte douce, et du haut-bois*. Paris, 1707. Trans. and ed. David Lasocki as *Principles of the Flute, Recorder, and Oboe* by David Lasocki. New York: Praeger, 1968.

————. *Méthode pour la musette*. Paris, 1738.

Houle, George. *Meter in Music, 1600–1800*, Bloomington: Indiana University Press, 1987.

Howey, H. E. *A Comprehensive Performance Project in Trombone Literature, with an Essay Consisting of a Translation of Daniel Speer's "Vierfaches musikalisches Kleeblatt."* D.M.A. dissertation, University of Iowa, 1971.

Hsu, John. *A Handbook of French Baroque Viol Technique*. New York: Broude, 1981.

————. "The Use of the Bow in French Solo Viol Playing of the 17th and 18th Centuries." *Early Music* 6 (1978): 26–29.

Hucke, Helmut. "Die Besetzung von Sopran und Alt in der Sixtinischen Kapelle." In *Miscelánea en homenaje a Monseñor Higinio Anglés* 1: 379–96. Barcelona: Consejo superior de investigaciones científicas, 1958–61.

Hudson, Richard. *The Allemande, the Balletto, and the Tanz*. 2 vols. Cambridge: Cambridge University Press, 1986.

Hughes, Charles W. "The Music for Unaccompanied Bass Viol." *Music and Letters* 25/3 (July 1944): 149–63.

Hunt, Edgar. *The Recorder and its Music*. London: Herbert Jenkins, 1962; New York: Norton, 1963.

Husk, W. H. *An Account of the Musical Celebrations on St. Cecilia's Day*. London: Bell and Duldy, 1857.

Huygens, Constantin. *Musique et musiciens du XVIIe siècle: Correspondence et oeuvre musicales*. Ed. W. J. A. Jonckbloet and J. P. N. Land. Leyden: Brill, 1882.

Iacobilli, Ludovico. *Modo di ballare*. Ms., ca. 1615.

Il corago o vero alcune osservazioni per metter bene in scena le composizioni drammatiche (ca. 1630). Florence: Olschki Editore, 1983. Trans. Olga Termini in "Baroque Operatic Acting: The Role of Diction and Gesture in Italian Baroque Opera." *Performance Practice Review* 6 (1993): 146–57.

Inns of Court manuscripts. Bodleian Library, Rawl. Poet. 108, ff. 10v–11r; British Library, Harley 367, 178–9; Bodleian, Douce 280, ff. 66av–66bv (202v–203v); Bodleian, Rawl. D. 864, f. 199v, ff. 203r, 204r; Royal College of Music, Ms. 1119, title page and ff. 1–2, 23v–24r; Inner Temple, Miscellanea Vol. 27. See Cunningham–*Dancing*.

Jacobs, René. "The Controvery Concerning the Timbre of the Countertenor." *Alte Musik: Praxis und Reflection*. Winterthur: Amadeus Verlag, 1983.

Jambe de Fer, Philibert. *Epitome musical*. Lyon, 1556. Facs. ed. François Lesure, *"Epitome musical* de Philibert Jambe de Fer (1556)." *Annales Musicologiques* 6 (1958-63): 341–86.

Jander, Owen. "Concerto Grosso Instrumentation in Rome in the 1660's and 1670's." *Journal of the American Musicological Society* 21 (1968): 168–80.

Janowka, Thomas Balthasar. *Clavis ad thesaurum magnae artis musicae . . . .* Prague, 1701.

Jaque, Juan Antonio. *Libro de Danzar de Baltasar de Rojas Pantoia*. Late seventeenth century. Transcription by José Subirá in *Anuario musical. Barcelona* 5 (1950): 190–98.

Jean-Baptiste Bérard. *L'art du Chant*. Paris, 1755. Trans. Sidney Murray. Milwaukee: Pro Musica Press, 1969.

Jones, Edward Huws. "'To Sing and Play the Base-Violl Alone': the Bass Viol in English 17th-Century Song." *Lute Society Journal of Great Britain* 17 (1975): 17–23.

————. *The Performance of English Song 1610–1670*. New York: Garland, 1989.

Jones, Pamela. *The Relation between Music and Dance in Cesare Negri's "Le gratie d'amore" (1602)*. Ph.D. dissertation, King's College, University of London, 1989.

Jürgens, Jürgen. "Die Madrigale Alessandro Scarlattis und ihre Quellen." In *Scritti in onore di Luigi Ronga*, 279–85. Milan: Riccardo Ricciardi, 1973.

Kämper, Dietrich. *Studien zur instrumentalen Ensemblemusik des 16. Jahrhunderts in Italien. Analecta Musicologica* 10. Vienna: Böhlau Verlag, 1970.

Karstädt, Georg. *Zur Geschichte des Zinken und seiner Verwendung in der Musik des 16.-18. Jahrhunderts.* Inaugural dissertation, University of Berlin, 1935. Extracts in *AMf* 2 (1937): 385–432.

Kazarow, Patricia. "Luther's Small Catechism: Liturgical Transformations." Paper read at the International Congress for Medieval Studies, Kalamazoo, 1989.

Kendrick, Robert. *Genres, Generations and Gender: Nuns' Music in Early Modern Milan, c. 1550–1706.* Ph.D. dissertation, New York University, 1993.

Kenton, Terry Meyer: *The Crumhorn: Its History, Design, Repertory, and Technique.* Ann Arbor: UMI Research Press, 1983.

Kenyon de Pascual, Beryl. "A Brief Survey of the Late Spanish Bajón." *Galpin Society Journal* 37 (1984): 72–79.

———. "A Late Sixteenth-Century Portrayal of the Jointed Dulcian." *Galpin Society Journal* 43 (1990): 150–53.

———. "The Wind-Instrument Maker, Bartolomé de Selma (†1616), His Family and Workshop." *Galpin Society Journal* 39 (1986): 21–34.

Kinkeldey, Otto. *Orgel und Klavier in der Musik des 16. Jahrhunderts.* Leipzig: Breitkopf & Härtel, 1910. Reprint. Hildesheim: Olms, and Wiesbaden: Breitkopf & Härtel, 1984.

Kinney, Gordon J. "A 'Tempest in a Glass of Water', or a Conflict of Esthetic Attitudes." *Journal of the Viola da Gamba Society of America* 14 (1977): 42–52.

———. "Problems of Melodic Ornamentation in French Viol Music." *Journal of the Viola da Gamba Society of America* 5 (1968): 34–50.

———. "Writings on the Viol by Dubuisson, De Machy, Roland Marais, Étienne Loulié." *Journal of the Viola da Gamba Society of America* 13 (1976): 17–55.

Kinsky, Georg. "Alessandro Piccinini und sein Arciliuto." *Acta Musicologica* 10 (1938): 103–18.

Kirby, P. R. "The Kettle-Drums: An Historical Survey." *Music and Letters* 9 (1928): 37–43.

Kirchner, Gerhard. *Der Generalba[ß] bei Heinrich Schütz.* Kassel: Bärenreiter, 1960.

Kirk, Douglas. "Cornett." In Kite-Powell–*Renaissance*, 79–96.

Kirnbauer, Martin. *Verzeichnis der Europäischen Musikinstrumente im Germanischen Nationalmuseum Nürnberg, Band II: Flöten- und Rohrblattinstrumente bis 1750.* Wilhelmshaven: Heinrichshofen, 1994.

Kite-Powell, Jeffery. "Crumhorn." In Kite-Powell–*Renaissance*, 63–68.

———. "Large Ensembles." In Kite-Powell–*Renaissance*, 228–32.

———. "Racket." in Kite-Powell–*Renaissance*, 76–78.

———, ed. *A Performer's Guide to Renaissance Music.* New York: Schirmer Books, 1994.

Klitz, Brian. "A Composition for *Dolzaina*." *Journal of the American Musicological Society* 24 (1971): 113–18.

———. "The Bassoon in Chamber Music of the Seventeenth Century." *Journal of the American Musical Instrument Society* 9 (1983): 5–20.

Kopp, James B. "Notes on the Bassoon in Seventeenth-Century France." *Journal of the American Musical Instrument Society* 17 (1991): 85–114.

Kreitner, Kenneth. "Minstrels in Spanish Churches, 1400–1600." *Early Music* 20 (1992): 532–46.

Krummel, D. W. *English Music Printing, 1553–1700.* London: Bibliographical Society, 1975.

Kuhn, Max. *Die Verzierungs-Kunst in der Gesangs-Musik des 16.-17. Jahrhunderts (1535–1650).* Leipzig: Breitkopf & Härtel, 1902. Reprint. Wiesbaden: Publikationen der Internationalen Musikgesellschaft. Beiheft VII, 1969.

Kurtzman, Jeffrey G. *The Monteverdi Vespers of 1610: Music, Context, Performance.* Oxford: Oxford University Press, forthcoming.

Lacroix, Paul. *Ballets et mascarades de cour.* Geneva: J. Gay et fils, 1868–70.

La Fontaine, Jean de. "Epître à M. de Niert sur l'opéra." In *Oeuvres diverses.* Vol. 2. Paris, 1677. Reprint. Paris, 1958.

Lambrechts-Douillez, Jeannine. "Een contrabas blokfluit in het Museum Vleeshuis te Antwerpen: curiosum en wereldunicum." In *Miscellanea Josef Duverger*, 907–19. Ghent: Vereniging voor de Geschiedenis der Textielkunsten, 1968.

Lampl, Hans. "A Translation of *Syntagma Musicum* III by Michael Praetorius." D.M.A. dissertation, University of Southern California, 1957. Selected excerpts with commentary by S. E. Plank in *Historic Brass Society Journal* 6 (1994): 244–68.

Langwill, Lyndesay G. *The Bassoon and Contrabassoon.* New York: Norton, 1965.

Lasocki, David. "The French Hautboy in England, 1673–1730." *Early Music* 16 (1988): 339–57.

———. "The Recorder Consort at the English Court 1540-1673, Part 2." *The American Recorder* 25/4 (November 1984): 132–35.

———. "The Recorder in the Elizabethan, Jacobean and Caroline Theater." *The American Recorder* 25/1 (February 1984): 3–10.

Lauze, F. de. *Apologie de la Danse.* Trans., with original text, additional commentary, and music, by Joan Wildeblood. London: Frederick Muller, 1951.

Lauze, F. de. *Apologie de la danse.* [London], 1623. Facs. rep. Geneva: Minkoff, 1977.

Laver, James. *Costume in the Theatre.* London: Harrap, 1964.

Lawrence-King, Andrew. "'Perfect' Instruments." In *Companion to Medieval & Renaissance Music.* Ed. Tess Knighton and David Fallows, 354–64. New York: Schirmer Books, 1992.

Le Bègue, Nicolas. *Les pièces de clavecin.* Paris, 1677.

Le Cerf de Vieville. *Comparaison de la Musique Italiene et de la Musique Francoise.* Brussels, 1704.

Le Gallois, Jean. *Lettre de M. Le Gallois à Mademoiselle Regnault de Solier touchant la musique.* Paris, 1680. Transcribed by François-Joseph Fétis in "Histoire de la musique." *Revue Musicale* 8/39 (September 1834): 305–08.

Ledbetter, David. *Harpsichord and Lute Music in 17th-Century France.* Bloomington: Indiana University Press, 1987.

Lesure, François. "Die 'Terpsichore' von Michael Praetorius und die französische Instrumentalmusik unter Heinrich IV." *Die Musikforschung* 5 (1952): 7–17.

———. "Le traité des instruments de musique de Pierre Trichet." *Annales musicologiques* 4 (1956): 175–248.

———. "Une querelle sur la jeu de la viole en 1688: J. Rousseau contre DeMachy." *Revue de Musicologie* 46 (December 1960): 181–99.

Lindley, Mark. "Early 16th-Century Keyboard Temperaments." *Musica Disciplina* 28 (1974): 129–51.

———. "Renaissance Keyboard Fingering." In Kite-Powell–*Renaissance*, 189–99.

———. "Tuning Systems for 12-Note Keyboard Instruments." *The English Harpsichord Magazine* 2 (1977): 13–15.

Linfield, Eva. "The Viol Consort in Buxtehude's Vocal Music: Historical Context and Affective Meaning." In *Church, Stage, and Studio: Music and Its Contexts in 17th-Century Germany.* Ed. Paul Walker, 163–92. Ann Arbor: UMI Research Press, 1990.

Lionnet, Jean. "Performance Practice in the Papal Chapel during the Seventeenth Century." *Early Music* 15 (1987): 3–15.

Locke, Matthew. *Matthew Locke: Anthems and Motets.* Transcribed and ed. Peter LeHuray. *Musica Britannica* 38. London: Stainer & Bell, 1976.

———. *Melothesia, or Certain Rules for Playing Upon a Continued-Bass.* London, 1673.

Loewenberg, Alfred. *Annals of Opera, 1597–1940.* Totowa, NJ: Rowman & Littlefield, 1978.

Lorimer, Michael. *Saldívar Codex No. 4.* Santa Barbara, CA: Lorimer, 1987.

Lorin, André. *Livre de contredance du Roi.* Ca. 1685. Facs. rep. with trans. by Julia Sutton. Stuyvesant, NY: Pendragon, forthcoming.

Loulié, Étienne. *Élémens ou principes de musique.* Paris: C. Ballard, 1696.

Lowe, Michael. "Renaissance and Baroque Lutes: A False Dichotomy; Observations on the Lute in the Seventeenth Century." *Proceedings of the International Lute Symposium, Utrecht 1986, 124–39.* Utrecht: Stimu, 1988.

———. "The Historical Development of the Lute." *Galpin Society Journal* 29 (1976): 11–25.

Lundgren, Stefan. *New Method for Renaissance Lute.* Munich: Lundgren Musik-Edition, 1986.

Lupi, Livio. *Mutanze di gagliarda, tordiglione, passo è mezzo, canari e passeggi.* Palermo, 1600.

———. *Libro di gagliarda, tordiglione . . . .* 2d ed. of *Mutanze di gagliarda, tordiglione, passo è mezzo, canari e passeggo.* Rev. and enl. Palermo, 1607.

Lutij, Prospero. *Opera bellissima nella quale si contengono molte partite, et passeggi di gagliarda.* Perugia, 1587, 1589.

MacClintock, Carol. *Readings in the History of Music in Performance.* Bloomington: Indiana University Press, 1979.

Mace, Thomas. *Musick's Monument.* London, 1676. Facs. rep. Paris: Éditions du Centre Nationale de la echerche Scientifique, 1958.

Maffei, Giovanni Camillo. *Libri due, Discorso . . . i cantar di garganta senza maestro.* Naples, 1562.

Mancini, Giulio. *Del originne et nobiltá del ballo.* Ms., ca. 1623–30.

Mangsen, Sandra. "*Ad libitum* procedures in Instrumental Duos and Trios." *Early Music* 19 (1991): 29–40.

Martini, Jean-Paul. *Mélopée moderne.* Paris, 1792.

Marvin, Bob. "Recorders & English Flutes in European Collections." *Galpin Society Journal* 25 (July, 1972): 30–57.

Marx, Joseph. "The Tone of the Baroque Oboe." *Galpin Society Journal* 4 (1951): 3–19.

Mason, Kevin. *The Chitarrone and its Repertoire in Early Seventeenth-century Italy.* Aberystwyth, Wales: Boethius, 1989.

Massip, Catherine. *La vie des musiciens de Paris au temps de Mazarin (1643–1661).* Paris: Picard, 1976.

———. "Paris, 1600–61." In *Music and Society: The Early Baroque.* Ed. Curtis Price. Englewood Cliffs, NJ: Prentice-Hall, 1993.

Mattheson, Johann. *Der vollkommene Capellmeister.* Hamburg, 1739. Trans. Ernest Harriss. Ann Arbor: UMI Research Press 1981.

Maugars, André. *Response Faite á un Curieux sur le Sentiment de la Musique d'Italie.* Facs. ed. with intro., trans., and notes by H. Wiley Hitchcock. Geneva: Minkoff, 1993. Also trans. Walter H. Bishop, *Journal of the Viola da Gamba Society of America* 8 (1971): 5–17.

Mazzocchi, Domenico. *Dialoghi, e sonetti.* Rome, 1638. Facs. ed. Bologna, n.d.

———. *Partitura de' madrigali a cinque voci, e altri varii concerti.* Rome, 1638.

McDowell, Bonney. *Marais and Forqueray: A Historical and Analytical Study of their Music for Basse de Viole.* Ph.D. dissertation, Columbia University, 1974.

McGee, Timothy, ed. *Singing Early Music: An Introductory Guide to the Pronunciation of European Languages in the Middle Ages and Renaissance.* Bloomington: Indiana University Press, 1996.

McGowan, Keith. "The World of the Early Sackbut Player: Flat or Round?" *Early Music* 20 (1994): 441–66.

McGowan, Margaret M. *L'art du ballet de cour en France, 1581–1643.* Paris: Centre Nationale de la Recherche Scientifique. 1963.

Ménestrier, Claude-François. *Des ballets anciens et modernes selon les régles du théâtre.* Paris, 1682. Facs. rep. Geneva: Minkoff, 1972.

Merck, Daniel. *Compendium musicae instrumentalis chelicae.* Augsburg, 1659.

Mersenne, Marin. *Correspondance du P. Marin Mersenne, religieux Minime.* 13 vols. Ed. Cornelis de Waard. Paris: Beauchesne, 1933–1977.

————. *Harmonie universelle.* Paris, 1636-7. Facs. rep. of copy in Bibliothéque des Artes et Métiers containing Mersenne's annotations. 3 vols. Ed. and with intro. by François Lesure. Paris: C.N.R.S., 1963.

————. *Harmonie universelle: The Books on Instruments.* Trans. Roger Chapman. The Hague: Nijhoff, 1957.

Meylan, Raymond. *The Flute.* Portland, OR: Amadeus, 1988. This work is a translation by Alfred Clayton of *Die Flöte* (Bern: Hallwag AG, 1974), which in turn is a translation from the French.

Mirimonde, A. Pomme de. "La musique dans les oeuvres flamandes du XVIIe siècle au Louvre." *Revue de Louvre* 13 (1963): 167–82.

Mischiati, Oscar. "Documenti sull' organaria padana rinascimentale." *L'Organo* 22 (1984): 23–160.

————. *L'Organo di Santa Maria di Campagna a Piacenza.* Piacenza: Cassa di Risparmio di Piacenza, 1980.

Mitchell, Nicholas. "Choral and Instrumental Pitch in Church Music, 1570–1620." *Galpin Society Journal* 48 (1995): 13–32.

Moens-Haenen, Greta. *Das Vibrato in der Musik des Barock: Ein Handbuch zur Aufführungspraxis für Vokalisten und Instrumentalisten.* Graz: Akademische Druck und Verlagsanstalt, 1988.

Monson, Craig. "Consort Song and Verse Anthem: A Few Performance Problems," *Journal of the Viola da Gamba Society of America* 13 (1976): 4–11

Monson, Craig. *Voices and Viols in England, 1600–1650.* Ann Arbor: UMI Research Press, 1982.

Montagu, Jeremy. "Choosing Brass Instruments." *Early Music* 4 (1976): 36.

————. *Making Early Percussion Instruments.* London: Oxford University Press, 1976.

————. *The World of Baroque and Classical Musical Instruments.* Woodstock, NY: Overlook, 1979.

————. *The World of Medieval and Renaissance Musical Instruments.* New York: Overlook, 1976.

Montéclair, Michel Pignolet de. *Nouvelle méthode pour apprendre la musique.* Paris, 1709.

————. *Principes de Musique.* Paris, 1736,

Moore, James. "The *Vespero delli Cinque Laudate* and the Role of *Salmi Spezzati* at Saint Mark's." *Journal of the American Musicological Society* 34 (1981): 249–78.

————. "Venezia favorita da Maria: Music for the Madonna Nicopeia and Santa Maria della Salute." *Journal of the American Musicological Society* 37 (1984): 323–24, 345–46.

————. *Vespers at Saint Mark's: Music of Alessandro Grandi, Giovanni Rovetta, and Francesco Cavalli.* 2 vols. Ann Arbor: UMI Research Press, 1981.

Morehen, J. "The English Consort and Verse Anthem." *Early Music* 6 (1978): 381–85.

Moreno, Ignacio. *Music and Its Symbolism in Seventeenth-Century Dutch Painting.* Ph.D. dissertation, University of Maryland, 1990.

Morley, Thomas. *A Plaine and Easie Introduction to Practicall Musicke.* London, 1597. Modern ed. by R. Alec Harman. New York: Norton, 1963.

Morley-Pegge, R. *The French Horn: Some Notes on the Evolution of the Instrument and of its Technique.* 2d ed. London: Benn, 1973.

Moroney, Davitt. "The Performance of Unmeasured Harpsichord Preludes." *Early Music* 4 (1976): 143–51.

Murata, Margaret. *Operas for the Papal Court, 1631–1668.* Ann Arbor: UMI Research Press, 1981.

————. "Pier Francesco Valentini on Tactus and Proportion." *Frescobaldi Studies.* Ed. Alexander Silbiger, 327–50. Duke Studies in Music 1. Durham, NC: Duke University Press, 1987.

Murray, Russell. "On the Teaching Duties of the *Maestro di Cappella* in Sixteenth-Century Italy: The *Processo* against Pietro Pontio." *Explorations in Renaissance Culture* 14 (1988): 115–28.

Myers, Herbert. "Harp." In Kite-Powell–*Renaissance,* 154–60.

———. "Renaissance Flute." In Kite-Powell–*Renaissance,* 56–62.

———. "Pitch and Transposition." In Kite-Powell–*Renaissance,* 248–56.

———. *The Practical Acoustics of Early Woodwinds.* D.M.A. dissertation, Stanford University, 1980.

———. "Recorder." In Kite-Powell–*Renaissance,* 41–55.

———. "Three Seventeenth-Century Recorder Tutors. *The American Recorder* 7/2 (Spring, 1966): 3–6.

Mylius, Wolfgang. *Rudimenta musices.* Gotha, 1686.

Nagler, A. M. *A Source Book in Theatrical History.* New York: Dover, 1952.

———. *Theatre Festivals of the Medici, 1539–1637.* New Haven: Yale University Press, 1964. Reprint. New York: Da Capo, 1976.

Naylor, Tom. *The Trumpet and Trombone in Graphic Arts, 1500–1800.* Nashville: Brass Press, 1979.

Negri, Cesare. *Le Gratie d'Amore.* Milan, 1602. Reissued as *Nuove Inventione di balli.* Milan, 1604. Facs. rep. of 1602 edition. New York: Broude, 1969; also Bologna: Forni, 1969. Trans. in Gustavia Yvonne Kendall, *Le Gratie d'Amore by Cesare Negri: Translation and Commentary.* D.M.A. dissertation, Stanford University, 1985. Ms. trans. of *Le Gratie d'Amore* into Spanish by Don Balthasar Carlos for Señor Conde, Duke of St. Lucar, 1630. Madrid: Bibloteca Nacional, MS 14085.

Ness, Arthur. See *New Grove,* s.v. "Lute Sources."

Neumann, Berthold. ". . . kommt pfeift und trombt . . . On the Use of Percussion Instruments in the Dance Music of the Renaissance." Trans. Herbert W. Myers. *Historical Performance* 4/2 (Fall 1991): 87–93.

Neumann, Frederick. *Ornamentation in Baroque and Post-Baroque Music.* Princeton: Princeton University Press, 1978.

Neumann, Karl. "Captain Hume's 'Invention for Two to Play Upon One Viole.'" *Journal of the American Musicological Society* 22/1 (Spring 1969): 101–06.

The New Grove Dictionary of Musical Instruments. Ed. Stanley Sadie. London: Macmillan, 1980. See entries for individual instruments.

The New Grove Dictionary of Music and Musicians. 20 vols. Ed. Stanley Sadie. London: Macmillan, 1980.

The New Grove Encyclopedia of the Opera. Ed. Stanley Sadie. London: Macmillan, 1992.

Newman, William S. *The Sonata in the Baroque Era.* New York: Norton, 1972.

Newton, George. "Le Nuove Musiche of Caccini: A New Translation of the Preface." *NATS Bulletin* 19/2 (Dec. 1962): 14–18.

Nicoll, Allardyce. *Stuart Masques and the Renaissance Stage.* London: Harrap, 1937.

———. *The Development of the Theater.* New York: Blom, 1968.

Nivers, Guillaume-Gabriel. *Livre d'orgue.* Paris, 1665.

Nordstrom, Lyle. *The Bandora: Its Music and Sources.* Detroit Studies in Musicology 66. Warren, MI: Harmonie Park, 1992.

North, Nigel. *Continuo Playing on the Lute, Archlute and Theorbo.* Bloomington: Indiana University Press, 1987.

North, Roger. *Roger North on music, being a selection from his essays written during the years c. 1695–1728.* Transcribed from the manuscripts and edited by John Wilson. London: Novello, 1959.

"Notation." In *New Grove.*

Nurse, Ray. "On the Development of Renaissance Lute Construction." *Proceedings of the International Lute Symposium, Utrecht 1986,* 102–7. Utrecht: Stimu, 1988.

O'Brien, Patrick, and Paul O'Dette. *The Lute Made Easie: A Tutor for the Renaissance Lute.* In preparation.

O'Dette, Paul. "Plucked Instruments." In Kite-Powell–*Renaissance,* 139–53.

———. "Some Observations About the Tone of Early Lutenists." *Proceedings of the International Lute Symposium, Utrecht 1986,* 86–91. Utrecht: Stimu, 1988.

————, et al. "Continuo and Proto-Continuo Practices in Sixteenth- and Early Seventeenth-Century Music." Lecture-demonstration presented at Boston Early Music Festival, June 1991. Synopsis by Barbara Coeyman, "Continuo in the Historical Continuum." *Historical Performance* 4/2 (Fall 1991): 131–32.

Oldham, Guy. "Two Pieces for 5-Part Shawm Band by Louis Couperin." *Hinrichsen's Eleventh Music Book: Music Libraries and Instruments*, 233–38. London: Hinrichsen, 1961.

Olsson, Dorothy (under name Dorothy Rubin). "English Measures and Country Dances: A Comparison." *Proceedings. Society of Dance History Scholars. Eighth Annual Conference (1985)*, 156–64. University of California, Riverside: Dance History Scholars, 1985.

Orgel, Stephen. *The Jonsonian Masque*. Cambridge, MA: Harvard University Press, 1965.

Ornithoparcus, Andreas. [See Dowland, John.]

Orrey, Leslie. *Opera, a Concise History*. London: Thames and Hudson, 1987.

Otterstedt, Annete. "The Spoon to the Soup: An Approach to the Lyra Viol." *Chelys* 20 (1991): 43–51.

Otterstedt, Annette. *Die englische Lyra-Viol: Instrument und Technik*. Kassel: Bärenreiter, 1989.

Padouan, Maurizio. "La musica in Santa Maria Maggiore a Bergamo nel periodo di Giovanni Cavaccio (1598–1626)." In *Studi sul primo Seicento*. Como: Centro Ricerche dell' A.M.I.S. (Antiquae Musicae Italicae Studiosi), 1983.

————. "Un modello esemplare di mediazione nell'Italia del nord: Santa Maria Maggiore a Bergamo negli anni 1630–1657." *Rivista internazionale di musica sacra* 11 (1990): 115–57.

Paras, Jason. *The Music for Viola Bastarda*. Ed. George Houle and Glenna Houle. Bloomington: Indiana University Press, 1986.

Parisi, Susan Helen. *Ducal Patronage of Music in Mantua, 1587–1627: An Archival Study*. Ph.D. dissertation, University of Illinois, 1989.

Parrott, Andrew. "Getting It Right." *The Musical Times* (October 1995): 531–35.

————. "Transposition in Monteverdi's Vespers of 1610: An 'Aberration' Defended." *Early Music* 12 (1984): 490–516.

Paulsmeier, Karin. "Temporelationen in Frescobaldi." *Alte Musik, Praxis und Reflexion. Sonderband der Reihe Basler Jahrbuch für historische Musikpraxis*, 187. Zurich: Amadeus Verlag, 1983.

Payne, Ian. *The Almain and Other Measures in England, 1549–1675. Their History and Choreography*. Aldershot: Scolar Press, forthcoming.

————. "The Provision of Teaching on Viols at Some English Cathedral Churches, c. 1594–c. 1645: Archival Evidence." *Chelys* 29 (1990): 3–15.

Penna, Lorenzo. *Li primi albori musicali*. Libro 2. 4th ed. Bologna, 1684. Facs. rep. Bologna: Forni, 1969.

Pepys, Samuel. *The Diary of Samuel Pepys*. 11 vols. Ed. Robert Latham and William Matthews. Berkeley and Los Angeles: University of California Press, 1983.

Perrine, [first name unknown]. *Livre de musique pour le luth*. Paris, 1679.

————. *Table pour apprendre à toucher le luth sur la basse continüe*. Paris, 1682.

Peters, Gordon. *The Drummer–Man: A Treatise on Percussion*. Rev. ed. Wilmette, IL: Kemper-Peters, 1975.

Piccinini, Alessandro. *Intavolatura di liuto, et di chitarrone, libro primo*. Bologna, 1623.

Pinnock, Andrew, and Bruce Wood. "A Counterblast on English Trumpets." *Early Music* 19 (1991): 437–42.

Pinto, David. "The Fantasy Manner: The Seventeenth-Century Context," *Chelys* 10 (1981): 17–28.

Pisa, Agostino. *Breve dichiarazione della battuta musicale*. Rome: 1611. Facs. rep., ed. Walther Dürr. Bologna: Forni, 1965.

Planchart, Alejandro. "On Singing and the Vocal Ensemble II." In Kite-Powell–*Renaissance*, 26–38.

Playford, John. *The Division Violin*. London, 1684. Facs. rep. New York: Performer's Facsimiles, 1995.

————. *A breefe introduction to the skill of musick.* London, 1654. (Many subsequent editions, some with variant wording and spelling of title.) Facs. of 12th ed. *An introduction to the skill of musick.* London, 1694. New York: Da Capo, 1972.

————. "Directions for Singing after the Italian Manner." See Caccini–*Nuove musiche.*

————. *Musick's Recreation on the Viol, Lyra-Way.* London, 1682. Facs. rep. London: Hinrichsen, 1965.

————. *Musick's Delight on the Cithren.* London, 1666.

————. *The English Dancing Master: Or, Plaine and easie Rules for the Dancing of Country Dances, with the Tune to each Dance.* London, 1651; later editions to 1728. Annotated facs. rep. by Margaret Dean-Smith as *Playford's English Dancing Master 1651.* London: Schott, 1957. Modern transcription by Hugh Mellor and Leslie Bridgewater as *John Playford's The English Dancing Master.* London, 1933. Two facs. rep. editions. New York: Dance Horizons, n.d.; and London: Dance Books, 1984.

Polk, Keith. *German Instrumental Music of the Late Middle Ages.* Cambridge: Cambridge University Press, 1992.

Poulton, Diana. *A Tutor for the Renaissance Lute.* London: Schott, 1991.

————. *Lute Playing Technique.* London: The Lute Society U.K, 1981.

Praetorius, Michael. *Syntagma musicum.* Vol. 1. Wittenberg, 1614/1615. Vol. 2. Wolfenbüttel, 1618/1619. Vol. 3. Wolfenbüttel, 1619. Facs. rep. Kassel: Bärenreiter, 1958–1959. Trans. of vol. 2 by Harold Blumenfeld. New York: Bärenreiter, 1962.

————. *Terpsichore.* 1612. Ed. Günther Oberst in *Gesamtausgabe der Musikalischen Werke.* Vol. 15. Wolfenbüttel: Möseler Verlag, n.d.

Pressacco, Gilberto. *Sermone, Cantu, Choreis et — marculis: cenni di storia della danza in Friuli.* Udine: Società fililogica friulana, 1991.

Printz, Wolfgang Caspar. *Anweisung zur Singe-Kunst oder Bericht wie man einen knaben . . . konne singen lehren.* Guben, 1671.

————. *Compendium musicae signatoriae.* Dresden, 1689. Reprint. Hildesheim: Olms, 1974.

————. *Musica modulatoria vocalis, oder Manierliche und zierliche Sing-kunst.* Schwiednitz, 1678.

————. *Phyrnis Mytilenaeus oder satyrischer Componist.* Quedlinburg, 1676–77. 2d ed. Dresden and Leipzig, 1696.

Prizer, William. "Bernardino Piffaro e i pifferi e tromboni di Mantova." *Rivista italiana di musicologia* 16 (1981): 151–84.

Pruitt, William H. *The Organ Works of Guillaume Gabriel Nivers (1632–1714).* Ph.D. dissertation, University of Pittsburgh, 1969.

"Proportions." In *New Grove.*

Prynne, M. W. "James Talbot's Manuscript: The Lute Family." *Galpin Society Journal* 14 (1961): 52 ff.

Pugliese, Patri, and Joseph Casazza. *Practise for Dauncinge, Some Almans and a Pavan, England 1570–1650.* Cambridge, MA: Pugliese, 1980. (Book, dance reconstructions and practice tape.)

Puglisi, Filadelfio. "A Survey of Renaissance Flutes." *Galpin Society Journal* 41 (1988): 67–82.

Puliaschi, Giovanni Domenico. *Musiche varie a una voce.* Rome, 1618.

Purcell, Henry. *Choice Lessons for the Harpsichord.* London, 1696.

Pure, Michel de. *Idée des spectacles anciens et nouveaux.* Paris: Brunet, 1668. Facs. rep. Geneva: Minkoff, 1972.

Quantz, Johann Joachim. *Versuch einer Anweisung die Flöte traversiere zu spielen.* Berlin, 1752. Trans. Edward R. Reilly as *On Playing the Flute.* London: Faber & Faber, 1966.

Radke, Hans. "Beiträge zur Erforschung der Lauten-Tabulaturen des 16.-18. Jahrhunderts." *Die Musikforschung* 16 (1963): 34–51.

Rameau, P[ierre]. *Le Maître à danser.* Paris, 1725. Facs. rep. New York: Broude, 1967.

Raison, André. *Seconde livre d'orgue.* Paris, 1714.

Ranum, Patricia M. "Problems with Editing Loulié." *The American Recorder* 25/3 (August 1984): 19–21.

Rasch, Rudolf. "Nogmaals t'Uitnement kabinet." *Jaarboek van het Vlaams Centrum voor Oude Muziek* 2 (1986): 115–38.

———. Introduction to T. Lupo, I. Coperario, and W. Damian, *XX Konincklycke Fantasien en Noch IX Fantasien 3 Fioolen de Gamba* (1648). Facs. rep. by Eugeen Schreurs and Martine Sanders. Peer: Musica Alamire, 1987.

———. "Some Mid-Seventeenth Century Dutch Collections of Instrumental Ensemble Music." *Tijdschrift van de Vereniging voor Nederlandse Muziekgeschiedenis* 22/3 (1972): 160–200.

Reid, Cornelius. *Bel Canto: Principles and Practice*. New York: Patelson, 1972.

Remnant, Mary. *Musical Instruments: An Illustrated History from Antiquity to the Present*. London: Batsford, 1989.

Riedel, Friedrich W. *Kirchenmusik am Hofe Karls VI (1711–1740)*. Munich and Salzburg: Katzbichler, 1977.

Robinson, Trevor. "A Reconstruction of Mersenne's Flute." *Galpin Society Journal* 26 (1973): 84–85.

Roche, Jerome. *North Italian Church Music in the Age of Monteverdi*. Oxford: Clarendon Press, 1984.

Rodgers, Julane. *Early Keyboard Fingering, ca. 1520–1620*. D.M.A. dissertation, University of Oregon, 1971.

Rognoni Taeggio, Francesco. *Selva de varii passaggi*. Milan, 1620. Facs. ed. with preface by G. Barblan. Bologna: Forni, 1970. Trans. of *Avvertimenti* to vol. 1 in Carter–Francesco.

Rosand, Ellen. *Opera in Seventeenth Century Venice*. Berkeley and Los Angeles: University of California Press, 1991.

Rose, Gloria. "Agazzari and the Improvising Orchestra." *Journal of the American Musicological Society* 18 (1965): 382–93.

Rosow, Lois. "Performing a Choral Dialogue by Lully." *Early Music* 15 (1987): 325–35.

Rosselli, John. "The Castrati as a Professional Group and a Social Phenomenon." *Acta Musicologica* 60 (1988): 143–79.

Rostirolla, Giancarlo. "Policoralità e impiego di strumenti musicali nella basilica di San Pietro in Vaticano durante gli anni 1597-1600." In *La policoralità in Italia nei secoli XVI e XVII*. Ed. Giuseppe Donato, 11–53. Miscellanea Musicologica 3. Rome: Edizioni Torre d'Orfeo, 1987.

Rousseau, Jean-Jacques. *Dictionnaire de musique*. Paris, 1768.

Rousseau, Jean. *Méthode . . . pour apprendre à chanter*. Paris, 1683.

———. *Traité de la viole*. Paris, 1687.

Russell, Craig. *Santiago de Murcia's Codice Saldivar no. 4: A Treasury of Secular Guitar Music from Baroque Mexico*. Urbana: University of Illinois Press, 1995.

Sabbatini, Galeazzo. *Regola facile e breve per sonare sopra il Basso continuo nell' Organo, Manacordo, ò altro Simile Stromento*. Venice, 1628.

Sabol, Andrew J., ed. *Four Hundred Songs and Dances from the Stuart Masque*. Providence, RI: Brown University Press, 1982.

Sadie, Julie Anne. "Bowed Continuo Instruments in French Baroque Chamber Music." *Proceedings of the Royal Music Association* 105 (1978–9): 37–49.

———. "Charpentier and the Early French Ensemble Sonata." *Early Music* 7 (1979): 330–35.

———. *The Bass Viol in French Baroque Chamber Music*. Ann Arbor: UMI Press Research, 1980.

Sadie, Stanley. See *New Grove*.

Sadler, Graham. "The Role of the Keyboard Continuo in French Opera, 1673–1776." *Early Music* 8 (1980): 148–57.

Sage, Jack. "La música de Juan Hidalgo." In Juan Vélez de Guevara, *Los celos hacen estrellas*. Ed. J. E. Varey and N. D. Shergold, 169–223. London: Tamesis, 1970.

Saint Lambert, M. de. *Les principes du clavecin*. Paris, 1702. Facs. rep. Geneva: Minkoff, 1972. Trans. Rebecca Harris-Warwick as *Principles of the Harpsichord by Monsieur de Saint-Lambert*. Cambridge: Cambridge University Press, 1984.

————. *La manière de composer et faire réussir les ballets*. Paris, 1641. Facs. rep. Geneva: Minkoff, 1989. Trans. André Bergens as "How to Compose a Successful Ballet." *Dance Perspectives* 20 (1964): 26–37.

Sanders, Donald C. "Vocal Ornaments in Durante's *Arie devote* (1608)." *Performance Practice Review* 6 (1993): 60–76.

Sanford, Sally A. "A Comparison of French and Italian Singing in the Seventeenth Century." *Journal of the Society for Seventeenth Century Music* 1 (1995).

————. "A Guide to Singing the French Language According to the Principles in Seventeenth- and Eighteenth-Century Treatises." D.M.A. term project, Stanford University, 1979.

————. *Seventeenth & Eighteenth Century Vocal Style and Technique*. D.M.A. dissertation, Stanford University, 1979.

Santa Maria, Fray Tomas de. *Libro Ilamado Arte de taner fantasia*. Valladolid, 1565.

Sanz, Gaspar. *Instrucción de musica sobre la Guitarra española*. Zaragoça, 1674.

Sartori, Claudio. *Bibliografia della musica strumentale italiana stampata in Italia fino al 1700*. Firenze: Olschki, 1952 & 1968.

Satoh, Toyohiko. *Method for the Baroque Lute*. Munich: Tree-Edition, 1987.

Saunders, Steven. *Cross, Sword, and Lyre: Sacred Music at the Imperial Court of Ferdinand II of Habsburg (1619–1637)*. Oxford: Clarendon Press, 1995.

————. "Giovanni Valentini's 'In te Domine Speravi' and the Demise of the Viola Bastarda." *Journal of the Viola da Gamba Society of America* 28 (1991): 1–20.

Savage, Roger. "Producing *Dido and Æneas*, an Investigation into Sixteen Problems." *Early Music* 4 (1976): 393–406.

Sawkins, Lionel. "For and Against the Order of Nature: Who Sang the Soprano?" *Early Music* 15 (1987): 315–24.

Sayce, Linda. "Continuo Lutes in 17th- and 18th-Century England." *Early Music* 23/4 (1995): 666–84.

Scaletta, Oratio. *Scala di musica*. Verona, 1598. Facs. rep. of 1626 edition. Bologna: Forni, n.d.

Schneider, Herbert. *Die französische Kompositionslehre in der ersten Hälfte des 17. Jahrhunderts*. Mainzer Studien zur Musikwissenschaft 3. Tuzing: Schneider, 1972.

Schneider, Max. *Die Anfänge des Basso Continuo*. Leipzig: Breitkopf & Härtel, 1918.

Schnoebelen, Anne. "Performance Practices at San Petronio in the Baroque." *Acta musicologica* 41 (1969): 37–55.

Schünemann, Georg, ed. *Trompeterfanfaren Sonaten und Feldstücke. Das Erbe Deutscher Musik*. Vol. 7. Kassel: Bärenreiter, 1936.

————. "Mattaeus Hertel's theoretische Schriften." *Archiv für Musikwissenschaft* 4 (1922): 336ff.

Schütz, Heinrich. *Psalmen Davids 1619*, Nr. 1-9. Ed. Wilhelm Ehmann. *Neue Ausgabe sämtlicher Werke*. Vol. 23. Kassel: Bärenreiter, 1971.

Schwartz, Judith L., and Christena L. Schlundt. *French Court Dance and Dance Music: A Guide to Primary Source Writings, 1643–1789*. Stuyvesant, NY: Pendragon, 1993.

Schwendowius, Barbara. *Die solistische Gambenmusik in Frankreich von 1610 bis 1740*. Kölner Beiträge zur Musikforschung 59. Regensburg: Bosse, 1970.

Segerman, Ephraim. "English Pitch Standards, Mostly c.1600." *FoMRHI Quarterly* 65 (1991): 13–16

————. "English Viol Sizes and Pitches." *FoMRHI Quarterly* 38 (1985): 55–62.

————. "On Praetorius and English Viol Pitches." *Chelys* 18 (1988): 24–27.

————. "The Sizes of English Viols and Talbot's Measurements." *Galpin Society Journal* 48 (March, 1995): 33–45.

Selfridge-Field, Eleanor. "Bassano and the Orchestra of St. Mark's." *Early Music* 4 (1976): 153–58.

————. "Instrumentation and Genre in Italian Music, 1600–1670." *Early Music* 19 (1991): 61–67.

————. "Italian Oratorio and the Baroque Orchestra." *Early Music* 16 (1988): 506–13.

————. *Venetian Instrumental Music from Gabrieli to Vivaldi.* 3d rev. ed. New York: Dover, 1994.

Semmens, Richard. "A Translation of Etienne Loulié's Method for Learning How to Play the Recorder." *The American Recorder* 24/4 (November 1983): 135–45.

Severi, Francesco. *Salmi passaggiati per tutte le voci nella maniera che si cantano in Roma.* Rome, 1615.

Sherman, Bernard D., ed. *Inside Early Music: Conversations with Performers.* New York: Oxford University Press, 1997.

Sherman, Joy, and Laurence B. Brown. "Singing *Passaggi*: Modern Application for a Centuries-Old Technique." *Choral Journal* 36/1 (August 1995): 27–36.

Sherr, Richard. "Competence and Incompetence in the Papal Choir in the Age of Palestrina." *Early Music* 22 (1994): 606–29.

————. "Performance Practice in the Papal Chapel during the Sixteenth Century." *Early Music* 15 (1987): 452–62.

Sicard, Michel T. A. *L'École française de viole de gambe de Maugars á Sainte-Colombe.* Dissertation de doctorat de troisième cycle, École Pratique des Hautes êtudes. Paris, 1979.

Sicard, Michelle. "The French Viol School before 1650." *Journal of the Viola da Gamba Society of America* 18 (1981): 76–93.

————. "The French Viol School: The Repertory from 1650 to Sainte-Colombe (ca. 1680)." *Journal of the Viola da Gamba Society of America* 22 (1985): 42–55.

Silbiger, Alexander. *Italian Manuscript Sources of 17th Century Keyboard Music.* Ann Arbor: UMI Research Press, 1980.

————. "The Roman Frescobaldi Tradition, c. 1640–1670." *Journal of the American Musicological Society* 33 (1980): 42–87.

Simpson, Christopher. *A Compendium of Practical Musick.* London, 1667.

————. *The Division-Viol, or, The Art of Playing Extempore upon a Ground.* London, ²1665. Facs. rep. Huntingdon, England: King's Music, n.d.

Skeaping, Mary. "Ballet under the Three Crowns." *Dance Perspectives* 32 (Winter 1967).

Smith, Anne. "Die Renaissancequerflöte und ihre Musik: Ein Beitrag zur Interpretation der Quellen." *Basler Jahrbuch für historische Musikpraxis* 2 (1978): 9–76.

————. "The Renaissance Flute." In John Solum, *The Early Flute,* 11–33. Early Music Series 15. Oxford: Clarendon Press, 1992.

————. "Über Modus und Transposition um 1600." *Basler Jahrbuch für historische Musikpraxis* 6 (1982): 9–43.

Smith, Douglas Alton. "Baron and Weiss *contra* Mattheson." *Journal of the Lute Society of America* 6 (1973): 48ff.

————. "The Ebenthal Lute and Viol Tablatures: Thirteen new Manuscripts of Baroque Instrumental Music." *Early Music* 10 (1982): 462–67.

Smith, Kathryn E. *Music for Voices and Viols: A Contextual Study and Critical Performing Edition of Verse Anthems in Christ Church [Oxford] MSS 56-60.* D.M.A. thesis, University of Illinois, 1988.

Smithers, Don L. "The Baroque Trumpet After 1721: Some Preliminary Observations, Pt. 2." *Early Music* 6 (1978): 358–61.

————. "The Hapsburg Imperial *Trompeter* and *Heerpaucker* Privileges of 1653." *Galpin Society Journal* 24 (1971): 84–95.

————. *The Music and History of the Baroque Trumpet Before 1721.* Carbondale: Southern Illinois University Press, 1988.

Snyder, Kerala J. *Dieterich Buxtehude, Organist in Lübeck.* New York: Schirmer Books, 1987.

Soderlund, Sandra. *Organ Technique, An Historical Approach.* Chapel Hill, NC: Hinshaw, 1980.

Solum, John. *The Early Flute.* Early Music Series 15. Oxford: Clarendon Press, 1992.

Speer, Daniel. *Grundrichtiger Unterricht der musikalischen Kunst . . . oder ein vierfaches musikalisches Kleeblatt.* Ulm, 1697.

Spencer, Robert. "Chitarrone, Theorbo and Archlute." *Early Music* 4 (1976): 407–23.

Speth, Johann. *Ars magna consoni et dissoni*. Augsburg, 1693.

Spink, Ian. "English Cavalier Songs, 1620–1660." *Proceedings of the Royal Musical Association* 86 (1960): 62.

———. *English Song, Dowland to Purcell*. New York: Scribner's, 1974.

———. "Playford's Directions for Singing After the Italian Manner." *Monthly Musical Record* 89 (1959): 134.

———, ed. *The Seventeenth Century*. Vol. 3 of *The Blackwell History of Music in Britain*. Oxford: Blackwell, 1992.

Spitzer, John. "The Birth of the Orchestra in Rome: An Iconographic Study." *Early Music* 19 (1991): 9–27.

———. "Grammar of Improvised Ornamentation: Jean Rousseau's Viol Treatise of 1687." *Journal of Music Theory* 33 (1989): 299–332.

———. "Jean Rousseau and the Mechanics of Viol Playing." *Journal of the Viola da Gamba Society of America* 8 (1970): 5–12.

Spring, Matthew. *The Lute in England and Scotland after the Golden Age, 1620–1750*. Ph.D. dissertation, Oxford University, 1987.

Staden, Johann. *Kurzer und einfältiger Bericht für diejenigen, so im Basso ad Organum unerfahren, was bey demselben zum Theil in Acht zu nehmen*. Appended to his *Kirchenmusic, Ander Theil*. Nuremberg, 1626.

Stanley, Barbara, and Graham Lyndon-Jones. *The Curtal*. Available from the authors at 20 Queen Street, St. Albans, Hertfordshire AL3 4PJ, England.

Stark, Alan. "What Steps Did the Spaniards Take in the Dance? A Survey of Four Centuries of Documentary Sources." *Society of Dance History Scholars. Procedings. Fourteenth Annual Conference (1991)*, 54–64. Riverside: University of California, 1991.

Stein, Louise. "La Plática de los dioses: Music and the Calderonian Court Play, with a Transcription of the Songs from *La estatua de Prometeo*." Chapter 2 of Pedro Calderón de la Barca. *La estatua de Prometeo*, 13–92. Critical edition by Margaret Rich Greer. Reichenberger, 1986.

———. *Songs of Mortals, Dialogues of the Gods: Music and Theatre in Seventeenth-Century Spain*. New York: Oxford University Press, 1993.

Stevens, Denis, trans. *The Letters of Claudio Monteverdi*. Rev. ed. Oxford: Clarendon Press; New York: Oxford University Press, 1995.

Stevenson, Robert. Review of Pedro Cerone, *El Melopeo Tractado de Musica Theorica y Practica*. Facs. rep. in two volumes of *El Melopeo y Maestro* (Bologna, 1969). *Journal of the American Musicological Society* 24 (1971): 477–85.

Stradner, Gerhard. "The Evolution of the Pitch of Cornetts and Trombones at the Time of Scheidt and Buxtehude." *Dietrich Buxtehude and Samuel Scheidt: An Anniversary Tribute*. Proceedings of the International Buxtehude/Scheidt Festival and Conference at the University of Saskatchewan, November 1987, 106–16.

Strizich, Robert. "L'accompanimento di basso continuo sulla chitarra barocca." *Il Fronimo* (January 1981): 15–26; (April 1981): 8–24.

Strunk, Oliver, ed. *Source Readings in Music History: from Classical Antiquity through the Romantic Era*. New York: Norton, 1950.

Strunk, Oliver, ed. *Source Readings in Music History*. Vol. 3: *The Baroque Era*. London: Faber, 1981.

Stubbs, Stephen. "*L'armonia sonora:* Continuo Orchestration in Monteverdi's *Orfeo*. *Early Music* 22 (1994): 87–98.

Sullivan, Mary. *Court Masques of James I*. New York: Knickerbocker, 1913.

Sutton, Julia. "Dance. IV. Late Renaissance and Baroque to 1700." In *New Grove*.

———. "The Minuet: An Elegant Phoenix." *Dance Chronicle* 8 (1985): 119–52.

———. "Triple Pavans: Clues to Some Mysteries in 16th-Century Dance." *Early Music* 14 (1986): 175–81.

Tagliavini, Luigi. "The Art of 'Not Leaving the Instrument Empty': Comments on Early Harpsichord Playing." *Early Music* 11 (1983): 299–308.

Talbot, James. Oxford, Christ Church Mus MS 1187. See Baines–Talbot's Manuscript.

Talbot, Michael. "Tenors and Basses at the Venetian *Ospedali*." *Acta Musicologica* 66 (1994): 123–38.

Tarr, Edward H. *The Trumpet*. Trans. S. E. Plank and Edward H. Tarr. London: Batsford, 1988.

———. "Ein Katalog erhaltener Zinken." *Basler Jahrbuch für historische Musikpraxis* 5 (1981): 11–262.

Teplow, Deborah. "Rhetoric and Eloquence: Dramatic Expression in Marin Marais' Pièces de viole." *Journal of the Viola da Gamba Society of America* 24 (1987): 22–50.

Termini, Olga. See *Il corago*.

Thomas, Bernard, and Jane Gingell. *The Renaissance Dance Book: Dances from the Sixteenth and Early Seventeenth Centuries*. London: London Pro Musica Edition, 1987. (Dance reconstructions, music, and cassette tape.)

Tilney, Colin. *The Art of the Unmeasured Prelude*. London: Schott, 1991.

Titcomb, Caldwell. *The Kettledrums in Western Europe: Their History outside the Orchestra*. Ph.D. dissertation, Harvard University, 1952.

Titon du Tillet, Evrard. *Vies des Musiciens et autres Jouers d'Instruments du rägne de Louis le Grand*. Ed. with preface by Marie-Françoise Quignard. Collected from *Le Parnasse françois* (Paris, 1732) and supplements (1743, 1755). Paris: Gallimard, 1991.

Toft, Robert. *Tune Thy Musicke to Thy Hart: The Art of Eloquent Singing in England, 1597-1622*. Toronto: University of Toronto Press, 1993.

Tomlinson, Kellom. *The Art of Dancing*. London, 1735. Facs. rep. (with Tomlinson's *Six Dances*, London. 1720). [Brooklyn]: Gregg International Dance Horizons, 1970.

Tosi, Pier Francesco. *Observations on the Florid Song*. Trans. John Galliard, preface by Paul Henry Lang. New York: Johnson Reprint, 1968.

———. *Opinioni de' cantori antichi e moderni, o sieno osservazioni sopra il canto figurato*. Bologna, 1723. Facs. ed., Erwin R. Jacobi. Celle: Hermann Moeck Verlag, 1966.

Tourin, Peter. *Viollist: A Comprehensive Catalogue of Viole da Gamba in Public and Private Collections*. Duxbury, VT: Tourin Musica, 1979; with revisions and updates by Thomas MacCracken, forthcoming.

Trabaci, Gio. Maria. *Ricercate, canzone franzese, capricci, canti fermi, galliarde, partite diverse, toccate, durezze, ligature, consonanze stravaganti, et un madrigale passeggiato*. Naples, 1603.

———. *Il secondo libro de ricercate, & altri varij Capricci, Con Cento Versi*. Naples, 1615.

Traficante, Frank. "Lyra Viol Tunings: 'All ways have been tryed to do It'." *Acta Musicologica* 42/3–4 (1970): 183–205.

———. "Music for Lyra Viol: Manuscript Sources." *Chelys* 8 (1978–79): 4–22.

———. "Music for the Lyra Viol: The Printed Sources." *Lute Society Journal* 8 (1966): 7–24.

Trichet, Pierre. *Traité des instruments de musique*. Ms., ca. 1630–36. Ed. François Lesure in *Annales musicologiques* 3 (1955): 283–87, and 4 (1956): 175–248.

Tyler, James. *A Brief Tutor for the Baroque Guitar*. Helsinki: Chorus Publications, 1984.

———. *The Early Guitar: A History and Handbook*. New York: Oxford University Press, 1980.

———. "The Italian Mandolin and Mandola 1589–1800." *Early Music* 9 (1981): 438–46.

———. "The Mandore in the 16th and 17th Centuries." *Early Music* 9 (1981): 22–31.

———. "Mixed Ensembles." In Kite-Powell–*Renaissance*, 217–27.

———, and Paul Sparks. *The Early Mandolin: The Mandolino and the Neapolitan Mandoline*. New York: Oxford University Press, 1989.

Uberti, Mauro. "Vocal Techniques in the Second Half of the 16th Century." Trans. Mark Lindley. *Early Music* 9 (1981): 486–95.

Valentini, Pier Francesco. *Trattato della battuta musicale*. Ms. Rome, Vatican Library Ms. Barb. lat. 4417; 1643.

Van der Straeten, Edmond. *History of the Violoncello, the Viol da gamba, their Precursors and Collateral Instruments*. London, 1914. Reprint. London: Reeves, 1971.

———. *La musique aux Pays-bas*. 8 vols. 1867. Reprint. New York: Dover, 1989.

van Baak Griffioen, Ruth. *Jacob van Eyck's Der Fluyten Lust-hof*. Utrecht: Vereniging voor Nederlandse Muziekgeschiedenis, 1991.

van der Meer, John Henry. *Musikinstrumente von der Antike bis zur Gegenwart.* Munich: Prestel-Verlag, 1983.

Veilhan, Jean-Claude. *Les regles de l'interpretation musicale a l'epoque baroque (XVIIe-XVIIIe siècles), generales a tous les instruments.* Paris: Leduc, 1977. Trans. John Lambert as *The Rules of Musical Interpretation in the Baroque Era.* Paris: Leduc, 1979.

Viadana, Lodovico Grossi da. *Cento concerti ecclesiastici.* Rome, 1603. Trans. of preface in Strunk–*Source Readings*, 419–23.

Viles, Ann. "*New Grove* Index for Viol Players." *Journal of the Viola da Gamba Society of America* 27 (1990): 55–75.

Virdung, Sebastian. *Musica getutscht.* Basel, 1511. Trans. Beth Bullard. Cambridge: Cambridge University Press, 1993.

Virgiliano, Aurelio. *Il Dolcimelo.* Ms, Bologna (?), ca. 1600. Facs. rep. Florence: Studio per Edizioni Scelte, 1979.

"Von den Paucken, deren Gebrauch und Mißgebrauch in alten und neuen Zeiten." *Wöchentliche Nachrichten und Anmerkungen die Musik betreffend* 2 (1768).

von Ramm, Andrea. "Singing Early Music." *Early Music* 4 (1976): 12–15.

Walker, D. P. *Musique des Intermèdes de "La Pellegrina."* Paris: Centre National de la Recherche Scientifique, 1963.

Walker, Diane Parr and Paul. *German Sacred Polyphonic Vocal Music Between Schütz and Bach.* Warren, MI: Harmonie Park, 1992.

Walker, Thomas. "Castrato." In *New Grove.*

Walls, Peter. "London, 1603–49." *Music and Society: The Early Baroque.* Ed. Curtis Price. Englewood Cliffs, NJ: Prentice-Hall, 1993.

Ward, John. "Sprightly & Cheerful Musick: Notes on the Cittern, Gittern and Guitar in 16th- and 17th-Century England." *Lute Society Journal* 21 (1979–81): entire issue.

———. "The English Measure." *Early Music* 14 (1986): 15–21.

———. *Tudor and Stuart Dance and Dance Music.* Oxford University Press, forthcoming.

Wasielewski, Joseph Wilhelm von, comp. and ed. *Instrumentalsätze vom Ende des XVI. bis Ende des XVII. Jahrhunderts.* Bonn, 1874. Facs. rep. with notes by John Suess as *Anthology of Instrumental Music from the End of the Sixteenth to the End of the Seventeenth Century.* New York: Da Capo, 1973.

Waterhouse, William. "A Newly Discovered 17th-Century Bassoon by Haka." *Early Music* 16 (1988): 407–10.

Weaver, John. *Orchesography or the Art of Dancing.* Trans. of Feuillet, *Chorégraphie.* London, 1706. Facs. rep. in Richard Ralph, *The Life and Works of John Weaver.* New York: Dance Horizons, 1985.

Weber, Rainer. "Some Researches into Pitch in the 16th Century with Particular Reference to the Instruments in the Accademia Filarmonica of Verona." *Galpin Society Journal* 28 (1975): 7–10.

Weidlich, Joseph. "Battuto Performance Practice in Early Italian Guitar Music (1606-1637)." *Journal of the Lute Society of America* 11 (1978): 63–86.

Werckmeister, Andreas. *Die nothwendigsten Anmerckungen und Regeln wie der Bassus continuus oder General-Bass wohl könne tractiret werden.* Ascherleben, 1698.

Wigness, Clyde Robert. *A Comprehensive Performance Project in Trombone Literature with an Essay on the Soloistic Use of the Trombone in Selected Works of Eighteenth-Century Viennese Imperial Court Composers.* D.M.A. dissertation, University of Iowa, 1970.

Williams, Peter. "Basso Continuo on the Organ." *Music & Letters* 50 (1969): 136–52, 230–45.

———. "Continuo." In *New Grove.*

———. *Figured Bass Accompaniment.* 2 vols. Edinburgh: Edinburgh University Press, 1970.

Wilson, John. *Roger North on Music.* London: Novello, 1959.

Winkler, Klaus. *Selbständige Instrumentalwerke mit Posaune in Oberitalien von 1590 bis 1650.* Tutzing: Hans Schneider, 1985.

Woodfield, Ian. *The Early History of the Viol.* Cambridge: Cambridge University Press, 1984.

———, and Lucy Robinson. "Viol." In *New Grove.*

Woodfill, Walter L. *Musicians in English Society from Elizabeth to Charles I.* Princeton: Princeton University Press, 1953.

Worsthorne, Simon Townley. *Venetian Opera in the Seventeenth Century.* Oxford: Clarendon Press, 1954.

Wörthmüller, Willi. "Die Nürnberger Trompeter- und Posaunenmacher des 17. und 18. Jahrhunderts." *Mitteilungen des Vereins für Geschichte der Stadt Nürnberg* 45 (1954): 208ff; 46 (1955): 372–480.

Young, Phillip T. *The Look of Music: Rare Musical Instruments 1500–1900.* Vancouver: Vancouver Museums & Planetarium Association, 1980.

Zacconi, Lodovico. *Prattica di musica.* Venice, 1592. Facs. ed. Bologna: Forni, 1983. Partial German translation by F. Chrysander, "Lodovico Zacconi als Lehrer des Kunstgesanges." *Vierteljahrschrift für Musikwissenschaft* 7 (1891): 337–96; 9 (1893): 249–310; 10 (1894): 531–67.

Zaslaw, Neal. "When is an Orchestra not an Orchestra?" *Early Music* 16 (1988): 483–95.

———. "The Enigma of the Haut-Contre." *Musical Times* 115/11 (1974): 939–41.

Index

INDEX